INDIGENOUS SYMBOLS AND PRACTICES IN THE CATHOLIC CHURCH

Indigenous Symbols and Practices in the Catholic Church presents views, concepts and perspectives on the relationships among Indigenous Peoples and the Catholic Church, as well as stories, images and art as metaphors for survival in a contemporary world.

Few studies present such interdisciplinary interpretations from contributors in multiple disciplines regarding appropriation, spiritual and religious tradition, educational issues in the teaching of art and art history, the effects of government sanctions on traditional practice, or the artistic interpretation of symbols from Indigenous perspectives.

Through photographs and visual materials, interviews and data analysis, personal narratives and stories, these chapters explore the experiences of Indigenous Peoples whose lives have been impacted by multiple forces – Christian missionaries, governmental policies, immigration and colonization, education, assimilation and acculturation. Contributors investigate current contexts and complex areas of conflict regarding missionization, appropriation and colonizing practices through asking questions such as, 'What does the use of images mean for resistance, transformation and cultural destruction?' And, 'What new interpretations and perspectives are necessary for Indigenous traditions to survive and flourish in the future?'

VITALITY OF INDIGENOUS RELIGIONS

Series Editors

Graham Harvey, Open University, UK
Afeosemime Adogame, University of Edinburgh, UK
Ines Talamantez, University of California, USA

Ashgate's *Vitality of Indigenous Religions* series offers an exciting new cluster of research monographs, drawing together volumes from leading international scholars across a wide range of disciplinary perspectives. Indigenous religions are vital and empowering for many thousands of indigenous peoples globally, and dialogue with, and consideration of, these diverse religious life-ways promises to challenge and refine the methodologies of a number of academic disciplines, whilst greatly enhancing understandings of the world.

This series explores the development of contemporary indigenous religions from traditional, ancestral precursors, but the characteristic contribution of the series is its focus on their living and current manifestations. Devoted to the contemporary expression, experience and understanding of particular indigenous peoples and their religions, books address key issues which include: the sacredness of land, exile from lands, diasporic survival and diversification, the indigenization of Christianity and other missionary religions, sacred language, and re-vitalization movements. Proving of particular value to academics, graduates, postgraduates and higher level undergraduate readers worldwide, this series holds obvious attraction to scholars of Native American studies, Maori studies, African studies and offers invaluable contributions to religious studies, sociology, anthropology, geography and other related subject areas.

OTHER TITLES IN THE SERIES

Aboriginal Environmental Knowledge
Rational Reverence
Catherine Laudine
ISBN 978 0 7546 6430 7

Native Christians
Modes and Effects of Christianity among Indigenous Peoples of the Americas
Edited by Aparecida Vilaça and Robin M. Wright
ISBN 978 0 7546 6355 3

Caribbean Diaspora in the USA
Diversity of Caribbean Religions in New York City
Bettina Schmidt
ISBN 978 0 7546 6365 2

Indigenous Symbols and Practices in the Catholic Church

Visual Culture, Missionization and Appropriation

Edited by
KATHLEEN J. MARTIN
California Polytechnic State University, USA

ASHGATE

Published by
Ashgate Publishing Limited
Wey Court East
Union Road
Farnham
Surrey, GU9 7PT
England

Ashgate Publishing Company
Suite 420
101 Cherry Street
Burlington
VT 05401–4405
USA

www.ashgate.com

British Library Cataloguing in Publication Data
Indigenous symbols and practices in the Catholic Church : visual culture, missionization
    and appropriation. – (Vitality of indigenous religions series)
    1. Catholic Church – Missions. 2. Christianity and art – Catholic Church.
    3. Appropriation (Art) 4. Indigenous art. 5. Cultural property. 6. Indigenous
    peoples – Religion.
    I. Series II. Martin, Kathleen J.
    282'.089–dc22

Library of Congress Cataloging-in-Publication Data
Indigenous symbols and practices in the Catholic Church : visual culture, missionization,
    and appropriation / [edited by] Kathleen J. Martin.
        p. cm. – (Vitality of indigenous religions series)
    Includes bibliographical references and index.
    ISBN 978–0–7546–6631–8 (hardcover : alk. paper)
    1. Catholic Church – Missions. 2. Christianity and culture. 3. Indigenous
    peoples – Religion. 4. Christian art and symbolism.
    I. Martin, Kathleen J.

    BV2180.I53 2009
    282.089–dc22   2009019656

ISBN 9780754666318 (hbk)
ISBN 9780754697794 (ebk)

Mixed Sources
Product group from well-managed
forests and other controlled sources
www.fsc.org Cert no. SA-COC-1565
© 1996 Forest Stewardship Council

Printed and bound in Great Britain by
MPG Books Group, UK

For my *Cuwe*. ...

Contents

List of Figures

Notes on Contributors

Angela D. Blaver is Kutzadika'a (Mono Lake Paiute) and received her PhD in Educational Psychology, with emphases in Child, Adolescent, and Human Development, from the University of California, Santa Barbara. She currently is an assistant professor in the Bagwell College of Education at Kennesaw State University. Her dissertation is entitled "An Examination of Gender, Home Language, Self-appraisals, and Mathematics Achievement Among Hispanic Youth." She has published on such subjects as gender and ethnicity in education, retention and high school dropout, and achievement trajectories. Her primary teaching interests include action research, developmental studies, and social justice, equity, and culture in the classroom.

C. Kalani Beyer is currently the Dean of the School of Education at National University with the rank of Full Professor. He received his PhD from the University of Illinois at Chicago in Curriculum Design. His research interests are in multicultural education, Native American education, and the history of education for Hawaiians. His research consists of multicultural education articles, book reviews of Native American and Hawaiian education, and articles on topics related to the history of education for Hawaiians.

Herman Pi'ikea Clark is a member of the Faculty of the College of Education at Massey University in Palmerston North, New Zealand. A lecturer in Visual Art Education, Dr. Clark conducts research in the areas of Pacific Visual Epistemology, Critical Pedagogy, and Bicultural Teacher Education. A native of Hawaii, Dr. Clark initiated the first courses in Kanaka Maoli/Indigenous Hawaiian Visual Art/Design studies to be taught at the University of Hawaii. Following the completion of an MFA in Visual Communication Design, Dr. Clark joined the faculty of Applied Art and Design at Northtec in Whangarei, New Zealand in 1999 where he headed the Graphic Design program. A practicing artist, Pi'ikea Clark has exhibited internationally with his artwork housed in both private and public collections in North America and the Pacific. Together with his wife, Norfolk Island artist Sue Pearson, Pi'ikea established Pili, a design business specializing in the contemporary interpretation of Pacific culture and identity.

Bernardo P. Gallegos (Coyote/Genizaro/Pueblo), a career educator/scholar in the area of Social Foundations of Education, Professor Gallegos has published in the areas of Indigenous and Latino educational/cultural history and performance studies in education. He is the author of *Literacy, Education, and Society in New Mexico, 1692–1821*; co-editor and contributor to *Performance Theories in Education:*

Power, Pedagogy, and the Politics of Identity; co-editor of *Indigenous Education and Epistemologies in the Americas*, a special issue of *Educational Studies*; and co-editor of the forthcoming *Handbook of Research in Social Foundations*. Professor Gallegos has held the position of Professor at California State University, Los Angeles, the University of Illinois at Chicago, and Distinguished Professor at Washington State University. Currently he serves as Program Lead and Professor at National University, Los Angeles Campus.

James J. Garrett (Lakota) from Cheyenne River Reservation holds a PhD in Rangeland Ecosystem Science from the College of Natural Resources at Colorado State University, Fort Collins. His dissertation entitled, "A Triadic Relationship on the Northern Great Plains: Bison, Native Plants, and Native People," skillfully integrates the major components of the Northern Great Plains ecosystem, including the grassland ecosystem, bison, and Lakota People. His work addresses the relationship and importance of Lakota traditions, beliefs, and communities to an understanding of the complexity of the plains. Currently, he is an associate professor at Cankdeska Cikana Community College in North Dakota.

James B. Jeffries is Visiting Assistant Professor in the Department of History and Geography at Clemson University where he is a specialist in Colonial America and Native American history. His research interests in early Native American history center on understanding the impact of European colonization on the development of Native American religious orientations, which, in turn, exposes critical perspectives on the academic discourse of comparative religion. Jeffries received his PhD from the Department of Religious Studies at the University of California, Santa Barbara.

Kathleen J. Martin is an assistant professor at Cal Poly State University in the Ethnic Studies Department where she teaches courses in Indigenous Studies. She also is a mother of three and grandmother of five, and her family is from Minnesota and South Dakota. She is of German, Irish, Dutch, and Dakota heritage. She holds an MA in Native Traditions and a PhD in Educational Leadership with an emphasis in culture, language, and literacy from the University of California, Santa Barbara. Her research investigates historical relationships and issues of land, culture, and language, and educational issues in Native communities and has appeared in *Teaching and Teacher Education*, the *Journal of School Effectiveness*, *Santa Barbara Papers in Linguistics*, and the *Encyclopedia of Religion*.

Delvin J. Slick from Shonto, Arizona was born in Tuba City, Arizona. Introducing himself in a traditional way he says, "My clans are the Reed People Clan, born for the Bitterwater Clan, my maternal clan is the Red House Manygoats, and my paternal clan is the Ute. I was raised around Shonto and on Black Mesa. The majority of my youth, I was raised by my grandparents, not because my parents weren't there, but because they wanted me to understand our Navajo traditional culture. They strongly believed in our Navajo belief, 'The Way of Life.'"

Larry M. Taylor specializes in areas of modern and contemporary American art, particularly as they intersect with religious contexts. The subjects of his writings have ranged from nineteenth-century skepticism to contemporary artists, and these have been published in a variety of contexts. Recently he has written for *Reconstruction*, an online interdisciplinary journal for contemporary culture. He is currently a doctoral student at the Graduate Theological Union in Berkeley, California.

David Toole received his PhD in Theology and Ethics from Duke University in 1996. From 1992 until 2005, David lived in his native state of Montana, where he taught at Carroll College in Helena and at the University of Montana, Missoula, before leaving the academy to become general manager of a construction company that specialized in building custom homes throughout the Northern Rockies. With his wife, Nancy, and three sons (Gabe, Ben, and Finn), he left Montana and returned to Duke in 2005, where he now serves as the Associate Dean for Academic Administration and Strategic Initiatives in the Divinity School. He is the author of *Waiting for Godot in Sarajevo: Theological Reflections on Nihilism, Tragedy, and Apocalypse* and has written a variety of articles on theology, philosophy, and the environment.

Karen Willeto has been a faculty member at Diné College for more than twenty-five years, teaching in the areas of Art and Art History, and beginning and intermediate Photography and Composition. She holds an MA from Eastern Michigan University and has expertise in black-and-white and digital photography, art history, commercial art, and visual studies.

Preface

From the beginning of my interest in the topics presented in this volume, I have endeavored to address from multiple perspectives the challenges, dichotomies, expropriations, and symbolic idealistic contestations of appropriating and missionizing in Indigenous communities. I myself am a product of Catholic and ex-Catholic, Irish and German, Midwestern and Dakota, academic and motherly perspectives. This multiplicity of perspectives is part of all of our lives in various ways, and they exist simultaneously and effortlessly, as well as in active conflict with each other. Trickster's finest and most artful point is that contradictions and oppositions exist seamlessly, and certainly I have been accused of playing Coyote's role at times. This is notable since, as Lewis Hyde suggests, "the origins, liveliness, and durability of cultures require that there be space for figures whose function is to uncover and disrupt the very things that cultures are based on."[1]

Without even a challenge or raising a voice, innuendos and deceptions are afoot and afield since Trickster "attends the internal boundaries by which groups articulate their social life."[2] Trickster is contradictory and enlightening, and won't be ignored or unimagined once born and renewed. He is not evil, but can be cruel, a grandfather of lies, and a comic fool. Present in the world as "wild children on the inside, a red salute crossed with a white sparrow and a blue rose, one vast prairie that blooms on three hundred and thirteen words, exactly the number of panic holes a tribal trickster needs to be imagined in a wicked world."[3] He, if it is he, defies categories and descriptions and hopes to confuse, constrain, contradict, and illuminate. He is no Joan of Arc or Joseph of Arimathea; no Mary Magdalene or Pontius Pilot. He rears his head among dichotomous thinking and selective hearing, challenging those that would try to adopt and mold him. And yet, "Trickster is a communal voice in a comic worldview, not a tragic method in the social sciences, and the trickster needs ten times more lust to overcome your inhibitions to even imagine the world."[4] With this in mind, examining the differences between Indigenous and Catholic interpretations may cause us to struggle in the subjects of discussion; yet from it we will attempt to illuminate oppositions and contradictions, challenging inhibitions.

---

[1]   Lewis Hyde, *Trickster Makes This World: Mischief, Myth and Art* (New York, 1998), p. 6.

[2]   Ibid., p. 130.

[3]   Gerald R. Vizenor, *The Trickster of Liberty: Wild Heirs to the Baronage* (Minneapolis, 1988), p. x.

[4]   Ibid., p. xvi.

For some Catholics, the language of trickster is foreign, unimaginable, and just downright wrong. It is evil incarnate to be stamped out, not embodied in narratives and stories of heroic epic proportions; it is the "devil talking." For, as the characters in Gerald Vizenor's *Trickster of Liberty* contemplate, "Trickster mediates wild bodies and adamant minds; a chance in third person narratives to turn aside cold litanies and catechistic monodramas over the measured roads of civilization."[5] Maybe the wicked world needs to recognize trickster the most, and the Christianizing and assimilation policies of the past can no longer ignore his insistent voice. In this, the questions of where, what, and why with regard to the incorporation of symbols and traditions in the Catholic Church are significant. The most pressing question for me in this discussion is: How is it that Catholics come to desire to blend with Native traditions and incorporate traditional symbols and practices? The answer is unclear. Maybe it's the idea of "salvation for the heathen" in the one true God or helping those that need it to find the right path. Maybe it's tied to old notions of the noble savage in tune with nature that lures the imagination. In the past, "playing Indian offered a powerful tool for holding contradictions in abeyance,"[6] and maybe it still does today. Or is it a reflection of a culture that wants to pick and choose certain images to adopt and to ignore others at their whim, since, ultimately, isn't God by whatever name the same for all? Maybe it is even simpler than this. Traditional practices have inherent power, and wanting to acquire some of that power and efficacy is a policy recognized and aggressively asserted by those members of societies with the power and proclivity to do so.

The relationship between Indigenous communities in the New World and the Catholic Church has a long-standing and complex history, and the contributors to this volume examine a range of topics designed as interdisciplinary discussions, debates, and deliberations. They present perspectives regarding the missionizing efforts of the Catholic Church in Indigenous communities and the appropriation of images and symbols. They also suggest some interpretations and thoughts on the subject that come from community members and which may lead to further discussions as part of an ongoing dialogue. Their efforts reflect diverse understandings, backgrounds, and ideas that include the study of spiritual traditions and religion, art and art education, culture and visual studies, and the analysis and interpretation of qualitative data. Attempts at co-optation of any culture often carries with it a reinterpretation of symbols, the reconfiguration of contexts, and ultimately endeavors to acculturate or assimilate those who desire to maintain their own way of interpreting the world. It also assumes that those with "the best of intentions" are proceeding with that goal unaware or unconcerned of the harm to those they most desire to serve. A reinterpretation of motives and an examination of the similarities and differences of past policies and practices through studies of visual culture and the interpretations and commentaries of Native Peoples may provide us with a new lens to examine these issues.

---

[5]   Ibid., p. xiii.

[6]   Philip J. Deloria, *Playing Indian* (New Haven, 1998), p. 182.

The goal of this edited collection is to present a scholarly interpretation from people not in need of help, but in need of the opportunity to use and interpret their world from perspectives not dominated by Euroamerican politics or Catholic missionary actions. John Grant cautioned more than 25 years ago that:

> If one looks honestly at the record, one is nagged by a suspicion that what was embraced was so different from Christianity as the missionaries understood it as to be classified more properly as imitation of its externals or, at best, as a blend neither quite Christian nor quite traditional.[7]

We suspect that this is more than a "nagging question" regarding current contexts of missionization and that it is not part of the past, but very much of the present. More appropriately, we might ask: If we look honestly at the record, can we say that what is currently embraced by Catholicism is so very different from what is known and understood by Indigenous Peoples as to be merely a blend or imitation of externals? The efforts and goals of the Church regarding conversion have continued, and in some current contexts the blending of traditions is not quite Catholic and not quite traditional. Although some would argue that the times are different, in many ways they are similar to the past. The demands and influences of Christianity in general call for the "elimination of the culture and value system of the colonized and the imposition of values and culture of the colonizer."[8] In many ways, we are a product of the social systems, cultural patterns, and cognitive processes that are embedded in political and economic systems. And we often are incapable of acting outside of these same systems of thought even when we most desire to or even disagree with interpretations. Without conscious reflection and active attempts to understand the underlying processes at work, we are swept up by the very same processes we try to avoid. In other words we might say, "the more we try to change, the more we stay the same."

Some scholars have responded to critiques of the Church's position in Indigenous communities by saying the sacred is for everyone no matter how it is used or when, and "playing Indian," whether by Euroamericans in the early years or Christians in the later half of the twentieth century, is merely an attempt to honor traditions and peoples. Whatever the stated reasons, Euroamericans and Christians incorporate Indigenous symbols, images, and traditions seemingly as they pick and choose flowers to decorate altars, colored glass for stained-glass windows with images of prostrate young Indigenous women, or ceremonies in service of personal egos, wants, and desires. Abalone, sweet grass and drum-dressed altars, and anything that fits the goal of display, can be added or subtracted. It is supposed as part of a process, "one of conversion, and it needs to rise above any one particular cultural

---

[7] John W. Grant, *Moon in Wintertime: Missionaries and the Indians of Canada in Encounter since 1534* (Toronto, 1984), p. 246.

[8] George Tinker, *Missionary Conquest: The Gospel and Native American Cultural Genocide* (Minneapolis, 1993), p. 119.

worldview."[9] The justification is one of collection, a practice begun with Pope Pius XI and the Vatican Missionary Exhibition. This exhibition set the stage for a strategy of "Catholic mission propaganda using objects and artifacts based on the mission collections and exhibitions of the Society of Jesus (Jesuits)."[10] Collection and exhibition support picking and choosing, like the smorgasbords popular in America. Choose what is significant to Indigenous communities surrounding the missions, and then display them as is necessary to further the aims of the Church. The potential misconceptions of cultural inclusion and enculturation may be most egregious in the assumption that it is acceptable not only to pick and choose, but also to call it something sacred as in rising above petty "cultural worldview differences" for something greater. This seems to suggest little difference from earlier times when Native Peoples engaged in struggles to sustain traditional practices in light of oppression, assimilation, removal, and persecution. Maybe now it is of a more disturbing nature in the pick-and-choose mentality that breaks practices apart and creates piecemeal traditions within the larger Catholic tradition. If past assessments of Native and Catholic relationships are accurate reflections of current interactions, then "careful examination should be given to the nature of cultural and social disagreement and the origin of differences in both the religious and geographical dimensions of people's lives."[11] It is yet to be determined how these more recent efforts by the Church will be perceived either in terms of reconciliation, integration, or in the end abandonment.

The contributors and I hope the discussion can play a role in communicating and supporting a reinterpretation of the meaning of cultural change and destruction. As Marie Battiste eloquently conveys, we seek to "bring voices, analyses, and dreams of a decolonized context further into the academic arena, and to urge an agenda of restoration from a multidisciplinary context of human dignity."[12] This is not a definitive work by any means, but a cross-disciplinary investigation. When I initially became interested in the topic in 1996, I had no particular goal in mind for this work as a study per se, only that I felt compelled to investigate it. My efforts over the years have deeply affected me, and it is a project that continues to disturb me for the sense of cultural loss and oppression that I often feel when I listen to Indigenous and Native Peoples talk about their relations with the Catholic Church. My response is somewhat different when I listen to non-Indian Catholic

---

[9] National Catholic Educational Association, *The People: Reflections of Native Peoples on the Catholic Experience in North America* (Washington, DC, 1992), p. 2.

[10] Frances Lord, "The Silent Eloquence of Things: The Missionary Collections and Exhibitions of the Society of Jesus in Quebec, 1843–1946," in Alvyn Austin and Jamie S. Scott (eds), *Canadian Missionaries Indigenous Peoples: Representing Religion at Home and Abroad* (Toronto, 2005): 205–34.

[11] Vine Deloria, Jr., *For this Land: Writings on Religion in America*, ed. James Treat (New York, 1999), p. 145

[12] Marie Battiste (ed.), *Reclaiming Indigenous Voice and Vision* (Vancouver, 2000), p. xxi.

clergy and practitioners discuss the integration and "help" that is now provided as part of Catholic relations with Indigenous communities. In these conversations, I often am overcome with sadness. In one instance, a Native colleague waited outside as I visited a mission in South Dakota; he couldn't bring himself to come into the church because of its history. Inside, I spoke with lay ministers regarding community relations only to leave so disturbed by the language and discussion as to implore my colleague to stop the car as we drove across the Missouri River. I needed to visit the river, not just for its power, but also for the way it can sooth and move life along. Maybe this is what Trickster helps to do best—move and smooth (or make rough) life and this mixing of traditions for us to be better able to understand the meaning and significance of Indigenous symbols and practices in the Catholic Church. We shall see where Trickster takes us; he is not an artifact of a "long dead culture," but waiting at the boundaries for the time of winning.

Kathleen J. Martin

Acknowledgements

First and foremost, I want to acknowledge all the Native and Indigenous communities that are crowded with Catholic and Christian churches and yet endeavor to maintain traditional beliefs within the pressures that are exerted. Some of the contributing authors are from these communities and their work is most important to me. Often they did not see how their work "fitted" with the text, or if their scholarly ability was up to the task. Yet I believed in the power of their efforts and felt it was essential to provide cross-disciplinary perspectives and viewpoints within a framework of study and reflection. Therefore, I am most grateful for their work and dedication. Some are long-time friends and colleagues who, when first introduced to the topic, immediately provided good words and supportive insights. This is particularly true of Jim Garrett. He willingly let me "tag along" with him on his studies of tribal bison herds and gave me the confidence to continue in what I called my "interesting project". —*Pilamayaye*.

I am most indebted to Inés Talamatez for the careful and astute guidance and attention she has provided to me and to all her students over many years. As a mentor, she has the uncanny ability to cut to the heart of matters, but also to recognize what her students need in the moment, just as she did with me on a number of occasions. I am reminded of what Vine Deloria Jr. says about insightfulness: "Indians hone right in on a person's specific feats and personal quirks and make their point with considerable precision."[1] This is Dr. Talamantez, and I am grateful for her willingness to work with me as student with precision regardless of my personal quirks or specific feats.

I am also grateful to many Indigenous collaborators and colleagues for their thoughtful consideration when I asked them if this project was interesting to them, especially those that agreed to be interviewed. Sometimes their response was, "Wow, that was a hard interview!" I most heartily thank them. There are many to name, yet the comments of one in particular stay with me. Patrick Collins (Anishinaabe), who after seeing and hearing about the project told me simply, "I wish I had thought of it." —I say, *Megwetch*. I have appreciated all whose comments are similar to his and who have willingly thought about the topic with me in conversations even when difficult—listened through presentations with attention—and tried reading earlier, sometimes incoherent, drafts. With particular acknowledgment to my friend and colleague Linda Murray (Pima) who has worked at a major university for more than twenty-five years as an educational opportunity

---

[1] Vine Deloria, Jr., Samuel Scinta, Kristen Foehner, and Barbara Deloria (eds), with foreword by Wilma Mankiller, *Spirit and Reason: The Vine Deloria, Jr., Reader* (Golden: 1999), p. 29.

counselor in an effort to recruit and retain Native students. Her persistence for something she believed too important to ignore or quit working on in the face of prejudice and discrimination should humble us all.

A number of colleagues also have provided encouragement, thoughtful consult, careful consideration, and insights and commentaries. Since I first met Steven Athanases from the University of California, Davis in 1999, our relationship has been one of mutual "like" with interests far beyond that of the academy. His supportive guidance and willingness to see beyond the obvious is fabulous! Many thanks also to all my colleagues at California Polytechnic State University, particularly Elvira Pulitano. From the moment we began as new faculty at Cal Poly in the fall of 2006, our interests and commitments to equity have converged into an esteemed friendship and collaborative relationship. As well to Angela Blaver for all the long thoughtful conversations about this effort, and to Gabrielle Tayac whose intentional listening skills in the subject of art and visual images propelled me to look more deeply. I also must acknowledge the work of Rachel Cherny, Danielle Johnson, and Jonnie Reinhold, students at Cal Poly, for their dedicated assistance with the preparation of the manuscript and exceptionally insightful perspectives. We should watch for them in graduate school and beyond. In addition, a number of Catholic colleagues willingly let me explore this topic and provided me with friendly conversations in their communities, most especially my aunts who were members of religious orders. My own Catholic upbringing led me to explore these ideas and, from the time of high school catechism classes and my challenges to the presented dogma, I have been the contentious student. This does not seem to have changed, and I am grateful for the patience and assistance that I have received.

Most of all I want to recognize my family: my husband, John B. Martin, for his encouragement and support, even when he did not know what I was doing; grandparents, parents, siblings, aunts, uncles, sisters, cousins, and all my family by virtue of extended relations (some of whom have passed on), who represent a very diverse and eclectic group of people. Of these, my daughters are most important to me: Mariah, with her ability to systematically and succinctly come to the heart of an issue and care deeply about issues of justice; Dawn, for her exuberance and intense interest in things both political and unjust, and finally Nicole, whose perseverance and ability through observation to understand complex social matters intuitively is uncanny. And, of course, I am most grateful for and to my grandchildren in whom I see the hope for new possibilities in the future and who make my heart happy. Many thanks with heartfelt appreciation. — *Toksa.*

Abbreviations

ABCFM	American Board of Commissioners for Foreign Missions
AIFRA	American Indian Freedom of Religion Act
AIHEC	American Indian Higher Education Consortium
AIM	American Indian Movement
BHA	Black Hills Alliance
CRZ	Coronado Room, Zimmerman Library, University of New Mexico, Albuquerque
DOE	United States Department of Education
GOP	Grand Old Party (Republican Party in the US)
LITF	The Lakota Inculturation Task Force created for the Catholic Dioceses of Rapid City, South Dakota
ISDEAA	Indian Self-Determination and Educational Assistance Act
NARF	Native American Rights Fund
NCEA	National Catholic Educational Association
NMAI	National Museum of the American Indian
NMNH	National Museum of Natural History
OFM	Ordo Fratrum Minorum, first order of Franciscans, Friars Minor
OSBS	Oblate Sisters of the Blessed Sacrament
RFRA	Religious Freedom Restoration Act
SANM 1-II	Spanish Archives of New Mexico
SBS	Sisters of the Blessed Sacrament
SJ	Society of Jesus (Jesuits)
USCCB	United States Conference of Catholic Bishops

Note on Cover Photo

The cover photo, entitled 'Four Directions' was part of a larger painting and graffiti art composition on a retaining wall near Mescalero, New Mexico. Photographed in 2000, the artist(s) are unknown, but the work was reportedly completed as part of a local high school art program four to five years earlier. It expresses aspects of Apache beliefs and philosophies, as well as the representation of ethics evident in other Indigenous communities. Although Catholic communities may see the Christian cross in the headdress of the figures—as with any visual studies interpretation, those with the power to do so can see and interpret what they want to see—yet, in the reality of those who created it, the Indigenous philosophical allusions are apparent.

—Photograph courtesy of Kathleen J. Martin

Notes on Terminology

The contributors to this volume have made the choice how and in what ways to use terminology to challenge the dominant hegemony regarding language usage. Often facts, pronunciations, and spellings are distorted by small incremental changes so that the original is unrecognizable. Some scholars actively choose ways to deal with linguistic oppression. Western hegemony contributes to and supports cultural destruction through the use of language to minimize people's lives. The use of capitals has been one area contested within the dominant Euro-anglo hegemony and one that has not been fully resolved. In the case of White and Black groups, for instance, Black, in reference to a person of African descent, was not capitalized, yet White was seen as a noun and proper to capitalize; this has changed. Regarding terms such as Indigenous (indigenous), Native (native), American(s) or peoples (Peoples), Euroamerican (EuroAmerican), or Anglo-American, some changes have occurred, while others have not. Therefore, the choice of terms and capitalization has been left largely to the contributors' discretion. This includes the decision to italicize or not as is the convention with foreign terms. For instance, Kanaka Maoli and Kutzadika'a are largely considered foreign terms to Western Europeans, but certainly not to Native Hawaiians or Kutzadika'a Paiute.

Introduction

"You must be new here," says Young Man Walking On Water. "You don't seem to know the rules."
What rules, says Old Woman.
"I know, I know," says Coyote. "Young Man Walking On Water is talking about Christian rules."
"Yes," I says. "That's true."
"Hooray," says Coyote. "I love Christian rules."
Christian rules, says Young Man Walking On Water. And the first rule is that no one can help me. The second rule is that no one can tell me anything. Third, no one is allowed to be in two places at once. Except me.[1]

—Thomas King

Knowing the rules and understanding them often has been more of a challenge for Catholic missionaries than for Indigenous Peoples. The ability to look with irony and humor at situations has sustained peoples through more than 500 years of contact, and has provided multiple opportunities for teasing the serious-minded. Coyote says he "loves Christian rules," yet we know what he says must be taken with the proverbial grain of caution (salt). We recognize Coyote's ways from Indigenous narratives and stories, and this knowledge is embodied not only within oral traditions, but also within facets of the arts, education, history, and political and cultural contexts. This is the basis and purpose of this volume as well: to present a juxtaposition of views, concepts, and perspectives from multiple fields, and to present stories, images, and art as metaphors for survival in a contemporary world. In it, the contributors explore current contexts and complex areas of conflict regarding missionization, appropriation, and colonizing practices through the voices of Indigenous and non-Indigenous scholars and knowledgeable consultants. As a theoretically informed examination of the use and meaning of Indigenous symbols and practices, particularly in relation to Catholic churches and the education of Indigenous students, it is unusual. The organization of this volume is designed to present the use and interpretation of images, practices, and symbols beginning with theoretical investigations of the subjects and topics, and than providing perspectives, commentaries, and examples of educational practice. Few studies present a multidisciplinary interpretation of appropriation, spiritual and religious tradition, educational issues in the teaching of art and art history, the effects of government sanctions on traditional practice, or the artistic interpretation of symbols from Indigenous perspectives. Further, the study of the Catholic Church

---

[1]   Thomas King, *Green Grass, Running Water* (New York, 1993), p. 291.

and its institution, particularly in terms of Indigenous communities, often has been deemed politically incorrect and perceived as largely unimportant at secular research institutions, an attitude still prevalent today.[2]

Some scholars attempt to broach the subject of the use of Native symbols and traditions within churches yet provide little critical commentary on the practice. In fact, a number of authors, particularly Catholic clergy and scholars, write on the use of Indigenous practices as expressions of the holy and of the similarities of thought between the two traditions. Typically, this is accomplished without examination of the larger contexts, abstract and sensory influences, and cultural conditions and impositions that frame complex social dynamics. Yet, efforts to examine differences and preface the voices of opponents to a pan-Indian mythology often are not heard. There's no doubt cultural change and adaptation happens; however, without an examination of local contexts, the influences of media, art, and literature combined with issues of power and authority, how can we begin to interpret, decipher, or study such complex matters? Sometimes the larger systemic issues that affect cultures and prohibit adaptation often prove most resistant to change and, in fact, are exceptionally durable in the face of political and economic conditions regardless of intentions.

From the vantage point of visual culture and art as socially constructed acts that reflect and perpetuate dominant ideology and interpretation, the contributors to this volume work to problematize the study and use of visual culture in a number of ways. Some of the chapters may be of more interest to you as a reader than others. However, the conclusions come from an integration of multiple perspectives and disciplines posing new ideas for the discussion of symbols and images and of Indigenous and Catholic relations. Yet, the contributors recognize that no definitive and concise answers are possible within this complex and multifaceted topic. The chapters ask readers to engage in interdisciplinary discussions that includes Indigenous studies, Native and Christian religious traditions, visual studies, and history, and in fact may pose a challenge to readers. These fields are connected in often subtle and understated ways by virtue of the social and cultural links that frame the disciplines. Our hope in writing on the topics from these perspectives is that it will lead us to an engaging discussion of the effects of colonization, missionization, and appropriation with attention to nuance and thought. Similar to the experiences of North American Native Peoples whose lives have been impacted by multiple forces—Christian missionaries, governmental policies, immigration and colonization, education, assimilation, and acculturation—we ask

---

[2]   This idea is paraphrased from the recent work of Gastón Espinosa and Mario García regarding Mexican American religions in the United States, a significant and valuable contribution to the literature. Most certainly it can be applied, maybe with even more emphasis, to Indigenous and/or Native traditions in which the discussion can be more complex given the number and degree of Native traditions, and then coupled with colonial policies of assimilation and Christian conversion. See Gastón Espinosa and Mario García (eds.), *Mexican American Religions: Spirituality, Activism, and Culture* (Durham, 2008).

you the reader to think about the multiple disciplines that frame our understanding and knowledge of social conditions. It is not possible to simply look at Native and Catholic traditions and make comparisons regarding similarities and differences. It also is not possible to contextualize simply between the historical past and the evolving present. There are a number of factors that influence these conditions. However, from these perspectives, we ask that you explore connections, reflect on possibilities, and engage in an interdisciplinary discussion of Indigenous and Catholic relations. We endeavor to add more information and awareness to a topic that reflects a social experience in which some disdain and reject changes to traditional practices, but whose interpretations and voices typically are not heard.

Each of the chapters presents interpretations and commentaries on current contexts and missionary activities in relation to the study of visual culture, as well as to incorporate particular ideas of Native and Indigenous art and power as reflected in symbols and epistemologies. A number of the chapters break new ground and the authors speak from personal and cultural experiences regarding the topics. They keenly explore the critical intersections among visual studies, the impact of Christianity in Indigenous communities, and the educational paradigms that may foster success and relevance for Indigenous students and communities in the future. At the heart of their work is a desire to provide a context for discussion that illuminates the lives of people so that conscious choices can be made and awareness of the issues heightened. Some of the chapters set the context and history of the use of Indigenous symbols and practices within an historical and visual studies milieu, as well as to provide examples of differences between Native and Euroamerican interpretations and understandings. Others offer commentaries, research investigations, stories and personal experiences, and reflections on educational practice. Together they provide perspectives on appropriation, education, and the roles visual symbols play in instantiating the status quo and contributing to cultural destruction. In the discussions, the contributors pose questions such as: Have the Christianizing and educational policies toward Indigenous communities of the past changed in measurable ways? In what ways can personal and cultural narratives help further our understanding of social and political relationships? And, if, as has been noted, "art informs life" and instantiates beliefs, than what effects can be observed in photographs, language, and current educational and Christian contexts to provide evidence of either change or maintenance of the historical status quo?

Chapter 1 provides an introduction and overview to issues of resistance and change, missionization and visual studies. It offers a discussion of the ways that the past 40–50 years, and in particular the decades of the 1960s and 1970s, fostered a resurgence of Native traditions and activism, as well as the institution of the Catholic ecumenical movement. These movements often times acted in opposition to each other and, as such, provided necessary and important resistance and tension that helped to balance the politicizing and missionizing processes. Christians often suggest that both Native and Catholic traditions operate from similar underlying beliefs and cultural prescriptions. The chapter examines this assumption and provides a framework for the study of visual images as a way of analyzing and discussing differences, issues of appropriation and missionization, and the influences of Western ideology.

Chapters 2 and 3 by James Garrett and James Jeffries respectively, present a juxtaposition of centuries that stimulates an interesting comparative study of the difficulty of ideological change and the continuing contexts of conversion and appropriation. In Chapter 2, "Spiritual Freedom, Pious Appropriation", Garrett examines the current context and ironies of United States history, and the historical and political context of the American Indian Religious Freedom Act of 1978. Enhanced through a discussion based in personal experience and knowledge of the political struggles for equality and fairness of the 1970s specifically, Garrett presents current representations and policies explored through the lens of philosophical and epistemological differences. An image of the medicine wheel (Figure 2.1), as created in a garden at a tribal college, affords an example for comparison when discussing these differences. By way of contrast, Jeffries examines purposeful misinterpretations of manitou customs by Jesuits in the seventeenth century in Chapter Three. He takes on the problem of the comparative study of religion presented through the lens of seventeenth-century French accounts of Native Americans and sets it within the context of European thought and practice. Moreover, by reading the histories of New France and what the early French observers denied, scholars propagated a Christian missionary discourse under the false pretense of comparison. Yet, as Jeffries concludes, the Jesuits understood Native spirituality and practice. By contrasting the two chapters, we see evidence across the centuries of the same philosophies with little change to existing policies of conversion or co-optation, and the many similarities between Native beliefs across the centuries.

In Chapter 4, C. Kalani Beyer investigates the religious transformation of the Hawaiian culture during the nineteenth century in four sections: the traditional religion during the ʻāikapu era; the spread of Christianity during the ʻāinoa era; the interference from Christian rivals; and the decline of Calvinist influence. While early ethnographers concluded that Native Hawaiians were entirely devoid of religion, contemporary ethnohistorians and scholars of religion insist they were and are thoroughly religious. Beyer seeks to address this issue more specifically and answer the questions: Why does missionary influence decline among the Hawaiian people during the nineteenth and twentieth century? What has been the religious climate of Hawaiʻi? And, how did traditionalist practices survive until the more recent decades? Further, Beyer provides evidence that, although Native beliefs went "underground" for a period of time, Hawaiian families continued to worship the spirits and in some cases combined traditional practice with Catholic beliefs. With the rise and institution of *Ka Lahui Hawaiʻi*, the author concludes with an interpretation of the ways current generations of Hawaiians are seeking to regain their Native lands and re-establish themselves as a self-governing people.

Larry Taylor's investigation of archival imagery in Chapter 5 provides insights from the perspective of art history and the use of photography as a means of justifying cultural oppression. Taylor presents astute reinterpretations of two specific images (Figures 5.1 and 5.2) from before and after the 1890 Wounded Knee Massacre. As editor, I debated with Taylor the value of including images that reflect such a sensitive issue as that of the 1890 Ghost Dance, and we struggled with the representations of such a contested and heinous history. We contacted other Native academics and colleagues, particularly Lakota, seeking their feelings and impressions on the images and issues. Based on their input, we choose to utilize the two dance images as a way of countering the political context and cultural implications that remain part of the dominant ideology; one that maintains these images in their unanalyzed forms, seldom with any kind of reinterpretation in terms of Lakota constructs, ideas or beliefs. A goal of Chapter 5 is to do just this through the interpretive field of visual studies. It is designed to help us understand the power of images for their destructive and hurtful presence and power, and to work to provide more nuanced and accurate interpretations. The dance images illustrated with text inscribed on the original photograph most likely were taken without the knowledge and permission of the participants, and then they were mislabeled and misused by a non-Indian public in desperate need of justification for the killings and attempted eradication of Lakota People. Methods of visual studies critique and analysis illuminate the ways repositories such as the National Anthropological Archives continue to help maintain negative public images of Native Peoples, even if they attempt to dispel them. Of particular importance to this volume is the idea that explication of the visual is necessary and words alone cannot suffice to describe and explain. The visual needs descriptive and interpretive words, as well as visual images, and the two work together *intertexually*. Often— as with these images—words defined images of the past, and they continue to define interpretations of them in the present.

Chapter 6 by David Toole examines the ironic complexity of some of the very issues presented in this volume. It is a discussion both emotionally and realistically charged with thought-provoking dialogue regarding cultural change and social construction. Toole explores the ironies inherent in the power to describe and grapples with the multilayered dimensions of change. Embedded in the discussion are issues related to power, such as the power—to define—to discuss—to determine—and ultimately, to decide the language we use and the paradigm for discussion we choose both in textual and public spaces. Through a close examination of the work of Jonathon Lear's *Radical Hope* and Toole's more recent experiences at the National Museum of the American Indian (NMAI), he poses conflicting and somewhat disturbing interpretations of the current influence of textual and visual interpretations regarding Native America and the future of Christianity. Grappling with these issues is not easy, nor are they possible to ignore.

In Chapter 7, Kathleen Martin examines and investigates imagery displayed in Catholic churches through interviews with Native consultants who reflect on and discuss their interpretations and perceptions. Martin investigates visual culture and the study of art or image as objects that influence interpretations and contribute to socially constructed meanings. She poses ideas regarding visual culture and art as significant to the reinterpretation of cultural traditions and provides examples of community relations with the Catholic Church. Through consultants' interpretations and perspectives, and photographic examples from churches, the adaptation and use of objects and images by the Church can be seen as a way to access power for a specific purpose.

Chapters 8 and 9 work in tandem to specifically critique and pose alternatives to the education of Indigenous students in the areas of art and art history. Herman Pi'ikea Clark's discussion of 'Kauhale Theory' in Chapter 8 is an educational philosophy for visual theory based on research and grounded in Kanaka Maoli 'Indigenous Hawaiian' cultural metaphor. It supports the notion that Indigenous metaphors and meanings are reflected in art and cultural objects, and these meanings differ significantly from Western interpretations. Developed as a viable alternative to state and federally mandated approaches to art and art education that historically marginalize Kanaka Maoli knowledge, Clark imparts the Kauhale theory and offers the opportunity to learn and adapt the teaching of art within a traditional epistemology. The historical background against which Kauhale theory was developed and imagined is derived from cultural perspectives, values, and aspirations of Kanaka Maoli people; it is the "people speaking" and an expression of experience. Clark provides examples and specific ways of knowing, inquiry and investigation, and teaching and learning that reflect a viable medium and "doorway to knowing" that is fully integrated with life.

Karen Willeto and Delvin Slick present Diné interpretations of the sacred and educational practices that reflect the Diné educational philosophy of *Sá'ah Naagháí Bik'eh Hózhóó* in Chapter 9. Willeto and Slick focus on the teaching and learning of photography within this philosophy and the ways images in everyday life and the choice of images photographed reflect an awareness and comprehension of the sacred. They ask readers to reflect on questions from their own experiences such as: What do we see? How do we interpret what we see? What does the photographer's eye capture? And how does this relate to our perceptions of the sacred, particularly from a Diné perspective? By way of example the chapter includes several of Slick's black-and-white photographs and his corresponding interpretations of the sacred as evidenced in the images. This merging of Diné educational philosophy with coursework and assignments designed to engage the students and develop their expertise is firmly located within the Diné teaching and learning philosophy of *Sá'ah Naagháí Bik'eh Hózhóó*, a philosophy applicable for all courses and educational settings, as well as for life.

Angela Blaver explores the intersection between Christianity and the Mono Basin Paiute in Chapter 10 through personal experiences, narratives, and interviews with Kutzadika'a Paiute. Blaver specifically addresses issues regarding death and burial practices, and changes brought by Christians to the Mono Lake Paiute community in California in three successive waves of contact and incursion by the Spanish, Mexicans, and Americans as "the outsiders". Similar to instances in the southwest United States, Native contact with missionaries in California has been quite extensive and prolonged. Native Peoples of California have been used as cheap labor sources, portrayed as victims, missionized, and ultimately determined to be obstructions standing in the way of development, particularly that of land, water, and natural resources.

Bernardo Gallegos, in Chapter 11, enriches the discussion of Catholic and Indigenous identity by arguing that the Comanche dances and Genizaro practices of New Mexico are essentially impossible to separate into two components of hybrid identities and practices. The discussion of his family's experiences chronicles and documents elements of a long and complex history of relations among cultures in the southwest United States and the Catholic Church. Deeply embedded in the history of Pueblo and Catholic traditions and relations, when borders were not defined as in current constructions and the lives of people were often ignored or minimized, the discussion presents a theoretical interpretation grounded and focused in family and personal experiences. Gallegos' sensitive and nuanced discussions pay attention to the 'efficacy of ritual as pedagogy' from both Indigenous and Catholic Franciscan systems of practice.

Chapter 12, "Trickster's Art and Artifice," presents concluding thoughts on the contributors' efforts and poses interpretations for the future that provide recommendations and commentaries, recapitulation of the ideas, and suggestions for further study of the topics. Taken as a whole, the chapters represent the integration of multiple fields of study as a way to explore the issues from within a social and cultural context surrounded and enmeshed in political and contemporary issues.

A few qualifications prior to opening a dialogue around the topics presented in this volume are necessary and important to identify. First, this is not meant as a treatise for or against personally held beliefs either Native or Catholic since each individual has the right to choose their spiritual practice and to make assessments about their understanding of the world and life in general. Andrea Smith notes, "Even Natives raised with a more traditional worldview do not always feel the need to reject Christianity outright, even as they criticize its abuses."[3] It also is not meant as a challenge or critique of those who would engage in both Catholic and Indigenous practices, either fully integrated, side-by-side, or as separate practices. For many Native Catholics, there is limited or no conflict since there is an acceptance and flexibility in interpretation, and there are multiple ways of knowing or encountering the sacred.

A second qualification is that complete assessment of relations between Catholic dioceses in Indigenous communities is not the aim—or within the scope of possibility—of this volume. Instead, we desire to enrich the discussion with critical reflections through examples of Catholic Church contexts examined through the lens of historical and organizational theories, discussions of art and literature, theorizing from abstract ideas and concepts, and examples from real world communities. The discussions are set within a context of power and

---

[3]   Andrea Smith, "Walking in Balance: The Spirituality-Liberation Praxis of Native Women," in Jace Weaver (ed.), *Native American Religious Identity* (Maryknoll, 2002), p. 182.

hegemony that contributes to and maintains power over communities, as well as makes it difficult to examine without attention to these influences.

And finally, regardless of the efforts of Native, Catholic, or Indigenous peoples, the context for oppression and suppression of Indigenous philosophies and epistemologies is maintained through Christianizing and educational practices that foster and support a dominant Western ideology and that limits the exploration of those that are specifically Indigenous. We hope to address some of these conflicts, contexts, and inconsistencies, and provide interpretations and possibilities for the future, but certainly not all.

Kathleen J. Martin

Chapter 1

Resistance and Change: Visual Culture, Missionization and Appropriation

Kathleen J. Martin

In the past, Indigenous responses to a variety of evangelizing and conversion attempts have led to a complex set of conditions and differences between and among communities. Some Catholics and scholars have attributed the differences to the variety and number of Indigenous communities with their own belief systems and practices. Still others attribute it to the weather and climate (since in warmer climes it was easier for Church officials to "maintain oversight and supervision"); to the amount of destruction and death due to disease; to the length and degree of contact (as with tribal communities who first met the newcomers); to the number of Indigenous people who actively support and evangelize for the Church; to political policies and legal practices.[1] Yet these ideas concern past evangelizing processes. The purpose of this chapter is to look more recently at social, political, and visual contexts in a number of areas as particularly relevant for an examination and discussion of Catholic missionary and Indigenous relations over the past fifty years. Although some of the topics have been discussed in greater depth elsewhere, this chapter is designed to provide an overview of the discussions from an interdisciplinary perspective. It situates the discussion within social and historical movements by examining the topics through visual studies research to provide a grounding for the chapters, as well as a basis for investigating ideas and perspectives.

---

[1] For historical discussions of missionaries in the New World, see, for example: Gauvin Alexander Bailey, *Art on the Jesuit Missions in Asia and Latin America, 1542–1773* (Toronto, 1999); Carole Blackburn, *Harvest of Souls: The Jesuit Missions and Colonialism in North America, 1632–1650* (Montreal, 2000); Angelyn Dries, OSF, *The Missionary Movement in American Catholic History* (Maryknoll, 1998); John W. Grant, *Moon in Wintertime: Missionaries and the Indians of Canada in Encounter since 1534* (Toronto, 1984); Nicholas Griffiths and Fernando Cervantes, *Spiritual Encounters: Interactions between Christianity and Native Religions in Colonial America* (Lincoln, 1999); Alvyn Austin and Jamie S. Scott (eds.), *Canadian Missionaries Indigenous Peoples: Representing Religion at Home and Abroad* (Toronto, 2005); George Tinker, *Missionary Conquest: The Gospel and Native American Cultural Genocide* (Minneapolis, 1993); Christopher Vecsey, *On the Padres' Trail* (Notre Dame, 1996).

There is a continuous and lengthy stream of possibilities that are raised to suggest the complexity and variety of Indigenous and Catholic contexts arising from the impact of conquest and ongoing colonization and missionization. In the United States, it is stimulated and supported by a legal system that often serves its own motives and ends more than that of Native Peoples.[2] In the past, contact, conversion efforts, and legal mandates were largely instituted and applied to Indigenous Peoples with little opportunity for active decision-making and agency. More recently, viewpoints regarding these contexts and situations assume an end to racist attitudes regarding Indigenous beliefs, as well as the implied sense that changes have occurred regarding policies of colonization, assimilation, and missionization. Although there are conditions that have contributed to the perception of change as well as stimulated real change such as increased educational opportunities, political activism, influence in the courts, and increased control over natural resources, Indigenous communities continue to grapple with paternalism and parochial ideologies. The assumptions and perceptions of change that were initiated and stimulated may be attributed in part to the efforts of two organizations during the 1960s: the American Indian Movement and the Catholic Church. In some overt ways, these organizations worked in opposition to each other, which contributed to forms of active resistance. The efforts and current status of the two organizations continue to appear to be at crossed purposes, yet they somewhat mirror each other. The following provides a brief examination of these two movements as a way of setting the context for over the past forty-plus years and the history that has contributed to the perception that change is no longer needed and missionization is a thing of the past.

Organizational Movements in the 1960s: AIM and the Catholic Church

The formation and organization of movements in the 1960s such as the American Indian Movement and the ecumenical movement by the Catholic Church after the Second Vatican Council (1962–65) were designed to address the history of physical abuse and cultural genocide, prohibitions against traditional practices, mis-education of Native youth, and assimilation policies of the past. In Minneapolis in 1968, Clyde Bellacourt, George Mitchell, Eddie Benton Benai, and Dennis Banks founded the "Concerned Indian Americans," which soon became the American Indian Movement (AIM). The organization was founded out of concern for the desperation and deplorable conditions of Native Peoples living in some of the larger cities in the United States and Canada, but particularly those in the United States most affected by the relocation and termination programs of the 1950s and 1960s. Peter Matthiessen quoted a member of the movement as saying, "AIM wasn't so much an organization as a level of conscience, of commitment to our

---

[2]   See Jace Weaver (ed.), *Native American Religious Identity: Unforgotten Gods* (Maryknoll, 2002).

Indian People."[3] This commitment included addressing issues of employment, social services, legal rights, protection from police abuse and brutality, and the education of Native students initially in kindergarten through twelfth grades.[4] AIM also integrated into the education of Native students a revival of traditional practices and ceremonies by leaders such as Wallace Black Elk, Frank Fools Crow, Pete Catches, Leonard Crow Dog, and John Fire Lame Deer among others. For many, these efforts as well as others have contributed to a sustained revival of traditional practices aimed at the education and development of Native youth through programs such as Native-way Schools, Elders conferences, and the Indigenous Women's Network. Although it is not possible to name all of those who were influential, two examples are illustrative of Indigenous efforts. Eddie Benton Benai, a founder of the Red Schoolhouse and an Anishinaabe Midewiwin spiritual leader in Minneapolis, and Vern Harper and Pauline Shirt, founders of First Nations School (formerly Wandering Spirit Survival School) in Toronto, designed schools to provide Native and First Nations students with curriculums oriented toward Native culture and traditions. AIMs efforts and impact in education and traditional renewal are still in evidence today.

During this same period, the Catholic Church instituted changes in policies and practices designed to mitigate the negative effects of missionizing and assimilation policies, and to present a new attitude regarding its role in Indigenous communities. After the Second Vatican Council, the Church actively adopted policy changes designed to be reflective of "inclusion" and openness to the religious beliefs of others. These efforts, combined with the subsequent Roman Instruction of 1994, speak of enculturation with sincere approval, if not enthusiasm, albeit with cautionary language regarding any "syncretism" of traditions.[5] For some American Catholics, the changes instituted a crisis of identity that led to confusion about their faith and past relations with other spiritual and religious traditions. The call for better relations with nonbelievers, greater openness to the beliefs of others, and more democratic collegiality initiated this identity confusion and may have contributed to the loss of active participation by Catholics in general.[6] Efforts to apologize and engage in discussions with Indigenous Peoples, in some

---

[3]   Peter Matthiessen, *In the Spirit of Crazy Horse*, Afterword by Martin Garbus (New York, 1999), p. 577.

[4]   Within a short time, this also included postsecondary education at tribal colleges. The American Indian Higher Education Consortium (AIHEC) was founded in 1972 by the first six tribal college presidents, now totaling thirty-six. President Carter signed into law the Tribally Controlled Community College Act in 1978.

[5]   Joseph P. Swain, "Inculturating liturgical music," *America* (13 September 2004): 14.

[6]   Philip Gleason, "The Catholic Church in American Public Life in the Twentieth Century," *Logos*, 3/4 (Fall 2000): 85–99. For a more in depth discussion, see, for example: R. Laurence Moore, *Selling God: American Religion in the Marketplace of Culture* (New York, 1994); Michael L. Budde, *The (Magic) Kingdom of God: Christianity and Global Culture Industries* (Boulder, 1997).

cases, created an internal conflict for missionaries, as well as Catholics who tried to balance between the goals of a mission and conversion practices, and efforts toward ecumenism.[7]

The language of Vatican II affected missionaries in particular by charging them to reconsider "the attitude of Catholicism to non-Christian religious traditions, lessening the tone of condemnation toward them and seeking reconciliation."[8] In terms of organizational theory, the charge of Vatican II called for individuals who were vested in Church principles to change historical policies and practices, something difficult to do without "buy-in" from staff. In general, clergy remained reticent and skeptical of the changes, and, as Christopher Vecsey remarks:

> Even if missionaries were willing to acknowledge the integrity of cultures, they were not eager to espouse relativism when it came to the question of religions. The whole history of Christian missionization was bound up in the claim that Christianity as a system exists *sui generis*. According to the Church, the Indian should not be allowed to think that aboriginal religion was comparable to true faith.[9]

This thinking remains in evidence. However, some clergy in the 1970s and 1980s eagerly embraced the inclusion of Native traditions and practices in Church services. For instance, church buildings were remodeled and brought in line with traditional Native and Indigenous structures, and objects and images were used and employed as decoration. Native Catholics were actively recruited for spiritual orders, particularly the priesthood, something almost unheard of in the Catholic Church in previous decades with the exception of catechists, deacons, and oblates.[10] However, even in recent years the impact of recruitment efforts into the priesthood has been minimal. Few Native vocations exist, and reports of difficulty for Native people entering the ministry, such as hiding tribal affiliations while in the seminary, continue to surface.[11]

---

[7]   William K. Powers suggests that "ecumenism" is a process in which spiritual ideas are "freely transmitted to another with the hope or agreement that there will be some form of reciprocity, … and it is frequently associated with monotheistic movements whose leaders announce a movement is taking place for the sake of mankind." *Beyond the Vision: Essays on American Indian Culture* (Norman, 1987), p. 147.

[8]   Christopher Vecsey, *Where the Two Roads Meet* (Durham, 1999), p. 49.

[9]   Vecsey, *Where the Two Roads Meet*, p. 111.

[10]   Christopher Vecsey reports that currently there are no Oglala Lakota Catholic priests. Gerald Clifford and Emil Her Many Horses were seminarians, but they did not receive full ordination. C.P. Jordan, a Rosebud Sioux fluent in Lakota, served at Holy Rosary and St. Francis. For further discussion of the recruitment of Native Peoples to religious orders, and as an initial starting point, see Vecsey, *Where the Two Roads Meet*.

[11]   Rev. Donald Pelotte (Abenaki) rose from poverty and was ordained as the first Native Catholic bishop in 1986. However, even in this diocese, difficulties have existed

Critics have interpreted the policy changes initiated during Vatican II and continuing to the present as ways to "save faith (or face)" given the Church's historic role in Indigenous communities, especially those most affected by missionization.[12] They also have been interpreted as attempts at co-optation of AIM and subsequent groups who would actively strive to separate Indigenous and Catholic practices. For instance, some churches financially supported AIM during the civil rights era for what may have been politically expedient reasons. And some AIM members compared the Sundance with taking communion in the Christian denomination—a parallel that Vine Deloria charged has absolutely no validity whatsoever.[13] Yet, when examining these two organizations, the indication of conflict and resistance between the organizations and its members is evident even given the presence of colonialist mentality and efforts to accomplish directives surrounding religion and traditional practices. On the one hand, as an organization AIM attempted to separate from the effects of Christianity as an enemy of Indigenous Peoples, yet individuals continued to struggle with the internalized effects of missionization and colonization. On the other hand, the Catholic Church sought ecumenism as a way to apologize for the detrimental actions of the past. However, it did not want to eliminate standards and policies designed to preserve Catholicism and subsume Indigenous traditions, yet practicing Catholics were sometimes at a loss as to their roles and responsibilities. In both cases, individuals struggled with conflicting purposes, histories, and effects that challenged individual identities and called for the formation of new ones.

More recently, both the Catholic Church and AIM are perceived through different lenses than they were early in the civil rights movement of the 1960s. The Catholic Church continues to struggle with effectiveness due to recent court judgments and decisions regarding physical and emotional abuses, waning membership, and the increased need to respect and incorporate the beliefs of others. Physical abuses by clergy and resulting legal issues have diminished power and influence, as well as the financial resources of the Church significantly.[14] Most

---

that precluded individuals from acknowledging their Native heritage for fear of retribution. Rev. Pelotte resigned in April 2008 after suffering a "fall" under suspicious circumstances. *Las Cruces Sun News* (30 April 2008), www.lcsun-news.com/ci_9104967 (accessed 21 July 2008).

[12] Saving faith becomes an important idea for two reasons: one, the majority of churches in reservation communities in the United States are losing membership, and two, it can be interpreted as a way of getting more members. Saving faith and face in an era of apology becomes a likely metaphor to describe the Church's attempts at missionization.

[13] Vine Deloria, Jr., *God Is Red* (Golden, 1973/2003), p. 53.

[14] See, for example: "Legal Affairs Involving American Indians," *Dakota-Lakota-Nakota Human Rights Advocacy Coalition* (12 April 2003), www.dlncoalition.org/dln_issues/2003march12.htm (accessed 17 January 2009); "Sexual Abuse and Catholic Church's Civil Liability," *Religion Newswriters* (24 June 2002), www.religionlink.org/tip_020624c.php (accessed 17 January 2009).

importantly, the coming to light of these abuses has reduced the level of public trust and "faith" contributing to what can be described minimally as diminished organizational effectiveness. Yet the Church maintains a strong presence in Native communities if not from active Catholic participation, than from the standpoint of landholdings, educational facilities, and the sheer longevity of relations that continues to provide a presence hard to dispel or ignore.

On the other hand, the effectiveness of AIM as an organization and its presence in the public arena also has waned due to a variety of factors that include external pressures from largely US government agencies and internal organizational conflicts. Internal struggles affect the ability of an organization to deal with conflicts within and external to the group. This sometimes includes damage done to individuals by outside pressures and actions. As Andrea Smith notes:

> Native activists have found that it is impossible to maintain the fight for liberation without a simultaneous movement to heal the damage done by colonization. Much of the American Indian Movement's drug and alcohol abuse and mistreatment of women can be attributed to the fact that its male leadership did not deal with the impact of colonization on their psyches.[15]

However, AIMs goals of increased educational opportunities for children, knowledge and practice of traditions, and issues of sovereignty have continued. As John Trudell and a number of others have observed, "The lasting effect of it was that it made the spirit of the people stronger."[16] It also has provided a model for opposition and resistance to the continuing effects of colonization and marginalization, but possibly more significantly the impetus and foundation for the larger movement toward Indigenousness and Indigeneity in the twenty-first century.

It is within the contexts of these dual purposes and conflicts, and the complex forces at work for more than 40 years that these two organizations have played a significant role in the investigation, reframing, reinterpretation, and challenging of Catholic and Indigenous relations today. During the 1960s and 1970s, both organizations maintained high levels of credibility, active engagement, continuing challenges to each other's roles, and resistance. More recently, both are perceived as ineffective within a social context in which the need for resistance to missionization and colonizing activities is assumed to be minimal. With this background providing the impetus for change in relations and the subsequent efforts, we examine some of the current contexts and use of Indigenous symbols and practices in the Catholic Church with the idea that co-optation is never a direct line and that subtle influences over time are difficult to follow without the perspective of hindsight.

---

[15]   See Andrea Smith, "Walking in Balance: The Spirituality-Liberation Praxis of Native Women," in Weaver (ed.), *Native American Religious Identity: Unforgotten Gods* (Maryknoll, 2002), p. 194.

[16]   John Trudell in a film by Heather Rae, *Trudell* (Appaloosa Pictures, 2005).

Setting the Contexts for Discussion

Personal Context

A number of years ago, when I first began working on my dissertation on the Cheyenne River Sioux Reservation in South Dakota, I was living with a friend of my aunt's. They both are members of the Sisters of the Presentation of the Blessed Virgin Mary, a Catholic religious order that originated in Ireland. My aunt passed away in 1996 before seeing the completion of my dissertation, something she helped to start, and her friend recently retired from teaching at a college on the reservation. I discovered two interesting aspects while living with this small group of nuns in South Dakota. The first is the assumption by people in the community that I too am a nun with the incumbent attitude of "hands-off" or at least of differential respect and guarded communications. The second is the opportunity to hear what visiting Catholics think, encounter, or believe about the local community. Regarding the first, I did entertain the idea of becoming a member of my aunt's religious order when I was in high school, and I am no stranger to people thinking I followed that path. Therefore, this aspect proved less interesting to me, and now, as a non-practicing Catholic, it is something I am prepared to handle.

The second aspect proved more challenging since comments by Catholic visitors often reflected Eurocentric notions about the world. Some visitors wondered rhetorically, "Why isn't there any grass in the yards?" Or, "When will they ever move those old cars parked near the front door?" Others questioned, "When are 'they' going to learn to take care of things?" Lay catechists came to the reservation to "help" and simply believed that they could "whip people into shape," maybe even Christ's shape. (I may be struck down for blasphemy for this comment.) I remember one particular example in which a lay catechist who came for the summer went out to visit one of the full-blood communities on the reservation armed with ideas and directions for local Catholics to take to better themselves. With gusto and exuberance at the church meeting, she outlined her plan. However, she did not receive much indication of agreement or head-nodding from the audience members. Finally, after no small amount of effort, she turned to one of the Lakota leaders in the back of the room, and said, "You're behind me on this, right?" His response was quick-witted and to the point, "Yes, but waaaay back." In many ways, his response sets the stage for our discussion regarding the ideas and directions sent to and impressed upon Native and Indigenous communities both in the past and during the present time: "We're here, but way back." It also is indicative of concern for the demands of participation coupled with a patience that encourages an attitude of "Let's wait and see what happens." This may be particularly true regarding appropriation, missionization, and the Catholic Church since, like many things that can be ephemeral and short-lived, things change.

The idea of "way back" encompasses a number of conditions and situations that are reflective of almost five and a half centuries of contact in terms of government actions, education, and missionization. Sometimes these include coercive engagement in various institutions, meetings, and treaty signings in which the threats of physical harm were not only real but also imminent. Other times, it is indicative of situations when Native presence was solicited and encouraged by government agencies, but comments, suggestions, and leadership of the meeting itself were not. For example, in 2000 I attended a US Department of Education (DOE) meeting of American Indian and Alaskan Native educational leaders and scholars. By the end of the first morning of meetings, some of the Native scholars in attendance suggested that a change be made to the program agenda. They wanted it to be more relevant to current concerns of Native educators and the students their communities serve. DOE representatives, however, felt their agenda already was relevant and suggested that it might be possible to change it on the last day of the conference. This suggestion was met with little enthusiasm and many of the attendees stood up to leave. However, Dr. Michael Pavel (Skokomish) took the microphone and posed other considerations for the meeting, albeit utilizing the DOE original agenda.[17] He encouraged people to remain at the meeting and to continue to work toward ensuring fairness in the treatment and education of Native students. However, the agenda for the meeting changed little with the view from the "back" of the room. The conference culminated with a Pueblo educator pulling out his copy of the 1928 Merriam Report and asking when *these* educational recommendations for Native students would be addressed.

The history of Christian missionization in the "New World," like education issues, is far from simple or limited to one religious denomination. Yet, when we examine the history of Catholic evangelization, we can look at the specifics of one group and their actions in Native and Indigenous communities. Participation, if we can use this term, in Catholic missionization has proceeded through a series of stages and time periods such as violent conversion, government enforcement of assimilation policies, removal of children to Church-affiliated boarding schools, and a number of other policies and practices designed to eradicate Native identities and traditions. The oral and historical records provide examples of Native Peoples who adopted or were baptized as Catholics by force or preference. These records indicate severe abuse for associating with non-Catholic Natives in their communities. Missionaries justified this treatment by claiming Native traditions were the ignorant work of the devil, and those newly converted must be separated from those not yet civilized. Dancing was equated with the influence of Satan, and those who disobeyed by participating in or even speaking about traditional

---

[17]   Associate Professor at Washington State University, Dr. Pavel—along with his efforts to bridge the divide between Indigenous knowledge systems and contemporary society—is well known. Many in the audience were aware of his work on issues of American Indian and Alaska Native access and achievement in higher education. More recently, he is Tradition Bearer of the Southern Puget Salish and member of the Skokomish Tribal Nation, member of the Council of 100 Distinguished Native Scholars, Leaders and Elders, and 2007 Ecotrust award finalist. See www.ecotrust.org/indigenousleaders/2007/michael_pavel.html (accessed 17 January 2009).

ceremonies often were jailed.[18] This view was not only from the back, but from the outside. The opportunity to actually change or influence policy did not exist and was violently suppressed by Catholic authorities and government agents who sometimes were the same person.

Following the years since Vatican II and the policies of the 1990s, "new" processes of missionization have been the subjects of Native and Catholic relations. Inculturation and enculturation are terms now used in proselytizing or what some have referred to as appropriation and syncretism. Church representatives in Native communities attempt to include practices and traditions through dialogue and incorporation into services. However, the view remains somewhat from the back—Native Catholics have limited agency, and inculturation and enculturation come from adoption, not specifically collaboration and participation, in defining policies and practices. For example, William Stolzman's discussion of the "Medicine Men and Pastor's Meetings" in *The Pipe and Christ* attempts to balance multiple Native and Catholic perspectives respectfully.[19] The text details six years of dialogues between Rosebud medicine men such as Frank Picket Pin, Charles Kills Enemy, and George Eagle Elk, as well as others,[20] and the majority of the Catholic pastors stationed on the Rosebud and Pine Ridge Reservations at the time. The text underscores the differences between the two groups, while focusing on the commonalities. It attempts to present the ideas in a fair and equivocal manner based on the notion that the participants were there to understand one another.[21] This specifically was Stolzman's goal as chairman and a statement he used to begin the meetings to minimize conflict or disagreements among the participants. Given the fact that it was not one of the medicine men leading the discussions and acting as chairman, we are left with the feeling that the outcome of these meetings and the conclusions referred to in the text may have been different if conducted and written by one of the other participants. A comment by Ben Black Bear who participated in the meetings is illustrative. He found it ironic that the priests were embracing some Lakota beliefs that were becoming less important to contemporary Lakota, but were used to promote comparisons between the two traditions.[22]

---

[18]   Jordan Paper, *Offering Smoke: The Sacred Pipe and Native American Religion* (Edmonton, 1989), p. 110.

[19]   The meetings began in January of 1973 and ended in 1979. Meetings were typically held every other week for nine months of the year with from six to twelve medicine men attending. Often, there were 30 to 40 people present including community members, consultants, and clergy. See William Stolzman, *The Pipe and Christ: A Christian–Sioux Dialogue*, 5th edn. (Chamberlain, 1995).

[20]   Leonard Crow Dog's attendance is listed as sporadic due to his AIM association. However, Matthiessen indicates that Crow Dog advocated for the "running off of priests, in order that the Indians can return to original Indian religion and medicine men." Matthiessen, *In the Spirit*, p. 216.

[21]   Stolzman, *The Pipe and Christ*.

[22]   Vecsey, *Where the Two Roads Meet*, p. 56.

A goal of this volume is to present views, not from the back, but from authority, intention, and direction from perspectives of authorship and representation, and to pose theoretical and contextual examples that provide insight into the societal influences and complex forces at work. Although there have been discussions regarding the fluidity of culture and what some have called the "cultural turn," these abstract philosophical ideas typically do not refer to the actual lives of people. Rather, they present a view from the collective not based in people or their ways of being in the world. These philosophies often force individuals to take a "back seat" to the social, political, intellectual, and cultural forces acting upon them.[23] This includes the appropriation and syncretism of images and symbols in contexts removed from their source, and the argued validity of doing so as part of the natural process of fluidity of culture, cultural adaptation, and ecumenism. In this volume, we attempt to present another side of the discussion, not from out of the context or "way back," but from the center as a way to excavate the individual from this "predicament of marginality-billed as centrality."[24] One in which a closer examination of the forces of power and authority is needed to examine the process of change and the ways it is materially significant to the lives and actions of real people. This goal includes the presentation of perspectives often not heard due to a variety of factors: some withheld out of respect for people of both Native and Catholic traditions, others consciously silenced by those who would set guidelines for interaction.

Traditions and the Traditional

Past and present visual images, epistemologies, traditions, history, and social cognitive frameworks inform experience and construct the worlds we live in, as well as framing beliefs we hold about the world. Some scholars attempt to broach the subject of the use of Native symbols and traditions within churches yet provide little critical commentary on the practice itself. In fact, a number of authors, particularly Catholic clergy and scholars, write on the use of Indigenous practices as expressions of the holy and of the similarities of thought between Native and Christian religious traditions. Typically, this is accomplished with limited reflection or examination of the larger contexts and abstract influences and conditions in the communities most affected. Christians suggest that both traditions operate from similar underlying beliefs and cultural prescriptions. This assumption proclaims that Christians and Natives are worshipping the same thing, that which is holy and of the same God, effectively minimizing and limiting the exchange of ideas and interpretations. For Native Peoples, however, they "find it difficult if not impossible to protect their religious traditions under the laws of the United States … [and] do not split the sacred from any aspect of life."[25] Ironically for

---

[23] Caroline Knowles, *Race and Social Analysis* (Thousand Oaks, 2003), p. 28.
[24] Ibid., p. 29.
[25] Smith, *Walking in Balance*, p. 178.

Christians the subject often takes a different tone when it is politically expeditious or when it calls for a separation of church and state. For example, Jordan Paper suggests that a recent mode of suppression of Native traditions is designed to take reservation land, particularly sacred sites, and turn them into public parks. Perhaps the most notorious is "Bear Mountain" in the Black Hills. This was and is the most important sacred fasting site for several Native Peoples in the Plains. "The site has become Bear Butte State Park, where tourists can follow trails to watch Native people vision-questing. Lip service is given in the park literature to respect tobacco and cloth offerings, yet their very mention encourages tourists to look for them and take them home as souvenirs."[26] Thus, Native practices and traditions continue to be promoted as exoticized tourist attractions, and Western designations of the sacred are maintained and separated.

In reality, cultural change and adaptation does happen since cultures are not isolates and there is fluidity as cultures interact and respond to environmental, cultural, and historical conditions. However, without an examination of local contexts and the influences of music, art, and literature in combination with issues of power and authority, how can we begin to interpret, decipher, or study such complex matters? George Tinker in *Missionary Conquest* theorizes that the larger systemic issues that effect cultural adaptation often prove "resistant to change and durable in the face of political and economic conditions regardless of personal intentions."[27] In this, we are a product of the embeddedness of social structures, cultural patterns, and cognitive processes that are part of political and economic systems. Interestingly, theories of post-structuralism, post-colonialism, or postmodernism attempt to separate and identify processes; however, the embedded nature of the ideas and the methods of analysis use the very same theories of that which is to be analyzed and broken down. This circularity is difficult to avoid in any analysis. As Tinker remarked more than 15 years ago, the crux of the difficulty in this situation is rooted in the forms and types of analyses applied:

> The main difficulty is that Indian spiritual traditions are still rooted in cultural contexts that are quite foreign to white Euroamericans, yet Euroamerican cultural structures are the only devices Euroamericans have for any deep structure understanding of native spiritual traditions. Hence, those native traditions can only be understood by analogy with white experience.[28]

Indigenous methods of analysis and categories of thought are necessary and must be utilized to frame these difficulties and pose new interpretations.

---

[26]   Jordan Paper, *Native North American Religious Traditions: Dancing for Life* (Westport, 2007), p. 47.

[27]   George Tinker, *Missionary Conquest: The Gospel and Native American Cultural Genocide* (Minneapolis, 1993), p. 117.

[28]   Ibid., p. 122.

Any examination of complex social settings is difficult, and, similar to missionizing efforts, the history of contact influences responses and interpretations. Tinker provides two questions that are relevant to the discussion. First, he asks, in what ways are our actions and thoughts controlled by a systematic whole that includes political, economic, societal, institutional and intellectual realms? And second, "How can we begin to stand apart from this whole with some intentionality?"[29] The process of examination based on Euroamerican analogies with and to white experience supports multiple opportunities for misinterpretation, misappropriation, and "mis-sonization" to continue as they have in the past. Although there are valuable and significant discussions regarding the importance and presence of "Native voice" in the academy, we are in a difficult time. Homer Noley cautioned in 1998:

> We are entering an era in which eye witnesses to overt institutional moves against Native American culture will be unavailable. These overt institutional moves began to be phased out both by the church and state during the civil rights era of the '60s. New generations of Native Americans are born into a society that seeks to accomplish the same ends as the policies of the historical period prior to the civil rights era in a more studied and subtle way. These new generations, having not experienced the blatant public policies of church and state in the era prior to the '60s, are more vulnerable to these maneuvers. Yet, there are people who remember those years, and a way should be made for them to be heard.[30]

Noley's words of caution have gained more truth in the years since he wrote them. We are in a phase when "overt institutional moves" *are* unavailable and when the rhetoric from church and state is strategically designed to counter objections and resistance. Noley's imperative to access those with the memories and knowledge regarding the policies of the past is important. Covert institutional moves under the rubric of "inculturation" may still reflect the assimilation and missionization policies of the past, yet they are harder to identify and counter with resistance. There is a subtlety in covert institutional moves that is difficult to identify and actively resist, particularly in this era of ecumenism and apologizing, one that has continued even as voices from the opposition are raised.

Visual Culture and Images

Beginning in the 1970s, photography and elements of visual culture have been utilized as a social science research methodology for examining cultural construction and maintenance. There is a perceived realism and concreteness in

---

[29]   Ibid., p. 117.

[30]   Homer Noley, "The Interpreters," in Jace Weaver (ed.), *Native American Religious Identity: Unforgotten Gods* (New York, 1998), p. 53.

images that is difficult to refute or challenge. Visual sociologists argue that the use of images is significant for the study of social settings, and they raise questions regarding the use of photographs and visual representations in social science research and teaching.[31] A number of classic texts on the topic have emerged designed to reflect specific methodologies for the study of visual culture.[32] These efforts provide insights into the power of visual research and the use of images to tell a story, as well as some of the difficulties for researchers in using visual data.

The role of visual culture and its presence in the construction of relationships between Catholic and Indigenous communities assumes the perspective of art as a socially constructed act that reflects and perpetuates dominant ideology and interpretations. It also assumes the viewpoint that the use of images is an accurate and inclusive reflection of specific contexts, values, or religious beliefs, while at the same time excluding the interpretations of those it attempts to dominant, convert, or assimilate. David Morgan defines visual culture as:

> The images and objects that deploy particular ways of seeing and therefore contribute to the social, intellectual, and perceptual construction of reality; as a professional practice of study, visual culture is that form of inquiry undertaken in a number of humanistic and social scientific disciplines whose object is the conceptual frameworks, social practices, and the artifacts of seeing.[33]

Differences regarding the interpretation of images and visual representations, then, are critical to explore in discussions of power, oppression, and hegemony. "Art is a kind of concrete logic. And, this inscribing of the law within sensory existence is what Antonio Gramsci meant by hegemony."[34] When we view images in specific contexts such as churches, they acquire meaning and validity through a visual sensory experience that frames and constructs our understanding of the world. An important aspect of power and oppression is tied to the creative, and Martin Heidegger's work of the late 1930s onward suggests that technology becomes the shorthand for operations of power. Art and the visual world "instantiates, creates and represents

---

[31] Jon Wagner, "Contrasting Images, Complementary Trajectories: Sociology, Visual Sociology and Visual Research," *Visual Studies*, 17/2 (2002): 160–71.

[32] See Jon Wagner (ed.), *Images of Information: Still Photography in the Social Sciences* (Beverly Hills, 1979); Jon Prosser (ed.), *Image-based Research: A Sourcebook for Qualitative Researchers* (Bristol, 1998); Michael J. Emmison and Philip D. Smith, *Researching the Visual: Images, Objects, Contexts and Interaction in Social and Cultural Inquiry* (Thousand Oaks, 2000); Gregory C. Stanczak, *Visual Research Methods: Image, Society, and Representation* (Los Angeles, 2007); Marita Sturken and Lisa Cartwright (eds.), *Practices of Looking: An Introduction to Visual Culture* (New York, 2008).

[33] David Morgan, *The Sacred Gaze: Religious Visual Culture in Theory and Practice* (Berkeley, 2005), p. 27.

[34] Terry Eagleton, "The Fate of the Arts," *The Hedgehog Review*, 6/2 (Summer 2004): 7.

something, and it does so by employing technological modes of power, production making, and manipulation."[35] Terry Eagleton speaks of art almost as an alien who infiltrates, co-opts and works with the senses to overtake the unsuspecting through concrete symbols and tangible presence.[36] In other words, visual culture has the power to frame, manage, and manipulate our understandings of the world.

Visual representations and images in Catholic churches often are not the subject of critical analyses, explicit review, or interpretation by community members from inside or outside the Church. In fact, the Church maintains a powerful position within communities in terms of past histories, financial resources, continued government support of missionizing efforts, and the care and education of children, often with significant physical needs. Manipulation is more difficult to interpret and identify conclusively since it often is connected to the misuse of images and denial of behaviors designed to influence viewers. Yet certainly there are points of manipulation used in competition that are evident in the way churches in general recruit and proselytize. An underlying assumption of the study of visual culture is that it "concentrates on the cultural work that visual images do in constructing and maintaining (as well as challenging, destroying, and replacing) a sense of order in a particular place and time."[37] According to Susan Sontag, "in the real world, something *is* happening and no one knows what is *going* to happen. In the image-world, it happened and it *will* forever in that way."[38] Images then, have the power to convey, construct, and manipulate not only a sense of time but also feelings, sentiments, and attitudes, and to frame responses in a static form with some amount of permanence.

Early Euroamerican artists such as George Catlin, Edward S. Curtis, and others who wanted to obtain images of the "dying culture of the west" took turns at capturing images of the "vanishing Indian." These images seized the Euroamerican imagination and created stereotypical images that are hard to dispel.[39] Alfred Young Man observes, "If you don't look like that savage Indian in the window, mister, you might as well consider yourself an extinct Cree, Sioux, Crow, Assiniboin, or Gros Ventre."[40] Simon Ortiz, in discussing the work of Frank Rinehart and Adolph Muhr, presents another response to looking at past moments in these old photographs. Ortiz contends the photographs are valuable to Native Peoples for different reasons since they *hold* memories and stories of the past, yet the exact

[35]   Krzysztof Ziarek, "The End of Art as Its Future," *Hedgehog Review*, 6/2 (Summer 2004): 30.

[36]   Eagleton, "The Fate of the Arts", pp. 7–14.

[37]   Morgan, *The Sacred Gaze: Religious Visual Culture in Theory and Practice*, p. 29.

[38]   Susan Sontag, *On Photography* (New York, 1977), p. 168 (italics in original).

[39]   For more on this topic, see, for example: Philip Deloria, *Indians in Unexpected Places* (Topeka, 2004).

[40]   Alfred Young Man, "The Primitive White Mind," in Simon J. Ortiz (ed.), *Beyond the Reach of Time and Change: Native American Reflections on the Frank A. Rinehart Photograph Collection* (Tucson, 2004), p. 140.

time period is insignificant to the discussion. He notes: "We are experiencing them in the present. … The cultural aspect of story, namely the power of language in the Indian oral tradition, is what makes the picture vivid and alive. And this is what creates an Indian image as real."[41] The people photographed come alive through the stories and the mental images they invoke stimulating memories of the past— of communities—and of places. Western and Euroamerican interpretations add layers of meaning and interpretation to the images and reflect clearly different reasons for valuation. For Euroamericans, the images support the stereotypes and Western notions of the "vanishing Indian," while, for Native audiences, they preface Indigenous voices that continue to tell stories and recall memories as if happening in the present.

Visual images typically have functioned as illustration and were thought to enhance perspectives and understandings of social situations. This "reality as such is redefined—as an item for exhibition, as a record for scrutiny, as a target for surveillance."[42] Further, images and image making support the acquisition of information as part of a system, rather than real experiences furnishing knowledge. The point of research is to examine images for their ability to provoke questions in the study of social and relational issues. This generates questions such as: How and what do images convey? And, who makes decisions about the outcomes and use of images? These are not easy questions to answer; they suggest "images are not merely appendages to the research but rather inseparable components to learning about our social worlds."[43] The study of visual culture then contributes to an enriched understanding of contemporary culture and perceptions of reality that are mediated through material culture. When specifically studying the culture of religion and religious practices, the role of interpretation and perception is an essential element not only of belief, but also in the construction of belief. As David Morgan asks: "What do we learn about religion by investigating the power of images, that is, their capacity to frighten, seduce, deceive, influence, and inspire?"[44] This question is central to the work reported in this volume since the things we see, the ways objects and images are used and incorporated, can powerfully affect our perceptions and understanding of contexts, motives, meanings, and, ultimately, cultural change. Images as a visual text and physical record represent and reflect the integration of traditions and symbols.[45] Visual images are part of a cultural system of production and reception in a field that demands examination of not only the image itself but also of its role in narrative, perception, and display.

---

[41] Simon J. Ortiz (ed.), *Beyond the Reach of Time and Change: Native American Reflections on the Frank A. Rinehart Photograph Collection* (Tucson, 2004), pp. 3–4.

[42] Sontag, *On Photography*, p. 156.

[43] Stanczak, *Visual Research Methods*, p. 3.

[44] Morgan, *The Sacred Gaze*, p. 258.

[45] Ibid., p. 30.

Situating the study and investigation of images within the history of reception, refusing to see them as fixed, aesthetically permanent entities is significant.[46] Complex social phenomena emerge and are framed by an ongoing history and relationship of practice and thought. Looking at and seeing images within a specific context such as the reservation mission church serves particular functions that are difficult to separate from the colonial, historical, and social relationships of the past. Vine Deloria indicates that the procedure by which religious imagery arises is still the subject of great debate among theologians. And, he questions the problem of religious imagery by asking: How do people conceive of the symbols, doctrines, insights, and sequences in which we find religious ideas expressed? And, how do we come to conceive deity in certain forms and not others?[47] Displays separate images or symbols from specific traditions, features of the land, and knowledge given to individuals to which they are effectively tied. In fact, displays can fix them permanently in a particular time and location that may transform them into something not of the purpose they were intended, but for a new purpose. This may effectively change the inherent nature of the images and symbols from living animate beings to inanimate objects for display, a practice typical of Western Euroamericans who view objects as something to be arranged and displayed to suit specific purposes. The Catholic Church's practice of incorporating images into representations, providing accessibility and ensuring availability, particularly as conducted by the Jesuits,[48] is a Western perspective that often is antithetical to the communities they serve.

In Indigenous communities, beliefs, images, stories, and traditions are tied specifically to concrete features of the land, environment, and community.[49] Although new meanings can enhance understanding, images and symbols gain

---

[46]   Ibid.

[47]   Deloria, Jr., *God Is Red*, p. 70.

[48]   As Gauvin A. Bailey indicates, "A Jesuit missionary could be at once an accomplished scientist, doctor, botanist, musician, sculptor, painter, and architect, all the while devoting most of his energy to attending to the spiritual needs of his community. Without doubt the most visible of this panoply of skills involved the fine arts. Taking their cue from classical rhetoric, to which all good humanists were committed, the Jesuits envisioned art as the visual equivalent to sacred oratory." Bailey, *Art on the Jesuit Missions*, p. 8.

[49]   A number of authors address these issues and the significance for Native Peoples in terms of land given specifically to them by the Creator for their continued well-being. See, for example: Keith Basso, *Wisdom Sits in Places: Landscape and Language among the Western Apache* (Albuquerque, 1996); Vine Deloria, Jr., *For this Land: Writings on Religion in America*, ed. James Treat (New York, 1999); A. Oscar Kawagley, *A Yupiaq Worldview: A Pathway to Ecology and Spirit* (Prospect Heights, 1995); James. K. McNeley, *Holy Wind in Navajo Philosophy* (Tucson, 1981); Richard K. Nelson, *Make Prayers to the Raven: A Koyukon View of the Northern Forest* (Chicago, 1983); James Treat (ed.), *Native and Christian: Indigenous Voices on Religious Identity in the United States and Canada* (New York, 1996); Jace Weaver (ed.), *Native American Religious Identity: Unforgotten Gods* (New York, 1998).

power and meaning through specific contexts and cultural traditions that require respect, interaction in the environment, and care or caretaking. Knowledge and understanding emanate from the natural world, and images, symbols, or practices are reflections of that understanding designed not for display, but for accessing help and knowledge. For example, a basketweaver works to create a reflection of knowledge gained from the spirits, natural world, and plants gathered from specific locations. This knowledge is then fully integrated and mixed with the weaver's saliva, dexterity, and ability so that the design reflects this knowledge. It is not taken out of context as an exhibit and detached from the reality of place, the knowledge acquired there, or the potentiality for further insight. These perspectives are critical to the interpretation and study of visual culture and images, as well as an awareness of difference and culturally specific attitudes toward symbol usage, power, and spiritual practice.

Missionization and the Catholic Church

Missions no longer separate traditional and Christian practices by brutal force, damning Indigenous religious practice and calling it "the work of the devil." Now there is a "gentler liberalism in most mission contexts that nevertheless takes paternalism as its most common form and functions to subvert and co-opt the culture of an Indian community."[50] Syncretism and incorporation of Native images and symbols serve a number of functions for Catholic churches in Indigenous communities. These include: suggesting and maintaining the appearance of similarity and integration; fulfilling the directives of Vatican II; demonstrating like-minded beliefs, goals, and ideals; and providing a venue for expressions of belief by Native Catholics. Some churches employ non-Catholic Native artists to complete murals, frescos, sculptures, or images that reflect Christian ideals using Native themes to accomplish these functions. Commissioning non-Catholic artists who are Native in the creation of images can serve a specific purpose, but also releases the Church from negotiations with communities. Sometimes the incorporation occurs in subtle and automatic ways such as the construction of circular tipi-like churches to reflect Native sensibilities. Other times, it occurs more directly with traditional practices such as the use of the Pipe as central to practice. It is possible to envision the practice of incorporating traditional images and practices as emerging naturally from expressions of spirituality and experiences of the sacred by Native members of the Church. It also is possible to imagine these practices as reminiscent of past missionizing policies under a new demeanor and countenance, and as co-optation of images conducted under the auspices of "in service to" the local community without ostensibly a negotiation of boundaries, willingness to change policies, or letting Native Peoples assume full leadership for the community. Within the context of a "gentler liberalism," the processes of covert

---

[50] Tinker, *Missionary Conquest*, p. 114.

as well as "overt institutional moves"[51] are difficult to assess, recognize, decipher, and identify. However, some would charge that the actions of appropriation are evidence of the continuing cultural and religious genocide of the past. This occurs through the practice of equating Native and Catholic traditions as parallel and similar aspects of the same ideas of the sacred. Therefore, proselytizing efforts are interpreted only as organizing and arranging universal and underlying themes that are present in both Christian and Indigenous traditions.

Today, the Catholic Church often continues to maintain the notion of "mission" as it was understood in the past in Indigenous communities.[52] Scientific attitudes and beliefs remain even given the notion of "ecumenism" indicated in Vatican II and the ecumenical movement. Vatican II attempted to support and set in motion a more democratic system particularly in Latin America, East Asia, and Eastern and Central Europe,[53] not specifically, however, in Native North America. Overall, the Church retained much of its hierarchical traditions and conservative policies in North American churches historically created as missions, and the Pope affirmed the role of the missionary as the authority and power to make decisions over what actions are to be considered acceptable Catholic practice. As an emissary whose authority is vested by the Church, missionaries maintain policies of conversion and inclusion, the rewriting of history, and the maintenance of their role of authority. However, in communities such as the Society of Jesus, there has been a lessening of the priest's role and opportunities for lay catechists to influence and provide service have increased. For instance, in the Archdiocese of St. Paul and Minneapolis, the Office of Indian Ministry promotes innovative liturgy to include the burning of sage, use of tobacco from birch-bark baskets, and the blessing of water by a woman since "only women may bless the water, a sacred symbol."[54] For the most part however, Catholic and Christian missionaries continue to embrace the mission concept, albeit in the name of syncretism and unity.

A number of missionaries still consider the job "undone" and the people in need of "help." As is often quoted, Vine Deloria tells a story about asking a Presbyterian minister among the Shinnococks how long he thought mission activities would

---

[51]   Noley, "The Interpreters," p. 53.

[52]   Santeria and Catholic missions in Africa use almost exclusively Spanish and African languages for Church work and religious services. Beginning 100–150 years ago, this was true of Catholic missions in the United States, and in some cases continues to be evidenced. Certain priests in particular stand out for their translations of Catholic and Christian liturgy and hymns into Native languages (e.g. Lakota, Fr. Eugene Beuchel; Diné, Fr. Bernard Haile; Dakota, Rev. Stephen Riggs). Although the use of Native languages is important because it helps to stabilize language loss, it comes at a price since translation of Catholic doctrine does not equate to traditional practice and can misinterpret meaning.

[53]   Peter McDonough and Eugene C. Bianchi, *Passionate Uncertainty: Inside the American Jesuits* (Berkeley, 2002), p. 1.

[54]   Dawn Gibeau, "Sage Smudge, Sip of Water, a Consecrated Host," *National Catholic Reporter*, 30/7: 18.

continue. The minister's response was "until the job is done."[55] His response is reflective of Christian and Catholic attitudes regarding missions as places of permanent employment. The mission belief is framed within a hierarchy of authority that rests with the missionary or Church emissary as necessary for leadership. A priest at Pala Mission in California reasoned as recently as 1991 that Native people are not yet ready to assume leadership of the Church. For them, "Catholic spirituality is largely superstitious rather than an informed expression of faith," and they need to be better informed "before they can partake of the mysteries of the Church."[56] His attitude is reminiscent of earlier missionizing efforts that remain problematic and continue to support entrenched notions typical of previous generations.[57] Although these are the responses of only two pastors, they present striking examples of the paternalism that persists and supports parochial notions of power and hierarchy in terms of religious expression. Christopher Jocks contends: "the sharing of spiritual practices and knowledge can only rightly take place between equals, in a discourse of mutual respect, with the permission of both parties."[58] Unequal relationships of power and hierarchy support and maintain a system in which the practices and traditions of Indigenous Peoples are assumed and presumed by Euroamericans to be open for and to interpretation, usage, and appropriation. Often they fail to recognize or acknowledge an understanding of spirituality and the differences between Indigenous and Western Christian traditions.

Catholic Jesuit authors such as Paul Steinmetz write about the most significant traditions of Lakota people as "primal" expressions and archetypes of Christianity that will ultimately be subsumed under the Catholic Church: "The pipe stone as the blood of the buffalo is a beautiful archetypical image of Christ gathering the entire Sioux way of life unto Himself. Through this image the Lakota find their identity in Christ and the Church seeks final perfection of her nature, absorbing and transforming the Lakota tradition into herself."[59] Steinmetz's comments are deeply reflective of hegemonic assimilationist policies and practices. The use of the Sacred Pipe and Lakota ceremonies in church contexts indicates a surface incorporation, change, or alignment with Church policy. While at the same time, as George Tinker argues, "the pipe is being used in this case to enhance the power of the missionary spiritual form, that is, holy communion,"[60] the underlying structure of the Catholic Church remains intact. Discussion and analysis of the incorporation of the Pipe is examined within the context and structure of Catholic ideology. When expressed by

---

[55]   Vine Deloria, Jr., *For this Land: Writings on Religion in America*, p. 24.

[56]   Vecsey, *On the Padres' Trail*, p. 312.

[57]   Rupert Costo and Jeannette H. Costo (eds.), *The Missions of California: A Legacy of Genocide* (San Francisco, 1987).

[58]   Christopher Ronwanièn:te Jocks, "Spirituality for Sale: Sacred Knowledge in the Consumer Age," in Lee Irwin (ed.), *Native American Spirituality: A Critical Reader* (Lincoln, 2000), p. 62.

[59]   Steinmetz, *The Sacred Pipe*, p. 174.

[60]   Tinker, *Missionary Conquest*, p. 115.

Church representatives, lay people, and priests, these attitudes reflect an ideology that supports and maintains the hierarchy and hegemony of the past. Hence, "colonization continues to necessitate the political, military, social, psychoculture and value system of the colonized and the imposition of the values and culture of the colonizer."[61] Most significantly, it suggests the goal of absorption and transformation of traditions and practices into the Catholic Church.

Prior to Vatican II, conversion efforts by Catholic and Christian missionaries were the ultimate goal, and the means to achieve this goal could be somewhat flexible depending on a number of factors. For example, the use of images of Native people by Church emissaries was not unknown or repressed depending on the circumstances and image.[62] Decisions were made to seek images of converts from earlier periods who could be held up as role models in communities and by extension carry over to other conversion locales. Catherine "Kateri" Tekakwitha in the late 1880s and Nicholas Black Elk in the early 1900s are prominent examples. With the rise of nationalism in the United States and continuing efforts to define a uniquely "American" personality separated from Europe, Kateri would become a model of Native Catholicism. In 1884, Catholic bishops gathered for the Plenary Council in Baltimore and were interested in promoting and marketing a Native identity in an effort to support nationalism under a pan-Indian Catholicism. The "Lily of the Mohawk," as she became known, was the individual of choice as a potential national saint with shrines at places such as Kahnawake, Quebec and Fonda, New York.[63] Kateri, baptized in 1676 at the age of 20, was a Mohawk woman who fled to Kahnawake where a group of Native Christians lived. She reportedly fled because of threats of persecution from her own Native community regarding her Christian beliefs. She died a short four years later in 1680 and was beatified and accorded "Blessed" by the Pope in 1980, some three hundred years later. Yet the idea of using her image for "marketing," coupled with new conversion efforts of the time, began in 1880, almost one hundred years earlier. Clarence Walworth and his niece Ellen "Nelly" Walworth dedicated themselves to the Americanization of Tekakwitha in the 1880s. Nelly, in particular, worked to recapture the lost world of the "vanishing Indian." Their efforts generated for "the Catholic Church a symbol in the form of an Indian maiden from another century that could anchor this *foreign* religion in American soil."[64]

Images of Kateri would be used throughout Native communities in North America as a sign not only for the value of conversion, but also of her importance as a symbol of a uniquely North American image separate from Europe. Kateri

---

[61]   Ibid., p. 119.

[62]   See Deloria, *Writings for the Land*; Tinker, *Missionary Conquest*; Vecsey, *On the Padres' Trail*.

[63]   Ironically, French and Canadian Catholics had already been using the story of Catherine Tekakwitha since 1717. See Allan Greer, *Mohawk Saint: Catherine Tekakwitha and the Jesuits* (New York, 2005).

[64]   Greer, *Mohawk Saint*, pp. 266, 272. Italics added.

currently appears in posters, large and small cast statues, note cards, and a number of forms as remembrances. These materials seek to present the civilized—the converted—the committed—the saintly woman who voluntarily came to Christ and willingly suffered for her faith. The artistic quality and range of images is extensive; however, the similarities in the pose and demeanor of Kateri are striking (see Figures 1.1 and 1.2). Today, images of Kateri, such as the one illustrated in Figure 1.1, can be found in the majority of Native Catholic communities and churches. The National Kateri Tekakwitha Conference is held each year. At a recent Kateri conference, Mary Lou Smith, when interviewed, commented that the conferences were similar to the Indian congresses she attended as a child, and that "Blessed Kateri 'gave herself to the Lord, and she suffered for it.'"[65] Figure 1.2 illustrates another depiction of Kateri—a garden statue at a Catholic church in South Dakota. In both figures, the image of Kateri as a modest young Indian woman with braids and striking gaze encourages viewers to emulate this exemplar. Tellingly, the story of Kateri is largely unknown to non-Native Catholics in the United States who do not reside near Native communities.

Another example of a convert whose image is used extensively by the Catholic Church is that of Nicholas Black Elk.[66] He was born in 1863 along the Little Powder River and resided near Manderson, South Dakota for most of his life. At the age of nine, he received a vision that foreshadowed his lifetime role of dedication to curing and aiding his people. He was baptized a Catholic on 6 December 1904 and became a catechist who traveled extensively for the Church proselytizing among Plains Indian communities. Well known as a medicine man, he seemingly abandoned his traditionalist practices and became somewhat of a poster-boy whose conversion was touted by the Catholic Church as an example of the changes taking place. In 1925, "Nick" Black Elk was pictured in a photograph in the Catholic missionary journal *The Indian Sentinel* (Figure 1.3). The photograph appeared inside the edition as part of a short article on Indian catechists with Black Elk dressed in the suit of a Catholic catechist as he shows a young girl the rosary. This image is a sensitive reflection of Black Elk and a young girl whose face seems to indicate expressions of interest. Most significantly, it is a representation of a man as a deeply caring human whose attention is focused on this child.

---

[65] Emilie Lemmons, "Ojibway Catholic Finds Traditional Spirituality Woven into Faith," *The Catholic Spirit* (uploaded 24 June 2007), www.tcsdms.com/heritage/ojibway-catholic-finds.html (accessed 19 July 2008).

[66] The number of images of Black Elk is so extensive and they are used so often in ways to justify the Church's actions, particularly in Lakota communities, that his images are included here as a way to highlight the use, influence, and pervasiveness of his image in Catholic iconology. Figures 1.3 and 1.4 reflect examples of images used in marketing. Actual images of Kateri are unknown; however, images of Black Elk are widely distributed and well known. His image has also been used in ways that solidify the idea that he was a "real man" who was a "real Catholic"; however, this mentality that images can be used to support religious conversion by association is strange at best.

Figure 1.1   Photograph of a Kateri Tekakwitha poster that used to hang in a meeting room at All Saints Catholic Church, Eagle Butte, South Dakota, 1998. Photograph courtesy of author, and used with permission.

Figure 1.2   Exterior statue of Kateri Tekakwitha from a mission church in South
             Dakota, 1996. Photograph courtesy of the author.

Figure 1.3   Nicholas Black Elk as catechist, *The Indian Sentinel*, 5/2 (1925):
81. Courtesy of Department of Special Collections and University
Archives, Marquette University Libraries, image ID number, BCIM
09–147–14.

A year later, in 1926, the same image appeared on the cover of *The Indian Sentinel* except this time as an artist's rendition of "Nick" Black Elk in buckskin and headdress with long hair. As illustrated in Figure 1.4, it is difficult to know for certain that this is the same man identified in Figure 1.3 without the benefit of textual identification and the overwhelming similarity of the images. The image in Figure 1.4 typifies what some have termed the "pagan-turned-Christian, rosary beads in hand."[67] Unlike the photograph of Black Elk in Figure 1.3, this image is a fabricated characterization overlaid with interpretation to suit the needs of a public hungry for such images. However, some might argue that this image was a product of its time since it reflects the sensibilities of the first half of the twentieth century. Created by a visitor to the Black Hills from Wisconsin, it presents sentiments that are intertwined with notions of the Boy Scouts and "Indians as children of nature" to which Americans turned to understand their present.[68] Romanticized versions of Native Peoples living "traditionally" as Indians demonstrated these sentiments, now however they are living as Christians in both popular and "imagined" sentiments. For those reading the *Indian Sentinel* in 1926, the image conveys both the converted catechist and the possibility of returning to "the blanket" that underscores the man, notions popular at the time. Unlike the 1925 image that did not rate the cover of the journal, the 1926 figure poses an interpretation of America's understanding of Black Elk and Native Peoples in general, particularly as Christians who were different from other Christians.

In 1931, Black Elk did not attend the Catholic Sioux Congress held that year, meeting instead with John Neihardt for a number of interviews on Lakota traditions. Neihardt's goal was to present the life of a traditional Lakota in the widely popular *Black Elk Speaks*. Black Elk's absences from Catholic catechist duties led to a series of public displays and confrontations, specifically with Catholic clergy who wanted to maintain the image of their convert as no longer pagan and who characterized the discussions with Neihardt as erroneous. More recently, the idea of Black Elk as "walking two roads" fits with the current vernacular of the Church in that both traditions are worthwhile, and it is possible for an individual to participate in both. Yet Charlotte Black Elk, his great-granddaughter, recalls family stories that have been handed down of how Black Elk tricked the priests into thinking he was a convert.[69] Vine Deloria indicates that possibly the greatest significance for the text *Black Elk Speaks* may be for "contemporary generations of young Indians" to read about their roots. This may be true even with the "sporadic sniping of the Roman Catholic writers who subtly develop the posture that everything contained in *Black Elk Speaks* is actually good Jesuit teaching and that very little represents the old Sioux ways of religion."[70] The record of Black Elk's conversion to Catholicism is

---

[67] Vecsey, *Where the Two Roads Meet*, p. 38.

[68] Philip Deloria, *Playing Indian* (New Haven, 1998), p. 105.

[69] Vecsey, *Where the Two Roads Meet*, p. 43.

[70] Deloria, *For this Land*, p. 278.

Figure 1.4   Nicholas Black Elk on the cover of *The Indian Sentinel*, 6/4 (1926).
              Courtesy of the Department of Special Collections and University
              Archives, Marquette University Libraries.

not without controversy, and his motives are not as clear as the Church would like them to be.

Indigenous spiritual knowledge as worthy and equal to that of Christian theology continues to be misunderstood, and missionaries maintain the final authority in all decisions regarding Church doctrine and authentic expressions of faith.[71] Conflicts, disagreements, and challenges arise concerning interpretations of faith, the actions of clergy, and the conversions of "premier" Native examples such as Black Elk and Kateri. Another example of disagreement involves the proposed sainthood of Fray Junípero Serra, who was beatified and accorded "Blessed" by the Pope in 1988. The conflict centers around those who declare Serra creates miracles in their lives when they pray to him and should be canonized as a saint, and those who reply that his cruelty and inhuman treatment is legendary among Native Peoples. Michael Mathes counters that there is no written proof of Serra's cruelty, only "stories by Indian People."[72] The Western notion of history as written is significant in this discussion since it validates authenticity, while simultaneously denigrating oral histories and the lives and experiences of Native Peoples. In part, this may be attributed to continuing paternalism regarding, not only spirituality and knowledge, but also the need for dominance over "neophytes." Assessments of knowledge and comments regarding a task "still not done" are common. Similar to discussions of Black Elk's "true Catholic" nature, the power of one group to remain as the writer of history with certain forms more valid than others is evident. Images and visual culture hold the power to create a chain of documentary evidence as much as the written word. Catholic images are presented as open to interpretation and change, yet the Church utilizes the power to record, document, and structure events and activities through images and individuals such as those of Kateri, Black Elk, and Serra.

Appropriation and Adaptations

In more recent times, Catholic churches on American Indian reservations have typically presented a blending of Native and Catholic images and symbols unlike that found in other Catholic parishes in the United States. Some parishes incorporated new ideas and approaches to missionization and syncretism to fit the Vatican II decree,[73] such as "inculturation" and the community and religious syncretism that brought changes in the early 1990s. Inculturation is defined as "independent of the missionary, and … occurs as the Word interacts with the recipient culture to produce a unique response. This encounter produces a local Church, the place of a culturally new response to the Gospel," in which all members of the community

---

[71]   Raymond J.A. Huel, *Proclaiming the Gospel to the Indians and Métis* (Edmonton, 1996). Huel asserts, "once this encounter has taken place, the missionary must verify that the resulting church is an authentic expression of the faith" (Epilogue note, p. 357).

[72]   Costo and Costo, *The Missions of California*.

[73]   Huel, *Proclaiming the Gospel*.

contribute.[74] An Arizona parish publication describes inculturation as looking to find "God IN our culture. We ask, 'How is Christ found IN the good and authentic parts of any culture?'"[75] Others talk of the beneficial double effect since it reveals the Gospel in other cultures and introduces them to the Church. An interesting aspect of this is that the Church also becomes "inculturated" in the process, yet this point is often avoided.[76]

The Lakota Inculturation Task Force (LITF), created by Bishop Chaput in 1994 for the Catholic Diocese of Rapid City in South Dakota, emphasizes the need for evangelization, Native leadership, and inculturation. The LITF's goal is to accomplish "new methods of evangelization of Native Peoples," and, with this, there is some urgency. As noted by the Catholic Diocese of Rapid City, South Dakota, "it is very possible that in many places, this will be the last generation of Native American Catholics."[77] A variety of religious retreats for reflection and nondenominational spirituality have been designed to further this goal. For example, the Sioux Spiritual Center, founded by Fr. John Hatcher, S.J., Superior of the St. Francis Jesuit Center, provides Native Catholics opportunities to hear the Christian word and to involve Lakota Catholics in the evangelization process. Participation in decisions regarding evangelization is encouraged while Native Catholic leaders are enlisted to reach out to those who for one reason or another do not fully participate.[78] The LITF also works with Lakota Catholics to determine which Lakota ceremonies can be used in Catholic liturgy. The diocese's Office of Permanent Diaconate has prepared eight Lakota deacons working on four reservations and two working in parishes in Rapid City. However, any new mission or church configuration must be overseen and approved by priests and clergy so that it is consistent with Church theology. In an example of Oblates and First Nations negotiations in Canada, discussions are still unfolding and may be suggestive of an ongoing and continuing process. As Raymond Huel reports, it is difficult to predict the results of these discussions:

> Attractive as the concepts of the "Amerindian Church" and inculturation might
> be to the current generation of missionaries, these ideas cannot be imposed on
> the First Nations as a legitimate expression of spirituality. To do so would be to
> invite a far greater frustration and disenchantment than that brought about by

---

[74]   René Jaouen as cited in Huel, *Proclaiming the Gospel*, pp. 284–5.

[75]   Ibid., p. 285.

[76]   Swain, "Inculturating liturgical music," p. 16.

[77]   Catholic Diocese of Rapid City, *Inculturation Project Office* (established 1 September 1999), www.rapidcitydiocese.org/Ministries/Inculturation.htm (accessed 11 July 2008).

[78]   See comments by Fr. John Hatcher, SJ, Superior, St. Francis Mission, www.sfmission.org (accessed 22 July 2008).

the classical period of missionary activity. The First Nations themselves must decide if they are willing to accept Christianity.[79]

An aspect that appears most evident in any of these discussions is the continuing authority of the priest or emissary of the Church and the subsuming of the Native tradition under the Catholic rubric of an "Amerindian Church" designed for "Native Catholics."

According to the US National Conference of Catholic Bishops (USCCB), there is a wide range of self-identification by Native Peoples—from Native Catholic to Catholic Native to Catholic with many areas of gray in between. Responses to a 2002 survey of 51 dioceses serving Native communities in the United States (just under 30 percent of the total number of dioceses) described the ways Native symbols and rituals are currently used in the liturgy or communal prayer.[80] They include: smudging with cedar, sage, sweet grass and tobacco; use of an eagle feather in blessing; dancing and drumming as part of the liturgy; naming ceremonies; four-directional prayers; sweat lodge; medicine wheel and Native cross displays; and the use of the Pipe.[81] Hence the range and degree of inculturation, incorporation, and appropriation is complex and multifaceted. Furthermore, a number of Native Catholics who are members of religious orders including Marie Therese Archambault, Kateri Mitchell, Paul Ojibway, Donald Pelotte, and Charles Chaput, among others, attest to the complexity of this issue in their writings. They make a concentrated effort to achieve definitions and descriptions that present multiple interpretations and perspectives.[82] The USCCB survey results and statements by Native Catholics indicate that a mixing of Native and Catholic traditions has already created a new religion that may or may not be under the authority of the Church or specifically reflective of a particular Native tradition. However, it is yet to be determined the degree and form of "Native Catholicism."

In three separate volumes on the Catholic Church's relations with Native communities, Christopher Vecsey examines notions of syncretism with attention primarily on Native Americans influenced by Catholicism, yet he indicates that he tried not to ignore the motives and methods of the Church's Euroamerican

---

[79]   Huel, *Proclaiming the Gospel to the Indians and Métis*, p. 289.

[80]   For a sense of the magnitude of the number of parishes serving Native Catholics in a diocese, the Catholic Diocese of Rapid City in South Dakota has approximately ninety parishes that are part of the diocese; www.rapidcitydiocese.org (accessed 18 July 2008).

[81]   See USCCB, *Native American Catholics at the Millennium*, a report on a survey by the United States Conference of Catholic bishops ad hoc committee on Native American Catholics (Washington, DC, 2002), p. 11, www.usccb.org/education/nac.shtml (accessed 9 July 2008).

[82]   See National Catholic Educational Association, *The People: Reflections of Native Peoples on the Catholic Experience in North America* (Washington, DC, 1992); Weaver, *Native American Religious Identity*.

evangelists.[83] These volumes do, in fact, remain focused on perspectives and beliefs concerning Native Catholics with some commentaries that challenge the processes of appropriation and syncretism in and of themselves. According to Vecsey, many Catholic catechists and evangelizers today utilize Pope Paul VI's words from a 1975 encyclical on evangelization to target, transform, and, most importantly, Christianize. The appropriation and use of specific practices and symbols are designed to accomplish these goals, and to "make the people feel comfortable [and] place a superficial veneer on the gospel."[84] The USCCB survey provides evidence of this phenomenon with data to support the incorporation of Native symbols and rituals. The survey reports that it is more common in parishes and ministries serving Native Americans on reservations or in rural communities than in urban settings.[85] Few discussions indicate anything more than what is reported as "disagreements" over the use of the Pipe rather than serious objections by local Native community members. In fact, some theorized that the use of the Pipe in Catholic ceremonies at Pine Ridge during the late 1960s and early 1970s would not continue after the reassignment of the priests incorporating it, thus making the objections of local Lakota opponents a moot point by some. Yet this has not occurred. As a symbol of Christ, the Pipe currently is used in Catholic ceremonies such as funerals and weddings, and during the Mass, even as objections about its use continue to be voiced by traditional, as well as Catholic, Lakotas. Indicated and supported by the USCCB survey and examples from specific parishes in Minneapolis, the practice of incorporating the use of the Pipe in Catholic ceremonies seems to have become more widespread among Native Catholic dioceses in both urban and rural settings.[86] Ironically, or maybe expectedly as George Tinker notes, it is typically a non-Native priest who holds the Pipe, leads the prayers, and indicates that they are the same as Catholic traditions. All of this within the context of placing the Pipe under the authority and power of the Church to interpret and enhance Christian practices. It is from within this framework for discussion and introduction that the contributors to this volume examine social, political, religious, historical, and visual contexts. The ideas are framed within the context of resistance and change brought about by the American Indian and ecumenical movements since the 1960s. However, currently the relations are set within a context of apology and integration in which resistance may be harder to maintain particularly within a society that fosters "overt institutional moves."[87] Yet a number of Indigenous peoples—possibly a growing number—are convinced of the need for separation of these traditions for the health and well-being of their traditions and communities.

[83]   Vecsey, *Where the Two Roads Meet*, p. 367.

[84]   Christopher Vecsey, *On the Padres' Trail*, p. 381.

[85]   USCCB, *Native American Catholics at the Millennium*, p. 12.

[86]   See, for example, parishes in Rapid City, South Dakota, Minneapolis, Minnesota and Gallup, New Mexico.

[87]   Noley, "The interpreters," p. 53.

Chapter 2
Spiritual Freedom, Pious Appropriation

James J. Garrett

One of the most extreme of ironies in America's history is the fact that, although it was founded upon the principle of religious freedom for all, it has denied that freedom to the original inhabitants of the land. This is not idle thought. There is a long and rich body of research that documents this historical fact from the time the first Euroamericans settled on this continent's eastern shore.[1] Steve Talbot shows us that the Doctrine of Christian Nations, also known as the Right of Christian Discovery, has been the official policy of the colonizers ever since Europeans stumbled ashore.[2] This ancient doctrine dictates that any discovered lands found to be occupied by non-Christian people are subject to be taken by Christian nations as conquered land. This outlandish doctrine permitted explorers and government officials alike to violate Indians' human rights by infringing on their freedom to practice their own version of spirituality, religions, sacred practices, and ceremonies, and to do so at their accustomed sacred sites. It has also been at the heart of several court cases involving American Indian sacred sites such as the infamous *Lyng v. Northwest Indian Cemetery Protection Association* case where a logging road was allowed to go through a sacred area in order to facilitate economic exploitation of the forests in northern California.[3]

Fast-forward through a myriad of examples that are too numerous to cite of violations of the Indian religious freedoms from colonial America to the settling of the West in 1883, and we can look at an example that can give us an accurate picture of exactly how insidious America has treated Indian Nations' religious and human rights. In 1883, the US government promulgated rules through the Bureau of Indian Affairs for the Indian Courts known as the "Indian Religious

---

[1] See, for example: Lee Irwin, "Freedom, Law, and Prophecy: A Brief History of Native American Religious Resistance," *American Indian Quarterly*, 21/1 (1997): 35–55; and Lee Irwin, "Freedom, Law, and Prophecy: A Brief History of Native American Religious Resistance," in Lee Irwin (ed.), *Native American Spirituality: A Critical Reader* (Lincoln, 2001), pp. 295–316.

[2] Steve Talbot, "Spiritual Genocide: The Denial of American Indian Religious Freedom, from Conquest to 1934," *Wicazo Sa Review* (Fall 2006): 7–39.

[3] Jace Weaver, "Losing My Religion: Native American Religious Traditions and American Indian Religious Freedom," in Jace Weaver, *Other Words: American Indian literature, Law, and Culture* (Norman, 2001).

Crimes Code."[4] This code banned most, if not all, Native spiritual ceremonies and practices and made it a crime for those that refused to abandon their traditional ways. For most modern Americans, this may seem like an exaggeration or made-up tale about how terrible the government of this country can be; however, there is a clear and lengthy trail of documentation. All one has to do is to begin investigating this subject to prove beyond a doubt that suppression of Indian religious freedom is real. Furthermore, most Indian people today will tell you that it continues today, albeit in much more subtle methods than in the past.[5] It is an ongoing battle that Indian Nations fight many a day.

Although John Collier and the American Indian Defense Association fought valiant battles in the 1920s and 1930s to ensure cultural pluralism and that the American Indian enjoyed the right of religious freedom as did every American citizen, their battle only put the issue on the back burner and only minimally stopped the continuous attacks on Indian ceremonial practices. These efforts did literally nothing to protect sacred sites.[6] However, when Collier became Commissioner of Indian Affairs during the Franklin D. Roosevelt administration, he at least initiated rules by enacting BIA Circular 2970, entitled "Indian Religious Freedom and Indian Culture." It was the first specific policy made to protect Native American religious rights. This rule said that there would be no further interference with Indian religious life or ceremonial expression, and that harassment thereafter would not be tolerated. Although BIA Circular 2970 stopped government officials from blatantly harassing Native spiritual practitioners and allowed ceremonies to be conducted once again after a 50-year hiatus, there is some evidence that Collier had little if any concept of protecting sacred sites.[7] Not until the enactment of the American Indian Religious Freedom Act of 1978 (AIRFA) was the subject of religious freedom and rights seriously addressed by the federal government again. Many Indians thought AIRFA was going to be the panacea, but the protections it espoused proved to be very illusory.

Indian Civil Rights Issues

Through the hard work of many very dedicated Indian activists such as Vine Deloria, Jr., Suzan Shown Harjo, and Alan Parker, the concept of legislation to prohibit violation of Indian religious freedoms was to become real.[8] In fact, the

---

[4]   Irwin, "Freedom, Law, and Prophecy."

[5]   Steve Pavlik, "The U.S. Supreme Court Decision on Peyote in *Employment Division v. Smith*: A Case Study in the Suppression of Native American Religious Freedom," *Wicazo Sa Review*, 8/2 (1992): 30–39.

[6]   Talbot, "Spiritual Genocide."

[7]   Ibid.

[8]   Suzan Shown Harjo, "The American Indian Religious Freedom Act: Looking Back and Looking Forward," *Wicazo Sa Review*, 19/2 (2004): 143–51

1970s was alive with activism on many fronts by Native Peoples all over the country and AIRFA was only one of many legislative acts enacted that were meant to protect Indian rights. The Indian Self-Determination and Education Assistance Act (ISDEAA) was enacted in 1974, and the Indian Child Welfare Act was passed along with AIRFA in 1978, to name just a few of the most significant.[9]

During this time, I became involved in working in the area of Indian inmate rights. While working on a cattle ranch up the coast from Goleta, California, I grew into being a helper to a Lakota spiritual healer named Archie Fire Lame Deer who also resided in the area. Together, Archie, myself, and a score of other Indian and non-Indian activists around the Santa Barbara area protested the construction of a liquefied natural gas terminal that was to be constructed upon a Chumash Indian sacred site called Point Conception. Archie was also collaborating with another Lakota named Bear Ribs who was incarcerated in the Lompoc Federal Correctional Facility. Bear Ribs was suing the US federal government for violating his civil and religious rights by depriving him of the right to be able to consult with a medicine man freely and to have that person be able to come into the correctional facility to minister to Indian inmates' religious needs. The ultimate goal of the lawsuit was to be able to participate in traditional religious ceremonies inside the walls of a federal correctional facility. It seems that, although the feds would provide rabbis, priests, and so on to inmates, they would not allow medicine men to come in and work with Indian inmates. The Native American Rights Fund (NARF), a law firm from Boulder, Colorado, was representing Bear Ribs and eventually maneuvered the feds into settling the lawsuit out of court. The settlement allowed Bear Ribs to have a medicine man come inside the walls. The federal correction system began allowing Archie to come inside the walls and meet with Indian inmates in groups. When the feds relented, the state system followed suit. Inch by inch, we progressed. Although it seemed to be very slow progress indeed, we eventually were able to take a Sacred Pipe and a drum inside the walls of some facilities and conduct traditional ceremonies with the Indian inmates in groups.

I became involved in working with both the federal and the state correctional systems by hanging out with Archie. We went around to various correctional facilities up and down the coast where we would go inside the walls and meet with the Indian inmates. Eventually, Archie was given permission to build a sweat lodge and conduct a ceremony inside the fence at the Lompoc facility. We had to carefully calculate exactly what we would need inside the walls in order to conduct this ceremony. We had to calculate exactly how many rocks, how much wood, willows for the structure, tarps for covering, tools for hauling rocks, buckets, and so on. We loaded everything into my pickup truck and took it inside the facility. Archie also had to calculate how he would deal with federal officers going through his bundles of sacred objects and medicines that he wanted to bring in. All in all, it was a heck of a day and exciting beyond words. We loaded the pickup to the maximum and went to Lompoc. We had to go in the back gate where I had to

---

9   Irwin, "Freedom, Law, and Prophecy."

drive into a giant cage for inspection purposes. The federal officers spent over an hour going through the pickup looking at everything. We went in, constructed the lodge, conducted two sweat lodge ceremonies, and then the exact same inspection process occurred on our way out to make sure everything we brought in was going back out. It was also to check that nothing extra was going out, too. Although I knew the gravity of what the event meant, only after many years did I realize that we made history that day. Later on, it became apparent to many of us that often Indian offenders felt the same discrimination as did Mr. Bear Ribs, and years later only when describing our actions to a friend did it sink in that we had given Indian offenders at least a portion of their human rights back.

Soon after constructing the sweat lodge in the Lompoc facility, I moved home to South Dakota. The main reason for moving home was that uranium exploration was beginning in the Black Hills, and I went home to help defend our sacred land. Eventually, I hooked up with the Black Hills Alliance, which was an alliance of various groups that were located around the Black Hills. Representative groups within the Alliance were Indians, cowboys, homesteaders, loggers, miners, and students. The Alliance also had ties to other organizations in Minnesota, Wisconsin, etc. These were exciting times for Indian people. We were gaining significant recognition on a number of fronts. One was prisoner rights; another was protection of Indian children's rights not to be shipped off to outside non-Indian homes; another was on the environmental front, particularly surrounding the protection of our lands. We were demanding our rights and consequently we became the focus of many new Congressional legislative actions. However, I must add that my participation and contributions were minimal compared to other people's contributions.

Not long after I moved home, Archie called me and asked me to meet him at the airport, as he would be attending a meeting near my home. It was a meeting of the Presidential Advisory Task Force on the implementation of the American Indian Religious Freedom Act. The advisees consisted of medicine men and political leaders from many Tribal Nations and Archie Fire Lame Deer had been selected to sit on the panel. We went to this meeting that was held at the Swiftbird Pilot Project in Swiftbird village on the Cheyenne River Reservation. The Swiftbird Project was a newly funded pilot program that attempted to rehabilitate first-time Indian offenders through immersion in counseling, sacred ceremonies, vocational training, and support services. The AIRFA Advisors' meeting took place there and I remember that many reservation community members showed up to observe the proceedings. There were also officials there taking testimony about the significance of AIRFA and how it should be implemented. While there, Arvol Looking Horse, the Buffalo Calf Pipe Keeper, testified and then invited everyone to come to his home in Green Grass for a Pipe ceremony. Some of the advisees went; many did not. I remember being surprised at how many of the advisees did not attend the ceremony because I thought of the invitation as a tremendous opportunity. The Governor of an alliance of 19 Pueblo villages and his spokesman did attend and were great fun to be around because they had a very special sense of humor. The

Governor was about 92 years old and he said that he had brought a younger man to speak on his behalf. This younger man was only 78 years old.

While attending the meeting at Swiftbird, I applied for a job and was hired on as a coordinator. The background to the Swiftbird Pilot Project was that the Native American Rights Fund had determined through research that the State of South Dakota was not doing anything to rehabilitate American Indian inmates. It was also determined that the vast majority of Indian inmates were incarcerated because of some problem with alcohol. Therefore, it was thought that, if the inmates could have full access to medicine men and ceremonies, then they would be healed and would go straight. It was my job to interview potential clients within the prisons and to present their cases before a board for approval to bring them to the Swiftbird complex. They would spend their last year of incarceration at Swiftbird Project, a minimum-security facility, and have access to counselors and medicine men, and also maybe learn a trade from one of the vocational education programs. Towards the end of their stay at Swiftbird, I would begin lining up support people in the inmate's home community that could give support once they returned home. Since we accepted only first-time felons, it was felt that most, if not all, would need only a guiding hand to go straight if they could attend ceremonies and be healed. The project lasted only a few years and eventually went under because of reservation politics. A member of the board of directors wanted her son hired into an administrative position that he was not qualified for and, when the administration refused to hire him, she proceeded to destroy the whole effort. Eventually, I went into the family cattle business, remained around home, worked with the Black Hills Alliance (BHA), and contributed as much as I could to the protection of the Black Hills and the struggle for their return to the Lakota Nation. Eventually, I teamed up with Mario Gonzalez, an Oglala Lakota attorney, and we served as appellate court justices for the Cheyenne River Tribe.

Over a number of years, several lawsuits worked their way through the system up to the United States Supreme Court and the court issued negative positions regarding the protection of a sacred site in the *Lyng v. Northwest Indian Cemetery Protection Association* court case and also in the ceremonial use of peyote in *Employment Division v. Smith*. These two cases proved that AIRFA had "no teeth" for enforcement of protection[10] and actually might even be damaging to American Indian religious freedoms. American Indian religious rights were being trampled upon despite the fancy language in AIRFA. It was a cruel joke on American Indians to learn that the enactment of AIRFA was really only a policy statement that had "no teeth" for enforcement, and it was a big disappointment. As we witnessed court case after court case with outcomes that were against Indian religious rights, it appeared to be no protection of our rights at all and seemed like just another broken promise. Then, in 1993, Congress decided to introduce legislation that would attempt to address the shortcomings of AIRFA. It passed an amendment to AIRFA entitled the Religious Freedom Restoration Act (RFRA). However, with

---

[10]   Weaver, "Losing My Religion."

the Republican rise to power in 1994, Native issues fell by the wayside once again. Before long, the constitutionality of RFRA was challenged and any bite the RFRA might have had was taken out of it, too.[11]

Christian Neo-colonization

Colonization has many faces and the religious front is but just one. In fact, religious missionaries have always been out front in almost every colonial effort throughout history. It has always seemed that the doctrines of colonizing indigenous peoples wherever colonizers go is to do two things to the society they intend to colonize. The first method is to take away the victims' spiritual ceremonies by banning them from being performed any longer, and the second is to take away their language by the same means. After a generation or two, the people begin to lose their identity. They lose bits and pieces of their original identity until their cultural identities as nations are severely eroded to the point that the next generations don't really know what the original culture was all about. For example, today there is a whole generation of Lakota youngsters who have no understanding of the important role that bison once played in their nation's history and their teachers encourage this by telling a distorted "Americanized" version of our country's history. For example, contemporary Lakota Indian children do not understand that there were 20–50 million bison on the Prairies a little over a century ago (now there are only a few hundred thousand). They do not know that their ancestors depended entirely on bison for nearly every need. Schoolteachers, especially those teaching in Indian schools, should include this history in their lessons.

Colonizing processes have happened all over the world, specifically wherever Europeans and/or Christians went. It has happened wherever Catholic missionaries went and is happening wherever they remain today. The suppression of Native languages and ceremonies during the late 1800s was not just a government concept; it was also the brainchild of religious fanatics who sometimes disguised themselves as government officials. A very poignant story of a young Indian boy's arrival at a government boarding school is told by Luther Standing Bear in his 1934 classic book, *The Land of the Spotted Eagle*.[12] Mr. Standing Bear was among the first Lakota children to be taken away from their parents and sent to a government school that was located in Pennsylvania. When they arrived at Carlisle Indian School, their traditional clothing was taken away and they were made to wear White Man's clothing including their hard-soled shoes. They were forbidden to speak Lakota, their hair was cut off, and they were made to select a White Man

---

[11]   As Jace Weaver indicates: "Sadly, many of my fears about the future of First Amendment litigation … have been realized in subsequent events. On September 25, 1997, the Supreme Court handed down its decision in *City of Boerne v. Flores*. The 6-to-3 decision struck down RFRA as unconstitutional." See Weaver, "Losing My Religion," p. 177.

[12]   Luther Standing Bear, *The Land of the Spotted Eagle* (Lincoln, 1978).

name. Although he does not discuss the forbidden ceremonies, this process of forced education disrupted the ceremonial initiation into Lakota society that all children traditionally underwent. It deprived them of the invaluable *Hanblechiya* (Vision Quest) ceremony in which they were given a roadmap by the Creator to follow throughout their lives. This ceremony relieved the children of the anxieties of youth by giving them a defined purpose in life and by marking a clear boundary between childhood and adulthood.

When Catholic priests use traditional tribal symbols of the Indian culture such as the Sacred Pipe, their end goal is to get their tribal church members, or potential members, to believe that, when they see the Pipe, they equate this with Catholicism. It may be that some of the Catholic use and incorporation of the Pipe into Church ceremonies is because of a misunderstanding about exactly what the Pipe represents to tribal people. The Lakota Oyate understand that the red stone out of which the bowl of the Sacred Pipe is made represents the blood of the people as a nation, and that the ash stem of the Pipe is the backbone of the people. Obviously, the red stone (pipestone or Catlinite) is the same color as the people's blood and ash is known to be the hardest and strongest of all woods in North America; and thus the Pipe incorporates two natural symbols that the people live for and by. The Catholics may have mistaken the meaning of this philosophy, or just plain did not care, and projected their own meaning on to it in order to accomplish their complete takeover of the Native Peoples' belief system. From what I understand, Catholics place great store in equating the red wine they use in ceremony as the blood of Christ. However, this is very different from the Pipe bowl representing the blood of the entire nation and, thus, to interpret this as representing the blood of Christ is an offense. The appropriation of the Sacred Pipe into Catholic services is just hegemony at its best and is offensive to most Indian people who do not consider themselves to be Christian.

The appropriation of Indian spiritual materials, objects, and symbols into Christian churches is very disturbing because no one seems to understand why this is being done. The Catholic Church, for example, has never given an adequate explanation of their purpose for doing so despite the fact that many reservation churches and priests now regularly display Indian objects or symbols. This appropriation disturbs many Indian people because it appears to them as a new method of colonizing Native communities. When one visits a reservation church that has Native symbolism displayed, one can often see depictions of Jesus and Mary with brown faces, and sometimes even hear the priest singing Christian songs or saying prayers in an Indian language.[13] When this occurs, one gets the impression that the Church is desperately trying to hang on to their members. I guess, in a way, they are attempting to make Christianity relevant to Indian lives but the message remains the same—only true believers will go to heaven in the

---

[13] Many Catholic and Christian bibles have been translated into Indian languages, particularly by the Jesuits who are known to encourage a facility in language acquisition for the express purpose of encouraging conversions and proselytizing.

hereafter. It remains the exact same old guilt trip that the Catholic religion is so good at laying at the feet of their membership.

I remember attending Catholic services as a kid. It appeared that just about anything and everything one might do required repenting over so you would not die with sin attached to your soul. In those days, the churches were all full on Sundays but today many are not. The opposite is true about the annual Sundance ceremonies that are held throughout the reservations. Many people are attending the annual Sundance ceremony these days. When I was young, the Sundance ceremonies might have a only handful of spectators but today there are traditional Sundances on each reservation that are very well attended by the local people and also by visitors from afar. In fact, many Sundances are packed with urban Indians who have made their annual journey home to the reservation specifically to participate in or to support a dance. This is how many contemporary Native people spend their hard-earned annual vacations. The Sundance usually takes up their entire leave time, and those that actually participate in the dance usually have to return to work while still healing from the physical and spiritual sacrifices they have made. Many tribal governments and other tribal organizations grant special leave time to their employees in order for them to attend traditional ceremonies.

In pre-reservation times, there was only one Sundance ceremony held among the Lakota Nation and it took place during the annual gathering of the *Oceti Sakowin* (the Seven Council Fires of the Teton). This gathering was huge and consisted of all the Lakota bands coming together for a short period during the summer months when resources were plentiful. However, in modern times, some reservations have upwards of 30 Sundances. The popularity of these traditional Native ceremonies, and spiritualism in general, appears to be infringing upon the religious ceremonies held by the Christian denominations to the point where some churches struggle to remain alive on the reservations. I know of at least a half-dozen churches on my home reservation of Cheyenne River that have closed down completely within the past 40 years.

To a person who has participated in contemporary-traditional Lakota spiritual ceremonies all of my adult life, it is especially disturbing to witness the appropriation of Lakota spiritual symbols by reservation-based Christian religious organizations. It impedes the progress that has been made towards a united and sovereign nation once again. As a point of clarification to the terminology used above, I must explain what is meant by the term "contemporary-traditional," used here to describe the ceremonies that are practiced today in as close to their traditional way as is feasible given the significant changes that have occurred since the major disruption caused during the mid 1800s. These changes include the modern workday, clothes, cars, annual vacations, food, and so on. The circumstances are such that it is recognized that they have evolved with the times to a certain extent. Some would argue that they have changed significantly, which may be true; however, I believe the values expressed within the ceremonies remain intact. When I was in college, one of my university professors used to bait me over the fact that I, and many other modern-day Indians, drive a four-wheel drive pickup truck and therefore we were not "real" Indians. For some reason he honestly believed that driving a truck, any truck, was the determining factor of whether I was truly an Indian or not. The point here is that the Indian and his culture have changed, and so the question becomes how much change can happen before there is no semblance of the culture anymore? Or will it continually evolve into a whole new identity?[14] After all, it is thought that most languages evolve and change into completely new and different ones every so many generations. In 1934, Luther Standing Bear lamented over the tremendous erosion of Lakota culture at that time, and yet Indian people are still here participating in traditional Lakota ceremonies, speaking the languages and teaching values to their children.

From the grassroots perspective, it remains true that some contemporary Indians will always move back and forth between the Church and the traditional ceremonial way of living their lives. I know many Indian people who, when asked to pray, use both Lakota and English—which always sounds funny to me, even though I do it, too. This is mostly to do with the loss of language on the part of some, but it sounds funny when a native speaker of the Indian language uses English in their prayers. I sometimes listen to an Indian radio station where an unidentified elderly man gives a wonderful opening prayer in the Dakota language (of course it is taped) and then ends it by saying "Amen," which seems really awkward.

The Church's recent effort to incorporate traditional Indian symbols and sacred objects into their services represents a new wave of colonization. This takes place inside the church itself as well as out in the community when the priests are asked to officiate at funerals and other events. Although the clergy's use of Native languages is by no means new, the display of images of Jesus and Mary looking like they are Indians and burning sage is. When this is done, there seems to be a subtle message that says: "It's OK to believe this way for now, we will forgive you for this shortcoming. In the future, though, you will get over it, and sooner or later you will become a real Christian and forget about this nonsense." I cannot see that the Catholic Church will ever condone the incorporation of the traditional Indian philosophy into teachings of the Church. The use of Native sacred symbols in Catholic services is held in deep suspicion by some, and it is partly because the Church has never come forth and given an explanation of its reasoning and purposes for this appropriation. It appears likely, however, that the Church wants us to believe that the two religious philosophies are so closely related and similar that there may not even be any real differences. Since when did the Church ever really care about the physical environment that we live in? Or does it really understand or care about the relationship that may exist between the people and any other living organism? Since when did it really know anything of value about how familial relationships work and survive? Does the parish priest have any real

---

[14]   This is a significant issue and complex topic for Indian peoples since it calls for the acknowledgment and reaffirmation of cultural values, something of considerable value in the face of the extreme pressure to assimilate and "vanish," as Euroamericans have forcibly encouraged and demanded.

knowledge to contribute about a relationship between a man and a woman? It appears to me that the Catholics have appropriated these sacred symbols without any understanding of their true meaning, or even without attempting to do so.

Philosophical Differences

When one views the new-found concern with Native symbols and their incorporation into the Catholic Church from a Native perspective, it is clearly a patronizing attitude and is offensive. It is paternalistic in nature and most Indian people are fed up with patrimony. The two philosophies are not even remotely similar and never will be. The one is consumed by life in the hereafter and only cares about picking up points in this life to give to Saint Peter and gain entry on reaching the pearly gates of heaven. The other philosophy has always concerned itself with the well-being of earthly relatives and the continuation of harmonious relationships within the community. A blending of these diverse philosophies does not work because of a natural tendency on the part of the Christian to dismiss the value of plants and animals. It is very similar to attempting to blend water and oil. In fact, Christians have a long history of attempting to negate Native Peoples' spiritual belief systems by purporting that they are animistic. Apparently, in their view, animism is not good and should be outlawed and struck down. This has been the Christian philosophy throughout the entire age of colonization … and now they want us to believe they have changed? Their new idea about incorporating some of our symbols into their church services is just another ploy to get a few more bodies into their churches at a time when more and more individuals are questioning the validity of the Christian faith. These new-found attitudes amount to neo-colonization at best. A friend of mine says of a guy we know who is always attending events and singing sacred songs yet acts disrespectfully towards others: "He can sing all the sacred songs he wants, but it does not make him sacred until he begins treating others in a sacred manner." Much the same could be said of the recent Catholic attitude towards incorporating our symbols into their church services. They can use them all they want but, unless they change their behavior and attitudes towards all our relatives, they will never possess any meaning other than just being another physical object. The Sacred Pipe that the people carry is after all just another physical object with no meaning unless it is blessed, carried, and used in a sacred manner; only then does it become holy.

Is the Catholic Church asking Native people to forget the root philosophical underpinnings of traditional beliefs where all life is related? The Church's appropriation of these symbols and re-imaging of them trivializes their meaning. The images take on new meaning when used within a Catholic service. They do not hold the same powerful understanding of relations among living organisms and the spiritual entities they depict. For example, let us study and understand the meaning of the medicine wheel according to the Lakota Nation (Figure 2.1).

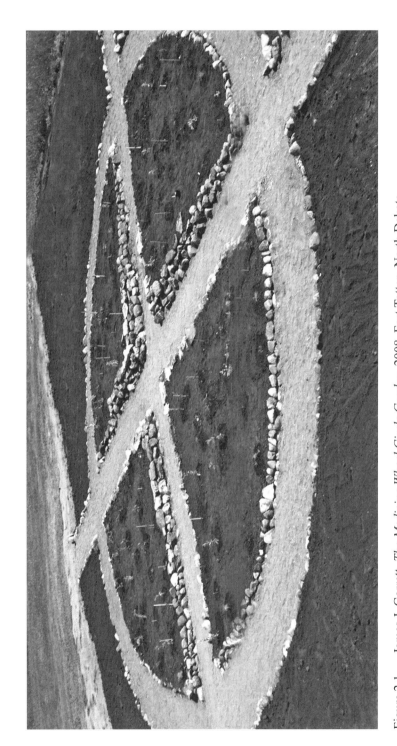

Figure 2.1   James J. Garrett, *The Medicine Wheel Circle Garden*, 2008. Fort Totten, North Dakota.

The symbol is the circle with north–south and west–east lines across the circle. The circle represents the universe that surrounds us and that we are a part of. The lines represent the four cardinal directions. The very center depicts two things: first is the Earth below us and, secondly, the Sky above us. We are but a very small part of the universe and yet where we presently stand is the center of that universe. The cardinal directions have separate and distinct meanings. They depict the spiritual entities that reside in those directions such as those beings that went to the spirit world before us, the cold freezing weather that comes from the north and purifies the Earth in the springtime, the direction from which the life-giving sun comes, and the direction from which the warm rains come. The below direction is honored because the Earth nurtures us just as a mother or grandmother does and is consequently revered just as one would a physical mother. The above direction is where the Creator and all the helper spirits reside and is where our prayers and songs go when they leave our mouths and are consequently heard by the Creator.

Catholic philosophy has never included any of these meanings of the medicine wheel nor has it ever attempted to understand the Sun, Wind, Water, Thunder, and Lightning as spiritual entities that assist us in our survival. The Lakota recognize the energy that makes the world move as *Taku Skan Skan*. It is understood that, without *Taku Skan Skan*, our heart would not beat, birds would not fly, or fish swim, and so forth. This sacred entity makes the Earth revolve around the Sun so that all other life may continue. Christians, and certainly not the Catholic Church, have never held such a holistic-type faith that might include the very environment in which humans reside and which contributes to our survival. The Christian faith is in direct conflict with this type of belief system. In fact, Christianity in general believes in the notion that human beings are above the rest of the creatures because of their capacity to reason and speak. This belief places human beings outside of the circle of life and thus characterizes the rest of life as something for them to exploit. This philosophy reeks with the arrogant attitude that human beings must be superior to all other living organisms and, consequently, all other life is treated with less respect. That is the nature of the relationship that the Christian faith has with the world and the rest of the living beings, including, oftentimes, other humans.

Only very recently has Christianity accepted the idea that the Native American might be a fellow human being. For ages, they thought of the Black man and the American Indian as less than human and actually placed a value of being a fraction of a full human upon them. The Indian was thought of as being savage because they practiced a so-called "voodoo" religion, one that has been practiced in the Caribbean for centuries. In fact, one can still look at place names today and gain an understanding of this Christian mentality of the past. For example, a sacred lake in eastern North Dakota is named "Devils Lake" because the local Dakota Indians believe the lake to be where spirits dwell. The true Dakota name for the body of water, however, is *Mni Wakan*—"sacred water" or "spirit water." This mistranslation of an Indian language was arguably a calculated misinterpretation.

In other words, anything that Indian people held sacred was labeled as "devil worship" and was of a savage nature.

Christians everywhere are completely and utterly disrespectful of Indians' sacred sites and their spiritual beliefs. There are numerous examples of them building their churches right on top of indigenous sacred sites in every part of the world. The most recent examples of disrespectful behavior is the construction of a saloon billed as the world's largest biker bar right next to the sacred site of Bear Butte in western South Dakota. This butte is held sacred by a number of Indian tribes who are indigenous to the area. In fact, at least two tribes have bought land surrounding the butte in attempts to protect its integrity. Yet, despite a large protest over the proposed construction, the town of Sturgis and the State of South Dakota decided that Indian beliefs about the holiness of the butte were of such insignificance that they allowed the construction to go forward. The local newspapers published editorials that referred to Indian communities as being physically dirty and therefore not worthy of holding anything sacred. This feeling is allowed and even encouraged, despite the fact that the town of Sturgis is overwhelmed by trashy bars and campgrounds that cater to partying bikers. The town condones the behavior of this wild bunch of people who spend their time during this summer event drugged and/or drunk raising holy hell in and around the sacred Black Hills and specifically Bear Butte. The people of South Dakota display such disrespect and contempt for Indians and their belief system that they hold this type of behavior in higher esteem than they do the desire for the surrounding Indian communities to go to the sacred site to pray. The non-Indian community allows this type of behavior in their community mainly because the annual summer motorcycle rally event brings in millions of dollars into the economy. Nothing makes people disrespect each other quicker than does money. Sometimes I have to shake my head in wonderment when Christian parents wonder why their children are so disrespectful of their parents despite all they have given their children. This mentality is endemic to the area. Another nearby sacred site called Devils Tower, or Bear's Lodge by the Lakota, is also a source of conflict. Traditional ceremonies are held there annually during June. Rock climbers continue to climb despite the request by the National Park Service to honor and respect the Indians' right to practice their religious ceremonies undisturbed.

Not only has our land been stolen, but now serious attempts are being made to steal our religion, too. American Indians have for a very long time strongly objected to the New Age Movement "borrowing" spiritual items and beliefs from them for the very same reasons that are listed in this chapter. The New Age Movement has a long history of this so-called borrowing. This movement attempts to adopt portions of traditional Indian ceremonies that they like and, when they do this, the adopted portions are thus placed out of context. The people who do the borrowing do not understand that they may end up hurting themselves and others by conducting ceremonies without totally understanding them. One time I was attending a music festival in San Francisco and a woman came up and asked if I was an Indian. When I responded that yes I was, she proceeded to tell me all about an all-lesbian Sundance that is held annually in the nearby mountains where they dance completely naked for four days. This is so out of context that it is laughable except for the fact that it is hurting Native Peoples' traditions by perpetuating the disrespect and disdain.

Native Peoples often do not speak out against the very same type of "borrowing" of their sacred objects by the Catholic Church. This may be due to the fact that many Indian families include members who consider themselves to be Christians and, out of respect for their beliefs, they say nothing. Many of these family members are Church members who attended mission schools and it has become ingrained into their psyche that they have to attend Sunday Mass no matter what or how they feel about it. This is a direct result of being punished if they did not show the proper respect for the Church. My mother told a great story about one of her classmates who received a severe punishment because he literally "poked fun" in class by asking the priest about Jesus Christ. My mother said:

> One of the boys asked the priest to reassure them all that God and Jesus were all around them. He asked if Jesus saw everything they did, and if he was in the room with them all right then? The priest replied, "Yes, Jesus is always present." So the boy responded by asking, "If this is true, then if I hold out my hand with my palm up, then maybe Jesus is in my hand?" The priest acknowledged again saying, "Yes, this is true." The boy quickly took the finger of his other hand and flicked at his upward facing palm and said, "Well, skidoo, little Jesus." All the other students laughed so hard that forever after the boy was known as "Skidoo," but he was ultimately punished for his disrespect.

Although this story comes from an earlier time, many of the same ramifications for perceived disrespect, conflicts, attitudes, and difficulties in interpretation and understanding remain today.

Conclusion

In summary, the American Indian Religious Freedom Act of 1978 has not really accomplished anything tangible for Native Peoples. If anything, it appears to have established parameters for those seeking to tromp American Indians' religious rights. Although in the *Lyng* case the court ruled that the case had merit, it ruled that public need was more important. Certain legal cases such as the one at Devils Tower that allows non-Indians to claim that Indians are just another special-interest group and should have no special claims to rights not granted to others are an abomination. The appropriation of American Indian spiritual symbols by the Catholic Church is unethical without the full consent of all Indians. Usually what happens in these types of cases is that the Church will ask only a few individuals for permission, and this enables them to claim that Indians have indeed given them the necessary consent. Neo-colonialism is occurring today throughout the entire world and is usually connected to violations of indigenous intellectual property rights. Sacred symbols and objects are the intellectual property of indigenous people. The appropriation of these items constitutes a violation of indigenous intellectual property rights and, consequently, they have not been properly acquired. However, no matter what, they are not for sale because most indigenous communities would never sell their sacred items. Until proper and appropriate permission is sought and received, the Church is conducting themselves in an unethical manner towards Native communities by their appropriation of sacred items and symbols. The attitude that no one will care is tantamount to a new and modern form of Old World–style colonialism.

Chapter 3

Denying Religion: Native Americans and French Missionaries in Early New France[1]

James B. Jeffries

> It cannot be said that the savages profess any doctrine; and it is certain that they do not, so to speak, follow any religion.[2]
>
> —Nicolas Perrot (explorer and fur trader), c.1660

From the time of their first contact with indigenous peoples of North America in the sixteenth century to the end of the seventeenth century, French observers consistently reported that the Natives of New France had no religion apart from the Christian faith that some had acquired from Europeans. What is interesting about these claims is that they occur beside descriptions of Native customs that appeared religious according to the Frenchmen's *own* definition. The numerous stories and ceremonies centered on spirits, or "manitous," that the French observed among Natives strongly resembled the kind of religiosity that other Europeans had reported in the New Word—namely idolatry. Nevertheless, explorers, fur traders, and missionaries alike in New France maintained that *their* Natives were uniquely irreligious. What complicates matters is that, while the early non-missionary observers assumed that Natives would be easily brought to Christianity, the missionaries discovered that Natives refused to abandon their local beliefs and practices. Despite this resistance to Christian conversion, however, the French continued to insist that these people had no religion of their own.

In this chapter, I recover two important problems for both the academic study of religion as well as Native American history that are conveyed in these French denials. First, why didn't the manitou customs of Native Americans qualify as religious? Second, why didn't the French change their minds about this once it became apparent—from the widespread failure of missionization—that Natives

---

[1] Aspects of this chapter, including the title, are drawn from an earlier project: James B. Jeffries, "Denying Religion: French and Native American Spiritual Crossroads in Seventeenth-century New France" (PhD diss., Santa Barbara: University of California, 2007).

[2] Nicolas Perrot, "Memoir on the Manners, Customs, and Religion of the Savages of North America (1864)," in Emma Helen Blair (ed.), *The Indian Tribes of the Upper Mississippi Valley and Region of the Great Lakes* (Cleveland, 1911), p. 47.

remained attached to these customs? To address these questions I trace the earliest missionary accounts of the Natives of Canada, which were made by the Récollets from 1615 to 1629. By considering the conceptual framework that the missionaries used to make sense of Montagnais and Huron resistance to conversion, I contend that the French based their understanding of Native irreligiousness on the lack of confidence that the indigenous peoples expressed about their local spiritual customs. Furthermore, what the missionaries asserted about Montagnais and Huron resistance to Christian conversion was that they refused to attach themselves to "factual" spiritual beliefs and practices. In other words, the Natives of New France were turned off by spiritual beliefs and practices that were framed authoritatively, like Christian customs, as the absolute truth. Thus, the French concluded that the Montagnais and Huron resisted Christian conversion not because they had their own opposing religious convictions, but because they refused to adopt any such convictions. Astonishingly, Natives knowingly preferred spiritual beliefs and practices that entailed fantastic—unbelievable—elements. It was not Natives' opposition to Christianity per se, but to religion qua spiritual conviction, that confused and befuddled the missionaries.

By recasting the quandary expressed by the missionaries (and overlooked by contemporary scholars) outside a Christian framework, this chapter offers a different explanation of the purported irreligiousness of Natives. Just as the Récollets noted, I contend that the Montagnais, Hurons, Algonquins, and the other indigenous peoples of New France preferred beliefs and practices about spirits that entailed fantastic elements. As in Christianity, such customs applied to existential mysteries of Creation and afterlife, of fortune and misfortune. As was often the case within Catholicism, they also applied to the interpretations of, and attempts to influence, chancy endeavors—such as hunting, fishing, healing, warfare, and gaming. What the missionaries failed to understand, however, was that Natives utilized these ambiguous and unpredictable facets of their lives in order to generate *poetic* insights into their humanity. It is in such distant, unknown places that fictional and semi-fictional art forms thrive in all cultures, except where stamped out by religious dogma. Thus, Natives expressed a lack of faith and conviction in the factualness of their spiritual beliefs and practices, but not in their significance. The poetic force generated by these customs was as undeniable to them as it was indispensable. For this reason, they would not yield ground to the authoritative claims of Christianity, or any other religion.

Scholarly Critiques of French Ethnographies

To the reader there is probably little worth pointing out about the assertions that Native Americans lacked religion, except the stupendous degree of cultural misunderstanding that they reveal about those who made them. In this vein, the French not only failed to recognize the obvious religiousness of Natives' manitou customs; they also failed to correct themselves even after it had become apparent that Natives refused to replace these local customs with Christian ones. Scholars of religion as well as Native American historians largely concur on these two points. Like other European explorers throughout the sixteenth and seventeenth centuries, we are told that French travelers denied that Natives had religion due to their inflexible Christocentric bias, which restricted religion to visible institutions. "What these early observers missed in Indian life, of course," explains James Axtell, "were the familiar signs of institutionalized religion … that codified national beliefs and prescribed ritual observances."[3] Like the Christian church, clergy, and bible, such visible institutions delineated the sacred beliefs and practices apart from ordinary, secular activities. Thus, the early Christian observers were insensitive to Native American religions, which entailed beliefs and practices that were not dictated by discrete, authoritative bodies of polity or scripture, but instead by systems of belief and practice that were integrated into their everyday lives. Such "social institutions existed," contends Peter Moogk, but "without the visible tokens that seemed essential to French eyes."[4] Regarding the earliest accounts about Native Americans, for example, Sam D. Gill writes:

> Columbus considered religion to be equal to "creed and church," as did Vespucci. They equated religion and Christianity, and while they probably did not expect to find Christianity among Indians, they appeared to expect some corruption of religion in the form of idolatry. Yet they reported finding not even that. For them, Native Americans had nothing that resembled religion.[5]

Even so, Gill explains, "Columbus described several cultural activities that *we* [my emphasis] cannot avoid considering as religious."[6] Similarly, cultural historian David Murray writes: "The realities of daily communication gave the lie to this idea of a complete absence of religion, though it is not uncommon to find confident statements of its absence followed immediately by quite detailed descriptions of what *we* [my emphasis] would certainly recognize as religious practices."[7]

Insisting that the French mistook the absence of visual forms of worship for the absence of religion sets the stage for some historians to assert that the French "later" came to realize their mistake and increasingly came to appreciate the

---

[3] James Axtell, *The Invasion Within: The Contest of Cultures in Colonial North America* (New York, 1985), p. 12.

[4] Peter N. Moogk, *La Nouvelle France: The Making of French Canada—A Cultural History* (East Lansing, 2000), p. 20.

[5] Sam D. Gill, *Native American Religions: An Introduction* (Belmont, 2005), p. 8.

[6] Sam D. Gill, *Native American Traditions: Sources and Interpretations* (Belmont, 2006), p. 3.

[7] David Murray, *Indian Giving: Economies of Power in Indian–White Exchanges, Native Americans of the Northeast* (Amherst, 2000), p. 176.

unwritten codes of a complex religious system.[8] The existence of such "invisible" religions is further supported by Natives' rejection of the Christian belief system. Why would Natives resist Christianity unless they were rooted in *their own* religious systems? For instance, Carole Blackburn writes:

> The Jesuits initially believed that the Huron did not have an organized religious system of their own and would therefore be easy to convert. ... It was only after they had devoted considerably more time and effort to the attempt to convert people that the Jesuits realized the extent to which religious beliefs and spiritual observances permeated the day-to-day activities as well as the annual and life cycles of Huron individuals.[9]

After quoting the French fur trader Nicolas Perrot's account of Menominee and Ottawa ritual activity (centered on the spirits of Hare and Sun), Cornelius Jaenen writes: "The French missionaries' and explorers' progressive realization of the high development of Amerindian religions is shown by such statements."[10] What Jaenen neglects to mention, however, is that his quotation occurs in a section Perrot titled: "Religion, or rather superstition, of the savage tribes," which begins with the sentence: "It cannot be said that the savages profess any doctrine; and it is certain that they do not, so to speak, follow any religion."[11]

While it may be natural for us to expect that the French must have (or should have) stopped insisting that Natives were without religion, their accounts throughout the seventeenth century indicate otherwise. Frenchmen—missionaries included—rarely, if ever, acknowledged the existence of an indigenous religion in New France (Acadia and Canada). Two exceptions were the Jesuit missionaries Paul Le Jeune and Jean de Brébeuf who initially declared that the Montagnais and Hurons acknowledged divinity, which accorded nicely with the theory that they carried to the New World that all human beings must.[12] Even so, the longer they spent in New France the more these two missionaries backtracked from

---

[8]   For example, see Denys Delâge, *Bitter Feast: Amerindians and Europeans in Northeastern North America, 1600–64*, trans. Jane Bierley (Vancouver, 1993), p. 71.

[9]   Carole Blackburn, "Harvest of Souls: The Jesuit Missions and Colonialism in North America, 1632–1650," in *Mcgill-Queen's Native and Northern Series* (Montreal, 2000), vol. 22, pp. 37–8.

[10]   Cornelius J. Jaenen, *Friend and Foe: Aspects of French–Amerindian Cultural Contact in the Sixteenth and Seventeenth Centuries* (New York, 1976), p. 44.

[11]   Perrot, "Memoir on the Manners, Customs, and Religion of the Savages of North America," p. 47.

[12]   Reuben Gold Thwaites and A.E. Jones, *The Jesuit Relations and Allied Documents; Travels and Explorations of the Jesuit Missionaries in New France, 1610–1791; the Original French, Latin, and Italian Texts, with English Translations and Notes* (Cleveland, 1896), vol. 5, p. 153; vol. 10, pp. 59–61.

this assessment.[13] The missionaries—contrary to Blackburn's claims—readily acknowledged both that their "spiritual observances" were commonplace, and that they permeated Natives' day-to-day activities. Of course, as Gill suggests, Native customs appeared ridiculous to the French. But the critical question is why the French *did not* change their minds about Native irreligion once they discovered that Natives remained attached to their own spiritual customs. Did not such conduct require revisions to earlier notions that these Natives had no form of religion at all? Likewise, the critical question left unanswered by Gill is why the French did not find in these customs what they expected to find: a crude form of religion that presented something minutely comparable to Christianity.

Seventeenth-century European Definition of Religion

For the French, religion was defined as the worship given to divinity according to one's recognition of divinity: *"Culte qu'on rend à la Divinité, suivant la créance que l'on en a."*[14] While anchored in monotheism and elaborated in ideas of Christian salvation, the term was frequently applied to Jews and Muslims: *"La Religion Juifve ... la Religion de Mahomet."*[15] Like other Europeans in the seventeenth century, however, the French also identified a fourth category of religion—idolatry—in which all others peoples were subsumed—that is, before the French encountered the peoples of Acadia and Canada.[16] Here, outside the three monotheistic belief systems, people misdirected their worship to false objects: *"Qui adore les idoles ou des créatures, and leur rend des honneurs qui n'appartiennent qu'à Dieu."*[17] As religion scholar Tomoko Masuzawa notes, this taxonomy of religion was consistently applied by Europeans throughout most of the early modern era: "Thus four seemingly well-marked categories—Christianity, Judaism, Mohammedanism, Idolatry (or heathenism, paganism, or polytheism)—recur in book after book with little variation from at least the early seventeenth century up to the first half of the nineteenth century."[18]

---

[13]   Ibid., vol. 8, p. 185; vol. 21, pp. 97–9.

[14]   Académie française, *Le Dictionnaire de l'Académie françoise, dedié au roy* (Paris, 1694), p. 391.

[15]   Ibid.

[16]   Thus, in Daniel Defoe's dictionary of "all religions," the entry for religion reads: "Religion is properly the Worship given to God, but 'tis also applied to the Worship of Idols and false Deities." Daniel Defoe, *Dictionarium Sacrum Seu Religiosum: A Dictionary of All Religions, Ancient and Modern. Whether Jewish, Pagan, Christian, or Mahometan* (London, 1704). This passage is quoted in Tomoko Masuzawa, *The Invention of World Religions, or, How European Universalism Was Preserved in the Language of Pluralism* (Chicago, 2005), p. 60.

[17]   Académie française, *Le Dictionnaire de l'Académie françoise, dedié au roy*, p. 582.

[18]   Masuzawa, *The Invention of World Religions*, p. 59.

What is important to note, however, is that three "other" examples of religion were viewed as false in this taxonomic system because their object(s) of worship obscured or qualified God's absolute beneficence as well as his sovereignty over creation.[19] This was especially so in the case of idolatry, where both divided (polytheistic) and embedded (anthropomorphic) notions of divinity condemned it to the low end of the religious spectrum.[20] As Vincent Milner wrote in his book (published in 1872) *Religious Denominations of the World*: "The true point of distinction [between non-idolaters and idolaters] is therefore to be placed in the recognition or denial of one universal, perfect Being."[21] Proper worship stemmed from the recognition of divinity, which in the Christian context, conveyed the idea of a wholly transcendent good and perfect creator in whom one was indebted for his equally transcendent, good and perfect (gratuitous) gift of redemption: Jesus. Thus, an imperfect understanding of divinity inhibited full and complete worship. Recognizing religion among the so-called idolaters enabled Christian observers to interpret a kernel of (their) "truth" in others, which verified the universality of Christianity as the one true religion.

Without presenting obvious notions of God, however, non-monotheistic settings forced Christians to adjust their focus in order to detect more subtle indicators of it. Without much if any written theology to work with, they probed the ethnographic accounts of European explorers and colonizers. In the descriptions of New World peoples generated during the sixteenth century, for example, theologians turned their attention to the Spanish accounts of Aztec and Mayan worship practices.[22] Here, the comparativists found the cultural attributes they needed to determine that religion was indeed present among these peoples. Here, too, they concluded divinity was represented, as in Judaism and Islam, in a corrupted form. Yet, in this case, the corruption was much greater since these peoples had, since the days of Noah's flood, presumably forgotten God. A sense of divinity—however muted—remained in their worship of false gods. According to this historical reconstruction, their worship divided and reduced divinity into multiple anthropomorphized forms. By the seventeenth century, French officials as well as Récollet and Jesuit missionaries would bring this

---

[19]   Comparative theologians would articulate this pejorative view of Judaism and Islam most forcefully in the nineteenth century, arguing that the "ethnic" qualities of their religious customs reflected a circumscribed understanding of God. Ibid., pp. 72–104.

[20]   Sabine MacCormack, "Limits of Understanding: Perceptions of Greco-Roman and Amerindian Paganism in Early Modern Europe," in Karen Ordahl Kupperman (ed.), *America in European Consciousness, 1493–1750* (Chapel Hill, 1995), pp. 87–8, 90, 93, 96.

[21]   Vincent L. Milner, J. Newton Brown, and Hannah Adams, *Religious Denominations of the World: A new and improved, with an appendix brought up to the present time*, ed. J. Newton Brown (Philadelphia, 1872), p. 518. Insertion added. Although it first appeared 1860, Masuzawa, who quotes this passage, argues that Milner's book reflected this "archaic taxonomy." Masuzawa, *The Invention of World Religions*, pp. 47, 48.

[22]   MacCormack, "Limits of Understanding."

comparative enterprise—with all of its expectations—to Acadia, then Canada. So, what happened? Why didn't they "find" what they *sought* and *expected* to find: religion?

The Récollets in Canada, 1615–1629

For a decade following their first arrival with Champlain in the spring of 1615, a handful of Récollets represented the sole missionary presence in New France. Operating within a Franciscan order that, unlike its Jesuit counterpart, provided little in terms of financial backing, coordination, or scholastic training, the Récollets functioned mainly in and around the vicinity of Quebec during this period. In the village they constructed a small chapel, the first church in Canada, where they performed regular religious services for the inhabitants. It is from this base that they reached out to nearby Montagnais at Tadoussac and passersby in what amounted to a limited campaign to educate and convert Natives to Christianity.[23] A few daring exceptions produced the richest ethnographic accounts of Natives by the Récollets. These were the incursions westward into Huronia initiated by Le Caron.

Le Caron, who arrived in Huron territory just prior to Champlain in 1615, returned with two more Récollet missionaries including Gabriel Sagard in 1623. The Récollets quickly apprehended both the impropriety and the meaninglessness of baptizing Natives before Christian indoctrination. And they came to recognize the same obstacles to conversion in Canada that the Jesuit Pierre Biard had identified among the Micmacs of Acadia (1611–13). Likewise, Le Caron and Sagard echoed their countryman's declarations about Native irreligiosity and, not surprisingly, painted a picture of an intractable savage condition that closely resembled Biard's account.

Le Caron was amazed at what he saw as a contradiction between the secular industry and the religious indolence of the Natives of Canada:

> We have thus far traversed more than six hundred leagues inland, and even wintered several years with the principal nations. They do not lack good sense in what concerns the public or private interest of the nation; they reach their end, and even adopt very fit means and measures; and it is the subject of my surprise that, being so enlightened for their petty affairs, they have nothing but what is extravagant and ridiculous when you treat of religious dogmas or rules of morality, laws, and maxims. We have visited eight or ten different nations down the river towards Tadoussac, and we have found that almost all the Indians of New France acknowledge no divinity, and are even incapable

---

[23] W.J. Eccles, *The French in North America, 1500–1783* (East Lansing, 1998), p. 28. Axtell writes: "The 115 Jesuit fathers who came to New France in the seventeenth century were among the best educated men in Europe." Axtell, *The Invasion Within*, p. 77.

of ordinary and common and natural reasonings on this point, so material and benighted is their intellect.[24]

Like Biard, Le Caron determined that the absence of rules reflected a conceptual awareness that was limited to the senses. In the same manner, he realized that building an understanding of Christianity was going to be especially difficult without the availability of useful Montagnais or Huron terms for translating its abstract ideas:

> I know not whether their ancestors knew any divinity, but the fact is that their language, natural enough for anything else, is so sterile on this point that we can find no terms to express the Divinity nor any of our mysteries, not even the most common. This is one of our greatest difficulties.[25]

The Récollets admitted, however, in creation stories and conjuring practices, the presence of "some confused sentiments of the Deity." Although such customs evoked notions of powerful nonhuman entities responsible for creation, bounty, wisdom, and other graces (vaguely reminiscent of the Frenchmen's own understanding of God), they were not "in the spirit of religion" for there was no corresponding faith or devotion paid to these entities. As Le Caron put it, they were "steeped in perfect indifference on the subject of religion" without "even exteriorly any ceremony for their worship—no sacrifice, temple, priest, or other mark of religion."[26]

The indifference that was expressed toward their so-called creator reflected, according to the Récollets' accounts, the Natives' own speculative, sometimes conflicting, understanding of the event itself. In other words, the lack of devotion that they displayed toward any divinity was a function of an acknowledged imprecision in their knowledge of such affairs. Consequently, although the stories of creation attributed to particular tribes differed in Le Caron's and Sagard's letters, the missionaries repeatedly underscored a common observation—namely, that such stories were to be distrusted. For example, upon hearing a Huron version—according to which, the grandmother of Yoscaha, the creator, stands as the source of evil—Sagard mockingly reported:

> If you tell them that there is no likelihood that a God could have a grandmother, and that this is an inconsistency, they have no answer, as in regard to all the other details. They say that they live far away, although they have no other

---

[24]   Chrestien Le Clercq, *First Establishment of the Faith in New France / Premier établissement de la Foy dans la Nouvelle France* (New York, 1881), p. 215.

[25]   Ibid., p. 221.

[26]   Ibid., pp. 389, 216.

sign or proof of it other than the story which they say was told them by an
Attiuoindaron, who made them believe that he had seen him.[27]

In the absence of definitive knowledge about these distant gods and events, there
were tremendous variations of belief as individuals drew their own opinions.
Thus, while the Récollets wrote that the Hurons generally viewed Yoscaha as the
source of good, Sagard added: "for though many speak in praise of their Yoscaha,
we have heard others speak of him scornfully and irreverently."[28] Similarly, after
summarizing a Huron creation story, Le Caron wrote: "If you make any objection
on the absurdity of this idea they answer that this is good for us [the French] and
not for them."[29]

Ironically, it was this refusal to refute that became a major source of annoyance
and frustration for the Récollets. If only the Natives had held religious convictions,
however false, such that they would deny Christian teaching, there would at least
have been something for the missionaries to upend through argument. Instead,
their reports suggest in the Natives of New France an awareness of spirits that was,
much like the linguistic incapacity for acknowledging essential qualities, adrift in
a sea of subjective relativity. Le Caron explained:

> As they believe that the French live in a different world from theirs, when we
> wish to disabuse them of their folly by telling the real creation and restoration
> they say that this seems to be true of the world we inhabit, but not of theirs. They
> often ask even whether there is a sun and moon in Europe, as in their country.[30]

Although the Hurons and Montagnais professed a disregard toward and uncertainty
about the creator, they did not question his existence. Likewise, according to the
Récollets' letters, the Natives assumed that the world was filled with such nonhuman
persons. Thus, although Yoscaha and his grandmother ("mother" in Le Caron's
account) are said to be sources of good and evil respectively, Le Caron wrote:

> Some acknowledge the sun, others a genius who rules in the air; others regard
> the heavens as a divinity, others a Monitou, good or bad. The nations up the river
> seem to have a universal spirit in everything, even in those which are inanimate,
> and they sometimes address them to conjure them.[31]

Besides the "god" associated with creation, according to the Récollets, the Hurons
and Montagnais made references to a seemingly limitless array of "geniuses" about

[27]   Gabriel Sagard, George McKinnon Wrong, and Hugh Hornby Langton, *The Long Journey to the Country of the Hurons* (Toronto, 1939), p. 169.
[28]   Ibid., p. 170.
[29]   Le Clercq, *First Establishment of the Faith in New France,* p. 217.
[30]   Ibid.
[31]   Ibid., pp. 215–6.

their world that felt and reasoned as humans did. Apparently, this was especially the case for those upstream from the Montagnais, the Hurons, whose world was teeming with spirits. For them, there was a soul operating not only in entities that the French considered alive (plants, animals, and humans), but in nearly all "non-living" things as well (thunder, lakes, rocks, tools, etc.). Le Caron wrote: "As they ascribe souls to all sensible things, they believe that men after death hunt the souls of beaver, elk, foxes, wild geese, seals, and that the soul of their snowshoes serves to keep them above the snow, and the souls of their bows and arrows to kill beasts."[32]

The missionaries were unexpectedly made aware of these beliefs while accompanying Natives during mundane activities such as canoeing, hunting, or preparing food. In the typical situation, the missionaries noted an abrupt interruption in the proceedings as their guides stopped to observe some sort of ritual. Consistent with Samuel Champlain's observations on the Ottawa River, for example, Le Caron learned while traveling with Hurons that they perceived a spirit person within dangerous water passages: "We remark that when there is any rapid difficult to pass, any peril to avoid, they throw in the very place a beaver robe, tobacco, wampum, and other things by way of sacrifice to conciliate the good-will of the spirit who presides there."[33] Similarly, Sagard wrote:

> They believe also that there are certain spirits which bear rule over one place, and others over another, some over rivers, others over journeying, trading, warfare, feats and diseases, and many other matters. Sometimes they offer them tobacco and make some kind of prayer and ritual observance to obtain from them what they desire.[34]

Likewise, Le Caron and Sagard extrapolated from their observations of Native hunting practices that animals as well were each ascribed with an anthropomorphic "spirit" or "soul." Thus, Le Caron wrote:

> These poor blind creatures also profess a thousand other superstitions with which the devils entertain them. They believe that many kinds of animals have reasonable souls; they have an insane superstition against profaning certain bones of elk, beaver, and other beasts, or letting their dogs gnaw them. They pretend that the souls of these animals come to see how their bodies are treated, and go and tell the living beasts and those that are dead; so that if they are ill-treated the beasts of the same kind will no longer allow themselves to be taken either in this world or the next.[35]

---

[32]   Ibid., p. 218.

[33]   Ibid., p. 216.

[34]   Sagard, Wrong, and Langton, *The Long Journey to the Country of the Hurons*, p. 171.

[35]   Le Clercq, *First Establishment of the Faith in New France*, pp. 219–20.

The absence of religion among the Natives of New France was not simply a reflection of their unchristian ways, for the disregard that the Natives displayed toward their *own* "gods" exceeded that of all known exotic peoples. Sagard drew from the Roman philosopher Cicero, as had Frenchmen before him,[36] to establish a comparative platform, albeit with a Christian superstructure, for describing the various religious beliefs that he expected to find in New France. For Sagard, while all false, non-Christian religious beliefs were fabricated according to a people's condition, they were, nonetheless, organized social expressions of an innate virtuous human desire to honor something higher than oneself. Such beliefs were indicators of civility:

> Cicero has said, in speaking of the nature of the gods, that there is no people so savage, so brutal, or so barbarous that has not some instinctive notion about them. Now as there are diverse nations and countries of barbarians so also are there different opinions and beliefs because each of them fashions a god suitable to its place.[37]

Accordingly, as missionary, Sagard hoped to arouse this impulse in the Natives, to usher the ignorant from their dark and miserable condition with the light of the Gospel, so that they would aspire to know and honor the true Divinity. Instead, the Récollets found that the Hurons, as the rest of the Canadians, had only vague and conflicting notions of a creator, and they treated the spirits in their surroundings with little distinction from humanity. In this way, Sagard conceded that there was nothing in their beliefs that reflected a religious instinct: "This actually reveals that they do not really know and adore any divinity or God, of whom they could give some account and whom we could recognize."[38] Rather than worshipping spiritual entities that mirrored the exalted characteristics of divinity—which the missionaries would have recognized as a confused and fragmented awareness of the True God—Huron and Montagnais imagined pseudo-deities with basic human qualities. In the same vein, Le Caron found that the religious instinct, which was apparent in all other known peoples, was uniquely squelched among the Natives of New France. He wrote: "They are naturally inconstant, mockers, slanderers,

---

[36] From his experiences in Acadia in 1607–8, the French author and lawyer Marc Lescarbot wrote: "Yet though Cicero has said, speaking of the nature of the gods, that there is no nation so savage, or brutish, or so barbarous, but is imbed with some faith in them; nevertheless there have been found, in these later ages, nations with no feeling thereof; which is some much the stranger, that among them there were, and still are, idolaters, as in Mexico and Virginia, and if we will, we may add Florida." Marc Lescarbot, *Histoire de la Nouvelle France*, Publications of the Champlain Society Publication 11, ed. Henry Percival Biggar and William Lawson Grant (Toronto, 1914), 90.

[37] Sagard, Wrong, and Langton, *The Long Journey to the Country of the Hurons*, p. 167.

[38] Ibid., p. 170.

unchaste—in fine, amid a host of vices in which they are swallowed up you can perceive no principle of religion or of moral or pagan virtue, which is a great drawback to their conversion."[39] Le Caron concluded that their indiscriminate, whimsical manner of conceiving and petitioning spirits had left them uniquely insensitive to the transcendent truths to which the rest of humanity aspires:

> Their sins have apparently spread a darkness and insensibility in their souls for all kinds of religion such as historians have never remarked in any other nation in the world. For amid their countless superstitions there seem to be none to which they cling from religious motives. It is pure fancy. When pressed on their reveries they make no answer; their mind remains, as it were, stupid and dull.[40]

The puzzle we face, like the early French observers, is in understanding the non-dogmatic basis for spiritual customs.

Reinterpreting Native Manitou Customs

In his study of missionization of the Montagnais by the Jesuits of New France, Kenneth Morrison relates the reported absence of religious convictions among Montagnais to the absence of a transcendental theological edifice in their worldviews. Drawing from the groundbreaking ethnographic interpretations of A. Irving Hallowell (who explained that the Ojibwa did not conceive of a *super-*natural), Morrison writes: "In effect, then, the idea of belief or faith in some sacred and transcendental otherness which we commonly associate with religion was not particularly relevant to Montagnais interests."[41] What the missionaries failed to understand as they questioned the Montagnais about their spiritual beliefs was that "Montagnais religious discrimination was everyday and practical."[42] While they reported that Natives expressed ingratitude about their manitous, the missionaries "did not understand that rituals attached to hunting ensured proper relations with these mythological beings."[43] He adds: "Since the Jesuits never really understood the Montagnais religious system, they could not eradicate it."[44]

By emphasizing the practical and effective principles directing their spiritual customs, Morrison allows us to appreciate how and why specific customs changed,

---

[39]   Le Clercq, *First Establishment of the Faith in New France*, p. 222.

[40]   Ibid., p. 220.

[41]   Kenneth M. Morrison, *The Solidarity of Kin: Ethnohistory, Religious Studies, and the Algonkian-French Religious Encounter*, Suny Series in Native American Religions (Albany, 2002), p. 119.

[42]   Ibid., p. 120.

[43]   Ibid.

[44]   Ibid., p. 129.

much the way Richard White does in his emphasis of the pragmatics of exchange.[45] Similarly, it allows Morrison to elucidate how Montagnais processed and gauged Christian customs. "One might say ... that they came to think of Jesus and Mary as additional other-than-human persons, admittedly very powerful persons who offered daily assistance."[46] On the other hand, in recognizing that there had to be some kind of theological presuppositions through which the Montagnais projected other-than-human benefactors, Morrison identifies three unconscious and unarticulated assumptions. He writes:

> Still, the religious outlook of the Montagnais people was systematic, and the system channeled their evaluation of the Jesuits' religious claims. While they did approach religious change pragmatically, they made largely unconscious and usually unarticulated assumptions about the character of reality. Three ideas are central to Montagnais reality assumptions, as they were to all Algonkian-speaking Native Americans. These are the concepts of Person, Power, and Gift, which dominated their perception, cognition and social behavior.[47]

Here Morrison elucidates the (non-doctrinal) principles governing the spiritual customs of New France. The non-dogmatic given-ness of the existence of spirits was comparable, and integrated, with the non-dogmatic given-ness of the common essential personhood of all life-forms and the non-dogmatic given-ness of the protocols of gift exchange. In light of this application, Morrison questions the notion of religious conversion in this context: "Whatever the Jesuits claimed about the preeminence of the Christian God, nothing in Montagnais religious practice constituted a dogmatic creed. So the fundamental problem with the term 'conversion' has to do with the assumption that to convert is to change traditions, to shift religious direction."[48] Instead, Morrison views their incorporation of Christian customs as "a process of rediscovery" in which "they came to reexperience and thereby revitalize the basic religious truths of their traditional life."[49]

Morrison's perspective is insightful because he points the way toward articulating *set principles* through which Natives developed *non-authoritative* spiritual customs—that is, the "unconscious" and "unarticulated" ideas that are brought to bear on "concrete experience."[50] He explains: "Any idea of impersonal cause was foreign to their thinking. Thus, natives" idea of power was also closely related to the concept of person. In fact, the word for power—manitou—was also

---

[45]   Richard White, *The Middle Ground: Indians, Empires, and Republics in the Great Lakes Region, 1650–1815* (Cambridge, 1991), pp. 25–7.

[46]   Morrison, *The Solidarity of Kin*, p. 128.

[47]   Ibid., p. 120.

[48]   Ibid., p. 129.

[49]   Ibid.

[50]   Ibid., p. 120.

synonymous with the concept of person, human and otherwise."[51] In this way, by anchoring these customs in concrete experience rather than set belief, Morrison allows us to see that Native spiritual customs were based on concrete experiences of natural (other-than-human) forces that were *automatically* interpreted as manitous—that is, other-than-human persons to whom human persons owe propitiatory gifts. Drawing from the theoretical perspective of Sam Gill, Morrison indicates that the beliefs and practices produced by these experiences carried weight because they oriented Montagnais meaningfully and purposefully to their world. Furthermore, because Montagnais society was egalitarian, individuals developed their own understanding of manitous from their individual experiences. As he explains: "Although the ideas of Person, Power, and Gift structured the Montagnais' overall tradition, the tradition itself was possessed unevenly."[52]

While this understanding of a "religious heterogeneity" is useful for explaining how and why manitou customs varied between individuals, Morrison's study downplays the lack of conviction and confidence that individual Montagnais conveyed about their own beliefs and practices.[53] Morrison claims that the French reports of Native religious indifference reflected their questioning, which centered on abstract religious beliefs and practices such as creation and redemption. Given the distant location of the creator's dwelling, not to mention the uncertainty surrounding his true identity, it follows that the Natives of Canada displayed a greater concern toward those who, according to their point of view, directly and presently impacted their environment rather than the one who might have created it.[54] This is confirmed repeatedly by the missionaries, who complained that Natives did not care about "the spirit," only "the flesh." Similarly, Sagard reported that, despite having heard about a creator, Hurons made "no prayer nor offering to their Yoscaha, at least not to our knowledge, but only to these special spirits I have just described, on suitable occasions."[55] Yet Morrison concludes from similar statements by the Jesuits that the French *did not* understand that what was important to Natives was everyday and practical. He suggests that, if they had looked, they would have found what was religiously important to them. This contention misrepresents the missionaries, who not only understood that Native customs applied to the concrete world, but also probed Natives' attitudes about them for any indication of religious convictions.

The problem was that, though Natives were certain of the existence and relative importance of spirits in general, they neither regarded them as wholly beneficent nor held fast to the particulars of their existence. Le Caron wrote, "If pressed on our mysteries they hear all with as much indifference as if they were relating their

---

[51]   Ibid., p. 121.

[52]   Ibid., p. 127.

[53]   Ibid., p. 128.

[54]   Ibid., p. 120.

[55]   Gabriel Sagard, *Long Journey to the Country of the Hurons*, Publications of the Champlain Society 25 (New York, 1968), pp. 171–2.

chimeras."[56] Likewise, Sagard noted: "When one begins to gainsay or dispute with them on these matters some make the excuse of ignorance, others desist for shame, and others who think of maintaining their position get confused immediately, and there is no consistency or likelihood in their assertions, as we have often seen and known by experience."[57] Thus, among people who "emphasized the immanent character of religion,"[58] we are left to think that individuals honored the individual conclusions that they drew from individual experiences of persons/powers.

What is misleading about this statement is that by conflating practical knowledge with spiritual knowledge, it conflates the different regard the Montagnais had for each. For example, while the hunter's techniques combined both forms of knowledge, he conveyed an uncertainty and indifference about the spiritual aspect of his craft. Likewise, the Natives of New France were highly suspicious of individual shamans, even though they steadily relied on shamanism. While Morrison applies a fairly flat and neutral definition of religion—"a human activity through which people assign responsibility for meaning, worldly and otherwise"—it should not surprise us that, in imputing it in the Montagnais context, a venerational regard for the beliefs and practices creeps into his discussion.[59]

I contend that the Jesuits, like the Récollets before them, knew far more about Montagnais spirituality than Morrison suggests. The missionaries understood that Natives always associated spiritual customs with practical endeavors. They understood that Natives doubted Christian beliefs as well as their local spiritual beliefs. Lastly, they understood that Natives refused to adhere to any discernable patterns of belief. Should we conclude from this that there must have been "hidden" patterns that the French did not understand? It is clear that we may come to know more about the "religious systems" of the Natives of New France once we come to appreciate what the missionaries knew about the peoples in which they found no such systems.

If the Natives of New France did not honor their beliefs and practices regarding manitous, it is because such honor had no currency in the system of exchange that they perceived with them. It is here where we can finally turn the corner on a problem presented by Natives' regard for spirits whose unquestioned existence is somehow not supported by dogma. We can see that such "regard" differed in the context of explaining verses implementing these customs (in a way that closely relates to the absence of dogma and unquestioned presence of spirits, respectively). The minimal regard that Natives paid their beliefs and practices was not perceived to undermine the exchange with spirits because it did not enter into it. In this, we can recognize a distinction that is largely absent in the Judeo-Christian perspective. The notion of God or gods based on a definition of transcendence conflates what in a single unified cosmos is clearly distinguished: spiritual knowledge verses spiritual tribute. Natives distinguished what they knew about manitous (including

[56]   Le Clercq, *First Establishment of the Faith in New France*, p. 220.
[57]   Sagard, *Long Journey to the Country of the Hurons*, p. 170.
[58]   Morrison, *The Solidarity of Kin*, p. 119.
[59]   Ibid.

how to placate them) from the business of honoring them. The distinction reflects an uncertainty they felt about the accuracy of this knowledge contrasted with the certitude they felt about the existence of manitous who demanded honor. Neither seventeenth-century French observers nor today's ethnohistorians fully appreciate this separation. Consequently, the early observers misinterpreted the indifference that Natives displayed toward their spiritual knowledge as an indication of disrespect for spirits themselves. This is precisely the aspect of French testimony widely dismissed by scholars who mistakenly assign Natives' spiritual conduct— that is, the ceremonial offerings Natives made to manitous before divining, hunting, fishing, warring, etc.—to a sacred belief system.

The French gauged false religions not by how their customs differed from particular Christian customs, but by the extent to which beliefs and practices about divinities were tainted with human contingency. The absence of dogma among Natives was assumed to be indicative of a disregard for spirits themselves. I hold that scholars have not recognized and tested this assumption expressed by seventeenth-century Frenchmen because they share it. "Religion," in both primary and secondary materials, entails faith and worship—that is, a system, undergirded by dogma, for paying tribute to God or gods.

In a Christian perspective, knowledge of and tribute to God are mutually implicating such that one speaks of faith (a worshipful knowledge) and worship (a faithful tribute) interchangeably. The conflation of knowledge and tribute reflects the historical development of a transcendent theology in the Judeo-Christian Western world, which drew certain beliefs and practices into its spiritual economy—beliefs and practices that were increasingly demanded by, because they are owed to (the idea of), a perfect, absolute Creator. Thus, a sense of certitude or conviction was generated about particular beliefs and practices that one owed God—that is, about the "truths" that acknowledge God's absolute power and beneficence. The role of belief and correspondingly the sense of debt, guilt, and conviction in this spiritual economy increased exponentially among Christians in the wake of Saint Paul's theological interpretation of Jesus Christ. As others have remarked, Christianity— a world religion centered on an interior and personal (psychological–theological) commitment to orthodoxy—was born from this seismic theological shift that occurred to the requirements of worship, which Paul, its first theologian, dislodged from the outer and communal (legal–scriptural) Jewish rubric of orthopraxy.[60]

On the basis of unconscious and unspoken principles of personal causality, Natives detected the presence of manitous in the self-evident other-than-human forces that they encountered in their environment. Such perception was brought into focus by the speculative claims about these forces, which went above and beyond the general impressions provided by the raw perception of things. By filling in the details about manitous—the origin, history, and scope of their powers—such knowledge sharpened the feelings of awe that were aroused in their presence. This

---

[60]   Patrick V. Reid (ed.), *Readings in Western Religious Thought: The Ancient World* (Mahwah, 1987), pp. 285–6.

leads to an important question: Why were such details about manitous filled in at all? The short answer is that they provided interesting ways of imagining them and, in so doing, responded in kind to the intriguing nature of these obscure powerful persons. This is comparable to speculation provoked by the unpredictability of the weather and the uncertainty of the forecasts themselves. The difference in this case, however, is that the speculation about manitous prompted fantastic possibilities about them. So, why did Natives knowingly project illusory notions about manitous? Possibly, the same reason we do in respect of tales, legends, or poetic metaphors: for their playful engagement with reality.

By leading one's thoughts beyond the probable or possible, Natives' ideas about manitous drove ceaseless speculation about mysteries that inspired them in the first place. By humanizing the mysterious events of other-than-human persons, such speculation created poetic reflections of their own humanity. As Dennis Tedlock explains, "Fantasy ... looks in one way or another for a distant place to happen."[61] Turning this around, perhaps it can be said that life's mysteries present natural frames in which we are drawn to insert fantastic explanations. It is not just that we utilize contexts of "long ago," "long from now," and "far away" to present fantasies already at hand; such opaque conditions inspire them. They inspire explanations that do not resolve the mystery—what actually occurs there—but that spin it in ways to meet the existential concerns of the audience. By calling upon one to imagine strange, improbable, impossible, or even absurd scenarios operating within the mystery, they endow such elusive domains, as Keith Basso explains about the Apaches' distant past, with "discernible applications."[62]

As they met different expectations than conveying facts, these fictional or semi-fictional aspects of Native spiritual customs did not reflect unintended misunderstandings of reality. It is expected within this genre of historic tale-telling that the actual past will be somewhat distorted. Considering Apaches' view of history, for instance, Basso explains:

> Apache tribal history as crafted by Anglo-Americans proceeds on different assumptions, produces a different discourse, and involves a different aesthetic. Mute and unperformed, sprawling in its way over time and space alike, it strikes Apache audiences as dense, turgid, and lacking in utility. But far more important is the fact that it does not excite. It does not captivate. It does not engage and provoke a measure of wonder. As Charles Henry said once in English, summing up quite a bit, "It's pretty mainly quiet. It stays far away from all our many places."[63]

---

[61] Dennis Tedlock, *The Spoken Word and the Work of Interpretation* (Philadelphia, 1983), p. 177.

[62] Keith H. Basso, *Wisdom Sits in Places: Landscape and Language among the Western Apache* (Albuquerque, 1996), p. 33.

[63] Ibid., p. 34.

In this way, objective explanations of, for example, rivers, journeying, trading, warfare, feats and diseases may have seemed as trivial and unsatisfying to the Hurons as historical treatments of their past seem to Apaches. Furthermore, it is the inherent uncertainty about such events—even when objective scientific inroads are afforded—that attracts fanciful speculation. Questions about the past and future as well as natural events present limits on what can be known or predicted about them with objective certitude anyway. This opens the possibility for fantastic explanations, which operate and thrive at the limits and in the gaps of factual knowledge. As these non-authoritative explanations apply to the fringes of what can be known with certitude, they do not necessarily conflict with, nor forestall efforts to expand, factual ones. Their purpose is in deriving "truths" other than the factual kind. In weighing explanations, the paramount issue for the Natives of this study, like the Apaches, was utility. Perhaps in some facets of their lives fantasy was more useful than fact. As Basso explains, the Apaches might not question the veracity of history books concerning their past, just their viability.[64] It is not necessarily that Anglo-Americans have been wrong about the distant past so much as they have wasted too much of this field of inquiry to dole out mere (lifeless) facts about it.

By examining the assorted references of Native spiritual beliefs in seventeenth-century New France, it is clear that Natives utilized nearly every conceivable domain of unpredictability and uncertainty in which to project fantastic explanations. The weather, hunting, gaming, warfare, birthing, child development, and other naturally unpredictable and precarious events and occupations, as well as the sun, moon, stars, past, future, and afterlife provided ready-made platforms on which to stage fantasy—unknowns through which one's thoughts easily transitioned, as in dark of night, from reality to unreality and back again. By calling upon one to imagine the presence of persons and places, operating behind such mysteries, ideas about manitous represented what Basso referred to in place-making as "a common response to common curiosities."[65]

Like the French, Montagnais and Hurons explained origins, ends, stars, storms, and other common curiosities by interjecting agency behind them. In sharp contrast with the French, Natives drew from ordinary and everyday examples of human conduct to describe capricious, ambiguous, and imperfect agents, in explanations that were regarded equally so. They filled in the gaps of knowledge about events that occurred by asking: Why did this happen? Why should it matter? Who was involved? Why did they do it to me or us? What did I or anyone do to provoke them? What should I or we do about it? Such speculation deepened the sense of wonderment about manitous not only by furnishing them with interesting characteristics, but by interpreting their actions—the natural events that they purportedly caused—in purposeful terms. As Tedlock discussed with regard to Zuni tales, "the real motive or trait is the

---

[64]   Basso, *Wisdom Sits in Places*, p. 34.

[65]   Ibid., p. 5.

taking-off point for behavior that would be extreme or nonexistent in real life."[66] This event-making utilized attributes of real interpersonal conduct as the taking-off point for imagining fanciful beings operating behind natural events. At the same time, from such fanciful strata, in which reality was deflected, Natives reached perspectives from which to ponder the nature of interpersonal conduct. In the absence of an omnipotent and omniscient arbiter, mysteries were made meaningful not by making them suit the ultimate concerns of dispensation, but by linking them to present, immediate, and manifold concerns of human survival. In this way, French and Native peoples bent the truth about mysteries so as to endow them with discernible applications. Yet, they did so in opposite directions. While the former sanctified them, the latter humanized them.

Applying Jonathan Z. Smith's understanding of myth as a "self-conscious category mistake" allows us to appreciate that Natives not only tolerated implausible aspects of their stories and rituals pertaining to manitous; they expected them.[67] Thus, we can recognize that the activities of divination, tobacco-offerings, storytelling, and so forth, marked occasions in which participants relaxed their regular, rational expectations of proceedings in order to entertain (in order to be entertained by) fantastic ones. As Mary Douglas explains, a ritual provides a frame: "The marked off time or place alters a special kind of expectancy, just as the oft-repeated "Once upon a time" creates a mood receptive to fantastic tales."[68] In this way, we further clarify our understanding of the class of activities and understandings pertaining to manitous in Native cultures, which stood apart from, as it interrupted, the flow of ordinary activities and understandings.

By viewing their world as filled with human beings in other-than-human forms, Natives utilized otherwise meaningless and unpredictable events as poetic metaphors of interpersonal conduct. By imagining the drama of strange and extraordinary persons operating behind uncontrollable events—on the margins of the ordinary, predictable world—Natives reached unique perspectives on their own social condition. Yet such imaginative understanding of rainfall, animals, disease, and other curiosities was continually upset by the reality of such occurrences, which generally repelled the anthropomorphic assertions about them. Jonathan Z. Smith's view of myth enables us to appreciate that it was the tension and interplay generated between the fit and misfit of spiritual beliefs and practices with reality that drove ceaseless speculation and rethinking about the mysteries to which they applied.[69] Because the final say about manitous was always out of reach, in thinking about them Natives were continually drawn

[66] Tedlock, *The Spoken Word and the Work of Interpretation*, p. 173.

[67] Jonathan Z. Smith, "Map Is Not Territory: Studies in the History of Religions," in Jacob Neusner (ed.), *Studies in Judaism in Late Antiquity* (Leiden, 1978), vol. 23, p. 299.

[68] Mary Douglas, *Purity and Danger: An Analysis of the Concepts of Pollution and Taboo* (New York, 1966), p. 64.

[69] Smith, "Map Is Not Territory," p. 300.

back to the drawing board to search for new ways to connect ordinary aspects of themselves with the unknowns about them. But having the final say about unknowns, about manitous, was never the point of these customs. It would be a mistake, therefore, to judge them—to assume they were judged—according to the extent to which they approximated reality, for the useful, meaningful insights that these customs generated depended on ideas that ventured beyond reality. Here was where they found their target. It is in this way that these customs served as vehicles of, and for experiencing,"what it is to be human."[70] By pondering the extraordinary persons of manitous, Natives of New France developed insights into their own humanity.

Unfettered by conventionality and absolutism, the speculation about manitous provided occasions not only for affirming social guidelines, but also for creatively redrawing them to meet current realities—to rethink them, as Basso says of place-making, "in ways different from what others have supposed".[71] The indomitably indeterminate nature of capricious events presented an inexhaustible resource for reviving and revising what it means to be human. The Natives of New France harnessed this resource by bending it back in such a way as to reflect themselves. By viewing fortuitous events as personal responses to human conduct, they deflected the capriciousness of physical nature back on human nature, and thus established discernable application in what were otherwise impersonal, cold, and meaningless events. In terms of metaphor, the capriciousness of humans provided suitable source images for projecting onto fortune and misfortune. To speculate about manitous, in this way, was to generate poetic metaphors between the two, altering perspectives on each. "Natural events," as we might call them, were transformed into barometers of human conduct—human virtue, vice, skill, and folly—while the events, in turn, came to be seen as personal, purposeful, and meaningful. In this way, the speculation about other-than-human kinds of persons served as a vehicle for understanding the human kind.

---

[70]   Ibid., pp. 290–91.

[71]   Basso, *Wisdom Sits in Places*, p. 6.

Chapter 4

Past and Present Transformation of Hawaiian Religious Participation

C. Kalani Beyer

The "discovery" of the Hawaiian Islands in 1778 by Captain James Cook began the rapid transformation of the Hawaiian culture. The rejection of the traditional religion in 1819 by the rulers of Hawai'i was an overt sign of this cultural transformation.[1] From the death of Kamehameha the Great until the beginning of the twentieth century, when a new religious equilibrium was established, it was the Calvinist and Roman Catholic missionaries who mainly attracted Hawaiians to Christianity. This chapter investigates the transformation of the Hawaiian culture with a focus on the religious participation of Native Hawaiians during the nineteenth century. There are four sections to this investigation: 1) the traditional religion and the initial transformation during the 'āikapu era; 2) the establishment of Christianity by Calvinist Christians during the 'āinoa era; 3) the erosion of Calvinist success as the result of the Roman Catholic challenge; and 4) the resistance and revival of the Native Hawaiian religion during the last 40 years of Hawaiian sovereignty, ending in the 1898 forcible annexation to the United States. A postscript concludes the chapter, which reports the modern transformation of Native Hawaiian religious participation from the 1960s to the present as the result of the Native Hawaiian sovereignty movement and the revival of Native Hawaiian culture and religion.

'Āikapu Era

For several centuries, the Hawaiian religion, which was imported from Tahiti, was the center piece for the 'āikapu era. Once this religion was adopted by Hawaiian rulers and imposed on the rest of the population, the 'āikapu era ensued. During this era, which lasted until 1819, religion through the *kapu* system was the paramount system for holding the social, political, and economic structures together. In its simplest form, the *kapu* system acted as a regulator, establishing

---

[1] Religion is briefly defined as a set of symbolic forms and acts that relate human beings to the ultimate conditions of their existence. Robert Bellah, "Religious Evolution," in W.A. Lessa and E.Z. Voght (eds.), *Reader in Comparative Religion* (New York, 1965), p. 78.

priorities for attention. On one hand, the *kapu* system determined the divine, pure, or impure; all else was forbidden (*kapu*) to persons or things not divine. This meant that people had to pay attention and relate to the divine in a prescribed way. On the other hand, if it was permitted behavior (*noa*), there was no need to pay attention. Consequently, *kapu* had the dual meaning of "forbidden" and "sacred." It was a prohibition, but also a privilege, accruing to someone of high rank.[2]

The Hawaiian form of religion has been termed archaic by anthropologists. Its characteristic feature was the emergence of a true cult with a complexity of gods, priests, worship, sacrifices, and divined and priestly kingship.[3] Moreover, it was made up of a mixture of spiritual, ceremonial, social, and political elements.[4] Gods were represented in Hawaiian legends as chiefs, living in far-off lands or in the heavens, and coming as visitors or immigrants to special localities in the Islands, which would then become sacred places of worship. For a long time, the gods, with their families and friends, lived with Hawaiians as visible personal gods but, when they became disgusted with humankind's evil ways, they left, leaving the promise that someday they would return speaking an unrecognizable language.[5]

The Hawaiian religion consisted of a multiplicity of gods. Each man could have a distinct god; women had their own female deities. The multitude of gods was organized into separate levels: the four great gods and the lesser gods.[6] All the people worshiped the great gods, Ku, Lono, Kane, and Kanaloa, and each god had a distinct form of worship with priests and *heiau* (temples) and particular symbols of ritual distinction. The worship of the god Ku was by far the most severe of the great gods for two reasons. First, Ku's ritual was practiced in *heiau* by a stricter class of priests and could be used only by the ruling chief to protect him from his enemies and to insure his own success. Thus, Kamehameha, as guardian of the god Ku, was the only one who could appeal to Ku in his venture to conquer the islands of Hawai'i. Second, the worship of Ku included the sacrifice of humans. In contrast, the worship of Lono, the god of the *Makahiki* (the harvest season), was milder in ritual and was practiced in inauspicious *heiau* without human sacrifices. Both Kane and Kanaloa were of negligible influence in Hawai'i; both were more powerful gods elsewhere in Polynesia.[7] The lesser gods belonged to

---

[2]   Martha W. Beckwith, *Hawaiian Mythology* (New Haven, 1940), p. 159; E.S.C. Handy, K.P. Emory, and Mary Pukui, *Polynesian Religion* (Honolulu, 1927), p. 43; David Malo, *Hawaiian Antiquities* (Honolulu, 1951), pp. 53–4, 58, 81–2.

[3]   Marshall Sahlins, *Historical Metaphors and Mythical Realities: Structure in the Early History of the Sandwich Islands Kingdom* (Ann Arbor, 1985), pp. 8–17; Valerio Valeri, *Kingship and Sacrifice: Ritual and Society in Ancient Hawaii*, trans. Paula Wissing (Chicago, 1985), pp. 20–30.

[4]   William F. Blackman, *The Making of Hawaii: A Study in Social Evolution* (New York, 1899), p. 43.

[5]   Beckwith, *Hawaiian Mythology*, pp. 4–5.

[6]   Ibid.; Malo, *Hawaiian Antiquities*, pp. 3, 5, 85.

[7]   Beckwith, *Hawaiian Mythology*, pp. 81, 120–21; Malo, *Hawaiian Antiquities*, p. 81.

families descended from one of the major deities or worshiped by those who pursued special occupations. These *'aumakua* (family gods) included the worship of animals, vegetation, objects (such as stones) that contained certain powers, or family spirits, and they were valuable as a family protector.[8] Samuel Kamakau explained how useful *'aumakua* were for Hawaiians:

> Thus did each person who had an *'aumakua* call upon his *'aumakua* and his ancestors – those directly related to him – for help in times of sickness, for the increase of fish and food, for the forgiveness of a specific wrong (*ho'okalahala*), or for the forgiveness of all his sins of commission and omission (*huikala*), or for help in the troubles that come to every family that calls upon the *'aumakua* (*ke ho'aumakua*).[9]

If worship was neglected and its *kapu* forgotten or disregarded, the *'aumakua* wreaked vengeance upon its keeper and his family. If the family god proved ineffective, however, it might be disregarded in favor of a stronger god.[10]

Not all of Hawaiian life was governed by the exactness of the *kapu* system. The celebration of the god Lono during the *Makahiki* festival, which lasted from October to January, was a period when neither work was performed nor religious *kapu* were observed. It was a time of rest, great feasts, games, sexual promiscuity, and the *hula*. Nathaniel Emerson, nineteenth-century historian of the *hula*, stated:

> The hula was a religious service, in which poetry, music, pantomime, and the dance lent themselves, under the forms of dramatic art, to the refreshment of men's minds. Its view of life was idyllic, and it gave itself to the celebration of those mythical times when gods and goddesses moved on earth as men and women and when men and women were as gods.[11]

While the *hula* epitomized the frivolity of the *Makahiki* season, when it ended in January all Hawaiian life returned to the rigid *kapu* system until the next fall season.[12]

The actual form of worship was not idolatrous as often claimed by the Calvinist missionaries. Two antiquarian Hawaiian historians, Samuel Kamakau and David Malo, both of whom were Christians in good standing with the Calvinist missionaries, have said that no actual idol worship existed before the advent of

---

[8]   Ibid.

[9]   Samuel Kamakau, *Ka Po'e Kahiko: The People of Old* (Honolulu, 1964), p. 30.

[10]   Beckwith, *Hawaiian Mythology*, p. 106.

[11]   Nathanial B. Emerson, *Unwritten Literature of Hawaii* (Washington, DC, 1909), pp. 11–12.

[12]   Beckwith, *Hawaiian Mythology*, p. 50; Kamakau, *Ka Po'e Kahiko*, pp. 19–24; Malo, *Hawaiian Antiquities*, pp. 47–8, 141.

Christianity.[13] According to Malo, the idol was carved "to resemble the description of an imaginary being, and not to give the actual likeness of a deity that had been seen."[14] Thomas Thrum, a descendent of Calvinist missionaries, concurred with the two Hawaiian historians: the idols were merely representations of an invisible god; furthermore, at ceremonial gatherings led by *kahuna* (priests), the congregation never bowed down to and worshiped the idols. In fact, some gods were worshiped without any concrete form.[15]

An important concept that explains the traditional Hawaiian religion during the *'āikapu* era was *mana*. Hawaiians believed *mana* was a quality that was divine in origin. It manifested itself in a person having power over people, animals, or inanimate objects. It was predicated on the gods and of the person or thing closest to them, such as *ali'i*, priests, prayers, temples, sacred houses within temples, images of gods, ritual objects, and omens. Humans became *mana* by descent. They passed *mana* on to another person and were dependent on feelings and dispositions that were connected to fellowship.[16] Certain of the *kahuna* were also concerned with the use of sorcery. Sorcery was commonly practiced when a person, in order to gain the power or *mana* of a god, obtained an object containing that god. Thus, sorcery began when the keeper sent the possessed spirits abroad to do his bidding. *Kahuna* who practiced sorcery employed several variants: *kahuna anaana*, praying to death; *kahuna ho'ounauna*, sending sickness or trouble; and *kahuna kuni*, divination by burning. Another type of *kahuna* was the *kahuna lapaau-laau*, medical practitioner. This class of *kahuna* expanded after the introduction of foreign diseases.[17] In spite of the disreputable deeds accorded *kahuna* by Calvinist missionary historians, the class of pre-missionary *kahuna* was made up of serious and greatly respected men. According to Kamakau, *kahuna* "was a person who lived quietly, was lowly, unassuming, humble of heart, not a gad-about, or covetous, but one who suppressed his lusts. This was the kind of man who represented the true sorcerer."[18] Based upon the use of the term sorcerer above, the "true sorcerer" was someone who claimed or was recognized as having magical powers used to heal, determine the future, or cast spells for the benefit of the person seeking his help.[19]

The social and political systems of Hawaiians were closely aligned with the religious system. The hierarchies of the gods corresponded with the social hierarchy; thus, each member of the society was ranked according to his proximate kinship with the gods. At the top of the social scale were the *ali'i*. Closely associated with them

---

[13]   Samuel Kamakau, *Ruling Chiefs of Hawaii* (Honolulu, 1961), pp. 200–202; Malo, p. 84.

[14]   Malo, *Hawaiian Antiquities*, p. 84.

[15]   Thomas Thrum, *More Hawaiian Folktales* (Chicago, 1923), p. 278.

[16]   Valeri, *Kingship and Sacrifice*, p. 150.

[17]   Ibid.

[18]   Kamakau, *Ruling Chiefs*, p. 214.

[19]   Mary Pukui, E.W. Haertig, and C. Lee, *Nana I Ke Kumo (Look to the Source)* (Honolulu, 1972), vol. 1, pp. 27–31, 81, 99.

were *kahuna*. Below the *ali'i* and *kahuna* were the mass of people collectively called *maka'āinana* (commoners).[20] As a class, the *ali'i nui* (high chiefs) were the highest on the social hierarchy claiming familial ties to one of the four great gods. They not only governed the people, but also led them in rigorous adherence to the ceremonies of religion and the worship of the four great gods. The *maka'āinana*, then, worshipped both their own *'aumakua* and the family god of the *ali'i nui*.[21]

Between Cook's "discovery" of Hawai'i in 1778 and 1819, when the *kapu* system and "idolatry" were abolished, traditional Hawaiian culture underwent a rapid transformation. Two factors explain the societal changes: one, the political consolidation of Hawai'i under Kamehameha the Great, and two, the impact of foreign influence. The ancient worship of the god Ku gave Kamehameha the support of Hawai'i's most powerful god. Correspondingly, while Kamehameha relied on tradition for power, he also procured foreign assistance in the form of weapons and advisors.[22] Hawai'i had never been united but rather had been organized in chiefdoms ruled by *mō'ī* (highest of the high chiefs). At the time that Kamehameha began his bid to extend his power to become *mō'ī* of all the Hawaiian Islands, there were six *mō'ī* in power throughout the archipelago. Kamehameha's unification of the Islands therefore caused a major dislocation for the defeated followers of the other *mō'ī*. Land was redistributed to the victors and to the warring adventurers. Moreover, Kamehameha continued to employ foreign ideas brought to him by his advisors or by the foreign trade that he encouraged. All these actions accelerated the transformation of the traditional culture.[23]

Even before the first missionaries arrived in 1820, *haole* influence, often unknowingly, paved the way toward the future Christianizing of Hawaiians.[24] The first aspect of this influence was the appearance of warships. Aarne Koskinen, the Finnish historian of missionaries to Hawai'i, labeled the impact of warships as the most successful factor in converting Natives to Christianity.[25] Lawrence

---

[20]   Handy, Emory, and Pukui, *Polynesian Religion*, p. 3; Kamakau, *Ruling Chiefs*, p. 208; Malo, *Hawaiian Antiquities*, pp. 60, 192.

[21]   Ibid.

[22]   Ralph S. Kuykendall, *The Hawaiian Kingdom: 1778–1854* (Honolulu, 1966), pp. 29–44; David Tynerman and George Bennett, *Journal of Voyages and Travels* (Boston, 1832), pp. 77, 81, 92, 351, 435–6.

[23]   Beckwith, *Hawaiian Mythology*, p. 8; Ephraim Eveleth, *History of Sandwich Islands* (Philadelphia, 1839), p. 78; Walter P. Frear, *A Century of Achievement* (Honolulu, 1920), p. 7.

[24]   Originally, Hawaiians applied the term *haole* to all foreigners; over time, it applied primarily to white people of Anglo-Saxon Protestant background. When Portuguese immigrants arrived in Hawai'i, they were not referred to as *haole*. Generally, the term has a neutral connotation, used to designate the background of a person. It can be used negatively, especially when dominance and subordination are involved in its use.

[25]   Aarne A. Koskinen, *Missionary Influence as a Political Factor in the Pacific Islands* (Helsinki, 1953), p. 26.

Fuchs, renowned Hawaiian social historian, claimed that Native religion proved impotent: "observing the superiority of *haole* cannon over Hawaiian clubs, of *haole* ships over native canoes, the Hawaiian *ali'i* began to doubt the power of their ancient gods."[26] Furthermore, many Hawaiians became sailors on foreign ships and, for the most part, gave up their belief in the ancient religion. Upon their return home, they began to refute the ancient *kapu* by blatantly disregarding them. Some sailors even adopted Christianity while traveling abroad. In fact, a few of the Hawaiian youths who emulated the Christian missionaries to Hawai'i had been sailors Christianized during their voyages.[27]

Even more important to the introduction of Christianity into Hawai'i were the anti-religious and religious *haole* settlers. The anti-religious *haole* settlers included sailors, adventurers, and merchants. They differed from the religious *haole* by their lack of adherence to Christian morality and teaching. The religious *haole* were identified by their "morality and decorum against prevalent lewdness, obscene *hula* dances, drunkenness, opium and the lottery, as espoused by the [*ali'i*] and reckless whites."[28] Both *haole* groups enhanced skepticism in the traditional Hawaiian religion when they disregarded the *kapu* and did not suffer the prophesized dangers. Ernest Beaglehole explained the resulting psychological effect: "the Hawaiian acceptance of this material culture meant an implicit, and sometimes explicit, recognition of the superiority over their own culture."[29]

The religious *haole*, of whom Isaac Davis and John Young are the most frequently mentioned, were considered good men by Natives and missionaries. The missionaries judged them as good because they lived according to Christian mores; Hawaiians considered them good because they married Hawaiian women and adopted Hawaiian customs and language. Their influence helped Hawaiians choose to adopt aspects of Western culture. For example, they advised Kamehameha during his unification efforts and were the sources of Western crafts introduced by Kamehameha into Hawaiian society. They also have been credited with the abolishment of human sacrifices and the overthrow of "idolatry."[30] By the final year of Kamehameha's life in 1819, *haole* influence had been so successful that the *kapu* system and "idolatry" were floundering. The destruction of idolatry in Tahiti precipitated Kamehameha's request to be instructed in the doctrines of Christianity, which none of his foreign advisers were qualified to teach. A further indication of the deteriorating situation was the general laxity with regard to *kapu*. Finally,

---

[26]   Lawrence H. Fuchs, *Hawaii Pono: A Social History* (New York, 1961), pp. 196–7, 212.

[27]   James J. Jarves, *History of the Hawaiian or Sandwich Islands* (Boston, 1843), pp. 206–7, 212.

[28]   Sereno E. Bishop, "Are Missionaries' Sons Tending to America a Stolen Kingdom?," *The Friend*, 52/1 (1894): 18–20.

[29]   Ernest C. Beaglehole, *Some Modern Hawaiians*, University of Hawai'i Research Publications 19 (Honolulu, 1937), p. 82.

[30]   Blackman, *The Making of Hawaii*, pp. 68–9.

upon his deathbed, Kamehameha proclaimed that all human life was sacred, thus disavowing the traditional human sacrifice.[31] With the death of Kamehameha, who had firmly continued to unite the rites of the traditional religion with the policy of government, the "keystone" was removed and the entire system rapidly dissolved. The skepticism that pervaded all ranks became manifest. None had a more hearty contempt for the traditional rituals than Kamehameha's successor, Liholiho. The new *mō'ī* had been tutored in English by foreign advisors and acquired a taste for Western alcohol. James Jarves, a nineteenth-century historian, spared no words in describing the state of Liholiho and the nation's wantonness at the death of Kamehameha: "In his love of sensual gratification, disregard of customs and traditions, sanctioned by usage immemorial, desire yet fear of change, and ignorance of the means of accomplishment, he embodied the general spirit of his nation."[32] In other words, with Liholiho's rule, conditions were ripe for the transformation of the Hawaiian religion and the end of the *'āikapu* era.

The coup de grâce to the *kapu* system and "idolatry" came during the traditional mourning period for the dead *mō'ī*. In practice, this period had been one of license; even women were free to eat with men, enter the *heiau*, and partake of the sacred foods.[33] Usually, at the end of the mourning period, a new set of *kapu* were issued. In this case, Liholiho, with the encouragement of his mother, Keopuolani, and aunt, Ka'ahumanu, both wives of Kamehameha, continued the practice of free eating. Ka'ahumanu gave the strongest clue as to why the *kapu* was broken: "The tabu is broken. Let us live as the white men do."[34] Without the old restraint of *kapu*, the people were left in a religious void and no laws, civil or religious, were issued to fill the void. Kamakau reported, "bitterness reigned everywhere and murder, theft, adultery, drunkenness, and deceit were commonplace."[35] The traditional orderly times of rest from work and opportunities for worship were destroyed. Mary Pukui, the renowned modern expert on Hawaiian culture, stated that domestic life "became helter-skelter …[and] it would be decades before a new order, based upon New England Congregationalist and French Roman Catholic mores, was really comprehended."[36] Since every activity in the daily life of Hawaiians was linked to their religion, they were at a loss as to how they should proceed with their life without the *kapu* religion.

---

[31]   Jarves, *History*, pp. 206–7, 212.

[32]   Ibid., p. 210.

[33]   Hiram Bingham, *A Residence of Twenty-one Years in the Sandwich Islands* (New York, 1847), pp. 77–9; Jarves, *History*, pp. 212, 213, 215–16; Kamakau, *Ka Po'e Kahiko*, p. 222.

[34]   Henry B. Restarick, *Hawaii, 1778–1920, from the Viewpoint of a Bishop* (Honolulu, 1924), pp. 40–41.

[35]   Kamakau, *Ruling Chiefs*, p. 288.

[36]   Handy, Emory, and Pukui, *Polynesian Religion*, pp. 233–4.

'Āinoa Era: Christianizing of the Kingdom

With the end of the *kapu* system, the *'āinoa* era began. As a term, *'āinoa* refers to freedom of choice or literally "free eating." Ultimately, it was the individual preference and conscious actions of Hawaiians that defined the early meaning of the *'āinoa* era. During the early years of this era, there was an acceptance and coexistence of beliefs old and new. Although many Hawaiians called themselves Christian, aspects of the traditional religion, particularly the worship of family deities (*'aumakua*) and the use of priests (*kahuna*), continued for some families. Consequently, throughout the nineteenth century, Hawaiian identity was in constant flux, as individuals at varying intervals adopted Western ways while continuing to follow many of the customs of the traditional culture.[37]

Judging from twentieth-century studies, there is evidence that Hawaiians continued to practice many traditional customs or merged their culture with Western practices.[38] From these sources and the occasional glimpses into Hawaiian identity by the missionaries, the following picture emerges. For most Hawaiians during the *'āinoa* era, the daily routine of life continued to be based on spending a small portion of their day in the production of food and the larger part of the day in playful pastimes. The work portion of the day involved the maintenance of taro or sweet potato fields, raising of pigs, and fishing in the sea. The arrival of the missionaries altered their playtime by including a couple of hours for missionary taught reading instruction (*palapala*). Every time the Calvinist missionaries set up literacy lessons, adult Hawaiians skipped their surfing, gaming, and other leisure activities to go to school.[39]

When the vast majority of the adult Hawaiian population was literate in their own language, they returned to the full-time pleasures of their leisure activities. Some differences in their leisure activities emerged and related to the end of the *kapu* system and the coming of the missionaries. When the *Makahiki* festival, part of the worship of the god Lono, ceased due to the end of the *kapu* system,

[37]   Lilikala Kameʻeleihiwa, *Native Land and Foreign Desires: Pehea La E Pono Ai?* (Honolulu, 1992), pp. 80–84, 142–3; George K. Young, "'Moʻolelo Kaukau Aliʻi: The Dynamics of Chiefly Service and Identity in 'Oiwi Society,'" (PhD diss., University of Hawaiʻi, Mānoa, 1995), pp. 109, 277–80.

[38]   See Ronald Gallimore, John W. Boggs, and Cathie Jordan, *Culture, Behavior and Education: A Study of Hawaiian-Americans* (Beverly Hills, 1974); George H.S. Kanahele, *Ku Kanaka Stand Tall: A Search for Hawaiian Values* (Honolulu, 1992); Joyce Linnekin, *Sacred Queens and Women of Consequence: Rank, Gender, and Colonialism in the Hawaiian Islands* (Ann Arbor, 2000); Pukui, Haertig, and Lee, *Nana I Ke Kumu*.

[39]   Other leisure activities included swimming, surf-riding, sledding, boxing and wrestling, foot-racing, a Hawaiian form of bowling, throwing darts, guessing games, a Hawaiian form of checkers, mock battles, and *hula* dancing. John P. Iʻi, *Fragments of Hawaiian History*, ed. Dorothy B. Barrere (Honolulu, 1959), pp. 63, 72–4.

Hawaiians stopped participating in many of the games that were related to warfare.[40] However, much to the chagrin of the missionaries, *hula* schools (*halau*) continued to train *hula* dancers, even as the religious significance of these dances declined. The *hula* became a source of pride for the performers and a form of entertainment for the observers. In addition, the luau replaced the *Makahiki* festival as the time for *hula* students to share what they had learned at the *halau*. Eventually, the luau was to become a celebration that could take place more than once a year, serving to sustain the Hawaiian values of *aloha* (love) and *kokua* (generosity). In continuing to perform and observe the *hula,* Hawaiians were celebrating a special part of their heritage, even if it prevented them from being both baptized and members of the Christian church.[41] My family was one of the few who kept the traditional *hula* alive during this time period. This required teaching and performing the *hula* out of the sight of the Christian *ali'i* and the Calvinist missionaries. Open display of the *hula* would not take place until the revival of Hawaiian culture during the last forty years of the nineteenth century.

Few Hawaiians were baptized and allowed to become members of the Calvinist churches because they continued to practice elements of the ancient religion.[42] Although worship of the four great gods of Polynesia (Ku, Lono, Kane, Kanaloa) had been abolished and their representations and temples destroyed by order of Kamehameha II, most Hawaiians continued to worship their *'aumakua* and, on the island of Hawai'i, the goddess of volcanoes, Pele. As pragmatic people, Hawaiians worshipped *'aumakua* that related to their daily activities such as fishing, hunting, acquiring materials such as rocks, plants, and feathers, as well as building, procreating, child-naming, *hula* dancing, swimming, tool making, and anything related to daily life. Moreover, the mysteries of nature, such as the volcanoes and other natural disasters, and death and birth, led them to continue to act on the religious beliefs of their traditional religion.[43] They might pray to a Christian God, but better to be sure rather than sorry, and they continued to practice ancient religious customs as well. Although *kahuna* (priests) were less visible during the *'ainoa* period, a person could easily acquire their services. Since Western medicine had not saved Hawaiians from the perils of the introduced diseases, *kahuna* were still sought out for their aid even as missionaries saw these services as an abomination. It had been their constant complaint that any practicing of the traditional religion by Hawaiians was backsliding.[44] However, according to Lilikala Kame'eleihiwa and George Young, contemporary Native Hawaiian scholars, in the minds of many

[40]   Nathaniel B. Emerson, 'Causes of Decline of Ancient Hawaiian Sports," *The Friend*, 50/8 (1892): 57–60.

[41]   Linnekin, *Sacred Queens and Women of Consequence*, pp. 113–14.

[42]   Gavan Daws, *Shoal of Time: A History of the Hawaiian Islands* (Toronto, 1968), pp. 104–5; Kuykendall, *The Hawaiian Kingdom*, p. 116.

[43]   Handy, Emory, and Pukui, *Polynesian Religion*, pp. 116–59.

[44]   William D. Alexander, *A Brief History of the Hawaiian People* (New York, 1891), pp. 1–20; James Bicknell, "Hawaiian Kahunas and Their Practices," *The Friend*, 48

Hawaiians, the people believed they could both worship the Christian God and practice aspects of the Hawaiian religion.[45] This was a logical deduction of the choices Hawaiians believed the *'āinoa* period allowed.

Family life continued to be centered upon the *'ohana* (the community). As people moved around more and as family members began to intermarry with other races, the *'ohana* was enlarged to encompass relatives and non-relatives alike who spoke Hawaiian or participated in reciprocal social relations with each other.[46] Due to missionary urging, the King decreed that marriage between a couple sharing time and sexual favors was to be the law. This did not prevent Hawaiians from continuing to share sexual favors with other adults. When ships docked in the Hawaiian archipelago, it was common practice for women to share sexual favors with sailors, even if they were married. This practice was a remnant of the sexual activity that was common during the ancient *Makahiki* festival. The Calvinist missionaries found this sexual promiscuity an abomination; however, the *'ohana* never negatively judged its members' sexual conduct even when it led to children born out of wedlock. Children were prized, although disease led to Hawaiians having fewer children. The practice of *hanai* (giving up adoption of a child to a favored relative or friend) continued to complicate genealogy records but managed to add more members to one's *'ohana*.[47]

The first Christian missionary group to arrive in Hawai'i was the American Board of Commissioners for Foreign Missions (ABCFM), an interdenominational religious body whose membership was predominantly Congregational and Presbyterian. This organization represented the last adherents to Calvinist theology.[48] Shortly before the abolition of the *kapu* system and "idolatry," the ABCFM sent the brigand *Thaddeus* abroad with the first company of Calvinist missionaries to Hawai'i. The attention of this organization was directed toward the Island Kingdom by reports of traders and by the presence in New England of several Native youths from the Islands. The Prudential Committee of the ABCFM outlined the missionaries' duties prior to their departure: their mission was not to be

---

(September 1890): 61–7; Sereno E. Bishop, "Why Are the Hawaiians Dying Out?," *The Friend*, 47 (March 1889): 18–20.

[45]   Kame'eleihiwa, *Native Land and Foreign Desire*, pp. 155, 165; George T.K. Young, *Rethinking the Native Hawaiian Past* (New York, 1998), p. 136

[46]   Handy, Emory, and Pukui, *Polynesian Religion*, p. 15; Linnekin, *Sacred Queens and Women of Consequence*, p. 33.

[47]   I'i, *Fragments of Hawaiian History*, p. 87; Linnekin, *Sacred Queens and Women of Consequence*, pp. 61–3; Houston Wood, "Displacing Native Places: The Rhetorical Production of Hawai'i" (PhD diss., University of Hawai'i, Mānoa, 1996), p. 1; Young, *Rethinking the Native Hawaiian Past*, p. 130.

[48]   John H. Bratt, *The Rise and Development of Calvinism* (Grand Rapids, 1959), pp. 122–8; Warren Candler, *Great Revivals and the Great Republic* (Nashville, 1904), pp. 189, 91–2; John T. McNeill, *The History and Character of Calvinism* (New York, 1954), p. 353.

for private and earthly gratification but rather for the good of the people of Hawaiʻi and for the glory of God. Upon their arrival on 30 March 1820, the missionaries learned of the downfall of the "idolatrous" system and were convinced that they had received God's grace, preparing the way for their mission.[49]

The Calvinist missionaries arrived at an opportune time. Not only had the *kapu* system and "idolatry" been abandoned, but the nation had already undergone forty years of Western influence. The fact that Calvinist missionaries from New England were the first organized Christians to direct a mission in Hawaiʻi gave them a decided advantage over other Christian sects that would arrive later. Liholiho or Kamehameha II and his aunt, Kaʻahumanu, welcomed with friendly caution the Calvinist missionaries.[50] The newcomers were allowed to stay one year according to a "wait and see" attitude. When the year was up, Calvinist missionaries had proven themselves to the *aliʻi* and were allowed to remain as long as they pleased. After the trial period, Native rulers were more than cooperative; indeed, they practically monopolized the efforts of the new religious leaders.[51]

The most potent factor for the success of converting Hawaiians to Christianity was the attitude and influence of the chiefs. In the early years of the Calvinist missionaries' work, *makaʻāinana* were reluctant to commit themselves to Christianity until they knew the attitude of their *aliʻi* toward the new religion. At first, only a few chiefs were willing to be instructed in the Christian faith. Keopuolani, Liholiho's mother, was the most important early convert. Liholiho also allowed himself to be instructed but remained a skeptical student until his mother requested his conversion on her deathbed. Before he could influence his people, however, he sailed for England, where he and one of his wives died in 1824.[52]

With the death of Liholiho and return of the royal bodies to Hawaiʻi, Kaʻahumanu, the regent for the new King (the nine-year-old Kauikeaouli), became the greatest exponent of Christianity. She began to travel around the various islands exhorting the people to become Christians and follow the laws of the Bible. She wanted to establish a civil code by declaring that the Ten Commandments be adopted as the law of the nation.[53] Thereafter, under her leadership, more *aliʻi* became Christian

---

[49]   Rufus Anderson, *History of the Mission of the American Board of Commissioners for Foreign Missions to the Hawaiian Islands* (Boston, 1872), pp. 10–12; Bingham, *A Residence of Twenty-one Years*, pp. 57–9; Kuykendall, *The Hawaiian Kingdom: 1778–1854*, pp. 100–102; Tynerman and Bennett, *Journal of Voyages and Travels*, p. 404.

[50]   Kaʻahumanu was elevated to the position of *kuhina nui* or premier of the Kingdom by Kamehameha the Great because he recognized her brilliance as a leader. Before the King died, it was an accepted fact that as *kuhina nui* she was second in command. After his death, she became the actual ruler of the kingdom. Jane L. Silverman, *Kaahumanu: Molder of Change* (Honolulu, 1987), p. 62.

[51]   Bingham, *A Residence of Twenty-one Years,* pp. 86–91.

[52]   William Ellis, *Journal of a Tour around Hawaii* (Boston, 1825), pp. 44, 161, 76, 79.

[53]   Timothy D. Hunt, *The Past and Present of the Sandwich Islands; Being of Lectures to the First Congregational Church* (San Francisco, 1853), pp. 91, 95; Kamakau, *Ruling*

and the people were directed to learn the written word of God and follow the laws of the land. Important among these laws were the prohibition of murder, robbery, cheating, adultery, prostitution, polygamy, distillation of alcohol, and idolatry.[54]

Following the example of the rulers, it became fashionable to become Christian. Other factors, however, aided the Christianization of Hawai'i such as the arrival in 1822 of Rev. William Ellis from Tahiti with several Christian Natives who greatly facilitated the conversion of several of the Hawaiian *ali'i*. In addition, Christianity seemed to offer Hawaiians a decided economic advantage. Hawaiians observed how well off materially were the Calvinist missionaries and other religious *haole*, and they believed that if they, too, were Christian that they would also have wealth. At several stops on his tour around the Hawaiian Islands, numerous persons who wished to become Christian so that they could enjoy all the comforts afforded the Christian *haole* confronted Ellis. The *palapala*, or reading and writing, offered the people both a new pastime and a way to receive the *mana* (the power) of the *haole*. The *ali'i* had at first been reluctant to allow their subjects this magic knowledge until they themselves possessed it. Once their concern dissolved, people flocked to Calvinist missionaries to be instructed. Finally, the healing power of the Calvinists demonstrated the power of the Christian God. Foreign diseases had increased the sickness and death rates among Hawaiians; when the medical *kahuna* failed to arrest the increasing tide of maladies, Native Hawaiians turned to the missionary, his medicine, and his God.[55]

For missionaries, the fruit of these influences was the Great Revival in 1837–38, and many Hawaiians became Christians during these years because their relatives and friends were doing so. According to Beaglehole, these converts were guided by curiosity, superstition, the power of suggestion, and imitation.[56] By the second decade of the Calvinists' mission, they realized the need for more than divine help to change the character of the people and lead Hawaiians towards developing their notion of a "civilized" society. Success to the Calvinists meant that Hawaiians had to exhibit Puritan values; missionaries had to control the lives of the people through control of the entire life of the Kingdom. Calvinist missionaries, more than other *haole*, were trusted by *ali'i*. Given this situation, they encouraged strong rulers and state building. Paradoxically, while the ABCFM viewed this political control by its missionaries as imperative for the further propagation of their faith, it strongly opposed the political activities of its missionaries. Even

---

Chiefs, pp. 75, 273.

[54]   Kamakau, *Ruling Chiefs*, pp. 298–9, 304, 307.

[55]   Bingham, *A Residence of Twenty-one Years,* pp. 76, 96–7, 164; Titus Coan, *Life in Hawaii* (New York, 1882), p. 63; Ellis, *Journal of a Tour*, pp. 43–4, 48, 165; Eveleth, *History of Sandwich Islands*, p. 104; Jarves, *History*, pp. 225, 99; Kamakau, *Ruling Chiefs*, pp. 261–2; Koskinen, *Missionary Influence*, pp. 27–8, 32; C. Stewart, *Private Journal of Voyage to and Residence in Sandwich Islands* (New York, 1828), pp. 164, 76, 96–7.

[56]   Beaglehole, *Modern Hawaiians*, p. 83; Blackman, *The Making of Hawaii*, p. 85; T. Coan, *Life in Hawaii*, pp. 52; Koskinen, *Missionary Influence*, pp. 28, 30.

so, by 1840, Calvinist missionaries were able to bring about the creation of a democratic government, which included a Privy Council, a codified Declaration of Rights, and a constitution. With the power of the government behind them, Calvinist missionaries sought to implement changes in the Hawaiian character through laws that enforced the Ten Commandments, chastity, temperance, and Sabbath consecration. But the key to their social changes was to be achieved by the Great Mahele of 1848, a land distribution policy enacted by the government. The Calvinist missionaries hoped the acquisition of a piece of property by each Hawaiian would enhance hard work, individualism, sobriety, and ultimately the spread of "true" Christian attitudes and values among Natives.[57] Thus, after 28 years of labor, Calvinist missionaries could look back upon the laws of the land, individual Native landholdings, and Native membership in their churches and claim that Hawai'i was a Christian nation at last.

Roman Catholic Missionaries

By the mid 1850s, the Calvinist missionaries were in a position to assess their progress. They had sown their seeds of Christianity in fertile soil and reaped a multitude of converts. However, they would not maintain their monopoly among the Natives for long. Statistics gathered by the government demonstrate that in 1853 Hawaiian membership in Calvinist churches was at 80 percent of the population (56,840 members). Roman Catholics were 16 percent of the population (11,401 members) with Mormons at 4 percent of the population (2,778 members). By 1896, Roman Catholic churches supplanted the Calvinist churches with 48 percent in membership compared with 43 percent who identified as Calvinist.[58] The challenge by Roman Catholics had begun within seven years of the Protestant missionaries' arrival. They were a part of the Roman Catholic order, the Sacred Hearts of Jesus and Mary, organized in France and directed to evangelize in some distant foreign country. Concurrently, John Rives, a French advisor and secretary to the Royal Hawaiian Court, requested that a Catholic mission be sent to Hawai'i. Rome granted approval and three priests, Fathers Alexis Bachelot, Abraham Armand, and Patrick Short, left for Hawai'i in November 1826.[59]

Although the first three years of the Catholic mission in Hawai'i were relatively quiet, the second three-year period proved to be more successful in gaining converts. However, this success led the Catholic mission to experience

---

[57]   A similar policy of land-base destruction would be applied to Native Peoples on the mainland in 1887 particularly with the passage of the Dawes Act and the parceling of Native lands.

[58]   Robert C. Schmitt, "Religious Statistics of Hawaii, 1825–1972," *The Hawaiian Journal of History*, VII (1973): 41–7.

[59]   Reginald Yzendoorn, *History of the Catholic Mission in the Hawaiian Islands* (Honolulu, 1927), pp. 29–31.

persecution against its priests and Hawaiian converts. The chiefs were hard-pressed to be cordial to Roman Catholics while the devout Calvinist Christian Kaʻahumanu controlled the government. As regent for Kamehameha III until he came of age to rule, Kaʻahumanu attended to all the affairs of the Kingdom and laid down all the laws of the land. The chiefs throughout the Hawaiian Islands, prominent persons, and land agents were all under her orders, and, because she adhered to the Calvinist faith, that faith became the religion of the state.[60] Kaʻahumanu denounced and persecuted Catholics for several reasons. First, she believed that the Kingdom had to be united under one faith, the faith of the chiefs. Second, as one of the most Christian of the Hawaiians, she objected to the Catholic religion because of its use of images, like the pagan Hawaiians. Finally, she also feared that a rival faith would cause a civil war. Indeed, in 1829, Governor Boki, uncle of the King and one of the few chiefs inclined toward Catholicism, became involved in an abortive coup d'état, confirming her fears.[61] Under Kaʻahumanu's bidding, the *aliʻi* set out to dispose of this interference. Church and state became tightly aligned when the Calvinist missionaries delivered sermons that attacked the Catholic Church, leading to the banishment of priests from Hawaiʻi in 1831.[62] Calvinist ministers were particularly attentive in their sermons to providing that Catholocism meant the worship of idols, and they tried to show through geography that Catholic nations, with the exception of France, were lazy, ignorant, pleasure loving and poor. In contrast, they presented Protestant nations as thrifty, skillful, learned people, all faithfully serving God.[63]

The French Roman Catholic mission was not strictly a religious affair. It was more of a government-supported venture, implementing national, commercial, and political influence in foreign nations. Consequently, France felt unjustly treated by countries that admitted American and English missionaries, but rejected those of French nationality. The Hawaiian rulers did not understand that their actions against the French priests would bring foreign intervention. This changed when France sent warships to Hawaiʻi and forced the repeal of legalized intolerance of Roman Catholics. One month before the frigate *Artémise* arrived, the Declaration of Rights was bestowed on the people, but it did not guarantee religious liberty. Following the *Artémise* visit, an incident of religious persecution caused the King to include within the Declaration of Rights full liberty to all his chiefs and subjects, allowing people to embrace whatever religion they thought proper;[64] thus did religious tolerance begin in Hawaiʻi.

During both periods of religious persecution and religious tolerance, the Roman Catholic Church attracted followers. Converts specifically were Hawaiians who had been unaffected by Calvinist influence, who were dissatisfied with the

---

[60]   "Supplement to the Sandwich Island Mirror," *Honolulu Spectator* (15 January 1840): 1–2.

[61]   Jarves, *History*, pp. 279–80; Kamakau, *Ruling Chiefs*, pp. 328–9.

[62]   Jarves, *History*, p. 281.

[63]   Yzendoorn, *History of the Catholic Mission*, pp. 45, 48–9, 51, 53.

[64]   Kuykendall, *Ruling Chiefs*, pp. 133–4, 149–52.

government, or who disagreed with the increased American influence as advisors to the Hawaiian monarchy. To Calvinist missionaries, Roman Catholic converts were attempting to disorganize society and were identified as liars, thieves, drunkards, and adulterers.[65] The Calvinists' real complaint was that the priests had placed doubt in many people's minds about the "True Church."[66] However, the priests were considerably more humble and simple than were Calvinist missionaries, and they were devoted to self-sacrificing work, often in lonely places where others refused to serve.[67] The Catholic historian Reginald Yzendoorn described them as often going barefoot because they had no money to buy shoes: "Like the people to whom they preached the Gospel, they lived in grass huts and dieted on poi and fish."[68] The similarity between the worship services of Hawaiian traditional religion and the Roman Catholic religion also was attractive to many Hawaiians, especially those unaffected by the Calvinist missionary propaganda against idolatry.[69] Even more important, the Roman Catholic missionaries were less doctrinaire than the Protestant missionaries, demonstrating a willingness to understand the people they were serving. For example, they extended lenient laws of fasting and abstinence because of the poor physical condition of many of their converts.[70] Probably the most important aspect of their appeal to Hawaiians was their effort to become a part of the *'ohana* (family) of Hawaiians. The Catholic missionaries, more than the Calvinists, worked at understanding and developing a relationship with their congregation.

The Catholic Church was solidly established in Hawai'i by the early 1850s, and persecution of priests and converts, except for minor difficulties, had passed. However, Calvinist missionaries continued to oppose their Catholic rivals. Although the conflicts between Calvinists and Catholics ceased to be dual when the Mormons and Anglicans arrived in Hawai'i to seek their own converts, neither of the latter groups posed a serious threat to either the prominence of the Calvinists nor the expanding reach of the Roman Catholic mission.

---

[65] Lydia Coan, *Titus Coan, a Memorial* (Chicago, 1884), pp. 61–2; T. Coan, *Life in Hawaii*, pp. 96–7; William Ellis, *The American Mission in Sandwich Islands* (London, 1825), pp. 55–7; Hunt, pp. 120, 132–3.

[66] Manley Hopkins, *Hawaii: The Past, Present, and Future of Its Island-Kingdom. An Historical Account of the Sandwich Islands* (London, 1862), pp. 391–2; Jarves, *History*, p. 332; Koskinen, *Missionary Influence*, p. 115.

[67] Koskinen, *Missionary Influence*, p. 115; Restarick, *Hawaii, 1778–1920*, pp. 71, 53.

[68] Yzendoorn, *History of the Catholic Mission*, p. 185.

[69] Hopkins, *Hawaii*, p. 396; James J. Jarves, *A Tradition of Hawaii* (Boston, 1857), pp. 83–4, 96–8; Arthur Korn, *The Victorian Visitors* (Honolulu, 1968), p. 68; Malo, p. 84.

[70] T. Coan, *Life in Hawaii*, p. 96; Yzendoorn, *History of the Catholic Mission*, pp. 141, 145–6, 185.

Hawaiian Religious Revival and the Nativistic Movement

By the time of the 1853 census, there were strong indications that Calvinist churches in Hawai'i had reached their zenith and were beginning to decline in influence. The Roman Catholics had made substantial inroads into the Hawaiian Islands, and the 1896 census conclusively documented the successful challenge made by the Catholic Church. A striking feature of the census figures is the large percentage of Native adherents to the Roman Catholic faith. When Mormon adherents, and Natives who did not return the census forms and were reported as presumably indifferent, were added to the Roman Catholic figures, the Calvinists were no longer the dominant religion among Hawaiians. There is no concrete evidence that the non-participating Hawaiians were practicing the traditional religion, but it is hard to believe that they were indifferent. Even today, most Native Hawaiians are very religious people in spite of not belonging to an organized religion. Moreover, Hawaiians also took their rights seriously and voted in high numbers, so it is unlikely that they were indifferent to taking part in the census. It is more likely that they did not belong to any of the religious groups in the census, and during the latter 40 years of the nineteenth century this meant that they had returned to practicing the traditional religion.

Although many Hawaiians found solace worshipping as Roman Catholics, in many areas of Hawai'i traditional beliefs continued. Alberto Bisin and Thierry Verdier propose an early learning hypothesis to explain this phenomenon. According to their theory, those values that have been learned in the earliest years of childhood tend to be the most persistent in the face of cultural change. This applies to the tenacity of the traditional Hawaiian religion because it was tied to family and *'ohana*, two institutions to which acceptable values and behaviors are taught early in childhood.[71] It is likely that this theory explains the persistence of the Hawaiian religion even when the monarchy under Kamehameha II and Kamehameha III and the Calvinist missionaries conspired to rid Hawai'i of the traditional religion.

From the available evidence of the persistence of Hawaiians worshipping their traditional religion, and following Bisin and Thierry's theory, three patterns of the tenacity of the traditional Hawaiian religion emerge.[72] First, the old beliefs were dormant except during times of crisis, and reversion occurred during the

---

[71]   Alberto Bisin and Thierry Verdier, "Beyond the Melting Pot: Cultural Transmission, Marriage, and the Evolution of Ethnic and Religious Traits," *The Quarterly Journal of Economics*, 115/3 (2000): 957, 968.

[72]   The following sources substantiate the tenacity of Hawaiians continuing to worship the traditional religion during the nineteenth century: Beckwith, *Hawaiian Mythology*, pp. 10, 107; Ellis, *The American Mission*, pp. 69–72, 161, 165–6, 176–7; Jarves, *History*, p. 262; Kamakau, *Ruling Chiefs*, p. 304; W.D. Alexander, *A Brief History*, p. 44; Hawaiian Church Mission, *Occasional Paper* (London, 1865), pp. 18, 28; Yzendorn, *History of the Catholic Mission*, p. 14.

crisis as a safeguard against possible harm. Second, a large group of Native Hawaiians hid their continuing beliefs in the traditional religion for fear of being branded as heathen. Finally, an even larger group of Hawaiians continued to practice traditional beliefs in their daily lives. Particularly persistent was the worship of 'aumakua, which aided Natives in fishing and planting or in explaining the mysteries of life (birth, death, ghosts, and natural disasters). These patterns merged into strong dynamic nativistic movements in Hawai'i beginning in the 1860s.[73] Nativistic movements are attempts by cultures undergoing acculturation due to the impact of Western cultures to revive and perpetuate certain aspects of their traditions in the face of the external pressure to change. Due to the religious systems of these types of cultures typically embodying the central values of their cultures, nativistic movements generally involve some type of religious rituals.[74] Since religion permeated all aspects of the traditional Hawaiian culture, it was not surprising that Hawaiian nativistic movements were mostly about reviving religious practices.

The first type of revival was a magical nativistic movement. Magical nativism occurs when worshippers continue to follow rituals that confer magic powers to any act to which they need help. The magical nativist movement occurred before there was a significant decline in Calvinist missionary influence. It began during the 1820s when the prophetess Kahapu'u founded the sect Hapu'uism in Puna, Hawai'i. This sect combined Christianity and elements of the traditional Hawaiian religion. Hapu'uism continued after Kahapu'u's death in 1832 and lasted until the arrival of the Roman Catholic priest, Father Walsh, in 1841. Subsequently, the majority of the sect's members became Roman Catholics. No sooner had Hapu'uism disappeared, a second sect was founded by another woman at Wailua, O'ahu. Calling herself Lono, after one of the great gods, she performed cures through a mixture of Hawaiian rites, Christian scriptures, prayers, and confession of sins.[75]

The second type of revival, the rational nativistic movement, resembles the magical type in its conscious effort to revive or perpetuate selected elements of culture. It differs however, in its motive. Ralph Linton states, "Rational revivalistic nativistic movements are, almost without exception, associated with frustrating situations and are primarily attempts to compensate for the frustrations of the society's members."[76] Usage of this type of revival is not magical but psychological,

---

[73]   Blackman, *The Making of Hawaii*, p. 90; Edward G. Burrows, *Hawaiian Americans* (New Haven, 1947), pp. 9–10; Thrum, *More Hawaiian Folktales*, p. 288.

[74]   Ralph Linton, "Nativistic Movements," in William A. Lessa and Evon Z. Vogt (eds.), *Reader in Comparative Religion* (New York, 1965), pp. 499–506.

[75]   Blackman, *The Making of Hawaii*, p. 33; Beaglehole, *Modern Hawaiians*, p. 78; Burrows, *Hawaiian Americans*, p. 151; L. Coan, *Titus Coan*, p. 44; Sheldon Dibble, *History of the Sandwich Islands* (Honolulu, 1854), pp. 105, 107; Hopkins, *Hawaii*, p. 215; Koskinen, *Missionary Influence*, pp. 100, 101, 104; Yzendoorn, *History of the Catholic Mission*, pp. 83–5.

[76]   Linton, "Nativistic Movements," p. 501.

and often assumes social and political proportions.[77] This movement began when Hawaiian monarchs came to power who distrusted the *haole* influence, particularly that of the American Calvinists.

By the early 1860s, the beginning of a rational nativistic movement was in the offing. It was fueled in 1863, when Kamehameha V ascended the throne and took steps to legalize licensing *kahuna* as doctors and permitting *kahuna* and *hula* dancers into the palace.[78] By 1880, when the nativistic movement was led by King Kalakaua, not only were traditional Hawaiian customs renewed, but the ideas of absolutism and divine rights were also restored. The latter act was accomplished by joining the King's family genealogy to the *Kumulipo*, the Hawaiian story of creation. Thus, he proclaimed his family to be descendents of the gods.[79] In 1881, he left for a trip around the world; upon returning he utilized the frustrations of his people by openly rejecting *haole* religion: "I have seen the Christian nations, and observed that they are turning away from Jehovah. He represents a waning cause. Shall we Hawaiians take up the worship of a god whom foreigners are discarding? The old gods of Hawaii are good enough for us."[80]

In 1886, Kalakaua held a grand political meeting where he formed the *Hale Naua,* an organization of sorcerers in which the King planned to unite the best powers of Hawaiian and Christian practice.[81] No doubt, to some extent, politics had some part in Kalakaua's beginning this organization. He had won a close election against Queen Emma, the wife of Kamehameha IV. As his adversary for leadership of the Hawaiian people, she had been involved with the Hawaiian religious revival.[82] But more than chiefly rivalry, the attachment of the highest *ali'i* and of many commoners to the ancient religion was another case of the century-old battle between Christianity and the traditional Hawaiian religion. Whereas, during the *'āinoa* era, Hawaiian *ali'i* and commoners allied with Christian missionaries, by this stage the battle had polarized between two groups: Hawaiians and *haole.* To

---

[77]   Ibid.

[78]   James M. Alexander, *The Islands of the Pacific* (New York, 1895), p. 190; Burrows, *Hawaiian Americans*, pp. 152–3.

[79]   Frear, *A Century of Achievement*, p. 13; Leilani Melville, *Children of the Rainbow* (Wheaton, 1969), pp. 11–12, 50.

[80]   Blackman, *The Making of Hawaii*, p. 90.

[81]   Beaglehole, *Modern Hawaiians*, 79–80; Sereno E. Bishop, *Reminiscences of Old Hawaii* (Honolulu, 1916), p. 22.

[82]   A cousin of Queen Emma had contracted leprosy and was removed to the Molokai settlement. In a series of letters, the two correspondents shed valuable evidence concerning their own and Kalakaua's motives for becoming involved in sorcery. Arthur Korn and Mary Pukui, the editors of the "Molokai Letters," state that the letters show "very clearly the way surviving native attitudes toward the supernatural continued in fairly recent times in Hawaii to reinforce one of the most characteristic features of the old social system, the custom of chiefly rivalry." Arthur Korn and Mary K. Pukui, "News from Molokai," *Pacific Historical Review*, 34 (February 1963): 17–19, 31–2.

most Hawaiians during the last forty years of the nineteenth century, the cause of all their woes was the dominant *haole* – the Calvinist missionaries. This included the rapid dwindling of a proud race, the disappearance of their land and culture, and the diminishing power of their *ali'i*. The rational nativistic movement represented the last stand against what they saw as the onslaught of the missionary way of life, which included narrow-minded morals, money seeking and land-monopoly, stinginess and hard-heartedness.[83]

Reversion to the traditional Hawaiian religion continued after Kalakaua's death with his successor, Queen Liliuokalani. She attempted to carry through politically what her brother had been doing socially. However, a *haole*-led revolution overthrew the monarchy, set up a republic, and petitioned for annexation to the United States, which was fulfilled in 1898 when Hawai'i was annexed. The reversion of the *ali'i* to elements of the Hawaiian religion was both cause and effect of the rational nativistic movement among Hawaiians. It was, in part, the cause because Natives were naturally inclined toward imitating the royalty. It also was in part the effect because the anti-*haole* reaction had brought forth in a political manner the reason for Hawaiians to come out from behind their fears to claim their right to their traditional religion. Their rulers assumed the leadership of the nativistic movement as a way to increase their power over the people. By means of the supernatural, the *ali'i* attempted to prevent the threat to their sovereignty by *haole* who desired annexation of Hawai'i to the United States. Regrettably, it accomplished the acceleration of what they most feared—the loss of Hawaiian sovereignty. The monarchy leadership in the Hawaiian nativistic movements solidified the *haole* community against what appeared to them as a threat to the "civilization," which they had worked so hard to create. Faced with this threat, the only deed that made sense was to end Hawaiian sovereignty.

Postscript

By the turn of the nineteenth century, Hawaiian culture was once again in equilibrium. Annexation of the islands to the United States crushed Native resistance. Hawaiian and *haole* antagonists ceased to battle. When the *haole* leaders (who were mostly descendants of Calvinist missionaries) established the Provisional Government, all elements of the Hawaiian nativistic movement were outlawed. Religious participation of Hawaiians, for the moment, was transformed as they could choose only between Christian religious groups. The traditional religion had its nineteenth-century heyday in the nativistic movement and, except for evidence of some Native beliefs in the traditional religion, went underground.

---

[83]   J.M. Alexander, *The Islands of the Pacific,* pp. 194–5; Blackman, *The Making of Hawaii,* p. 89; L. Coan, *Titus Coan,* p. 118; Hopkins, *Hawaii,* pp. 248–9; Kamakau, *Ruling Chiefs,* pp. 201–2, 370, 377, 399, 404, 408–9, 411, 416, 417; Koskinen, *Missionary Influence,* pp. 91, 94; Melville, *Children of the Rainbow,* pp. x–xi.

Some families continued to secretly worship the traditional spirits, often mixing Native beliefs with beliefs taught by Roman Catholics. Outwardly, Hawai'i was predominantly Christian, yet more religious sects, Christian and non-Christian alike, would establish communities in Hawai'i over the next 100 years. However, sectarian disputes ceased, and Hawai'i became one of the most religiously tolerant communities in the world.[84]

In the end, despite an initial increase in members during the early years of the twentieth century, Hawaiian members of Calvinist churches remained a small proportion of the total Hawaiian population. The Roman Catholic faith was particularly attractive to Hawaiians for a variety of reasons: less doctrinaire, more accepting of Hawaiian culture, and offering a more active religion connected to rituals and beliefs that seemed more similar to the traditional Hawaiian religion. Today, there are more than 900 religious organizations in Hawai'i. The state ranks as one of the most religiously diverse areas in the world. Christianity still ranks as the dominant religion. Of the residents who acknowledge a religion, three-quarters are Christian, and Roman Catholics represent half of this number.[85]

Throughout the twentieth century, aspects of the Hawaiian culture continued to be practiced. One of the most enduring of Hawaiian customs was the *hula.* Even when it was outlawed, Hawaiians secretly trained as *hula* dancers. The *hula* was always a source of pride for the performers, but with the spread of tourism it also became a form of entertainment for observers. The luau already replaced the *Makahiki* festival as the time for families to celebrate birth, marriage, and death. It also is a time for *hula* students to share what they had learned at the *halau.* In continuing to perform and observe the *hula,* Hawaiians celebrate a special part of their heritage. Chants, which are connected to the traditional religion, re-appeared as an introduction to *hula* performances. In many families, traditions that were continually practiced involve elements of the traditional religion. In my youth, two of my great grandaunts were *kahuna lapaau*, and they had regular customers for their services. Although my mother was less trained than her grandaunts, she practiced *lomi lomi* (Hawaiian massage) and used medicines derived from Hawaiian plants and herbs and traditional practices of *kahuna lapaau.*

Whether aspects of the Hawaiian culture were practiced in secret or openly, there was no organized effort to revive the Hawaiian culture throughout most of the first 60 years of the twentieth century. By the beginning of the 1960s, however, a Hawaiian cultural renaissance revived dance, music, and other Native cultural traditions. This revival was aided by the offering of the Hawaiian language at University of Hawai'i campuses during the 1970s. Language revival was given a further push when, in 1978, the Hawai'i Constitutional Convention declared Hawaiian one of the state's two official languages. With the opening in 1984 of the first Hawaiian language preschool, the spread of the Hawaiian language was further

---

[84]   Daws, *Shoal of Time*, p. 292.

[85]   Sonia P. Juvik and James O. Juvik (eds.), *Atlas of Hawai'i*, 3rd edn. (Honolulu, 1998), p. 201.

supported. Today, several Hawaiian Immersion High Schools are graduating their first students.

The traditional Hawaiian religion has also entered a new period of revival. The beginning of this religious revival occurred in 1976 when a community of Native Hawaiians gathered to use *Lonomakua* to bring life-giving water to reinvigorate the island of Kahoʻolawe, an island devastated by the United States as a military test ground between World War II and continuing until 1981. Practitioners who maintained their *ʻaumakua* connections surfaced to aid the Hawaiian community in reawakening the *ʻaumakua* religion. Moreover, in 1988, Native Hawaiians protested the insensitivity of the exhuming of more than one thousand skeletal remains of Native Hawaiians from an ancient burial site slated for a hotel. Natives who still practiced Hawaiian death rituals came forth to help bury the skeletal remains properly. As a result of these two events and many less dramatic ones, Hawaiian religion resurfaced, and even the practice of *laʻau lapaʻau* (curing medicine) is once again being practiced and taught openly. Hawaiian and non-Hawaiians are learning to grow taro using traditional practices including building *ahu* (altars) for offerings to *ʻaumakua* forms of the god Kane to ensure the continual flow of fresh water to *loʻi* (taro ponds). Finally, many families have always used the old *kuʻula* (gods of fishing) along shoreline trails, leaving offerings of appreciation for fish caught in the area. This practice is being emulated even by non-traditional fishermen.[86]

Even more important to the revival of Hawaiian culture and religion is *Ka Lahui Hawaiʻi,* a grassroots Native initiative to return Hawaiian sovereignty. Mililani Trask, one of the organizers of this initiative, refers to *Ka Lahui Hawaiʻi* as an evolutionary product of generations of Hawaiians who have sought to regain their Native lands and to re-establish themselves as a self-governing people. The sovereignty being sought includes the following five elements: a strong and abiding faith in the *Akua* (God); a people with a common culture; a land base; a government structure; and an economic base. The *Ka Lahui Hawaiʻi* Constitution sets forth a belief that Hawaiian cultural rights should include the rights to worship, fish, cultivate *kuleana* lands, and gather Native plants and herbs necessary to make Hawaiian medicines. Finally, the Constitution provides that Native Hawaiians have rights of access to the mountains and the sea, as well as the right to be buried on Hawaiian soil and to elect a government.[87] One of the first successful acts performed by *Ka Lahui Hawaiʻi* occurred in 1989 when its leaders set out to convince the Hawaiʻi Ecumenical Coalition that tourism was a major cause of threats to Hawaiian culture and the land, especially sacred sites. A call went out to the churches to initiate a process of reconciliation and reparations by acknowledging the harm done to the Native peoples of Hawaiʻi as well as an

---

[86]   Ibid., pp. 199, 201.

[87]   See Mililani B. Trask, "*Ka Lahui Hawaiʻi*: A Native Initiative for Sovereignty," *Turning the Tide: Journal of Anti-Racist Activism, Research & Education*, 6 (December 1993): 1–10.

apology to the Hawaiian people. The Roman Catholic Church has been the leading faith to acknowledge the needs of Hawaiians, and currently its clergy lead the Hawai'i Ecumenical Coalition in its effort to reconcile and repair the harm done to Hawaiians.[88]

Once again, Native Hawaiian religious participation seems to be in a state of transformation. It is unlikely that the revival of Native Hawaiian religion will involve all or even a majority of Native Hawaiians. However, the attacks on Native Hawaiian religious participation such as the ones by Christian groups during the *'ainoa* era will not return. Today, all religious groups in Hawai'i support the rights of Native Hawaiians, including their right to participate in the practices of their Native religion. Similar today, as in the nineteenth century, revival is being generated by issues involving sovereignty and the survival of Native Hawaiian culture and traditions.

---

[88] Haunani-Kay Trask, *From a Native Daughter: Colonialism and Sovereignty in Hawai'i* (Honolulu, 1999), pp. 245–7.

Chapter 5

Ghosts of Photography: The 1890 Ghost Dance and Afterimages of the Sacred

Larry M. Taylor

Indian guns and arrows were no longer the threat. The danger for whites was the power of ceremonial dance, a magic they could not control.[1]

—Jamake Highwater

We've always taken photographs as proofs of events, and we probably never should have.[2]

—Per Gylfe

Our dance is a religious dance.[3]

—Little Wound

The intersection of religion and the visual takes a highly particular form in the case of South Dakota reservations around 1890. That time and date, of course, is heavily shadowed by the violence culminating in the Wounded Knee Massacre. And to be sure, much exists in the way of histories of that massacre. Some attention has also been paid to the mission history of Dakota reservations. But one of the greatest symbols of that era is the Lakota Ghost Dance itself. Too often the Ghost Dance has been maligned—either associated too directly with violence, or not given enough attention in its own right (or both). Images of the Ghost Dance, be they reported, illustrated, or photographic, present another layer to the highly complex cultural dynamics at play at the time. To take a critical look at some of these images unlocks a door that is often not opened. Many of the images are problematic on a number of levels, and precisely how to regard such problematic images is a question that very much involves religious and ethnic identity. It can

---

[1]   Jamake Highwater, *Ritual of the Wind: North American Indian Ceremonies, Music and Dance* (Toronto, 1984), p. 161.

[2]   Per Gylfe, Manager Digital Media Lab at International Center of Photography, as quoted in the *New York Times*, Online Edition (17 August 2008), http://www.nytimes.com/2008/08/17/fashion/17photo.html?em (accessed 1 October 2008).

[3]   Little Wound as reportedly in a letter to Agent Royer received 23 November, corresponded in "Little Wound's Defiant Letters," a subheading to "Ghost Dancers Plot to Kill the Troops," in the *New York Herald* (24 November 1890): 3.

be helpful to first get a sense of how the Ghost Dance "looked" to mission eyes by examining the thoughts of some of the priests on site before moving on to images that impacted the surrounding culture at large.

The Clergy and the Dancers

The Catholic Church has had an extensive tradition of incorporating sacred painting and sculpture in its 2,000-year history. Such artistic formats have weathered seasons of high fashion and superstitious iconoclasms to finally rest fairly comfortably in modern liturgical environments. Yet the relationship towards other art forms such as dancing has presented a much less auspicious case.[4] Perhaps the closest historical antecedent might be the Passion plays that thrived in the Middle Ages before falling out of favor after the Protestant Reformation.[5] But by the time of the Victorian era, Euroamerican attitudes to dance were highly prescribed and had little to no relationship with ecclesiology. It was civic, formal, public and steeped in precise social codes, manners, and proscriptions. The clothing, the spaces, the movements were all very much determined in advance. Liturgical dance hardly existed at this time—the Liturgical Movement was only in its infancy.[6] Dance, suffice it to say, was not particularly a part of mainline Christian liturgy. Like so much else it was parceled away, compartmentalized as a society event or performing art. Therefore, when one reflects back at one of the greatest crises in Euroamerican and Native American relations, it is on the one hand not entirely surprising to find strained emotions over what might rather have been a point of greater spiritual connection, the Ghost Dance, and most particularly the Lakota Ghost Dance. That is, there seems a natural cultural–historical gap between the Indian understanding of dance as vital to and indicative of the holistic nature of life, and the West's potential uneasiness with any kind of dance outside of a small performative box.

Or perhaps it should still shock and surprise us—that is, it still should not make sense to observant minds that a genocidal attack ensued in large part over a sacred dance. If the cultural binaries are held in suspension for a moment, we

---

[4] The Ghost Dance, or dance in general, as will be brought out, is not thought of as a performance but part of the integration of the sacredness of all life. It could even be considered a mistake to call it "liturgical," as such binaries are a Euroamerican construction, however persistent and pervasive. Even "sacred dance" holds as its opposite "secular," and so some reclamation of terminology is in order.

[5] However, dance enjoyed a greater prominence in ancient history, as in various references to it in the Hebrew scriptures as well as its pervasiveness in Greek society.

[6] And at that, its origins were confined to Europe. The earliest sparkling of the movement was in 1832 at the Benedictine monastery of Solesmes in France, but it did not get underway until Pope Pius X issued a motu proprio in 1903 inviting a fuller participation of musical arts in worship.

find that the Ghost Dance actually held great potential in crossing boundaries. Alice Beck Kehoe wrote that the Lakota could conceive of a "fundamental agreement" between Christianity and their religion because of parallels between the omnipotent God and the traditional Power.[7] The dancers typically selected Sunday as the day for the ceremony.[8] James Mooney would compare the Ghost Dance movement's Paiute founder, Wovoka (Jack Wilson), to the great leaders of Western civilization. Wovoka, of course, was noted to have been in contact with Shakers and Mormons, as well as other Christians, and he himself attended church regularly.[9] Among his famous proscriptions regarding the Ghost Dance (from whom Lakota delegations were instructed directly) included: "You must not hurt anybody or do harm to anyone. You must not fight. Do right always."[10] Years later Dakota physician and author Charles Eastman would compare Ghost Dancing to the revivals of Billy Sunday.[11] While there was some accusation that leaders of the Lakota Ghost Dance distorted Wovoka's original message of peace into one of battle cry, that has been roundly contested. A caution remains not to gloss over the various understandings of the cosmos as conceived by Native or Christian; however, it is to say that the Ghost Dance has sometimes been so exoticized to the point that one could be led to think that any kind of ecumenical relationship was forestalled at the outset. Rather, as a great spiritual conduit, it held extraordinary potential to renew and transcend.

There was much in the way of contributing factors to the tensions that developed and ultimately ended in violence at Pine Ridge between the Lakota and non-Indians—broken treaties, government edicts, grossly incompetent agents, hunger—but remarkably the Ghost Dance movement still bore, however erroneously or implicitly, the greatest share of the blame, and it continues to do so into the present. Of course, the war was fomented by the government with its own ends in mind. But the Christian churches entered into the complex set of relationships at Lakota reservations, at times as a mediating factor. In 1889, just under half of the population at Pine Ridge reportedly attended Sunday services

---

[7] Alice Beck Kehoe, *The Ghost Dance, Ethnohistory and Revitalization*, 2nd edn. (Long Grove, 2006), p. 64.

[8] James Mooney, *The Ghost-Dance Religion and Sioux Outbreak of 1890* (Chicago, 1965), p. 69. Other accounts note ceremonies that would begin a day or two earlier and end on a Sunday.

[9] Alice Beck Kehoe reported that Wilson had heard of Smohalla, "The Preacher," a famed prophet of the Northwest who incorporated ritual elements from Catholicism including a bell ringer who accompanied a priestly procession: *Ethnohistory and Revitalization*, p. 35.

[10] "The Messiah Letter (free Rendering)" printed in Mooney, *The Ghost-Dance Religion*, p. 23.

[11] As noted by George R. Kolbenschlag in *A Whirlwind Passes: Newspaper Correspondents and the Sioux Indian Disturbances of 1890–91* (Vermillion, 1990), p. 30.

regularly.[12] And part of the appeal of the Ghost Dance lay not only in the return to the traditional way of life, but also the newer familiarity of messianic apocalypse. While Catholic priests were ultimately charged with conversion, we do have reports of some instances of connection regarding the dance. Perhaps the default understanding may have been that the Ghost Dance was out of orthodoxy as a kind of "pagan" remnant; still, a glimmer of enlightenment is detected in a diary entry that states that Fr. Francis M. Craft witnessed a Rosebud Ghost Dance and "found it to be all right, quite Catholic, and quite edifying."[13] That this account comes from someone who was sometimes sympathetic to the military should be all the more telling. Fr. Craft occupies a most anomalous historical place as he was appointed by the federal government on a clandestine mission precisely to investigate the dance. Compounding his identity yet more is his Indian blood.[14] One Fr. John Jutz was known to move freely among the Ghost Dance camp. On one occasion a conference between Jutz and leading chiefs ended with dancing.[15] Such incidences complicate notions of clearly drawn lines.[16] Later, as hostilities ultimately rose, the missions would be reassured by warriors that they would not become targets, a notable measure of some mutuality on the one hand and distinction between government and church on the other.[17] Opinions varied, and to be sure other priests were dismissive of the dance at best. Meanwhile, the Indian agents, even be they religious as in the case of James McLaughlin, a Catholic at Standing Rock, seemed to have a harder time finding religion in the dance.

----

[12]   Rani-Henrik Andersson, *The Lakota Ghost Dance of 1890* (Lincoln, 2008), p. 164 n. 7. This number accounts for all denominational Christian missions.

[13]   Father Amilius Perrig, diary [15 December 1890], Marquette University Library (MUL), Special Collections (transcribed by John M. Carroll), p. 36, quoted in William S.E. Coleman, *Voices of Wounded Knee* (Lincoln and London, 2000), p. 44. Fr. Francis M.J. Craft was also known as Hovering Eagle and had some Indian blood.

[14]   For more on Fr. Craft, see Thomas W. Foley, *Father Francis M. Craft, Missionary to the Sioux* (Lincoln, 2002), p. 85. He was at the service of the Secretary of War and Secretary of the Interior. His paternal great-grandmother was the full-blood daughter of a Mohawk chief. James Mooney would remark (*The Ghost-Dance Religion*, p. 121) that Craft "had given a large part of his life to work among the Sioux, by whom he was loved and respected." The author further noted that many of the soldiers were of his own faith.

[15]   As reported in Mooney, *The Ghost-Dance Religion*, p. 150, from a statement by Brigadier General L.W. Colby, commander of the Nebraska National Guard. The kind of dance is not specified other than as "an Indian dance."

[16]   And the Jutz example was not the only incident of such mediation. A Father Jule, for example, was asked by General Brooks to hold conference with a "hostile camp" at Pine Ridge as reported in the *New York World* on 7 December 1890. He was chosen because "it was thought that they might regard overtures from him with more favor than from any other available messenger."

[17]   See Mooney, *The Ghost-Dance Religion*, pp. 124–6, where also a warrior was reported to say that Fr. Jutz had earned the trust of Indians by virtue of taking care of refugees and binding the wounded.

Ultimately the Catholic Church can never escape its association with colonization. At times the Ghost Dance movement directly influenced the number of attendees at mass and other traditional demarcations of "conversion" and so presented a threat to the very concept of missionary activity. Still others mistrusted the dance entirely. Fr. Aemilius Perrig feared its waxing power and deemed it "more and more the appearance of deviltry."[18] A broad panoply of opinion has been documented, from the surprisingly open-minded to the predictably reactive and rigid. Within the Catholic camp alone there was a surprising variety of opinion, far from unanimous. Frs. Craft, Emil Perrig, and Florentine Digman are known to have had a heated exchange about the Ghost Dance, nearly causing Craft to up and leave the reservation. Though somewhat individualistic, Craft generally carried out his mission, but was still able to maintain some sense of perspective. And he was far from alone in looking past the dance to some of the more glaring causes of unrest—broken treaties, starving hunger, encroachment, to name but a few very serious problems. Episcopalian Bishop William H. Hare would not list the Ghost Dance as a cause of disaffection, but rather cited drought and hunger. He saw the dance as a "hallucination" but not without also stating that "the abuse here [i.e., abuse stemming from the spiritual poverty of 'hungry politicians'] has been shameful."[19]

The following question then presents itself: If opinion could range to such a degree within the Catholic clergy in an institution where unity of dogma was of prime value, what can account for the widespread suspicion of the Ghost Dance in the Christian population more generally? That is, if persons so close to the dance— some of whom would be among the privileged few to see it for themselves—could find "edification" in carrying out this sacred ritual (even as they were ostensibly charged with conversion), how could the Ghost Dance have provided such heightened charge in outlying audiences near and far from reservations? There are the occasional incidences of anxious settlers pushing the panic button (mainly after the arrival of troops). But such excitement, simply left alone, would have eventually dissipated altogether. Perhaps one needs to look beyond word—to the image—in order to better see how the Ghost Dance was so misrepresented to the Christian world.

What Do Images Want?

It is very true that histories of the Ghost Dance reside principally in words. There are volumes dedicated to testimonies and official reports. These are necessary and invaluable tools for any kind of analysis of the occurrences, be it historical, ethnographical or otherwise. However, still very much lacking is sufficient

---

[18]   Rani-Henrik Andersson, *The Lakota Ghost Dance of 1890*, p. 170 n. 23.

[19]   Statement to Secretary of the Interior John K. Noble printed in Mooney, *The Ghost-Dance Religion*, pp. 85–7.

attention to the images of the Ghost Dance and images deriving from the dance.[20] That means principally the medium of photography and all of its attendant forms of reproduction; in other instances, imagistic language could be called on when an actual picture wasn't available. In reality, very few Euroamerican persons ever saw a dance. Thus the Christian audience was dependent upon accounts disseminated most usually by the media (which itself depended on second-hand reports gleaned from near and far). Additionally, photographers sold their images to clients locally. With so much hearsay and varying information at the height of tensions, pictures— either seen or merely said to have been witnessed—could be authoritatively believed in a way that words alone could not always be. Contemporary society is learning just how visual human beings are now, but the privileging of the image is of course not a new invention.

When photographs are included in histories of Wounded Knee, they are almost always the familiar few. A more robust account, however, will ask how images of the Ghost Dance movement might have contributed and continue to contribute to persistently erroneous themes of violence, savagery, and otherness. Though familiar and seemingly innocent enough, images are said to have a "currency" by which they operate.[21] What should be further considered is just how visual analysis, as used in contemporary art history, can unravel the currencies of photographs and illustrations of Ghost Dancers and chiefs.[22] In doing so we go from treating the photograph as an illustration of a corresponding referent to a stance where the image does not simply perform what a text says—a stance where the image has a life and agenda of its own.

A number of scholars and writers have contributed to rethinking the way we view photography in general and its role in Native American life in particular. Susan Sontag reminded us that the photographer's actions are bound up with

---

[20] Thomas Kavanagh has recently noted the lack of attention specific to images, cautioning that, because the variety of images are so impacting, they must be "constantly examined; one must see as well as look." Further, photographs have not sufficiently been examined for "what they can say about ... imaging and imagining the Ghost Dance"; Thomas W. Kavanagh, "Reading Photographs: Imaging and Imagining the Ghost Dance: James Mooney's Illustrations and Photographs, 1891–1893," php.indiana.edu/~tkavanag/visual5.html (accessed 1 October 2008). Kavanagh references pictures taken of the Ghost Dance among the Southern Arapaho. He concludes that manipulation there has lead to "a misleading image of the Ghost Dance" on several accounts that has no less continued to "shape our visualization of that ceremonial."

[21] As suggested by John Tagg in "The Currency of the Photograph" (1978), reprinted in M. Alvarado (ed.), *Representation and Photography* (Basingstoke, 2000): pp. 87ff. Roland Barthes originally situated photography within a cultural "code" in the essay "The Rhetoric of the Image" (1964; translated in Barthes, *Image, Music, Text*, ed. and trans. Stephen Heath (New York, 1977), pp. 32–51) before retracting the idea later.

[22] That is to say, art history, as it has evolved in its "new" more postmodern stripes, involves social histories in contrast to formalist readings.

the limitations of his culture.[23] The era in question was steeped in Manifest Destiny's "colonization through photography."[24] Photographic shots transformed the very image of the human, "seeing [people] as they never see themselves."[25] Photographers who stole shots of Ghost Dancers were generally unaware that their dominant culture wasn't the only way from which to view the world. Thus, "We have seen Native Americans as we want to see them, rather than as they were and are."[26] Gerald Vizenor cautioned that pictures of Native Americans were never "the same as those nostalgic photographs of homesteaders and their families in a new constitutional democracy."[27] Such images commonly featured settlers in front of newly built homes, markers of domesticity, in contrast to the Native who was situated as an inseparable part of the wilderness.

In asking "for whom is the photographer working," Lee Clark Mitchell brings the matter closer to home:[28] photographs at Pine Ridge, as elsewhere, were not neutral but taken primarily for their salability—photographic agency filtered through the burning desire to excite potential clients and/or the readership of newspapers.[29] The "exotic" nature of Native dance was always of premium value. And newspapers nationwide began ratcheting up the rhetoric: the Indian was "ready for battle," a fear-stoking idea resulting in a "monetary snowball" for paper and photographer alike.[30] It is also worth bearing in mind in this context that throughout the nineteenth century photographers had been commissioned by the US government and railroad companies to assess the land and the threat that the Native might pose to the desires for expansion.

---

[23] Notably, almost all photographers of Indian culture are male at this time.

[24] Susan Sontag, *On Photography* (New York, 1977), pp. 14 and 64, respectively.

[25] Ibid.

[26] William E. McRae, "Images of Native Americans in Still Photography," *History of Photography*, 13/4 (1989): 321.

[27] Gerald R. Vizenor, *Fugitive Poses: Native American Indian Scenes of Absence and Presence* (Lincoln, 1998), p. 155.

[28] Lee Clark Mitchell, "The Photograph and the American Indian", in Alfred L. Bush and Lee Clark Mitchell (eds.), *The Photograph and the American Indian* (Princeton, 1994), p. xiii. He continues, "What is the audience meant to see, and at the same time, not to see?"

[29] Many have noted the depraved kind of reporting found in the newspaper articles. For example, David Humphreys Miller (*Ghost Dance* (Lincoln and London, 1985; reprint of 1959 edn.), p. 167): "By and large, these accounts were highly colored and sensational reports which exaggerated Indian savagery and touted the various military commanders and Indian agents … Behind them all lay an almost universal ignorance of Indian psyche."

[30] Many have noted this textual side of the exaggeration. One, among a few, treating the photographic intersection is Lynn Marie Mitchell in "George E. Trager: Frontier Photographer at Wounded Knee," *History of Photography*, 13/4 (1989): 305.

"Authenticity" at Pine Ridge

The photograph of the Lakota Ghost Dance at Pine Ridge by J.E. Meddaugh (see Figure 5.1) is representative of one of very few taken of the ceremony.[31] Indeed, genuine pictures of the Ghost Dance at any Dakota or Lakota reservation are extraordinarily rare. By this time, the Lakota had begun to suspect the motives of outsiders keenly, and many Natives were suspicious of the camera in general.[32] Moreover, the dance was part of sacred ceremony and was not the kind of event meant to be photographed. Photographing as a way of documenting was a concept that wore well in the Euroamerican mindset (long steeped in linear perspective), but Native attitudes tended to be more nuanced, embracing the camera at occasions, utilizing it at others, and resisting it altogether in many other instances.

It is not abundantly clear that this picture was made with the participants' knowledge and permission. When another photographer came to White Clay Creek to try to steal a shot of the dance, he was quickly discovered and his camera destroyed.[33] Meddaugh was a commercial photographer based in Rushville, Nebraska and he did take many pictures at Pine Ridge Agency in his short career, including a portrait of Oglala Tribal Police Chief George Sword and his wife, Lucy Different Eagle. However, just how he would have earned the trust of the Ghost Dancers at such a time remains an open question. In any case, the picture actually tells us quite little. Some foreknowledge reveals the sacred tree that the dance was centered around (at far right). Vague but still discernable is the circular pattern of the dance. If one looks closely, one can see that many dancers are joined arm in arm as they dance.[34] But that is about all that can positively be said; purporting total omniscience, the picture fails to elucidate in many ways.

---

[31]   This photograph also has appeared in the work of Richard E. Jensen, R. Eli Paul, and John E. Carter, *Eyewitness at Wounded Knee* (Lincoln, 1991). Meddaugh was from Rushville, Nebraska and traveled to Pine Ridge expressly to see the Ghost Dance. He took the only known photographs of the Lakota in the Ghost Dance at Pine Ridge: John E. Carter, "Making Pictures for a News-hungry Nation," in *Eyewitness at Wounded Knee*, p. 43. Carter suggests that the dance took place at No Water's camp, north of the Agency. The number of authentic Ghost Dance photographs at Pine Ridge has been listed as three.

[32]   For its ability to "capture" one's spirit, among other concerns—broken treaties and a general mistrust not withstanding.

[33]   John Carter believed the photographer to be Clarence Morledge, *Eyewitness at Wounded Knee*, p. 7. The account of the destroyed camera comes from Keeps the Battle; see Willis Fletcher Johnson, *Life of Sitting Bull, History of the Indian War, 1890–91* (Philadelphia, 1891), pp. 342–5.

[34]   The dance was performed in a circular motion. At certain points individuals might break free from the circle in order to experience a vision. Though there are "spectators" in this picture, Lynn Huenemann cautions that in Lakota dance there is not the kind of separation between dancer and "audience" found in Anglo-European dance; "Northern Plains Dance", in *Native American Dance: Ceremonies and Social Traditions* (Washington, DC, 1992), p. 131.

Figure 5.1   J.E. Meddaugh, "Ghost Dance, Pine Ridge" (1890), used with permission of the National Anthropological Archives, Smithsonian Institute, INV. 09859900.

Due to the desire to capture all, there is an enormous distance between camera (i.e., you) and the dancers. While not entirely chosen, that separation functions to reinforce the physical and psychic divide between two cultures. Each figure that is legible has his back to the viewer and, to the Western eye, for whom the view was likely meant, Native remains inextricably "other." What the viewer does see is that there are "many." The number might not be so great as would seem, but the ambiguous viewpoint, repeated anonymous figures and tipis, and tight cropping, coupled with hazy focus, could easily be misinterpreted by the naïve. James Faris has equated framing with "censoring," and certainly many possibilities are extinguished by this particular view.[35] The photo does not fully communicate the religion of the Ghost Dance; in essence, it cannot. Western culture tends to strongly prize the represented over the unseen, the result being that "all that is *not* recorded is implicitly devalued."[36] And such representationalism does not always translate well across cultural and ethnographical boundaries. One cannot see the prayers and the visions, the offerings, the solemn cries to *Wakan Tanka*. No particular indication of the prayer that "our hearts are now good" comes forth.[37] The figures are most certainly present to the average viewer, but is their full "existential posture"?[38] Left unaided, the uninitiated and non-Indian mind is fairly free to wander and interpret. Misinterpreted the picture could become evidence of a mysterious cult—other, outside of the set cultural norms, a thing to hold suspect.

"Ghost Dance" and "War Dance" Pictures

The drive for money and recognition would cause photographers to *create* Ghost Dance images when they were unable to observe the actual ceremony. Thus, pictures of other dances were often passed off as a either a Ghost Dance or a War Dance (see Figure 5.2). Such fakes offer a vantage point more proximate, but present a whole host of new problems. Here again the total information provided is quite little. While dance is especially hard to photograph in the first place, what this picture presents is fairly unclear to the uninitiated eye. Individuals appear to have no prescribed orchestration. Whole bodies are cropped off, making for a

---

[35]   James A. Faris, *Navajo and Photography: A Critical History of the Representation of an American People* (Albuquerque, 1996), p. 13.

[36]   Scott McQuire, *Visions of Modernity* (London and Thousand Oaks, 1998), p. 166.

[37]   The recitation "Great Wakan Tanka: We are ready to begin the dance as you have commanded us. Our hearts are now good" was reported by ethnologist Warren K. Moorehead who visited the Indians, as relayed in Coleman, *Voices of Wounded Knee*, p. 36.

[38]   Here I borrow Barthes's terminology, though admittedly just slightly out of context. He complained that most pictures lacked this quality whereas a tiny few contain "animation." However, rather than making a sheer aesthetic judgment we might consider the spiritual merits of such photographs. See Barthes, *Camera Lucida*, pp. 18–20.

Figure 5.2 "Rosebud and Sioux Indian War Dance at Pine Ridge," dated 25 December 1890, from the collection at the Western History/Genealogy Department, Denver Public Library.

jarring, disorienting view. Neither is there a visual entry point, pathway, or clear focus for the viewer—compositional choices that would seem curiously poor.

Adding to the confusion is the nomenclature. This particular photograph has been presented as a "War Dance."[39] The title, with spurious date, is written right on the plate. A picture of this same dance was called a "Ghost Dance" (Nebraska State Historical Society). Of course, there are several reasons why this scene could not be a War Dance, not to mention a Ghost Dance. It is highly unlikely that any white photographer would have been privy to a War Dance at this time (25 December 1890)—on this reservation and at such proximity. Guards kept strict watch on private dances for one, and multiple factors point to the fallacy. More to the point, the Lakota were not concerned with a War Dance. While other tribes sometimes were, the closest for the Lakota would have been the Victory Dance performed only after the battle in thanksgiving and in honor of the fallen.

Arguments of why the picture cannot be read as evidence of a Ghost Dance follow the same logic with an addition. Namely, the doctrine of Ghost Dance Religion strictly espoused peace and good works; any action was left to the Messiah Himself.[40] The "holy shirts" of the dance were to be bulletproof. What is seen in Figure 5.2 is more likely an Omaha Dance (or Grass Dance), a commonly photographed social dance that took place on the reservation.[41] One writer in *Frank Leslie's Illustrated Newspaper* unconsciously made reference to such free conflation of "ghost or grass dances."[42] The phony titles and frenetic appearance of

---

[39]   The photograph is still listed under this title at the Denver Public Library, Western History and Genealogy Department, its repository.

[40]   Dancer Weasel, for example, states, "we did not carry our guns nor any weapon, but trusted to the Great Spirit to destroy the soldiers"; cited by Raymond J. DeMallie, "The Lakota Ghost Dance: An Ethnohistorical Account," *Pacific Historical Review*, 51/4 (1982): 394 n. 27; James P. Boyd, *Recent Indian Wars, Under the Lead of Sitting Bull, and Other Chiefs; with A full Account of the Messiah Craze, and Ghost Dances* (Philadelphia, 1891), pp. 194–5.

[41]   Multiple sources have noted the discrepancy in the identifications of dance pictures. Jamake Highwater states in particular how the Omaha Dance was mistaken for a war dance in *Ritual of the Wind*, pp. 12, 144, and 153. She clearly states that the Omaha Dance (or Grass Dance) has "never been performed in connection with war," p. 153. Reginald and Gladys Laubin further stated that the Lakota "had no real war dance"; *Indian Dances of North America: Their Importance to Indian Life* (Norman, 1979; reprint of 1977 edn.), p. 148. Among others, Thomas Kavanagh puts the origin of the Grass dance with tribes south of the Dakotas, particularly the Omaha, Kansa, Ponca, and Pawnee (hence the Omaha moniker); it was termed Grass Dance for the braids of sweet grass: "Southern Plains Dance: Tradition and Dynamism," in Charlotte Heth (ed.), *Native American Dance: Ceremonies and Social Traditions* (Washington, DC, 1993): pp. 190ff.

[42]   Frank Leslie's *Illustrated Newspaper*, 20 December 1890, p. 372. In an article signed by "an officer," the writer claimed to have witnessed "several of these dances" and noted that newspapermen dubbed them "ghost or grass dances." Despite the instability of the source, the apparent systemic conflation of terms is of note.

the dancers in the image suggests that the ritual dance of the Indian was meant to foment battle. Dr. James J. Garrett, noting that the clothing of the dancers doesn't coincide with the freezing temperatures of South Dakota winters, suggests a more accurate interpretation of this picture: mislabeled as such it may have been used by the photographer or another entity as a "calculated mis-statement designed to support and justify the massacre, incite a riot, and secure stolen lands."[43]

While the Ghost Dance religion was noted for its many parallels with Christianity, in such images one begins to see how a Christian public was misled. Even in the twenty-first century there is an astonishing credulity when it comes to the photographic image, but in the nineteenth, the century of its birth, it was "taken to be an automatic record of reality."[44]

Some might argue that photographers cannot be blamed for the deficiencies of their medium. However, comparisons with James Mooney pictures of the Ghost Dance at the Cheyenne and Arapaho Reservation provide an alternative explanation.[45] While the cultural dynamics of the Ghost Dance might have been quite different there, Mooney produced pictures in a way that makes it clear he took the time to better understand the culture before photographing. In one instance, he highlights an Arapaho woman standing in prayer—the ancient Orant gesture that Catholic Christians would readily recognize from the liturgical prayer of the Our Father.[46] Mooney would include figures near the viewer's space, thoughtfully looking on; the viewer is better able to identify with them and is thus led to feel more included, if not physically then psychologically. The overall mood conveyed is one of far greater subtlety and peace, with depth privileged over spectacle.[47] While one does have to look past Mooney's limited cultural understanding it was

---

[43] That is, calculated by the photographer or another entity misusing a photograph already taken. As further noted by Dr. Garrett, it is significant that 120 years later the image is still mislabeled as "Rose Bud and Sioux Indian, War Dance at Pine Ridge" with no discussion. Personal communication with editor, 29 January 2009.

[44] Victor Burgin, "Something about Photography Theory," in A.L. Rees and Frances Borzello (eds.), *The New Art History* (Atlantic Highlands, 1986), p. 46.

[45] He was studying Eastern tribes including the Cherokee, when he was summoned to investigate the South Dakota tragedy just after it happened. His pictures of the Cheyenne and Arapaho that are dated range from 1891 to 1893. For further illumination on the thorniness of Mooney's imagery, refer to Thomas Kavanagh's "Reading Photographs."

[46] Smithsonian National Anthropological Archives, #06081600, "Ceremony, Ghost Dance," n.d. Mooney took extensive photographs of the Arapaho dance, many of which are found at the same repository.

[47] He would notably condemn the actions of government officials at Wounded Knee in his report. For example, Mooney wrote, "The Ghost dance [sic] itself, in the form which it assumed among the Sioux was only a symptom and expression of the real causes of dissatisfaction, and with such a man as [agent] McGillycuddy or McLaughlin in charge at Pine Ridge there would have been no outbreak, in spite of broken promises and starvation"; *The Ghost-Dance Religion*, p. 828.

he who would note that the Ghost Dance had parallels in the biblical King David dancing before the Lord or the moral codes given by the Buddha.[48]

For a somewhat more direct comparison, we can look to Frederic Remington, who sketched the Ghost Dance on scene at Pine Ridge. His illustrations are more cleaned up by the very nature of his medium (drawing naturally edits with even the best of hands); but at the end of the day they would seem to win out over any of the photographs taken there as they effectively "show" more; spirituality is rendered visible in his famous image of "The Ghost Dance by the Ogallala [sic] Sioux at Pine Ridge Agency, Dakota" shown in the *Harper's Weekly* of 6 December 1890.[49] Community is witnessed by carefully interwoven dancers; sacredness by draped figures; and especially in a lone seeker whose upturned gaze connotes supplication, which is the ultimate aim here: communion with the Great Mystery. Such an image may not be perfect, yet the contrast is quite telling.

Spawned Images

There is much more at stake than the artistry or accuracy of one picture over another. Images have a half-life. Because most reporters on the scene in South Dakota likely never saw an actual Ghost Dance, certainly not close up, photography was a key means of dissemination. For newspapers, it was still more common to feature illustrations. A crude sketch (in every sense) pretending to be of the Ghost Dance was placed in a front-page *Chicago Daily Tribune* article that reported "Sitting Bull Placed in Irons." Spurious headlines dotted the page: "Redskins," "Bloody Work," "Settlers Fleeing for Safety."[50] The Ghost Dance is indicted by association with such text; a reminder that images always "have to be mediated by words," even though they are at the same time "pre-linguistic."[51] Moreover, the illustrations have to come from somewhere, and we are left to wonder about the dissemination of photographs purporting to be of a War Dance or Ghost Dance.

Similarly depraved was an illustration featured in the *Phrenological Journal* in January 1891, and its existence suggests just how widespread interest in the Ghost Dance was. Phrenology is now infamous for its use of photography to undermine

---

[48]   Mooney, *The Ghost-Dance*, pp. 24–5. Sadly, Mooney also held the belief that the Indians' natural instinct had in the past been for war; uniquely, he saw the Ghost Dance as "civilizing."

[49]   Some have noted, for example, that the image appears anglicized. Remington had a peculiar stance toward the Indian that was surely influenced by their supposed "vanishing" condition. He traveled to Pine Ridge Agency with General Miles in October and December of 1890. *Harper's Weekly*, in which his image appeared, was more above the fray than the newspapers and was often sympathetic.

[50]   And "Indians Ready to Give Attack," 20 November 1890.

[51]   According to Max Kozloff, as recounted by Clive Scott, *The Spoken Image: Photography and Language* (London, 1999), p. 10; "pre-linguistic" is Scott's term, p. 20.

the capacities of certain ethnic groups, such as African American slaves.[52] In other instances, images did not pretend outright to be illustrations of the Ghost Dance. Rather, political cartoons appropriated the dance iconography to lampoon political figures, as a *New York World* cartoonist did in order to poke fun at GOP politicians' spending.[53] Illustration, like photography, cooperates in "a perfect crime" that is "simply the trace left behind" for "a world which projects only illusion."[54]

When news stories were not illustrated, imagistic headlines and reports could present just as much guilt-by-association. An intrepid journalist on 26 November 1890 recounted his alleged journey, passing "Uncle Sam's defense posts," and his "alarm" at finding no Indians on ration day.[55] Against orders, he "ran the guards" into the reservation to view "a weird scene"; "wild and weird wailing" could be heard "ten miles away."[56] A "mammoth ghost dance [sic]" was being carried on: "fires … lit up the surroundings and showed the brown, naked bodies of fully six thousand Sioux warriors."[57] "Ghost Dancers Plot to Kill the Troops" screamed the first column of the second page of the *New York Herald* two days earlier (24 November 1890). The Ghost Dance was part of a "plan" to lure General Brooke and his command "into an ambush and shoot them down"; the outlook was "ominous." Daily headlines raged off the page, often the front page: "Indians Insolent, Settlers Terrified"[58]; "Sioux … Crazed by the Ghost Dances, Ready to Go on the Warpath at Any Moment."[59] Spurious reports from locals, such as Mrs. James A. Finley, wife of the postmaster at Pine Ridge, served to reinforce the otherwise entirely impracticable: Ghost Dancers were dancing with all their guns and weapons.[60] In the *Chicago Tribune* the notion that Indians were "Dancing with Guns" merited

---

[52]   As in the case of Harvard scientist Louis Agassiz's use of daguerreotypist J.T. Zealy to document plantation slaves in order to establish different ancestral origins for different races. See, for example: Alan Trachtenberg, "Illustrious Americans," in *Reading American Photographs* (New York, 1989).

[53]   On its front page, 4 December 1890. "GOP" refers to the "Grand Old Party"—the Republican political party in the United States.

[54]   Jean Baudrillard, "The Art of Disappearance," in Nicholas Zurbrugg (ed.), *Art and Artefact* (London, 1997), p. 28.

[55]   A journey from Pierre, South Dakota under the headline: "Painted Savages in the Ghost Dance," *New York Herald*, 26 November 1890, p. 3.

[56]   Ibid.

[57]   Ibid.

[58]   Headline: "Indians Insolent, Settlers Terrified"; subheading: "Sioux Defy the Authorities and Say They Will Resist an Attempt to Stop Their Ghost Dances"; *New York Herald* , 28 November 1890, p. 10.

[59]   Headline: "Sioux Threatening, Troops Concentrating"; subheadings: "Sitting Bull May Provoke an Immediate and Bloody Indian War If So Disposed"; "General Miles Gathering Forces"; *New York Herald*, 22 November 1890, p. 1. And so it continued on and on: "Sioux Rascals Dance and Steal," *New York Herald*, 13 December 1890, p. 4 …

[60]   *New York Herald*, 22 November 22, 1890, p. 2. Under the headline "The Ghost Dance Described," she aimed to do just that: "Every Indian has about four clubs made out

a headline.[61] Mooney clarified such glaring accusations in his book saying: "No weapon of any kind was allowed to be carried in the Ghost dance [sic] by any tribe, north or south."[62] Readers of newspapers were taken on a constant back-and-forth ride between mildly reassuring and grossly scare-mongering print from day to day and week to week. Sometimes buried in the page was a bit of truth, far less salable. General Miles: "[Indians] have as much right to have an Indian Messiah as the whites have to have a white Messiah. The situation is not alarming in any way."[63]

Newspapermen were perhaps the greatest contributors to religious and cultural divisions. Much of this was simply in the labeling: "the Messiah craze" was probably the second-most used moniker after "Ghost Dance." In the late nineteenth-century, such terminology was not without qualification, for indeed evangelical movements had swept the country earlier under the Second Great Awakening. From Methodists to Quakers to Adventists ecstatic visions and physical convulsions were not uncommon. Later, by the time of the Ghost Dance, Spiritualism—wherein spirits of the dead could be channeled—was in its heyday, mostly among wealthier classes. With so little in the way of any kind of real understanding, the *New York World* conflated the dance with the latter movement. The Ghost Dance had even more powerful an effect on Indians than "the communications made by mediums have upon spiritualists."[64] Meanwhile, other pages would regularly report a who's who of high-society dancers in cosmopolitan life as a matter of edification. Typical *New York World* headlines of the day included: "The Herrigan Association Members had a Gay Time" and "The Lady Lafayette Members of the White High Hat Association On the Floor."[65] In another instance the gap between two stridently different worlds of "dance" was unwittingly laid bare: the Cheyenne and Arapaho had had "several dances of late, but they were like those of white people, for pleasure merely."[66]

A Ghost Dance "Portrait"

Not just past history, the Ghost Dance continued to be conflated with violence. It was not simply the dance itself but figures associated with it: Sitting Bull, Kicking

---

of round stones twisted in raw hide. They throw these around during the dance, strew the ground with them and beat their heads against them."

[61] *Chicago Tribune*, 20 November 1890, p. 1.
[62] Mooney, *The Ghost-Dance*, p. 30.
[63] "The Indian Messiah," *St. Louis Post-Dispatch*, 7 November 1890, p. 2. Robert M. Utley (in the *Last Days of the Sioux Nation* (New Haven, 2004), p. 212) would report another side of Miles's opinion; on one occasion Miles characterized warriors' plans as a "comprehensive plot."
[64] *The New York World*, 18 November 1890, p. 1.
[65] See front-page headlines, *The New York World*, 1890.
[66] *The New York Herald*, 4 December 1890, p. 3.

Bear, and Standing Bear were persistently painted (in both word and image) as tyrants that had to be dealt with.[67] A series of photographs were taken of Kicking Bear, likely while he was on delegation in Washington, DC to petition for rights on behalf of his people (1896).[68] The photographer, William Dinwiddie, titled many of these pictures so as to connote Kicking Bear as "Former Chief High Priest" of the Ghost Dance—more trophy pictures no doubt. (Sitting Bull, Short Bull, and Kicking Bear were variously given the title of high priest of the dance when it was convenient.) The first word of the title contributes to a "disappearing" identity— his essence is implied to exist only in his past. And the pictures illuminate nothing of the Ghost Dance: for one, he does not wear the typical Ghost Dance shirt.[69] More damaging is that in more than one instance the photographer poses Kicking Bear with a gun—guns were certainly not a part of the dance.[70] Kicking Bear was a zealous advocate of the Ghost Dance; his actions, though, were peaceful prior to his provocation by the army. Yet Dinwiddie showed him as if ominously staring down the enemy. It has been pointed out that the language of photography often uses the verb "to take"—one takes and the other gives away something of their identity. Questions, ultimately unanswerable, about photographic agency rise to the surface: though Kicking Bear obviously assented to have his picture taken, it is more than doubtful that he would have had it be as representative of the Ghost

---

[67]   They were chiefs and seen as the leaders of the Ghost Dance at Standing Rock, Cheyenne River, and Rosebud Reservations, respectively. Kicking Bear was part of a delegation from the Dakota reservations that went to Nevada to hear from Wovoka, the Paiute holy man who originated the Ghost Dance (see above). David Humphreys Miller writes that Kicking Bear was chosen at Red Cloud's council to lead the first Sioux Ghost Dance at Pine Ridge: in Mooney, *The Ghost-Dance*, pp. 56–8.

[68]   Out of respect for Kicking Bear and his family, and because of the controversial nature of some of the pictures, they will not be illustrated here. The full title of one of these is "Portrait (Front) of Mato-Wa-Nahtaka (Kicking Bear), Former Chief High Priest of Sioux Ghost Dance, in Native Dress with His Scalp Shirt and Holding Rifle 1896"; the others are similarly titled. The repository is the Smithsonian National Anthropological Archives, NAA INV 06539300. Notably, Dinwiddie has chosen to combine the Ghost Dance (and its distinctive clothing) with the scalp shirt.

[69]   While Ghost Dance shirts were considered by the Lakota to be bulletproof, Richard E. Jensen (among others) points out that the prophecy Wovoka preached was that whites would simply disappear at the appointed time; "Another Look at Wounded Knee," in *Eyewitness at Wounded Knee*, p. 10. With their v-shaped neck and celestial designs, muslin Ghost Dance shirts were very different from the kind of clothing worn here. Many photographers kept stock clothing in their studios to enhance the outcome of the picture. Also, in contrast to the iconic westerner with gun at his side, any Indian arms used for defense were kept in common.

[70]   Again, James Mooney writes that Wovoka instructed followers to "put away all old practices that savored of war"; *The Ghost-Dance*, p. 772. He stated to Short Bull of the Brule Sioux: "They may try to kill you, Short Bull. Even so, do not fight back. You must live in peace"; David Humphreys Miller, *Ghost Dance*, p. 45.

Dance—a further reminder that even the most savvy of subjects (then as now) sacrifices a measure of control the moment the picture is taken. With both title and scene not suited for context, one has to wonder if such a portraitist isn't guilty of "falsifying forever a person's place in the world."[71]

The unreality of such images is thrown into high relief when it is compared to a picture on the reservation dated 30 January 1891 or shortly thereafter.[72] One would hardly recognize that he is the same man. However, in it Kicking Bear resembles a person Lakotas would recognize as a "common man," a leader intent on helping and serving his people with wisdom and compassion. He wears slightly Western clothing and appears modest, humble, and unpretentious. Though the picture is far closer to the time of the massacre, and we might expect anger, sadness, and bitterness from any Lakota, it is not evident in the image. Kicking Bear appears altogether human, whereas years later Dinwiddie would cast him as fearsome. It is not simply the lens that "disfigures and decimates character,"[73] there is a highly active photographer, conveniently unseen. Baudrillard's finding that the "human being is masked" presents itself as true.[74] He was speaking of the mask as the inner identity of the person, which is ultimately unavailable to us, but that mask is also layered by a second false mask that the photographer imprints on another. So close to observed reality and yet disembodied from lived experience, photography has quite rightly been described as a mask having a "secular aura."[75]

Afterimages

It is important for us to consider just how much the imagistic may have contributed to the "crisis"—a physical, cultural, and religious crisis—at Pine Ridge one tragic winter; it was not just words. The influence of the pictures that were disseminated through newspapers, magazines, and private means did not suddenly end; the images remain "dramatic by virtue of [their] silence."[76] No wonder there was an

---

[71] Lucy Lippard, *Partial Recall: Photographs of Native North Americans* (New York, 1992), p. 15.

[72] A second photograph, also in the Denver Library, Western History and Genealogy Department collection shows "Kicking Bear with Young Man Afraid of His Horses and Standing Bear at Pine Ridge" and is dated 30 January 1891. It is most likely that the photographs were taken the same day—shadows, outfits, and backgrounds all corroborate—but it is unclear why the repository has dated the two pictures separately.

[73] Miller, *Ghost Dance*.

[74] Baudrillard, "Art of Disappearance," p. 29.

[75] "Mask as Descriptive Concept" is used repeatedly in Mary Price, *The Photograph: A Strange, Confined Place* (Stanford, 1997).

[76] Jean Baudrillard, *The Transparency of Evil* (Paris, 1990), p. 155; quoted in Zurbrugg, *Art and Artifact/Artefact*, p. 161.

"outbreak"—it was pre-staged, pre-invented by and for a "Society of Spectacle."[77] Perhaps religion could not thwart the power of the image magicians. It was not and remains not evident that the photograph is a "fluid, mobile," and "unstable medium," with propensity toward "dispossession … discontinuity."[78]

News photographs have a way of later being translated into History.[79] That, of course, is dangerous because of the relatively high degree of visual illiteracy. And there is also an uncomfortable democratic nature to photographs, something that Umberto Eco attests to: "It is of no interest to know if it was posed (and therefore faked), whether it was the testimony of an act of conscious bravado, if it was the work of a professional photographer who gauged the moment, the light, the frame, or whether it virtually took itself … At the moment it appeared, its communicative career began."[80] Rather than viewed as documentary, a better stance might be to ask what the utilization of a picture truly intends. For many of them stand less as historical ciphers and more as indicators of the work we have left to do. What must be *seen* is "Ghost Dance as a creative response," one that did not die but was born and contributes yet still to the "story of religion in America."[81] Images have been produced—appropriately, uninformed or otherwise—and have an afterlife. But any negative powers they contain can be used against them—to show their very inadequacy and the limits of the monocular point of view that persists yet today. Inadequacies identified, identities reclaimed, one can begin to point to something greater. For the true religious task—or challenge—in seeing, be it a breathing or represented human, is to peel away the layers that always exist and unknowingly stand between the eye and the Thou. "Put another way, we must reveal the mask or the figure which haunts a person, and withdraw it from their identity—the masked divinity which inhabits every one of us, even the most insignificant, for an instant, one day or another."[82]

---

[77] *Avant la lettre*: While television, movies, and other forms of mass communication arising in the twentieth century are often seen as the origins of spectacle, it is worthwhile to reconsider earlier formats, which perhaps had a different power precisely because of the lesser competition.

[78] Scott, *The Spoken Image*, pp. 14, 55.

[79] A common yet often overlooked fact well put in print by Mary Price in *The Photograph*, p. 1.

[80] Umberto Eco, "A Photograph," in Liz Wells (ed.), *The Photography Reader* (New York and London, 2003), p. 128.

[81] A welcome change of approach from past to prophetic is so outlined by Joel W. Martin in "Before and beyond the Sioux Ghost Dance: Native American Prophetic Movements and the Study of Religion," *Journal of the American Academy of Religion*, 59/4 (1991): 694. General books, encyclopedias, and websites often consider the Ghost Dance as a past event; it rather has occurred and continues long after the 1890–91 circumstances. Åke Hultkrantz some time ago noted its continuity among the Shoshoni, for example, in *Belief and Worship in Native North America* (Syracuse, 1981), pp. 264–81. Another classic example is the revival among the Kiowa, 1894–1916.

[82] Baudrillard, "The Art of Disappearance," p. 31.

Chapter 6

Negotiating the Evidence: Christianity and the Ruins of Native America

David Toole

Let me begin with a brief explanation of the key words in the title.[1] First, the phrase "ruins of Native America" names for me something quite specific: the eastern plains and western mountains of Montana, Wyoming, and the Dakotas, because, quite simply, this is home for me. And to speak of ruins in this context is to say that both the native peoples and the native flora and fauna of this region are in ruins, when compared, say, to their state in 1803, to pick an easy marker—the year Lewis and Clark left St. Louis. "The ruins of Native America" is for me a straightforward descriptive statement of the place where I grew up and that I call home.

More difficult to name are the realities of what it means for people to live in ruins—and to speak of "negotiating the evidence" is my way of naming this difficulty. This title came to me after visiting the National Museum of the American Indian (NMAI) on the mall in Washington, DC, where one of the exhibits gathers around the theme of "evidence." At the entrance to this exhibit stands the declaration, "We are the evidence of this Western Hemisphere." Instructions for how to interpret the exhibit follow: "Think of the exhibition as an excavation site, where evidence that has been buried, ignored, and denied is finally brought to light. For us ... the evidence suggests that the history of this hemisphere is written in the lives of Native people."[2] This statement raises many questions about what it might mean for human beings to be "evidence." Consider the case of the Lakota holy man: Black Elk (1863–1950).

Black Elk became famous, of course, because of John Neihardt's book *Black Elk Speaks*—the result of interviews Neihardt conducted in 1931.[3] The book was published in 1932, reprinted in 1961 and 1979, and became something of a cultural phenomenon in America in the late 1970s and early 1980s, long after Black Elk himself was dead. Then, in 1984, Raymond DeMallie published the transcripts

---

[1]   This essay is a revision of a paper I presented, using the same title, at the annual meeting of the American Academy of Religion, for a session of the Native Traditions of the Americas Group on the theme of "Sacred Spaces and Sacred Places," Chicago, Illinois, 1 November 2008.

[2]   My descriptions of exhibits at the NMAI come from visits on 12 January 2007 and 3 October 2008.

[3]   John G. Neihardt, *Black Elk Speaks* (New York, 1972; reprint of 1932).

of the 1931 interviews that Neihardt used as the basis for *Black Elk Speaks.*[4] What some had suspected became readily apparent; namely, Neihardt had used significant poetic license to create his portrait of Black Elk—which raised many questions: about Neihardt and his intentions and methods, about Black Elk and who he really was, and about the encounter between the colonial powers of the West and native peoples everywhere. Since 1984, a minor publishing industry has developed around Black Elk and these questions, and to read through this literature is to be schooled in what it means to negotiate the evidence when the evidence in question is a person, now dead, and people still living, but in ruins.[5]

One of the central debates about Black Elk concerns the disparity between Neihardt's account of him as a Lakota holy man steeped in Lakota traditions, and the fact that he became a Catholic in 1904, and then for the decades following served as a Catholic catechist. What does this mean? Was he a Lakota who used Catholicism as a means of cultural survival? Was he a Catholic who rejected central features of Lakota culture? Was he a Lakota Catholic who found a way to be both at once? All of these "Black Elks" exist in the literature, and more.[6] These questions about Black Elk frame what I take to be the larger issue of what we are up to when we find ourselves negotiating the evidence. Once we make Black Elk the evidence, then we have to ask ourselves: What is he evidence of? Is he evidence of the ruins of what once was? Is he evidence of what might be possible for the Lakota amid the ruins? Is he evidence of what might be possible for us all in the face of cultural devastation? Is he evidence of Christian complicity in colonialism? Is he evidence of the future of Christianity once it comes to terms with the ways in which it is has been transformed by people like Black Elk? Is he evidence of all these things and more? The reason we must negotiate the evidence is precisely because the evidence is not self-evident—nor are our negotiations of it neutral and objective. We find ourselves negotiating the evidence, once we have encountered it as such, for various reasons, and these reasons matter.

My own reasons for negotiating the evidence bring me to the last term in my title: "Christianity." My copy of *Black Elk Speaks* still carries the inscription my mother wrote when she gave it to me for Christmas in 1973, when my eleven-year-old imagination was formed more by stories of Chief Joseph, Sitting Bull, and Crazy Horse than by anything else. Well into my adult life, Christianity was only a negative presence—that which had ruined the native cultures I so admired. But

---

[4]   Raymond DeMallie (ed.), *The Sixth Grandfather: Black Elk's Teachings Given to John G. Neihardt* (Lincoln, 1984).

[5]   See Clyde Holler (ed.), *The Black Elk Reader* (Syracuse, 2000); Damian Costello, *Black Elk: Colonialism and Lakota Catholicism* (Maryknoll, 2005); and Roger Dunsmore, "Nicholas Black Elk: Holy Man in History," in *Earth's Mind: Essays in Native Literature* (Albuquerque, 1997), pp. 69–90.

[6]   The best overview of the scholarship on Black Elk's Lakota Catholic identity is Costello, *Black Elk*. Costello also stakes out his own views on the character of Black Elk as a Lakota Catholic, which I find largely persuasive.

now I am a Catholic, and it is certainly not accidental—indeed, it seems especially fitting—that I find myself returning to Black Elk and finding in his story the difficulties of negotiating the evidence of the encounter between the Christian West and indigenous people everywhere. There was a time when the only evidence I was interested in was anything that added to the proof of the ways in which whites (and especially Christians) had systematically destroyed native peoples. But now I am interested in the ways in which native peoples might be the salvation of Christianity, and, even more, how a Christianity so saved might in turn be the salvation of a world that otherwise is ruined.

Let me now deepen what I have started with these introductory comments by focusing on three things: first, a long excursus concerning Jonathan Lear's attempt to negotiate the evidence of Plenty Coups and the Crow in his book *Radical Hope: Ethics in the Face of Cultural Devastation*;[7] second, the way this negotiation of evidence plays out in one of the inaugural exhibits of the NMAI; and finally, what such negotiations might suggest about the future of both Christianity and the ruins of Native America.

Dancing as If Nothing Has Happened: Plenty Coups and the Crow

Frank Linderman published his account of the life of the Crow chief Plenty Coups in 1930. In an author's note at the end of the text, Linderman says:

> Plenty-coups refused to speak of this life after the passing of the buffalo, so that his story seems to have broken off, leaving many years unaccounted for. "I have not told half that happened when I was young," he said, when urged to go on. "I can think back and tell you much more of war and horse stealing. But when the buffalo went away the hearts of my people fell to the ground, and they could not lift them up again. After this nothing happened. There was little singing anywhere. Besides," he added sorrowfully, "you know that part of my life as well as I do. You saw what happened to us when the buffalo went away."[8]

In *Radical Hope*, Jonathan Lear offers an extended interpretation of this passage, and in particular of the words, "After this nothing happened."[9] Because Plenty Coups's words hinge on "the passing of the buffalo," let me begin with a reminder of the startling reality of this historical moment.

---

[7]   Jonathan Lear, *Radical Hope: Ethics in the Face of Cultural Devastation* (Cambridge, 2006).

[8]   Frank B. Linderman, *Plenty-Coups: Chief of the Crows* (Lincoln, 2000; reprint of 1930 edn.).

[9]   Parts of the following discussion appeared in Stanley Hauerwas and David Toole, review of *Radical Hope: Ethics in the Face of Cultural Devastation* (Cambridge, 2006) by Jonathan Lear, *The Christian Century*, 124 (13 November 2007): 43.

When Lewis and Clark polled and pulled their way up the Mississippi and through the Great Plains of North America in 1803, the plains teemed with tens of millions of American bison, known more commonly as "buffalo." For the southern herd, which ranged from Colorado and Kansas south into Texas, this time ended in November 1879, when Jack Harris, an accomplished buffalo hunter, scoured the plains of Texas and found only twenty-two animals, twelve of which he killed.[10] Just six years before, in 1873, the railroads running through Kansas and Nebraska had hauled more than 700,000 hides, 2,400 tons of meat, and 4,000 tons of bones (for fertilizer and sugar refineries) to markets in the east. With the southern herd gone, but with markets thriving, hunters like Jack Harris moved north.

The northern herd, which ranged in Wyoming, Montana, and the Dakotas, had not been immune to the mass killings (by no means all of which were market-driven) that had been carried out on its southern counterpart. But the Indians of the northern plains, particularly the 15,000 or so members of the various tribes known collectively as the Sioux, were still enough of a military presence to check the wholesale expansion of white settlements into the heart of the northern plains. Even at the relatively late date of 1876, Sitting Bull, Crazy Horse, and other chiefs of the Sioux, Cheyenne and Arapahoe were able to hand the Seventh Calvary its decisive defeat on the Little Big Horn. But for the Sioux and the other tribes this was a victory in a war that had already been lost. Crazy Horse was killed, in captivity, a year later; Sitting Bull surrendered in 1880; and the Northern Pacific Railroad expanded into Montana in 1881. In 1882, shipments of buffalo hides from the northern plains peaked at 200,000. In 1883, only 300 hides found their way onto trains headed east; and railroad records indicate that the last carload of buffalo robes left the northern plains from Dickinson, North Dakota, in 1884. Retrospectively, the years from 1879 to 1884 became known as the "Great Slaughter." In Yellowstone Park, which would become home to the last of the buffalo in the wild, only 200 remained in 1885, and by 1902 this number had dropped to just over twenty.

About the time the last shipment of buffalo hides left Dickinson, North Dakota, Frank Linderman arrived in Montana.[11] Two decades later, as the nineteenth century turned into the twentieth, and as Linderman saw that the life he had come to experience on the "frontier" had played out, he began to collect the stories and record the lives of the native peoples who had lived on the other side of the divide, before "the buffalo went away." Linderman's "as-told-to" story of Plenty Coups was his best-known record of Indians and Indian life. A Crow warrior and chief born in 1846, Plenty Coups told Linderman his story through a translator just

---

[10]	See David A. Dary, *The Buffalo Book: The Full Saga of the American Animal*, revised edn. (Athens, 1989); Dale F. Lott, *American Bison: A Natural History* (Berkeley, 2002).

[11]	See, in particular, this chapter by Sherry L. Smith, "Native Son: Frank Bird Linderman," in her *Reimagining Indians: Native Americans through Anglo Eyes, 1880–1940* (New York, 2000), pp. 95–118.

a few years before he died in 1932, the same year John Neihardt published his story of Black Elk. Indeed, Linderman and Neihardt were part of a larger effort in the early twentieth century to preserve a record of the life Indians had once led. Linderman was convinced that all would be lost when the last of the Indians like Plenty Coups died. As he put it in 1930, "The real Indians are gone."[12]

Plenty Coups, still holding on in 1930, said it better with the words already quoted above: "When the buffalo went away the hearts of my people fell to the ground, and they could not lift them up again. After this nothing happened." The buffalo of the northern plains "went away" between 1879 and 1884. Thus the part of Plenty Coups's story that "seems to have broken off" and remains unaccounted for amounts to more than forty years of his life. Although he lived on after the passing of the buffalo, and in fact remained an engaged leader of his people, Plenty Coups apparently had nothing to say, because after the buffalo were gone "nothing happened."[13] Jonathan Lear is transfixed by this declaration. What did Plenty Coups mean when he said, "After this nothing happened"? "It would seem," Lear notes, "to be the retrospective declaration that history has come to an end. But what could it mean for history to exhaust itself?"[14] The answer to this question requires that we think carefully about what a "happening" is. Lear's book is an exploration of how such language works, and he conducts this exploration by looking closely at Crow culture, both as it would have existed in Plenty Coups's youth in the 1840s and 1850s, and as it existed when Linderman interviewed Plenty Coups in the late 1920s.

---

[12] Linderman, *Plenty-Coups*, xxvii. Linderman was not simply stating his own nostalgic judgment about the fate of Native Americans but in fact voicing deep cultural assumptions about "the vanishing American." Though it is not the task of this chapter to do so, it is important to situate Linderman, Neihardt, and others like them within the historical moment of 1920s. See both Brian W. Dippie, *The Vanishing American: White Attitudes and U.S. Indian Policy* (Middletown, 1982), and Smith, *Reimagining Indians.*

[13] Sherry L. Smith notes in her article on Linderman: "Given Plenty Coups' active involvement in reservation politics, it is quite possible that Linderman was the one who preferred to ignore contemporary life. It did not fit his romantic image" (see "Native Son," p. 108). Moreover, the appearance of a similar declaration in the "as-told-to" story of Two Leggings, a Crow who was a contemporary of Plenty Coups, raises additional questions about the meaning of Plenty Coups's words. During interviews conducted between 1919 and 1923, Two Leggings told William Wildschut, "Nothing happened after that. We just lived. There were no more war parties, no capturing of horses from the Piegans and the Sioux, no buffalo hunt. There is nothing more to tell." See Peter Nabakov (ed.), *Two Leggings: The Making of a Crow Warrior* (Lincoln, 1967), p. 197. Lear takes Linderman at his word that Plenty Coups did not talk about contemporary life. Even more, neither Lear nor Linderman are sensitive to the possibility that declarations like "nothing happened" were coded pronouncements that the Crow offered to outsiders as a "public transcript" of "hidden" acts of resistance to white exploitation. See James C. Scott, *Domination and the Arts of Resistance: Hidden Transcripts* (New Haven, 1990).

[14] Lear, *Radical Hope*, p. 3.

Before the buffalo went away, the Crow were a warrior culture in which the practice of "counting coups" was paradigmatic for their whole life. Counting coups stood as the proof of courage and honor. To count coups, warriors had to touch an enemy with a coup stick before killing them or darting away to safety. In the midst of a fight, a warrior would also plant the coup stick in the ground to indicate an unwillingness to retreat—a visible indication of a last line of defense (and of cultural preservation), beyond which the enemy would not be allowed to pass, come what may. This same display of risk and courage was also evident in horse stealing, whereby Crow warriors would sneak into an enemy camp and steal horses that were often tethered just outside enemy lodges. Plenty Coups (*A-Lek-Chea-Ahoosh* in Crow) received his name because he was particularly adept both at stealing horses and at counting coups in battle. For the Crow, stealing horses and battling their enemies were not simply matters of courage and honor. They were activities required to secure Crow territory, which, stretching as it did across what is now southern Montana and northern Wyoming, was the heart of buffalo country. To secure this territory was to secure access to the great herds upon which everything depended: food, clothing, lodging, and a whole host of daily activities (dancing, singing, storytelling) associated with both the hunt and its fruits. When Plenty Coups told Linderman that after the buffalo went away the hearts of his people fell to the ground and "there was little singing anywhere," he was not being poetic but naming the fact that the very practices that had sustained Crow culture had ceased to exist.

Lear notes that there are many ways that we might try to make sense of Plenty Coups's declaration, but what he wants us to entertain is the possibility that when Plenty Coups said, "After this nothing happened," he was "making as radical a claim as is humanly possible to make. And we want to ask, what would it be for such a claim to be true?"[15] Lear's answer to this question is displayed with particular clarity in his discussion of the Crow Sun Dance, an elaborate ceremony that was used to prepare for war (and also the hunt). The Crow stopped performing this ceremony about 1875. Therefore, Lear says, it is possible to hear in Plenty Coups's declaration a description of what it was like after the Crow moved on to the reservation:

> No traditionally important events like the Sun Dance happened any more. But it is also possible to hear him as bearing witness to a deeper and darker claim: namely, that no one dances the Sun Dance any more because it is no longer possible to do so. Once planting a coup-stick loses meaning, so, too, does the Sun Dance. One might still teach people the relevant steps; people might learn how to go through the motions; and they can even call it the "Sun Dance"; but the Sun Dance itself has gone out of existence. The Sun Dance itself was a prayer-filled ritual asking God's help in winning military victory. This is not something that can be intelligibly performed now. … Concepts get their lives

---

[15]   Ibid.

through the lives we are able to live with them. If nothing any longer can count as dancing a Sun Dance or planting a coup-stick, then the tribe has lost the concepts Sun Dance and coup-stick. ... [This] loss is not itself a happening, but is the breakdown of that in terms of which happenings occur.[16]

When the Crow could no longer live lives rooted in the practices of warfare and the hunt, their concepts were emptied of significance, and their own lives became unintelligible to them. Indeed, as something of a counterpart to his story of Plenty Coups, Frank Linderman told the story of a Crow woman named Pretty Shield, who expressed just this loss of intelligibility when she said of her life on the reservation, "I am trying to live a life I do not understand."[17]

Lear suggests that Plenty Coups's declaration about the end of happenings marks the total unintelligibility of Crow life for the Crow. But that is only half the story, because, although Pretty Shield could no longer understand her life in the 1930s, and although Plenty Coups refused to talk about his life after the 1880s, the Crow tribe itself persisted into the twentieth century (and persists still in the twenty-first). This persistence ultimately drives Lear's plot. If with the end of the buffalo, the cessation of intertribal war, and the creation of the reservation, Crow life as such was no longer intelligible, then how is it that the Crow persist as Crow? Obviously, the answer must be that in spite of the destruction of their culture, something Crow remained, something substantial enough to be still recognizably Crow. But what could that be if the central forms of Crow life were gone? Much of Lear's book is an attempt to answer this question, and he does so with recourse to an account and analysis of a dream that Plenty Coups had when, in 1855 or 1856, as a boy of nine or ten, he journeyed into the Crazy Mountains to seek a vision—a normal right of passage for young Crow boys.

Plenty Coups reported his vision to Crow leaders, and the vision and its interpretation became part of the public life of the tribe. As Lear reports, "The tribe relied on what it took to be the young men's capacity to receive the world's imaginative messages; it relied on the older men to say what the message meant."[18]

---

[16] Ibid., p. 37. Lear's judgments about the unintelligibility of the Sun Dance in changing cultural circumstances are overdrawn, as he himself seems to know, given what he says later in the text. As with all such practices, their performance and its meaning can change with time and remain intelligible. For a good account of the Sun Dance and its transformation over time, see Clyde Holler, *Black Elk's Religion: The Sun Dance and Lakota Catholicism* (Syracuse, 1995). I offer this as a caution about Lear's argument but do not mean to take issue with his larger point, namely, that practices and the conditions that render them (and the lives they make possible) intelligible can be so thoroughly destroyed that, indeed, they no longer make sense.

[17] Frank B. Linderman, *Pretty-Shield: Medicine Woman of the Crows* (Lincoln, 2003; reprint of 1932 edn.), p. 8.

[18] Lear, *Radical Hope*, p. 71. Lear recounts and discusses Plenty Coups's dream on pp. 66–100. Linderman records Plenty Coups's account of the dream and the tribal elders'

In his dream, Plenty Coups saw all the buffalo disappear into a hole in the ground and then watched as spotted buffalo emerged to take their place. He then saw a powerful storm descend upon a forest, and when the storm had passed only one tree remained standing. A voice then told him to take notice that in this tree was the lodge of the Chickadee:

> The lodges of countless Bird-people were in that forest when the Four Winds charged it. ... Only one is left unharmed, the lodge of the Chickadee-person. ... He is least in strength but strongest of mind among his kind. He is willing to work for wisdom. The Chickadee-person is a good listener. ... He gains successes and avoids failure by learning how others succeeded or failed. ... Develop your body, but do not neglect your mind, Plenty Coups. It is the mind that leads a man to power.

When Plenty Coups returned to his village and reported this dream to the tribal elders, Yellow Bear offered the following interpretation:

> [Plenty Coups] has been told that in his lifetime the buffalo will go away forever and that in their place on the plains will come the bulls and the cows and the calves of the white man. ... The dream of Plenty Coups means that the white men will take and hold this country. ... The meaning of the dream is plain to me. I see its warning. The tribes who have fought the white man have all been beaten, wiped out. But listening as the Chickadee listens, we may escape this and keep our lands.

Because of this dream and its interpretation, Lear notes, "the tribe decided to ally with the United States against its traditional enemies. ... This fact did not stop the United States from repeatedly revising treaties at will and from encroaching on Crow lands. But, unlike other tribes, ... they could correctly say of themselves that they were never defeated."[19] Lear argues that Plenty Coups's dream embodied a "radical hope" that "facilitated a courageous response to the new challenges the Crow would face."[20] He notes that "what makes this hope radical is that it is directed toward a future goodness that transcends the current ability to understand what it is."[21] In other words, it is a hope that materializes out of circumstances that leave participants like Plenty Coups and Pretty Shield saying, "After this nothing happened," and "I am living a life I do not understand." For Lear, these statements involved the "stark recognition that the traditional ways of structuring significance—of recognizing something as happening—had been devastated."[22]

---

interpretation of it in *Plenty-Coups*, pp. 34–43. This account is drawn from both texts.

[19]   Lear, *Radical Hope*, p. 136.
[20]   Ibid.
[21]   Ibid., p. 103.
[22]   Ibid., p. 152.

Evidence of the cultural devastation of the Crow arrived when it was no longer possible to count coups (or steal horses)—which was simply an indication that the concepts, as embodied in narratives and practices, that made counting coups intelligible no longer existed. This issue of intelligibility was embodied in the actions of a young Crow warrior named Wraps His Tail, who led a band of warriors in a horse-stealing raid against the Blackfeet, a historic enemy to the north. This raid took place in the fall of 1887, three years after the last shipment of buffalo hides left North Dakota. In response to the raid, the US military pursued Wraps His Tail and the other Crow men, captured most of them, and killed Wraps His Tail. These events and others they spawned launched a series of competing narratives about Wraps His Tail and his exploits. Wraps His Tail and others insisted that the Crow men were simply responding to the tribal insult leveled at the Crow by the Blackfeet, who had recently stolen Crow horses. The raid was thus a classic case of counting coups against an enemy. The government agent on the Crow reservation, however, ordered the arrest of Wraps His Tail and the other men for "horse stealing," refusing to accept "counting coups" as a description of the event. Lear notes that it is tempting to focus on how these competing narratives lead to such radically different interpretations of the event. But he counsels us to avoid this temptation:

> Once the U.S. government forbids intertribal warfare—and demonstrates that it has the power to enforce this prohibition—the possibility of counting coups evaporates. Counting coups makes sense only in the context of a world of intertribal warfare; and once that world breaks down, *nothing* can count as counting coups. …. We do not grasp the devastation that the Crow endured so long as we think that the issue is who gets to tell the story. For the problem goes deeper than competing narratives. The issue is that the Crow have lost the concepts with which they would construct a narrative. This is a *real loss,* not just one that is described from a certain point of view. It is the *real loss of a point of view*. This is the confusion of the young man who takes the horse: he has not yet recognized the loss.[23]

What makes Plenty Coups such a fascinating figure for Lear is that, unlike Wraps His Tail, he recognized that the destruction of Crow culture had changed everything, and in so doing he charted a course for the Crow into an impossible future. Plenty Coups remained hopeful "in the face of the recognition that, given the abyss, one cannot really know what survival means":

> From the perspective of this commitment, the rebellion of Wraps His Tail isn't just futile; it is nostalgic evasion. … Wraps His Tail tried to hold onto this position in spite of the fact that it became unintelligible. Plenty Coups's position, by contrast, was ironic: the only way for a Crow to go forward was to

---

23   Ibid., pp. 31–2.

acknowledge that the traditional way of life was going to be blown away in a storm. Only after the storm would new Crow possibilities open up.[24]

Lear displays the difference between this futile nostalgia and ironic hope by once again using a dance as an example—now not the Sun Dance but the Ghost Dance, which was part of a movement that swept through many of the tribes of the American West in the late 1880s and 1890s.[25] The dance stemmed from the dream of a holy man named Wovoka. To perform the dance was to bring the dream to life and to usher in a time when all whites would be wiped out, Indian ancestors would be raised and the buffalo would return. Lear explores the meaning of this dance by contrasting Plenty Coups's response to the Ghost Dance with that of his great Sioux rival Sitting Bull.

Sitting Bull supported the Ghost Dance, but Plenty Coups opposed it. Lear says that the men "had the same vision, but they interpreted it in opposite ways. Both saw the ghosts of the buffalo, but for Plenty Coups the vision signified they were going away forever; for Sitting Bull and his Sioux followers, it signified that they were coming back."[26] For Lear, Sitting Bull's willingness to support the Ghost Dance was not unlike Wraps His Tail's raid against the Blackfeet—it was a futile attempt to hold on to things already lost. Plenty Coups, by contrast, refused to support the dance because he recognized that in circumstances where a dance as rich and culturally central as the Crow Sun Dance was no longer intelligible, a new dance was not the answer. Yet if a new dance is not the answer and if traditional dances are no longer intelligible, then what does the future hold for the Crow? Lear answers this question by jumping ahead to 1941, nine years after the death of Plenty Coups, when the Crow reintroduced the Sun Dance.

Since it had been more than fifty years since they had performed the dance, the Crow had to learn the steps from their Shoshone neighbors; and in the absence of intertribal warfare they had to reinterpret its meaning. The question that looms is whether or not this reintroduction of the Sun Dance is anything more than nostalgia, as Lear implies: "One might still teach people the relevant steps; people might learn how to go through the motions; and they can even call it the 'Sun Dance'; but the Sun Dance itself has gone out of existence."[27] However, as he reflects on what Plenty Coups leadership has bequeathed to the Crow, Lear seems to offer another possibility with regard to the reintroduction of the Sun Dance to the Crow:

> What is valuable about Plenty Coups's declaration is that it lays down a crucial fact that needs to be acknowledged if a genuinely vibrant tradition is to be

---

[24] Ibid., pp. 97–8.

[25] See Alice B. Kehoe, *The Ghost Dance: Ethnohistory and Revitalization* (Long Grove, 2006; reprint of 1989 edn.).

[26] Lear, *Radical Hope*, p. 151.

[27] Ibid., p. 37.

maintained or reintroduced. It is one thing to dance as though nothing has happened; it is another thing to acknowledge that something singularly awful has happened—the collapse of happenings—and then to decide to dance.[28]

When trying to summarize the radical nature of the hope that Plenty Coups's vision seems to have made possible for the Crow, a hope that enabled them to exist without the Sun Dance and, years later, to recover it, Lear says: "Precisely because Plenty Coups sees that a traditional way of life is coming to an end, he is in a position to embrace a peculiar form of hopefulness. It is basically the hope for revival: for coming back to life in a form that is not yet intelligible."[29] This summary description of Plenty Coups's contribution to Crow culture, with its images of things coming to an end and things coming back to life, is an apt place to turn to a consideration of a museum exhibit.

We Are the Evidence

The exhibit "Our Peoples: Giving Voice to Our Histories" at the NMAI in Washington, DC, gathers around the theme of evidence, as I noted briefly at the start.[30] Not only do the instructions at the entrance to the exhibit say that visitors should "think of the exhibition as an excavation site, where evidence that has been buried, ignored, and denied is finally brought to light," but the exhibit itself keeps the theme visually central. Just inside the entrance, visitors encounter an opaque glass wall with the word "EVIDENCE" stamped upon it in big block letters. Buried within this wall are various artifacts that are identifiable (a peace pipe, a lacrosse stick) and yet blurred by the opacity of the glass. Inside the exhibit, most of the display cases, which extend from the floor to well over head, are backed with similar opaque material. Thus, from the front, through the clear glass of a display case, visitors might see masks of gold, swords, guns; but as they follow the

---

28   Ibid., pp. 152–3.

29   Ibid., pp. 94–6.

30   For an overview the museum, see Duane Blue Spruce (ed.), *Spirit of a Native Place: Building the National Museum of the American Indian* (Washington, DC, 2004). For critical perspectives, see Mark Hirsch and Amy Pickworth (eds.), *The Native Universe and Museums in the Twenty-first Century: The Significance of the National Museum of the American Indian* (Washington, DC, 2005). With regard specifically to the exhibit I describe here, see the essay by Richard W. Hill, Sr., "In Search of an Indigenous Place: Museums and Indigenous Culture," pp. 97–117. Hill says, 'I saw too many Bibles, too many guns, and too much gold stripped of its identity,' p. 113. What I describe here favorably, Hill hated—just another reminder of how difficult it is to negotiate the evidence, and also that the NMAI, no less than any of the texts I have discussed, is contested. See also Amanda J. Cobb (guest ed.), "The National Museum of the American Indian," special issue of *The American Indian Quarterly*, 29, 3/4 (Summer/Fall 2005).

flow of the exhibit and find themselves a few steps farther on, now looking at the back of the same case, they see the objects again—buried in opacity and in need of excavation. Moreover, a thin chest-high case perhaps two feet tall and filled with sandy soil runs along most of the walls in the space—a constant reminder of the themes of evidence and excavation.

The displays themselves are arranged to guide visitors on a walk that, at least initially, follows a chronological order. The first display contains hundreds of clay figurines representing the indigenous peoples of the Americas prior to 1492; then come displays of beautifully crafted gold artifacts that date back to 1490, followed by Spanish swords. At this point, visitors are near the center of the exhibit space and have choices about which direction to take, but the most natural path leads to what turns out to be the central display—three curved cases, each full of its own artifacts, and together serving as the exterior walls of a small circular room.

The first case is titled "God's Work: Churches as Instruments of Dispossession and Resilience" and contains bibles in dozens of native languages. After passing a doorway into the small room, visitors then encounter the second case, which contains treaties and is titled "Stated Intentions: Treaties as Instruments of Dispossession and Survival." After continuing around the curve of the circle and passing a second entrance into the small room, visitors see the case titled "Coiled Dragon: Guns as Instruments of Dispossession and Resistance," which displays the full history of weaponry in the Americas. Upon entering the small room, which stands in semi-darkness, visitors encounter video screens scattered across the walls and an audio tape that is synchronized to the changing scenes on the screens. This video/audio narrative runs on a continuous loop that takes several minutes from start to finish and is divided into three parts, each of which matches one of the exterior displays. This part of the exhibit is titled "The Storm: Guns, Bibles, and Governments," and the video/audio loop begins and ends with the images and sounds of a hurricane and a narrator noting that storms are forces of creation and destruction. Paired with the displays of guns, bibles and treaties on the exterior, this video/audio production is deeply ironic and profoundly unsettling. Storms are forces of creation and destruction; churches, treaties, and guns are instruments of dispossession, but also of resilience, survival, and resistance. Thus, with pictures of churches and worship flashing on the screens, the Indian narrator says, "We know Jesus; he has been with us for a very long time. … Today, many of us are Christian, and many are not." And then, most tellingly, church bells give way to gunfire and images of violence, and the narrator says, "What could be more Indian than a Winchester rifle, except maybe a horse?"

Here we find, at the center of a pivotal exhibit in the NMAI, the same deep irony that Lear identifies as the defining characteristic of Plenty Coups's leadership of the Crow. Recall that Lear defined Wraps His Tail's raid against the Blackfeet as nostalgic. "Plenty Coups's position, by contrast," says Lear, "was ironic: the only way for a Crow to go forward was to acknowledge that the traditional way of life was going to be blown away in a storm. Only after the storm would new

Crow possibilities open up."[31] No doubt following a path different from Lear, the curators of the exhibit discovered this same link between storms and irony and were clearly aware that to be ironic instead of nostalgic is to be open to the surprises of possibility: "What could be more Indian than a Winchester rifle, except maybe a horse?" Such irony is accentuated by one additional part of the exhibit: around the outside of the large exhibit space, in small eddies that stand to the side of the central flow of the displays, are eight exhibits devoted to eight different tribes, each of which has used the exhibit space to display its understanding of its historical identity in light of the present. Taken together, these exhibits accompany the voice of the Indian narrator in the inner room and declare, in the words that stand above the Cherokee exhibit, "We're still here." Here again is the irony Lear recognized in Plenty Coups: "It is no longer possible to be Crow. And yet somehow the Crow will survive their own death."[32]

Black Elk, the Re-enchantment of the World, and Christianity as Fairy Tale

Let me return briefly to Black Elk, whose relationship to Christianity is worth placing within the context of the ironic as it is displayed in both Lear's account of Plenty Coups and at the NMAI—a task that returns us to the Sun Dance. In his careful analysis of the Lakota Sun Dance, Clyde Holler notes the ways in which Black Elk's accounts of the Sun Dance and other Lakota rituals are influenced by his engagement with Catholicism.[33] Even more, as Damian Costello argues, drawing on Holler, Black Elk's account of the Sun Dance disassociates it from war and violence.[34] Costello also goes a step farther and argues, via a painstaking exegesis of Black Elk's vision, that even here he blends Lakota traditions with Christian teachings.[35] Costello comes close to the position Lear develops in his engagement with Linderman's account of Plenty Coups, namely, that a profound sense of irony became the best way for figures like Black Elk and Plenty Coups to advance their culture in the face of its destruction.

One way to name the shortcoming of Neihardt's depiction of Black Elk in *Black Elk Speaks* is to note the way in which nostalgia trumps irony. Thus Neihardt's now infamous ending, in which Black Elk reflects upon the massacre at Wounded Knee and declares:

---

[31]   Lear, *Radical Hope*, pp. 152–3.

[32]   Ibid.

[33]   Holler, *Black Elk's Religion*, and Joseph Epes Brown, *The Sacred Pipe: Black Elk's Account of the Seven Rites of the Oglala Sioux* (New York, 1971; reprint of 1953 edn.).

[34]   Costello, *Black Elk*, p. 81.

[35]   Ibid., pp. 91–132. I think Costello forces some of his links between Black Elk's vision and Christian influence; however, he shows the depths of Black Elk's Christian commitments, even as he embodies Lakota commitments.

> And so it was all over. I did not know then how much was ended. … A people's
> dream died there. It was a beautiful dream. And I, to whom so great a vision was
> given in my youth,—you see me now a pitiful old man who has done nothing,
> for the nation's hoop is broken and scattered. There is no center any longer, and
> the sacred tree is dead.[36]

Pure nostalgia, and thanks to DeMallie's publication of the transcripts, we know
that both these words and the decision to end the narrative with Wounded Knee
belong wholly to Neihardt. But there is also something more than nostalgia here;
or, rather, this passage serves as a reminder of why nostalgia is dangerous. Thomas
Couser sees the issue clearly:

> To end the narrative so *conclusively* with the Battle of Wounded Knee is the
> literary equivalent of killing off the survivors; it is a subtle but insidious form
> of cultural genocide. The effect is to encourage white readers to indulge in an
> uncomplicated pathos at the demise of a noble way of life rather than to compel
> them to contemplate its survival in assimilated forms.[37]

I would go one step farther and say that the challenge is not to contemplate the
survival of the Crow or the Lakota in assimilated forms (which gives up too
much ground), but to recognize the ironic character of their existence, which
is indeed complicated. In his account of Black Elk, Neihardt left us only with
"an uncomplicated pathos"; to do otherwise, he would have had to compel us to
contemplate Black Elk's Catholicism. Of course, one can argue, as Julian Rice and
Clyde Holler do (in quite different ways),[38] that we are left with neither assimilation
nor irony because Black Elk's Catholicism did not fundamentally transform what
it meant for him to be Lakota, but it seems a better description to say that Black Elk
accepted Catholicism as an ironic surprise—and nothing was more of a surprise
than the fact that to become Catholic was also to become nonviolent.[39]

Perhaps the most difficult aspect of negotiating the evidence of the encounter
between Christianity and native peoples is the fact that, in destroying the cultural
penchant for violence, Christianity could not help but destroy practices like
counting coups and the Crow Sun Dance. Of course, to speak of the way in which

---

[36]   Neihardt, *Black Elk Speaks*, 230.

[37]   G. Thomas Couser, "*Black Elk Speaks* with Forked Tongue," in James Olney (ed.),
Studies in Autobiography (New York, 1988): 73–88.

[38]   See Julian Rice, *Black Elk's Story: Distinguishing Its Lakota Purpose* (Albuquerque,
1991); Holler, *Black Elk's Religion*, esp. pp. 204–23. Costello, *Black Elk*, provides something
like an ironic reading of Black Elk that is a persuasive alternative to the views of both Rice
and Holler. He also provides a good account of the components of Black Elk's thought that
tend toward nonviolence.

[39]   Speaking theologically, this surprise is called the resurrection, and there is nothing
more ironic. Indeed, Christianity is founded on irony. Jesus died, and yet he lives.

the Gospel would have necessitated the end of practices that rested on violence is not to ignore the accompanying fact of Christian complicity in the violence of colonialism that was, at the same time, wiping out people like the Lakota. The right response to this latter fact, however, is not to dismiss Christianity as nothing more than a ruse for violence. Rather, the question to press is: In what way was a person like Black Elk a better Christian than the Christians who introduced him to the Gospel? Moreover, to what extent was he able to be a better Christian precisely because he was Lakota? Again, it is the irony that these questions point toward that leads us past the impasse of having to argue that Black Elk was or was not Catholic or Lakota. There is an important sense in which it would have been impossible for Black Elk and others like him to embrace the Gospel without having this embrace destroy traditional culture. Thus we should not underestimate the fact that Black Elk's Sun Dance was a dance for the survival, and revival, of the people instead of a dance for war.

In part thanks to Black Elk, the Lakota Sun Dance did survive the years in which it was banned by the US government. Unlike the Crow, the Lakota did not have to relearn the dance from another tribe, but continued to dance—which leads us back to Lear. Recall that Lear preferred Plenty Coups to Sitting Bull because Sitting Bull supported the Ghost Dance, which Lear interpreted as a nostalgic refusal to recognize that a divide of unintelligibility had been crossed. And recall too that the Crow gave up the Sun Dance about 1875. Lear does not consider the possibility that the Crow lost the Sun Dance precisely because they refused to adopt the Ghost Dance. Indeed, what if the Ghost Dance was already part of restoring intelligibility to Lakota practice and in fact was integral to both the preservation and transformation of the Sun Dance? [40] Such a possibility would turn Lear on his head because now the Crow would appear nostalgic when they sought to recover the dance after 50 years, and the Lakota would be the masters of irony who kept dancing in the face of cultural devastation. It may well be, of course, that both the Lakota and the Crow were equally ironic and simply pursued different courses, but Lear's preference for Plenty Coups over Sitting Bull points to the ways in which he sometimes betrays his own best insights.

Charitably considered and engaged constructively, Lear's book is an extended reflection about how not to kill off the survivors; it serves as a kind of catechesis concerning the difficulty of thinking about what it means for us white folk to continue to live alongside the people we have killed. Lear fails, ironically (of course), to the extent that he himself is really up to something altogether different. He gives some indication of this early on when he says, "I am not primarily concerned with what actually happened to the Crow tribe or to any other group. I

---

[40]   Holler, in *Black Elk's Religion*, notes just this connection between the two dances in Black Elk's account of the Sun Dance: "The influence of the Ghost Dance, with its theme of revival, is omnipresent in Black Elk's dance, for his dance is essentially conceived as a revival, a response to the need to restore the center of the religious life of the people," p. 150.

am concerned rather with the field of possibilities in which all human endeavors gain meaning."[41] In the end, Lear's book is not really about Plenty Coups and the Crow but about post-9/11 America.[42] Framed as it is by this concern, Lear's catechesis for how not to kill off the survivors in fact kills them off after all.

The NMAI takes up the same catechetical task with more success: its exhibits are unsettling because they refuse nostalgia, provoke irony, and leave visitors contemplating the survivors. Both the museum and Lear at his best, however, accomplish something even more significant than simply compelling whites to remain unsettled by the ongoing consequences of colonialism. Indeed, the reason I invoke "catechesis" as a description of Lear's book and the museum's exhibit is that both are initial steps in the training required to see that the world is fundamentally ironic, which has profound implications for the relationship between Christianity and the ruins of Native America.

I can best unpack these implications by noting one aspect of the museum exhibit that so far I have skipped over. The words that frame the exhibit—"We are the evidence"—are ascribed to "Henry Crow Dog (Lakota), 1974." Because these words appear on a relatively small plaque off to the side of the entrance, it is possible to miss them, and in fact I walked right past them the first time I went through the exhibit. I saw them only when I returned a second time. Having already experienced the exhibit and come to appreciate the careful way in which "evidence" was used to frame everything, I was astounded to learn that these words had provided the inspiration for the exhibit; for I had encountered Henry Crow Dog in a different context more than twenty years earlier.

One of my professors in college posted a photograph on his door in the spring of 1985. I found the photograph so striking that I commented at length to him about it. My comments apparently made an impression because years later, when he retired and was cleaning out his office, he came upon the photograph, tracked me down, and offered it to me as a gift. I have carried it around ever since, and now it hangs on my office wall. This photograph appeared in the *Oyate Wicaho*, a publication of the Dakota American Indian Movement, in March 1985.[43] It is part of an obituary for a "longtime medicine man and spiritual leader of the Sicangu Lakota"[44] named Henry John Crow Dog (born 2 September 1900; died 2 February 1985). The photo depicts Henry Crow Dog standing on a hillside in South Dakota, in knee-high prairie grass, hand on his hips, with a big seemingly toothless grin, and looking down toward his feet. Just in front of him, perhaps three feet away, stands a bald eagle. The caption to the right of the photo says, "On the hill behind his house at Spring Creek, Henry John Crow Dog blew an eagle bone whistle

---

[41]   Lear, *Radical Hope*, p. 7.

[42]   Thus Lear says, "We live at a time of a heightened sense that civilizations are themselves vulnerable" (ibid.).

[43]   *Oyate Wicaho*, Volume 5, N 1. I have only partial information about this publication. The address listed for the publication is Box 99, Porcupine, South Dakota, 57772.

[44]   Ibid.

and waited. The eagle in the picture circled high above, then slowly descended, landing at Henry Crow Dog's feet. It has been said that he was one of the last who knew how to catch eagles."[45]

The photograph reminds me of the words with which Michel Foucault opens his book *The Order of Things*:

> This book first arose out of a passage in Borges, out of the laughter that shattered, as I read the passage, all the familiar landmarks of my thought—*our* thought, the thought that bears the stamp of our age and our geography—breaking up all the ordered surfaces and all the planes with which we are accustomed to tame the wild profusion of existing things. ... The thing we apprehend in one great leap, the thing that, by means of [Borges's] fable, is demonstrated as the exotic charm of another system of thought, is the limitation of our own, the stark impossibility of thinking that.[46]

Foucault names for me why this photograph is so startling, and why Jonathan Lear is so captivated by the radical divide apparent in Plenty Coups's words, "After this nothing happened": the glimpses of the world in which counting coups made sense and the wonder of the scene depicted in the photograph establish in stark relief the limits of our own system of thought. Placed in theological context, what this photograph does is raise profound questions about the encounter between the Christian West and native peoples like Plenty Coups, Sitting Bull, Black Elk, and Crow Dog. For me, the photograph represents that the true promise of Christianity is lost just to the extent that Henry Crow Dog was indeed one of the last who knew how to catch eagles. In a word, Christianity is lost and the world with it insofar as it has delivered us into a *disenchanted* existence.[47] We are in desperate need of recovering an enchanted world, and if we take the long view, it strikes me that it may well be that the future of Christianity rests amid the ruins of Native America. Of course, many people would argue that this recovery of an enchanted world does not involve Christianity at all—but that is just the kind of disjunctive (and nostalgic) thinking rejected by both Plenty Coups and the NMAI, as well as by Black Elk.

Surely Black Elk's ironic embrace of the Gospel made new things possible within Christianity, even if those things remain latent and in need of excavation.

---

[45]   Ibid.

[46]   Michel Foucault, *The Order of Things: An Archaeology of the Human Sciences*, a translation of *Les Mots et les choses* (New York, 1970; reprint of 1966 edn.), p. xv.

[47]   The description of our existence as "disenchanted" is linked most famously to Max Weber: "The fate of our times is characterized by rationalization and intellectualization and, above all, by the 'disenchantment of the world.'" See "Science as a Vocation," in *From Max Weber: Essays in Sociology,* ed. and trans. H.H. Gerth and C. Wright Mills (New York, 1946), p. 155. For a good discussion of disenchantment and its opposite, an "enchanted world," see Charles Taylor, *A Secular Age* (Cambridge, 2007).

Just what that might mean is suggested in a fascinating essay by John Milbank, in which he argues that books like the Harry Potter series and Tolkein's *Lord of the Rings* are part of a re-envisioning of Christianity and a re-enchantment of the world that in fact is true to the Truth of the Gospel, insofar as the Gospel itself is best understood as a fairy tale, not in the pejorative sense, but in the sense of its narrative form:

> Properly understood, monotheism concerns an ultimate unified source beyond mere numerical unity and diversity—and it is a consequence of this very plenitude at the origin that there should be multiple and diverse spiritual mediators, some of whom can only locally be understood. It is the mark of true apophatic acknowledgment of the one God that one approaches him by multiple mediations of gods, angels, daemons, spirits, and fairies. … It is conceivable that Christianity properly understood is the metahistory of sending-helping [fairy figures] which should rescue and not imperially overrule local tales and revelations."[48]

Framed in these terms, the question about Christianity and the ruins of Native America becomes how we might discern the ways in which Christianity "rescues" local traditions and revelations, even as it also is itself rescued by them.

For Milbank, to speak of Christianity as fairy tale is in part to note that objects and not subjects move the plot: the tree of knowledge and its fruit, God's rainbow, the stone tablets, the ark, bread and wine—just as in fairy tales we find glass slippers, gingerbread houses, rings, swords in stones, the holy grail, and the like. The centrality of objects in such stories, says Milbank, causes us to heed the "ineliminable positivity of things" and to see "transcendence first of all within the material sphere." It is this privileging of the material world and of the transcendence within things that characterizes fairy tales. "Therefore," says Milbank, "if the Christian narrative can be taken as a fairy tale that mainly concerns the proper use of material things and their sacramental nature, it remains truer than we have suspected to the magical nature of the fairy tale":

> Perhaps then, the fictionalization of Christianity in imaginative children's literature is … but a harbinger of a new and truer re-imagination of Christianity as such. And it may be time to bid farewell to the monotheism of the grown-up, disenchanted cosmos. … Most people cannot understand—and with good reason—a worldview where one acknowledges no mysteries until one suddenly stumbles upon the ultimate one of the one God. … By contrast, belief in God and in the triune God can perhaps only be revived if we re-envisage and re-imagine the immanent enchantments of the divine creation which appropriately

---

48   John Milbank, "Fictioning Things: Gift and Narrative," at http://www. theologyphilosophycentre.co.uk/papers/Milbank_FictioningThings.doc. Unpaginated.

witnesses to the transcendent One through a polytheistic profusion of created enigmas.

If some mediators can be only locally understood, as Milbank suggests, it is no doubt because certain material objects bound wholly to a particular locality serve as the medium of transcendence—for example, eagle-bone whistles and cottonwood trees. Apparently Black Elk could imagine, as perhaps many of us cannot, that such particularity was at the same time part of the universal tradition of the Gospel. The full weight of Milbank's suggestion, however, is not simply this exchange of the particular and the universal; rather, his point is that the Truth of Christianity is precisely its ability to *rescue* the particular—local tales and revelations—which then populate the universal. The irony is obvious: those sent on a mission to rescue the world have ruined it. Insofar as Christianity has instead imperially overruled local tales and revelations, Henry Crow Dog was one of the last who knew how to catch eagles. Milbank's logic suggests that this loss is not simply an occasion for nostalgia. It is a real loss—like a species extinction—it is a failure to rescue a particular thing, a thing without which our access to the universal is somehow less than it might have been, so that sustaining the universal requires an increasingly radical hope. Such hope is increasingly radical because the real lesson here is that hope itself is always rooted in the particular even as it aims at the universal, and so every loss makes hope more difficult.

If we take Milbank seriously that the Truth of Christianity is best conceived in terms of a fairy tale rooted in the local and the particular, then Christianity's ability to proclaim the truth rests in the continued existence of the local tales and revelations of native peoples like the Crow and Lakota. And how ironic is that? Those who were meant to be saved may now be in a position to offer salvation in return. But there is a need for caution here, a caution embodied perfectly in the exhibit at the NMAI. This exhibit refuses to let you come to rest on one side or the other. It disallows the judgment that Christianity ruined Native America, even as it also says exactly that. And so it would be wrong to say that the Lakota and the Crow are now in a position to rescue the rest of us, but right to say that the Lakota and the Crow are in a position to rescue the rest of us, if at the same time this rescue is conducted within the metahistory of Christianity. I know that will not satisfy those who resent Christianity, and nor will it satisfy many Christians. All I can say to this dissatisfaction is that it is irony all the way down.

Chapter 7

"Jesus was not an Indian": Encountering Native Images in the Catholic Church

Kathleen J. Martin

The context of religious beliefs is complex and diverse, yet a goal of this chapter is to highlight key aspects of the Catholic Church's relationship with Native communities as reflected in visual culture and discussed through interviews with Native consultants.[1] Set within a research context identified by Linda Tuhiwai Smith as an approach situated in the decolonization politics of the Indigenous Peoples Movement, it is focused on self-determination.[2] The intention is to present a "perspectival accounting' of what currently exists and to arrive on the "believably firm ground of interpretation."[3] In this process as Oscar Kawagley notes, "basic philosophical questions are raised in the course of observing and questioning people with respect to notions of inquiry, explanation, technology, science, and religion, as they relate to particular lifeways."[4] In fact, central to ethnographic investigation is its ability to make and substantiate interpretations, and to make a point that is useful and interesting for individuals to reconstrue, recognize, or, in the end use, resist relationships. Significant in these assumptions is the notion that "respect is a reciprocal, shared, constantly interchanging principle which is expressed through all aspects of social conduct."[5] This chapter represents part of the results of examination into the visual culture of Catholic churches in mission and reservation contexts, and presents the interpretations and perspectives of Native interview consultants who viewed and discussed photographs of images

---

[1] An earlier version of this chapter entitled "American Indians and Appropriation: Cultural and Visual Interpretations" was presented at the 2007 annual meeting of the American Academy of Religion to the Indigenous Religious Traditions Group. It also is a revision of an earlier essay entitled, "Why don't they leave? Saving faith and other issues of Catholic missionization," In *Ayaangwaamizin: The International Journal of Indigenous Philosophy*, 3/2 (2007): 223–67.

[2] Linda Tuhiwai Smith, *Decolonizing Methodologies: Research and Indigenous Peoples* (New York, 1999), p. 116.

[3] Alan Peshkin, "Nature of Interpretation in Qualitative Research", *Educational Researcher*, 29/9 (2000): 5.

[4] A. Oscar Kawagley, *A Yupiaq Worldview: A Pathway to Ecology and Spirit* (Prospect Heights, 1995), p. 7.

[5] Tuhiwai Smith, *Decolonizing Methodologies*, p. 120.

from the various churches that were visited.[6] It also situates the discussion within Native and Indigenous perspectives and ethics of place as embedded in a system of thought that perceives the world as animate and connected. Photographic and interview data frame the discussion as a way of explicating perspectives and providing insights. In effect, these data may illuminate multiple interpretations and understanding.

Personal Reflections

In 1994, during a visit with my mother to family in Wagner, South Dakota, I was struck by the images displayed in the St. Paul the Apostle of the Nations Catholic Church at Marty. My great-aunt taught at the school and was a member of the order of the Sisters of the Blessed Sacrament. Her parents, my mother's grandparents, moved to South Dakota from an area outside of Chicago in 1910, and my aunt joined the order in February 1919. At the time, the Sisters of the Blessed Sacrament (SBS) served only American Indian and African American communities, and all monies raised went to provide services for the communities. In fact, when my aunt joined the order, her father had to agree to provide her with essentials such as clothing, soap, and food, and she had to agree never to enter a white person's home again. When her father was near death, he went to the local hospital to die so that she could visit him. My aunt served in communities in New York and Chicago until 1928, then returned to South Dakota until about 1949, when she left for reservation communities in Arizona and New Mexico. A Lakota Oblate Sister of the Blessed Sacrament (OSBS) who knew my aunt, and who was one of the first to join the order under her guidance, still resided at the mission in 1994. She recalled my aunt fondly as Sister B. Jo, and told my mother and me a story about a mural behind the altar that included a representation of our aunt.

    The mural in St. Paul Apostle of the Nations encompasses hundreds of figures and images. Many of them were unfamiliar to me as someone who grew up in a predominately Catholic Irish and German family in Minnesota. I was accustomed to "traditional" Catholic iconography, not images of birds, animals, and depictions of unknown saints. Some of these same images were published on holy cards and posters, indicating they were not just representations specific to one community, but part of a larger contingent within the Catholic Church. Most unusual to me was the depiction of my aunt standing next to an Oblate and a child in Indian-styled clothing painted on the wall behind the altar.[7] Why was she pictured? What

    [6]   Initial research for this project was supported by a grant from the American Academy of Religion in 1998, and a grant in 2000 from the National Endowment for the Humanities. Also with grateful appreciation to all the interview consultants who willing shared and provided their insights and commentaries.

    [7]   According to Francis Bernie who wrote a description of the mural for *The Wagner Post*, 9 October 1991, it is an anonymous Sister of the Blessed Sacrament, Oblate Sister of

did it mean? And how was this a reflection of Catholic ideology? I wondered if it mattered to Catholics and Native Peoples alike if symbols and signs were interpreted and changed, and if similar instances of image usage occurred in other mission churches? I continued to consider these questions, and visited other mission and reservation Catholic churches.

There are a number of dilemmas that contribute to the complexity of this investigation: respect for Native and Catholic communities; my personal history and experience within the Church, now as a non-Catholic; and the high regard with which some clergy and lay ministers are held in Native communities and still talked about, as with my aunt. Furthermore, as Andrea Smith reports: "Many Indians tend to relate to both Christianity and to their Native traditions along a continuum."[8] And finally, Catholic communities supported my efforts through access, willingness to supply information, and allowing me to photograph the churches. Several questions arise from these dilemmas. What are the motives for the blending of traditions? What do people from the communities that witness these changes think and feel about them? And what effects does it have on traditions, particularly those of Native communities? The incorporation and adoption of images allude to a Western ethic that supports the combining of traditions to make a point as opposed to an Indigenous ethic that explores spiritual ideas for further understanding of life and the sacred.

Visual Culture and the Use of Images

Visual art, symbols, and images are argued to be ambiguous and designed to acquire meanings not specific to the original intent of the symbol, thus leading to new interpretations within a culture or group.[9] Yet, the idea of using symbols in ambiguous ways detached from specific places is antithetical to Native philosophies that recognize power and knowledge as emanating from particular places. However, adaptation, syncretism, and blending of images are viewed and discussed positively by Catholics.[10] Altering what is considered a "typical" Christian image does not reflect a change in the concept of God, but rather a reinterpretation of the same concept not specifically tied to the environment,

---

the Blessed Sacrament, and Indian child who are pictured. But according to the Oblate my mother and I met, the sister depicted is our aunt; the Oblate pictured is unknown.

[8]   Andrea Smith, "Walking in Balance: The Spirituality-Liberation Praxis of Native Women," in Jace Weaver (ed.), *Native American Religious Identity: Unforgotten Gods* (Maryknoll, 2002), p. 182.

[9]   See Chapter 1 of this volume for additional discussion of the topic.

[10]   See, for example: Angelyn Dries, OSF, *The Missionary Movement in American Catholic History* (Maryknoll, 1998); National Catholic Educational Association, *The People: Reflections of Native Peoples on the Catholic Experience in North America* (Washington, DC: 1992).

cultural beliefs, or communities, but rather open to individual abstraction. This can be accomplished through the use of a sign or symbol as a decorative element, with the Indigenous meaning and interpretation obscured or reinterpreted. When we view images in specific contexts such as churches, they "encode data about values, norms, and practices that are often inaccessible to other forms of collecting and reporting information."[11] And the images acquire meaning and validity through the visual sensory experience when displayed within the context in which they are embedded. As Susan Sontag clarifies, photographs and images often are used as aids to understanding; however, they do not explain, they acknowledge.[12] Thus, it is difficult for viewers to separate experience from acknowledgment, one that confirms and reaffirms a connection between ideas and relations from personal experiences as opposed to simply viewing images and recognizing depictions. This may be particularly true in religious contexts since there is an implicit understanding regarding the authority of religious institutions which individuals are reluctant to challenge. These same images are deeply embedded in a particular philosophy that provides for interpretation. For instance, as noted by a Catholic clergy member, "changing a familiar image such as the physical appearance or dress of Jesus or Mary to coincide with a particular community does not reflect a change in the concept of God or even a challenge of faith, but essentially comes from God as a way to further understanding."[13] Yet, image making such as this can be a principal means of producing qualities ascribed to things, events, and situations that erases distinctions and makes things analogous.[14] Thus, images have the potential to limit differences, to take on meaning by and through isolation and focus, and to do so within specific agendas.

Scholars of religion point out that images and meanings are understood momentarily, with some of the meaning unnoticed, implicit, or embedded in the image. From a Western Euroamerican perspective, altering, changing, or appropriating images tied to specific communities is acceptable practice and insignificant in relation to understanding or interpreting religious beliefs. William Stolzman, in *The Pipe and Christ*, argues, "the nature of God and all things holy, life and history are pluralistic. ... It is not we who establish and define true religion but it is God and His spirits."[15] Images and symbols are perceived to be abstractions and not located in particular places. Any new reflection of God can be reinterpreted to suit the time, place, or situation. This idea suggests a belief that objects, images, or material forms do not have power in and of themselves, but

---

[11]   John Grady, "Sociology's New Workshop: The Visual Challenge of Sociology," *Sociological Imagination*, 38/1–2 (2001): 4.

[12]   Susan Sontag, *On Photography* (New York, 1970), p. 111.

[13]   Personal communication with author, South Dakota, June 2003.

[14]   Sontag, *On Photography*, p. 175.

[15]   William Stolzman, *The Pipe and Christ: A Christian–Sioux Dialogue*, 5th edn (Chamberlain, 1995), p. 220.

can be adapted and used to access power for any purpose necessary. Indigenous beliefs, however, support a living universe regarding not only notions of what is animate and inanimate, but also regarding the centrality of communities and the significance of place in daily life. Images and symbols are reflections of places, spirits, knowledge, and meaning that is inherently connected to specific places.

Art and photographs provide representations about cultural contexts and social values by way of visual experience, and they inscribe meaning through representation. As a "concrete logic, this inscribing of the law within sensory existence is what Antonio Gramsci meant by hegemony."[16] Experience and validity is supported and privileged through the use of power by a dominant group's ability to access and utilize images in combination with ideas of subordinate groups. These same images are not the subject of critique from Catholics, possibly because they are tied to the religious beliefs of a dominant group and the subject of religion typically is seen as "normal" and value free. For many Catholics, missionary efforts and the structure of the past no longer exist, but now are based on a process of "inculturation" and inclusion that respects Native traditions as partners. In recent Church and parish literatures, all cultures are recognized as necessary for understanding the text of the Gospel. According to Christopher Vecsey in *On the Padres' Trail*, the Church's missionary method today emphasizes contextualization or inculturation within a pan-cultural context.[17] Inclusion and inculturation are viewed as a "bringing together" of traditions into the Catholic family as it were. Catholic images and symbols are designed to highlight conditions for all people united under the one true Church.

The definition of inculturation implies that the use of culturally specific material is designed for the purpose of helping believers find Christ. Further, appropriation often is characterized as a benign activity and presupposes the power and ability to do so, with Church representatives often making the determination. George Tinker indicates two areas of concern regarding the mixing of Native and Christian traditions. First, "placing a native religious symbol adjacent to the Christian focus of worship elevates the white religious expression of the gospel as superior to traditional native spiritual forms," and second, "misappropriation of native spirituality is usually performed in a context where the pastoral leadership is characteristically non-Indian."[18] The first area subsumes the symbol and the second allows for its use by someone outside the community, fully appropriating and changing the meaning and use. Native symbols are co-opted by members of the dominant group, and the missionaries' power to use Native symbols is justified as an acceptable practice since their effort is designed to "help" those in need as spiritual leaders.

---

[16] Terry Eagleton, "The Fate of the Arts," *Hedgehog Review*, 6/2 (Summer 2004): 7.

[17] Christopher Vecsey, *On the Padres' Trail* (Durham, 1996).

[18] George Tinker, *Missionary Conquest: The Gospel and Native American Cultural Genocide* (Minneapolis, 1993), p. 115.

An early example of appropriation in the name of inculturation began with Paul Steinmetz in 1961, as a recently ordained Jesuit priest stationed in South Dakota. Under his supervision, Benjamin Black Elk and other Lakota Catholics designed the church's painted symbols and images to include the incorporation of various wall murals of tipis, buffalos, and other images from the natural world. The altar cloth read, "*Wakan Wakan Wakan*,"[19] alluding to Catholic liturgy with a similar refrain, "Holy Holy Holy." Within a few years, Steinmetz was actively using the Pipe as a symbol of Christ and, reportedly by request of Lakota Christians, saying Mass following the Pine Ridge Sundance. In 1971, the Mass followed the piercing of the dancers, even over Leonard Crow Dog's objections and attempts to expel Christians from the ceremony and reservation.[20] Steinmetz, however, reported he saw "no good cause to keep these dual identities and ceremonies separate."[21] He began to actively advocate using the Pipe "as a symbol of Christ" in the Church, and theorized that the Pipe is "derived from a common religious substratum expressed through primal religions [designed to] ... keep one in touch with the basic instincts of humankind."[22] Christopher Vecsey reports that Steinmetz continued to promote the use of the Pipe even over Lakota objections:

> Many Sioux preferred to keep the two forms of religious practice separate. They didn't mind comparing them and understanding one in terms of the other, but in practice they wanted them segregated (Black Bear, August 4, 1988). ... Some feared that syncretism and dialogue promoted by Jesuits would undermine their traditional Lakota religious identity.[23]

Although use of the Pipe did not become a sacrament in the traditional Catholic sense as Steinmetz advocated, the Pipe is and has been used as a sacramental in Christian and Catholic ceremony. *The Sacred Pipe: An Archetypal Theology* defends not only the use of the Pipe and the similarities between Catholicism and Native tradition, but places the analysis within the Western philosophies and epistemologies of Karl Rahner, Carl Jung, and Mircea Eliade.[24]

Michael Steltenkamp and William Stolzman, like Steinmetz, were Jesuits at Holy Rosary Mission-Red Cloud Indian School on the Pine Ridge and Rosebud Reservations from approximately 1962 through the early 1980s. In *The Pipe and Christ*, Stolzman asks the question: Can a single individual practice reflect both religions authentically without any real conflicts or contradictions? And if so,

---

[19]   Christopher Vecsey, *Where the Two Roads Meet* (Notre Dame, 1999).

[20]   Matthiessen, *In the Spirit of Crazy Horse* (New York, 1992).

[21]   Vecsey, *Where the Two Roads Meet*, p. 53.

[22]   Paul B. Steinmetz, SJ, *The Sacred Pipe: An Archetypal Theology* (New York, 1998), pp. 167–8.

[23]   Vecsey, *Where the Two Roads Meet*, p. 56.

[24]   Steinmetz, *The Sacred Pipe*.

how would this be accomplished?[25] These questions focus on connecting the two traditions and practices, and resolving the conflict for Native Catholics. It does not address the underlying assumption that a discussion should be held or that it was held even over the objections of some Lakota characterized as "militants from the 60s." In fact, at one meeting, to the dismay of the Native and Christian participants alike, one priest stood up and declared, "Let's slice through everything that has been said tonight and get to the heart of things. *Wanikiya cannupa kin he e* [Christ is the Pipe]."[26] A number of the Lakota men involved in the meetings repeatedly voiced concerns over the effects of combining Lakota and Christian religious ceremonies, the resultant loss of spirit contacts and powers, and the subjugation and suppression of Lakota spirits. Their concerns did not seem to be addressed or resolved except for an assurance by Stolzman that the meetings were not designed to combine traditions. It remains unclear what evidence there is to support with certainty that the combining of these traditions will not or does not occur in Catholic contexts. The historical paradigm of a dominant group with the ability to co-opt, prescribe, describe, and analyze from the viewpoint of Western traditions remains largely intact and unchallenged.

Viewing images within a specific context such as a church serves multiple functions that are difficult to separate from historical oppression and the missionization of the past. An important aspect of power and oppression is tied to the creative and the methods used to access, display, and transmit power and authority. Krysztof Ziarek notes, "when art instantiates, creates, or represents something, it does so by employing technological modes of power, production-making and manipulation."[27] Images and art are not fixed aesthetically permanent entities, but rather can be interpreted as social phenomena defined by an ongoing history of thought, interpretation, and practice.[28] Within this, the idea of a pan-cultural or pan-Indian Church is spoken of positively in terms of inculturation, while the thoughts and feelings of traditional and Native Catholics are not as readily known, particularly as they relate to ideas of pan-Indian identity.[29] Vine Deloria indicates, "Indian symbolism is not symbolic in the same way that Christian symbolism

---

[25] Stolzman, *The Pipe and Christ*, p. 13.

[26] William Stolzman himself was surprised by the declaration during the meeting and reported, "Upon hearing that, one wondered if this man had heard the many ways in which the Pipe and Christ functioned differently." See ibid., p. 208.

[27] Krysztof Ziarek, "The End of Art as Its Future," *Hedgehog Review*, 6/2 (Summer 2004): 30

[28] Morgan, *The Sacred Gaze: Religious Visual Culture in Theory and Practice* (Berkeley, 2005).

[29] Christopher Vecsey relates that Holy Rosary Mission in South Dakota began a process of "inculturation" that included curriculum development, and, although it was understood that many traditional Lakota Catholics would be scandalized by innovations, "certain priests decided to cross the boundaries between Catholic and Lakota religious expressions." See Vecsey, *Where the Two Roads Meet*, p. 52.

is; therefore, mixing liturgical objects has become anathema to many Indians."[30] In fact, many Lakota have resisted liturgical innovations during the more recent decades. Others, however, adopted them with the idea that it would be the easiest way to avoid conflict, and Steinmetz and other Jesuits would eventually move on to new assignments and abandon the Lakota traditions. Yet the practice of mixing and integrating has continued by Church clergy in a variety of forms, but now under new terminology and within a context of apology.

Ethnographic Study of Visual Images in Churches

David Morgan poses a question specifically relevant to the investigation of cultural and visual research. He asks: "How can we study images to find out what they tell us about cultural encounters and the process of religious migration, change, and resistance that follows?"[31] Visual culture can function to shape interpretations and understandings of the world in complex ways similar to that of narratives and texts. Hilary Wyss, in an examination of early Christianity and Native communities, suggests the missionary tracts and narratives glorify endurance, while the conversion narratives are stories of surrender. "The conceptual base of the religious conversion narrative is the rejection of one's previous identity following a transformative moment that grants new religious experience."[32] Thus, the willpower, determination, and strength of the missionaries are glorified, while the "neophytes" surrender to a more powerful god. Similar to texts, but possibly more ambiguous, visual images provide a space for interpretations through pictorial representations about conversion narratives and religious experiences. Images shape meaning and construct new identities by working in tandem with other elements such as artifacts, documents and texts, forms of representation and rituals. The investigation of churches seeks to discover what the encounter with Native Peoples tells us about the use of images and its relationship to change, appropriation, and resistance.

Native consultants' perceptions and attitudes regarding the use of Native symbols and practices seldom are readily accessible. In some cases, church missionaries and leaders ask Native Catholics about their use of, opinions about, or ideas regarding symbols and images. However, these encounters often occur within certain guidelines, and typically only positive perspectives are presented to support the Church's position, while negative assessments receive a brief footnote or disclaimer. This does not adequately address the more serious problem of the appropriation of symbols and the practice of Native traditions in Catholic contexts, and the continuing fascination with Native spirituality and traditions even over

[30]   Deloria, *God Is Red: A Native View of Religion* (Golden, 2003), p. 38.

[31]   Morgan, *The Sacred Gaze*, p. 148.

[32]   Hillary Wyss, *Writing Indians: Literacy, Christianity and Native Communities in Early America* (Amherst, 2000), p. 14.

objections by Native Peoples who were not able to practice their own traditions.[33] For some, the use of Native traditions and comparisons between Catholic and Native traditions are intensely disliked. Therefore, not only is it important to photograph and document the contexts of use, but also to hear the opinions, ideas, and feelings of Native consultants regarding the topic. Like myself when I first came across the representations on that altar in South Dakota, during the interviews consultants often were surprised and dismayed by what they saw in the photographs.

Photographic and Interview Data

Between 1997 and 2005 more than 45 churches and missions in Arizona, California, Montana, Nebraska, New Mexico, South Dakota and Alaska were photographed, representing a visual record of approximately 600–650 photographs. Visual and extant data were also gathered from posters, pamphlets, holy cards, weekly announcements, and other church artifacts. This collection provides a substantial visual record regarding the context and use of symbols within churches, and ties ideas to the world we live in as a way of pursuing a reflective and somewhat elusive undertaking.[34] To begin organizing and interpreting the visual and photographic data, themes and categories emerged to reflect the variety of churches and geographical locations. Photographs were organized around Catholic and Native images and contextual similarities between and across church sites. Analyses of photographs revealed general categories of use such as symbols specific to the Native or Indigenous community in which the church is located, as well as symbols associated with a Christian application of an image such as representations of Kateri Tekakwitha and Nicholas Black Elk.

Consultants examined church imagery in photographs and reflected on the meanings of images in the interviews, which illuminated personal perspectives not typically heard.[35] The ten interview consultants, eight women and two men, represent Batwat Wiyot, Pomo/Miwok, Lakota, Huichol/Mayan, Akimel O'odham, Yaqui, Mexican/Veracrúz, Mexican/Apache, and Mexican/Zapatecas Nations and communities. They also represent various age groups (approximately 20 to 60 years of age), and live in a variety of settings and contexts (rural, city, or reservation).[36] A goal of the interviews was to provide the opportunity for thorough

---

[33]   Clara Sue Kidwell, Homer Noley, and George Tinker, *A Native American Theology* (New York, 2001), p. 173.

[34]   Jon Wagner, *Images of Information: Still Photography in the Social Sciences* (Beverly Hills, 1979), p. 199.

[35]   Jaber F. Gubrium and James A. Holstein, *The New Language of Qualitative Method* (Oxford, 1997).

[36]   The number of consultants is small; however, as Andrea Smith points out, few Native people engage in these types of discussions unless they are Native academics, and not surprisingly few Native people find themselves in academic theological professions. See Smith, "Walking in Balance."

discussions with knowledgeable consultants.[37] For the most part, consultants were raised as Catholics or have family members who are Catholic, and have bachelor and/or advanced educational degrees. Their candid and thoughtful reflections, particularly in light of the Native ethic of respect for the beliefs of others, provided significant insights. During the summer of 2000, consultants were interviewed using a photo elicitation interview protocol that provided a framework for discussions, and offered a means of "grounding cultural studies in the mundane interpretations of culture users."[38] Consultants and interviewer had the opportunity to "explore the photographs together, and the images invited people to take the lead in inquiry, making full use of their expertise."[39] As Douglas Harper indicates, this process prefaced the authority of consultants rather than the researcher.[40] The responses were then organized to exhibit patterns, illuminate categories, and draw conclusions,[41] and compared with the photographic data. Through the constant-comparative method of visual and interview data,[42] analysis proceeded until a useful understanding emerged.

Perspectives from Interview Consultants

Although the complete photo elicitation interview protocol included ten photographs, a few images provided general interpretations with specific insights in three areas of response: limited, mixed, and strongly negative. Consultants provided limited responses to images that displayed minimal attempts to integrate

---

[37] Pseudonyms were used unless requested by the consultants. Further information on the interviews and photo elicitation interview protocol are available by request of the author. Ethical considerations are important, and consents for interviews, observations, and photographs have been obtained and are maintained. Honorariums provided a small compensation for participation, and consultants played an active role in the review of photographs, transcriptions, and manuscripts.

[38] Douglas Harper, "Talking About Pictures: A Case for Photo Elicitation," *Visual Studies*, 17/1 (2002): 19.

[39] John Collier, Jr. and Malcolm Collier, *Visual Anthropology: Photography as a Research Method* (Albuquerque, 1986), p. 105 (italics in the original).

[40] Harper, "Talking About Pictures."

[41] Transcripts were read and reviewed for emergent themes; then, themes from each interview were put into charts so that they could be compared across and between interviews. Preliminary data analysis revealed categories and themes related to issues of context and presentation, differences in women's perspectives, and the purpose for using symbols and images. For further discussion, see: James Spradley, *Participant Observation* (New York, 1980); Robert. K. Yin, *Case Study Research: Design and Methods* (Thousand Oaks, 1994); and Norman K. Denzin, Yvonna S. Lincoln, and Linda Tuhiwai Smith, *Handbook of Critical and Indigenous Methodologies* (Thousand Oaks, 2008).

[42] See Gubrium and Holstein, *The New Language*, and Spradley, *Participant Observation*.

ideas or traditions. They often indicated the images attempted to "utilize symbols from both cultures to create an association that these two symbols are similar" (Teresa). Still displayed on the tabernacle stand in 2009, Figure 7.1 presents an image described as the "*Chi-Rho* Cross and Feathers" that evoked a limited response from consultants.[43]

"There's something that's comforting looking at this picture and knowing the symbol of the four directions. It's like honoring the people that are there" (Sara). Others were skeptical regarding the integration, yet elaborated on the significance of the union of both symbols. "It's really interesting because they're trying to combine the Catholic symbol for peace with the Native American symbol of the four directions for harmony and world balance" (Teresa). Consultants wanted to know "who put it there?" and stated, "It would make a difference if it were someone from the clergy or if it was an Indian kid who said, 'Hey, I'm going to do this.'" And they often added, "I would have to look at who the congregation is and see who they are trying to get in." Amanda interpreted it as a way to "Indian it up ... almost as an afterthought [like] classrooms that are having Indian week."

Another image in the protocol was named a "Native Church" by consultants, and this image generated mixed responses, both positive and negative. Unlike most Catholic churches, which are rectangular with the altar at the far end opposite the front door, the "Native Church" is circular with sixteen ceiling beams that meet in the center to support the roof. The main altar is set off to one side of the large open interior with pews on three sides and people enter through a circular corridor that surrounds the pews. The altar is draped in a Pendleton blanket that changes with the church liturgical calendar. It is decorated by one of the clergy who believes it is important to present both cultures, and he tries to make an "artistic inside of a Lakota/Dakota Catholic Church as an expression of who the people are." A poster of the "Lakota Trinity," distributed by Bridge Building Images,[44] hangs on the right side of the altar with an abalone shell and sage on the floor in front of it. Interpretation and comments by consultants related to decoration, sense of comfort, and presentation; they also reflected confusion, irritation, and uncertainty about the purpose. They asked clarifying questions such as "Is this their representation of God?" Amanda commented, "I would say I like it better than the other images. I think it's definitely more inclusive—the intimidation factor's not there. You know, that's more palatable to me the way that it's not overtly Christian or overtly Catholic."

---

[43]   According to Lawrence Martin, the *Chi-Rho* is an ancient Greek Christian monogram that represents the beginning of the Greek word *CHRistos*, or Christ. Email communication with author, 21 January 2008. Additionally, although not technically a cross, the *Chi-Rho* invokes the crucifixion of Jesus and was used by the Roman emperor Constantine as an emblem for his military. See www.seiyaku.com/customs/crosses/chi–rho.html. It also is used as a symbol for *Pax Vobis (cum)* in Latin meaning "peace be with you," a symbolic blessing made with the sign of the cross. See www.newadvent.org/cathen/11595a.htm.

[44]   Bridge Building Images, "Religious Cards and Gifts," www.bridgebuilding.com (accessed 27 February 2009).

Figure 7.1   "*Chi-Rho* Cross and Feathers" as displayed on a tabernacle stand
in All Saints Catholic Church, Eagle Butte, South Dakota, 1998.
Photograph courtesy of author, and used with permission.

Teresa went further saying, "I don't see anything Catholic about this church. This is a Native Church." Other consultants concurred with this assessment, believing it to evidence "more powerful influences of Native" (Sonya), and "a place that invites you to think" (Amanda). Sheila noted, "I respond more favorably to this knowing it is a *ho'gan* or *tipi* structure."

Although some consultants saw this church as an integration of the two traditions, it presented troubling images of blended traditions for others, and they were reluctant to speak, carefully choosing their words. Cory, the only Lakota interviewed, indicated:

> It's hard for me to talk about. I know a lot of Indian people who have a strong belief in this. So it's hard for me to go against their right to believe the way they want. But, I keep going back to the idea that I don't believe it's right to mix the two belief systems. That is what the spirits told us.

Rosa's comments were based on experiences with her parish church in California. "My response is, 'What happened to the church?' [Mine] is devoid of everything except Jesus Christ and God and Mary and the Apostles and the steps to crucifixion." Elena felt that she would "feel comfortable," but stated, "I could never see anything like this in my church because they keep themselves separate, so to see it combined—just seems like a contradiction." Sara felt that it reflected a policy of integration and negotiation of images typical of the Catholic Church, and commented, "That's what is interesting about Catholicism because you wouldn't necessarily find the same thing in Protestant churches." For Elida, it revealed "local culture with decorations that reflect people's interest," while for Sheila, "I don't know—not so sterile—maybe that's what it is. It seems more welcoming." Cory saw the 16-pole structure of the church as an attempt to give the impression of going home. "I have some strong feelings, but negative feelings about this. They're trying to give the idea of 'welcome into my home.' You're welcome in my home, that's a traditional way of inviting people into your house."

Finally, some images in the protocol generated strong negative responses and were considered offensive by all consultants. They expressed ambiguity regarding the meaning of the images and the purpose behind them, and perceived the blending of traditions as confusing the meaning of the symbol or image for both traditions. These images included *Holding up Christ* by Father John Giuliani[45] and *The Apache Christ* by Robert Lentz, OFM.[46] They both were perceived as "disrespectful" or "loathsome," representing "a suffering of perhaps a way of life being transformed into something that it never was." The *Holding up Christ* image by Father Giuliani is reprinted and sold as greeting cards, posters, and holy cards

---

[45]   Fr. John B. Giuliani, *Holding up Christ* (distributed through Bridge Building Images, Inc., Burlington, VT), www.bridgebuilding.com (accessed 27 February 2009).

[46]   Brother Robert Lentz, OFM, *The Apache Christ* (Courtesy Trinity Stores, 1990), http://www.trinitystores.com/?detail=3&artist=1 (accessed 27 February 2009).

through Bridge Building Images. It presents the crucifixion of Jesus Christ as he is being taken down from the cross, floating above the ground with a ring of sage under his feet. A description next to the image indicates that his body is supported on the left by "Blessed Kateri Tekakwitha, a seventeenth century Mohawk," and on the right by Nicholas Black Elk a Lakota medicine man who, when baptized, became a catechist on the Pine Ridge Reservation. All are encircled by an image of Mary with her cloak wrapping around Kateri, Jesus and Black Elk. By far, this image was the most troubling for all consultants. It evoked the swiftest response and was viewed for the shortest period of time during the interviews. It marked a transition point during the interviews from one of viewing images with little emotional response to personalizing the discussion.

Consultants felt the *Holding up Christ* image incorporated a variety of themes not often seen in Catholic iconography. Some equated the image of Mary with "the Virgin of Guadalupe, the woman who stands above and embraces all … and Spanish or Mexican images of Catholicism" (Teresa). Others were surprised by the modern attire of the characters in the picture that presented "someone in modern clothes dressed in a picture with an ancient theme" (Rosa). Elena voiced some of the questions, sentiments, and ambiguity expressed by others: "Maybe that's supposed to be Christ? Is he supposed to be Jesus because Jesus was a Jew? So they're confusing people. I don't know who these people are supposed to be." Mikal indicated, "It's disturbing. I see a suffering brought on here. I mean it seems abnormal. It represents suffering of people. It represents suffering of perhaps a way of life being transformed into something that it never was." Sheila's comments are instructive: "That really bugs me a lot. And Jesus was not an Indian." She continued, "Well, that's fine, but why aren't the things that Indian People have already done sacrificially adequate?" Amanda's response is pointed and poignant:

> I just loathe that. It reminds me of stuff that actually happened over here in this land of people being tortured and lynched and put through a lot of pain against their will—and the sorrow of the parents. Oh, I just loathe that. I really do. This is just a real painful strange image, and he's just so naked and you don't usually see Indian men like that. I mean we're not very body shy, but more modest, and it's just kind of startling to see that, and it's kind of hard to tell what happened, you know? I don't know what it's trying to say. It's a painful picture—it's a strange picture too. It's almost like there's a story there, but I don't know what it is.

For Teresa it evoked images of bloodshed: "If I came into a church and I saw these things it would … I would immediately associate it with massacre." Sonya continued this theme of suffering during her interview. "It's very disturbing. Mary at the top—poles of the cross are Indian People—Indian Jesus being held up by two converted Indians both wearing crosses. … I really don't like it." Cory's descriptive response is important in its entirety:

I really don't know what to think of it. I understand that Black Elk was a lay priest or preacher, but you know the Indian people were persecuted so badly because of their own religious understanding of the world. Their own ceremonies were banned by law—these healers—these medicine people among my people—the only way they could continue to minister to their own people and make sure they were OK was to act as if they threw away the Lakota way and picked up the Christian way. Then, they had the freedom to go out among the people and hold gatherings and try to soothe them in their suffering. But not suffering in the sense of how Christianity looks at suffering. They're suffering because they lost their homes. They lost everything they had including their livelihoods—their culture—live on one piece of land—wear foreign clothes—speak a foreign language. So, I mean that kind of suffering, not the suffering that Jesus and Tekakwitha and whoever else is in this picture tries to portray of poor Jesus. I think that's crazy that they'd have Black Elk in there because certainly he is not as well known as a Christian minister. That was just kind of incidental to what his life was all about. Now the Catholic Church is trying to use that to bring Lakota people in—manipulating people into saying. "Well, if Black Elk was part of us, then you should be part of us too."

The second image to evoke a negative response, illustrated in Figure 7.2, is *The Apache Christ* by Robert Lentz, OFM. It presents an Apache man in traditional dress with minimal representations of Catholic iconography except for the halo and inscriptions above the man's head. A large poster-sized version hangs above the main altar in a church in New Mexico. Responses to this image varied from amazement to disbelief and generated the largest number of rhetorical questions during the interviews. Most were incredulous that such an image existed. Elena wondered, "There was an Apache Christ? He was like Christ or are they saying he was Christ?" Amanda declared, "What a strange thing to be saying, 'Apache Christ.' Do we all get one? Is there a Norwegian Christ and a Pomo Christ? You start wondering." When asked if she was familiar with the Apache Christ or believed in the image as a practicing Catholic, Rosa speculated, "I wouldn"t believe in it, but I guess there could be. They have him, and if maybe a lot of Apache People are around and felt that this one person, the Apache Christ, was the one that God made for them, then maybe?" A notation that accompanies the image of the Apache Christ on the holy card references the "reconciliation of the spiritual vision of Native and Christian peoples" and "the icon celebrates the beauty of Apache culture."[47] Sonja indicated, "This icon was not imaged by Native Peoples. What does [it] mean 'reconciliation'? That they made him look Indian? Sacred power is always there. The Christ image does not reveal sacred power. What makes that Christ a prophetic sign?" Other consultants were judicious and circumspect about the image. Mikal stated, "Well, I did not know there was an Apache Christ.

---

[47]   See *The Apache Christ* by Br. Robert Lentz (Trinity Stores, 1990).

Figure 7.2   Br. Robert Lentz, OFM, *The Apache Christ* (1990), used with permission and courtesy of Trinity Stores (www.trinitystores.com), in the United States (800.699.4482).

It seems like a fabrication. ... I don't think you can change a religion and tailor it to meet demographics of certain people."

Consultants touched upon issues of respect for revered individuals regardless of Native or Christian background regarding *The Apache Christ*. Changing the image of someone was viewed as disrespectful. Teresa declared, "I would think a Catholic person would think this was sacrilegious." Cory commented, "Why would they do that? I mean if they were really true to their belief systems, why would they disrespect Christ?" Others discussed the importance of "reality in representation," and they raised issues of how symbols and images are understood. Elena's comment regarding truthfulness is illustrative. "I believe Jesus was supposed to be a Jew. So if somebody doesn't know that and sees this I don't think it's OK to misrepresent it. I just think let the truth show whatever it is." Elida was more critical of the Church's representations. "I almost wonder if there wasn't some kind of manual that these priests got that said three things you have to do. 'You're going to find some holy person that's from that group, and build it up as an icon, and then display it.'" During the interviews, photographs from the churches provided real-life contexts for examination, posed initial categories, and stimulated discussions.

Interpretations of Visual Culture and Power

The following section incorporates a discussion of the photographic data with the advantage of interpretations, insights, and perspectives from the interview consultants. The act of seeing and categorizing images reflects differences in the functions photographic images play within contexts and provides a useful framework for analysis. Some images and symbols in the churches are used in minimal ways and are reflective of missionary purposes that include the goals of teaching and preaching the Gospel.[48] An analysis of photographic data in two areas is revealing: first, images or structures used on the landscape or in display, and, second, printed materials, either photographic or artistic renditions of Catholic iconography. Images on the landscape are reflective of the colonizing efforts of the past and suggest domination upon the land for the purpose of missionization. In contrast, "Natives traditionally do not relate to the land as landscape. ... It is a word rooted in a belief that the earth must be subdued by human effort."[49] Photographic data from a number of reservations reveals a typical practice of placing a cross or building in a prominent position or on open landscape that overlooks the community and church grounds. Utilizing a central location for maximum exposure and dominance upon the landscape, Figures 7.3 and 7.4 provide examples of this often-used technique and presence.

[48]   See, for example, Figure 7.1, *Chi-Rho* sign.

[49]   Jace Weaver (ed.), *Native American Religious Identity: Unforgotten Gods* (Maryknoll, 2002), p. 20.

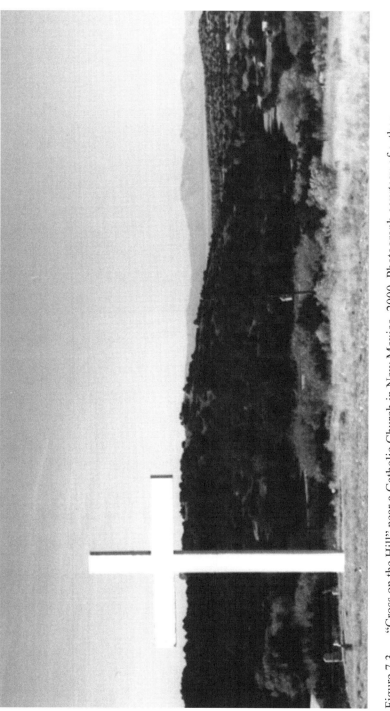

Figure 7.3   "Cross on the Hill" near a Catholic Church in New Mexico, 2000. Photograph courtesy of author.

Figure 7.4 "Abandoned Mission Church on a Hill," South Dakota, 2004. Photograph courtesy of author.

Throughout the number of churches visited, this application of images and buildings located on significant and dominating positions on the land is apparent. Further, cultural displays such as those found in California missions arrange and present a particular perspective and interpretation of history that includes a transformation of the local community. Catholic churches typically are built on the land in a way that supports Jace Weaver's critique of Christians and the meaning of landscape as something to be transformed.[50] The land itself must reflect the ideology, and the display of images employs Western attitudes, beliefs, actions, and behaviors to make a point.

Catholic missions across Canada and the United States—California as one example in particular—are unique in that they serve as museums as well as sites of missionary practice. Imagery utilized for display reveals the suggestion of ownership of objects and display of such as acceptable practice because they are inanimate. Often objects for display can be described and characterized as serving two goals: first, to attract interest largely from and for non-Indians for the preservation of the missions through donations; and second, to give the appearance of similarity and beneficence between the two groups in terms of the history of spiritual practice. As one priest explained, "The Catholic Church's mission on reservations is to be a constant beacon of hope ... for the people so they feel welcome."[51] This is accomplished through church decorations such as signs presenting the mission story, a Pendleton blanket draped across the altar, or the display of objects such as abalone shells as holy water receptacles, headdresses, and wall hangings. Display, however, reduces the object or image to the Western notion of possession, artifact, or something to be owned. Vine Deloria points out that religion today reflects this element of the American psyche—the possibility to create our own reality and the freedom to do so, suggesting "there is no reality and that we live in a completely intellectual world where the free choice of the individual determines the values and emotional content of experiences."[52] Thus, it is possible not only for New Age adherents to mix and match religions as they choose, it also is possible for the Catholic Church to incorporate and display objects as part of freedom of religious expression justified as in service to and helping the people.

Printed materials are designed to promote and recruit new Church members, as well as encourage recognition of similarities of thought. They can be used for fund-raising and publications designed to promote the Church and mission activities, and the "you are just like us" emphasis continues. As one consultant noted, images of Kateri as a Mohawk woman were "very carefully planned and balanced to appeal to Indian people." Statues and images of Kateri Tekakwitha, as illustrated in Figure 7.5 and Figures 1.1 and 1.2, are significantly similar and reflective of other forms of advertising and marketing designed for conversion. Furthermore, images of Kateri and Black Elk lend themselves to the idea that

---

[50]   Ibid.

[51]   Personal communication with author. South Dakota, July 2000.

[52]   Deloria, Jr., *God Is Red*, p. 57.

Figure 7.5   Exterior statue of Kateri Tekakwitha near a reservation Catholic
church in New Mexico, 2003. Photograph courtesy of the author.

"you too can be a saint" and the notion of a pan-Indian Catholicism. Kateri is utilized by the Church in Native communities with the implicit and explicit goals of conversion and creating a pan-Indian Catholicism. It is a way of conducting outreach to non-Indian communities under similar efforts of the past, "helping the Indian" and displaying images of Native converts and the progress of conversion efforts. Further, images of Kateri Tekakwitha and Black Elk indicate an example of holiness utilized in reservation churches, but typically unknown in non-Indian Catholic communities with the exception of fund-raising events.

Often the message of Christianity, and by extension Catholic images, appears to subsume issues of power and oppression present in the relationship and assume the age-old notion of conversion to Christianity as a logical evolutionary progression.[53] Cultural oppression and hegemony can be examined through "revisionist or expropriated imagery"[54] that is used to promote the Catholic Church and the communities from which the images emanate. The Church is viewed as having the power to unify all peoples under the ideology of the Church—highlighting the idea that "you are like us." David Morgan indicates that this consists of the use of images, styles, objects, and visual rituals that come to stand for the postcolonial religion and its significance for a national identity.[55] For example, in the image of *The Apache Christ* (Figure 7.2) an implicit understanding and inference suggests that Christ was an Apache, and he can be envisaged as such without harm or detriment to the notion of the Catholic Christ. His visage and suffering becomes comparable to the suffering of Apache people, creating an implicit link to Catholic tradition. Christ and the image of the cross compare to the lives of Native Catholics, and sacrifice is an expression of faith that is here on earth, with redemption and the attainment of heaven for the future. In other words, the image implies that Christ not only was Apache, but that Apache and Catholic holy people and ideas are the same. However, as the consultants noted, changing the image of someone so important to Catholicism "was a strange" and "disrespectful" thing to do, and they wondered if Catholics would think it sacrilegious. They did not make or interpret a connection to their lives as Native people.

As indicated by consultants in response to John Guiliani's *Holding up Christ*, the suffering of Christ also is implicitly linked to that of Apache and Native Peoples. For consultants, the image compares the plight of disadvantaged and marginalized people today to the suffering of Christ. They will be vindicated and redeemed, but they will have to wait until the next life. Christ as the definitive social outcast provides a redemptive message for those who wait until after death. This particularly Catholic notion incorporates suffering for something better in the future that not only discounts current suffering, but is antithetical to Native and Indigenous traditions who view the world as actively present and personal. With

---

[53]   Jerry D. Meyer, "Profane and Sacred: Religious Imagery and Prophetic Expression in Postmodern Art," *Journal of the American Academy of Religion*, LXV/1 (1997): 19–46.

[54]   Morgan, *The Sacred Gaze*.

[55]   Morgan, *The Sacred Gaze*, p. 151.

some considerable irony, a number of postmodern artists have assumed a prophetic stance. Artists use a variety of mediums to reexamine religious and cultural attitudes that foster persecution and exploitation in the present.[56] Altering images in ways that challenge the Catholic context, Native artists critique colonization and oppression and invite audiences to rethink and reinterpret images based on a combination of ideas and meanings in the representations. They create imagery that is reflective of the past and challenges the expropriation and appropriation of Indigenous images as well, often reflecting the first line of resistance and re-imagining of a social condition.

The reinterpretation of imagery by Native artists counters the purposes of the missionary, and explores reinterpretations of contexts and the hierarchical relationship of the Church to communities. As Tomson Highway indicates, "the most potent kind of art is that which is inseparable from religion."[57] Artistic works as commentaries reflect oppression and dominance, and incorporate and recall the historical colonial past of war, genocide, and the destruction of Native ways of life. The work of Carl Beam exemplifies ironic intensity in his sharply titled image *Calvary to Calvary*. It juxtaposes an archival photo of five Native men as militant members defending their nation with an image of Christ's crucifixion at Calvary. It has been described as "searing commentary on the harrowing military-missionary alliance," but also reflective of the common ground of persecution.[58] In another example of commentary regarding persecution and oppression, Ojibway artist Ron Noganosh presents a work entitled *Dominus Vobiscum*,[59] a rosary constructed out of bullets and mounted against a red background behind a sheet of Plexiglas with bullet holes and Christ as a G.I. Joe doll. Noganosh interprets his work as a commentary on the emotional and psychological distance between Native and Western cultures:

> It's visually appealing, but there is a lot going on in it. It actually started with a Jacques Cartier dollar. That was the scapular medal I put on top. And then I made the rosary. ... Beads out of bullets, because of the wars—about fighting the Indians, fighting all kinds of wars. And then, of course, G.I. Joe's hangin' on the cross because of the senselessness of war, if you want. It's set out in a heart shape because they used to do that in the mission schools. ... And [the frame's] made out of walnut because when they gave medals away for bravery or killing people you got a nice walnut case with a medal in it.[60]

---

[56]   Meyer, "Profane and Sacred," p. 44.

[57]   Tomson Highway, "Tomson Highway: Native Voice," dir. Robert Sherrin (*Adrienne Clarkson Presents*, 2002), Videotape, CBC.

[58]   Allan J. Ryan, *The Trickster Shift: Humour and Irony in Contemporary Native Art* (Vancouver, 1999), p. 194.

[59]   Noganosh's commentary in its entirety is in Ryan, *The Trickster Shift.*

[60]   In Ryan, *The Trickster Shift*, p. 197.

Native and Indigenous artists ask viewers to interpret Catholic images through the lens of political and social commentary, and often indirectly address George Tinker's questions regarding appropriation and power. First, "How are our actions and thoughts today controlled by this systematic whole? And second, how can we begin to stand apart from it with some intentionality?"[61] Both questions call for actions and efforts that deconstruct the power and authority of images as social constructions that reflect and frame interpretations of relationships.

Interpreting "Jesus was not an Indian"

Photographic and visual research examines the space between what is seen and what is felt, and inquiry into the contexts of visual images is important for confronting issues of hegemony. Contemporary power constitutes today's reality in visual images for their ability to represent, access, and provide information.[62] When images are displayed, meanings are acquired through a visual sensory experience that employs aspects of power to shape the meaning and interpretation of images. Often, consultants reflected on the history of Native Church associations and experiences of the past, and they made interpretations regarding the continuing social context of missionization. Examining the images together became a "form of inquiry" about a topic personally relevant and emotionally difficult since it evoked memories of a genocidal history. It also made explicit the context of continuing missionization that has been submerged and covered in subtle ways. The use of images as a form of colonization, power, and manipulation for changing the meaning of images is a complex process of deep concern. "The question that the so-called world religions have not satisfactorily resolved is whether or not religious experience can be distilled from its original cultural context and become an abstract principle that is applicable to all peoples in different places and at different times."[63] Yet attempts by Catholic churches to complete this distillation process take place subtly, and the creation of images and representations is evident. The process is meant to change and transform the "communal cultural values of Indian people by those who do not even begin to see the cultural imposition that has occurred."[64]

An important theme to surface during this project was the sense of confusion and ambiguity as consultants encountered familiar images displayed in unfamiliar contexts, reflecting Tinker's concerns. Examination of church contexts focused consultants' awareness on the issues and images, specifically providing the opportunity for careful attention to the subjects and topics presented. Thus, changing the focus from one of passive reception to active engagement increased

---

[61] Tinker, *Missionary Conquest*, p. 117.
[62] Ziarek, "The End of Art."
[63] Deloria, Jr., *God Is Red*, p. 65.
[64] Tinker, *Missionary Conquest*, p. 122.

consultants' recognition and awareness of what and how images influence viewers, as well as the ways they contribute to confusion and/or ambiguity. An alternative explanation posed in Christian theological circles is that confusion takes place in the minds of "ordinary lay people" who don't understand the images. Yet this attitude regarding knowledge and religious symbols negates the active role viewers take when they encounter symbols, images, or texts presented in unfamiliar ways. Using images and symbols in contexts that are dislocated from place also negates Native beliefs that recognize objects and places as powerful and appropriating them for use in unfamiliar contexts as disrespectful. This ethic recognizes the material physical world as a dynamic animate and living world. Most significantly, in a social context such as a church, ideas and beliefs are subtly and with innuendo changed to suit new interpretations in the minds of people who view them.

The impact of hegemonic practice that limits confrontation and disagreement over the appropriation of images to only those that concur, while discounting the critiques of those who do not, also has significant impact. Using Native images and symbols transforms the worlds in which people live, and these images are meant to configure "agents, practices, conceptualities, and institutions that put images to work."[65] Consultants revealed conflicting emotions and implicit assumptions regarding the misuse of images for both Natives and Catholics. Yet the confusion and uncertainty they evidenced regarding the meaning of the images emanate from knowledge and understanding of both belief systems. In reality, the images themselves may be confusing and ambiguous, and are so purposefully as part of continuing Christianizing efforts. From these interpretations, we might conclude that missionization and colonization are not ideas of the past, but efforts that continue today. As noted by one of the consultants, "It is evidence that we must increase the forms and level of resistance."

As we return to David Morgan's question regarding what images can tell us about cultural encounters and the "process of religious migration, change and resistance," we see from the comments of consultants and the images presented a number of significant issues. On the one hand, the Catholic Church participates in acts that can be characterized as conversion violence against Native Peoples through the integration of Native images and domination upon the land. Objects, images, and material forms do have power in and of themselves, and the adaptation and use of them by the Catholic Church is a way to access power for a specific purpose. Actions are validated under the guise of service and consent by some Native Catholics. Yet, changing the context, theme or persona of images is in direct opposition to Native perspectives, but supported by Church efforts designed for conversion. Resistance efforts designed to counter the force of co-optation by Native artists actively explores critique and commentary of practice.

Native traditions are different in character from Catholic religious expression. They are traditions of "ritual practice" that permeate "every aspect of daily life and

---

[65]   Morgan, *The Sacred Gaze*, p. 33.

existence."[66] And, they are intimately connected to the living world. On the other hand, missionary teachings continue to misinterpret and appropriate the practices and images of Native communities, while simultaneously changing Catholic traditions to suit a local audience. Most telling regarding the phenomena is the response by one consultant: "And, Jesus was not an Indian. Native people already sacrifice and their sacrifices should be enough." Maybe resistance to and outrage at the practice asks that we question and challenge repeatedly the appropriation of images in the Catholic Church. In any case, one aspect that seems evident is that the character–application–presence or use of Native images is not well known outside of specific communities, and that efforts by the Catholic Church to influence Native practices continues.

---

[66]   Weaver, *Unforgotten Gods*, p. 219.

Chapter 8

Ke Kauhale O Limaloa: A Kanaka Maoli Approach to Teaching through Image Making

Herman Pi'ikea Clark

The "Kauhale Theory" is a pedagogical model derived from a Kanaka Maoli, an indigenous Hawaiian cultural metaphor.[1] Designed to offer an alternative approach to the dominant mainstream teaching conventions in the visual arts in Hawai'i, the Kauhale Theory draws upon ancestral knowledge, values, and cultural perspectives to provide teachers and learners the opportunity to engage an educational setting where Kanaka Maoli knowledge, ways of knowing, and expressing knowledge are prioritized. This chapter describes the process by which the Kauhale Theory was conceptualized and developed for the purposes of facilitating a discussion of the importance of an indigenous Hawaiian learning experience through image making. It is derived from the cultural perspectives, values, and educational aspirations of Kanaka Maoli people, and provides a means by which contemporary images and objects are utilized and engaged in a manner consistent with the place of visual culture in a customary setting.

I was born and raised in Hawai'i, my ancestral homeland. As a first-born son of my family, I remember being taken to stay with my great-grandmother for periods of time at her home in Ka'a'awa, O'ahu. As was the practice within the Kanaka Maoli tradition of Hawai'i, first-born sons were often raised by elders who possessed knowledge that was important to our family heritage. This practice of handing down knowledge would have occurred through a holistic process of teaching that could well have taken place over the course of a lifetime.[2] First-born children were often looked upon by elders to care for genealogical knowledge, as well as other skills and understandings that were of importance to their family. This practice of education has been a consistent feature of Kanaka Maoli families for generations. My great-grandmother, born in the late 1800s as a citizen of the

---

[1]   An earlier version of this chapter was presented in 2007 at the American Educational Research Association annual meeting in Chicago, Illinois for the Indigenous Peoples of the Pacific Special Interest Group.

[2]   See, for example: David Malo, *Hawaiian Antiquities*, 2nd edn., trans. Nathaniel Emerson (Honolulu, 1903/1951); Mary K. Pukui, E.W. Haertig, and C. Lee, *Nana I Ke Kumu (Look to the Sour ce)* (Honolulu: Hui Hanai, 1972).

Kingdom of Hawaiʻi, lived much of her life in a traditional way. Although witness to incredible changes in society brought about by advances in technology, two world wars and the Americanization of Hawaiʻi, my great-grandmother remained steadfast in her quiet adherence to Kanaka Maoli culture and values.

My great-grandmother's home was located at Lae o ka Oʻio point across the road from the beach at Kaʻaʻawa, a deep valley on the windward side of the island of Oʻahu. Our family had lived in Kaʻaʻawa for many generations and my great-grandmother's life there from childhood was a continuation of this legacy. Each morning, she would get up before dawn to gather *limu*, shellfish and other ocean delicacies from the offshore reef. Whenever I visited her, my great-grandmother would take me out to the reef to teach me how to fish and read the ocean environment. When the tide was right, we would walk out to the furthest edge of the reef where she would take me to the places where the *muheʻe* or squid would live. *Muheʻe* are a prized delicacy in Hawaiʻi and, while our walks to the reef were intended to gather fresh seafood, my great-grandmother used these occasions to teach me the things I needed to know. Standing on the edge of a deep blue opening in the reef, the waves swirling around her feet, my grandmother recited to me the words of an *ʻolelo noʻeau*, an ancient proverb. "*Ka muheʻe, he iʻa hololua. Muheʻe* are fish that can swim in two directions," she said. "They can change their color to match the rocks of the reef. When they swim, they move with the flow of currents yet they are able to quickly change direction in order to avoid the fisherman's nets." Even then as a young boy, I knew that my great-grandmother was trying to teach me something of importance that extended beyond the intricacies of a fishing lesson. That day, my great-grandmother taught me as children in my family had been taught for generations. This educational process differed greatly from the teaching I had experienced at school. In the many decades since her passing, I have often reflected upon that morning on the reef at Kaʻaʻawa. As much as her lesson was about fishing, I've come to understand that there was a much deeper message in my great- grandmother's story that day. Anticipating the unpredictable and potentially ominous future I would experience as a Kanaka Maoli living within the context of Hawaiʻi and the Pacific in the twenty-first century, I believe my great-grandmother offered to me a strategy for survival through the metaphor of the *muheʻe*. It was for its cunning, its capacity for camouflage, and its ability to maneuver through difficult passages to elude capture that my great-grandmother chose the *muheʻe* as the example for me to emulate in whatever direction my life would take. As an artist, educator, and Kanaka Maoli—a descendant of the first people of Hawaiʻi—my research has long focused on the development of teaching approaches through the visual arts that facilitate an understanding of indigenous Hawaiian cultural perspectives and knowledge(s). This objective aims to improve the educational experience not just for indigenous Hawaiians, but also for all people who connect with an educational experience in Hawaiʻi. To engage with this process, I have found myself at times needing to emulate the characteristics of the *muheʻe* in my attempts to introduce and advance this indigenous culture based pedagogy within mainstream educational contexts, which are at times reluctant to adopt approaches considered alternative or experimental into its norm.

At the foundation of my research has been a desire to connect with pedagogical and curricular approaches that are derived from the cultural perspectives and values of my ancestors. Fueling this work has been a desire to reinterpret Kanaka Maoli cultural concepts into relevant methods for teaching so as to offer alternatives to national and state education policies that have historically marginalized indigenous knowledge in Hawai'i.[3] An example of this practice can be seen in the school curriculum of the State of Hawai'i. In this very important policy document, Kanaka Maoli knowledge is presented for study within an edited subsection of the school curriculum as opposed to finding broad inclusion within the entire range of subject studies for public schools in Hawai'i. Beyond its aim to resist the assimilative aims of state and federal education policies, the work of this research has sought to contribute to the continued evolution of Kanaka Maoli knowledge and culture within the twenty-first-century context of Hawai'i's occupation as the fiftieth American state.

Confronting my work have been the academic disciplines of visual art and art education, which steadfastly occupies the territory for aesthetics and visual-based teaching within all levels of education globally. As a reflection of indigenous research generally, my work attempts to connect with ancestral knowledge as a way of establishing an approach to teaching that is grounded in the indigenous culture of Hawai'i, and that is distinct from the conventions of Western academic traditions and epistemology. This includes, for instance, an understanding of the integrated role that visual arts played within the social and cultural context of Kanaka Maoli society as contrasted against its position in the west. thesis?

Art Education in Hawai'i

The content and perspective of visual art education in Hawai'i schools have historically followed the point of view of European and American art, art history and aesthetics.[4] These fields teach from the dominant paradigm that has served to support state hegemony through the vehicle of education. Whether state interests lie in maintaining the status quo of social relations and hierarchies within society, insuring the economic vitality of business and government, or transmitting the moral and cultural values that underpin society, mainstream education in art has adjusted over time to convey the economic, social, and political interests of the dominant in society.

---

[3]   Maenette K.P. Benham and Ronald H. Heck, *Culture and Educational Policy in Hawai'i: The Silencing of Native Voices* (New Jersey, 1998), pp. 111–13.

[4]   Herman Pi'ikea Clark, "Kukulu Kauhale o Limaloa: A Kanaka Maoli Culture Based Approach to Education through Visual Studies" (PhD diss., New Zeeland: Massey University, 2006), pp. 3–6.

Following practices in the United States, the visual arts are transmitted in schools within terms, values, and conditions defined principally by American art education theories and practice nationally.[5] Owing its existence historically to the works of European and American artists, teachers, and educational theorists, and the field of visual arts education cannot help but reflect the Euroamerican cultural perspectives and values. The field of art education owes much to the work of Professor Arthur Efland who has written extensively of the underlying social, economic, and political pressures, which have influenced Art Education's development through time. Efland's book *A History of Art Education*[6] is particularly useful to this chapter in that it details and contextualizes some of the primary factors and interests that have influenced the trends and developments for teaching and learning within the field of art education. Underlying this history, Efland reveals the case for art education's use by the powerful in society to establish and reinforce their political, economic, and moral interests through public education in the United States. Efland's work, therefore, is supportive of my assertion that art education in Hawai'i, particularly in the period following the annexation of Hawai'i as a territory of the United States in 1898, has been and continues to be an instrument to advance the political, cultural, and economic interests of America in Hawai'i.

Overlooking this cultural bias, education policies widely celebrate art education for its capacity to cultivate the senses and encourage higher-order thinking, as well as provide students with a tangible link between their logical and emotional selves. This belief in the positive effect of visual arts education has been particularly cogent in Hawai'i where national developments and projects have long been welcomed and adopted in school curricula, and in programs for teacher education. Juxtaposed against a history of American imperialism in Hawai'i, however, the affirmative and beneficial intent of visual arts education takes on a less than benevolent character. Despite claims of multicultural inclusion, visual arts education in Hawai'i appears to have been broadly defined by the language, values, and cultural perspectives of Europe and America.

As with much of the rest of the world, the practice of art and art education in Hawai'i has offered few opportunities through which the viewpoint of cultural "others" are allowed voice to authentically shape curriculum and pedagogy. The arts typically have not included diverse perspectives, values, and knowledge(s), with the exception of particular examples of indigenous mark or pattern making that can be appropriated out from its original cultural context to support the aims of the "mainstream" curriculum. This "additive"[7] approach to cultural diversity

---

[5]   Richard Cary, *Critical Art Pedagogy: Foundations for Postmodern Education* (New York, 1998) pp. 59–61.

[6]   Arthur D. Efland, *A History of Art Education: Intellectual and Social Currents in Teaching the Visual Arts* (New York, 1990).

[7]   James Banks, "Approaches to Multicultural Curriculum Reform," in James Banks and C. McGee-Banks (eds.), *Multicultural Education; Issues and Perspectives*, 3rd edn.

through art study provides little beyond a superficial engagement with cultural difference to enable students' learning outside the mainstream centrism of the official curriculum. Of primary concern to my work has been the exclusion from art and art education practice in Hawai'i of the cultural perspectives and expressions of Kanaka Maoli—the indigenous people of this land. Over the last 100 years, with little or no Kanaka Maoli cultural influence within Hawai'i's art and art education settings to introduce and engage an indigenous way of knowing and seeing, people in Hawai'i have been conditioned to perceive and represent the world through a foreign lens. Like a cultural Trojan horse, visual arts education in Hawai'i has served as a subtle vehicle of cultural assimilation through which the values, aesthetics, and visual pedagogies of American society have been transmitted.

Western Exclusion of Knowledge

Specific to the discussion in this chapter is the exclusion of Kanaka Maoli knowledge from visual arts education as a symptom of the exclusion of Kanaka Maoli knowledge more generally from education in Hawai'i. Beyond the art curriculum, Kanaka Maoli knowledge, ways of knowing, and aesthetics—a knowledge base that extends from a culture nearly two thousand years old—have been edited and apportioned for teaching practice in Hawai'i.

The modern concept of art as taught, envisioned, or practiced coalesced as an independent category for aesthetic objects in Western European society during the eighteenth century. From this period forward, the concept of art as a separate and autonomous class of objects and images made for the explicit purposes of aesthetic engagement and market trade was established.[8] For as much as I have been able to determine, no other pre-industrial society or culture in the world has established a disassociated category for aesthetic objects as has Western European society. The broad adoption of the art concept by nations throughout the world had perhaps more to do with the success of the European colonial enterprise than with art's claim of a universal appeal. Education in art, whether applied to classrooms in Europe, Asia, America, Africa, or the Pacific, has largely been shaped by the ideals of Modernism that support the notion that art is an individual expression that is self-referencing, aesthetically focused and disassociated from social interrelation.[9]

Despite the intensive attention to material, technique, and form in the creation of visual objects created, Kanaka Maoli culture did not produce art as it is conceptualized in the Western world. No word in the Kanaka Maoli language, in fact, fits the definition that we today give to the word "art." The closest Kanaka

(Hoboken, 1997), pp. 121–6.

[8] L.E. Shiner, *The Invention of Art: A Cultural History* (London, 2001), pp. 80–86.

[9] Ibid., pp. 88–9.

Maoli word, *maiau*, which means skillful, ingenious, expert, correct, careful (as in speech), is indicative of the culture's aesthetic standard in workmanship, which is thorough, meticulous, and tidy. Although aesthetics are of vital concern, the objects and images created within a Kanaka Maoli cultural setting are designed to function within an interconnected social context. Beyond utility, images and objects created within a Kanaka Maoli cultural context often serve as identifiers and visual representations of genealogical history and knowledge. Through these objects and images, the character and nature of Kanaka Maoli society as an interrelated whole is expressed.

The *`Ahu`ula,* or the sacred chief's feather cloak, provides a useful example of the role of visual images and objects in Kanaka Maoli society and culture. Composed of the selected feathers of thousands of native birds, the *`Ahu`ula* was one of the highest material achievements of Kanaka Maoli society. By virtue of its elegant design and meticulous construction through a precious medium, the *`Ahu`ula* could easily sit within the definition generally attributed in the West to a work of art. Unlike "art," however, the *`Ahu`ula* was more than a well-crafted aesthetic object. Within the context of Kanaka Maoli society, the *`Ahu`ula* functioned to represent and manifest the sacredness of the chief who wore it, as well as of the collective identity and *mana* (prestige, status, and power) of the community to which he or she was responsible. In contrast to its designation as an artifact or tribal object by Western art and art history, the *`Ahu`ula* served as an edifying component within a Kanaka Maoli system of images and objects that evidenced the sacredness and secular authority of chiefs.[10]

Let me take a moment to say that my critique of Western interpretations and understanding of art and art education should not be equated with dismissal of its value and contribution to the human experience. Quite to the contrary, I have long respected the historic developments and achievements of Western art and its particular aesthetic interpretation and view of the world. My objection, however, lies rather with national and state education policies in Hawai'i and other former colonial countries in the world that draw upon the theories and conventions of European and American art history to define teaching and learning for art and aesthetic education exclusively. It is as though the nineteenth-century colonial imperative to impart Western knowledge and culture to the far reaches of the world continues as a directive for educational practice today. This is testament to Western knowledge and the cultural hegemony that is practiced in the field. My ancestors understood and valued the importance of a diversity of views in what is comprised of knowledge as expressed in the well-known *`Ôlelo No`eau,* or proverb, *"A'ole pau ka ike I ka hâlau ho'okahi"* (Not all knowledge is contained in one school).[11] It is unfortunate that education policy in Hawai'i as related to the arts has seemed

[10] Peter H. Buck, *Arts and Crafts of Hawaii* (Honolulu, 1964), pp. 215–31.

[11] Mary K. Pukui, *`Ôlelo No`eau: Hawaiian Proverbs and Poetical Sayings* (Honolulu, 1984), p. 34.

to have overlooked this very ancient appreciation for difference that the Kanaka Maoli culture recognizes, supports, and values.

Wisdom of the Ancestors

Through the work of indigenous education research, the wisdom of our ancestors reaches across the generations to raise us all above this constricted path to learning that we find ourselves confronted by today. Beyond a concern for the assimilative effect of standards-based educational practice, I question the capacity of the current fields of art and art education to adequately engage and represent the complex and interdisciplinary nature of Kanaka Maoli knowledge and visual ways of knowing.

In my work to develop an indigenous approach to education through visual image and object making, I have found opportunity, through the absence of the word or concept "art" in the Kanaka Maoli language, to demarcate new territory for knowledge making beyond that established and occupied by Western art history, aesthetics and art education. Traditionally, Kanaka Maoli culture was principally oral based. All knowledge and history was recorded and transmitted through oral-based genealogical compositions and through `Ôlelo No`eau, or "proverbs," and *Mo`olelo*, "stories." As repositories of traditional values and cultural perspectives, genealogies and `Ôlelo No`eau today provide an avenue of access through which contemporary Kanaka Maoli can connect with the beliefs and values of their ancestral culture.

Although the concept and place of "art" as understood in the Western cultural context was absent from traditional Kanaka Maoli culture and society, the role of visual culture was of vital importance. In contrast to the rarified place of art within Euroamerican societies following the eighteenth-century, Kanaka Maoli visual culture served specific functions within society, at times providing an important means by which information was visually recorded, codified, and transmitted. Beyond its role as repository and transmitter of knowledge, Kanaka Maoli visual culture also was recognized within its own cultural context as an important vehicle in the exploration and construction of knowledge as well. A traditional proverb from the island of Kauai describes in a subtle way the important role that images and objects served within Kanaka Maoli society in the formulation of new ideas and knowledge. "*Ho`onohonoho i Waineki Kauhale O Limaloa*"[12] is a traditional saying that describes the workings of the god Limaloa, the Kanaka Maoli god of mirage making. According to the proverb, Limaloa was known to construct mirages of *kauhale* "houses" along the plains at Waineki on the island of Kauai during the earliest hours of the morning. As soon as the rising sun began to crest the horizon, Limaloa would complete the building of his *kauhale* and cause them to disappear. As with so much in Hawaiian language, *kaona*, or hidden meaning,

---

[12] Ibid., p. 200.

served an important function within Kanaka Maoli language compositions. *Kaona* challenges listeners to engage in the complexity of meanings within Kanaka Maoli language and signs to gain access to the underlying meaning of a proverb. The underlying meaning of this Kauai proverb lies in analogizing the act of Limaloa's mirage making with the intellectual and creative activity of developing ideas and the ordering of plans. According to Pukui's commentary on the proverb story, Limaloa's play through the building and arranging of *Kauhale* mirages is equated to the use of imagination and clarification of ideas one accomplishes through the making of models, mind maps, or concept drawings.[13] It was the act of visually interpreting and giving form to concepts and ideas through images and objects that Limaloa was engaging in with his building and arranging of *Kauhale* structures over Waineki in the early-morning hours.

Limaloa's building of *kauhale* at Waineki offers evidence of another function that visual images and objects provide in traditional Kanaka Maoli culture, and that is a tool to engage the development of new ideas and knowledge. Within the context of the proverb, Limaloa's mirage house constructions provide him with a visual-based process through which to employ and develop new knowledge. From the viewpoint of this proverb, it is the process of coming to ideas through the construction and arrangement of the *kauhale*, rather than the creation of *kauhale* itself that is important. The philosophical principles underpinning this Hawaiian philosophy and understanding of the story stands in contrast to the focus of conventional art education. As a discipline, conventional art education maintains a strong belief in Modernism, which, at its core, never conceived of art as a socially situated practice, but rather as an expression of an individual artist's creativity and inspiration. Within this epistemological framework, the artistic product is the artist's object. Even postmodern influences in art education, with their embrace of multiple viewpoints, critique of empiricism and formalism, and inherent challenge to power and authority, still (to a large extent) privileges the art image or object as its ultimate objective and focus.[14]

Indigenous education research could be viewed primarily as a strategy created and undertaken by indigenous researchers and teachers as a way of combating the assimilative and homogenizing effect of state schooling on indigenous children. Given the experience of indigenous people in Eurocentric education, it would be justified to view the project of indigenous education as a resistance strategy alone. This interpretation, however, would allow only a partial if not disparaging understanding of the field's aim and purpose. The perception of indigenous education research as a resistance strategy alone may, in fact, serve to normalize mainstream educational theories and practices by virtue of its critique and reaction against it. From this viewpoint, indigenous education research could not escape the influence of Eurocentric cultural perspectives and values reflected

[13]   Ibid.

[14]   Cary, *Critical Art Pedagogy*, pp. 336–8.

in conventional practices, even as it aims to resist it, since the act of resistance is within the dominant paradigm.

Indigenous education research also must undertake to critically assess conventional practices to establish and validate space for culturally specific constructions of knowledge and pedagogical approaches that are particular to people and cultures indigenous within a given place. This educational paradigm emerges from the beliefs and practices of the culture, not as imposed by Western educational pedagogy. Implicit within this is an underlying assumption that space for educational approaches from indigenous perspectives has been denied a position within conventional mainstream education. A cursory review of conventional educational practice, particularly in countries that have been created over colonized indigenous populations, concludes that indigenous epistemology, cultural perspective, and language are, under the very best of situations, placed at the margins of school curricula and teaching practices. Schools, curriculum, and education preference normalize Eurocentric knowledge, history, and culture over all else. Since the nineteenth century, British and European colonization of Asia, Africa, North and South America, and the Pacific have resulted in European domination over not just indigenous people, their lands, political systems, and economic resources but the form, content, and structure of indigenous knowledge, language, and culture as well. According to Linda Tuhiwai Smith: "The nexus between cultural ways of knowing, scientific discoveries, economic impulses and imperial power enabled the West to make ideological claims to having a superior civilization. The 'idea' of the West became a reality when it was re-presented back upon indigenous people."[15] In many instances, the primary method by which the colonial powers accomplished and exerted their influence, beyond military force and the church, was through the program of colonial education.

The actuality of practice and theory in indigenous education research is that it is engaged simultaneously on multiple levels. For indigenous art education, one of its objective streams has been aimed at resisting the assimilative and homogenizing effect of state-sponsored art education upon Kanaka Maoli people in Hawai'i. This critique has sought to deconstruct academic practice, and the system of beliefs, values, and perspectives that support it, so as to reveal the Eurocentric cultural bias that underlies the institution and practice of art education. Through this critique, space for Kanaka Maoli and indigenous knowledge within the discipline of art education is argued to broaden the monocultural foundation that currently underpins its educational practice.

The other stream, and perhaps the more challenging one, has been to reengage the development of knowledge making, and teaching and learning approaches, of Kanaka Maoli society that has been interrupted by 200 years of US occupation in Hawai'i. Researchers in the field attempt to puzzle together surviving fragments of indigenous knowledge so as to construct a knowledge system that is distinctly

---

[15]   Smith, *Decolonizing Methodologies: Research and Indigenous Peoples* (Dunedin, 2001), p. 64.

Kanaka Maoli. This kind of theorizing is challenging in that it compels researchers and theorists to exit the thought processes, knowledge base, culture, language, and history of European academic inquiry that have been imposed upon Kanaka Maoli and other colonized indigenous people. Instead, it is necessary to engage the question of what does knowledge, teaching, and learning mean from a native and indigenous perspective, and what are the important criteria for assessing the transmission and use of such knowledge. The project to resurrect indigenous knowledge so as to enable its continued evolution within the twenty-first-century context involves recognition of the conditioning of Eurocentric epistemology. It also demands a will to expand beyond the limitation of its borderlines to engage authentically with knowledge construction from a Kanaka Maoli and indigenous cultural perspective.

For Kanaka Maoli students and researchers who have been compelled to ascribe to the conventions and perspectives of the academy in order to conduct research, the exiting of Eurocentric structures of knowledge to engage an indigenous perspective poses a challenge. To engage Kanaka Maoli knowledge, students and researchers must disengage from the conventions and conditioning of their academic upbringing and connect with the specificity of indigenous knowledge(s) and ways of knowing. This disengagement from Eurocentric academic traditions, though liberating, is often undertaken within spaces fractured and depleted by the generational assault of colonialism upon indigenous people, their lands, languages, and culture. The effort to reconstruct indigenous knowledge(s) and methodologies must be undertaken within a process that recognizes and embraces indigenous epistemologies and ways of knowing. The temptation to disguise Eurocentric disciplinary knowledge under an indigenous cultural veneer in order to validate its worth against conventional standards, particularly where there is no equivalency in the European tradition, must be avoided. Kanaka Maoli and other indigenous knowledge(s) are valid in their own right and as a worthy expression of a people's response to their particular environment and social condition. The resurrection of indigenous knowledge(s) gives evidence to the resilience of indigenous peoples and the rich diversity that characterizes the human experience globally.

Kauhale Theory in Practice

The Kauhale Theory, based upon a Kanaka Maoli metaphor for knowledge making as envisioned within the story of Limaloa, prioritizes the process of thinking through image and/or object making to focus the students upon the development of community and the interrelationships of people within that community. While individual achievement and growth is of interest within this approach, it is the growth of the individual as a component of a community that underlies this indigenous philosophical approach.

Linked by genealogy, Kanaka Maoli share a common source of knowledge, which extends from the time of their ʻaumakua, or ancient god ancestors.

Interpreted, built upon, and transmitted over the generations, these knowledge(s) evidence the multiple ways in which Kanaka Maoli, as individuals of a group or community, have come to know and understand their changing world. This indigenous approach to teaching and learning through image and object making encourages students and teachers to orient their visual studies toward an investigation and translation of knowledge contained within genealogy. In contrast to the homogenizing objective and effect of standards-based curriculum, indigenous genealogy based pedagogy offers students a means to construct their individuality, while re-establishing connections with land, family history, and community. Through this coming to knowledge of self, students understand their relationship to community and environment, as well as their duties and obligations within it. The process of thinking through images allows students the space to investigate, translate, and communicate their stories into mnemonic images and objects that aid in the recall of genealogical knowledge. Unlike Western art, these visual objects and images are produced primarily as "knowledge devices" whose intended purpose is for the recall and preservation of knowledge(s) contained within genealogy.

In the struggle to find our own paths to knowledge and meaning outside that already occupied by Western philosophical and academic frameworks, Kanaka Maoli and other indigenous educational research initiatives globally aim to serve the needs of the communities from which they extend. In doing so, indigenous education research offers the world one of few viable alternatives to the increasing homogenization and commoditization of knowledge within the neoliberal context of education globally. To establish its function as an indigenous knowledge vehicle, a Kanaka Maoli approach to education must exploit the absence of Western cultural concepts such as that of art in the Kanaka Maoli language and culture in order to engage its own visual ontology and epistemological methods. In doing so, art and art education will expand beyond their cultural bias to reflect an authentic voice of the island's geographic, historic, and cultural reality.

Chapter 9

The Photographic Vision of Delvin Slick: Beauty and Power in Sacred Places

Karen Willeto and Delvin J. Slick

The notion of the sacred made visible in this chapter emphasizes the beauty, power, and essential spiritual nature present in the interconnectedness of all beings. The idea of the sacred in everyday life, present in mountains, rivers, and other-than-humans, is integral and intimately connected to all relationships. As Steve Talbot indicates:

> Many Native people find it difficult to relate to the word *religion* to explain their beliefs, traditions, and spiritual practices, a Navajo Community College text published in 1977 recommended using the concept "The Sacred". The Sacred, or spirituality, lies at the heart of Indian culture and is not separate from indigenous institutions of government, the family, or even the economy.[1]

In these ways, Diné photography artist Delvin Slick is deeply influenced by his culture and the land of his people. As a student at Diné College in Arizona, the visual representations and imagery present in his black-and-white photographs illuminate these aspects of his life. It impressively ties to the land, livestock, and Diné traditions, and is a dominant and powerful reflection of the artistic and perceptive autobiographical statements inherent in his photographs. The combination of these elements is sacred and life-defining to the Diné, and Delvin's work reflects his daily living experiences, photographic vision, and interpretation of "Sacred Places."

Using the Diné College educational philosophy—one designed to advance quality student learning—Karen Willeto teaches beginning and intermediate photography. An important aspect for all of the faculty at Diné College is the training we receive in this philosophy—*Sá'ah Naagháí Bik'eh Hózhóó*. The philosophy and ethic is a significant traditional paradigm used to approach teaching and learning. It starts in the East with the concept of thinking (*Nitsáhákees*), moves to the South and planning (*Nahatá*); then West and living (*Liná*); and finally North and assuring (*Siih Hasin*). It is a logical usable approach to teaching

---

[1]   Steve Talbot, "Spiritual Genocide: The Denial of American Indian Religious Freedom, from Conquest to 1934," *Wicazo Sa Review* (Fall 2006): 7–39 (italics in the original).

that incorporates the principles of think, plan, live/do, and assure/reflect. "The philosophy provides principles both for protection from the imperfections in life and for the development of well-being, and it guides all aspects of Diné College's educational planning activities, as well as priority setting and implementation of research projects."[2] From my perspective as a teacher, it is applicable for all courses and educational settings, as well as for life.

In photography classes, during the thinking stage, Karen's students view the works of artists such as Hulleah Tsinhnahjinnie (Seminole/Muscogee/Diné), Shelly Niro (Mohawk Nation), and other Native photographers, as well as a number of other famous photographers. She believes it is important for them to have examples of others' work for inspiration. Then, she encourages them to plan what they will study and photograph based on a series of class assignments. Light and the use of light in photography is the first lesson, followed by composition. In subsequent lessons, students engage in the study of portrait photography, and they examine elements of time as reflected in photographs such as narrative time and conceptual time. In class assignments, students are also encouraged to take photos that are meaningful to them and that reflect their culture. During the planning stage, Delvin Slick's photographic work for the class was specifically designed to engage a study of sacred space and places with elements of narrative and time. Through the assuring and reflective process, he sought out places and utilized active reflection of the meaning of space. Represented in his photography, we the viewers are able to gain insight from his living participation, understanding, and photographic interpretations.

To begin, light is an important aspect of Delvin's photographs, especially in the images *Sacred Place*, *Morning Twilight*, and *The Renegades*. These three photographs are mysterious, hinting at memory and cultural foundations that characterize elements of the sacred. As a traditional Diné, Delvin values the practice of waking at dawn, facing the sun, and running to the east. Finding a special quality of light and recording it reflects this respect. His photographs *Sacred Place* and *Morning Twilight* are serious and spiritual in their quality of light. As illustrated in Figure 9.1, *Sacred Place* shows light shining through the ceiling of a traditional *ho'gan*, recalling images that are uplifting and reflective of a Navajo cathedral.

According to Delvin, this image holds memories that remind him of who he is today:

> This picture I think is very sacred to me because it reminds me of my grandparents. As a young boy I stayed most of my lifetime with my grandparents. After a long day of herding sheep, it's time to bed down. And when I mean bed, it is my sheepskin and a blanket. In the summertime when the moon is out you look up

---

[2]   Diné College, "Educational Philosophy," www.dinecollege.edu/about/philosophy. php (accessed 8 February 2009).

Figure 9.1   Delvin J. Slick, *Sacred Place*, black-and-white photograph, 24.5 x 16 cm, 2008. Reproduced with permission of the photographer and author.

along the stovepipes and see the stars in the sky. This image reminds me of my childhood and who I am today.

Life and the lessons learned as a young child in the care of dear grandparents remains present in the physical world through space and time and is reflected in the smoke opening of the *ho'gan*.

Morning Twilight invites the viewer to greet the morning sun in the tradition of the Diné. As we see in Figure 9.2, Delvin illuminates the meaning presented in the image:

> As a Navajo we pray outside towards east before sunrise. This was one of the things I've learned to do as a young boy and especially during ceremonies. The sun has to shine on you so you can be recognized by our holy people to grant our wishes, our prayers and to be thankful. And, it is important to add to the stories of how we are in the glittering world now.

This photograph captures the morning sun as it illuminates the "glittering world" in all its radiance. Delvin encourages viewers to "take a look at the picture. Look at the rock formation. See the sparkle or the glittering from the morning sunlight."

Sometimes photographs reflect humor and a sense of play possible in the world. The photograph entitled *The Renegades* presented in Figure 9.3 is humorous and charged with expectation of something mysterious.

The Renegades belong to Delvin's mother. He gave the photograph this title because "they [the goats] may look innocent, but looks can be deceiving." The personality and character of each goat is visible in the image, and yet the black goat, named Jurassic Park, towers over the others with a strong stance, his head held high. Delvin says, "he looks like one of the Raptors in a movie, more like he is the leader of the pack." All of the goats seem to be standing at attention, perhaps in anticipation of dinner or in preparation for getting their picture taken with their best foot forward. They are ready for whatever comes their way. In reality, they are all looking at Delvin because they want to be released out of the corral, especially Jurassic Park. "They are naughty goats and were being punished because they would just run away to where ever they saw fit. That's why they go out last of all the herds, mostly around noon." He says that his mother's goats serve as examples and lessons to live by:

> I've been raised around sheep, goats, cattle, and horses so they are very sacred to me because these animals can teach you something about life. For example, they might teach you how to be responsible and always try to do the right thing, otherwise later you will deal with the consequences. They also might teach you to accept your responsibilities in life.

life lessons through pictures

Figure 9.2   Delvin J. Slick, *Morning Twilight*, black-and-white photograph, 23 x 34 cm, 2008. Reproduced with permission of the photographer and author.

Figure 9.3   Delvin J. Slick, *The Renegades*, black-and-white photograph, 24 x 16 cm, 2008. Reproduced with permission of the photographer and author.

Goats and other animals present lessons, sometimes humorously and with a tinge of eagerness, sometimes with the ramifications of misbehavior evident in consequences.

Shonto Canyon, pictured in Figure 9.4, communicates the ruggedness and beauty of the landscape, and we are presented with another aspect of the sacred. Delvin's memories come from here. "The canyon is like the backyard of where I live in Arizona. As a young boy I used to herd sheep in this canyon." Shonto Canyon is sacred for Delvin and for Navajo people. In fact, he adds, "Not just for me, but for the ancestors, the Anasazi." There are ruins that they left of their existence in this canyon, and their lives continue to be remembered and cared for here. This photograph illustrates the complexity of the land, its history, and the multiplicity of senses it conveys and carries.

With the beauty and power of the land carved out in the canyon come challenges and hardships of life on the reservation. Delvin indicates that the water in the photograph is important for its life giving, but water can also become deadly: "The [Shonto Canyon] water was like the most used water resource for the livestock. And sometimes during the monsoon season, it would flood and create a very muddy place. This was a problem for our livestock. They would always be stuck in the mud, and the mud was like quicksand, but slower." The land holds contradictions, blessings, and dangers, stories of the people from the past and present, all within a balance that is connected and whole.

Finally the photograph *T'aa' Łíí'* [Three Horses], illustrated in Figure 9.5, indicates a peaceful and restful moment in Delvin's photographic journey. "I was driving around one evening to take pictures and I came across these horses grazing peacefully by the lake. When I took this picture, there was a beautiful sunset to my left and the color was just too beautiful to miss." Taken at Wheatfields Lake, the photograph is soothing and reflects the comfort both horse and human can find in this land near lake and mountains with rainfall and abundant forests. With the Chuska Mountains in the background, the photograph reflects a sense of place intimately connected to and part of the Navajo Nation. Diné viewers will recognize the landmarks, feel the solace and peacefulness of the land, and remember the stories of the people. Delvin tells us, "This picture is sacred to me because of how peaceful, colorful, and beautiful the world can be if you just take a moment to see it for yourself."

Through the powerful teaching philosophy of *Sá'ah Naagháí Bik'eh Hózhóó*, one grounded in cultural traditions, we are able glimpse at concepts and values connected with "natural processes, and the daily cycle of day and night, and the annual cycle of the seasons."[3] In these ways, Delvin helps us to glimpse sacred places and the world of memories, lessons, and traditions through his photographs. As the land itself holds them to remember and contemplate, his photographs encourage us to "drink" from places and gain knowledge from our surroundings through close observation and relationship. "Wisdom sits in places," says Dudley Patterson:

---

3   Diné College, "Educational Philosophy."

Figure 9.4   Delvin J. Slick, *Shonto Canyon*, black-and-white photograph, 24 x 16 cm, 2008. Reproduced with permission of the photographer and author.

Figure 9.5　Delvin J. Slick, *T'aa' Łii'* [Three Horses], black-and-white photograph, 24.5 x 16 cm, 2008. Reproduced with permission of the photographer and author.

It's like water that never dries up. You need to drink water to stay alive, don't you? Well, you also need to drink from places. You must remember everything about them. You must learn their names. You must remember what happened at them long ago. ... Then you will see danger before it happens. You will walk a long way and live a long time.[4]

There is wisdom, knowledge, and relationships evident in places. Similar to the work of Laura Pérez regarding Chicana and Indigenous art and images, Delvin's photographs "teach us to perceive and imagine differently, and that seeing is a learned, revealed, ever-changing, and transformative process, whether we do so through the mind, the eyes, the heart, or the spirit."[5] They help us to encounter moods, presence, and the spirit (sacred quality) of place. In these ways, the sacred and sacred places are "not only something made or declared holy; [they are] also something shared, a collective experience necessary in order to keep oral traditions and sacred ways vital."[6] Just as for Delvin, they reveal the ancestors and holy people, instructions and lessons for living, and stories of the animals that live in sacred places. The visual images and photographs coupled with interpretations are powerful statements that reflect the interconnectedness of all beings, and are a concrete recognition of the importance of beauty and power in sacred places.

---

[4]   Dudley Patterson quoted in Keith Basso, *Wisdom Sits in Places* (Albuquerque, 1996), p. 127.

[5]   Laura E. Pérez, *Chicana Art: The Politics of Spiritual and Aesthetic Altarities* (Durham, 2007), p. 306.

[6]   Talbot, "Spiritual Genocide," p. 7.

Chapter 10

California Imagery in Context: The Mono Basin Kutzadika'a Paiutes

Angela D. Blaver

This chapter is organized thematically and chronologically, beginning with the context of the indigenous tribes in North America and then focusing on the Kutzadika'a Paiute of the Mono Basin in California. The intersection between the Kutzadika'a and the outsiders was rife with conflict, but more importantly this confluence contributed to cultural changes and a diminishment of traditional practices. Three successive images of indigenous peoples are discussed, which were influenced by three waves of the outsiders: Spanish, Mexicans, and Americans. While there were multiple intersections between the outsiders and the indigenous, the two of concern herein are that of the changing image of indigenous in relation to the land and water, as well as the care and treatment of the dead.

The history of Native Peoples' inhabitation of the landmass now known as the United States (US) existed for thousands of years prior to the arrival of successive modern-day incursions of the Spanish (1769), Mexicans (1821), and Americans (1848). More specifically, the peoples living in the western US in the state of California had distinct regional civilizations, cultural beliefs and practices, ecosystems and foods, and languages prior to interactions with outsiders. While there can be no definitive assessment of population numbers, it is certain that before "discovery" there were tens of thousands of California natives, perhaps even hundreds of thousands, with some estimates significantly higher.

Christianity, especially Catholicism, was pivotal in California in the intersection of what some might call a "collision" between the indigenous communities and the outsiders. The mission system had its greatest impact on coastal California and its Native Peoples, but the reverberations were felt throughout the state. In the 1700s, the Catholic hierarchy, in conjunction with the various militaries, influenced the initial perception of the Native Americans as starving, immoral, and uncivilized. These opinions encouraged several responses on the part of the settlers, including the introduction of formal agriculture and religious training, as well as the suppression of native cultures, practices, and languages. Violence, including beatings, rapes, and even murder against indigenous peoples, was routinely condoned and often sanctioned.

The inland central California Indians, particularly those living in the Eastern Sierra Mono Basin, were somewhat protected from outsiders due to the mountainous topography, harsh winters, and a seeming lack of natural resources.

Interactions with non-Indians were brief and transient. This changed over time as exploration and settlement moved further and further inland and precious metals were discovered. Mining was introduced in the mid 1800s, particularly in Dog Town, Monoville, Main Lundy, Aurora, Bodie, and Masonic. Thus began more complex interactions, exchanges, and influence between the native peoples and those arriving on the land known as the Mono Basin.

Native Americans in the United States

At the time that Juan Ponce de Léon and the Spanish landed in what is now known as Florida in 1513, there was great diversity present among the Native Peoples in North America. There were distinct language groups, cultural practices, and belief systems. Depending on the ecosystem and land sustainability, the people could be nomadic, seminomadic, or agrarian and this might vary according to the seasons of the year. Most Native Peoples drew on subsistence support from hunting, fishing, and the gathering of natural fruit and vegetables, as well as more sedentary forms of agriculture and horticulture. Communities exhibited advanced "political and social refinement, as well as sophisticated control of resources,"[1] and the design and construction of advanced forms of architecture. The communities that they created could be informally or formally organized based on family, village, clan, band, and/or tribe. These groupings could be smaller than a hundred members or number in the thousands. While there is no definitive and universally accepted way of determining the overall population in the 1500s at first European contact, it is thought that the Native American population at the time was upwards of 1.8 million[2] and quite possibly even as high as 20 million[3] with approximately 8–12 million north of Mexico.[4] However, due to disease, relocation, changes in nutrition and diet, forced labor and murder, these numbers dropped considerably, and Native Peoples were reduced to approximately 530,000 by the twentieth century.[5] This decline was uneven and regional, as the initial contacts with outsiders were concentrated on the east and west coasts, spreading inland.

Although the various Native Americans did not have a universal culture, there were several similar characteristics regarding major life events across the

[1]   For more detailed discussion of the advanced civilizations in what became known as the "New World," see David E. Stannard, *American Holocaust: The Conquest of the New World* (New York, 1992), p. 18.

[2]   Douglas H. Ubelaker, "North American Population Size, A.D. 1500 to 1985," *American Journal of Physical Anthropology*, 77 (1988): 289–94.

[3]   S. Ryan Johansson, "The Demographic History of Native Peoples of North America: A Selective Bibliography," *Yearbook of Physical Anthropology*, 25 (1982): 133–52.

[4]   Stannard, *American Holocaust*, p. 11.

[5]   Clark S. Larsen, "In the Wake of Columbus: Native Population Biology in the Postcontact Americas," *Yearbook of Physical Anthropology*, 37 (1994): 109–54.

peoples.[6] There was usually an acknowledgment of birth, naming, entry into adulthood, pairings or marriage, and death. Many of these pivotal events were signified by custom or ceremony, and kinship was key. There were traditions that surrounded the social aspects of gender, age or generational status, family, food, games, musical instruments, dancing, and celebrations. Work roles were loosely or firmly prescribed between men and women including cooking, childcare, hunting, cultivation, harvesting and gathering, medicine, and tool making and use.[7] While clothing was often utilitarian and seasonal, individuality or status could be indicated by adornment, jewelry, and headgear. Hair length, styling, shaving, plucking, piercings, tattoos, and/or ritualized scarring were also used to enhance beauty, indicate a pivotal event such as a death, or signify an advancement in rank or standing.

There were a variety of belief systems, with oral history and storytelling common, including a variation of one or more creation narratives of the people, the land, natural phenomena, and primary food sources such as fish or buffalo. In fact, Native Peoples often had a unique conception or understanding of "place and space," where the people were perceived as integral to the land and responsible for its caretaking.[8] Attention to animals and forces of nature were not unusual, nor was an acknowledgment and interpretation of the power of prophecy, omens, and dreams.[9] The peoples "observed the elements, watched for disturbances to animal and plant life and took these as good signs or warnings because any disruption could threaten our lives."[10] These were opportunities for a greater understanding of values, how the world works, and the relationship between nature, humans, and the supernatural. Shamans and medicine people were often consulted for clarification, as these individuals were considered mediators and interpreters between and among the various levels of existence. The range and degree of power was significant, and as Vine Deloria, Jr. notes:

> Our ancestors invoked the assistance of higher spiritual entities to solve pressing problems, such as finding game, making predictions of the future, learning about medicines, participating in healings, conversing with other creatures, finding lost objects, and changing the course of physical events through relationships

[6] Angie Debo, *A History of the Indians of the United States* (Norman, 1984), pp. 3–18.

[7] Ibid.

[8] Rupert Costo, "The Indians Before Invasion," in Rupert Costo and Jeannette H. Costo (eds.), *The Missions of California: A Legacy of Genocide* (San Francisco, 1987), pp. 9–28.

[9] Jon Butler, Grant Walker, and Randall Balmer, *Religion in American Life: A Short History* (New York, 2008), pp. 1–20.

[10] Freda McDonald, "No Longer an Indian," in Jace Weaver (ed.), *Native American Religious Identity: Unforgotten Gods* (Maryknoll, 2002), p. 72.

with the higher spirits who controlled the winds, the clouds, the mountains, the thunders, and other phenomena of the natural world.[11]

There were a variety of beliefs regarding death and the removal of the body, as well as whether there was some type of afterlife, including a return of the dead or rebirth. Inheritance, mourning rites, cremation/burial practices, and how to speak of the dead were regulated in one way or another.

The various groups, bands, tribes, and societies interacted with each other, due to proximity or seasonal migrations. There is evidence of coinage, sharing, bartering and trade, competition over resources and warfare. Disease was not unknown, including toothache, arthritis, parasites, infectious disease, bacterial infections, and even tuberculosis.[12] It should also be noted that the indigenous peoples of North America did not have domesticated animals that were used as food supplies. As such, Native Americans did not produce or consume dairy products such as milk or cheese, resulting in a physiology that does not tolerate these food sources well. Instead, indigenous peoples evolved tailored diets based on the nutrition available in their milieu. This would prove to have a detrimental impact on Native Americans over time as contact with colonizers increased, natural food sources dwindled, and non-native and dairy-based alternatives proved to be inadequate or even harmful.[13]

While this summary of US Native Peoples is brief and intended to provide an overall context, it can be generalized that the indigenous civilizations were complex, multidimensional societies prior to European contact. After outsider encounters, each community's ability to adapt and survive over time has been influenced more by accident of location or isolation than by any kind of colonizer intent. Given the episodic waves of foreign infectious diseases, forcible relocation, disruption of social mores, and physiological stress from inappropriate diet,[14] it is apparent that indigenous peoples possessed a highly adaptive and intelligent approach to life that enabled survival to the present time under such overwhelming and destructive pressures.

---

[11]   Vine Deloria, Jr., *The World We Used to Live In* (Golden, 2006), p. xix.

[12]   Some scholars argue that the presence of tuberculosis co-occurs with high population, which suggests that the populations of indigenous peoples in the Americas were significant prior to European contact. For further information, see Larsen, "In the Wake of Columbus."

[13]   Thomas L. Jackson, "Father Serra Meets Coyote," in Rupert Costo and Jeannette H. Costo (eds.), *The Missions of California: A Legacy of Genocide* (San Francisco, 1987), pp. 99–110.

[14]   Florence C. Shipek, "Saints or Oppressors: The Franciscan Missionaries of California," in Rupert Costo and Jeanette H. Costo (eds.), *The Missions of California: A Legacy of Genocide* (San Francisco, 1987), pp. 29–48.

Native Americans in California

Located on the west coast of the United States, California is unique in many ways as it is an uncommonly large state encompassing a multitude of flora and fauna, climates, and topography within a landmass of over 160,000 square miles. The California Native Americans had particular food sources, clothing, tools, storage technologies, and homes distinct to each region, including the coast, forest areas, deserts, and the mountains. Scholars have delineated the various tribal groupings based on particular locales as well as shared social conventions such as language because state lines drawn on a map do not take into account sovereignty or group membership. Using this measurement, the core California cultural areas include tribes inhabiting the Northwest, Northeast, Central, and South, with the Great Basin and Colorado River regions maintaining language and tribal ties that blended further east and north.[15] The following are examples of tribal groups within each region: Northwest—Yurok and Shasta; Northeast—Modoc; Central —Pomo, Miwok, and Yokut; South—Chumash, Luiseño, and Cahuilla; Great Basin—Paiute and Chemehuevi; and Colorado River—Mohave and Yuma.

Just as there was no universal indigenous civilization in what became known as the United States, there was no uniform society in the California region. However, there are two distinct generalizations that can be made. First, none of the California tribes practiced nomadism[16] in the fashion of the Apache in the Southwest or the Plains Indians. These peoples followed the buffalo as they migrated, which were a central source of food, clothing, fuel, and tools. Instead, California tribes were land-based and established in their respective regions, with some moving in a seminomadic fashion within those boundaries or sharing overlapping regions with others.[17] Thus, they developed niches and specialties particular to their local ecosystems. For instance, acorns were gathered from mature oak trees and could be stored for up to two years in sophisticated storage systems, including woven baskets and clay pottery containers. Using a water-leaching method, the acorn tannins were removed for better taste and digestion. Resource management was engaged with controlled fire burning of debris, underbrush, and other trees, which reduced moth and weevil infestations and encouraged adequate spacing,

---

[15] See Alfred L. Kroeber, *Handbook of the Indians of California* (Washington, DC, 1925) and

James J. Rawls, *Indians of California: The Changing Image* (Norman, 1986).

[16] In relation to Native Peoples, the term "nomadism" is used here to describe communities that moved in cycles based on resource availability, and seasonal and familiar locales where they knew their needs could be met. For further discussion, see Theodore Binnema, *Common & Contested Ground: A Human Environmental History of the Northwest Plains* (Norman, 2001), p. 37.

[17] Robert F. Heizer, *Languages, Territories, and Names of California Indian Tribes* (Berkeley, 1966).

fertilization, and growth of the oaks.[18] In fact, "indigenous peoples of California had a profound influence on many diverse landscapes—in particular, the coastal prairies, valley grasslands, and oak savannas, three of the most biologically diverse rich plant communities in California."[19]

Second, California Native Americans engaged in only two general funerary practices regarding the dead. The indigenous of the California region did not preserve their deceased, nor engage in water, exposure, or tree burials. Instead, they ritually burned the bodies, also known as cremation, or buried the dead.[20] This included partial burials with cairns, or stones placed over the body, especially during winter months. Over time the gravesite or burning place was often indistinguishable from the natural topography. Gravesites were not identified or visited as it was believed that the spirit had left the body. There were strong prohibitions surrounding the dead. Possessions, including treasured tools, jewelry, and housing, might be buried, burned, given away, inherited, or some combination thereof. Speaking the name of the dead could be prohibited, especially if it was believed that the deceased's spirit would be disturbed or return.[21] This was also done so that the grief-stricken could forget their sorrow. In the Great Basin region, this practice may have contributed to the linguistic diversity found in California as the people would have to generate new or alternative words for their deceased relative's name as well as the construct, element, or animal that they were named after. For instance, if someone was named "Rabbit" and they passed away, another term would have to be generated to mean the animal "rabbit."

Colonization and Missionization in California

While the land that became known as the United States was "discovered" by Europeans in 1513, formal expansion and colonizing of the west coast did not occur until the 1700s. Initially, the Jesuits and the Spanish military began settling what is now called Baja California in present-day Mexico. The Jesuits were replaced with the Franciscan order in 1643, and these missionaries were largely

---

[18]   Stephen J. Pyne, *Fire in America: A Cultural History of Wildland and Rural Fire* (Princeton, 1982).

[19]   M. Kat Anderson, *Tending the Wild: Native American Knowledge and the Management of California's Natural Resources* (Berkeley, 2005), p. 2.

[20]   See Omer C. Stewart, "The Northern Paiute Bands," in *Anthropological Records* (vol. 2:3, Berkeley, 1939); and Omer C. Stewart, "Culture Element Distributions: XIV. Northern Paiute," in *Anthropological Records* (vol. 4:3, Berkeley, 1941).

[21]   See, for example, Robert F. Heizer, *The Natural World of the California Indians* (Berkeley, 1980); Kroeber, *Handbook of the Indians of California*; and Alfred L. Kroeber, "Culture Element Distributions: XI. Tribes Surveyed," *Anthropological Records*, 1/7 (1939): 435–40.

responsible for colonizing coastal California.[22] There was a systematic way that the missions were established in cooperation with the militia. The missionaries were representatives of the Spanish government, whose goal was to develop this region.[23] The military was present to protect Spanish interests and enforce Spanish law. However, the Spanish did not have adequate resources, human or financial, to settle the area properly. Thus, conveniently, while educating and converting the indigenous peoples to Catholicism, the Spanish crown would gain a foundation of laborers in California with these new neophyte workers to assist in farming, herding, and ranching.[24] Essentially, indigenous peoples would be used to colonize their own land.

However, the invaders moved beyond baptism and newly altered work roles. In practice, the baptized Native Americans were kept segregated from the unbaptized and often were required to live near the mission in cramped quarters.[25] There was segregation based on gender and marital status. Children were separated from parents so as to limit the transmission of savage ways and ensure proper training. The indigenous people were exposed to new infectious diseases that were the result of exposure, transmission, and their new living situation. Contributing to the decline of their health was the consumption of dairy-based products, such as milk and cheese, which could not be digested properly. The Native Americans' movements and liberty were increasingly limited as farming, herding, and ranching spread over greater and greater tracts of land.[26] Non-native species began replacing the local plants and trees, thus transforming the landscape and bounty of the land that the indigenous had previously known. Wildlife was impacted as well, as domesticated herds and farm animals altered or destroyed natural habitats, game, and migration patterns. The health of the "conquered" peoples suffered as their diet and nutrition changed dramatically.[27]

The life situation of Native Peoples did not improve when the Spanish ceded the land to Mexican control. In fact, it often grew worse in some regions of California with the people essentially enslaved. As exploration and settlement encroached inland, the experiences and lifeways of the Native Americans were increasingly

---

[22] Sydney E. Alstrom, *A Religious History of the American People* (2nd edn., New Haven, 1972).

[23] Jeannette H. Costo, "The Sword and the Cross: The Missions of California," in Rupert Costo and Jeannette H. Costo (eds.), *The Missions of California: A Legacy of Genocide* (San Francisco, 1987), pp. 49–66.

[24] James A. Lewis, "The Natives as Seen by the Missionaries: Preconception and Reality," in Rupert Costo and Jeannette H. Costo (eds.), *The Missions of California: A Legacy of Genocide* (San Francisco, 1987), pp. 81–98.

[25] Florence C. Shipek, "California Indian Reactions to the Franciscans," *The Americas*, 41/4 (1985): 480–92.

[26] J. Costo, "The Sword and the Cross."

[27] Shipek, "Saints or Oppressors."

altered.[28] The immigration of the Anglo-Europeans in the 1800s brought some respite from outright slavery; however, the gold rush, mining, ranching, and other commercial interests ensured that the original peoples of California were pushed aside at best.

Intersection of Outsider and Native Beliefs – Imagery of the California Indians

The indigenous in the California region have been described in many ways by invaders, sea captains, politicians, traders, colonizers, geographers, writers, and historians over time as: mission—gentile—tame—wild—useful and hostile.[29] It should be noted that these observers were not disinterested or unbiased. There was little to no effort expended in understanding the customs or lifeways of the Native Americans.[30]

The various waves of colonizers conceptualized the Native Americans in California in three distinct and successive ways: as uncivilized and godless; as cheap labor; and finally as exploited victim, which rapidly turned into unwitting obstruction. Each image was based primarily on the needs of the outsiders, regardless of how the indigenous people internalized layered perceptions of themselves and their world. Initially, California Indians were called "diggers," a pejorative that was applied to some groups in particular such as the Hupa, Karok, and Trinity River tribes.[31] The name also indicated harvesting and gathering activities, without perceiving or acknowledging the complexity of these short-term primary actions (nutrition and storage) and their long-term secondary purposes (maintenance, fertilization, and cultivation).[32] The intricate social, political, and technological development of these peoples were largely invisible to non-Indians, particularly to Spanish soldiers and missionaries.[33] This contributed to the first image of Native Americans in this region as savage, primitive, and in need of civilizing and religious conversion.[34] At this time, unbaptized Native Americans were considered gentiles, whereas the baptized were termed neophytes. Conceptually, the indigenous were "free," yet it was their duty to "work" or engage in meaningful enterprise, as

---

[28]   Jack Norton, "The Path of Genocide: From El Camino Real to the Mines of the North," in Rupert Costo and Jeanette H. Costo (eds.), *The Missions of California: A Legacy of Genocide* (San Francisco, 1987), pp. 111–30.

[29]   Rawls, *Indians of California*, p. 13.

[30]   Norton, "The Path of Genocide"; Shipek, "California Indian Reactions to the Franciscans."

[31]   Stephen Powers, *The Tribes of California: Introduction and Annotations by Robert F. Heizer* (Berkeley, 1976), p. 90.

[32]   Norton, "The Path of Genocide."

[33]   Lewis, "The Natives as Seen by the Missionaries."

[34]   Rawls, *Indians of California*.

defined by the Spanish. The ultimate goal was to transform the Native American into something "better," ignoring and even denying the complexity from which they originated.

The second evolution of image of California Native Americans occurred after Mexican independence in 1821, where they were exploited as cheap labor in an extension of the hacienda–peon society from further south.[35] Whatever minimal communal or reciprocal relationship was present at the missions became nonexistent during this time. This was essentially a feudal society, where the Native Americans continued to be subjugated, and even fined and restricted in their movements. Many Native Americans who fell under this system lost fluency in their language and became inexperienced in their own cultural mores and ways, including hunting and gathering skills.

The third image of the indigenous occurred after the Anglo-European expansion into California in the mid 1800s, and initially was that of an exploited victim of Mexican subjugation. However, this view changed rapidly to that of the discovery of a useful class of workers already "trained" by the missionaries and rancheros. After further immigration, ranching, the gold rush, and the advent of mining in California, Native Americans became more of a threat and even an obstruction to further expansion and enterprise.[36] In essence, the indigenous were perceived as standing in the way of the appropriate and legitimate use of the rich natural resources of the new land known as California.[37]

Paiutes in the Mono Basin

The Mono Basin is located in the north central part of California, flanked by the Eastern Sierras on one side and Nevada on the other (see Figure 10.1). The topography in this region includes high desert, the Eastern Sierras, and the only salt lake in California (Mono Lake), fed by freshwater streams, which has two islands that are crucial for over 200 nesting and migrating bird species. It is an arid region of high altitude (approximately 6,781 feet) with four distinct seasons. There are several freshwater springs, creeks, streams, and lakes in the area.

There were a variety of tribes that lived or traveled in the Mono Basin area. This included the Mono Lake Paiutes (originally termed as *Cuzavi-dika*, now known as Kutzadika'a), the Bridgeport Paiutes (originally called *Paxai-dika*[38] and now identified as *Pogaiticutta*[39]), and the Coleville Paiutes (called the *Onabe*

---

[35] Rawls, *Indians of California.*

[36] Ibid.

[37] Norton, "The Path of Genocide."

[38] Julian H. Steward, "Ethnography of the Owens Valley Paiute," *Publications in American Archaeology and Ethnology*, 33/3 (1933).

[39] Grace Dick, personal communication, 9 March 2009.

Figure 10.1   Angela Blaver, Map of California with insert photograph of Mono
Lake, California, 2009. Used with permission of the author.

dukadu[40] or *Onaticutta*[41]). These groups were regarded as part of the Paiute tribal
family because of their physical location and language base of Uto-Aztecan, most
particularly the Numic branch.[42] It is of some debate as to whether these bands or
tribes should be considered Northern,[43] Southern,[44] or Owens Valley Paiutes,[45] as

---

[40]   Alan D. Blaver, personal communication, 9 March 2009.

[41]   Grace Dick, personal communication.

[42]   Some people say "Shosonean." Numic is a large group encompassing most of
the Great Basin, and the term comes from the word "Numa" or "the people." Catherine
S. Fowler, "Northern Paiute" and "Owens Valley Paiute," in Mary B. Davis (ed.), *Native
America in the Twentieth Century* (New York, 1994).

[43]   Stewart, "The Northern Paiute Bands"; Stewart, "Culture Element Distributions."

[44]   Harold E. Driver, "Culture Element Distributions: VI. Southern Sierra Nevada," in
Anthropological Records (vol. 1:2, Berkeley, 1937).

[45]   Steward, "Ethnography of the Owens Valley Paiute."

they were seminomadic peoples who were mutually influenced by their surrounding communities. For the purposes of this writing, band or tribe names will be used.

Great Basin Indians, which included the Mono Basin, have been described by early ethnologists as among the "poorest" indigenous encountered by outsiders, who believed these people existed on a subsistence level, especially when compared to coastal California Indians.[46] This must have been based on limited data or perceptual inaccuracy, at least in the case of the Mono Basin indigenous. The original peoples of the Mono Basin were successful fishermen and hunters of antelope, deer, rabbit, and waterfowl. Pine nuts, berries, seeds, roots, and other plants were harvested. Pandora moth larvae were also gathered, cooked, and prepared, which were a delicacy called *piyaga*.[47] They were excellent spear and arrowhead makers, using local obsidian. These peoples were also weavers. The making of nets, traps, mats, sacks, and blankets, and several variations of baskets, including those for hats, cradles, storage, carrying, winnowing, sifting, and cooking were serious occupations of women and men that demanded high degrees of skill.[48] In addition, there were social and leisure activities such as singing, storytelling, music (from several instruments including drums, flutes, etc.), and games involving chance, guessing, dice, wrestling, and target skills. All of these areas of existence indicate a high degree of success and satisfaction in multiple areas of social and cultural life.

Mono Basin Intersection – Land, Water, and Death

The Mono Lake Paiute were known as Kutzadika'a, or "fly eaters," in their native language. This is because they made a salty, protein- and calorie-rich soup or small biscuits from the dried pupae of the brine flies, called *kutsavi*, which are harvested from Mono Lake. The following story illustrates how the Kutzadika'a people internalized the centrality of the lake and its resources into their personal history.

> Many years ago, a giant trout jumped from lake to lake, leaving little fish behind
> him in the water to feed the people, the coyotes, and the bears. When the giant
> fish came to Mono Lake, the Kutzadika'a people tried to keep him there so that
> he would give them little fish forever. The giant trout was very slippery and
> hard to hold, so the people journeyed into the mountains and found two unusual

---

[46] Kroeber, *Handbook of the Indians of California*; Rawls, *Indians of California: The Changing Image*.

[47] My grandmother provided me with a number of conversations on these topics over the years.

[48] Although in the past it was often presented in anthropological and historical literature as the task of women, the men in our tribe did basket making and weaving also, mostly nets, strainers, and "catchers." See also Steward, "Ethnography of the Owens Valley Paiute."

rocks, a big black rock and a big white rock, which they carried to the lake and heaved on top of the giant trout to hold him down in their lake:

> The giant trout thrashed about and was able to escape from under the rocks. As he angrily splashed away to another lake, he declared that the Kutzadika'a would never have fish or sweet water from the lake. The giant trout looked over his shoulder and felt sorry for the Kutzadika'a when he saw their sad faces, so he whispered that he would still feed the people with kutsavi, from Mono Lake.

> The rocks left behind then became the Black (Negit) and White (Paoha) Islands in the lake. As the giant trout promised, the Kutzadika'a never went hungry, the water of Mono Lake became too salty to drink, and no fish has ever been seen there since.[49]

The Kutzadika'a were a seminomadic people who moved from the west side of the lake, near the freshwater creeks and streams in the spring, to the east side of the lake in the fall for the annual pine nut gathering, greater sunshine, less snow, and availability of winter waterfowl. They developed distinct oral histories, origin stories, and belief systems. They also traveled many miles in the summers traversing the Sierras to Yosemite Valley to interact and trade with the Miwok.[50]

The Kutzadika'a were renowned and esteemed basket makers in their time, and these baskets continue to be prized today as excellent examples of combined artistry and utility as the following story details:[51]

> From our house overlooking the Mono Basin I can visualize the life that was. Everywhere I look are paths or campsites, which my relatives used, and it brings back such fond memories. Now there is no campsite or grandparents, this makes me sad. … My grandparents were Young Charlie and Nellie. I remember when we were children we would be delighted to visit our grandmother. She lived in a tent-like house near a beautiful meadow; further away was Rush Creek. I can still smell the sage and smoke from the campfire and the smell of willows being prepared for making baskets. … Our own Mono Lake baskets were considered the finest at the time. We would sit for hours watching the women with their

---

[49]   Angela D. Blaver, "Negit and Paoha: How the Black and White Islands Came to Be in Mono Lake," in Jonnie Reinhold, Rachel Cherny, and Kathleen J. Martin (eds.), *Osiyo: The Work of Indigenous Scholars* (San Luis Obispo, 2008), vol. 10, pp. 20–21. Reprinted with permission of the editors.

[50]   See B.W. Aginsky, "Culture Element Distributions: XXIV. Central Sierra," in *Anthropological Records* (vol. 8:4, Berkeley, 1943); Driver, "Culture Element Distributions."

[51]   Craig D. Bates and Martha J. Lee. *Tradition and Innovation: A Basket History of the Indians of the Yosemite–Mono Lake Area* (Yosemite National Park, 1991).

skilled hands, perfecting their masterpieces, each with their own design and technique.[52]

A partial list of basket makers includes: Nellie and Tina Charlie, Lula Charlie Hess, Daisy Charlie Mallory, Carrie Bethel, Minnie Mike, and Maggie Howard. Various collections of basketry, including the very large gift baskets to the smaller burden baskets, of the Mono Lake and Yosemite areas are housed and on display at the Yosemite Museum in Yosemite National Park, California.

It is unknown exactly when the outsiders first encountered indigenous peoples in this territory. However, with the advent of mining in 1852, including Dog Town, Monoville, Main Lundy, Aurora, Bodie, and Masonic mines, immigrants, miners, ranchers, and storekeepers flooded the area.[53] This was in conjunction with various land acts in the state of California that enticed farmers and ranchers to the Owens Valley and beyond, which was increasingly sectioned off for ranching and sheepherding. Even the precious and valuable pine and piñon trees in the Mono Lake area were cut down and used for lumber and fuel, particularly for Bodie, permanently altering the landscape and diminishing the local pine nut sources. Religious groups and sects also followed contributing to change and loss, including Mormons, Catholics, and several other Christian denominations.[54] Apparently, few of the Kutzadika'a were converted at this time.

Because the Kutzadika'a relied on seasonal movement and the maintenance of their various ecosystems, the coming of the outsiders with ideas about spiritual practice, land ownership, and domesticated animals significantly changed their lifeways. They were unable to sustain their communities when they were restricted to areas too small to support their way of life. Similar to James Rawls's image of the California Indian as an obstacle, and ever more relegated to the margins of their previous existence, the Kutzadika'a were forced to adapt. Unfortunately, consistent with the missionization legacy of the indigenous as cheap labor, many of the Kutzadika'a men became workers in the local mines, or adapted their livelihoods in the service of the outsiders as ranchers, sheepherders, and shopkeepers.[55] Some of the women became cooks, cleaners, and such, also for the benefit of the outsiders.

---

[52] Elma C. Blaver, "Prologue," in Craig D. Bates and Martha J. Lee, *Tradition and Innovation: A Basket History of the Indians of the Yosemite–Mono Lake Area* (Yosemite National Park, 1991).

[53] Earl W. Kersten, "The Early Settlement of Aurora, Nevada, and Nearby Mining Camps," *Annals of the American Association of Geographers*, 54/4 (1964): 490–507.

[54] Butler, Walker, and Balmer, *Religion in American Life: A Short History*.

[55] Emil M. Billeb, *Mining Camp Days* (Berkeley, 1968).

Land and Water

Corresponding with James Rawls's image of the Native American as exploited victim, there was belated federal recognition that the indigenous people of California were the original inhabitants of the land. The US Congress did reach the conclusion that non-reservation Native Americans should be compensated with public domain land of their own. This was the direct result of three acts of Congress in 1887,[56] 1891,[57] and 1910.[58] Several of the adult Kutzadika'a men of identifiable families applied for and were given federal land grant allotments near Mono Lake in the early part of the twentieth century. The application procedure was a formal and lengthy process, involving a substantial amount of paperwork and the assistance of third parties. A letter dated 1 February 1919 from the Superintendent in Bishop, California to a local Mono Lake rancher's family member states:

> I enclose a form of affidavit wanted from Young Charlie, Indian of Mono Lake. I wish you to please write on the blank lines, using the first person, describing the kind of improvements, such as a house, fences, etc., constructed by Young Charlie on his own land, also the date which he located on the land, which date should be before he made application for it, also what he has raised, and whether he has occupied it continuously. ... If you write this for Young Charlie, I wish you to please write it as though he was writing it himself. ... Young Charlie must sign the affidavit, also two other persons, either white or Indian as corroborative witnesses. ... The whole matter should be sworn to and signed by an officer of some capacity, either a postmaster or Notary Public. ... The securing of this affidavit is very important, and I wish you to obtain it for me if possible, as I must forward it to the U.S. Land Office for their information.

Interestingly, there were no valuable mineral deposits in or on the land that was deeded back to the indigenous people, and this was explicitly spelled out in writing on the land grant allotment. "The Geological Survey has reported that these lands are non-mineral in character and that they should not be withheld from allotment on account of any valuable power-site or reservoir capability."[59] For instance, Young Charlie, the head of a large family, applied for and was given a land grant allotment near a freshwater creek that emptied into Mono Lake. He was issued a paper deed to forty acres. Young Charlie lived on the land with his family, growing and harvesting hay. Still navigating the new economy, he in turn sold this land in the latter 1920s, as he was getting older and was unable to grow crops in the high altitude. Young Charlie's "X" and thumbprint on the deed of sale was used

---

[56]   Indian General Allotment Act (Dawes Act).

[57]   Allotment Act of 1891.

[58]   Acts of Sixty-first Congress, Second Session, 1910, Chapter 431.

[59]   Further mention of Young Charlie and the Paiutes during the mining era can be found in Billeb, *Mining Camp Days*.

to identify him. However, he was not given the price of the land outright. Instead, the money was kept by the Walker River Agency in Schurz, Nevada, and he was issued monthly payments of $25–$50 by check until he was paid in full.

The land that Young Charlie owned and the fresh water that flowed through it would eventually become part of the Mono Basin Project of the Los Angeles Aqueduct after World War II. The Owens River section of the Aqueduct had already been completed during Young Charlie's lifetime, having begun in 1908 with support from President Theodore Roosevelt. This project, as with earlier incursions by the outsiders, would have yet another significant effect on the lake-based ecosystem in the region. With increasing diversion and limited fresh water from its tributary streams, Mono Lake began to shrink. This caused a steep rise in the salinity of the lake and a land bridge emerged to the Black Island (*Negit*), allowing carnivores to negatively impact the previously protected nesting and migration resting places for many migratory birds. With the assistance of scientific research coupled with public outcry, Mono Lake's importance to the region was recognized and the water level has been allowed to rise closer to its target level.[60]

Death and Burial Practices

Before the advent of outsiders, there were several customs that were followed after the death of one of the indigenous people. A "cry dance" began after sunset, where the people would tend a fire near the home of the dead person and dance and sing around it.[61] The clothes and possessions of the deceased would be burned in a prescribed and ritual fashion, as well as their traditional dwelling, usually made of sagebrush. The cry dance would continue until dawn of the next day, when the people would eat a meal together, which signified the end of the ceremony. Food was also put into the fire or placed nearby to feed the spirits of those that had died before. The deceased person was then buried and the people would move their camp. This was primarily done so as to avoid disturbing the recently deceased.

Burial in the ground was the most common for the Kutzadika'a, with stones used in the winter when the ground was frozen. While there is some evidence of cremation among Great Basin Indians,[62] it may have been under certain circumstances, such as when someone died far away[63] or if one was a warrior.[64] After the outsiders came, the indigenous people had to fundamentally change their customary burial ways. Because the Kutzadika'a were limited to where they could camp or live due to the ranches and landowners, they no longer could bury their dead as they had before the arrival of the outsiders. The Kutzadika'a were aware

---

[60]   David Policansky, "Science and Decision Making for Water Resources," *Ecological Applications*, 8/3 (1998): 610–8.

[61]   Grace Dick, personal communication.

[62]   Driver, "Southern Sierra Nevada."

[63]   Steward, "Ethnography of the Owens Valley Paiute."

[64]   Stewart, "The Northern Paiute Bands."

of the cemetery that had been created by and for the settlers, and they considered it with some consternation and caution. However, an "Indian cemetery" was dedicated by one of the Kutzadika'a landowners in the 1920s. It would seem that burial and treatment of the dead, like other changes wrought by the outsiders, contributed to changes in the lives of Kutzadika'a people even in the final farewells to loved ones.

One of the last traditional cry dances and burial ceremonies to take place occurred in the 1950s.[65] After this time, the cry dance was adapted. Now, it ends much earlier in the evening than before, usually around midnight.[66] Yet, this is still a mourning ceremony lasting six hours or more. Clothes and belongings are still burned, but houses and dwellings are not. Valuable and prized items are now inherited or given away to relatives and friends of the deceased. However, before a Kutzadika'a person is buried, a traditional Anglo-European funeral is often held at one of the two local churches, one of which is Presbyterian and the other Catholic. People come from far and wide to attend the ceremonies, so there are often several other groups of indigenous peoples in attendance. Christian and Catholic clergy and officials have viewed the funeral as an opportunity for the conversion and further education of people in attendance, a captive audience so to speak.[67] This has caused discomfort for people attending as there is a plurality of beliefs among the various individuals who have come with the goal of honoring the family and the departed. After the funeral, the person is buried, and thus, the final public farewell is that of a formal institution – quite far removed from the integrative and community-based release of yesteryear.

The necessity of creating a cemetery and largely adapting death customs is yet another example of how the Kutzadika'a were victimized by the outsiders. Although these practices were disrupted long ago, the goals of change and conversion to a Christian ethic continue. Burial customs and practices have great meaning to the societies that engage in them. This is a sadly ironic mirror image of the view of the California Indian as an obstruction to civilization, where instead the settlers were the obstruction for the Kutzadika'a civilization as they were unable to continue a key aspect of their lifeways, that of honoring the dead.

Missed Opportunities

The imagery of the Native Americans of California underwent three successive transformations, beginning with Spanish missionization in the 1700s where the indigenous were in need of civilizing and Christian instruction.[68] Subsequently, Native Americans were used as cheap labor sources under the brief Mexican regime.

---

[65]   Alan D. Blaver, personal communication, 9 March 2009.

[66]   Vicki Beasley, personal communication, 11 March 2009.

[67]   Alan D. Blaver, personal communication.

[68]   Rawls, *Indians of California: The Changing Image.*

This gave way to the Anglo-European's initial image of the indigenous as victims, but soon progressed to a perception of indigenous peoples as obstructions standing in the way of development, particularly that of land and natural resources.

Until the advent of outsiders, abrupt change was uncommon for the Kutzadika'a, as it was for most Native Americans. The Kutzadika'a were surrounded by predictable and consistent events, including seasons, migration patterns, hunting and harvesting cycles, family life, and even death. The mountains, the basin, the water, and the flora and fauna were permanent fixtures in their world. And, there was no need to abruptly change or disturb this pattern since it provided for all the peoples' needs. This thoughtful and measured existence was and is a hallmark of indigenous life. The people were accustomed to possessions as something that one could physically transfer to another person, as in the trading activities that they had previously known. The Kutzadika'a understood that one could move a stone, but not a rock or a mountain. It was a significant shift in worldview to imagine the possession and restriction of immense and permanent resources such as land or vast amounts of water.

Today, the Kutzadika'a are seeking federal recognition of their tribal status. This would have an immense impact on their ability to deal with local land issues as there is no reservation set aside specifically for them. This may also solidify their rights to the land upon which the "Indian cemetery" rests. Secondary outcomes of federal recognition would be increasing the tribe's ability to care for their elderly, boosting healthcare access, and securing funding for the education of Kutzadika'a youth, particularly post secondary schooling. All of these issues deserve recognition and the responsibility of care so that the Kutzadika'a can reclaim and reaffirm that which has been suppressed and supplanted by the outsiders.

Chapter 11

"Dancing the Comanches": The *Santo Niño*, *La Virgen* (of Guadalupe), and the Genizaro Indians of New Mexico

Bernardo P. Gallegos

She was looking forward to her yearly holiday celebration of praying, singing, dancing the Comanche dances, and eating with family on Christmas Eve. Ologia, Mom, Grandma, "Gram", Sister, Auntie, and Friend will be forever missed. As we continue on with our lives we will carry her strength, love, faith, and joy for life with us always.

—Obituary of Ologia Sanchez, *Albuquerque Journal*, 14 December 2007

The obituary for Ologia Sanchez, who passed away just over a year ago, speaks to her importance as the matriarch of a large family, which includes my own children, Bernardo, Mario, and Rosalea, and my granddaughter, Janelle. It also provides an entrée into the following essay, which explores the complex and now inextricably connected relationships between Catholicism, colonialism, education, and Indigenous practices.

Among nostalgic memories of Christmas pasts are those of the Comanche dances at the Sanchez/Sarracino home in the community of Atrisco in Albuquerque's South Valley. Referred to fondly as the *Heya Heyo* dances by the grandchildren, the ceremony, organized and led by Ologia and her sisters, took place in the living room transformed into a sacred space for the occasion. The songs and dances were passed down from their mother, Lucarita Sarracino of the village of Cabezon, located in the Rio Puerco Valley about seventy miles northwest of Albuquerque.

At the north end of the room, in front of a large picture window, a blanket with an image of "*La Virgen*" (of Guadalupe) was draped over the television set. On top of the blanket rested the *Santo Niño* ["holy child"] *de Atocha* in a small dark wooden cradle. Standing in front of the makeshift altar, Ologia and her sisters began the ceremony by praying a rosary. The sisters then led the family members and guests in singing and dancing "los Comanches." The subtly festive nature of the evening was characterized by family from distant places catching up on recent events, and an awaiting culinary feast of tamales, posole, red chili, and cloud nine salad. The celebratory mood, however, was overshadowed by the somber and serious energy with which the Sarracino sisters prayed, sung, and danced. The moment was solemn, as it was crystal clear that they took this time to ask the *Santo Niño* and *la Virgen* to assist their families in whatever way they could, and that was very serious business.

The Comanche songs were organized into four-line stanzas sung in Spanish with an Indian chorus in between that was distinct to the Sarracino sisters. Among the beginning verses are the following:

> *Del cielo viene bajando*
> *Un arco lleno de Flores*
> *Y en el medio del arco viene*
> *La Senora de mis Dolores*
> [Descending from the Heavens
> Comes a rainbow of flowers
> and in the middle of the rainbow arrives
> the Goddess/Lady of my Pain]

> *Heya, Heyo*
> *Heya, Heyo,*
> *He yayne yayne yayne ooo*

> *De el cielo viene bajando*
> *un arco con tres artoches*
> *y en medio del arco viene*
> *el Santo Niño de Atocha*
> [Descending from the Heavens
> Is a rainbow with three arrows
> and in the middle of the rainbow arrives
> the *Santo Niño de Atocha*]

> *Heya, Heyo*
> *Heya, Heyo,*
> *He yayne yayne yayne ooo*

> *Viva el sol vive la Luna*
> *Y la rosa de Castilla*
> *Y al Santo Niño de Atocha*
> *Que anda en Nuestra compania.*
> [The Sun lives, and so the Moon
> And the rose of Castilla
> and so the *Santo Niño de Atocha*
> who is in our company]

> *Heya, Heyo*
> *Heya, Heyo,*
> *He yayne yayne yayne ooo*[1]

---

[1]   The songs in this chapter are from the Sanchez/Sarracino clan's songs used with permission of the author.

The dances are performed with a rhythmic two-step character similar to Plains Indian round-dance steps. Hands are extended outward with palms up. The dancers act out the words with their arms and bodies, reaching up when talking about the sky. The verses speak to the relationship between "las Comanchitas," the *Santo Niño de Atocha*, and *La Virgen* (of Guadalupe). All of these three form a relationship that results from the colonial encounter between the Catholic Spanish empire and the communities of Indigenous peoples from Mesoamerica to the United States Southwest.[2]

Las Comanchitas, Captivity and Slavery

If one were to take the word *Comanchita* literally, it would signify a young Comanche girl. However, as the saying goes, context is everything, and in this case that is ever so correct. In New Mexico and in particular in the Sanchez/Sarracino Comanche ceremony, *Comanchita*, as the following verse attests, does not necessarily signify a young Comanche girl. The term speaks more to a young girl who was sold into servitude by Comanches, a practice that dominated the New Mexican landscape in the latter half of the eighteenth and the beginning of the nineteenth century:[3]

> *El Comanche y La Comancha*
> *Se fueron a Santa Fe*
> *Pa Vender Los Comanchitos*
> *Por azucar y café*
> [The Comanche and the Comancha
> Took a trip to Santa Fe
> To exchange the Comanchitos
> For some Sugar and Coffee]
>
> *Heya, Heyo*
> *Heya, Heyo,*
> *He yayne yayne yayne ooo*

---

[2]   Ramon A. Gutierrez, *When Jesus Came, the Corn Mothers Went Away, Marriage, Sexuality, and Power in New Mexico, 1500–1846* (Stanford, 1991); Robert Ricard, *The Spiritual Conquest of Mexico: An Essay on the Apostalate and the Evangelizing Methods of the Mendicant Orders in New Spain, 1523–1572* (Berkeley, 1966); José M., Kobayashi, *La educación como conquista* (Mexico City, 1985).

[3]   James Brooks, "'This Evil Extends Especially … To the Feminine Sex': Negotiating Captivity in the New Mexico Borderlands," *Feminist Studies*, 22/2 (Summer, 1996): 279–309; Gutierrez, *When Jesus Came*; Estevan Rael-Gálvez, "Identifying Captivity and Capturing Identity: Narratives of American Indian Slavery, Colorado, and New Mexico, 1776–1934" (PhD diss., Ann Arbor, 2004).

Although this verse most likely does not describe a typical "slave trading scenario," it does function as a sort of metaphor and reminder to family members of their own origins. Thus, embedded in the ceremony is a family and community history of sorts.

Indian slavery was a prominent feature of the New Mexican cultural and demographic landscape during the Spanish (1598–21), Mexican (1821–46), and early American periods (1846–80s).[4] Comanches were the most prominent suppliers of Indian slaves whom they captured from other weaker tribes in the Plains.[5] Customary yearly fairs were held in Pecos, Taos, and Tome, and the primary commodity that the Comanches brought to trade were young Indian captives, mainly girls. As Brooks explains:

> Ransomed captives comprised an important component in colonial society …
> especially in peripheral villages [like Cabezon], where they may have represented
> as much as 40 percent of the "Spanish" residents. Girls and boys under the age
> of fifteen composed approximately two-thirds of these captives, and about two-
> thirds of all captives were women "of serviceable age" or prepubescent girls.[6]

Speaking to the origins of the captives, Fray Atanacio Dominguez, in the latter half of the eighteenth century, explained that the Comanches came to trade many objects including "pagan Indians whom they capture from other nations."[7] Robert Archibald notes that "in 1776 a young female Indian between twelve and twenty years old could be traded for two good horses and some trifles while a male slave was worth only half as much."[8] Interestingly, the above verse from the Sanchez/ Sarracino Comanche ceremony is testimony to the accuracy of folk history as articulated in this case through ritual performance. It may not have been Santa Fe, and perhaps not coffee and sugar they were trading for, and they were definitely not selling their own children, but in fact Comanches were certainly selling young Indigenous captives.

During the colonial period in New Mexico, the purchasing of slaves from the Comanches was a contested issue with officials both supporting and opposing the trade. According to Charles Kenner, "Most New Mexican Governors believed that it was a good idea because the redeemed captives were educated and

---

[4]   Lynn R. Bailey, *The Indian Slave Trade in the Southwest* (Los Angeles, 1973); Rael-Gálvez, "Identifying Captivity"; Gutierrez, *When Jesus Came*; James Brooks, Captives *& Cousins, Slavery, Kinship, and Community in the Southwest Borderlands* (Chapel Hill, 2002).

[5]   Brooks, "This Evil Extends …" p. 6; Charles Kenner, *A History of New Mexican-Plains Indian Relations* (Norman, 1969).

[6]   Brooks, *Captives & Cousins*, p. 283.

[7]   Ibid., p. 282.

[8]   Robert Archibald, "Acculturation and Assimilation in Colonial New Mexico," *New Mexico Historical Review*, 53 (July 1978), p. 208.

Christianized." Moreover, he explains, "clerics defended the trade as a potential means to save souls."[9]

Most often the young children that were sold into slavery had spent significant time among the Comanches. Moreover, the majority of the captives were women, and thus "Comanchitas" became a common endearing term to refer to the servant girls. In fact, in the Sanchez Comanche ceremony, the term *Comanchitas* is used in a highly affectionate way that serves as a sort metaphor for servant girls in general. Since the Sanchez/Sarracino clan, like many others in Atrisco, Armijo, Los Padillas, and Pajarito, in Albuquerque's south valley, are themselves descendants of Indian servants (mainly of Navajo origin). Their use of the term *Comanchitas* has become a signifier for their own servant/matriarchs who taught them the songs. As the following verses attest, the ceremony clearly highlights the spirituality of the family and places the Comanchitas (servant/matriarchs) at the center:

> *De los presentes del campo*
> *Te ofresemos florecitas*
> *Ya te pido niño Dios*
> *Que cuides las comanchitas*
> [Of those present here
> We offer you little flowers
> And we ask you Child-God
> Take care of the Comanchitas]

> *Santo Niño de Atocha*
> *Ay de digo a ti Niñito*
> *No te a podido pasiar*
> *La Comanchita un ratito*
> *Santo Niño de Atocha*]
> [I tell you my child
> The Comanchita has yet to hold you
> Even for a little while

> *Heya, Heyo*
> *Heya, Heyo,*
> *He yayne yayne yayne ooo*

> *Se retiran las Comanchitas*
> *Cumpleron su devocion*
> *Este niño chiquitito*
> *Lo llevo en mi Corazon*
> [The Comanchitas retire
> They completed their devotion

---

[9]   Kenner, *A History of New Mexican-Plains Indian*, p. 38.

This tiny child (*Santo Niño*)
I carry in my heart]

Heya, Heyo
Heya, Heyo,
He yayne yayne yayne ooo

The Indigenous servant girl/matriarchs were part of a larger category of Indian slave descendants most often referred to as *Genizaros* in the eighteenth and nineteenth centuries. Indian slavery was widespread in New Mexico, and by 1776 Genizaros and their descendants, most often referred to as *Coyotes* (mixed-bloods), are estimated to have comprised at least a third of the entire population of the province.[10] Musicologist and researcher Brenda Romero describes the relationship between Genizaro descendants and Comanche dances as follows:

> Comanche ceremonials in former genizaro villages in rural New Mexico are being "discovered", having been preserved for an unknown length of time by particular families who identified with their Indian ancestry and were not ashamed to preserve their heritage through yearly performances of songs and dances.[11]

The Sanchez/Sarracino clan, representative of the families to which Romero[12] refers, like my own, and countless others, are Genizaro descendants who, in 2007, were granted official recognition as Indigenous peoples by the New Mexico Legislature.[13] Ologia often spoke with great pride and affection for her Native American background, as did her daughter, Mary Jane, the mother of my children. Their narratives strongly align with the explanation by Romero above. Moreover, Ologia's husband, Guadalupe Sanchez, likewise is a descendant of a Navajo servant/matriarch whose name according to Lupe's father (Grandpa Theodosio) was Petra. She is pictured below with daughter and grandson.

Genizaro Indians of New Mexico

Antonio Casados of the pueblo of Nuestra Señora de Belén was, in the eyes of the Spanish Governor, a dangerous man. It was 1746 in the Royal Villa of Santa

---

[10]   Gutierrez, *When Jesus Came.*

[11]   Brenda Romero, "The Indita Genre of New Mexico: Gender and Cultural Identification," in Norma Ella Cantú and Olga Nájera-Ramirez (eds.), *Chicana Traditions: Continuity and Change* (Urbana, 2002), p. 73.

[12]   Ibid.

[13]   See New Mexico Legislature, House Bill 40, Senate Bill 59, "Genizaros, In Recognition," 2007.

Figure 11.1 Family photo of Petra Chavez (center), Navajo captive and matriarch of the Sanchez family of Atrisco, with her daughter and grandson Theodosio (right). Used with permission of the author.

Fe, and Don Pedro Meninduata, Governor of the province, ordered him confined in the Royal Guardhouse, for fear of the disruption of the peace that he might cause. Casados along with Luis Quintana, also of Belén, had walked to Santa Fe accompanied by over seventy other Indians from the pueblos south of Santa Fe. They carried with them a petition and letter that they had secured in person from the representative of the Viceroy in Mexico City. This urged the Governor of New Mexico to heed the complaints of the Christianized Indians in the province, and to negotiate with them—as there were so many enemy surrounding the province— that it was in the interests of the Crown to have the friendly Indians as allies. Casados had traveled to Mexico City where he by chance met Luis Quintana, also from New Mexico, and together they presented a petition to the *audencia* of the Viceroy, through the *abogado* [attorney] for the *Indios* "Cordova."

Casados was, by birth, a Kiowa Apache, purchased from other Apaches at an early age by a *Genizaro criado* [servant] named Miguelillo, at Ojo Caliente. He lived out most of his childhood as a servant in a Spanish household, like countless thousands of other Indian captives including Luis Quintana, also a Kiowa Apache, throughout the eighteenth and nineteenth centuries, in what is today considered the US Southwest and northern Mexico. The petition he was presenting to the Governor was on behalf of himself and several other "*Indios Genizaros*" of the pueblo of Belén, who had elected him as their captain. He argued:

> The Indians of Belen should have rights that other Indians had and their lands should be respected as they have given themselves in defense of the province, the King, and God, against the enemy gentiles surrounding the province. Moreover, Indians have occupied the Belén area since time immemorial, and it was just recently that the Spanish settlers had arrived and to the Indians detriment, encroached on their lands.[14]

More specifically, Casados asserted, he was "present in this court on account of two Spaniards who are residing in our pueblo, causing great injury by their *perjuicios* [prejudices] and devaluations [insults]."[15] As a result of the scarcities caused by the Spaniards presence many Natives had been obliged to leave to distant territories. "We therefore request that you order the Lieutenant Alcalde or the Alcalde Mayor to notify the said Antonio de Salazar to vacate our pueblo and return to his previous place of residence."[16]

In their testimony, the Spaniards of Belén told a very different story. According to them, there was no such pueblo as the petition stated. Belén was nothing more than a small *paraje* [hamlet]. Casados and Quintana, and the people they represented, were not a group of Indians but, rather, destitute people, with no

---

[14]   Spanish Archives of New Mexico (SANM I), Twitchell document 183, trans. Bernardo Gallegos.

[15]   Ibid.

[16]   Ibid.

language or semblance of culture. They were ungrateful servants, who had been rescued from paganism, educated in Spanish language and customs, and brought into the Christian world at the expense of the very Spaniards whose names they slandered in their petition. Moreover, the petitioners were liars, knaves, thieves, and fugitives from their masters, most notably, Diego Torres and Antonio de Salazar (Rio Abajo) who had recently brought them to the area.

The Governor, angered by the embarrassment that Casados and Quintana had caused him by appearing before his superiors in Mexico City, paid little heed to the Viceroy's letter and instead focused his questions on the actions of Casados and Quintana:

> By what right did you leave the province to go and cause this scandal when the proper venue for expressing a complaint was here [Santa Fe]? Why are you referring to the pueblo of Nuestra Señora de los Dolores de Belén when you know that such a pueblo does not exist, and what is the motive for bringing over seventy Indians of various pueblos with you?[17]

At the end of the hearing Casados and Quintana were ordered to be held in jail for the potential trouble that they could cause by inciting the other friendly Indians to protest against the Spanish.

Isleta Pueblo, 25 December 1994

I am standing inside of the adobe walls of the courtyard of the church of San Augustín in the Tiwa pueblo of Isleta waiting for the singers and dancers to enter. The courtyard, which sits inside a large dusty square at the center of the pueblo, is beginning to fill with mostly Tiwa people from the pueblo and a small contingent of Euroamericans, who for the most part look like tourists, getting out of their Saabs and Volvos and wearing lots of turquoise and nice sunglasses. The Isleta people are mostly well dressed as they come to celebrate Christmas Day in the traditional way. I was leaning on the wall when a man and woman approached me and asked if I knew where they could buy *"un hamburger."*[18] I pointed to a small trailer parked at the northwest corner of the large dusty plaza, which was currently serving as a parking lot. The woman, who looked as though she were in her late fifties, seemed very familiar. She wore a stocking cap over her shoulder-length black wavy hair and an old tattered and torn brown coat that covered a worn and loose pair of polyester pants. Her companion was short and walked with a cane, as it appeared that one of his legs was shorter than the other. He was poorly dressed as well, and together they clearly looked out of place.

---

[17] Ibid.

[18] Isleta Pueblo is known for delicious green-chili hamburgers during fiesta time.

She was brown-skinned and looked very Indian, but not Pueblo, more like the Ojibway (Chippewa) and Ho-Chunk (Winnebego) I had known while I attended college in LaCrosse, Wisconsin. He looked like a mixed-blood, or perhaps a light-skinned Mexican. I thought that I recognized her. She looked like a woman from Barelas, the neighborhood where I grew up and where both my maternal and paternal families had lived since the turn of the century, just south of downtown Albuquerque. Upon returning from the hamburger trailer, they got back into their car, which was parked right up against the adobe wall surrounding the courtyard, just next to the gate where the dancers, singers, and everyone else would enter. They were in a very large and old Plymouth with faded gold paint except for the left front fender that was brown. I could tell that they were very poor.

A while later, as the crowd began to gather, the couple entered the courtyard and stood next to me. As our eyes met, we greeted each other. I asked her if she was from Barelas and told her she looked familiar. They were both from Barelas and after identifying my family they moved closer to me and began to talk. People in South Barelas (fondly referred to as Tortilla Flats by its residents) know each other, and she knew both my mother's and father's families. She recalled that my (paternal) grandpa Amadeo was the janitor at West San Jose Elementary School, which I confirmed, and she remembered my mother, father, and uncles. She told me that she very much liked to come to the dances; she comes every year. She declared enthusiastically and with conviction, "*Yo soy India*" [I am Indian]. I asked her where her people were from. "*Vienen de Belén*" (They come from Belén), she responded. Actually, most of the people in Barelas came from Belén, Tome, Valencia, and the surrounding areas, or from the Manzano Mountain communities of Chilili, Tajique, or Torreon. My mother's family was from Tome, which was across the river from Belén and about thirty miles south of Albuquerque.

When I asked what kind of Indian she was, she said her father was a Mescalero Apache. Now, the Mescalaro reservation is quite far from Belén, and I thought it highly unlikely that her father was from the reservation, although I didn't want to ask any further for fear of being intrusive, impolite, and disrespectful. Interestingly, I know other people from Tome who likewise identify themselves as Mescalero, even though I know their families have no recent ties to the federally recognized Mescalaro tribe in southern New Mexico. It was, it seems, the way of Indian slave descendants to hang on stubbornly to an Indigenous identity by naming the closest Apache group they knew; perhaps, though, she was correct.

What Antonio Casados, Luis Quintana, the woman in the tattered jacket, and families like the Sanchez's have in common is a relentless desire to name themselves, even in the face of official opposition. In Santa Fe, in 1746, the attempt by the Belén Genizaros to assert themselves as an Indigenous group failed. More recently, the woman in the tattered jacket and the Sanchez/Sarracino clan are representative of people who proudly and stubbornly assert their Indianness in the face of official narratives that have authored the descendants of the captive Indian servants invisible. There is no federal tribal recognition or nation-to-nation sovereign status for the Indian slave descendants. We are on our own! Thus the

Comanche dances, as Romero asserts, function not only as religious ceremony and a collective exercise in maintaining a collective memory, but, moreover, as a declaration of Indian identity not granted in the dominant culture.[19]

Genizaros were central to the northward, eastward, and westward expansion of the Spanish empire and later the Mexican settlements in New Mexico.[20] After the reoccupation of New Mexico in 1692, following a twelve-year retreat south to El Paso del Norte, the purchase of young Indian captives by the *vecinos* [villagers] and Pueblo Indians began in earnest. In 1733, several adult Genizaros, the first generation, wrote and presented a petition to the Governor for permission to settle in the abandoned Tiwa Pueblo of Sandia, just north of present-day Albuquerque.[21] Their petition began as follows: *"Nosotros Los Hijos Genizaros de este Reino* ..." [We the Genizaro Children of this Kingdom, humbly ask ...]. They were not awarded the land grant, but a few years later the Governor did allow some Genizaros to settle in Valencia and Tome. These settlements were described as follows by a Spanish religious official, Fray Menchero, in the 1740s:

> This is a new settlement, composed of various nations, ... the Indians are of the various nations that have been taken captive by the Comanche Apaches, a nation so bellicose and so brave that it dominates all those of the interior country ... They sell people of all these nations to the Spaniards of the kingdom, by whom they are held in servitude, the adults being instructed by the fathers and the children baptized. It sometimes happens that the Indians are not well treated in this servitude, no thought being given to the hardships of their captivity ... Distressed by this, the missionaries informed the governor ... [who] ordered by proclamation throughout the kingdom that all the Indian men and women neophytes who received ill-treatment from their masters should report it to him. ... In fact a number did apply to him, and he assigned to them for their residence and settlement, in the name of his Majesty, a place called Valencia and Cerro de Tome, thirty leagues distant from the capital to the south, in a beautiful plain bathed by the Rio (del) Norte. There are congregated more than forty families in a great union, as if they were all of the same nation.[22]

In 1778 Fray Morfi, an ecclesiastical observer who chronicled the state of affairs, described Genizaros as follows:

---

[19]   Romero, "The Indita Genre of New Mexico." See also Hermanitos Comanchitos, *Indo Hispanic Rituals of Captivity and Redemption, Enrique Lamadrid* (Albuquerque, 2003).

[20]   Kenner, *A History of New Mexican-Plains Indian*; Gutierrez, *When Jesus Came.*

[21]   Spanish Archives of New Mexico (SANM I), Twitchell document 1208; trans. Bernardo Gallegos.

[22]   Declaration of Fray Miguel de Menchero from Charles W. Hackett, *Historical Documents Relating to New Mexico, Nueva Vizcaya, and Approaches Thereto* (Washington, DC, 1937), vol. 1, p. 395.

In all the Spanish towns of New Mexico there exists a class of Indians called genizaros. These are made up of captive[s] ... who were taken as youngsters and raised among us, and who have married in the province ... They are forced to live among the Spaniards, without lands or other means to subsist except the bow and arrow which serves them when they go into the back country to hunt deer for food ... They are fine soldiers, very warlike ... Expecting the genizaros to work for daily wages is a folly because of the abuses they have experienced, especially from the alcaldes mayores in the past ... In two places, Belen and Tome, some sixty families of genizaros have congregated.[23]

The practice of purchasing Indian children as servants persisted in earnest well into the American period in New Mexico. In the nineteenth century, almost all of the captives were of Navajo origin as most of the slave-taking expeditions were conducted in *Dinétah*—"Navajo Land"—by either Spanish/Mexican or Genizaro/ Pueblo troops or by certain Navajo groups themselves such as that of the Navajo rancher Antonio Cebolla Sandoval. David Brugge's examination of baptismal records indicates that most of the child servants during the Mexican period, which began in 1821, were Navajos.[24] An entry in the Albuquerque baptismal record for 6 May 1824 chronicles a typical scenario: the five-year-old Jose Antonio Aragon and four-year-old Maria Gertrudis, both identified as Navajos of Alameda, of unknown parents, were baptized in Albuquerque. Both had been purchased by Ramon Aragon.[25]

The extent of the Navajo slave trade perhaps is characterized best in the 1868 treaty negotiations between the Navajos and the US military at Fort Sumner. After the discussion of various issues, Barboncito, one of the Navajo negotiators, said, "I want to drop this conversation now and talk about Navajo children held as prisoners by Mexicans. Some of those present have lost a brother or a sister and I know that they are in the hands of Mexicans. I have seen some myself."[26] When asked by Colonel Samuel Tappan, "How many Navajos are among the Mexicans now?" the response was, "Over half the tribe."[27] In 1877, Navajo Agent Alexander G. Irvine wrote that, despite a more than ten-year-old US statute abolishing peonage, "Navajo Indians especially women are held as servants all over New Mexico and Southern Colorado receiving no compensation for their services except board and clothing."[28] Moreover, speaking of the Spanish American communities in 1907,

---

[23]   Juan Agustín Morfi, *Account of Disorders in New Mexico, 1778*, trans. Marc Simmons (Isleta: San Augustin Press, 1968), p. 34.

[24]   University of New Mexico, available in Coronado Room Zimmerman Library (CRZL), "Navajos in the Catholic Church Records of New Mexico," in David Brugge, *Research Report # 1* (Window Rock, 1965).

[25]   Archives of the Archdioceses of Santa Fe, Albuquerque Baptisms 1824, Reel 1.

[26]   "Navajos in the Catholic Church Records of New Mexico," p. 92.

[27]   Ibid.

[28]   Ibid.

it was reported that "pure blood Navajos who pass for Mexicans are still to be found in these communities."[29] In fact, as Estevan Rael-Galvez documents in his landmark dissertation, a multitude of full-blood Navajos were living in Spanish communities well up to the close of the nineteenth century.[30] Their descendants, moreover, continue to live in many of those communities. The Sanchez/Sarracino clan described earlier originated from the villages of Cabezon and San Ignacio, both located on the Rio Puerco (west of Albuquerque) and well into *Dinétah.*

Santo Niño de Atocha, the Santuario de Chimayo, and the Holy Dirt

mood?

The scent of adobe and illuminated candles permeated the dark room. A few rays of sunlight traveled through the two small side windows, allowing the persons inside to see. It was the last stop on our regular trip to the Santuario de Chimayo and the *Santo Niño* was the object of our journey. He was our reason for making the nearly two-hundred-mile round trip every couple of months at my grandma's insistence. The climax of our trip lay in his glass case on a chair wearing a light-blue cape and a hat with feathers. On his feet were white baby shoes with soiled soles. Besides candles that you could light for some change, the only other objects on the table, which was covered with a white linen cloth, were more baby shoes waiting in line for their own turn to be worn. They were left by anxious parents petitioning the *Santo Niño* to take care of their own newborns.

gifts.

My (maternal) grandma, Libradita, who raised me, was a devout believer in the powers of *Santo Niño* and the Holy Dirt of the Santuario de Chimayo. The *Santo Niño*, in fact, always occupied a central place in her home and, later, her room in my mom's house. Candles were regularly lit to the *Santo Niño*. Our frequent trips to the Santuario de Chimayo began with prayer in the larger of the two adobe chapels. We would enter the below-ground-level floors, a galaxy of candles, and the musty scent of adobe walls and earthen floors. After some prayer, we would walk up to the altar and genuflect in front of Our Lord of *Esquípulas*, a Guatemalan version of Jesus Christ on the cross with brown skin. The tradition of *Esquípulas* was imported to northern New Mexico from the Valley of *Esquípulas* (Guatemala), named after a highly respected Mayan icon that had dominion over the area. The figure, also known as the "Black Christ," and the chapel that housed it, built on the remains of a pre-Catholic Mayan shrine, went a long way toward the successful Christianization of the Mayans.[31] *Esquípulas*, a Chorti word, means "raised water or spring."[32] In fact, many hot springs can be found in the area, which have been

place

---

29   Ibid.

30   Rael-Gálvez, *Identifying Captivity*.

31   Stephen de Borhegyi, "The Miraculous Shrines Our Lord of *Esquípulas* in Guatemala and Chimayo, New Mexico," in The Spanish Colonial Arts Society, *El Santuario de Chimayo* (Santa Fe, 1956), pp. 2–4.

32   Ibid., p. 3.

the site of Indigenous pilgrimages since before the arrival of Europeans. Today, in Guatemala, pilgrims continue the practice of paying reverence to our Lord of *Esquípulas*, which now serves as a Catholic shrine housed in a large church on the same site as the previously mentioned pre-Columbian Mayan temple.[33]

Upon making the sign of the cross in front of Our Lord of *Esquípulas*, we turned to our left and walked into a small area through a wall so thick and door so short it almost resembled a tunnel. On the other side was a long and narrow room with walls populated by paintings of the *Santo Niño*, *la Virgen de Guadalupe*, and a multitude of saints. Taped to many of the paintings were photos of loved ones brought by devotees. On the bottom of each photo were words that described the petitions that were made by the believers to the site. "*Santo Niño*, please take care of my Daddy in prison"; "Please save my child from drug addiction"; "Please, *Virgen*, help my mother who has cancer!" It was clear that people made their trips to the *santuario* for very serious and specific reasons.

Years later, as an adult, I found myself participating in the same ritual. Dazed by the fate of my beloved daughter Rosalea, who, as the result of doctor and hospital errors at birth, was blind, severely retarded, and prone to regular and severe seizures, we were left helpless to assist our daughter/granddaughter/sister. As the prospects of Rosalea's hopes for improvement dimmed daily, the Santuario de Chimayo became our last and only hope. Her image on a Polaroid photo was added to the chorus of other pleas taped to the walls and paintings of the *Santo Niño* and *la Virgen*. Our own plea for the intervention of the *Santo Niño* and *la Virgen* on behalf of our beloved Rosalea, suffering for no fault of her own, became a part of the symphony of hope and despair that crowded the room.

Among the pictures, saints, and candles were many crutches and orthopedic braces, apparently left by believers who had been healed. Our visit to that chapel concluded by gathering the Holy Dirt from the hole that was said to mysteriously never grow deeper no matter how much dirt was taken from it. My grandmother and mom would take a couple of jars each of the dirt that they kept at home for use as necessary. It is believed to have healing powers, and my grandma was a staunch believer. The belief in the healing powers of the Holy Dirt and the practice of making pilgrimages to Chimayo go back to a time long before the coming of Europeans or Catholicism. The site was sacred to the Tewa and other Pueblo peoples of New Mexico long before the arrival of the Spaniards. According to Indigenous sources, "the site of the present *Santuario De Chimayo* was originally an Indian Shrine."[34] The original pit of the sacred earth was a pool called Tsimajopokwi. According to Tewa history, "When the twin war Gods killed the giant, fire burst out at many places, and the healing, hot mud springs atop Black Mesa, at Tsimmayo, and Obuhegi dried up and only mud was left. Natives

---

[33]   Ibid., pp. 3–4.
[34]   De Borhegyi, "The Miraculous Shrines," p. 8.

continued to visit the site of the hot spring and used the mud for healing calling it *nam po'uare* (blessed earth)."[35]

We concluded our visit by a short walk to the smaller chapel of the *Santo Niño* described earlier. It was at this chapel that my grandma engaged in intense and serious prayer often accompanied by tears and a myriad of emotions. The weathered massive carved door hanging on the thick adobe walls of the small chapel enclosed in a walled courtyard ushered us from the brightness of the day into the darker, candlelit space no bigger than a large living room. Inside was a small altar in front and two smaller altars on each of side extensions of the cross-shaped chapel. The aroma of candle flames coming from all three of the areas set a somber tone. The chairs and pews that occupied the central area were used by families awaiting their turn to visit the *Santo Niño*.

It was this altar, located on the left wing of the chapel that I have previously described, that was the center of activity and attention. It was the reason that people came from far and wide. In the middle of a glass enclosure the *Santo Niño* sat, his feet contained in worn baby shoes. It was widely held that at night he wandered the earth. Believers, including my grandma and mother, explained that if you put unworn shoes on him they would be soiled the next day from his wandering the countryside. It was a story that neither I nor any of my cousins dared question, like the power of the Holy Dirt, which I keep a jar of wherever I go until this very day. In fact, as several of my colleagues and friends will attest, I continue to distribute the Holy Dirt to this day.

La Virgen de Guadalupe and the Cerro de Tepeyac

> *Que gusto tiene la Virgen*
> *Con todos las Comanchitas*
> *Al sagrado Corazon*
> *Se los encargo toditas*
> [*La Virgen* (of Guadalupe) is so pleased
> With all the *Comanchitas*
> In the Sacred Heart
> She places their care]

> Heya, Heyo
> Heya, Heyo,
> He yayne yayne yayne ooo[36]

I recently completed a promise with a visit to the Cerro de Tepeyac and to petition on behalf of my family. My petition and visit was to *la Virgen de Guadalupe*, or to

---

[35]   Ibid., p. 18.

[36]   These are verses of the Sanchez/Sarracino Comanche songs.

Tonántzin, the pre-Catholic Indigenous goddess, or perhaps they are one in the same. Also joining me in the visit was my son, Mario, and my friend and former student, Father Eduardo Rivera, a native Mixtec Indian and a priest of the order of Saint Paul living in the Coyoacan delegation of Mexico City. Years ago, upon her request, I had taken my former mother-in-law, Ologia, to Tepeyac for her to fulfill a promise that she had made to *la Virgen*. Mario wanted to go where his grandmother had been and also had his own petitions. I had been to Tepeyac only a year previously, in 2008, to fulfil a promise for a petition that was granted. Tonántzin/*la Virgen* came through for me, and I will be forever grateful.

Each year millions of devotees, mainly Indigenous, visit the *Cerro de Tepeyac*, considered by many as the holiest of religious sites in the Americas. To many, la *Virgen de Guadalupe* is considered the patron saint of Native American peoples. To others she is known as the "Goddess of the Americas."[37] Yet others believe her to be the Virgin Mary, mother of Jesus, in a brown-skinned body.[38] The visits I described place me in the company of those participating in one of the oldest and most widely performed Native American rituals in North America. The *Cerro de Tepeyac* has been the destination of devout pilgrims since long before the arrival of the Europeans in Mexico. The site has for time immemorial been associated with an all-powerful female spirit. Before Our Lady of Guadalupe, it was *Tonántzin*, considered by the *Mexica*—"Aztecs"—to be their mother as well as that of all of the gods and goddesses.[39] Just as importantly for the purpose of this chapter, the site has often been at the center of great controversy. During the sixteenth century, the religious authorities in the capital of New Spain (Mexico City) were highly conflicted in regard to what was then referred to as the "cult of Our Lady of Guadalupe" and the pilgrimages to the *Cerro de Tepeyac*.[40]

Fr. Bernardino de Sahagún, one of original and the most influential of all the early Franciscan missionaries to come to the Americas, had great concerns over the "Cult of Guadalupe." According to Robert Ricard, "He [Sahagún] was acutely afraid that the Indians, on the pretext of honoring the Holy Virgin … would really continue to render homage to the pre-Hispanic goddess Tonántzin, whose shrine had been at Tepeyac itself."[41] The identity of the object of adoration at Cerro de Tepeyac continues to be complex and open to multiple interpretations, an issue I explored in a recent article examining the identity of Our Lady of Guadalupe.[42] As I sat in my (recently deceased) mother's kitchen a few years

---

[37]   Ana Castillo, *Goddess of the Americas: Writings on the Virgin of Guadalupe* (New York, 1996).

[38]   Bernardo Gallegos, "Whose Lady of Guadalupe? Indigenous Performances, Latina/o Identities, and the Postcolonial Project," *Journal of Latinos and Education* (Fall 2002).

[39]   Castillo, *Goddess of the Americas*; Miguel León-Portilla, *Tonantzin Guadalupe: pensamiento náhuatl y mensage cristiano en el* Nican Mophua (Mexico City, 2000).

[40]   Ricard, *The Spiritual Conquest of Mexico*.

[41]   Ibid., p. 191.

[42]   Gallegos, "Whose Lady of Guadalupe?"

Figure 11.2   Image of la Virgen de Guadalupe/Tonántzin and her Mexica devotees at the Cerro de Tepeyac. Photograph by author and used with permission.

his mom

ago, while I was engaged in the writing of the piece, I asked her if she thought that the Virgin of Guadalupe and the Blessed Virgin Mary were the same? Her response was that she always thought they were two separate persons. Her voice contributed to the myriad of sometimes conflicting interpretations presented in the article. Moreover, Mom's take on the identity of *la Virgen de Guadalupe* adds credence to the preoccupation of Fr. Bernardino Sahagún nearly half a millennium earlier. To explore the relationship of the Pre-Hispanic goddess Tonántzin and the contemporary Lady of Guadalupe, both female, both located on the Cerro de Tepeyac, and both the object of adoration by millions, and especially to Indigenous peoples, I turn to the first European university in the Americas.

During the third decade of the sixteenth century, shortly after the culmination of the conquest of Mexico-Tenochtitlán by the Spanish–Tlascalan Indian alliance, the Franciscan order established the *Colegio de Santa Cruz de Tlaltelolco*, the first college for Indigenous youth, in what was then probably the largest urban center in the world and the capital of the Mexica empire. The college, based on humanistic ideals championed by Erasmus and others, exemplified the Franciscan belief in the complexity of Mexica (Aztec) culture and the capacity for Natives to become priests.[43] While the mission of creating a native priesthood was not realized, the college did succeed in producing a large group of erudite scholars. At one point, the college was educating more than eighty students at a time in the classical works of Quintillian, Cato, Cicero, and other well-known and important authors of the time. The work that the students were doing was so impressive that even the poorest of the local Indians contributed what ever they could for the maintenance of the college. Taking pride in the scholarship of her people, Ana, a local Indian, and a group of other poor women who earned whatever they could with their hands, contributed significant amounts of money to support the students of the college.[44] The college was located in the neighborhood of Tlaltelolco, not far from Cerro de Tepeyac.

It was at the college that the story of the aspiration of *la Virgen de Guadalupe* first surfaced, in the form of a written narrative. The *Nican mopohua*, authored in the mid sixteenth century by native students under the supervision of the Religious at the *Colegio de Santa Cruz*, was a play about the apparition of a brown-skinned woman to Juan Diego (*Diegotzin*), a native of Tlaltelolco. In the narrative she appears three times to Juan Diego as he is at the Cerro de Tepeyac. In the play, she is referred to as both the Mother of the Christian God and as Tonántzin, the all-powerful Goddess of the Mexica.[45] [46] The narrative is highly ambiguous in relation to the identity of *la Virgen*. An image, according to the narrative, miraculously appeared on the *tilma* (a sort of poncho) of Juan Diego

---

[43]   Kobayashi, *La educación como conquista*.

[44]   Ibid., p. 249.

[45]   Léon-Portilla, *Tonantzin Guadalupe*.

[46]   Castillo, *Goddess of the Americas*.

after he emptied the roses the woman had given him to convince an unbelieving bishop. The image itself incorporates several ambiguous Indigenous images. She, for example, is in front of the sun and covers it. She is standing on the moon. Her shawl is made up of stars. Thus, the image subsumes some of the most important symbols from the Mexica cosmology. The document is filled with linguistic ambiguities that would easily leave open to interpretation the identity of the Lady who appeared to Juan Diego.[47] For the purposes of this essay, it is suffice to note that it is possible that the *Nican mopohua* written in Nahuatl (the language of the Mexica) represents one of the first translations of Western religion into the Native American worldview.

Over the centuries, the play was performed throughout New Spain as a means of introducing Christianity to the Natives. To this day, Mexicans and Indigenous people from all over the Americas continue the pre-Catholic practice of making pilgrimages to Cerro de Tepeyac to petition, or to keep a promise at the chapel dedicated to *la Virgen de Guadalupe* built on the site of the temple to Tonántzin.[48]

Conclusion

> Ahora si niños chiquitos
> Niño lindo y soverano
> Hay se nos presta la vida
> Te bailaremos el otro año
> [Take heed now little children
> Oh Beautiful and sovereign child
> If you loan us life
> We will dance for you in a year]

Ologia Sanchez, as her family wrote in her obituary, "was looking forward to her yearly holiday celebration of praying, singing, dancing the Comanche dances." She didn't get to dance again, but the legacy and the memories that she left for her family are clear. "As we continue on with our lives we will carry her strength, love, faith, and joy for life with us always." The Comanche dances of the Sanchez/Sarracino clan, like the family members themselves, represent a cultural articulation by a people born from the womb of Spanish imperialism. The Sanchez/Sarracinos, like countless other families, including my own, descendant from captive Indigenous girls, are truly the children of Imperialism. Without any claim to a non-Western Indigenous knowledge base, or religious practices outside of those inextricably connected to Catholicism such as the Comanche ceremonies, we are a people without a lengthy history.

---

[47]   Léon-Portilla, *Tonantzin Guadalupe.*

[48]   Ibid.

For many Genizaro descendants, genealogies began when their first young servant/matriarch was taken from her Indigenous Nation and sold into servitude in New Mexico. If you are fortunate, as is the Sanchez/Sarracino family, you at least know what nation your servant/matriarch came from. But most families don't have a photo of their own Nana Petra and her story to go with it. More familiar are the families that don't have a clue which Indigenous nations their servant/matriarchs—Comanchitas—came from.

The hybridity and ambiguity of Genizaro descendants are evident in their characterization as *Coyotes*, a term most often used to describe children of Indian servant women during the Spanish period. Aside from the better-known Native American Coyote stories most often featuring the ambiguity of Coyote as trickster, the term also referred to racial hybridity. In Spanish colonial New Mexico, *Coyote* was an ethnic identity, associated with ambiguity, much like the religious practices heretofore described. As I have demonstrated, pilgrimages to Chimayo and Cerro de Tepeyac constitute a continuation of Indigenous ritual that predates the European and Catholic presence in the Americas. Yet at the same time, they also constitute Catholic ritual performance, even though they are in the realm of Folk-Catholicism.

The question of appropriation is a difficult and complex one to address in this context. One could say that the Spanish missionaries appropriated the Indigenous sites of worship and replaced them with Catholic shrines. Yet, in the case of the Holy Dirt from the Santuario de Chimayo, or that of the valley of *Esquípulas* in Guatemala, this assertion can easily be called into question. That is, Holy Dirt is not a part of any official Catholic tradition. It is clearly a Native American practice, at least in these two regions. Yet, when one goes to the Santuario for the purpose of completing a promise or to petition the *Santo Niño* or to Tepeyac to petition *la Virgen*, it is difficult if not impossible to rationalize whether it is an Indigenous or a Catholic ritual one is performing.

During an interview with renowned filmmaker, scholar, and professor of anthropology, Dr. Beverly Singer (Diné/Tewa) of the Tewa Pueblo of Santa Clara, just across the highway from the Santuario de Chimayo, I posed the following question: "Do you consider a visit to gather dirt at the Santuario de Chimayo a Catholic or a Tewa ritual?" Her response was complex yet to the point. "Does it matter? It's in our cultural memory bag to practice these ways. We know when we need the dirt and your intuition just takes you there."[49] Indeed, Professor Singer's response resonates in my psyche and that of family members. We go the chapel of Our Lady of Guadalupe at Tepeyac or to the Santuario de Chimayo to fulfill a promise, present a petition, or to bring home Holy Dirt because we know we need it. It's not necessarily with the intention of practicing either a Catholic or an Indigenous ritual. It is much more visceral. I never heard the Sarracino sisters, nor any one of their families, including my own children, ever entertain

---

[49]   Interview with Beverly Singer, Albuquerque, New Mexico, 13 February 2009.

the idea of the origin of the Comanche dances. They just did them because they knew they were supposed to.

> *Niño chiquitito y bonito*
> *Niño de me corazon*
> *Lla me voy a retirar*
> *Echo me tu bendicion*
> [Beautiful little Child
> Child of my Heart
> I am leaving now
> Bestow your blessing on me]

Chapter 12
Trickster's Art and Artifice: Concluding Thoughts

Kathleen J. Martin and Angela D. Blaver

> The Indigenous Nations have resolved, here at the base of *Mato Paha*, that the Pope
> of the Catholic Church, the Queen of England and the Archbishop of Canterbury
> rescind these Doctrines of Discovery for having served to justify and pave the way
> for the illegal dispossession of aboriginal land title and the subjugation of non-
> Christian peoples to the present day.[1]

The examination of Indigenous images and symbols in the Catholic Church has
taken us to multiple places and through multidisciplinary fields. The contributors
have asked readers to consider a number of questions and issues such as: What
can we understand from the examination of representations of the sacred and the
differences between Indigenous and Catholic interpretations? In what ways do
visual images defy and disgrace, while simultaneously supporting expectations
and ideologies regarding appropriation and missionization? What can the ironies
of being tell us about recognizing and reconnecting with the mysteries of life?
What does the use of images mean for resistance, transformation, and cultural
destruction? And finally, what new interpretations and understandings are
necessary? The questions examined may be more important than any truth we
might hope to find, and yet the questions themselves also shape how they are
considered and ultimately answered.

The use of visual images in religious and social contexts continues to pose
numerous complexities for Indigenous self-expression, self-representation, and
self-determination. Whether visual images are caricatures designed as Indian
mascots with negative connotations, interpretations of Indigenous art that
frame political commentary or social conditions, or have supposedly uplifting
and positive connotations in churches, they fix and perpetuate historical and
social contexts within a dominant ideology. In fact, "photography's vision thus
articulates and recirculates a history in relation by which meaning is reconstituted
in historically constructed power relations."[2] Gordon Henry's prose illuminates the
corporeal and active role viewers can take when encountering and using images

---

[1]   Brenda Norrell, "Indigenous in Americas Just Say 'No' to Papal Bulls," *Indian Country Today*, 26/10 (16 August 2006): 5–7.

[2]   Kalli Paakspuu, "Winning of Losing the West: The Photographic Act," *Bulletin of Science, Technology and Society*, 27/1 (2007): 58.

for interpretation, articulation or abandonment, or sometimes, in the end, using them for our own purposes:

> There were the images, the cowboy killings, the product faces, figures giving authenticity to their smoke, their Sunday heroes. For a long time I swallowed it all and grew sick with anger, knowing the images inside can kill you and put faces on you that you can't get off, and it was the old man inside there sleeping and his companion, my mother, who washed those angry faces off. They taught me different, greater things about images, about the imagination, and growing toward healing. And I found I could turn images inside out from the mind to the hand, and the images in turn could replay healing images inside someone.[3]

Images and ideas of the sacred are present in life—all of life's moments—and sometimes the representations of these moments communicate aspects of the sacred, but they can never stand as true representations of the sacred or the spirits. In an animate universe that encompasses living beings in multiple forms, any representation pales in comparison to the living reality.

Indigenous Experiences of the Sacred

Native and Indigenous scholars pose that "American Indian theology involves a process of remembering and dreaming"[4] that others often cannot do. Spirituality continues to be "rooted in the land on which they lived and each people knew their territory in an intimate way."[5] Further, rootedness is tied to places and contexts, and beliefs and traditions are specific to concrete features of the land and environment. New knowledge can enhance understanding, and symbols gain power and meaning through specific contexts and cultural traditions that employ images. According to Inés Talamantez, "people create symbols out of the world they formulate. For Indian peoples, they create symbols out of the land, so when the land is taken away, their symbols and the meaning in their world perish as well."[6] Ironically, Christian form and function acts to subvert and co-opt the culture of the Indian community by detaching practices from the land and the places to which they belong. George Tinker theorizes that perhaps the most blatant form of this comes from those "liberal" and "open white missionaries who usurp native cultural forms, particularly with descriptions and justifications of authority to do

---

[3]   Gordon Henry, *The Light People* (East Lansing, 1994), p. 25.

[4]   Clara Sue Kidwell, Homer Noley, and George Tinker, *A Native American Theology* (Maryknoll, 2001), p. 126.

[5]   Ibid.

[6]   Inés Talamantez, personal communication with Kate Martin, 2000.

so as designated by spiritual leaders."[7] Christianity, as such, is detached from New World lands for specific reasons including: its own dislocation from Old World contexts; the facilitation of the primary goal of conversion; and the separation from current contexts that must occur in order to supplant existing beliefs. These interpretations highlight not only the differences in perceptions and assumptions, but also the reception of images when they are taken out of the community context from which they gestated and were born.

In combination with specifics of the land, Native Peoples hold a "religious view of the world that seeks to locate species within a fabric of life that constitutes the natural world, the land and all its various forms of life."[8] For example, the Ojibwa ethic of *pimadaziwin*, loosely translated as "well-spirited," reflects a desire for the well-being of humans that is inseparable and indistinguishable for all beings in the environment including plants, animals, spirits, and forces of nature.[9] The ethic of *pimadaziwin* is reflected in respect for places as sacred in and of themselves. Humans assume responsibility to and respect for places as caretakers with reciprocity to and for what is offered. Ethical behavior and responsibility to those who inhabit places, those considered sacred as well as others, include mountains, other-than-humans, and all entities that originate from each place. For instance, stories of *Mato Tipila* are specific to a place considered sacred—sturgeon live in specific places—water nourishes places—and humans, as the younger sibling, are given specific places to care for all those who live in that area. For Native Peoples the attitude of humans toward places "was thought to be as important as action; one was to be careful in thought and action so as not to injure another's mind or offend the spirits of the animals and surrounding environment.'[10] This is taught very early in life. As Vine Deloria recalls:

> When I was very small and traveling with my father in South Dakota, he would frequently point out buttes, canyons, river crossings, and old roads and tell me their stories. ... Gradually, I began to understand a distinction in the sacredness of places. Some sites are sacred in themselves, others had to be cherished by generations of people and were now part of their history and, as such, revered by them and part of their being.[11]

[7] George Tinker, *Missionary Conquest: The Gospel and Native American Cultural Genocide* (Minneapolis, 1993), p. 114.

[8] Vine Deloria, Jr., *God Is Red: A Native View of Religion* (Golden, 1994/2003), p. 303.

[9] J. Baird Callicott and Michael P. Nelson, *American Indian Environmental Ethics: An Ojibwa Case Study* (New Jersey, 2004).

[10] Oscar Kawagley, *A Yupiaq Worldview: A Pathway to Ecology and Spirit* (Prospect Heights, 1995), p. 4.

[11] Deloria, *God Is Red*, p. xv.

The ethic of place as sacred is embedded in a system that perceives the world as animate and interconnected. All components of the world have the power to recall, hold, teach, and provide for humans if they demonstrate worthiness, respect, responsibility, and care.

Praying is accomplished with dancing, Ghost Dance, Sundance and dance as a metaphor for life itself.[12] It is a physical movement and an engagement with the world and forces that carries the individual to new connections and interactions with the sacred. Native traditions are not ones of passivity, of sitting quietly singing prearranged hymns, or facing forward all in one direction, or listening to a religious professional sermonize or pray. Rather these are "traditions of dynamic religious lives, where one actively involves all of oneself, including the body."[13] People dance barefoot to be in touch with the earth.[14] They are intimately connected with the flow of air and physical contact with the earth. Tribal religious practices "are actually complexes of attitudes, beliefs, and practices fine-tuned to harmonize with the lands on which people live."[15] When we view Delvin Slick's images (Figures 9.1–9.5), we see a visible representation of the sacred that incorporates the living others in the world. *The Renegades* is a "here and now" image, not one lost in the translation of a messiah metaphor. It is a tangible image that captures in a photograph, if that is possible given the static quality, "the principle of respect for the sacred."[16]

Indigenous symbols and practices used in churches, educational settings, or historical discussions often are done in ways that are confusing, misleading, irritating, and disheartening, ambiguous and generally responsible for contributing to internal conflicts and external misinterpretations. Alternatively, they pose no conflict, are comforting, reassuring, dynamic, and the basis for cultural and spiritual memory. In many cases, the contributors provide evidence for the mixing of these two traditions as well as the continuing legacy of colonization, assimilation, and appropriation. More significantly, they address the diametrically opposed systems of belief. Missionaries in the past enjoined Native Peoples "to leave behind irrational dependency upon unseen spirits and accept the true faith with its individual responsibility for salvation and its

---

[12]   Christian religions needed to eliminate dancing since it was so central to practice and traditions, and anathema for many in its sensuality.

[13]   Jordan Paper, *Native North American Religious Traditions: Dancing for Life* (Westport, 2007), p. 4.

[14]   Inés Talamantez, response to the Native Traditions in the Americas special interest group session on the theme of "Sacred Spaces and Sacred Places," American Academy of Religion annual conference, Chicago, Illinois, 1 November 2008.

[15]   Vine Deloria, Jr., *For this Land: Writings on Religion in America* (New York, 1999), p. 69.

[16]   Barbara Deloria, Kristen Foehner, and Samuel Scinta (eds.), with a foreword by Wilma Mankiller, *Spirit and Reason: The Vine Deloria, Jr., Reader* (Golden, 1999), p. 327.

attempt to follow the injunction, taken to its extreme in the influential."[17] Yet the underlying assumption of this philosophy remained the same: the so-called primitive would advance and recognize the true and proper direction in search of the Almighty. Sometimes missionaries and Christians did not understand the histories and contexts of their own beliefs, nor the misunderstandings that they were unable or unwilling to acknowledge and rectify. Historical interpretations that closely examine the records of missionaries are seen as just that—*historical*—not of the current reality. Yet conceivably this argument is mired, as some would say, in the past, and it is time to move on for hope in the future to return us to what has been lost of this animate living world.

Philip Deloria suggests, in his work on ideology, our expectations can reinforce stereotypes, and ideology can offer "both truthful pictures of the world as it exists and falsely prescriptive understandings of the world as it might (or should) be."[18] In this way, visual culture can reaffirm, not only expectation, but also continue to support misinformation in the present from the dictates of the past. The creation of images such as *The Apache Christ* (Figure 7.3) exemplifies the ways Catholic imagery supports the continuing ideology of missionization and assimilation of the past. It illustrates the qualities inherent in static representation and Western individualism within the context of religious experience, and affirms the similarities of experience between Christ and his followers, and Apaches. At once, this image is truthful in that for Catholics it is a representation of Christ, and in any form, this image affirms the Catholic ideal that we are all children of the "one true God." At the same time, it presents a lack of understanding from Indigenous and Apache perspectives since Catholic and Christian beliefs and practices are largely centered around one individual, or at best the triune figure, God the Father, Son, and Holy Spirit—all males—with an absence of female representatives. Indigenous Peoples recognize, seek, and affirm a multiplicity of spirits, with female and male figures, who provide for the people. It is less about the individual receiving recognition and more centered on the well-being of the community. Western culture, Vine Deloria Jr. concludes, produces something completely different from Indigenous understandings:

> Both the scientific and religious postures produce an extreme individualism, the solitary atomic structure that constitutes the ultimate substrata of our physical world and the solitary sinner who needs first religious salvation and now in our time, therapy. Neither of these beliefs is found as a dominant motif in aboriginal societies.[19]

---

[17]   Ronald Neizen, *Spirit Wars: Native North American Religions in the Time of Nation Building* (Berkeley, 2000), p. 224.

[18]   Philip J. Deloria, *Indians in Unexpected Places* (Topeka, 2004), p. 9.

[19]   Deloria, Foehner, and Scinta, *Spirit and Reason*, p. 22.

The adoption and creation of images such as *The Apache Christ* vividly portray the theory and promise of reward in the afterlife, a world yet to come, as well as the possibility of religious salvation envisioned in a static form. To understand and accept this image is to accept that the world is no longer visibly alive, and evidence of the sacred no longer present through current and new understandings or revelations from the power of places. In fact, if we accept this image, there is no need of the Indigenous Trickster since now he is figured as a messiah, largely understood and interpreted as a psychological archetype or mythological figure. However, "for aboriginal peoples, there is not only no need for a messiah, there is really no place for him in the cosmos. ... We cannot validly find the Trickster as a prefigured messiah except insofar as the figure occurs in Western cultural tradition."[20]

Today, perhaps more than in the past, there is a need for "dialogical resistance."[21] The collecting of photographic artifacts "by government or private collectors [has] made new uses and created epistemologies within ruling relations external, and sometimes in contradiction"[22] to the original encounter, as in the exhibitions at the 1904 World's Fair.

The incorporation of the Pipe may be attributed to cultural changes and influences of evangelization since Vatican II; yet, individuals, such as Steinmetz, continue to defend their actions through various writings and printed texts. It is a powerful message to read in print or see reflected in photographs the use of Native traditions and practices within Catholic Church contexts, thus providing support in ways that are difficult to ignore from a Western ideological viewpoint. Steinmetz quotes individuals such as George Plenty Wolf by saying, "He accepted me as a Catholic priest praying with the Sacred Pipe. At least one time he believed that the power of the priest was stronger than his own power as a yuwipi man."[23] This is a compelling affirmation and impressive justification for those wishing to incorporate Native traditions, particularly when presented in combination with a photo of a priest using the Pipe. The combination of text and visual image contains a powerful "intertexual" message in light of assumptions and attitudes. When we examine the influence of Steinmetz's work and continuing record of publications on the subject of the Pipe, we see changes and adaptations to Native and Catholic traditions alike. This leads us to the conundrum investigated in this volume: What does the future hold in the way of Native and Catholic relations? Is it possible to move forward either separately or together when the two have been so intricately associated and combined? And, if so, can there be a new way of listening, knowing, acting and understanding—an innovative harmony that is simultaneously one, yet built collaboratively out of many with reciprocity at the forefront?

---

[20]   Ibid., p. 23.

[21]   We take this phrase from the important work of Dale Turner, *This Is Not a Peace Pipe: Towards a Critical Indigenous Philosophy* (Toronto, 2006).

[22]   Paakspuu, "Winning or Losing the West," p. 56.

[23]   Paul Steinmetz, *The Sacred Pipe: An Archetypal Theology* (New York, 1998), p. 178.

Insights, Art, and Artifice

Studies such as these are significant for the ways they contribute to the "social, intellectual, and perceptual construction of reality," and as a professional practice of study "undertaken within a number of humanistic and social scientific disciplines whose object is the conceptual frameworks, social practices and the artifacts of seeing."[24] Examining the use of images and symbols are ways to study representation and social and cultural construction. Perhaps, Trickster can continue to help us understand these complex fields by reflecting back on the work of this volume.

The contributors have tried to present the contexts of missionizing activities both from the historical past and the evolving present through the medium of visual and artistic expression and understanding. Chapters 1 through 4 engage specifically in the study of dualities within and surrounding Indigenous imagery, practices, and symbolism. As an overview, Martin juxtaposes resistance and tension within an historical context. Echoing a trickster theme that subverts linearity, she notes the theories of post-structuralism, post-colonialism, or postmodernism attempt to separate and identify processes, yet there is a circularity difficult to avoid in any analysis. Entering into another time and place, the struggles of Indigenous peoples in the 1970s in the United States are underscored through Garrett's description of the American Indian Freedom of Religion Act of 1978. The explanation of the medicine wheel—yet another symbol that overlays that of the Trickster—to draw comparisons is artfully accomplished so that we see the reflection of the past mirrored in the present. Stretching further back in time, Jeffries examines Indigenous experiences in New France in the seventeenth century, and notes that the fantastical exists for Native Peoples and Christians alike. He contends the Indigenous Peoples of New France preferred beliefs and practices about spirits that entailed extraordinary elements. And, in Chapter 4, Beyer notes a more playful side of the trickster theme with the discussion of "the celebration of the god Lono during the *Makahiki* festival, which lasted from October to January. ... It was a time of rest, great feasts, games, sexual promiscuity, and the *hula*."[25]

Dealing directly with imagery and the complexity that surrounds a powerful visual medium is captured in Chapters 5 through 7. Taylor notes the ways people experienced a nuanced duality in their relationship with the camera and in the creation of images, something Trickster would not only understand, but also encourage. Yet, Taylor reminds us that "Native attitudes tended to be more nuanced, embracing the camera at occasions, utilizing it at others, and resisting it altogether in many other instances."[26] In Chapter 6, Toole artfully discusses irony, nostalgia, and the paradoxes of life with no small amount of Trickster contrariness. He poses that Native Peoples "might be the salvation of Christianity," while at

[24]   David Morgan, *The Sacred Gaze: Religious Visual Culture in Theory and Practice* (Berkeley, 2005), p. 27.

[25]   Beyer, Chapter 4.

[26]   Taylor, Chapter 5.

the same time wondering if Christianity so saved will still remain as such, or might it be the "salvation of a world that otherwise is ruined." Yet Martin offers evidence in Chapter 7 that imagery can shape identity and the social construction of beliefs in ways that are confusing and misleading. Interview consultants revealed conflicting emotions regarding the misuse of images for both Natives and Catholics, and yet their confusion and uncertainty emanated from knowledge and understanding of both belief systems. Interestingly, cognitive dissonance of this sort in not uncommon in Trickster mythology as well.

The last set of chapters embrace educational and humanistic perspectives beginning with Clark's discussion of teaching art through Hawaiian metaphor. He concludes that "through the work of indigenous education research, the wisdom of our ancestors reaches across the generations to raise us all above this constricted path to learning that we find ourselves confronted by today."[27] Irony again, not lost on Trickster who finds it amusing that Western teaching and learning is now influenced by the wisdom of Indigenous Peoples who had been thought unremarkable and uncivilized. Yet, as presented in Chapter 9, we see the ways these paradigms are most effectively utilized and maintained at a tribal college.

As Blaver explains in Chapter 10, the Indigenous in the Mono Basin understood that "one can move a stone, but not a rock or a mountain. It was a significant shift in worldview to imagine the possession and restriction of immense and permanent resources such as land or vast amounts of water."[28] Although Trickster displays and is capable of fantastic feats, he also is the bearer of cautionary tales. A fascination with the power to hold land and move water would exist, yet Trickster would be the first to advise prudence in such an endeavor. Finally, Gallegos reminds us that songs and dances continue to hold stories, dreams, and blessings, and there is more to the sacred than we can imagine, yet always is it there for the imagining. When believers participate in Matachine, Comanche, and Posada celebrations performed on 12 December, the Feast of the Lady of Guadalupe and on Christmas Day, the long-lasting effects of the early friars is evident all across Mexico and the US Southwest, yet the dance continues without analysis or conflict for participants.

From these efforts, we suggest the contributors' work promotes the following four ideas and conclusions as significant. First, it is necessary to challenge dominant paradigms and investigate aspects of power. This may be evident in the ways the legal and political systems continue to support injustice, as well as marginalization in educational settings. Second, new forms of resistance and explorations of what visual studies can do to promote "dialogical resistance" are needed to frame ongoing discussions. Research in the areas of visual studies and art has the power to challenge the status quo, and "decolonize the theory and method of landscape within the broader context of visual art to construct what might be

---

27   Clark, Chapter 8.
28   Blaver, Chapter 10.

named as *artistic sovereignty*."[29] Further, photography as a means of investigating, challenging, and reinterpreting past and present contexts is significant since images are routinely "recontextualized for new uses in journalism, advertising, art, propaganda, anthropology, and entertainment."[30]

A third idea is that physical engagement with the sacred in the forms of dance and art continues without conscious attention to where or from whom it came. It is the physical expression, with feet in touch with the earth, or carried in a jar, that continues to reveal aspects of the spiritual world. This leads us to our final conclusion: experiences of the sacred are necessary for encouraging the possibility of "calling eagles" and discouraging the conflation, comparison, or coordination of beliefs systems into a homogenized "we're all the same" mentality of Western ideology. Yet, at the same time, it requires the recognition that new spiritual traditions have been formed over the past five hundred years, and people continue to bring home Holy Dirt when they need it. Most importantly, we must continue to explore, utilize, and support educational paradigms that seek to liberate students, teachers and communities from colonialist and neocolonialist ideals. This idea may begin to address the dislocation, loss, and disrespect many feel when symbols and practices are taken out of context and used without permission and agreement.

Concluding Thoughts

It is not enough to recognize and study the ways appropriation and missionizing continues to take place. Active resistance and confrontations occurred in the past, yet time marches on just as demonstrations against abuse marched on. Although contributing to a strengthening of the people, they no longer take place with the same degree of resistance as they did in the 1960s and 1970s. Yet perhaps now there is better articulation in a world more ready to hear what "the dreamers" have to say. "Contemplation. Reverence. Admiration. Inspiration. … It makes places sacred."[31] Native Peoples continue to speak out at *Mato Paha*, Celilo Falls, *Cerro de Tepeyac*, *Mato Tipila* and any number of other places that are impacted by Western encroachment, development, and disregard for sacred places. Actions may need to be politically and philosophically framed to not only look at what is, but also to address and actively articulate resistance to Western hegemony. As Dale Turner contends, "a 'Crazy Horse' approach to protecting indigenous philosophies is necessary for our survival as indigenous peoples. Yet at the same time, we must continue to assert and protect our rights, sovereignty and nationhood within an ongoing colonial

---

[29] Karen Ohnesorge, "Uneasy Terrain: Image, Text, Landscape, and Contemporary Indigenous Artists in the United States," *American Indian Quarterly*, 32/1 (Winter 2008): 43. Italics added.

[30] Paakspuu, "Winning or Losing the West," p. 53.

[31] Joseph C. Dupris, Kathleen S. Hill, and William H. Rodgers, Jr., *The Si'lailo Way: Indians, Salmon and Law on the Columbia River* (Durham, 2006), pp. 370–71.

relationship."[32] Can we afford to continue to believe that change has already happened or resistance is no longer possible, or maybe more disturbing, no longer necessary?

We have tried to present and pose alternatives for understanding symbols and practices specifically that challenge–articulate–stimulate and discern the meaning of sacred in our lives through the avenues of visual studies. The foundations of difference are substantive and resistance to appropriation serious business. "The problem of assimilation is always close at hand."[33] As a powerful construct that exemplifies duality, Trickster is embedded in oral histories, beliefs, actions, and expectations of Native Peoples into the present day. There is no linearity, convenience, or simplicity to the Trickster. This paradigm is consciously and unconsciously threaded throughout this volume, as each contributor portrays the complex directions in which the various collectives have collided, aligned, intersected, dominated, and resisted. As we began, "the trickster mediates wild bodies and adamant minds; a chance in third person narratives to turn aside the cold litanies and catechistic monodramas over the measured roads to civilization."[34] Thus, through the lens of the trickster, we can approach an understanding of the spectacles that consumed whole peoples under the guise of missionization, colonization, and Christianity, and ultimately what was believed to be "civilization" at various times and eras.

Trickster's art and artifice is most acute when he is out "just going along," and, just as in stories, we might laugh and walk away, or we might choose a path with new degrees of resistance and knowledge for what it means to be human and to learn from the stories that he chooses to tell. "The Messiah, unlike the North American Trickster, comes on the clouds and takes the faithful to a blessed land indescribably different than anything we have here."[35] Yet, for Indigenous Peoples, the sacred is here—in the homelands, the earth—and the sacred places that matter most. For Christians, it is Eve who brings about the downfall of the world with her disobedience as she eats the apple and corrupts the complicit and impressionable Adam. Yet Thomas King's ironic display of relationships is useful here:

> Anybody who eats my stuff is going to be very sorry, says that GOD. There are rules, you know.
> I didn't eat anything, says Old Coyote.
> I was just looking around.
> Is that chicken I see hanging out of your mouth? says that GOD.
> No, no, says Old Coyote. It must be my tongue. Sometimes it looks like chicken.

---

[32] Turner, *This Is Not a Peace Pipe*, p. 110.

[33] Ibid., p. 117.

[34] Gerald R. Vizenor, *The Trickster of Liberty: Native Heirs to a Wild Baronage* (Norman, 2005), p. x.

[35] Deloria, Foehner, and Scinta, *Spirit and Reason*, p. 31.

Christian Rules

What a stingy person, says First Woman, and that one packs her bags. Lots of nice places to live, she says to Ahdamn. No point in having a grouchy GOD for a neighbor. And First Woman and Ahdamn leave the garden.

All the animals leave the garden.

Maybe I'll leave a little later, says Old Coyote.

You can't leave my garden, that GOD says to First Woman. You can't leave because I'm kicking you out.

But First Woman doesn't hear him. She and Ahdamn move west. They go looking around for a new home.[36]

Maybe it will be in the rewriting that First Woman—with the equal support and participation of Adhamn—will move west (or return and restore our homelands) and again regenerate the powers of the world, while Coyote stays behind with "that GOD." We'll just have to wait and see, and watch out for images and ironies along the way.

[36] Thomas King, *Green Grass, Running Water* (New York, 1993), p. 57.

Bibliography

Manuscript sources

Académie Française, *Le Dictionnaire de l'Académie françoise, dedié au roy* (Paris: J.B. Coignard, 1694).

Archives of the Archdiocese of Santa Fe, NM: Albuquerque Baptisms 1824, Reel 1.

Catholic Diocese of Rapid City, South Dakota: *Inculturation Project Office* (1 September 1999), www.rapidcitydiocese.org/Ministries/Inculturation.htm (accessed 11 July 2008).

Dakota American Indian Movement, *Oyate Wicaho*, 5/1 (March 1985) (partial missing citation).

New Mexico State Legislature, Regular Session, *House Memorial 40; Senate Memorial 59 (SM59)* "Genizaros, In Recognition" (Santa Fe, NM, 2007).

Honolulu Spectator, "Supplement to the Sandwich Island Mirror" (15 January 1840): 1–2.

Spanish Archives of New Mexico (SANM I), Twitchell document 183, 1208, trans. by Bernardo Gallegos.

United States Conference of Catholic Bishops, "Native American Catholics at the Millennium," a report on a survey by the ad hoc committee on Native American Catholics, (Washington, DC: Report by the Ad Hoc Committee on Native American Catholics), www.usccb.org/education/nac.shtml (accessed 9 July 2008).

University of New Mexico, available in Coronado Room, Zimmerman Library (CRZL), "Navajos in the Catholic Church Records of New Mexico," in David Brugge, *Research Report # 1* (Window Rock, AZ: Research Section, Parks and Recreation Department, Navajo Tribe, 1968).

Printed primary sources

Aginsky, Bernard W., "Culture Element Distributions: XXIV. Central Sierra," in *Anthropological Records* (vol. 8:4, Berkeley: University of California Press, 1943), pp. 393–468.

Alexander, James M., *Islands of the Pacific* (New York: American Tract Society, 1895).

Alexander, William D., *A Brief History of the Hawaiian People* (New York: American Book Company, 1891).

Allen, Charles W. and Richard E. Jensen, *From Fort Laramie to Wounded Knee: In the West That Was* (Lincoln: University of Nebraska Press, 1997).

Alstrom, Sydney E., *A Religious History of the American People*, 2nd edn. (New Haven, CT: Yale University Press, 1972).

Anderson, M. Kat, *Teaching the Wild: Native American Knowledge and the Management of California's Natural Resources* (Berkeley: University of California Press, 2005).

Anderson, Rufus, *History of the Mission of the American Board of Commissioners for Foreign Missions to the Hawaiian Islands* (Boston: Congregational Publishing Board, 1872).

Andersson, Rani-Henrik, *The Lakota Ghost Dance of 1890* (Lincoln: University of Nebraska Press, 2008).

Archambault, Marie T., Mark Theil, and Christopher Vecsey, *The Crossing of Two Roads: Being Catholic and Native in the United States* (Maryknoll, NY: Orbis, 2003).

Archibald, Robert, "Acculturation and Assimilation in Colonial New Mexico," *New Mexico Historical Review*, 53 (July 1978).

Austin, Alyvn and Jamie S. Scott (eds.), *Canadian Missionaries Indigenous Peoples: Representing Religion at Home and Abroad* (University of Toronto Press, 2005).

Axtell, James, *The Invasion Within: The Contest of Cultures in Colonial North America* (New York: Oxford University Press, 1985).

Bailey, Gauvin Alexander, *Art on the Jesuit Missions in Asia and Latin America, 1542–1773* (University of Toronto Press, 1999).

Bailey, Lynn R., *The Indian Slave Trade in the Southwest* (Los Angeles: Westernlore Press, 1973).

Banks, James, "Approaches to Multicultural Reform," in James Banks and C. McGee-Banks (eds.), *Multicultural Educational Issues and Perspectives*, 3rd edn. (Hoboken, NJ: Wiley, 1997).

Barthes, Roland, *Image, Music, Text*, ed. and trans. Stephen Heath (New York, 1977), pp. 32–51.

——,, *Camera Lucida: Reflections on Photography*, trans. Richard Howard (New York: Hill and Wang, 1981).

Basso, Keith, *Wisdom Sits in Places: Landscape and Language among the Western Apache* (Albuquerque: University of New Mexico Press, 1996).

Bates, Craig D. and Martha J. Lee, *Tradition and Innovation: A Basket History of the Indians of the Yosemite–Mono Lake Area* (Yosemite National Park, CA: Yosemite Association, 1991).

Battiste, Marie (ed.), *Reclaiming Indigenous Voice and Vision* (Vancouver: UBC Press, 2000).

Baudrillard, Jean, "The Art of Disappearance," in Nicholas Zurbrugg (ed.), *Art and Artefact* (London, 1997), p. 28

Beaglehole, Ernest C., "Some Modern Hawaiians," *University of Hawai'i Research Publications*, 19 (1939): 76–83.

Beasley, Jr., Conger, *We Are a People in This World: The Lakota Sioux and the Massacre at Wounded Knee* (Fayetteville: University of Arkansas Press, 1995).

Becker, Howard S., "Visual Evidence: A Seventh Man, the Specified Generalization, and the Work of the Reader," *Visual Studies*, 17/1 (2002): 7–11.

Beckwith, Martha W., *Hawaiian Mythology* (New Haven, CT: Yale University Press, 1940).

Bell, Catherine M., *Ritual Theory, Ritual Practice* (New York: Oxford University, 1992).

Bellah, Robert, *Religious Evolution*, in William A. Lessa and Evon Z. Vogt (eds.), *Reader in Comparative Religion* (New York: Harper and Row, 1965), pp. 73–87.

Benham, Maenette, K.P. and Ronald H. Heck, *Culture and Educational Policy in Hawaii: The Silencing of Native Voices* (Mahwah, NJ: L. Erlbaum Associates, 1998).

Berkhofer, Robert F., "Protestant Indian Missions," in F.P. Prucha (ed.), *The Indian in American History* (Hillsdale, IL: Dryden Press Inc., 1971), pp. 75–84.

——, *The White Man's Indian: Images of the American Indian from Columbus to the Present* (New York: Alfred A. Knopf, 1978).

Bicknell, James, "Hawaiian Kahunas and Their Practices," *The Friend*, 48 (September 1890): 61–7.

Billeb, Emil M., *Mining Camp Days* (Berkeley: University of California Press, 1968).

Bingham, Hiram, *A Residence of Twenty-one Years in the Sandwich Islands* (New York: Sherman Converse, 1847).

Binnema, Theodore, *Common and Contested Ground: A Human and Environmental History of the Northwestern Plains* (Norman: University of Oklahoma Press, 1963).

Bishop, Sereno E., "Why Are the Hawaiians Dying Out? Or, Elements of Disability for Survival among the Hawaiian People," *The Friend*, 47 (March 1889): 18–20; (April 1889): 26–7.

——, "Are Missionaries' Sons Tending to America a Stolen Kingdom?," *The Friend*, 52/1 (1894): 2–3.

——, *Reminiscences of Old Hawaii* (Honolulu, HI: Hawaiian Gazette Co., 1916).

Bisin, Alberto and Thierry Verdier, "'Beyond the Melting Pot': Cultural Transition, Marriage, and the Evolution of Ethnic and Religious Traits," *The Quarterly Journal of Economics*, 11/3 (2000): 957–68.

Black Elk, Nicholas, *Black Elk Speaks: Being the Life Story of a Holy Man of the Oglala Sioux. John G. Niehardt* (Reprint, Lincoln: University of Nebraska Press, 2000).

Blackburn, Carole, *Harvest of Souls: The Jesuit Missions and Colonialism in North America, 1632–1650* (Montreal: McGill-Queen's University Press, 2000).

Blackman, William F., *The Making of Hawaii: A Study in Social Evolution* (New York: The Macmillan Company, 1899).

Blair, Emma Helen (ed.), *The Indian Tribes of the Upper Mississippi Valley and Region of the Great Lakes as Described by Nicolas Perrot, French Commandant in the Northwest; Bacquevile de La Potherie, French Royal Commissioner to Canada; Morrell Marston, American Army Officer; and Thomas Forsyth, United States Agent at Fort Armstrong* (Cleveland, OH: The Arthur H. Clark Company, 1911).

Blanchard, Kendall A., *The Economics of Sainthood: Religious Change among the Rimrock Navajo* (Cranbury, NJ: Associated University Presses, Inc., 1977).

Blaver, Angela D., "Negit and Paoha: How the Black and White Islands Came to Be in Mono Lake," in Jonnie Reinhold, Rachel Cherny, and Kathleen J. Martin (eds.), *Osiyo: The Work of Indigenous Scholars*, 10 (San Luis Obispo, CA: Ethnic Studies Department, Cal Poly State University, 2008): 20–21.

Blaver, Elma, "Prologue," in C.D. Bates and M.J. Lee (eds.), *Tradition and Innovation: A Basket History of the Indians of the Yosemite–Mono Lake Area* (Yosemite National Park, CA: Yosemite Association, 1991), p. xv.

Blue Spruce, Duane (ed.), *Spirit of a Native Place: Building the National Museum of the American Indian* (Washington, DC: Smithsonian Institution, 2004).

Borges, Jorges Luis, *Other Inquisitions: 1937–1952*, trans. Ruth L.C. Simms (Austin: University of Texas Press, 1975).

Borhegyi, Stephen de, "The Miraculous Shrines of Our Lord of *Esquípulas* in Guatemala and Chimayo, New Mexico," in *El Santuario de Chimayo* (Santa Fe, NM: The Spanish Colonial Arts Society, 1956), pp. 2–4.

Bowden, Henry Warner, *American Indians and Christian Missions: Studies in Cultural Conflict* (University of Chicago Press, 1981).

Boyd, James P., *Recent Indian Wars, Under the Lead of Sitting Bull, and Other Chiefs with A Full Account of the Messiah Craze, and Ghost Dances* (Philadelphia, PA: Kessinger Publishing, 1891).

Bratt, John H., *The Rise and Development of Calvinism* (Grand Rapids, MI: William B. Eerdmans Publishing Co., 1959).

Brooks, James, "'This Evil Extends Especially … to the Feminine Sex': Negotiating Captivity in the New Mexico Borderlands," *Feminist Studies,* 22/2 (Summer 1996): 279–309.

——, *Captives & Cousins, Slavery, Kinship, and Community in the Southwest Borderlands* (Chapel Hill: University of North Carolina Press, 2002).

Brown, Joseph E., *The Sacred Pipe: Black Elk's Account of the Seven Rites of the Oglala Sioux* (New York: Penguin Books, 1971; reprint of 1953 edn.).

Buck, Peter H., *Arts and Crafts of Hawaii* (Honolulu, HI: Bishop Museum Press, 1964).

Budde, Michael L., *The (Magic) Kingdom of God: Christianity and Global Culture Industries* (Boulder, CO: Westview Press, 1997).

Burgin, Victor, "Something about Photography Theory," in A.L. Rees and Frances Borzello (eds.), *The New Art History* (Atlantic Highlands, NJ: Humanities Press, 1986): 41–54.

Burrows, Edward G., *Hawaiian Americans* (New Haven, CT: Yale University Press, 1947).

Bush, Alfred L. and Lee Clark Mitchell, *The Photograph and the American Indian* (New Jersey: Princeton University Press, 1994).

Butler, Jon, Grant Walker, and Randall Balmer, *Religion in American Life: A Short History* (New York: Oxford University Press, 2008).

Cajete, Gregory, *Look to the Mountain: An Ecology of Indigenous Education* (North Carolina: Kiwaki Press, 1994).

Calhoun, Margaret, *Pioneers of Mono Basin* (Lee Vining, CA: Artemisia Press, 1984).

Callicott, J. Baird and Michael P. Nelson, *American Indian Environmental Ethics: An Ojibwa Case Study* (New Jersey: Pearson Prentice Hall, 2004).

Candler, Warren, *Great Revivals and the Great Republic* (Nashville, TN: Publishing House of the M.E. Church, 1904).

Carter, John E. "Making Pictures for a News-Hungry Nation," in Richard E. Jensen, R. Eli Paul, and John E. Carter (eds.), *Eyewitness at Wounded Knee* (Lincoln: University of Nebraska Press, 1991):

Cary, Richard, *Critical Art Pedagogy, Foundations for Postmodern Education* (New York: Garland Publishing, Inc., 1998).

Castillo, Ana, *Goddess of the America:,Writings on the Virgin of Guadalupe* (New York: Riverhead Books, 1996).

Caughey, John W., "California in Third Dimension," *The Pacific Historical Review*, 74/1 (1959): 111–29

Cazimero, Momi, David J. de la Torre, and Manulani Meyer, *Na Maka Hou: New Visions, Contemporary Hawai'ian Art* (Honolulu, HI: Honolulu Academy of Arts, 2001).

Clark, Herman Pi"ikea, "A Native Hawaiian Visual Language Project," *Art Journal*, 57/3 (1998): 3.

——, *"A'u Ka Lehua," Hiteemlkiliiksix: Within the Circle of the Rim* (Olympia, WA: Hemlock Press, 2002).

——, "Kûkulu Kauhale o Limaloa: A Kanaka Maoli Culture Based Approach to Education Through Visual Studies" (PhD diss., New Zealand: Massey University, 2006).

Coan, Lydia, *Titus Coan a Memorial* (Chicago: Revell, 1884).

Coan, Titus, *Life in Hawaii* (New York: Anson D.F. Randolph, 1882).

Cobb, Amanda J. (guest ed.), "The National Museum of the American Indian," special issue of *The American Indian Quarterly*, 29, 3/4 (Summer/Fall 2005).

Coleman, William S. E., *Voices of Wounded Knee* (Lincoln: University of Nebraska Press, 2000.)

Collier, Jr., John and Malcolm Collier, *Visual Anthropology: Photography as a Research Method* (Albuquerque: University of New Mexico Press, 1986).

Columbus, Christopher, Lionel Cecil Jane, and Bartolomé de las Casas, *The Journal of Christopher Columbus* (New York: Bonanza Books, 1989).

Comanchitos, Hermanitos, *Indo Hispanic Rituals of Captivity and Redemption, Enrique Lamadrid* (Albuquerque: University of New Mexico Press, 2003).

Costello, Damian, *Black Elk: Colonialism and Lakota Catholicism* (Maryknoll, NY: Orbis Books, 2005).

Costo, Jeanette H., "The Sword and the Cross: The Missions of California," in Rupert Costo and Jeanette H. Costo (eds.), *The Missions of California: A Legacy of Genocide* (San Francisco: Indian Historical Press, 1987): 49–66.

Costo, Rupert, "The Indians before Invasion," in Rupert Costo and Jeanette H. Costo (eds.), *The Missions of California: A Legacy of Genocide* (San Francisco: Indian Historical Press, 1987): 9–28.

Costo, Rupert and Jeanette H. Costo (eds.), *The Missions of California: A Legacy of Genocide* (San Francisco: Indian Historian Press, 1987).

Couser, G. Thomas "Black Elk Speaks with Forked Tongue," in James Olney (ed.), *Studies in Autobiography* (New York: Oxford University Press, 1988): 73–88.

Curtis, Georgina Pell, "Early Conversions to the Catholic Church in America (1521–1830)," *The Catholic Historical Review*, 1/3 (1915): 271–81.

Dary, David A., *The Buffalo Book: The Full Saga of the American Animal* (Athens: Swallow Press, Ohio University Press, 1989).

Daws, Gaven, *Shoal of Time: A History of the Hawaiian Islands* (Toronto: The Macmillan Company, 1968).

Debo, Angie, *A History of the Indians of the United States* (Norman: University of Oklahoma Press, 1984).

Delâge, Denys, *Bitter Feast: Amerindians and Europeans in Northeastern North America, 1600–64, trans. Jane Bierley* (Vancouver: UBC Press, 1993).

De la Torre, David, "Introduction: Reflections on the Group Exhibition," in Momi Cazimero, David De la Torre, and Manulani Meyer (eds.), *Na Maka Hou: New Visions, Contemporary Hawaiian Art* (Honolulu, HI: Honolulu Academy of Art, 2001): 7–9.

Defoe, Daniel, *Dictionarium Sacrum Seu Religiosum: A Dictionary of All Religions, Ancient and Modern. Whether Jewish, Pagan, Christian, or Mahometan* (London: Printed for James Knapton, 1704).

Deloria, Barbara, Kristen Foehner, and Samuel Scinta, (eds.), with a foreword by Wilma Mankiller, *Spirit and Reason: The Vine Deloria, Jr., Reader* (Golden, CO: Fulcrum Publishing, 1999).

Deloria, Philip J., *Indians in Unexpected Places* (Topeka: University of Kansas, 2004).

——, *Playing Indian* (New Haven, CT: Yale University Press, 1998).

Deloria, Jr., Vine, *For this Land: Writings on Religion in America* (New York: Routledge, 1999).

——, *God Is Red: A Native View of Religion* (Golden, CO: Fulcrum Publishers, 2003).

——, *Red Earth White Lies: Native Americans and the Myth of Scientific Fact* (New York: Scribner, 1995).

——, *The World We Used to Live In: Remembering the Powers of the Medicine Men* (Golden, CO: Fulcrum Publishing, 2006).

DeMallie, Raymond J., "The Lakota Ghost Dance: An Ethnohistorical Account," *Pacific Historical Review*, 51/4 (1982): 385–405.

—— (ed.), *The Sixth Grandfather, Black Elk's Teachings Given to John G. Newhart* (Lincoln: University of Nebraska Press, 1984).

Denzin, Norman K., Yvonna Lincoln, and Linda Tuhiwai Smith, *Handbook of Critical and Indigenous Methodologies* (Thousand Oaks, CA: Sage Publications, 2008).

Dibble, Sheldon, *History of the Sandwich Islands,* (Honolulu, HI: T.G. Thrum, 1854).

Dippie, Brian W., *The Vanishing American: White Attitudes and U.S. Indian Policy* (Middletown, CT: Wesleyan University Press, 1982).

Douglas, Mary, *Purity and Danger: An Analysis of the Concepts of Pollution and Taboo* (New York: Rutledge, 1966).

Dries, Angelyn, *The Missionary Movement in American Catholic History* (Maryknoll, NY: Orbis Books, 1998).

Driver, Harold E., "Culture Element Distributions: VI. Southern Sierra Nevada," in *Anthropological Records* (vol. 1:2, Berkeley: University of California Press, 1937), pp. 53–154.

Duncan, David Ewing, "The Object at Hand: A Famed Sioux Warrior-Prophet Named Kicking Bear," *Smithsonian*, 22/6 (September 1991): 22–7.

Dunsmore, Roger, "Columbus Day Revisited: American Indian Literature and Historical/Linguistic Truth," in *Earth's Mind: Essays in Native Literature* (Albuquerque: University of Nebraska Press, 1997): 193–213.

——, "Nicholas Black Elk: Holy Man in History," in *Earth's Mind: Essays in Native Literature* (Albuquerque: University of New Mexico Press, 1997): 69–90.

Dupris, Joseph C., Kathleen S. Hill, and William H. Rodgers, Jr., *The Si'lailo Way: Indians, Salmon and Law on the Columbia River* (Durham, NC: Carolina Academic Press, 2006).

Eagleton, Terry, "The Fate of the Arts," *The Hedgehog Review*, 6/2 (Summer 2004): 7–17.

Ebright, Malcolm and Rick Hendricks, *The Witches of Abiquiu: The Governor, the Priest, the Genizaro Indians, and the Devil* (Albuquerque: University of New Mexico Press, 2006).

Eccles, William J., *The French in North America, 1500–1783* (East Lansing: Michigan State University Press, 1998).

Eco, Umberto, "A Photograph," in Liz Wells (ed.), *The Photography Reader* (New York: Routledge, 2003), pp. 126–9.

Efland, Arthur D., *A History of Art Education: Intellectual and Social Currents in Teaching the Visual Arts* (New York: Teachers College Press, 1990).

Elide, Micea, *The Sacred and the Profane* (New York: Harcourt, 1959).

Ellis, William, *Journal of a Tour around Hawaii* (Boston, MA: Crocker and Brewster, 1825).

——, *The American Mission in the Sandwich Islands* (London: Whitney, 1866).

Emerson, Nathaniel B., "Causes of Decline of Ancient Hawaiian Sports," *The Friend*, 50/8 (1892): 57–60.

——, *Unwritten Literature of Hawaii* (Washington, DC: Smithsonian Institution, 1909).

Emmison, Michael J. and Philip D. Smith, *Researching the Visual: Images, Objects, Contexts and Interaction in Social and Cultural Inquiry* (Thousand Oaks, CA: Sage Publications, 2000).

Erdoes, Richard, *The Sundance People: The Plains Indians, Their Past and Present* (New York: Alfred A. Knopf, 1972).

Espinosa, Gastón and Mario García (eds.), *Mexican American Religions: Spirituality, Activism, and Culture* (Durham, NC: Duke University Press, 2008).

Eveleth, Ephraim, *History of Sandwich Islands* (Philadelphia, PA: American Sunday Schools, 1839).

Farella, John R., *The Main Stalk* (Tucson: University of Arizona Press, 1984).

Faris, James C., *Navajo and Photography: A Critical History of the Representations of an American People* (Albuquerque: University of New Mexico Press, 1996).

Foley, Thomas W., *Father Francis M. Craft, Missionary to the Sioux* (Lincoln: University of Nebraska Press, 2000).

Forsyth, Susan, *Representing the Massacre of American Indians at Wounded Knee, 1890–2000* (Lewiston, NY: Edwin Millen Press, 2003).

Foucault, Michel, The *Order of Things: An Archaeology of the Human Sciences*, a translation of *Les Mots et les choses* (New York: Vintage Books, 1970; reprint of 1966 edn.).

Fowler, Catherine S., "Northern Paiute," in Mary B. Davis (ed.), *Native America in the Twentieth Century: An Encyclopedia* (New York: Garland Publishing, 1994), pp. 422–6.

——, "Owens Valley Paiute," in Mary B. Davis (ed.), *Native America in the Twentieth Century: An Encyclopedia* (New York: Garland Publishing, 1994), pp. 426–8.

Frear, Walter, *A Century of Achievement* (Honolulu, HI: Mission Association, 1920).

Fuchs, Lawrence, *Hawaiian Pono: A Social History* (New York: Hancourt, Brace, and World, 1960).

Gallegos, Bernardo, *Literacy, Education, and Society in Colonial New Mexico, 1693–1821* (Albuquerque: University of New Mexico Press, 1992).

——, "Schools and Schooling in the Spanish Borderlands," in Jacob E. Cooke (ed.), *Encyclopedia of the North American Colonies* (New York: Macmillan Publishing, 1993).

——, "Theories of Education in the Spanish Borderlands," in Jacob E. Cooke (ed.), *Encyclopedia of the North American Colonies* (New York: Macmillan Publishing, 1994).

——, "Whose Lady of Guadalupe? Indigenous Performances, Latina/o Identities, and the Postcolonial Project," *Journal of Latinos and Education* (Fall 2002).

Gallimore, Ronald, John W. Boggs, and Cathie Jordan, *Culture, Behavior and Education: A Study of Hawaiian-Americans* (Beverly Hills, CA: Sage Publications, 1974).

Gateau, Dawn, "Sage Smudge, Sip of Water, a Consecrated Host," *National Catholic Reporter*, 30/7 (10 December 1993): 18.

Geertz, Clifford, *The Interpretation of Cultures* (New York: Basic Books, 1973).

—— (ed.), *Myth, Symbol and Culture* (New York: Norton, 1971).

Gendzel, Glen, "Pioneers and Padres: Competing Mythologies in Northern and Southern California (1830–1930)," *The Western Historical Quarterly*, 32/1 (2001): 55–79.

Gerth, Hans H., and C. Wright Mills (eds. and trans.) "Science as a Vocation," in *From Max Weber: Essays in Sociology* (New York: Oxford University Press, 1946).

Gill, Sam D., *Native American Religions: An Introduction* (Belmont, CA: Wadsworth Publishing Company, 2005).

——. *Native American Traditions: Sources and Interpretations* (Belmont, CA: Wadsworth Publishing Company, 2006).

Gleason, Philip, "The Catholic Church in American Public Life in the Twentieth Century," *Logos*, 3/4 (Fall 2000): 85–99.

Grady, John, "Sociology"s New Workshop: The Visual Challenge of Sociology," *Sociological Imagination*, 38/2–3, (2001): 4–6.

Grant, John W., *Moon in Wintertime: Missionaries and the Indians of Canada in Encounter since 1534* (University of Toronto Press, 1984).

Green, Kenneth J., *An Invitation to Social Construction* (Thousand Oaks, CA: Sage, 1999).

——, *Realities and Relationships: Soundings in Social Relationships* (Cambridge, MA: Harvard University Press, 1994).

Greer, Allan, *Mohawk Saint: Catherine Tekakwitha and the Jesuits* (New York: Oxford University Press, 2005).

——, "Natives and Nationalism: The Americanization of Kateri Tekakwitha," *Catholic Historical Review*, 90/2 (April 2004): 260–72.

Griffiths, Nicholas and Fernando Cervantes, *Spiritual Encounters: Interactions between Christianity and Native Religions in Colonial America* (Lincoln: University of Nebraska Press, 1999).

Grinde, Jr., Donald A., "Learning to Navigate in a Christian World," in Jace Weaver (ed.), *Native American Religious Identity: Unforgotten Gods* (Maryknoll, NY: Orbis Books, 1998/2002), pp. 124–33.

Grinde, Donald A. and Bruce E. Johansen, *Ecocide of Native America: Environmental Destruction of Indian Lands and People* (Santa Fe, NM: Clearlight, 1995).

Gubrium, Jaber F. and James A. Holstein, *The New Language of Qualitative Method* (Oxford University Press, 1997).

Gutierrez, Ramon A., *When Jesus Came, the Corn Mothers Went Away: Marriage, Sexuality, and Power in New Mexico, 1500–1846* (Stanford, CA: Stanford University Press, 1991).

Hackett, Charles W., *Historical Documents Relating to New Mexico, Nueva Viscera, and Approaches Thereto* (vol. 1, Washington, DC: Carnegie Institute, 1937).

Handy, E. S. Craighill, K. P. Emory, and Mary Pekoe, *Polynesian Region* (Honolulu, HI: Bishop Museum Press, 1927).

Harjo, Suzan Shown, "The American Indian Religious Freedom Act: Looking Back and Looking Forward," *Wicazo Sa Review*, 19/2 (2004): 143–51.

Harper, Douglas, "Talking about Pictures: A Case for Photo Elicitation," *Visual Studies*, 17/1 (2002): 14–26.

Hauerwas, Stanley and David Toole, "Radical Hope: Ethics in the Face of Cultural Devastation (Book Review)," *The Christian Century*, 124/23 (13 November 2007): 43.

Hawaiian Church Mission, *Occasional Paper* (London: Rivington, 1865).

Heizer, Robert F., *Languages, Territories, and Names of California Indian Tribes* (Berkeley: University of California Press, 1966).

——, *The Natural World of the California Indians* (Berkeley: University of California Press, 1980).

Henry, Gordon, *The Light People* (East Lansing: University of Michigan Press, 1994).

Highwater, Jamake, *Ritual of the Wind: North American Indian Ceremonies, Music, and Dance* (Toronto: Methuen Publications, 1984).

Highway, Tomson, "Tomson Highway: Native Voice," *Adrienne Clarkson Presents*, VHS, dir. Robert Sherrin (Canadian Broadcasting Company, 1999).

Hill, Richard W., Sr., "In Search of an Indigenous Place: Museums and Indigenous Culture," in Mark Hirsch and Amy Pickworth (eds.), *The Native Universe and Museums in the Twenty-first Century: The Significance of the National Museum of the American Indian* (Washington, DC: Smithsonian Institution, 2005), pp. 97–117.

Hirsch, Mark and Amy Pickworth (eds.), *The Native Universe and Museums in the Twenty-first Century: The Significance of the National Museum of the American Indian* (Washington, DC: Smithsonian Institution, 2005).

Holler, Clyde, *Black Elk's Religion: The Sun Dance and Lakota Catholicism* (Syracuse, NY: Syracuse University Press, 1995).

—— (ed.), *The Black Elk Reader* (Syracuse, NY: Syracuse University Press, 2000).

Hopkins, Manley, *Hawaii: The Past, Present, and Future of Its Island Kingdom. A Historical Account of the Sandwich Islands* (London: Longman, 1862).

Huel, Raymond J. A., *Proclaiming the Gospel to the Indians and Métis* (Edmonton: University of Alberta Press, 1996).

Huenemann, Lynn F., "Northern Plains Dance," in *Native American Dance: Ceremonies and Social Traditions* (Washington, DC: National Museum of the

American Indian, Smithsonian Institution, with Starwood Publishing, Inc., 1992), pp. 125–48.

Huffstetter, Stephen, *Lakota Grieving: A Pastoral Response* (Chamberlain, SD: Tipi Press Printing, 1998).

Hunt, Timothy D., *The Past and Present of the Sandwich Islands; Being of Lectures to the First Congregational Church* (San Francisco, CA: Whitton, Townsend and Co., 1862).

Hyde, Lewis, *Trickster Makes this World: Mischief, Myth and Art* (New York: Farrar, Strauss and Giroux, 1998).

I'i, John P. *Fragments of Hawaiian History*, ed. Dorothy B. Barrere (Honolulu, HI: Bishop Museum Press, 1959).

Irwin, Lee, "Freedom, Law, and Prophesy: A Brief History of Native American Religious Resistance," in

——, "Freedom, Law, and Prophesy: A Brief History of Native American Religious Resistance," *American* Indian Quarterly, 21/1 (1997): 35–55.

——, The Dream Seekers: Native American Visionary Traditions of the Great Plains (Norman: University of Oklahoma Press, 1994).

—— (ed.), *Native American Spirituality: A Critical Reader* (Lincoln: University of Nebraska Press, 2000), pp. 295–316.

Jackson, Thomas L., "Father Serra Meets Coyote," in Rupert Costo and Jeanette H. Costo (eds.), *The Missions of California: A Legacy of Genocide* (San Francisco, CA: Indian Historical Press, 1987), pp. 99–110.

Jaenen, Cornelius J., *Friend and Foe: Aspects of French–Amerindian Cultural Contact in the Sixteenth and Seventeenth Centuries* (New York: Columbia University Press, 1976).

Jaouen, René, "Condition for the Authentic Inculturation: Some Observations of a Missionary in Cameroun," *Kerygma*, 19 (1985): 4–6.

Jarves, James J., *History of the Hawaiian or Sandwich Islands* (Boston, MA: James Munroe, 1843).

——, *A Tradition of Hawaii* (Boston, MA: James Munroe, 1875).

Jeffries, James B., "Denying Religion: French and Native American Spiritual Crossroads in Seventeenth-century New France" (PhD diss., Santa Barbara: University of California, 2007).

Jennings, Francis, *The Invasion of America: Indians, Colonialism, and the Cant of Conquest* (New York: W.W. Norton and Company, Inc., 1975).

Jensen, Richard E., "Another Look at Wounded Knee," in Richard E. Jensen, R. Eli Paul, and John E. Carter (eds.), *Eyewitness at Wounded Knee* (Lincoln: University of Nebraska Press, 1991), pp. 1–21.

Jensen, Richard E., R. Eli Paul, and John E. Carter (eds.), *Eyewitness at Wounded Knee* (Lincoln: University of Nebraska Press, 1991).

Jocks, Christopher Ronwanièn:te, "Spirituality for Sale: Sacred Knowledge in the Consumer Age," in Lee Irwin (ed.), *Native American Spirituality: A Critical Reader* (Lincoln: University of Nebraska Press, 2000), pp. 61–77.

Johansson, S. Ryan, "The Demographic History of Native Peoples of North America: A Selective Bibliography," *Yearbook of Physical Anthropology*, 25 (1982): 133–52.

Johnson, Willis Fletcher, *Life of Sitting Bull, History of the Indian War, 1890–91* (Philadelphia, PA: Edgewood Publishing Company, 1891).

Juvik, Sonia P. and James O. Juvik, *Atlas of Hawaii*, 3rd edn. (Honolulu, HI: Bishop Museum Publications, 1998).

Kamakau, Samuel, *Ruling Chiefs of Hawaii* (Honolulu, HI: Kamehameha School Press, 1961).

——, *Ka Poʻe Kahiko: The Peoples of Old* (Honolulu, HI: Bishop Museum Special Publications, 1964).

Kamakau, Samuel M., *The Works of the People of Old-Na Hana a Ka Poʻe Kahiko*; trans. from the newspaper *Ke Au ʻokoʻa* by Mary K. Pukui and ed. Dorothy B. Barrère (Honolulu, HI: Bishop Museum Press, 1976).

Kameʻeleihiwa, Lilikala, *Native Land and Foreign Desires: Pehea La E Pono Ai?* (Honolulu, HI: Bishop Museum, 1992).

Kanahele, George H.S., *Ku Kanaka Stand Tall: A Search for Hawaiian Values* (Honolulu, HI: University of Hawaiʻi Press, 1992).

Kanaʻiaupuni, Shawn. M., "Kaʻakalai Ku Kanaka: A Call for Strength Based Approaches from a Native Hawaiian Perspective," *Educational Researcher*, 34/5 (2005): 32–9.

Kavanagh, Thomas W., "Reading Photographs: Imaging and Imagining the Ghost Dance: James Mooney's Illustrations and Photographs, 1891–1893," http://php.indiana.edu/~tkavanag/visual5.html (accessed 1 October 2008).

——, "Southern Plains Dance: Tradition and Dynamism," in Charlotte Heth (ed.), *Native American Dance: Ceremonies and Social Traditions* (Washington, DC: National Museum of the American Indian, Smithsonian Institution, with Starwood Publishing, Inc., 1992), pp. 105–24.

Kawagley, A. Oscar, *A Yupiaq Worldview: A Pathway to Ecology and Spirit* (Prospect Heights, IL: Waveland Press, Inc., 1995).

Kehoe, Alice Beck, *The Ghost Dance: Ethnohistory and Revitalization* 2nd edn. (Long Grove, IL: Waveland Press, 2006).

Kelly, Isabel T., *Southern Paiute Ethnography* (New York: Garland Publishing Inc., 1976).

Kenner, Charles, *A History of New Mexican–Plains Indian Relations* (Norman: University of Oklahoma Press, 1969).

Kersten, Earl W., "The Early Settlement of Aurora, Nevada, and Nearby Mining Camps," *Annals of the American Association of Geographers*, 54/4 (1964): 490–507.

Kidwell, Clara Sue, Homer Noley, and George Tinker, *A Native American Theology* (Maryknoll, NY: Orbis Books, 2001).

King, Thomas, *Green Grass, Running Water* (New York: Houghton Mifflin Company, 1993).

Knowles, Caroline, *Race and Social Analysis* (Thousand Oaks, CA: Sage Publications, 2003).

Kobayashi, José M, *La educación como conquista* (Mexico City: El Colegio de Mexico, 1985).

Kolbenschlag, George R., *A Whirlwind Passes: News Correspondents and the Sioux Indian Disturbances of 1890–1891* (Vermillion: University of South Dakota Press, 1990).

Korn, Arthur, *The Victorian Visitors* (Honolulu, HI: University of Hawai'i, 1968).

Korn, Arthur and Mary Pukui, "News from Molokai," *Pacific Historical Review*, 34 (February 1963): 17–32.

Kosasa, Karen, "Pedagogical Sights/Sites: Producing Colonialism and Practicing Art in the Pacific," *Art Journal*, 57/3 (Fall 1998): 46–54.

Koskinen, Aarne A., *Missionary Influence as a Political Factor in the Pacific Islands* (Helsinki: Seurah Kirjapainon, 1953).

Kroeber, Alfred L., *Handbook of the Indians of California* (Washington, DC: Smithsonian, 1925).

——, "Culture Element Distributions: XI. Tribes Surveyed," in *Anthropological Records* (vol. 1:7, Berkeley: University of California Press, 1939), pp. 435–40.

Kuykendall, Ralph S., *The Hawaiian Kingdom: 1778–1854* (Honolulu, HI: University of Hawai'i Press, 1966).

Lahontan, Louis Armand de Lom d'Arce and Henri Coulet, *Dialogues de Monsieur le Baron de Lahontan et d'un sauvage dans l'Amèrique* Collection xviiie siècle (Paris: Editions Desjonquères, 1999).

Lane, Belden C., "Giving Voice to the Place: Three Models for Understanding American Sacred Space," *Religion and American Culture*, 11/1 (2001): 53–81.

Larsen, Clark S., "In the Wake of Columbus: Native Population Biology in the Postcontact Americas," *Yearbook of Physical Anthropology*, 37 (1994): 109–54.

Lathrop, Alan K., "Another View of Wounded Knee," *South Dakota History*, 16/3 (Fall 1986): 249–68.

Laubin, Reginald and Gladys Laubin, *Indian Dances of North America: Their Importance to Indian Life* (Norman: University of Oklahoma Press, 1979; reprint of 1977).

Lawlor, Mary, *Public Native America: Tribal Self-representations in Casinos, Museums, and Powwows* (New Jersey: Rutgers University Press, 2006).

Lear, Jonathan, *Radical Hope: Ethics in the Face of Cultural Devastation* (Cambridge, MA: Harvard University Press, 2006).

Le Clercq, Chrestien, *First Establishment of the Faith in New France/ Premier Establissement de la Foy dans la Nouvelle France* (New York: John Shea, 1881).

Lemmons, Emilie, "Ojibway Catholic Finds Traditional Spirituality Woven into Faith," *The Catholic Spirit* (uploaded 24 June 2007), http://www.tcsdms.com/heritage/ojibway–catholic–finds.html (accessed 19 July 2008).

Lentz, Robert, "The Apache Christ," *Trinity Stores* (1990), www.trinitystores.com.

Léon-Portilla, Miguel, *Tonantzin Guadalupe:¸Pensamiento náhuatl y mensage cristiano en el* Nican Mophua (Mexico City: El Colegio de Mexico, 2000).

Lescarbot, Marc, *Histoire de la Nouvelle France*, Publications of the Champlain Society Publication 11, ed. Henry Percival Biggar and William Lawson Grant (Toronto: The Champlain Society, 1914).

Lewis, James A., "The Natives as Seen by the Missionaries: Preconception and Reality," in Rupert Costo and Jeanette H. Costo (eds.), *The Missions of California* (San Francisco, CA: Indian Historical Press, 1987), pp. 81–98.

Lewis, Thomas H., *The Medicine Men: Oglala Sioux Ceremony and Healing* (Lincoln: University of Nebraska Press, 1990).

Linderman, Frank B., *Plenty-Coups: Chief of the Crows* (Lincoln: University of Nebraska Press, 2000; reprint of 1930).

——, *Pretty-Shield: Medicine Woman of the Crows* (Lincoln: University of Nebraska Press, 2003; reprint of 1932,).

Linnekin, Joyce, *Sacred Queens and Women of Consequence: Rank, Gender, and Colonialism in the Hawaiian Islands* (Ann Arbor: University of Michigan Press, 2000).

Linton, Robert, "Nativistic Movements," in William A. Lessa and Evon Z. Vogt (eds.), *Reader in Comparative Religion* (New York: Harper and Row, 1965), pp. 499–506.

Lippard, Lucy, *Partial Recall: Photographs of Native North Americans* (New York: The New Press, 1992).

Long, Charles, *Significations: Signs, Symbols, and Images in the Interpretation of Religion* (Philadelphia, PA: Fortress Press, 1986).

Lord, Frances, "The Silent Eloquence of Things: The Missionary Collections and Exhibitions of the Society of Jesus in Quebec, 1843–1946," in Alvyn Austin and Jamie S. Scott (eds.), *Canadian Missionaries Indigenous Peoples: Representing Religion at Home and Abroad* (University of Toronto Press, 2005), pp. 205–34.

Lott, Dale F., *American Bison: A Natural History* (Berkeley: University of California Press, 2002).

MacCormack, Sabine, "Limits of Understanding: Perceptions of Greco-Roman and Amerindian Paganism in Early Modern Europe," in Karen Ordahl Kupperman (ed.), *America in European Consciousness, 1493–1750* (Chapel Hill: University of North Carolina Press, 1995), pp. 79–129.

Malo, David, *Hawaiian Antiquities, Second Edition*, trans. Nathaniel Emerson (Honolulu, HI: Bishop Museum, 1903/1951).

Manners, Robert A., *Southern Paiute Chemehuevi: An Ethnohistorical Report* (New York: Garland Publishing Inc., 1974).

Margolin, Malcolm, *The Way We Lived: California Indian Stories, Songs, and Reminisces* (Berkeley, CA: Heyday Books and the California Historical Society, 1993).

Martin, Joel W., "Before and beyond the Sioux Ghost Dance: Native American Prophetic Movements and the Study of Religion," *Journal of the Academy of Religion*, 59/4 (1991): 677–701.

Martin, Kathleen J., "Why don't they leave?" Saving faith and other issues of Catholic missionization," *Ayaangwaamizin: The International Journal of Indigenous Philosophy*, 3/2 (2007): 223–67.

Mason, Bernard A., *Dances and Stories of the American Indian* (Ann Arbor: University of Michigan Press, 1992; reprint of 1944).

Masuzawa, Tomoko, *The Invention of World Religions, or, How European Universalism Was Preserved in the Language of Pluralism* (University of Chicago Press, 2005).

Matthiessen, Peter, *In the Spirit of Crazy Horse* (New York: Penguin Books, 1992).

Maus, Marion P., "The New Indian Messiah," *Harper's Weekly*, 34/1772 (6 December 1890): 947.

McDonald, Freda, "No Longer and Indian," in Jace Weaver (ed.), *Native American Religious Identity: Unforgotten Gods* (Maryknoll, NY: Orbis Books, 2002), pp. 69–73.

McDonough, Peter and Eugene C. Bianchi, *Passionate Uncertainty: Inside the American Jesuits* (Berkeley: University of California Press, 2002).

McNeill, John T., *The History and Character of Calvinism* (New York: Oxford University Press, 1954).

McNeley, James. K., *Holy Wind in Navajo Philosophy* (Tucson: University of Arizona Press, 1981).

McQuire, Scott, *Visions of Modernity* (London and Thousand Oaks, CA: Sage Publications, 1998).

McRae, William E, "Images of Native Americans in Still Photography," *History of Photography*, 13/4 (October/December 1989): 321–42.

Meyer, Jerry D., "Profane and Sacred: Religious Imagery and Prophetic Expression in Postmodern Art," *Journal of the American Academy of Religion*, LXV/1 (1997): 19–46.

Melville, Leilani, *Children of the Rainbow* (Wheaton, IL: Theosophic Publishing House, 1969).

Merbs, Charles F., "A New World of Infectious Diseases," *Yearbook of Physical Anthropology*, 35 (1992): 3–42.

Milbank, John, "Fictioning Things: Gift and Narrative," http://www.theologyphilosophycentre.co.uk/papers/Milbank_FictioningThings.doc.

Miller, David Humphreys, *Ghost Dance* (Lincoln: University of Nebraska Press, 1985; reprint of 1959).

Milner, Vincent L., J. Newton Brown, and Hannah Adams, Religious Denominations of the World. A new and improved edition with an appendix brought up to the present time (Galesburg, IL: W. Garretson and Co., 1872).

Mitchell, Lee Clark, "The Photograph and the American Indian," in Alfred L. Bush and Lee Clark Mitchell (eds.), *The Photograph and the American Indian* (New Jersey: Princeton University Press, 1994), p. xiii.

Mitchell, Lynn Marie, "George E. Trager: Frontier Photographer at Wounded Knee," *History of Photography*, 13/4 (October/December 1989): 303–9.

Moogk, Peter N., *La Nouvelle France: The Making of French Canada—A Cultural History* (East Lansing: Michigan State University Press, 2000).

Mooney, James, *The Ghost-Dance Religion and the Sioux Outbreak of 1890*, ed. Raymond J. DeMallie (Chicago, IL: Kessinger Publishing, 1965).

Moore, R. Laurence, *Selling God: American Religion in the Marketplace of Culture* (New York: Oxford University Press, 1994).

Morfi, Juan Agustin, *Account of Disorders in New Mexico in 1778*, trans. Marc Simmons (Isleta, NM: San Augustin Press, 1968).

Morgan, David, *The Sacred Gaze: Religious Visual Culture in Theory and Practice* (Berkeley: University of California Press, 2005).

Morrison, Kenneth M., "Montagnais Missionization in Early New France," in Albert L. Hurtado and Peter Iverson (eds.), *Major Problems in American Indian History: Documents and Essays* (Lexington, MA: DC Heath and Company, 1994), pp. 104–16.

——, *The Solidarity of Kin: Ethnohistory, Religious Studies, and the Algonkian/ French Religious Encounter* (New York: SUNY Press, 2002).

Murray, David, *Indian Giving: Economies of Power in Indian–White Exchanges, Native Americans of the Northeast* (Amherst: University of Massachusetts Press, 2000).

Nabakov, Peter (ed.), *Two Leggings: The Making of a Crow Warrior* (Lincoln, University of Nebraska Press, 1967).

National Catholic Educational Association, *The People: Reflections of Native Peoples on the Catholic Experience in North America* (Washington, DC: NCEA, 1992).

Neihardt, John G., *Black Elk Speaks* (New York: Pocket Books, 1972; reprint of 1932).

Neizen, Ronald, *Spirit Wars: Native North American Religions in the Time of Nation Building* (Berkeley: University of California Press, 2000).

Nelson, Richard K., *Make Prayers to the Raven: A Koyukon View of the Northern Forest* (Chicago, IL: University of Chicago Press, 1983).

Noley, Homer, *First White Frost: Native Americans and United Methodism* (Nashville, TN: Abingdon Press, 1991).

——, "The Interpreters," in Jace Weaver (ed.), *Native American Religious Identity: Unforgotten Gods* (Maryknoll, NY: Orbis Books, 1998), pp. 48–60.

Norrell, Brenda, "Indigenous in Americas Just Say 'No' to Papal Bulls," *Indian Country Today*, 26/10 (16 August 2006): 5–7.

Norton, Jack, "The Path of Genocide: From El Camino Real to the Mines of the North," in Rupert Costo and Jeanette H. Costo (eds.), *The Missions of California: A Legacy of Genocide* (San Francisco, CA: Indian Historical Press, 1987), pp. 111–30.

Ohnesorge, Karen, "Uneasy Terrain: Image, Text, Landscape, and Contemporary Indigenous Artists in the United States," *American Indian Quarterly*, 32/1 (Winter 2008): 43–69.

Ortiz, Simon J. (ed.), *Beyond the Reach of Time and Change: Native American Reflections on the Frank A. Rinehart Photograph Collection* (Tucson: University of Arizona Press, 2004).

Paakspuu, Kalli, "Winning of Losing the West: The Photographic Act," *Bulletin of Science, Technology and Society*, 27/1 (2007): 48–58.

Paper, Jordan, *Offering Smoke: The Sacred Pipe and Native American Religion* (Edmonton: University of Alberta Press, 1989).

——, *Native North American Religious Traditions: Dancing for Life* (Westport, CT: Praeger Publishers, 2007).

Pavlick, Steve, "The Supreme Court Decision on Peyote in *Employment Division vs. Smith*: A Case Study in the Suppression of Native American Religious Freedom," *Wicazo Sa Review*, 8/2 (1992): 30–9.

Pelotte, Donald, "Native American Catholics at the Millennium," *Presentation to the Spring Assembly of the United States Conference of Catholic Bishops*, http://www.usccb.org/education/statement.shtml (accessed 20 March 2007).

Pérez, Laura E., *Chicana Art: The Politics of Spiritual and Aesthetic Altarities* (Durham, NC: Duke University Press, 2007).

Perrig, Amilius and John M. Carroll (trans.), "Diary [December 15, 1890]" (Marquette University Library, Special Collections), cited in William S.E. Coleman, *Voices of Wounded Knee* (Lincoln: University of Nebraska Press, 2000), p. 36.

Perrot, Nicolas. "Memoir on the Manners, Customs, and Religion of the Savages of North America (1864)," in Emma Helen Blair (ed.), *The Indian Tribes of the Upper Mississippi Valley and Region of the Great Lakes* (Cleveland, OH: Arthur H. Clark, 1911), p. 47.

Pesantubbee, Michelene, "Beyond Domesticity: Choctaw Women Negotiating the Tension between Culture and Protestantism," *Journal of the American Academy of Religion*, 67/2 (June 1999): 387–409.

Peshkin, Alan, "The Nature of Interpretation in Qualitative Research," *Educational Researcher*, 29/9 (2000): 5–9.

Peters, Michael, *Education and Culture in Postmodernity: The Challenges for Aotearoa/New Zealand* (Christchurch, New Zealand: Macmillan Brown Lectures, 2000).

Policansky, David, "Science and Decision Making for Water Resources," *Ecological Applications*, 8/3 (1998): 610–8.

Pollock, Della, "Introduction," in Della Polluck (ed.), *Exceptional Spaces: Essays in Performance and History* (Chapel Hill: University of North Carolina Press, 1998).

Powers, Stephen, *The Tribes of California: Introduction and Annotations by Robert F. Heizer* (Berkeley, CA: University of California Press, 1976).

Powers, William K., *Oglala Religion* (Lincoln: University of Nebraska Press, 1977).

——, *Sacred Language: The Nature of Supernatural Discourse in Lakota* (Norman: University of Oklahoma Press, 1986).

——, *Beyond the Vision: Essays on American Indian Culture* (Norman: University of Oklahoma Press, 1987).

Prakash, Gyan, "Subaltern Studies as Postcolonial Criticism," *American Historical Review*, 99 (December 1994): 1475–90.

Price, Mary, *The Photograph: A Strange Confined Space* (Stanford, CA: Stanford University Press, 1997).

Prosser, Jon (ed.), *Image-based Research: A Sourcebook for Qualitative Researchers* (Bristol, PA: Falmer, 1998).

Pukui, Mary K., E.W. Haertig, and Catherine Lee, *Nana I Ke Kumu (Look to the Source)* (Honolulu, HI: Hui Hanai, 1972).

——, *`Ôlelo No`eau: Hawaiian Proverbs and Poetical Sayings* (Honolulu, HI: Bishop Museum Press, 1984).

Pyne, Stephen J., *Fire in America: A Cultural History of Wildland and Rural Fire* (New Jersey: Princeton University Press, 1982).

Rael-Gálvez, Estevan, "Identifying Captivity and Capturing Identity: Narratives of American Indian Slavery, Colorado, and New Mexico, 1776–1934" (PhD, diss., Ann Arbor, University of Michigan, 2004).

Ramsey, Jarold, "The Bible in Western Indian Mythology," *Journal of American Folklore*, 90/358 (1977): 442–54.

Rawls, James J., *Indians of California: The Changing Image* (Norman: University of Oklahoma Press, 1986).

Reichard, Gladys, "The Navajo and Christianity," *American Anthropologist*, 51 (1949): 35–41.

Reid, Patrick V. (ed.), *Readings in Western Religious Thought: The Ancient World.* (Mahwah, NJ: Paulist Press, 1987).

Restarick, Henry B., *The Story of the Mission* (Honolulu, HI: Hawaiian Mission Association, 1920).

——, *Hawaii, 1778–1920, from the Viewpoint of a Bishop* (Honolulu, HI: Paradise of the Pacific, 1924).

Ricard, Robert, *The Spiritual Conquest of Mexico: An Essay on the Apostolate and the Evangelizing Methods of the Mendicant Orders in New Spain: 1523–1572* (Berkeley: University of California Press, 1966).

Rice, Julian, *Black Elk's Story: Distinguishing Its Lakota Purpose* (Albuquerque: University of New Mexico Press, 1991).

Rivera, Luis N., *A Violent Evangelism: the Political and Religious Conquest of the Americas* (Louisville, KY: Westminster/John Knox Press, 1992).

Robotham, Tom, *Native Americans in Early Photographs* (San Diego, CA: Thunder Bay Press, 1994).

Rodríguez, Sylvia, *The Matachines Dance: Ritual Symbolism and Interethnic Relations in the Upper Río Grande Valley* (Albuquerque: University of New Mexico Press, 1996).

Romero, Brenda M., "The Indita Genre of New Mexico: Gender and Cultural Identification," in Norma Ella Cantú and Olga Nájera-Ramírez (eds.), *Chicana Traditions: Continuity and Change* (Urbana: University of Illinois Press, 2002), pp. 56–80.

Ryan, Allan J., *The Trickster Shift: Humour and Irony in Contemporary Native Art* (Vancouver: UBC Press, 1999).

Sagard, Gabriel, "Long Journey to the Country of the Hurons," *Publications of the Champlain Society*, xlvii/25 (New York: Greenwood Press, 1968): 411.

Sagard, Gabriel, George McKinnon Wrong, and Hugh Hornby Langton, *The Long Journey to the Country of the Hurons* (Toronto: The Champlain Society, 1939).

Sahlins, Marshall, *Historical Metaphors and Mythical Realities: Structure in the Early History of the Sandwich Islands Kingdom* (Ann Arbor: University of Michigan Press, 1985).

Sayre, Gordon Mitchell, *Les Sauvages Américains: Representations of Native Americans in French and English Colonial Literature* (Chapel Hill: University of North Carolina Press, 1997).

Schmitt, Robert C., "Religious Statistics of Hawaii, 1825–1972," *The Hawaiian Journal of History*, VII (1973): 41–7.

Schurr, Theodore G., "The Peopling of the New World: Perspectives from Molecular Biology," *Annual Review of Anthropology*, 33 (2004): 551–83.

Scott, Clive, *The Spoken Image: Photography and Language* (London: Reaktion Books, 1999).

Scott, James C., *Domination and the Arts of Resistance: Hidden Transcripts* (New Haven, CT: Yale University Press, 1990).

Seymour, Forrest W., *Sitanka: The Full Story of Wounded Knee* (West Hanover, MA: Christopher Publishing House, 1981).

Shiner, Larry E., *The Invention of Art: A Cultural History* (London: University of Chicago Press, 2001).

Shipek, Florence C., "California Indian Reactions to the Franciscans," *The Americas*, 41/4 (1985): 480–92.

——, "Saints or Oppressors: The Franciscan Missionaries of California," in Rupert Costo and Jeanette H. Costo (eds.), *The Missions of California: A Legacy of Genocide* (San Francisco, CA: Indian Historical Press, 1987), pp. 29–48.

Silverman, Jane L., *Kaahumanu: Molder of Change* (Honolulu, HI: Friends of the Judiciary History Center of Hawaii, 1987).

Smith, Andrea, "Walking in Balance: The Spirituality-Liberation Praxis of Native Women," in Jace Weaver (ed.), *Native American Religious Identity: Unforgotten Gods* (Maryknoll, NY: Orbis Books, 2002), pp. 178–98.

Smith, Graham Hingangaroa, "The Development of Kaupapa Maori: Theory and Praxis" (PhD diss., New Zealand: University of Auckland, 1997).

Smith, Jonathan Z., "Studies in Judaism in Late Antiquity," in Jacob Neusner (ed.), *Map Is Not Territory: Studies in the History of Religion* (Leiden: E.J. Brill, 1978).

Smith, Linda Tuhiwai, *Decolonizing Methodologies: Research and Indigenous Peoples* (New York: Zed Books Ltd., 1999).

Smith, Rex Alan, *Moon of Popping Trees* (New York: Reader's Digest Press, 1975).

Smith, Sherry L., "Native Son: Frank Bird Linderman," in S. Smith (ed.), *Reimagining Indians: Native Americans through Anglo Eyes, 1880–1940* (New York: Oxford University Press, 2000), pp. 95–118.

Sontag, Susan, *On Photography* (New York: Farrar, Strauss and Giroux, 1977).

Spradley, James, *Participant Observation* (New York: Harcourt Brace Jovanovich College Publishers, 1980).

Stanczak, Gregory C., *Visual Research Methods: Image, Society, and Representation* (Thousand Oaks, CA: Sage Publications, 2007).

Standing Bear, Luther, *The Land of the Spotted Eagle* (Lincoln: University of Nebraska Press, 1978).

——, *My People the Sioux*, ed. E.A. Brininstol (Lincoln: University of Nebraska Press, 1975; reprint of 1928,).

Stannard, David E., *American Holocaust: The Conquest of the New World* (New York: Oxford University Press, 1992).

Steinmetz, Paul B., *Pipe, Bible, and Peyote among the Oglala Lakota* (Knoxville: University of Tennessee Press, 1990).

——, *The Sacred Pipe: An Archetypal Theology* (New York: Syracuse University Press, 1998).

Steward, Julian H., "Ethnography of the Owens Valley Paiute," *Publications in American Archaeology and Ethnology*, 33/3 (1933): 233–350.

——, "Two Paiute Autobiographies," *Publications in American Archaeology and Ethnology*, 33/5 (1933): 423–38.

Steward, Julian H., and Erminie Wheeler-Voegelin, *The Northern Paiute Indians* (New York: Garland Publishing Inc., 1974).

Stewart, Omer C., *Private Journal of Voyage to and Residence in Sandwich Islands* (New York: John P. Haven, 1828).

——, "The Northern Paiute Bands," in *Anthropological Records* (vol. 2:3, Berkeley: University of California Press, 1939), pp. 127–49.

——, "Culture Element Distributions: XIV. Northern Paiute," in *Anthropological Records* (vol. 4:3, Berkeley: University of California Press, 1941), pp. 361–446.

Stolzman, William F., *The Pipe and Christ: A Christian–Sioux Dialogue* (Chamberlain, SD: Tipi Press, 1989/1995).

Sturken, Marita and Lisa Cartwright (eds.), *Practices of Looking: An Introduction to Visual Culture*, 2nd edn. (New York: Oxford University Press, 2008).

Sullivan, Lawrence E., "Song and Dance: Native American Religions and American History," *Religion and American Culture*, 4/2 (1994): 255–73.

Swain, Joseph P., "Inculturating Liturgical Music," *America* (13 September 2004): 14–7.

Tagg, John, "The Currency of the Photograph," in Manuel Alvarado, Edward Buscombe, and Richard Collins (eds.), *Representation and Photography* (Basingstoke: Palgrave Macmillan, 2000), pp. 87ff.

Talbot, Steve, "Spiritual Genocide: The Denials of American Indian Religious Freedom, from Conquest to 1934," *Wicazo Sa Review* (Fall 2006): 7–39.

Taylor, Charles, *A Secular Age* (Cambridge, MA: Belknap Press, 2007).

Tedlock, Dennis, *The Spoken Word and the Work of Interpretation* (Philadelphia, PA: University of Pennsylvania Press, 1983).

Thornton, Russell, *We Shall Live Again: The 1870 and 1890 Ghost Dance Movements as Demographic Revitalization* (Cambridge University Press, 1986).

Thrum, Thomas, *More Hawaiian Folktales* (Chicago, IL: A.C. McClure and Co., 1922).

Thwaites, Reuben Gold and A.E. Jones, *The Jesuit Relations and Allied Documents; Travels and Explorations of the Jesuit Missionaries in New France, 1610–1791; The Original French, Latin, and Italian Texts, with English Translations and Notes* (Cleveland, OH: Burrows Bros. Co., 1896).

Tinker, George, *Missionary Conquest: The Gospel and Native American Cultural Genocide* (Minneapolis, MN: Fortress Press, 1993).

Trachtenberg, Alan, "Illustrious Americans," in *Reading American Photographs* (New York, 1989).

Trask, Mililani, "Ka Lahui Hawaii: A Native Initiative for Sovereignty," *Turning the Tide: Journal of Anti-racist Activism, Research and Education*, 6 (December 1993): 1–10.

Trask, Haunani-Kay, *From a Native Daughter: Colonialism and Sovereignty in Hawaii* (Honolulu, HI: University of Hawai'i Press, 1999).

Treat, James (ed.), *Native and Christian: Indigenous Voices on Religious Identity in the United States and Canada* (New York: Routledge, 1996).

Turner, Dale, *This Is Not a Peace Pipe: Towards a Critical Indigenous Philosophy* (Toronto: University of Toronto Press, 2006).

Tynerman, David and George Bennett, *Journal of Voyages and Travels* (Boston, MA: Crocker and Brewster, 1832).

Ubelaker, Douglas H., "North American Population Size, A.D. 1500 to 1985," *American Journal of Physical Anthropology*, 77 (1988): 289–94.

Underhill, Ruth, *The Northern Paiute Indians of California and Nevada* (New York: AMS Press, 1980).

Utley, Robert Marshall, *The Last Days of the Sioux Nation* (New Haven, CT: Yale University Press, 1963).

USCCB, *Native American Catholics at the Millennium*, a report on a survey by the United States Conference of Catholic bishops ad hoc committee on Native American Catholics (Washington, DC, 2002), p. 11, www.usccb.org/education/nac.shtml (accessed 09 July 2008).

Valeri, Valerio, *Kingship and Sacrifice: Ritual and Society in Ancient Hawaii*, trans. Paula Wissing (Chicago: University of Chicago Press, 1985).

Vecsey, Christopher, *On the Padres' Trail* (Notre Dame, IN: University of Notre Dame Press, 1996).

——, *The Paths of Kateri's Kin* (Notre Dame, IN: University of Notre Dame Press, 1997).

——, *Where the Two Roads Meet* (Notre Dame, IN: University of Notre Dame Press, 1999).

Vespucci, Amerigo, *Vespucci Reprints, Texts, and Studies*, trans. George R. Northrup (vol. 5, New Jersey: Princeton University Press, 1916).

Vizenor, Gerald R., *The Trickster of Liberty: Wild Heirs to the Baronage*, new edn. (Norman: University of Oklahoma Press, 2005).

——, *Fugitive Poses: Native American Indian Scenes of Absence and Presence* (Lincoln: University of Nebraska Press, 1998).

Voget, F.W., *The Shoshoni–Crow Sundance* (Norman: University of Oklahoma Press, 1984).

Wagner, Jon, "Contrasting Images, Complementary Trajectories: Sociology, Visual Sociology and Visual Research," *Visual Studies*, 17/2 (2002): 160–71.

—— (ed.), *Images of Information: Still Photography in the Social Sciences* (Beverly Hills, CA: Sage Publications, Inc., 1979).

Walker, James R., *Lakota Belief and Ritual*, ed. Elaine A. Jahner and Raymond J. DeMallie (Lincoln: University of Nebraska Press, 1980).

Walls, Andrew, *The Missionary Movement in Christian History: Studies in the Transmission of Faith* (Maryknoll, NY: Orbis Books, 1996).

Warrior, Robert Allen, *Tribal Secrets: Recovering American Indian Intellectual Traditions* (Minneapolis: University of Minnesota Press, 1995).

Weaver, Jace, "Losing My Religion: Native American Religious Traditions and American Religious Freedom," in Jace Weaver (ed.), *Other Words: American Indian Literature, Law, and Culture* (Norman: University of Oklahoma Press, 2001).

—— (ed.), *Native American Religious Identity: Unforgotten Gods* (Maryknoll, NY: Orbis Books, 1998).

Weber, Max, "Science as a Vocation," in H.H. Gerth and C. Wright Mills (trans. and eds.), *From Max Weber: Essays in Sociology* (New York: Oxford University Press, 1946), pp. 129–58.

White, Richard, *The Middle Ground: Indians, Empires, and Republics in the Great Lakes Region, 1650–1815* (New York: Cambridge University Press, 1991).

Witherspoon, Gary, "A New Look at Navajo Social Organization," *American Anthropologist*, 72 (1970): 55–65.

Wood, Houston, "Displacing Native Places: The Rhetorical Production of Hawai'i," (Honolulu, HI: University of Hawai'i, Manoa, 1996).

Wyss, Hillary, *Writing Indians: Literacy, Christianity and Native Communities in Early America* (Amherst: University of Massachusetts Press, 2000).

Yin, Robert K., *Case Study Research: Design and Methods* (Thousand Oaks, CA: Sage Publications, 1994).

Young, George T.K., *Mo'olelo Kaukau Ali'i: The Dynamics of Chiefly Service and Identity in "Oiwi Society"* (Honolulu: University of Hawai'i, Mānoa, 1995).

———. *Rethinking the Native Hawaiian Past* (New York: Garland Publishing, 1998).

Young Man, Alfred, "The Primitive White Mind," in Simon J. Ortiz (ed.), *Beyond the Reach of Time and Change: Native American Reflections on the Frank A. Rinehart Photograph Collection* (Tucson: University of Arizona Press, 2004), p. 140.

Yzendoorn, Reginal, *History of the Catholic Mission in the Hawaiian Islands* (Honolulu, HI: Star Bulletin, 1927)

Zeilinger, Ron, *Lakota life* (Chamberlain, SD: Tipi Press Printing, 1984).

Ziarek, Krzysztof, "The End of Art as Its Future," *Hedgehog Review*, 6/2 (Summer 2004): 23–35.

Zurbrugg, Nicholas (ed.), *Jean Baudrillard: Art and Artefact* (London: Sage Publications, 1997).

Index

Some passing references, particularly for frequently used terms such as Christian, Catholic Church, Indigenous, Hawaiian, missionizing, Native Peoples, spiritual, etc., are omitted. Page references in **bold** relate to extensive treatments of a particular subject; those in *italic* refer to illustrations. Affiliations to religious orders are given as follows: PVM=Sisters of the Presentation of the Blessed Virgin Mary; OFM=Franciscan; OSB=Order of Saint Benedict; OSF=Sisters of St. Francis; SBS=Sisters of the Blessed Sacrament; SJ= Society of Jesus. The preface and introduction are indexed.

A Treasury of Wall Street Wisdom

Edited by
Harry D. Schultz
&
Samson Coslow

1975~2001

Traders Press, Inc.®
PO Box 6206
Greenville, SC 29606

Cover Design
Teresa Darty Alligood
&
Cathy Rubert
Traders Press, Inc.®

1975~2001

**Traders Press, Inc.®
PO Box 6206
Greenville, SC 29606**

TRADERS PRESS, INC.®
PO BOX 6206
Greenville, SC 29606

Publishers of:

A Complete Guide to Trading Profits (Paris)
A Professional Look at S&P Day Trading (Trivette)
Ask Mr. EasyLanguage (Tennis)
Beginner's Guide to Computer Assisted Trading (Alexander)
Channels and Cycles: A Tribute to J.M. Hurst (Millard)
Chart Reading for Professional Traders (Jenkins)
Commodity Spreads: Analysis, Selection and Trading Techniques (Smith)
Comparison of Twelve Technical Trading Systems (Lukac, Brorsen, & Irwin)
Complete Stock Market Trading and Forecasting Course (Jenkins)
Cyclic Analysis (J.M. Hurst)
Day Trading with Short Term Price Patterns (Crabel)
Exceptional Trading: The Mind Game (Roosevelt)
Fibonacci Ratios with Pattern Recognition (Pesavento)
Futures Spread Trading: The Complete Guide (Smith)
Geometry of Markets (Gilmore)
Geometry of Stock Market Profits (Jenkins)
Harmonic Vibrations (Pesavento)
How to Trade in Stocks (Livermore & Smitten)
Hurst Cycles Course (J.M. Hurst)
Investing by the Stars (Weingarten)
Jesse Livermore: Speculator King (Sarnoff)
Magic of Moving Averages (Lowry)
Market Rap: The Odyssey of a Still-Struggling Commodity Trader (Collins)
New Concepts in Support and Resistance (Droke)
Pit Trading: Do You Have the Right Stuff? (Hoffman & Baccetti)
Planetary Harmonics of Speculative Markets (Pesavento)
Point & Figure Charting (Aby)
Point & Figure Charting: Commodity and Stock Trading Techniques (Zieg)
Profitable Grain Trading (Ainsworth)
Profitable Patterns for Stock Trading (Pesavento)
Short-Term Trading with Price Patterns (Harris)
Stock Market Trading Systems (Appel & Hitschler)
Stock Patterns for Day Trading (Rudd)
Stock Patterns for Day Trading 2 (Rudd)
Stock Patterns for Day Trading Home Study Course (Rudd)
Stock Trading Based on Price Patterns (Harris)
Study Helps in Point & Figure Techniques (Wheelan)
Tape Reading for the 21st Century (Droke)
Technically Speaking (Wilkinson)
Technical Trading Systems for Commodities and Stocks (Patel)
The Amazing Life of Jesse Livermore: World's Greatest Stock Trader (Smitten)
The Opening Price Principle: The Best Kept Secret on Wall Street (Pesavento)
The Professional Commodity Trader (Kroll)
The Taylor Trading Technique (Taylor)
The Traders (Kleinfeld)
The Trading Rule That Can Make You Rich* (Dobson)
Trading Secrets of the Inner Circle (Goodwin)
Trading S&P Futures and Options (Lloyd)
Understanding Bollinger Bands (Dobson)
Understanding Fibonacci Numbers (Dobson)
Viewpoints of a Commodity Trader (Longstreet)
Wall Street Ventures & Adventures Through Forty Years (Wyckoff)
Winning Market Systems (Appel)

PLEASE CONTACT TRADERS PRESS TO RECEIVE OUR CURRENT 100 PAGE CATALOG DESCRIBING THESE
AND MANY OTHER BOOKS AND GIFTS OF INTEREST TO INVESTORS AND TRADERS.
800-927-8222 ~ Fax 864-298-0221 ~ 864-298-0222
http://www.TradersPress.com~catalog@TradersPress.com

Publisher's Foreword

When one wishes to become successful in any venture, he is well advised to observe and to learn from the most successful individuals in that field. Those who would become successful in the fascinating and challenging subject of investing and trading are given the opportunity, in this classic book of yesteryear, to learn from the brightest and the best minds ever to "play the game." They share with the reader the wisdom they have accumulated through many years of study, hard work, and experience in the investment arena.

While many books are available giving the latest and most modern information and advice, there are few which provide information from the investment giants from the past. Knowledgeable experts concur that the advice and knowledge which may be gained from the individuals who contributed to this book is of great value, perhaps more so than that which is currently being published.

When I personally became interested in and involved in investing, in the early 1960's, I read dozens of books on the subject. Of these, only a handful come to mind as outstanding and stand out in my memory as being especially noteworthy. One of these is the book you are reading, *A Treasury of Wall Street Wisdom*. I hope that you find it to be as helpful and as valuable as I myself did.

Edward Dobson

Edward D. Dobson, President   **March 15, 2001**
Traders Press, Inc.®
Greenville, South Carolina

"IF I WANTED TO BECOME A TRAMP I WOULD SEEK INFORMATION AND ADVICE FROM THE MOST SUCCESSFUL TRAMP I COULD FIND. IF I WANTED TO BECOME A FAILURE I WOULD SEEK ADVICE FROM MEN WHO HAD NEVER SUCCEEDED. IF I WANTED TO SUCCEED IN ALL THINGS, I WOULD LOOK AROUND ME FOR THOSE WHO ARE SUCCEEDING AND DO AS THEY HAVE DONE."

JOSEPH MARSHALL WADE

TABLE OF CONTENTS

PART I

PART V

Introduction

You have in your hands the refined and filtered nectar from some of the keenest minds who have ever played an important role in Wall Street since its inception.

To bring you this Anthology of Wall Street Wisdom we have searched the libraries and private book collections; scanned microfilm, contacted living relatives of some of the Greats, and generally unearthed and uprooted everything and everybody who could be helpful in our all-out effort.

Books about investing are great in number, but few are wholly satisfactory. Still, it is seldom possible to skim through the most uneven of stock market manuals without emerging with at least one or two workable ideas. It was this paradox that led to the anthology of writings on investment philosophy presented here. In each case, the fat was carefully pared away, and the meat of the argument was left. Recognizing that one man's meat is another man's poison, a great variety of techniques and methods is included, from the earliest days on Wall Street to the present day.

At one stage or another in the career of almost every stock market trader, he devours stock market "methods" books—all sorts and sizes, from the classic writings of Dow to the most obscure "sure-fire" trading technique of some anonymous operator of the Twenties. From this reading program, the inquisitive investor will often discover refinements that can greatly improve his own methods.

Successful buying and selling of stocks is usually a lonely business. Behind consistent success, there usually lies a plan. And a plan able to sustain a profitable trading program is usually the result of a step-by-step thinking through of the sequences and signals that can guide the day-to-day execution. The working out of such a systematic program is often assisted by placing it alongside the detailed methods of other successful traders and critically evaluating each stage.

The selections which follow are presented, more or less, in chronological order. Over the years, the rules change and the types of actual operations are radically overhauled to match the new conditions in each era. But the objectives and motivations of the great Wall Street writers remain remarkably constant. It is the insights into these changeless aspects of market trading that are anthologized. In our final compilation, we endeavored to select the **essence**—the most important things and thoughts that these brilliant financial minds have recorded for posterity.

As Wall Street began to develop its characteristic methods around the time of the Civil War, trading was dominated by the Great Operators. These operators sought to carve out transportation empires and used the stock market as one of their critical battlefields. There are still some who go to Wall Street today seeking empires— such as the raiders shopping among the corporate shells and the closely held companies with relatively few shares outstanding.

Of more interest to the present day investor or trader are the efforts of the earlier stock market operators to follow the ebb and flow of market values through "readings" or signals taken periodically. The nature of these signals varies widely. One trader favors buying "undervalued" stocks or those with high yields, while another would buy only those stocks moving up on volume or forming a particularly "favorable" chart pattern. It was the development of these "methods" by Charles Dow and the other pioneers that established the necessary groundwork for the Cult of Common Stocks, as it first fully blossomed in the Twenties and has continued to flow right up to the present.

Without these guide lines, that at least on paper held out some promise of ultimate success, it is doubtful whether many small investors would have ventured so boldly into Wall Street. Therefore, it might be said that the leading approaches to investing that have stirred the public and motivated their purchases are introduced in this anthology. Each of these methods is presented in the exact words of the person who gave it its most eloquent and convincing expression. Together, they provide a review of the basic wisdom of Wall Street as it has appeared to several generations of market observers. It is hoped that this storehouse will add to the wisdom of Wall Street operators of today, and of those yet to come.

Part I

The Dow Theorists...

CHARLES H. DOW . . The Grandfather of Technical Analysis.

SAMUEL A. NELSON . . Author and Dow Theory Compiler.

WILLIAM P. HAMILTON . . Pioneer Technician and Successor to Dow.

ROBERT RHEA . . Dow Historian and Record Keeper.

RICHARD RUSSELL . . Leading Present-Day Dow Theorist.

CHARLES
H. DOW

A cornerstone name . . .

The Grandfather of Technical Analysis

One of the most frequently spoken words on Wall Street **any** day is DOW. "How is the Dow today?" is the commonest question put to brokers. The man who contributed his name to this (Dow-Jones Average) and to the equally famous "Dow Theory" was Charles H. Dow, who was born in Sterling, Connecticut on November 6, 1851.

Records of the New York Stock Exchange indicate that Dow was a partner of Goodbody, Glynn and Dow from December 1885 to April 1891. This, however, was a technicality. Dow became a partner merely because Robert Goodbody was not yet a naturalized citizen, and Dow held the seat only until Goodbody's citizenship came through. Even so, Dow executed orders on the floor and held the seat for several years, which was long enough to get an insider's view and feel of the market. (Goodbody & Company is still a major Wall Street house.)

But Dow was primarily a newspaper man, earning his income from this calling all of his working life. Starting on several New England newspapers, in 1880 he came to New York City as a financial reporter, writing articles and editorials for the *New York Mail* and *Express*. Thereafter he joined the Kiernan News Agency, where he met Edward D. Jones, a fellow worker. The two soon left Kiernan to form their own firm—Dow, Jones and Company—

3

which started by delivering "flimsies" or "slips" to financial institutions of Wall Street. July 8, 1889 saw the first edition of *The Wall Street Journal* with Dow as editor and founder.

Dow's editorials were written as just that, and not as a series of articles putting forth a specific theory. Since these editorials accurately reflected Dow's remarkably analytical thinking, S. A. Nelson put them together and called them, in toto, "Dow's Theory," of which Nelson became the first disciple.

Dow was modest in dress, in speech and in manner. He was a typical New Englander, intelligent, self-repressed, ultra-conservative, and he knew his business. He was said to be almost judicially cold in the consideration of any subject, whatever the fervor of discussion. His co-worker, William Hamilton, said of him, "It would be less than just to say that I never saw him angry, I never saw him even excited. His perfect integrity and good sense commanded the confidence of every man in Wall Street, at a time when there were few efficient newspaper men covering the financial section, and of these fewer with any depth of knowledge of finance."

An early associate on the Journal, Thomas F. Woodlock, said, "Dow was a tall, black-bearded, slightly stooping man, with a grave air and the measured speech of a college professor."

Hamilton once gave a fair and balanced appraisal of Dow's approach to the market:

"Knowing and liking Dow, with whom I worked in the last years of his life, I was often, with many of his friends, exasperated by his over-conservatism. It showed itself particularly in his editorials in *The Wall Street Journal,* to which it is now necessary to allude because they are the only written record of Dow's theory of price movement. He would write a strong, readable and convincing editorial, on a public question affecting finance and business and in the last paragraph would add safeguards and saving clauses which not merely took the sting out of it but took the 'Wallop' out of it. In the language of the prize ring he pulled his punches.

4

CHARLES H. DOW

"He was almost too cautious to come out with a flat, dogmatic statement of this Theory, however sound it was and however close and clear his reasoning might be. He wrote, mostly in 1901 and the first half of 1902, a number of editorials dealing with methods of stock speculation.

"But what may be commended is Dow's clarity and sterling good sense. What he had to say was worth saying and he stopped when he had said it—a rare virtue in editorial writing. His feeling for the essential fact and for the underlying truth, without which the fact is bare and impertinent, will be readily remarked. He dealt with speculation as a fact, and could still show forth its truth without profitless moralizing, or confusing it with gambling. It will be well to imitate his point of view in further discussion, both on his Theory and on the immense and useful significance of the stock market generally."

Dow died at the age of 51, in December 1902.

It is a matter of regret that Dow spoke to the world solely through his few editorials written within a three-year period early in the century for *The Wall Street Journal*. Poring through this scant supply of wordage now, one wonders whether perhaps the entire Dow legend may have been magnified all out of proportion by his later followers, and whether they have read into it more than its author actually conceived. Nevertheless, there is no doubt that Dow's source material provided the germ—as microscopic as it was—for the Theory which was later amplified by others into the now familiar concepts: The three market movements that go on simultaneously (major, secondary, and minor); the "higher tops and bottoms" and "lower tops and bottoms" that constitute the cornerstone of Dow Theory signals; the confirmations of the Industrial and Rail Averages, and the other well known theorems. Dow himself would probably have been the last one to suspect that an entire forecasting philosophy would evolve from his fragmentary day-to-day market comments, yet as crude as they may sound now, they were new and original in their day. They opened up new worlds and new horizons for his successors: S. A. Nelson, the first man to recognize

5

this breakthrough in stock market thinking, and who first "organized" Dow's writings in book form in 1903; Hamilton, Dow's successor as editor of *The Wall Street Journal,* an astute understudy who continued the tradition and who possibly contributed more to Dow Theory as it is known today than Dow himself; Rhea, who took Dow and Hamilton's basic principles and formulated them into an actual "system"; and Russell, who clarified much of the Theory's ambiguities and integrated them with the market concepts of today.

A few well-remembered examples of Charles Dow's writings of the early 1900's follows.

The Wisdom of
CHARLES H. DOW

Three General Lines of Reasoning...

W E HAVE SPOKEN in a preceding article of the fact that the experience of great interests in the market seems to have crystallized into three general lines of reasoning.

The first is that the surface appearance of the market is apt to be deceptive. The second is that it is well in trading to cut losses short and let profits run. The third is that correctly discounting the future is a sure and easy road to wealth. The problem is how these rules, which are undoubtedly sound, can be operated in a practical way.

Let us take first the action of the general market with reference to the time to buy. The market is always to be considered as having three movements, all going on at the same time. The first is the narrow movement from day to day. The second is the short swing, running from two weeks to a month or more; the third is the main movement covering at least four years in its duration.

The day to day movement should be disregarded by everybody, except traders, who pay no commissions. The medium swing is the one for ordinary consideration.

8

The outside trader should not attempt to deal in more than two or three stocks at a time. He should keep a chart of the price movements of these stocks so as to know their swings for months or years, and thus be able to tell readily where in the general swing his particular stocks appear to be.

He should keep with his price movement a record of the volume of transactions and notes of any special facts bearing on that property, such as increases or decreases in earnings, increases in fixed charges, development of floating debt, and above all the actual dividend earnings as shown from month to month. He should observe the movement of the general market as indicated by the averages published daily, as this shows the market more clearly than it is shown by any one stock.

The main purpose of this study is to enable the trader to determine, first, the value of the stock he is in; whether it is increasing or decreasing and, second, when the time to buy seems opportune. Assuming the thirty day swing to be about 5 points, it is in the highest degree desirable not to buy when three of these points have passed, as such a purchase limits the probable profits to about two points.

It is therefore generally wise to look for a low point on a decline. Suppose, for instance, that Union Pacific was the stock under consideration; that it was clearly selling below its value, and that a bull market for the four-year period was under way. Assuming further that in a period of reaction Union Pacific had fallen four points from the previous highest. Assume earnings and prospects to be favorable and the outlook for the general market to be about normal.

This would be the time to begin to buy Union Pacific. The prudent trader, however, would take only part of his line. He would buy perhaps one-half of the stock he wanted and then give an order to buy the remainder as the price declined. The fall might go much further than he anticipated. It might be necessary to wait a long time for profit. There might even be developments which would make it wise to throw over the stock bought with the hope of replacing it materially lower.

9

These, however, are all exceptions. In a majority of cases this method of choosing the time to buy, founded upon clear perception of value in the stock chosen and close observation of the market swings under way will enable an operator to secure stock at a time and at a price which will give fair profits on the investment.

Swings Within Swings

A CORRESPONDENT ASKS: "For some time you have been writing rather bullish on the immediate market, yet a little bearish in a larger sense. How do you make this consistent?"

We get this question in one form or another rather frequently. It denotes a lack of familiarity with fluctuations in prices when viewed over considerable periods. Many people seem to think that the change in prices in any one day is complete in itself and bears no relation to the larger movements which may be under way. This is not so.

Nothing is more certain than that the market has three well defined movements which fit into each other. The first is the daily variation due to local causes and the balance of buying or selling at that particular time. The secondary movement covers a period ranging from ten days to sixty days, averaging probably between thirty and forty days. The third move is the great swing covering from four to six years.

In thinking about the market, it is necessary to think with reference to each of these periods in order to take advantage of opportunities. If the main move is up, relapses are speculators' opportunities, but if the main move is down, rallies furnish these opportunities.

Losses should not generally be taken on the long side in a bull period. Nor should they generally be taken on the short side in a bear period. It is a bull period as long as the average of one high point exceeds that of previous high points. It is a bear period when the low point becomes lower than the previous low points. It is often difficult to judge whether the end of an advance has come because the movement of prices is that which would occur if the main tendency had changed. Yet, it may only be a pronounced secondary movement.

The first thing for any operator to consider is the value of the stock in which he proposes to trade. The second is to determine the direction of the main movement of prices. We know of nothing more instructive on this point than the course of prices as printed daily. The third thing is to determine the position of the secondary swing.

Assume for instance that the stock selected was Union Pacific; that the course of prices afforded clear evidence of a bull market under way; that the high point in Union Pacific thirty days ago was 108; that the price had slowly declined in sympathy with the market and without special new features to 98. The chances would be in favor of buying a part of the line wanted at that price with the intention of buying a little more if the stock had further decline or if the price showed a well defined advancing tendency. It would then be wise to watch the general market and wait for an advance.

A 10-point decline under such conditions would be almost certain to bring in a bull market more than 5 points recovery and full 10 points would not be unreasonable; hence if the general market maintained a good tone, it would be wise to wait for 5 points and then begin to think about stop orders.

Even in a bear market, this method of trading will usually be found safe, although the profit taken should be less because of the liability of weak spots breaking out and checking the general rise.

Methods of Reading the Market

A CORRESPONDENT WRITES: "Is there any way of forecasting the course of the market from the tape, from your records of transactions or from the summarized movement of prices? Transactions must mean something, but how can a trader tell what they mean?"

This is an old question. There have been a variety of answers but it is doubtful if any have been or can be wholly satisfactory. Several methods, however, are in practical use and at times afford suggestions.

There is what is called the book method.* Prices are set down, giving each change of 1 point as it occurs, forming thereby lines having a general horizontal direction but running into diagonals as the market moves up and down. There come times when a stock with a good degree of activity will stay within a narrow range of prices, say 2 points, until there has formed quite a long horizontal line of these figures. The formation of such a line sometimes suggests that stock has been accumulated or distributed, and this **leads other people** to buy or sell at the same time. Records of this kind kept for the last fifteen years seem to

* One of the earliest descriptions of point-and-figure.

support the theory that the manipulation necessary to acquire stock is often times detected in this way.

Another method is what is called the theory of double tops. Records of trading show that in many cases when a stock reaches top it will have a moderate decline and then go back again to near the highest figures. If after such a move, the price again recedes, it is liable to decline some distance.

Those, however, who attempt to trade on this theory alone find many exceptions and a good many times when signals are not given.

There are those who trade on the theory of averages. It is true that in a considerable period of time the market has about as many days of advance as it has of decline. If there come a series of days of advance, there will almost surely come the balancing days of decline.

The trouble with this system is that the small swings are always part of the larger swings, and while the tendency of events equally liable to happen is always toward equality, it is also true that every combination possible is liable to occur, and there frequently come long swings, or, in the case of stock trading, an extraordinary number of days of advance or decline which fit properly into the theory when regarded on a long scale, but which are calculated to upset any operations based on the expectation of a series of short swings.

A much more practicable theory is that founded on the law of action and reaction. It seems to be a fact that a primary movement in the market will generally have a secondary movement in the opposite direction of at least three-eighths of the primary movement. If a stock advances 10 points, it is very likely to have a relapse of 4 points or more. The law seems to hold good no matter how far the advance goes. A rise of 20 points will not infrequently bring a decline of 8 points or more.

It is impossible to tell in advance the length of any primary movement, but the further it goes, the greater the reaction when it comes, hence the more certainty of being able to trade successfully on that reaction.

A method employed by some operators of large experience is that of responses. The theory involved is this: The market is always under more or less manipulation. A large operator who is seeking to advance the market does not buy everything on the list, but puts up two or three leading stocks either by legitimate buying or by manipulation. He then watches the effect on the other stocks. If sentiment is bullish, and people are disposed to take hold, those who see this rise in two or three stocks immediately begin to buy other stocks and the market rises to a higher level. This is the public response, and is an indication that the leading stocks will be given another lift and that the general market will follow.

If, however, leading stocks are advanced and others do not follow, it is evidence that the public is not disposed to buy. As soon as this is clear the attempt to advance prices is generally discontinued. This method is employed more particularly by those who watch the tape. But it can be read at the close of the day in our record of transactions by seeing what stocks were put up within specified hours and whether the general market followed or not. The best way of reading the market is to read from the standpoint of values. The market is not like a balloon plunging hither and thither in the wind. As a whole, it represents a serious, well considered effort on the part of far-sighted and well-informed men to adjust prices to such values as exist or which are expected to exist in the not too remote future. The thought with great operators is not whether a price can be advanced, but whether the value of property which they propose to buy will lead investors and speculators six months hence to take stock at figures from 10 to 20 points above present prices.

In reading the market, therefore, the main point is to discover what a stock can be expected to be worth three months hence and then to see whether manipulators or investors are advancing the price of that stock toward those figures. It is often possible to read movements in the market very clearly in this way. To know values is to comprehend the meaning of movements in the market.

The "Ten Year Cycle" Theory

A CORRESPONDENT WRITES: "Is it true that commercial or stock exchange panics are approximately periodic in their occurrence?"

The facts point distinctly in that direction, and there is reason back of the facts. The reason is that the business community has a tendency to go from one extreme to the other. As a whole, it is either contracting business under a belief that prices will be lower or expanding under a belief that prices will be higher. It appears to take ordinarily five or six years for public confidence to go from the point of too little hope to the point of too much confidence and then five or six years more to get back to the condition of hopelessness.

This ten-year movement in England is given in detail by Professor Jevons in his attempt to show that sun spots have some bearing upon commercial affairs. Without going into the matter of sun spots and their bearing upon crops, commerce, or states of minds, it may be assumed that Professor Jevons has stated correctly the periods of depression as they have occurred in England during the last two centuries.

16

The dates given by him as the years in which commercial crises have occurred follow: 1701, 1711, 1712, 1731-2, 1742, 1752, 1763, 1772-3, 1783, 1793, 1804-5, 1815, 1825, 1836, 1847, 1857, 1866 and 1878.

This makes a very good showing for the ten-year theory, and it is supported to a considerable extent by what has occurred in this country during the past century.

The first crisis in the United States during the nineteenth century came in 1814, and was precipitated by the capture of Washington by the British on the 24th of August in that year. The Philadelphia and New York banks suspended payments, and for a time the crisis was acute. The difficulties leading up to this period were the great falling off in foreign trade caused by the embargo and non-intercourse acts of 1808, the excess of public expenditures over public receipts, and the creation of a large number of state banks taking the place of the old United States bank. Many of these state banks lacked capital and issued currency without sufficient security.

There was a near approach to a crisis in 1819 as the result of a tremendous contraction of bank circulation. The previous increases of bank issues had promoted speculation, the contraction caused a serious fall in the prices of commodities and real estate. This, however, was purely a money panic as far as its causes were concerned.

The European crisis in 1825 caused a diminished demand for American products and led to lower prices and some money stringency in 1826. The situation, however, did not become very serious and was more in the nature of an interruption to progress than a reversal of conditions.

The year 1837 brought a great commercial panic, for which there was abundant cause. There had been rapid industrial and commercial growth, with a multitude of enterprises established ahead of the time. Crops were deficient, and breadstuffs were imported. The refusal of the government to extend the charter of the United States Bank had caused a radical change in the banking business of the country, while the withdrawal of public deposits and their lodgment with state banks had given the foundation for abnormal speculation.

The panic in Europe in 1847 exerted but little influence in this country, although there was a serious loss in specie, and the Mexican war had some effect in checking enterprises. These effects, however, were neutralized somewhat by large exports of breadstuffs and later by the discovery of gold in 1848-9.

There was a panic of the first magnitude in 1857, following the failure of the Ohio Life Insurance & Trust Company in August. This panic came unexpectedly, although prices had been falling for some months. There had been very large railroad building, and the proportion of specie held by banks was very small in proportion to their loans and deposits. One of the features of this period was the great number of failures. The banks generally suspended payments in October.

The London panic in 1866 precipitated by the failure of Overend, Guerney & Co., was followed by heavy fall in prices in the Stock Exchange here. In April there had been a corner in Michigan Southern and rampant speculation generally, from which the relapse was rather more than normal.

The panic of September, 1873, was a commercial as well as a Stock Exchange panic. It was the outcome of an enormous conversion of floating into fixed capital. Business had been expanded on an enormous scale, and the supply of money became insufficient for the demands made upon it. Credit collapsed and the depression was extremely serious.

The year 1884 brought a Stock Exchange smash but not a commercial crisis. The failure of the Marine Bank, Metropolitan Bank and Grant & Ward in May was accompanied by a large fall in prices and a general check which was felt throughout the year. The Trunk Line war, which had lasted for several years, was one of the factors in this period.

The panic of 1893 was the outcome of a number of causes—uncertainty in regard to the currency situation, the withdrawal of foreign investments and the fear of radical tariff legislation. The anxiety in regard to the maintenance of the gold standard was undoubtedly the chief factor, as it bore upon many others.

Judging by the past and by the developments of the last six years, it is not unreasonable to suppose that we may get at least a stock exchange flurry in the next few years. This decade seems to be the one for the small crisis instead of the large one—a type of 1884 rather than a recurrence of 1837, 1873 or 1893.

Cutting Losses Short

WE HAVE SPOKEN in previous articles of methods of trading. Experience proves that every operator should adopt one of two methods: Either cut losses short, or take an investment position. We propose to point out today some of the advantages of cutting losses short.

The buyer of any stock has some reason for his action. He has heard that the stock is going up; he believes that it is selling below its value, he sees that a bull market is under way and believes that this stock will go up as much as any other. These and similar reasons lead to buying.

It is obvious that in all but one of these cases the buyer does not profess to know anything definitely about the stock he buys. He acts on the suggestions or advice of others. Points are good when they are good, and under some conditions can very wisely be followed. There is nothing better in trading than to know that a great operator or a great syndicate intends for good reasons to move the price of a stock from a lower to a higher figure.

But almost everybody learns by sad experience that the

"best laid plans of mice and men gang aft agley." Great operators change their minds about the expediency of market movements and most of them have learned that it is one thing to will and another to do in stock speculation. Hence the trader who takes a point, even from good sources, has only partial assurance of profitable results.

His true protection in such a case lies in a stop order. If the price advances, well and good, but if it declines his stop order cuts his loss short, while those who do not stop the loss, but who listen to assurances that the market is all right, often see larger losses in the end.

The general rule is to stop losses within a range of two or three points from the purchase price. All purchases on points, tendencies and rumors should be regarded as guesses and protected by stop orders. Traders, looking over their accounts, seldom lament the losses of $200, which they find scattered through their books as the result of stops, but they deeply lament the $1,500 or the $2,500 losses which reflect overconfidence in a position which proved unsound.

The difficulty with stop orders is that they are frequently exercised when the event shows that the loss need not have been taken. There is no help for this, but the placing of a stop order can be wisely varied by the circumstances of a given case. Suppose that the 5-year movement showed a bull market to be in progress; that there has come in this advance a 5-point reaction in a stock like Union Pacific and that a purchase had been made 5 points from the previous highest.

If the price declined 2 points more in such a case, it would probably be wise to exercise the stop order as the fall would suggest a down swing of larger proportions than had been anticipated. It might be such a move as occurred in December, 1899, when stop orders proved exceedingly profitable in bull accounts. If the price subsequently recovered the 2 points, and the stock was repurchased at about the original price, it would probably be wise to put the stop order the next time about 3 points away, under a belief that the stock would not go quite so low as it went before and that the stop order would therefore not be executed.

21

If this reasoning proved sound, and the price advanced, the stop order could wisely be kept 3 points below the market price until the stock had advanced several points and showed signs of what is called "toppiness." Then it might be well to advance the stop order to 2 points and await developments. The stop order is of primary importance when a purchase is first made and when its wisdom is in doubt. It is also of primary importance in pyramiding; that is, where stock is being bought on an advancing market every point up, because in such a case the stop order is relied upon to prevent the turning of a profit into a loss. It is of importance when a stock has had its normal swing for the purpose of saving most of the profit if a reaction comes, while leaving a chance open for further advance. It is of least importance when a stock has been well bought and is slowly advancing. It should be set further away from the market at such a time than any other so as to avoid being caught on the small setbacks which occur in an advancing period.

By means of a stop order, an operator can trade freely in active stocks of uncertain value, which he would not venture to touch as an investment. By it, he can trade in much larger amounts than he could otherwise undertake to protect. The stop order is the friend of the active speculator, who wants to make a quick dash for a large profit and who is willing to make small losses in the hope of getting a good run once in four or five attempts. It is the friend of the small operator, the out-of-town operator and the timid operator. It should be applied, however, only in active stocks where there is a large market. Stop orders should not be given in inactive stocks, as the seller may be slaughtered in their execution.

A stop order to sell 100 shares of Union Pacific at 75 means that the stock must be sold at the best price obtainable as soon as there has been a transaction at 75. If the best price were 74 or 73, it would still be the duty of the broker to sell. Hence the importance of not giving such orders in stocks where wide differences in quotations may be expected.

Selling Short

I N PICKING OUT a stock to sell short, the first consideration ought to be that the price is above value,
and that future value appears to be shrinking. It
should be an active stock and, if possible, a stock of large
capital. It should be an old stock by preference, which
means having wide distribution instead of concentrated
ownership. By preference it should be a high-priced stock
with a reasonable probability that dividends will be reduced or passed.

Such a stock should be sold on advances and bought on
moderate declines, say 4 or 5 points, as long as the market
seems to be reasonably steady. But, if the market becomes
distinctly weak, only part of the short stock should be
bought in with the hope that some short interest may be
established at a price so high as to be out of reach of
temporary swings. **The best profits in the stock market are
made by people who get long or short at extremes and
stay for months or years before they take their profit.**

SAMUEL
A. NELSON

Author and Dow Theory Compiler

It is generally agreed that the man who first compiled Charles Dow's writings and thus "launched" the Dow Theory, was S. A. Nelson. However Nelson's image has been somewhat smothered by that reputation, for his writings on trading tactics offer a great deal, apart from Dow concepts. It is this more or less unknown side of Nelson that is presented here. Adequate coverage of Dow's views can be found elsewhere in this volume, but only here can we present the real S. A. Nelson.

It was shortly after Dow's death that Nelson wrote his *ABC of Wall Street* and the *ABC of Stock Speculation*. In 1907 he wrote *The Consolidated Stock Exchange of New York*.

He tried to get Dow to write a book on Dow's ideas and when he failed to persuade him, Nelson wrote it himself, compiling all he could find of what Dow had said on stock speculation in *The Wall Street Journal*.

Very little biographical information is available on Nelson. He was described as a conscientious and sensible little man, one whom his co-workers both liked and laughed at for they could not take him quite as seriously as he took himself.

He was slowly dying of tuberculosis at the time of his most important writing (1902 to 1907) and died not long thereafter, a great distance from the Wall Street he loved.

Though some called him a pathetic, sickly, little figure with an earnest and strained face, he was active and vibrant with his pen, as the following pages reveal, and it was he who coined the term "Dow's Theory."

The Wisdom of
SAMUEL A. NELSON

A Trader's Apprenticeship

T HE SUCCESSFUL TRADER is obliged to serve an apprenticeship as a trader. This usually requires 6-12 months of close application. It is almost a tradition that novices who plunge successfully in the first year are very often failures in the second or third year. Early success is misleading and deceptive. A queer thing about this trade is that you may acquire it very slowly and gradually or you may stick at it and work away for months when suddenly in the most mysterious way the whole thing opens up to you and what seemed very difficult becomes comparatively simple. **You learn by a process of elimination.** You are bound to make mistakes. In some instances it takes quite a long time to find out that three profits of $25 each do not balance a loss of $100.

As to whether the work is harder and more dangerous than other trades . . . why no. It all depends on the man.

The object of all business is the "making of money" and nothing else. Wall Street is certainly no different from any other place or center of business activity, in this respect.

A healthy skepticism is seldom out of place in Wall

Street, so far as speculation is concerned. Money is very seldom lost thereby. People who have had experience covering one or two panics know very well that the first lesson that has to be learned by the successful speculator is the avoidance of the disaster always caused by a panic. The very essence of a panic is that it sweeps away everyone who is overtrading—whether it be to a large or to a small extent. Of what use is it to pile up imposing paper profits if they are all to be swept away when the tidal wave strikes? The only way whereby people can avoid being caught in a panic is by the exercise at all times of great conservatism and considerable skepticism. The successful speculator must be content at times to ignore probably two out of every three apparent opportunities to make money, and must know how to sell and take his profits when the "bull" chorus is loudest. When he has learned that much, he has learned a great deal.

Speculative Fever

TO STAND IN the office of a commission firm all day and hear the market opinions expressed and the reasons for making commitments is to understand why so much money is lost. The man who "guesses," who has a "fancy for a particular stock," "who wishes to make a bit," who has "a tip," is in the majority. He has the speculative fever, and having contracted the disease he has not the time nor the mood to adopt the reasoning dictated by ordinary common sense.

"Buy," says a customer to his broker, "100 shares of Metropolitan at 150."

The stock is bought at a cash cost of $15,000. The customer's equity in the stock is $1,000. The stock is capable of wide fluctuations.

"What did you buy it on?" the customer is asked.

"My friend Smith told me that it is going up."

"Who is Smith?"

"Oh, a neighbor of mine. He heard it was a good thing from Jones, whose cousin is a director in the company."

Would this man, who is a type, have invested $15,000

(equity $1,000) in his own business (mercantile) without a most careful investigation of conditions, and consequences, profits and losses, present and prospective? Would Smith and Jones influence him in such a transaction? Certainly not. And yet thousands of stock market ventures are made annually without any more justification.

Therefore if about to speculate in stocks, it behooves you to ask yourself if you possess the temperament and accurate and swift reasoning powers necessary to cope with the ablest money getters in the world. If you do, you will find that hardly a day passes that Wall Street does not present great opportunities for your skill in money making.

Market Panics

P ANICS IN THE stock market have a well defined course. The record since 1873 shows only two exceptions to the rule, the rule prevailing in all other cases. A panicky market usually lasts during parts of three days, although this is not invariable. The lowest prices are usually made on the second day. From those prices there is a recovery amounting usually to more than half the amount of the decline from the level of prices prevailing before the panic. This recovery culminates within a week and sometimes not for thirty days, but in all cases prior to the May 9, 1901 panic, within thirty days. After that comes a slow decline during which prices lose at least half of their recovery and in case of a bear market all the recovery and more is lost.

Nothing is more common than to hear people say that the big bankers can do what they please with the stock market, and yet nothing is further from the truth. The stock market is in the end made by the public and by no one else, if the smaller fluctuations and minor "swings" be disregarded. Traders can move prices within narrow limits; bankers can move them within wider limits, but without the public the market tends constantly to equilibrium. Stocks go off when traders sell and rally when they cover; stocks advance when bankers bid them up, but decline unless the public buys on the advance. Both traders and bankers can and generally do anticipate the public in its operations, but if the public does not do what is expected of it nothing is gained thereby.

The investor determines the prices of stocks in the long run. This statement is sometimes disputed by those who point to the fluctuations which are confessedly made by manipulators without regard to value. It is true that such fluctuations occur, but when the manipulation is over the voice of the investor is again heard. If he decides that a given stock is worth only so much, the manipulator will ultimately be compelled to accept that valuation because manipulation cannot be kept up. The object of manipulation is to buy below value and sell above value. The experience of all traders will afford many illustrations of how stocks have recovered after artificial depression and relapsed after artificial advances to the middle point which represented value as it was understood by those who bought or held as investors.

The Role of Value

VALUE HAS LITTLE to do with temporary fluctuations in stock prices, **but is the determining factor in the long run.** Values when applied to stocks are determined in the end by the return to the investor, and nothing is more certain than that the investor establishes the price of stocks. The manipulator is all-powerful for a time. He can mark prices up or down. He can mislead investors, inducing them to buy when he wishes to sell, and to sell when he wishes to buy; but manipulation in a stock cannot be permanent, and in the end the investor learns the approximate truth. His decision to keep his stock or to sell it then makes a price independent of speculation and, in a large sense, indicative of true value. It is so indicative because the price made is well known to insiders, who also know better than anyone else the true value of the stock. If the price is too low, the insiders will buy; hence stability is the price of a stock means that insiders do not think the stock especially cheap or dear.

The reason why in a bull market, dullness is followed by advance, is that a bull market is the exponent of increasing values. Values go on increasing, while the market rests, and prices start up because it becomes apparent to cliques or individuals that values are above prices, and that there is margin for use. Exactly the reverse argument applies to declines after dullness in a bear period.

Prices fall because values are falling, and dullness merely allows the fall in value to get ahead of the fall in prices. The start after a period of inactivity is generally due either to some special event or to manipulation. In the former case, the reason for acting is obvious. In the latter case, manipulators begin by studying the situation and reach a conclusion that it will pay them to move prices.

They then scrutinize the speculative situation, and learn something of the position of traders; whether they are carrying a good many stocks or not; whether they seem disposed to deal; whether margins appear to be large or small; and whether specialists have large scale orders to either buy or sell. This gives a basis on which manipulation begins. The public often follows the lead given, sometimes to its own advantage and sometimes to the advantage of the manipulators. All this, however, is merely an incident in the main tendency of prices, which, as a whole, is in accord with the values which grow out of changes in earnings. Temporary movements in the market should always be considered with reference to their bearing on the main movement. The great mistake made by the public is paying attention to prices instead of values.

Whoever knows that the value of a particular stock is rising under conditions which promise stability, and the absence of developments calculated to neutralize the effect of increasing earnings, should buy that stock whenever it declines in sympathy with other stocks, and hold it until the price is considered high enough for the value as it is believed to exist.

This implies study and knowledge of the stock chosen, but this marks the difference between intelligent trading and mere gambling. Anybody can guess whether a stock will go up or down, but it is only guessing and the cost of guessing will eat up most of the net profits

A Treasury of **Wall Street Wisdom**

of trading on pure guesses. Intelligent trading begins with study of conditions, and a justified opinion that the general situation is either growing better or worse.

If general conditions are improving, ascertain if the particular stock to be dealt in is having a fair share of that general improvement. Is its value rising? If so, determine whether the price of the stock is low or high with reference to that value. If it is low, buy the stock and wait. Do not be discouraged if it does not move. The more value goes on increasing, the greater the certainty that rise in the stock will come. When it does come, do not take two or three points profit and then wait for a reaction, but consider whether the stock is still cheap at the advance, and if so, buy more, rather than sell under the assumption that the expected rise is under way. Keep the stock until the price appears to be up to the value and get a substantial profit. This is the way the large operators make their money; not by trading back and forth, but by accurate forecasts of coming changes in value, and then buying stocks in quantity and putting the price up to value. The small operator cannot put prices up, but if his premises are sound, he can hold stock with assurance that large operators and investors will put the price up for him.

The Universal Laws of Speculation

A CLOSE STUDENT of speculation in all its forms as conducted on the exchanges of this country has arrived at the following conclusions, which, he says, in application to speculation are "universal laws." He divides his conclusions into two groups, laws absolute and laws conditional.

LAWS ABSOLUTE

1. Never overtrade. To take an interest larger than the capital justifies, is to invite disaster. With such an interest, a fluctuation in the market unnerves the operator, and his judgment becomes worthless.

2. Never "double up"; that is, never completely and at once reverse a position. Being "long," for instance, do not "sell out" and go as much "short." This may occasionally succeed, but is very hazardous, for should the market begin again to advance, the mind reverts to its original opinion and the speculator "covers up" and "goes long" again. Should this last change be wrong, complete demoralization ensues. The change in the original position should have been made moderately, cautiously, thus keeping the judgment clear and preserving the balance of mind.

3. "Run quick" or not at all; that is to say, act promptly at the first approach of danger, but failing to do this until others see the danger hold on or close out part of the "interest."

4. Another rule is, when doubtful **reduce the amount of the interest;** for either the mind is not satisfied with the position taken, or the interest is too large for safety. One man told another that he could not sleep on account of his position in the market; his friend judiciously and laconically replied: **"Sell down to the sleeping point."**

RULES CONDITIONAL

These rules are subject to modification, according to the circumstances, individuality and temperament of the speculator.

It is better to "average up" (pyramiding) than to "average down." This opinion is contrary to the one commonly held and acted upon; it being the practice to buy and on a decline buy more. This reduces the average. Probably four times out of five this method will result in striking a reaction in the market that will prevent loss, but the fifth time, meeting with a permanently declining market, the operator loses his head and closes out, making a heavy loss—a loss so great as to bring complete demoralization, often ruin.

But "buying up" is the reverse of the method just explained; that is to say, buying at first moderately and as the market advances adding slowly and cautiously to the "line." This is a way of speculating that requires great care and watchfulness, for the market will often (probably four times out of five) react to the point of "average." **Here lies the danger. Failure to close out at the point of average destroys the safety of the whole operation.**

WILLIAM P. HAMILTON

Pioneer Technician, and Successor to Dow

Famous as the man whose October 25, 1929 *Wall Street Journal* editorial "The Turn of the Tide" correctly identified the termination of the great bull market of the 1920's, William Peter Hamilton considerably furthered the theory first evolved by Charles Dow with thorough organization and formulation of the leading concepts.

Born in England and trained there as a newspaperman, he arrived in America in 1899 and joined *The Wall Street Journal* that same year. There is no proof that Hamilton was ever a close intimate of Dow, his editor, but rather the evidence points to relationship of employer and employee, or editor and reporter. Five years after Dow's death Hamilton became editor of *The Wall Street Journal*, where, in addition to taking up where Dow left off in the field of technical stock market interpretation, he undertook to expound Dow's views in an organized manner, which became "The Dow Theory."

To Hamilton should go much credit, because Dow did not deliberately set forth his ideas for use as a market tool. Dow used the market to predict business; but Hamilton put together these various findings for use as a method of predicting the stock market, which for investors was probably more to the point.

Hamilton had a better score of hits and misses than

many modern day market analysts. His only notable miscalculation was in 1926 when he incorrectly announced that a bear market was at hand, which turned out later to have been a severe secondary reaction instead.

He was able to pass sound judgment upon the action of the stock market for almost three decades until his death in 1929, with his views constantly in the public eye through the medium of his articles in *The Wall Street Journal*. That he was able to do this speaks a testimony of the highest eloquence.

Hamilton wrote an incisive book in 1922, entitled *The Stock Market Barometer,* in which he formed Dow's ideas and his own into just what his book calls itself—a "barometer," by which stock market weather was predicted. This book has come to be regarded as the "Bible" of the Dow Theory.

The Wisdom of
WILLIAM P. HAMILTON

Dow's Theory, Applied to Speculation

W E HAVE SEEN in past discussions of Dow's theory of the stock-market price movement that the essence of it could be summed up in three sentences. In an editorial published December 19, 1900, he says, in *The Wall Street Journal*:

"The market is always to be considered as having three movements, all going on at the same time. The first is the narrow movement from day to day. The second is the short swing, running from two weeks to a month or more; the third is the main movement, covering at least four years in its duration."

It has already been shown that his third and main movement may complete itself in much less than Dow's assumed four years, and also how an attempt to divide the ten-year period of the panic cycle theory into a bear and bull market of approximately five years each led to an unconscious exaggeration. That, however, is immaterial. Dow had successfully formulated a theory of the market movements of the highest value, and had synchronized those movements so that those who came after him could construct a business barometer.

This is the essence of Dow's theory, and it need hardly be said that he did not see, or live to see, all that it implied. He never wrote a single editorial on the theory alone, but returns to it to illustrate his discussions on stock-market speculation, and the underlying facts and truths responsible not only for speculation (using the word in its best and most useful sense) but for the market itself.

It is not surprising that *The Wall Street Journal* received many inquiries as to the assumptions it made on the basis of Dow's major premise. On January 4, 1902, Dow replies to a pertinent question, and any thoughtful reader of these pages should be able to answer it himself. The correspondent asks him, "For some time you have been writing rather bullish on the immediate market, yet a little bearish in a larger sense. How do you make this consistent?" Dow's reply was, of course, that he was bullish after the secondary swing but that he did not think, in view of stock values from earnings of record, that a bull market which had then been operative sixteen months could run much further. It was a curious contraction, incidentally, of his own minimum four-year estimate, but that major upward swing as a matter of fact ran until the following September. It may be said that such a swing always outruns values. **In its final stage it is discounting possibilities only.**

In the same editorial Dow goes on to give a useful definition from which legitimate inferences may be drawn. He says:

"It is a bull period as long as the average of one high point exceeds that of previous high points. It is a bear period when the low point becomes lower than the previous low points. It is often difficult to judge whether the end of an advance has come because the movement of prices is that which would occur if the main tendency had changed. Yet, it may only be an unusually pronounced secondary movement."

This passage contains, by implication, both the idea of "double tops" and "double bottoms" (which I frankly confess I have not found essential or greatly useful) and the idea of a "line," as shown in the narrow fluctuation of the averages over a recognized period, necessarily one either of accumulation or distribution. This has been found to be of the greatest service in showing the further persistence of the main movement, or the possible termination of the secondary movement, so apt to be mistaken for the initiation of a new major trend.

It has been said before that Dow's theory is in no sense to be regarded as a gambler's system for beating the game. Any trader would disregard it at his peril, but Dow himself never considered it in that light, as I can testify from many discussions with him . . . It would perhaps be well to point out here that a knowledge of the major movement of the market, whether up or down, is necessary for the successful flotation of any largely capitalized enterprise.

It is essentially the business of a barometer to predict. In that lies its great value, and in that lies the value of Dow's Theory. The stock market is the barometer of the country's and even the world's business, and the theory shows how to read it . . . **The sum and tendency of the transactions in the Stock Exchange represent the sum of all Wall Street's knowledge of the past, immediate and remote, applied to the discounting of the future.** There is no need to add to the averages, as some statisticians do, elaborate compilations of commodity price index numbers, bank clearings, fluctuations in exchange, volume of domestic and foreign trade or anything else. Wall Street considers all these things. It properly regards them as experience of the past, if only of the immediate past to be used for estimating the future. They are merely creating causes of the weather predicted.

The Nature of Secondary Swings

REVIOUS DISCUSSIONS HAVE shown how it was possible successfully to diagnose a major swing in its incipient stages. But the **secondary** movement postulated in Dow's Theory is a different matter. We have proved by analysis the correctness of the theory of the market as containing three distinct and, in a way, simultaneous movements—the great primary swing up or down; the secondary movement, represented by reactions in a bull market and corresponding rallies in a bear market; and the daily fluctuation. It may be that this discussion will seem to be addressed more to the speculator or embryo investor than to those who consider using the stock market barometer as a guide and warning to business.

It may be conceded at once that if it is hard to call the turn of a great bear or bull market it is still harder to say when a secondary movement is due, although there are no insuperable difficulties in the way of showing the termination of the secondary movement and the resumption of the main market trend. We cannot dogmatize about the depth of such movements, in duration or extent. We have seen, from a study of what was really a secondary reaction in a bull market aggravated by the San Francisco calamity in 1906, that such a reaction can look deceptively like the real thing—the development of a new major swing. It can look so vigorous and convincing, as in the case of the Northern Pacific panic of 1901, that even experienced traders will rashly assume that the bull market is over.

Dow estimated the length of a counter movement at from forty to sixty days, but subsequent experience has shown that this longer range is exceedingly rare and that the duration may be appreciably less than forty days. The daily fluctuation might be so considerable as to constitute almost a secondary reaction in itself, if the extent of it were all we were considering. When it was known that the government would take over the railroads, at the end of December, 1917, there was an advance in a single day in the railroad average of over six points. There have been true secondary movements which did not carry even so far as this. It is a tried rule, which will help to guide us in studying the secondary movement, that the change in the broad general direction of the market is abrupt, while the resumption of the major movement is appreciably slower. The latter is frequently foretold by a line of accumulation in a bull market or a line of distribution in a bear market.

Dow's Theory True of All Stock Markets

THE LAW THAT governs the movement of the stock market, formulated here, would be equally true of the London Stock Exchange, the Paris Bourse or even the Berlin Boerse. But we may go further. The principles underlying that law would be true if those Stock Exchanges and ours were wiped out of existence. They would come into operation again, automatically and inevitably, with the re-establishment of a free market in securities in any great Capital. So far as I know, there has not been a record corresponding to the Dow-Jones averages kept by any of the London financial publications. But the stock market there would have the same quality of forecast which the New York market has if similar data were available.

It would be possible to compile from the London Stock Exchange list two or more representative groups of stocks and show their primary, their secondary and their daily movements over the period of years covered by Wetenhall's list and the London Stock Exchange official list. An average made up of the prices of the British railroads might well confirm our own. There is in London a longer and more diversified list of industrial stocks to draw upon. The averages of the South African mining stocks in the Kaffir market, properly compiled from the first Transvaal gold rush in 1889, would have an interest all their own. They would show how gold mining tends to flourish when other industries are stagnant or even prostrated. The comparison of that average with the movement of securities held for fixed income would be highly instructive to the economist. It would demonstrate in the most vivid way the relation of the purchasing power of gold to bonds held for investment. It would prove conclusively the axiom that the price of securities held for fixed income is in inverse ratio to the cost of living, as we shall see for ourselves in a later chapter.

The San Francisco Earthquake

THE YEAR 1906 presents an interesting problem of an arrested main bull movement or an accentuated secondary reaction, according to the way you look at it. It has been said that major bull markets and bear markets alike tend to overrun themselves. If the stock market were omniscient it would protect itself against this over-inflation or over-liquidation, as it automatically protects itself against everything which it can possibly foresee. But we must concede that, even when we have allowed for the further established fact that the stock market represents the sum of all available knowledge about the conditions of business and the influences which affect business, **it cannot protect itself against what it cannot foresee.** It could not foresee the San Francisco earthquake of April 18, 1906, or the subsequent devastating fire.

The Wall Street Barometer...

(Written June 29, 1906)

SPECULATION IS ESSENTIAL not merely in the market for stocks but in any market. Somebody must take chances. The pound of coffee sold across the counter contains greater or less profit to the retailer as he judges the wholesale market correctly. Every market must therefore adjust itself not merely to present conditions but to future conditions. In this respect stocks are like any other commodity, but they cover so wide a range of interests that a general movement in them may, and frequently does, reflect a change in general conditions outside.

In this respect the Wall Street market is something of a rational barometer. It is the constant phrase of the street that a movement is over "when the news is out." Stockholders and intelligent speculators operate not on what everybody knows, but on what they alone know or intelligently anticipate. We have often had the spectacle of a general decline in the market, only followed six months afterwards by a contraction in business, or a general advance in the market anticipating by an equal time improving industrial conditions not then obvious.

It is the business of Wall Street to sell securities to the public. Wall Street anticipates that when the business improvement it expects matures, the public will take stocks off its hands. This is really what establishes a bull market. Favorable conditions inside and out of Wall Street act and interact until the necessary impetus for a stock boom is developed. In the summer of 1904 when the unskilled observer was convinced that the McKinley boom was over and industry on the down grade, professional Wall Street was buying stocks. It correctly estimated the vast recuperative power of business. The average price of twenty active railroad stocks advanced nearly thirty points in that year with a continuous gain between the latter part of May and the beginning of December.

It must always be remembered, however, that there is a main current in the stock market, with innumerable cross currents, eddies, and backwaters, any one of which may be mistaken for a day, a week, or even a longer period for the main stream. The market is a barometer. There is no movement in it which has not a meaning. That meaning is sometimes not disclosed until long after the movement takes place, and is still oftener never known at all; but it may truly be said that every movement is reasonable if only the knowledge of its source is complete.

What the barometer needs of course is expert reading. At the present time the stock market, which, touching the highest point ever recorded on January 22 of this year, has made an irregular reaction. The decline at one time extended in the case of twenty active railroads to over eighteen points, and in the case of twelve active industrials, to almost as much. Even now after very substantial rallies the market has worked off from the recovery point of last April and is even six points below the best quotation of the current month. On the surface, crop prospects, industrial conditions and the money market are all as favorable as ever. Here is an opportunity for the amateur reader of the barometer. Is the market, or is it not, reflecting some change in fundamental conditions which shall justify the present quotations six months hence?

Causes of the 1907 Panic

THESE BEAR ARGUMENTS were given on March 15, 1907, and they read curiously now. (1922) They were:

"1. Excessive prosperity.
2. High cost of living, due largely to the effect upon prices of a great gold production.
3. Readjustment of values to the higher rates of interest.
4. Speculation in land absorbing liquid capital that might otherwise be available for commercial enterprises.
5. Roosevelt and his policy of government regulation of the corporations.
6. Anti-railroad agitation in the various states.
7. Progress of socialistic sentiment and demagogic attacks on wealth.
8. Harriman investigation of exposure of bad practices in high finance.
9. War between big financial interests.
10. Over-production of securities.
11. Effect of San Francisco earthquake."

There were other causes quoted of only momentary consequence, in which possible bear manipulation was put last. It has been said already that there never was a bear market which was not justified by the facts subsequently disclosed. Are we not entitled to say that some of these influences became permanent, to an extent which even the stock market could not possibly foresee, conceding that it is, at least theoretically, of longer and larger vision than any of us? As after events proved, the over-regulation of the railroads alone was sufficient to justify investors in protecting themselves, whatever the consequences to the stock market might be.

In retrospect, the year 1907 seems to be the most interesting I have ever spent in Wall Street, and perhaps the most instructive. It is full of lessons and warnings.

(Editor's Note: *The following piece, from* The Wall Street Journal *of October 25, 1929, in Hamilton's most celebrated editorial, the one in which he announced that the 1929-1932 bear market had been confirmed by major Dow Theory signals, and giving a hint of the depression that was to come. The article was greeted with great disbelief by the boom-conditioned public of that day, most of whom thought that the market surely must be close to bottoming out after its violent slide of September and October. Later events, however, proved Hamilton's historic pronouncement was well-founded though he underestimated the scope of the coming business contraction.)*

A Turn in the Tide

O N THE LATE Charles H. Dow's well known method of reading the stock market movement from the Dow-Jones averages, the twenty railroad stocks on Wednesday, October 23 confirmed a bearish indication given by the industrials two days before. Together the averages gave the signal for a bear market in stocks after a major bull market with the unprecedented duration of almost six years. It is noteworthy that Barron's and the Dow-Jones NEWS service on October 21 pointed out the significance of the industrial signal, given subsequent confirmation by the railroad average. The comment was as follows:

"If, however, the market broke again, after a failure to pass the old highs, and the decline carried the price of the industrials below 325.17 and the railroads below 168.26, the bearish indication would be strong, and might well represent something more than a secondary reaction, however severe. It has often been said in these studies of the price movement that the barometer never indicates duration. There was a genuine major bear market in 1923, but it lasted only eight months. One good reason for not taking the present indications too seriously is that they have all been recorded in a most unusually short space of time. The severest reaction from the high point of the year had just one month's duration. In view of the nationwide character of the speculation, this seems a dangerously short period to infer anything like complete reversal in public sentiment."

There was a striking consistency about the market movement since the high figure of September 3. There were at least four rallies in the course of the decline in the industrials before the definite new low point was established and each of these was weaker than the last. Dow always considered this a danger signal, but for the past thirty years it has been the custom in discussing the stock market as a barometer of business to require that one average should confirm the other. Failure to agree has been found deceptive.

There are people trading in Wall Street, and many all over the country who have never seen a real bear market, as for instance, that which began in October, 1919, and lasted for two years, or that from 1912 to 1914 which predicted the Great War if the world had then been able to interpret the signs. What is more material is that the stock market does forecast the general business of the country. The big bull market was confirmed by six years of prosperity and if the stock market takes the other direction there will be contraction in business later, although on present indications only in moderate volume.

Some time ago it was said in a *Wall Street Journal* editorial that if the stock market was compelled to deflate, as politicians seemed so earnestly to wish, they would shortly after experience a deflation elsewhere which would be much less to their liking.

Insiders Are Poor Traders

THESE SO-CALLED "INSIDERS," the real men who conduct the real business of a corporation, are too busy to spend their time over the stock ticker. They are far too limited, too restricted to their particular trade, to be good judges of the turn of the market. They are normally bullish on their own property, in the respect that they believe it to be a growing concern with great possibilities. But of the fluctuations of business which will affect their stock, together with the rest in the same group or all other railroad and industrial stocks in the same market, their view is singularly limited. It is not mere cynicism but truth to say that **sufficient inside information can ruin anybody in Wall Street.**

High Volume in Bull Markets

T IS WORTH while to note that the volume of trading is always larger in a bull than in a bear market. It expands as prices go up and contracts as they decline. A moment's thought will reveal the reason. When the market has been under long depression many people have lost money, actually and on paper, and the fund for speculation or speculative investment is correspondingly contracted. On the advance, however, many people are making money, actually and on paper, and the well nigh universal experience has been that in the last stages of a bull market they trade in stocks beyond their real resources. This is uniformly true of major bull swings, but is subject to great modification in the secondary movements. A sharp reaction in a bull market will often stimulate the volume of business.

59

Averages No Blabbermouth

THE DOW JONES averages . . . have a discretion not shared by all the prophets. They are not talking all the time.

Labor Versus Brains

WE KNOW NOW that, far from labor creating everything (the preposterous major premise of Karl Marx) labor creates only a fraction of the sum of human wealth compared with the product of brains.

ROBERT RHEA

Dow Historian and Record-Keeper

Robert Rhea, the third in a line of celebrated Dow disciples, was born in 1896 in Nashville, Tennessee. His father ran a river boat line on the Mississippi, loved the stock market, and had been rich and poor, alternately, several times.

Before Robert was out of school his father gave him W. P. Hamilton's *Wall Street Journal* editorials on Dow Theory, and told him "to master them or get spanked."

After a short stay in college, Robert started a river boat line that nearly ran his father's out of business. He carried his savings in his pocket. On his father's advice he sent his funds to Henry Clews in New York with instructions to buy some good stock, and 10 shares of U. S. Steel were purchased at 14. This transaction was the start of Rhea's real interest in stocks; thereafter, he subscribed to *The Wall Street Journal*.

Later, Robert contracted tuberculosis and went to Colorado. But tuberculosis didn't prevent Rhea from enlisting in the Air Corps in 1917. His plane crashed, however, a piece of propeller pierced a lung, and Rhea returned to Colorado a permanent invalid.

In bed he began to average and chart stock prices and study Dow Theory again. He found he could forget his physical pain by concentrating heavily on this work so that at the day's end he was exhausted and could sleep.

When Hamilton died in 1929 the Dow Jones Company needed a new "high priest" for the Dow cult and published some of Rhea's "notebooks" in *Barron's*. The next year Rhea put his ideas on Dow lore into a book, and when publishers refused to print it, he published it himself and sold over 90,000 copies.

Letters began to stack up at the foot of his bed. Unable to answer them individually, he mailed a notice that if and when he had anything to say, he would mimeograph it and send it to anyone who wanted it.

By 1938 Rhea was selling his mimeographed "Dow Theory Comments" opinions to 5,000 clients at $40 a year. Soon he had 25 assistants and his bedroom became a statistical storehouse. He did **not** want to be a tipster; however, he reputedly averaged $436 gain as against every $100 he lost. He often composed tirades against Franklin D. Roosevelt, which were included at no extra charge in his letters.

Rhea wrote three books: *Dow's Theory Applied to Business and Banking* in 1938, *The Dow Theory* in 1932, and *The Story of the Averages* in 1932 published by Rhea, Greiner & Co.; in connection with the last-named work he compiled a book of graphic charts of the daily Dow Jones Averages from their commencement.

Rhea died in 1939, at the age of 43.

The Wisdom of
ROBERT RHEA

Determining the Trend

S UCCESSIVE RALLIES penetrating preceding high
points, with ensuing declines terminating above
preceding low points, offer a bullish indication.
Conversely, failure of the rallies to penetrate previous
high points, with ensuing declines carrying below former
low points, is bearish. Inferences so drawn are useful in
appraising secondary reactions and are of major importance in forecasting the resumption, continuation, or
change of the primary trend. For the purpose of this discussion, a rally or a decline is defined as one or more daily
movements resulting in a net reversal of direction exceeding three per cent of the price of either average. Such
movements have but little authority unless confirmed in
direction by both averages, but the confirmation need not
occur on the same day.

The significance of rallies in a secondary reaction in a
bull market is explained by Hamilton as follows: ". . . On
the well-tested rule of reading the averages, a major bull
swing continues so long as the rally from a secondary reaction establishes new high points in both averages, not

necessarily on the same day, or even in the same week, provided only that they confirm each other." (Dec. 30, 1921)

It should always be remembered that a new high or low by one average, unconfirmed by the other, is deceptive. Such action frequently denotes a change of a secondary nature, although sometimes proving to be of primary importance.

The authority of new highs or lows which are properly confirmed remains in force until cancelled by some later definite confirmed action. If, for instance, new highs are made in a primary bull market, the prediction is valid that the bull market will continue for a considerable time. Moreover, if one average later retraces its advance to a point below its old high, or even below a previous low point, but the other average fails to confirm the action, it is proper to infer that the previous bullish indication is still in force. Hamilton explains this as follows: "The barometer does not give indications every day and all the time; according to Charles H. Dow's theory, an indication remains in force until it is cancelled by another, or re-inforced in some way, as, for instance, when the industrial average confirms the railroad average or vice versa." (Sept. 23, 1929)

If, after a severe secondary reaction in a primary bull market, the ensuing rallies fail to go to new highs within a reasonable time and a further drastic decline occurs extending below the low points of the previous reaction, it is generally safe to assume the primary trend has changed from bullish to bearish. Conversely, when, after a decline has carried both averages to new low ground in a bear market, an important secondary reaction has taken place and the next decline fails to carry either average to a new low, one may infer that the primary trend has changed from bear to bull if the next rally carries both averages above the high points of the last important rally. Few exceptions to this rule can be found in the charted averages when examined over a 35-year period.

Many traders try to apply this rule to minor reactions, forgetting that a normal secondary reaction generally lasts from three to 12 weeks and retraces from one-third to two-thirds of the primary movement since the last important secondary reaction. The best way for the students to gain a complete understanding of the significance of small rallies and declines is to study the charted daily movements over the entire record of the averages.

According to Hamilton, "Dow always ignored a movement of one average which was not confirmed by the other, and experience since his death has shown the wisdom of that method of checking the reading of the averages. His theory was that a downward movement of secondary, and perhaps ultimately primary, importance was established when the new lows for both averages were under the low points of the preceding reaction." (June 25, 1928)

Because a lucid explanation of the significance of rallies and declines was always proved so difficult, and because a proper understanding of the rise and fall of prices as compared to previous similar movements is of such vital importance when using the averages as a forecasting device, it is perhaps wise to offer a second quotation which is merely a repetition, although phrased differently: "Whenever a series of rallies and declines have occurred in the day to day movement, always confirmed by both rail and industrial averages, and the rallies carry above immediately preceding high points, with declines failing to penetrate recent lows, the implication is bullish for the immediate future, but not necessarily indicating a primary bull trend."

When a series of such rallies and declines of both averages have penetrated the highest points previously attained in a primary bull market, it is generally safe to infer that the primary bull trend will continue for a considerable period of time. Conversely, successive rallies and declines, with highs failing to penetrate the immediately preceding high points, and the ensuing declines carrying below previous low prices, afford a bearish implication for the immediate future, although not necessary implying a primary bear trend. On the other hand, when a series of rallies and declines break through the lowest prices of a primary bear trend, the probability of much lower prices is generally a reasonable inference. When declines in a primary bull market result in violating the lowest points encountered during the last major secondary reaction of that market, it may generally be assumed that the primary trend has changed from bullish to bearish; the converse, of course, is usually a dependable means of determining when a bear primary movement has changed to the beginning of a bull market.

Occasional exceptions can be found, and it is proper that this should be true, for otherwise these rules would constitute a sure way of beating the stock market. Such a method would, of course, very quickly result in there being no market.

Characteristics of Bull Market Peaks

T HE TERMINATION OF a bull market is much harder to recognize than the end of a bear market. At the peak, both averages are, of course, in new high ground. Without exception, bull markets of the past have ended in periods of relatively heavy activity; moreover, near the top, pools have always been active, and comparatively worthless stocks have been advanced rapidly. Eager speculators, inoculated with the virus of greed and excitement, buy anything that is going up, regardless of earnings or of intrinsic worth. Truly, the termination of bull markets represents a period when nothing can justify the prices at which stocks are changing hands except the hope and expectation of those who are suffering from excessive speculative temperature.

When stocks are nearing the peak, call money is sometimes high but at other times it is not particularly so. **It is seldom that anything is apparent in the current business statistical situation to indicate that a collapse is imminent. Almost invariably, the opinions of newspaper writers, services, and brokers are rampantly bullish.**

At first thought it might seem that the conditions described would not be very hard to recognize, but in active practice it proves to be most difficult, for the reason that while more or less uniform conditions, as described, exist at bull peaks, it does not follow that whenever such situations develop a market collapse occurs. It is a case where unhealthy conditions have been gradually building up over the months, and that operator is shrewd indeed who can identify the exact day when public excitement reaches its zenith.

HOW TO AVOID GETTING CAUGHT IN BEAR MARKETS

Without meaning to imply that I am an expert on trading tactics, and with the full consciousness that trading methods which serve one man may appear foolish to another, I shall, nevertheless, try to outline methods which have, on more than one occasion in the past, preserved the greater portion of my modest speculative capital from the ravages of bear markets.

One method of avoiding bear market disaster is to get out of the market when a bull period has run for a normal length of time, **provided speculation is then rampant,** and if a long advance into new primary high ground has taken place without being interrupted by a secondary correction—all this, provided prices appear to have discounted present and future earnings for a great many years to come.

Investors may ask how they can determine the point when stocks are selling far above value and probable earnings. That, indeed, is a hard question to answer because no two men appraise values on the same basis. I can only say that sometime before the peak was reached in 1929, American Telephone and Telegraph common stock was selling around $300 per share. It had a book value of about $128, and its best recorded earnings were in 1929 when the reported net for common was $12.67 per share. Now in 1926 the stock had sold for $151 when its book value was $126, with earnings of $11.95. With its dividend at $9.00, a comparatively small amount was carried to surplus each year. At the price first noted above, the advance in the quoted value of this stock had obviously discounted earnings for many years in the future; moreover, it was selling far above its intrinsic value. Similar conditions existed in the stocks of General Motors, Sears Roebuck, Consolidated Gas, and hundreds of other well-managed corporations, while the price situation in Radio and other such favorites was absurd. These remarks are made only to show how one factor, always existing near the peak, and one which was understood and explained by Hamilton, could be detected by any one understanding elementary arithmetic. This speculator, for one, sold out partly in 1928 and partly in the Spring of 1929. These sales were premature, as later developments showed, but prices received for securities later proved to be most attractive, and, having once retired, I did not again re-enter that market. My next venture was on the short side after the prices had "turned the corner."

I presume that the indications upon which my decision to sell was based might have been said to exist in the Fall of 1927. However, at that time the market was showing no signs whatever of losing any steam.

Short Selling

A S A GENERAL THING, when speculators begin to understand something about primary trends of the stock market, they start to make plans for shorting stocks in bear markets. Few traders have found the short side profitable over a long period of time. I think that more than 75 per cent of my own losses have resulted from short sales.

Many people seem to think that there is something immoral about short selling. I, for one, have always thought that the difference between long and short operations is about the same as the difference between betting on black and red flushes in a poker game, at least so far as morality is concerned.

Perhaps one reason for my frequent bad luck on the short side was the fact that I never really got ahead of the market until I learned to let margin trading alone, but when I short stocks I am conscious of the fact that I am **technically** on margin from the minute the trade is made. You can't take a short transaction out of a broker's office and lock it up in your box, as can be done when long stocks are purchased. The liability behind an investment of $100,000 in stocks is limited to that amount. If declines should occur, the certificates would still be owed. But an "outright" short commitment on $100,000 worth of stocks, backed by $100,000 cash, would be completely wiped out by an advance of 100 per cent. Many old traders have told me that when short they are under a nervous tension which militates against success, and that this strain does not exist when trading for long account.

I have known men who have operated extensively on the short side, but who abandoned that practice without really understanding why their profits were so disappointing. There is a simple arithmetical explanation of this. Consider that a bull buys 100 shares of stock for $10,000, and that the stock advances 100 points. He has made 100 per cent on his capital. Then a bear shorts $10,000 worth of the same stock at $200. The bear will only be short 50 shares. When the stock goes down to $100 again, the bear will have a profit of $5,000 as compared with the $10,000 gained by the bull, notwithstanding the fact that both operators have traded in the same stock over an identical price range, and with the same capital.

A bear shorting a million dollars worth of the Dow-Jones Industrial averages on September 3, 1929, at 381.17, and holding his position until July 8, 1932, when the price was 41.22, would have gained $891,859, or 89.19 per cent, on his capital on an operation extending nearly three years. A bull buying the same stocks on July 8, 1932 with a like amount of capital would have realized the same profit as did the bear, in 49 trading days, when the averages had advanced through 77.98.

In spite of the unfavorable arithmetical odds and other factors, I persist in shorting stocks occasionally, but generally confine operations for a decline to a mere fraction of commitments for long account. If there is any sound reason for fooling with the short side at all, it is the fact that familiarity with and the practice of occasional short selling seem to prevent the development of the bull complex which causes traders to think that stocks are cheap after each decline in bear markets. I had friends during 1930 and 1931 who would never short a stock, and who were so impatient to get into the market that they persisted in buying for an advance in every rally as it occurred. Disaster overtook them. There is no more certain method of going broke than to make a habit of shorting stocks in bull markets or buying for a rally in bear periods. Success in both speculation and investment depends upon one's ability to swim with the tide rather than against it.

I was so fortunate as to be holding no stocks at the peak in '29 and shortly thereafter carried small short lines intermittently until June, 1932. Without doubt, the short position enabled me to refrain from developing a bull complex during the long decline, and, had I done so, my speculative funds would have been sadly impaired.

ℭhe Dow ℭheorems

THE AVERAGES DISCOUNT EVERYTHING

THE FLUCTUATIONS of the daily closing prices of the Dow-Jones rail and industrial averages afford a composite index of all the hopes, disappointments, and knowledge of everyone who knows anything of financial matters, and for that reason the effects of coming events (excluding acts of God) are always properly anticipated in their movement. The averages quickly appraise such calamities as fires and earthquakes.

THE THEORY IS NOT INFALLIBLE

The Dow theory is not an infallible system for beating the market. Its successful use as an aid in speculation requires serious study, and the summing up of evidence must be impartial. The wish must never be allowed to father the thought.

If these essential elements, around which the theory has been built up, cannot be accepted as axioms, then further study of the subject will prove to be confusing, if not actually misleading.

Reducing the theory to definite **theorems** proved to be a difficult task, but this was done in 1925. Subsequent study together with application of these theorems to trading operations, has not indicated the advisability of altering them now.

DOW'S THREE MOVEMENTS

There are three movements of the averages, all of which may be in progress at one and the same time. The first, and most important, is the primary trend: the broad upward or downward movements known as bull or bear markets, which may be of several years duration. The second, and most deceptive movement, is the secondary reaction: an important decline in a primary bull market or a rally in a primary bear market. These reactions usually last from three weeks to as many months. The third, and usually unimportant, movement is the daily fluctuation.

PRIMARY MOVEMENTS

The primary movement is the broad basic trend generally known as a bull or bear market extending over periods which have varied from less than a year to several years. **The correct determination of the direction of this movement is the most important factor in successful speculation.** There is no known method of forecasting the extent or duration of a primary movement.

PRIMARY BEAR MARKETS

A primary bear market is the long downward movement interrupted by important rallies. It is caused by various economic ills and does not terminate until stock prices have thoroughly discounted the worst that is apt to occur. There are three principal phases of a bear market: the first represents the abandonment of the hopes upon which stocks were purchased at inflated prices; the second reflects selling due to decreased business and earnings, and the third is caused by distress selling of sound securities, regardless of their value, by those who must find a cash market for at least a portion of their assets.

PRIMARY BULL MARKETS

A primary bull market is a broad upward movement interrupted by secondary reactions, and averaging longer than two years. During this time, stock prices advance because of a demand created by both investment and speculative buying caused by improving business conditions and increased speculative activity.

There are three phases of a bull period: the first is represented by reviving confidence in the future of business; the second is the response of stock prices to the known improvement in corporation earnings, and the third is the period when speculation is rampant and inflation apparent—a period when stocks are advanced on hopes and expectations.

SECONDARY REACTIONS

For the purpose of this discussion, a secondary reaction is considered to be an important decline in a bull market or advance in a bear market, usually lasting from three weeks to as many months, during which intervals the price movement generally retraces from 33 per cent to 66 per cent of the primary price change since the termination of the last preceding secondary reaction. These reactions are frequently erroneously assumed to represent a change of primary trend, because obviously the first stage of a bull market must always coincide with a movement which might have proved to have been merely a secondary reaction in a bear market, the contra being true after the peak has been attained in a bull market.

DAILY FLUCTUATIONS

Inferences drawn from one day's movement of the averages are almost certain to be misleading and are of but little value except when "lines" are being formed. The day to day movement must be recorded and studied, however, because a series of charted daily movements always eventually develops into a pattern easily recognized as having a forecasting value.

BOTH AVERAGES MUST CONFIRM

The movements of both the railroad and industrial stock averages should always be considered together. The movement of one price average must be confirmed by the other before reliable inferences may be drawn. Conclusions based upon the movement of one average, unconfirmed by the other, are almost certain to prove misleading.

DETERMINING THE TREND

Successive rallies penetrating preceding high points, with ensuing declines terminating above preceding low points, offer a bullish indication. Conversely, failure of the rallies to penetrate previous high points, with ensuing declines carrying below former low points, is bearish. Inferences so drawn are useful in appraising secondary reactions and are of major importance in forecasting the resumption, continuation, or change of the primary trend. For the purpose of this discussion, a rally or a decline is defined as one or more daily movements resulting in a net reversal of direction exceeding three per cent of the price of either average. Such movements have but little authority unless confirmed in direction by both averages, but the confirmation need not occur on the same day.

LINES

A "line" is a price movement extending two to three weeks or longer, during which period the price variation of both averages move within a range of approximately five per cent. Such a movement indicates either accumulation or distribution. Simultaneous advances above the limits of the "line" indicate accumulation and predict higher prices; conversely, simultaneous declines below the "line" imply distribution and lower prices are sure to follow. Conclusions drawn from the movement of one average, not confirmed by the other, generally prove to be incorrect.

THE RELATION OF VOLUME TO PRICE MOVEMENTS

A market which has been overbought becomes dull on rallies and develops activity on declines; conversely, when a market is oversold, the tendency is to become dull on declines and active on rallies. Bull markets terminate in a period of excessive activity and begin with comparatively light transactions.

DOUBLE TOPS AND DOUBLE BOTTOMS

"Double tops" and "double bottoms" are of but little value in forecasting the price movement and have proved to be deceptive more often than not.

INDIVIDUAL STOCKS

All active and well distributed stocks of great American corporations generally rally and decline with the averages, but any individual stock may reflect conditions not applicable to the average price of any diversified list of stocks.

Points to Remember About Dow's Theory

Number 1. They profit most from Dow's Theory who expect least of it.

2. The Theory is no sure method of beating the market, and no such theory or system will ever be devised.

3. Trading based upon an impartial reading of the averages as implied by the Theory will net frequent losses, but gains will outnumber them to a reasonable extent.

4. Do not try to work the Theory too hard.

5. Do not try to inject innovations until they have been tested over the 37-year record of the averages.

6. Do not try to trade with thin margins and Dow's Theory at the same time.

7. If the Theory is worth following, then study it—learn to form independent opinions, checking them against those of others who have learned to use Dow's methods through several bull and bear cycles.

8. Do not allow your position in the market, or current business statistics, to influence your reading of the averages.

Average Up Rather Than Down

HAMILTON BELIEVED THAT it was much better to increase a line (i.e. one's holdings) on rising prices than to average down on falling prices, and the advice is worth remembering. No trader should buy a stock unless he believes it due for an advance. There are, of course, some men who buy stocks on a declining market to put away as permanent investments. No criticism is intended of that market operation.

The first thing a trader must learn is that his commitments should at all times be limited to an amount which he can, if fate decrees, afford to lose.

Hamilton often said that the majority of opinion in the Street was seldom right. Assuming him to have been correct, then the trader who understands the Dow Theory should not hesitate to put out a short line of stocks if the market action indicates to him that this would be a wise move, even though sentiment on Wall Street is overwhelmingly bullish. Many times when Wall Street was bullish Hamilton would remark that there was entirely too much company on the constructive side; at other times, when public opinion was extremely bearish, he would warn his readers that there was too much company on that side and that the Dow-Jones averages were saying that the market was perhaps oversold.

Seven Winners Out of Ten

T HE QUESTION IS frequently asked, "What percentage of trades, timed in accordance with a reasonably competent interpretation of the Dow Theory, will be profitable?" It is the writer's belief that any trader endowed with ordinary market sense and plenty of patience who has studied and used the averages as a guide through the complete cycle of a bull and bear market should be able to make at least seven profitable turns out of every 10 efforts—and each profitable trade should net a gain in excess of the loss on a trade improperly timed. Many men have consistently bettered this record, but they seldom make more than four or five trades a year. They do not watch the tape but play for the important movements and are not concerned with a few points loss or gain.

The "Line" Formation

THERE ARE PEOPLE who insist on trying to place an exact mathematical interpretation on the duration of a "line," but this cannot be done successfully. The allowable price variation must be considered in connection with the prevailing activity of speculation and be compared with the violence or lack of violence of preceding fluctuations. This is one of the reasons why the successful application of the Dow Theory to speculation must be considered both an art and a science. Anyone attempting an exact mathematical interpretation of the Dow Theory is placing himself on a parity with the surgeon who tried to remove an appendix by cutting two inches deep at a point 38 inches above the patient's instep, regardless of the age, sex, height, or contour of his patient.

Students were warned that a line in one average alone has no forecasting value when Hamilton wrote that ". . . all past experience of the average has shown that unless such a line is made simultaneously by both the industrials and the railroads it is more apt to be deceptive than not." (3/20/1916)

Don't "Always" Be in the Market

ANY PERSON WHO tries to be in the market at all times is almost certain to lose money, for there are many periods when even the most skillful trader is in doubt as to what will happen.

A wise man lets the market alone when the averages disagree.

Confirmation of the Averages

THE AUTHORITY OF new highs or lows which are properly confirmed remains in force until cancelled by some later definite confirmed action. If, for instance, new highs are made in a primary bull market the prediction is valid that the bull market will continue for a considerable time. Moreover, if one average later retraces its advance to a point below its old high, or even below a previous low point, but the other average fails to confirm the action, it is proper to infer that the previous bullish indication is still in force.

RICHARD RUSSELL

Leading Present–Day Dow Theorist

During market crises or critical turning points the press associations and *Barron's* have often turned to Richard Russell for his interpretation of the stock market picture in terms of the Dow Theory. Although not alone in this field, Russell seems to have been thrown into the role of heir apparent to the Dow Theory sceptre.

Russell was born July 22, 1924 in New York City, where he was also educated. He began his market studies in the mid-1940's and began his market education the hard way, investing his own money.

At first, like most beginners in Wall Street, he had expensive lessons to learn. But over the years he bore down on his technical studies and has since fared well.

He began writing occasional articles in *Barron's*, starting in December, 1958, which is also around the period he began publishing his periodic "Dow Theory Letters."

Russell wrote one book, entitled "The Dow Theory Today" in 1960. More recently, he moved from New York to San Diego, California for the sake of his daughter's health, and still operates his service there.

The Wisdom of
RICHARD RUSSELL

Relative Strength

THE FIRST DISCUSSION of the use of relative strength (R.S.) techniques as an aid in stock selection appeared in *Barron's* in the issue of May 8, 1933. The article was written by Robert Rhea and was entitled "Stock Habits." In this article Rhea explained how he computed (during a given advance) the percentage of appreciation in the Industrial Average and the percentage of appreciation in a varied list of stocks. By comparing the **percentage of change** in each stock with the percentage of change in the Dow, Rhea was able to establish whether the stock was performing better or worse than the "market."

Furthermore, Rhea concluded that if a stock performed consistently better or worse than a market over a few swings, that relative strength or weakness was very likely to continue.

If we divide the price of a stock by the price of any convenient Average, we will obtain a ratio figure. If the stock (over a period of time) outperforms the Average, the ratio figure will rise; the converse is true if the stock performs worse than the Average. These two statistics (i.e. the price of the stock and the ratio figure) are then plotted on **semi-logarithmic** graph paper. One line of the graph will show the stock's actual movements in terms of percentages (since "log" paper deals in percentages), and the other line will show whether the stock is performing better or worse than the Average (and this too will be shown in percentages). This second line is the R.S. line, and conclusions drawn from the trend of R.S. can be extremely important in the selection of stocks.

I have noted that since 1959 each broad market movement seems to have been increasingly difficult from the technical standpoint. Stocks that "acted" beautifully during the 1953-56 and 1958-59 rises began (after 1959) to behave erratically, as far as technical analysis was concerned. I have little doubt that part of the difficulty stemmed from the astounding rise of technical analysis and charting throughout the nation. It seemed as if "too many cooks were spoiling the broth," and the more converts to charting, the more misleading the charts seemed to become. Finally, the 1961 "top" materialized into a classic of "false breakouts," erratic starts, and costly rises and reversals. After the 1962 collapse, the market started up with many stocks having failed to form any recognizable base of accumulation or, for that matter, any orthodox pattern at all. One simply had to buy them with the hope that they would continue to rise.

During the period since 1959 and particularly since 1961, I tested every conceivable method in a continuing search for a tool which might aid in stock selection. Technical analysis of individual stock charts were proving inadequate.

From my own experience, I believed that relative strength studies might be the answer. I know that R.S. trends were persistent, often lasting as long or considerably longer than a given movement in the general market. Furthermore, if the market was rising or simply moving sideways, and a stock was showing improving R.S., then obviously that stock was on its way up. **It did not matter whether the stock was break-**

ing out of a triangle or any other pattern, since improving R.S. in a static or rising market means appreciation.

From this, the following progression seemed logical: (1) Start with those stock groups which show the best R.S.—preferably groups which are in the act of definitely turning up after long R.S. declines. (2) Pick the stocks with the best R.S. within the strong R.S. groups. (3) Then pick the stocks with the best actual technical patterns from the strong R.S. stocks. These final choices can be expected to outperform during any market movement. But when they stop outperforming, when their R.S. line reverses or when the general market registers a "sell signal"— they should be sold.

The D.J. 30-Week Moving Average

THE RELATIONSHIP OF the Industrial Average to its own long-term (30-week) moving average is a meaningful one. During a major bull swing, Industrials tend to hold above their moving average (M.A.) and the opposite is true during a major decline. The manner in which the Industrial Average penetrates its own M.A. at the beginning of a move is also significant—and this whole relationship is worth studying.

Follow the Industrial Average and its M.A. (weekly) from early 1958 to the present. The 1958-59 rise traced a bullish pattern (with Industrials holding continuously above their M.A.) until 1959. In September, 1959, the senior Average turned down and penetrated its M.A. A few weeks later, Industrials embarked on a new rally above the M.A., but here we note that the M.A. was tending to "flatten out." A **second downward penetration** by Industrials through the M.A. occurred in January, 1960, and this proved to be the final bearish signal. The second penetration was followed by ten months of generally lower prices.

Another major rise began in October, 1960. The new

93

bull movement continued until January, 1962. In January, the Industrial Average turned down and penetrated its M.A. An attempt at a rally followed, but by February, 1962, the M.A. was seen to be moving sideways again. In March, the Industrial Average plunged below its M.A. for the **second time,** and this action was followed by the famous 1962 collapse.

The market struck bottom in June, 1962. A new bull movement took hold—then gathered momentum towards the end of the year. The rise continued until well into 1963. In July, 1963, Industrials turned down and violated their M.A. A rally started on July 24, and the first week of August saw the Industrial Average rise above its M.A. again.

Of interest is the fact that Industrials bettered their M.A. in April, 1958, and held above the M.A. until September, 1959—a period of **17 months.** Following the 1959-60 decline, Industrials pushed above their M.A. in December, 1960, and held above the M.A. until January, 1962—a period of **13 months.** Subsequent to the 1962 "crash," Industrials moved above the M.A. in October, 1962, and held above the M.A. until July, 1962—a period of **9 months.** Each of the swings since 1949 seems to have produced less upward force and less upward momentum.

D.J. Industrial Yields

DOW AND HAMILTON always attached the utmost importance to values. "Stocks fluctuate together," wrote Dow, "but prices are controlled by values in the long run." Again he observed, "The tendency of prices over a considerable period of time will always be towards values."

A study of market history reveals that the cycles of stock values tend to extremes. At the bottom of the 1932, 1942, and 1949 bear markets, the average yield on the Dow-Jones industrials was 10.3%, 7.9% and 6.9% respectively. The bull market highs of 1929 put the average yield of the D-J industrials at 3.1%, 1937 at 3.7% and 1946 at 3.3%.

It is obvious, then, that bull markets have usually ended when values, as measured by the average yield on the D-J industrials, enter a zone of about 3.5% or less. In 1902 Dow wrote, "When a stock sells at a price which returns only 3½% on the investment, it is obviously dear, except there be some special reason for the established price. In the long run, the prices of stocks adjust themselves to the return on the investment, and while this is not a safe guide at all times, it is a guide that should never be laid aside or overlooked." Dow's words concerning stock values have proved amazingly accurate as a guide for the investor who buys and sells values.

Bull Peaks

T HE DEGREE OF public participation and speculation have proved helpful gauges with which to measure the market. Here is Robert Rhea's description of the great 1929 top: "All the usual indications of inflation were present. Volume of trading was excessive and broker's loans were making new peaks regularly—in fact, call money rates were so high that many corporations were finding it profitable to liquidate inventories and lend their cash equivalent to Wall Street at fantastic returns. Pool activities were being conducted on a disgraceful scale, brokerage houses were hanging out S.R.O. signs, and leading stocks were yielding less than the best grade bonds.

"Worthless equities were being sky-rocketed without regard for intrinsic worth or earning power. The whole country appeared insane on the subject of stock speculation. Veteran traders look back at those months and wonder how they could have become so inculcated with the 'new era' view as to have been caught in the inevitable crash. Bankers whose good sense might have saved the situation had speculators listened to them, were shouted down as destructionists, while other bankers, whose names will go down in history as 'racketeers' were praised as supermen."

During such times, it is obvious that, regardless of the fact that the averages may be indicating the continuance of a bull market, the end cannot be far off. Most Dow Theorists would gladly sell out of a market which has all the earmarks of a third phase climax; they never wait for the actual bear signal. Often, on the advent of a bear signal, stocks drop so fast that it is impossible to obtain quotes on securities.

Dow Theory Js Technical, but Reveals Fundamentals

THE DOW THEORY is a completely technical approach to the market. It derives nothing from business statistics, indexes of production, economic reports, or any of the other thousands of facts that make up a study of the fundamental condition of the country. Operating on the principle that the averages take all these systems and much more into consideration, the Theory becomes a study of the movements of the averages themselves. The Dow Theorist believes that most of the fundamentalist's facts are already history. The market is not interested in yesterday or today; it is concerned only with tomorrow. It is the nature of the averages to contain all of the fundamentalist's facts plus the judgments and opinions of thousands of insiders, speculators, investors and businessmen, each viewing the market from the standpoint of his own business and general economy.

Hamilton illustrated this when he wrote, "The farmers say . . . 'what does Wall Street know about farming?' Wall Street knows more than all the farmers put together ever knew, with all that the farmers have forgotten. It can, moreover, refresh its memory instantly at any moment. It employs the ablest of the farmers, and its experts are better even than those of our admirable and little appreciated Department of Agriculture, whose publications Wall Street reads even if the farmer neglects them." Against this knowledge contained in the averages, says the Dow Theorist, the fundamentalist can seldom, if ever win.

Market Philosophy

EFORE PURCHASING STOCKS for my own account, I ask myself the following questions. Are stocks great "values," and are leading investment-grade issues now providing historically attractive yields? Can I buy good stocks in a quiet market, stocks which offer hopes of appreciation over the years (with but little risk of decline because of high, well-covered dividends)? Is the prevailing opinion dead bearish in the face of a market that grows dull and refuses to decline? Obviously, these are **ideal** (or bear market bottom) conditions, and we can forget them for now.

In the absence of the above conditions, I ask myself the next series of questions: is this the bottom of a full correction in what I assume to be a continuing and technically strong bull market? Are stocks (or at least many stocks) still attractive values? Has the bull market progressed without showing any signs of a third phase "top"? Are most stocks in good basing patterns, and do they show signs of having been under strong accumulation? These conditions describe markets such as late 1953-early

1954 or late 1957-early 1958. We must also try a third series of criteria.

Is the advance still "strong" from the technical standpoint? Are the two Averages, Industrials and Rails, rising to successive confirmed highs? Is volume tending to rise with higher prices? Are the majority of stocks (as measured by the Advance-Decline ratio) confirming the rise by taking the A-D ratio to fresh new highs? Are daily new highs tending to expand as the Averages push higher? Do stocks rise, hold their gains relatively well, then push out again to new highs? Is there general skepticism regarding the rise, and are the odd-lotters selling in the face of the advance? Is the short interest ratio (a gauge of relative skepticism) holding above 1.5 and preferably above 1.75? Is the rise tending to "spread out" among the laggard and secondary issues or is it confined to a handful of strong stocks and a few strong groups? If these questions add up on the positive side, I am willing to call it a "good speculative market" and I am willing to commit a portion of my funds.

The Stock–Bond Yield Relationship

THE YIELD DIFFERENTIAL between the D-J Industrials and Barron's 10 Highest-Grade Bonds measures values.

Historically, common stocks have been priced to yield more than fixed debt instruments or bonds. On infrequent occasions, common stocks have yielded less than bonds, but these areas have usually coincided with the formation of important market tops. Consciously or unconsciously, "big money" tends to move out of equities when the yield on equities is less attractive than the yield on bonds. The **"normal"** or historical stock-bond yield relationship is therefore expressed by a positive (or plus) yield differential, a differential in favor of bonds.

This positive yield differential held in effect during most of the 1940's (except for 1945-46) and most of the 1950's. But in late-1958 the yield on the D-J Industrial Average dropped below 4% and also below the yield on Barron's 10 Highest-Grade Bonds. Thus the stock-bond yield spread turned **negative.**

The negative spread reached —1.6 in late-1959; at the

same time the average Industrial yield dropped to approximately 3%. These **extremes** in the stock-bond yield relationship and in stock yields proved too much for the market, and a major decline followed. This decline, which carried to the lows of 1960, did not correct the negative yield spread, but despite this a new market advance occurred. Toward late 1961 the Average Industrial yield dropped to 3.2% while the negative stock-bond yield spread widened to —1.5. Important distribution took place in that area, and the resultant collapse took Industrials below their 1960 low.

Nevertheless, at no time during 1962 did the negative-yield-spread reverse, and except for a few weeks in June the average Industrial yield remained in the 3.2 to 3.9% area. In mid-1962 another advance began. The 1963-64 advance again pushed the yield relationship to extremes. As of 3/1/64, the average yield on the D-J Industrials stood at 3.3% while the negative stock-bond yield differential was approximately —1.06. Thus average Industrial yields were back in the adverse 3 to 3.5% area, and the negative stock-bond yield returned to the very negative —1. to —2.% zone. Under these conditions it becomes difficult to talk about "investing" in equities, and it should be understood that the historical yield and stock-bond yield relationships put equities in the upper range of what must be considered an area of overvaluation.

New Highs and Lows

D URING A MAJOR bull movement, it is normal to see stock after stock push out of their established patterns and rise to new highs for the year. If the upward momentum continues, those stocks which recorded new highs will continue to rise, and they will be joined by fresh "breakouts" which will also augment the "new high parade."

But when a bull movement shows a steady decrease in the number of new highs, it is a sign that the original rallying strength is ebbing. Such a market, regardless of temporary rallies or confusing fluctuations, may be said to be "living on borrowed time." It is axiomatic that diminishing strength during a market advance will gradually turn into increasing weakness. By the same token, decreasing weakness during a market decline will materialize into a growing strength.

Part II

Wisdom From The Big Boom Of...
...The Twenties

In the Twenties, the Great Operators and the Big Plungers were conspicuously active. At the same time, they were joined by increasing numbers of small investors, people from all walks of life, many of whom had never owned, let alone traded, common stocks before. The result was one of the great speculative eras in Wall Street. That it ended in grief does not detract from its heyday. While it was roaring along, the market of the Twenties was the most active, most exhilarating boom ever witnessed, and from it emerged a new market literature written by those attempting to understand its flights and to profit from them.

FREDERICK DREW BOND . .
Commentator of the Teens
and Twenties.

JESSE L. LIVERMORE . . The
Last of the Big Plungers.

WILLIAM D. GANN . . Advisor
to Traders of the Twenties.

FREDERICK DREW BOND

Wall Street Commentator of the Teens and Twenties

It's not altogether a pun to say that Bond was a "bonded writer" of Wall Street; i.e. he was guaranteed to do a good job by his background; he was a "newspaperman's newspaperman." His schooling was superb and his jobs led him to perfect order up the ladder, in precise and proper stages. He was correctly groomed for the role he was to play.

Born in Philadelphia on May 22, 1876, Frederick Drew Bond attended private schools, La Salle College and the University of Pennsylvania where he earned a B.S. degree.

In the business world he became first a newspaper reporter, then a copy reader, and finally a city editor. This was in Philadelphia and New York from 1899 to 1905.

Soon after, his interests turned exclusively to Wall Street, and by 1910 he was widely known as a financial consultant.

Bond became a prolific author on a wide range of financial subjects. His books include: *Stock Prices*, (published by Moody's Magazine, 1911, the forerunner of Moody's Investors' Service); *The Need for Currency Reform,* 1911; *Stock Movements and Speculation,* 1928; *Success in Security Operations* (Copyright 1931, Chilton Books, Phila. and N.Y.); he also contributed financial articles to periodicals.

He died in 1951 at the age of 75.

The Wisdom of

FREDERICK D. BOND

Bull Market Factors

TO SAY THAT nothing affects stock prices save through the minds of buyers and sellers might seem a mere platitude, but as a matter of fact, it is common to hear a rise in the rate of interest, the defeat of a nation in war, an earthquake or some other notable event ascribed as a cause of stock movements; the seeming implication being often, that in some vague way these facts do, of themselves, make the prices. In a sense, indeed, such statements, as well as the metaphor which speaks of the stock market as the "barometer of business" are convenient shorthand expressions, but, in another sense, they are not infrequently the token of a confusion of thought.

Stock prices may thus be regarded as the resultant of three general factors; there is, the psychological factor of hopes and fears of the participants conjoined with the capital which they are financially able to move. Secondly, there is the relation of the banks to the market, and this relation, as will be seen, not only limits in general the extent of price swings from the presumed investment point but it makes possible these speculative swings themselves by the extension and withdrawal of credit. Finally we have to consider the third factor, the manner in which, at a given time, the shares of a company are actually distributed and held in the market.

No more mischievous advice has ever been given than the counsel to make money in the stock market by selling when the public buy. There are a handful of alert bears who in a bull market are able to make money but they are exceptions. Professional and semi-professional speculators in a bull market are backing the same belief as the public speculator—namely, that prices will go higher. The essential difference between the professional bull and the amateur lies in how and when and what and how much each buys for the rise.

Since the public are always willing to buy when they think prices will go higher, a bull market terminates when, and only when, the public have no more funds with which to take on additional stock; or to put the matter from a slightly different angle, when public bids at a given price level are less than the combined offerings of stock by previous speculative holders, syndicate and investors who have decided to sell out.

This fact leads to the observation that thoughtful and well-informed speculators sometimes seriously under-estimate the duration of a bull market. By the time the market is half-way up, this class concludes with entire correctness that prices are too high when judged from an investment standpoint; hence, they believe that the bull market is near its termination. The basic error in this reasoning is due to lack of recognition of the acquisitive motives and intentions which are the propelling causes behind a bull market. The error here lies in forming a judgment of speculative movement on a basis of investment conditions. It is true that investment and banking conditions ultimately limit the great swings of the market both up and down; but within these widely extended swings it is, in general, speculative factors which cause the price movements.

Bears Can Never Be Out of Touch

URNING TO THE question of operations in a bear market, the first thing which invites notice is that the speculator must be in constant and immediate touch with the market and with his broker.

This is partly due to the fact that the market may move both abruptly and quickly, but it is also due to the fact that a bear can rely fully on no one else for information. Brokerage firms, and especially the managers of customers' rooms, are inveterately bullish, with extremely few exceptions. To await information from men in this frame of mind may cause a bear to miss good opportunities of selling short, may cause him to be caught in a sudden rally, or to miss the bottom of the decline. This means that the bear must either take up speculation as his profession, or must, at least, be entirely free from confinement to any other business calling. There are few things more bitter than to foresee correctly the course of a great break and yet make out of it little or nothing.

114

Traders Follow Trends, They Do Not Make Them

AS CUSTOMERS ASSEMBLE to watch the ticker it is on the current fluctuations of the market that their commitments are based. Whether they discern its immediate course correctly or not, all traders can always see one thing—whether the market is advancing or declining. It is on this single unequivocal fact that the great majority of the commitments in customers' rooms are made. The longer the market keeps going up and, consequently, the nearer it must be to its top, the more speculators—the more of the "public"—enter on the scene and buy shares, attracted by the great activity and by stories of gains and all hoping for still higher and higher prices. Thus whether successful or not, the great mass of commission house traders who attempt to discern the coming trend of the market simply from what it is doing at the moment, do not make the current trend themselves. They follow it. It is true that by this trailing behind the market, an ever growing mass of speculators have, at rather rare intervals, become responsible by their combined buying for a rise of prices to heights which, otherwise, they could not have touched. An instance of this sort of thing was in April 1901, though, even here, their uniform, if incoherent, action was sustained and directed by the concerted activity of wealthy individuals and interests concerned in the course of prices. But in any event, no matter how the speculative "public" may enhance and protract the trend of the market, they **follow** it as it presents itself to them; they do not **make** it.

But if the public do not make the trend of the market, neither do the few hundred room traders on the Exchange floor, whose commitments are usually cleaned up overnight. Of course, individuals among them may anticipate the course of prices and by acting on this anticipation help to create it. Moreover, it is true that this picked body of speculators discern the signs of the day-to-day trend earlier and far better than the average commission house customer; but generally speaking, the fact that room traders are usually thus alert to seize the course of prices is, in itself, a statement that though they may reinforce this course, they do not make it.

JESSE L. LIVERMORE

The Last of the Big Plungers

One of the most colorful of the legendary speculators in Wall Street history, Jesse L. Livermore, was born in West Acton, Massachusetts, in 1877. He started work as a marking boy, chalking up prices on the board for Paine Webber, and began to speculate with the first few dollars he earned. By the age of 15 Livermore had made $1,000 in the stock market. He also completed four years of mathematics in one year while holding down his job at the brokerage house.

He continued his all-or-nothing type of manoeuvring and made a fortune while still a boy. On Wall Street he was called "The Boy Plunger" and the name stuck for the rest of his picturesque life. His first killing was made selling short.

Eventually, Livermore became a big-time operator, with his own private boardroom and 30 direct-to-broker telephones, and he spread his action among all of them. When he was a bear trader after the 1929 crash he had a bodyguard, for bears were (and still are) unpopular.

He went bankrupt four times, but bounded back each time. His market philosophy is contained in a single book authored by Livermore, "How to Trade in Stocks" published by Duell, Sloan & Pearce early in 1940, reprinted with permission of Duell, Sloan & Pearce, Inc. by Investors Press Inc.

Apparently in a state of melancholy, he shot himself in

the cloakroom of the Sherry Netherlands Hotel, 5th Avenue at 59th, New York, on November 28th, 1940. He died the next day, at the age of 63. It was front page news in the New York *Times,* even though it was more than a decade since Livermore had been a daily byword on Wall Street, for Livermore had been one of the biggest of the big guns in the famous bull market leading up to 1929 and the infamous bear market which followed.

Although often called the "Bear of Bears" Livermore claims to have made more money, and more easily, as a bull than a bear. And ironically, many give him a large part of the credit for starting the long bull market which preceded the 1929 crash. He had a private telegraph operator presiding over a system of private wires, and played both the long and short side of the market. A squad of expert statisticians waded daily through mountains of data and libraries of books in order to keep the boss informed on the outside world.

But although he was often a bear, especially during the 1929-1932 crash, there never was any evidence that he ever headed any bear raids or worked with others to drive a price down. He was content to **ride** a stock down, rather than **force** it down.

Livermore could speak from strength, for he was a speculator for an entire generation. After the 1907 panic he walked out of the wreckage of Wall Street with $3,000,000.

Though bankrupt and owing $4,000,000 in 1915, he borrowed more capital, speculated on the bull side in Bethlehem and U.S. Steel and by 1917 had made enough to pay off his creditors and buy $1,000,000 in Liberty Bonds.

He also correctly predicted the vigorous 1921 and 1927 market advances. In 1929 he felt the market was overvalued but finally threw in the sponge (and became bullish), much too prematurely, in November. But he quickly cut his losses and switched to the short side.

Livermore listed two major points for success:

1. Sensitiveness to mob psychology.
2. Willingness to take a loss.

He chain-smoked cigars, wore dark suits and drove gaily colored Rolls Royces, preferably dazzling yellow. He was ever-willing to venture his entire fortune in one transaction.

It is reputed that Livermore had no regular brokerage accounts but called or dropped into this brokerage house and that, leaving orders to buy or sell. He would sell 5,000 shares of a stock one day in a Palm Beach branch office and buy the next morning in Miami, baffling those who tried to follow his movements.

By 1929 Livermore was just about the only "pure" titanic speculator left. Most of the other legendary names of that year were giants of industry **first** and giants of Wall Street **second.** Also, by 1929 the stock market had grown too large for "raids" to be truly successful.

He was almost always both long and short in the stock market at the same time. It was his practice not to get into any stock positions that could not be sold in 15 minutes. This implies he limited the size of his positions to what could be readily sold without a large price sacrifice, and that he usually traded in large or popular issues. The 15-minute principle was sacrosanct.

Additionally, it is interesting to note he usually bought and sold "at the market," not at fixed prices.

Livermore has left his mark on the Street as few others have done before or since; old-timers remember him as the most daring speculator of the century.

The Wisdom of
JESSE L. LIVERMORE

Take Small Losses

PROFITS ALWAYS TAKE care of themselves, but losses never do. The speculator has to insure himself against considerable losses by taking **the first small loss.** In doing so he keeps his account in order, so that at some future time, when he has a constructive idea, he will be in a position to go into another deal, taking on the same amount of stock as he had when he was wrong.

Uptrend Patterns

T MAY SURPRISE many to know that in my method of trading, when I see by my records that an upward trend is in progress I become a buyer as soon as a stock makes a new high on its movement, after having a normal reaction. The same applies whenever I take the short side. Why? Because I am following the trend at the time. My records signal me to go ahead!

I never buy on reactions or go short on rallies . . . Never average losses. Let that thought be written indelibly upon your mind.

At the beginning of the move you will notice a very large volume of sales with gradually advancing prices for a few days. Then what I term a "Normal Reaction" will occur. On that reaction the sales volume will be much less than on the previous days of its advance . . .

In a day or two activity will start again, and the volume will increase. If it is a real movement, in a short space of time the natural, normal reaction will have been recovered, and the stock will be selling in new high territory. That movement should continue strong for a few days with only minor daily reactions. Sooner or later it will reach a point where it is due for another normal reaction. When it occurs, it should be on the same lines as the first reaction, because that is the natural way any stock will act when it is in a definite trend.

At the first part of a movement of this kind the distance above the previous high point to the next high point is not very great. But as time goes on you will notice that it is making much faster headway on the upside . . .

When it resumes its advance again in a few days, you will notice that the volume of sales at that time is not nearly as large as it was at the beginning of the move. The stock is becoming harder to buy. That being the case, the next points in the movement will be much more rapid than before.

Don't Trade Every Day

THERE ARE ONLY a few times a year, possibly four or five, when you should allow yourself to make any commitment at all. In the interims you are letting the market shape itself for the next big movement.

If you have timed the movement correctly, your first commitment will show you a profit at the start. From then on, all that is required of you is to be alert, watching for the appearance of the danger signal to tell you to step aside and convert paper profits into real money.

Remember this: When you are doing nothing, those speculators who feel they must trade day in and day out, are laying the foundation for your next venture. You will reap benefits from their mistakes.

Most people are so engrossed with the minor ups and downs that they miss the big movements.

Some Livermore "Pearls of Wisdom"

A GAMBLER IS A man who doesn't know the market. He goes to a broker and says "What can I do to make a thousand dollars?" He is only an incident. The speculative investor buys or sells against future conditions on his knowledge of what has happened in the past under a similar set of conditions.

From my viewpoint the investors are the big gamblers. They make a bet, stay with it, and if all goes wrong, they lose it all. . . .

Do not have an interest in too many stocks at one time. It is much easier to watch a few than many. . . .

I know but one sure tip from a broker. It is your margin call. When it reaches you, close your account. You are on the wrong side of the market.

One major mistake of all speculators is the urge to enrich themselves in too short a time. Instead of taking two or three years to make 500% on their capital, they try to do it in two or three months.

A speculator should make it a rule each time he closes out a successful deal to take one-half of his profits and lock this sum up in a safe deposit box. The only money that is ever taken out of Wall Street by speculators is the money they draw out of their accounts after closing a successful deal. . . .

Stock market intuition is like that of a bridge player. After a man has played bridge all his life he knows when to finesse instinctively.

Stay With a Winner

EXPERIENCE HAS PROVED to me that the real money made in speculating has been in commitments in a stock or commodity showing a profit right from the start.

You immediately become fearful that if you don't take the profit the next day you may see it fade away—so out you go with a small profit, when that is the very time you should entertain all the hope in the world. Why should you worry about losing two points' profit which you did not have the previous day?

If you can make two points' profit in one day, you might take two or three the next, and perhaps five more the next week. As long as the stock is acting right, and the market is right, do not be in a hurry to take a profit. You know you are right, because if you were not, you would have no profit at all. Let it ride and ride along with it. It may grow into a very large profit, and as long as the action of the market does not give you any cause to worry, have the courage of your convictions and stay with it.

Wait for the Breakout

IN A NARROW market when the prices are not getting anywhere to speak of, but move within a narrow range, there is no sense in trying to anticipate the next big movement, whether it is going to be up or down. The thing to do is watch the market to determine the limits of the get-nowhere prices and make up your mind that you will not take an interest until prices break through the limits in either direction.

WILLIAM
D. GANN

Adviser to Traders of the Twenties

William D. Gann, born and educated in Texas, arrived in New York in 1903, working as a registered representative, a stock market letter writer, and an analyst until 1919.

In that year, Gann launched forth with his own advisory organization publishing a market letter called "Supply and Demand."

He is remembered chiefly because of eight books for investors, widely known in their day.

The best known were *Wall Street Stock* Selector (Financial Guardian Publishing Co., 1930); *45 Years in Wall Street* (Lambert Gann Publishing Co., 1949); and *Truth of the Stock Tape* (Financial Guardian Publishing Co., 1923).

Gann died June 14, 1955, at the age of 77.

The Wisdom of
WILLIAM D. GANN

Twenty-four Rules for Traders

IN ORDER TO make a success trading in the stock market, the trader must have definite rules and follow them. The rules given below are based upon my personal experience and anyone who follows them will make a success.

1. Amount of capital to use: Divide your capital into 10 equal parts and never risk more than one-tenth of your capital on any one trade.

2. Use stop loss orders. Always protect a trade when you make it, with a stop loss order 3 to 5 points away.

3. Never overtrade. This would be violating your capital rule.

4. Never let a profit run into a loss. After you once have a profit of 3 points or more, raise your stop loss order so that you will have no loss of capital.

5. Do not buck the trend. Never buy or sell if you are not sure of the trend according to your charts.

6. When in doubt, get out, and don't get in when in doubt.

7. Trade only in active stocks. Keep out of slow, dead ones.

8. Equal distribution of risk. Trade in 4 or 5 stocks, if possible. Avoid tying up all your capital in any one stock.
9. Never limit your orders or fix a buying or selling price. Trade at the market.
10. Don't close your trades without good reason. Follow up with a stop loss order to protect your profits.
11. Accumulate a surplus. After you have made a series of successful trades, put some money into surplus account to be used only in emergency or in times of panic.
12. Never buy just to get a dividend.
13. Never average a loss. This is one of the worst mistakes a trader can make.
14. Never get out of the market just because you have lost patience or get into the market because you are tired of waiting.
15. Avoid taking small profits and big losses.
16. Never cancel a stop loss order after you have placed it at the time you make a trade.
17. Avoid getting in and out of the market too often.
18. Be just as willing to sell short as you are to buy. Let your object be to keep with the trend and make money.
19. Never buy just because the price of a stock is low or sell short just because the price is high.
20. Be careful about pyramiding at the wrong time. Wait until the stock is very active and has crossed Resistance Levels before buying more and until it has broken out of the zone of distribution before selling more.
21. Select the stocks with small volume of shares outstanding to pyramid on the buying side and the ones with the largest volume of stock outstanding to sell short.
22. Never hedge. If you are long of one stock and it starts to go down, do not sell another stock short to hedge it. Get out at the market; take your loss and wait for another opportunity.

23. Never change your position in the market without a good reason. When you make a trade, let it be for some good reason or according to some definite plan; then do not get out without a definite indication of a change in trend.
24. Avoid increasing your trading after a long period of success or a period of profitable trades.

"Targets"– A Bad Practice

THE MAJORITY OF people have a habit when they buy or sell a stock, of fixing in their minds a certain figure at which they expect to take profits. There is no reason or cause for this. It is simply a bad habit based on hope. When you make a trade, your object should be to make profits and there is no way that you can determine in advance how much profit you can expect on any one particular trade. The market itself determines the amount of your profit, and the thing that you must do is to be ready to get out and accept a profit whenever the trend changes, and not before.

Part III

Learning From 1929...

At first, it was still possible to believe that 1929 was only a "healthy" shake-out. And prices did rally in early 1930. But then they turned down decisively, and the great reappraisal began. One of the basic assumptions of the Cult of Common Stocks was that stock prices always did better, over time, than other traditional investments. But the seemingly endless depression of stock prices in the early Thirties began to raise some doubts, and there was a flood of investment writing trying to explain what had gone wrong and "what to do now."

JOHN K. GALBRAITH . . Historian
of MARKET PANICS

BERNARD M. BARUCH . . Wall Street
Elder Statesman

GLENN G. MUNN . . Bear Market
Technician

JOHN K. GALBRAITH

Historian of Market Panics

It fell upon a noted contemporary economist and author, John Kenneth Galbraith, to supply the first comprehensive view of 1929 in perspective, to thoroughly research the real reasons behind the spectacular fall in prices. Galbraith has summed up his studies in his classic work *The Great Crash* (published by Houghton Mifflin, 1955).

John Galbraith is many things: economist, diplomat, government administrator, writer, university professor.

Interspersed with teaching were appointments as an economic advisor to the National Defense Advisory Commission 1940-41; assistant administrator in charge of Price Division, Office of Price Administration, 1941-42; Directing Officer of Economic Security Policy, State Department, 1946, etc.

Few writers in the fields of economics and the stock market have enjoyed greater success on so broad a scale as Galbraith. His books include: *American Capitalism*, 1951; *A Theory of Price Control*, 1952; *The Great Crash* (Houghton Mifflin, Publishers), 1955; *The Affluent Society*, 1958; *The Liberal Hour*, 1960. His career has been full of such varied jobs, as those listed above, and also included membership on the Board of Editors of Fortune Magazine, from 1943-48. He lectured at Harvard in 1948-49 where he has been Professor of Economics since 1949, although he has been on special leave from Harvard for such tasks as American Ambassador to India in the Kennedy administration, with extraordinary assignments.

The quotations here are selected from *The Great Crash*, with its vivid portrayal of one of Wall Street's blackest periods.

The Wisdom of
JOHN K. GALBRAITH

ℭhings Become More Serious

(Story Of the 1929 Panic)

N THE AUTUMN of 1929 the New York Stock Exchange, under roughly its present constitution, was 112 years old. During this lifetime it had seen some difficult days. On September 18, 1873, the firm of Jay Cooke and Company failed, and, as a more or less direct result, so did fifty-seven other Stock Exchange firms in the next few weeks. On October 23, 1907, call money rates reached 125 per cent in the panic of that year. On September 16, 1920—the autumn months are the off-season in Wall Street—a bomb exploded in front of Morgan's next door, killing thirty people and injuring a hundred more.

A common feature of all these earlier troubles was that, having happened, they are over. The worst was reasonably recognizable as such. The singular feature of the great crash of 1929 was that the worst continued to worsen. What looked one day like the end proved on the next day to have been only the beginning. Nothing could have been more ingeniously designed to maximize the suffering, and also to insure that as few as possible escaped the common misfortune. The fortunate speculator who had funds to answer the first margin call presently got another and equally urgent one, and if he met that there would still be another. In the end all the money he had was extracted from him and lost. The man with the smart money, who was safely out of the market when the first crash came, naturally went back in to pick up bargains. (Not only were a recorded 12,894,650 shares sold on October 24; precisely the same number were bought.) The bargains then suffered a ruinous fall. Even the man who waited out all of October and all of November, who saw the volume of trading return to normal and saw Wall Street become as placid as a product market, and who then bought common stocks would see their value drop to a third or a fourth of the purchase price in the next twenty-four months. The Coolidge bull market was a remarkable phenomenon. The ruthlessness of its liquidation was, in its own way, equally remarkable.

II

Monday, October 28, was the first day on which this process of climax and anticlimax **ad infinitum** began to reveal itself. It was another terrible day. Volume was huge, although below the previous Thursday—nine and a quarter million shares as compared with nearly thirteen. But the losses were far more severe. The *Times* industrials were down 49 points for the day. General Electric was off 48; Westinghouse, 34; Tel and Tel, 34. Steel went down 18 points. Indeed, the decline on this one day was greater than that of all the preceding week of panic. Once again a late ticker left everyone in ignorance of what was happening, save that it was bad.

On this day there was no recovery. At one-ten Charles E. Mitchell was observed going into Morgan's, and the news ticker carried the magic word. Steel rallied and went from 194 to 198. But Richard Whitney did not materialize. It seems probable in light of later knowledge that Mitchell was on the way to float a personal loan. The market weakened again, and in the last hour a phenomenal three million shares

147

—a big day's business before and ever since—changed hands at rapidly falling prices.

At four-thirty in the afternoon the bankers assembled once more at Morgan's, and they remained in session until six-thirty. They were described as taking a philosophical attitude, and they told the press that the situation "retained hopeful features," although these were not specified. But the statement they released after the meeting made clear what had been discussed for the two hours. It was no part of the bankers' purpose, the statement said, to maintain any particular level of prices or to protect anyone's profit. Rather the aim was to have an orderly market, one in which offers would be met by bids at some price. The bankers were only concerned that "air holes," as Mr. Lamont dubbed them, did not appear.

Like many lesser men, Mr. Lamont and his colleagues had suddenly found themselves overcommitted on a falling market. The time had come to short on premises. Support, organized or otherwise, could not contend with the overwhelming, pathological desire to sell. The meeting had considered how to liquidate the commitment to support the market without adding to the public perturbation.

The formula that was found was a chilling one. On Thursday, Whitney had supported prices and protected profits—or stopped losses. This was what the people wanted. To the man who held stock on margin, disaster had only one face and that was falling prices. But now prices were to be allowed to fall. The speculator's only comfort, henceforth, was that his ruin would be accomplished in an orderly and becoming manner.

There were no recriminations at the time. Our political life favors the extremes of speech; the man who is gifted in the arts of abuse is bound to be a notable, if not always a great figure. In business, things are different. Here we are surprisingly gentle and forbearing. Even preposterous claims or excuses are normally taken, at least for all public purposes, at the face value. On the evening of the 28th no one any longer could feel "secure in the knowledge that the most powerful banks stood ready to prevent a recurrence" of panic. The market had reasserted itself as an impersonal force beyond the power of any person to control, and, while this is the way markets are supposed to be, it was horrible. But no one assailed the bankers for letting the people down. There was even some talk that on the next day the market might receive organized support.

III

Tuesday, October 29, was the most devastating day in the history of the New York stock market, and it may have been the most devastating day in the history of markets. It combined all of the bad features of all of the bad days before. Volume was immensely greater than on Black Thursday; the drop in prices was almost as great as on Monday. Uncertainty and alarm were as great as on either.

Selling began as soon as the market opened and in huge volume. Great blocks of stock were offered for what they would bring; in the first half-hour sales were at a 33,000,000 a-day rate. The air holes, which the bankers were to close, opened wide. Repeatedly and in many issues there was a plethora of selling orders and no buyers at all. The stock of White Sewing Machine Company, which had reached a high of 48 in the months preceding, had closed at 11 the night before. During the day someone—according to Frederick Lewis Allen it was thought to have been a bright messenger boy for the Exchange—had the happy idea of entering a bid for a block of stock at a dollar a share. In the absence of any other bid he got it. Once again, of course, the ticker lagged—at the close it was two and a half hours behind. By then, 16,410,030 sales had been recorded on the New York Stock Exchange —some certainly went unrecorded—or more than three times the number that was once considered a fabulously big day. (Only on the best days during the 1954 boom did volume go above three million.) The *Times* industrial averages were down 43 points, cancelling all of the gains of the twelve wonderful months preceding.

The losses would have been worse had there not been a closing rally. Thus Steel, for which Whitney had bid 205 on Thursday, reached 167 during the course of the day, although it rallied to 174 at the close. American Can opened at 130, dropped to 110, and rose to 120. Westinghouse opened at 131—on September 3 it had closed at 286—and dropped to 100. Then it rallied to 126. But the worst thing that happened on this terrible day was to the investment trusts. Not only did they go down, but it became apparent that they could go practically to nothing. Goldman Sachs Trading Corporation had closed at 60 the night before. During the day it dropped to 35 and closed at that level, off by not far short of half. Blue Ridge, its offspring once removed, on which the magic of leverage was now working in reverse, did much worse. Early in September it had sold at 24. By October 24 it was down to 12, but it resisted rather well the misfortunes of that day and the day following. On the morning of October 29 it opened at 10 and promptly slipped to 3, giving up more than two-thirds of its value. It recovered later but other investment trusts did less well; their stock couldn't be sold at all.

The worst day on Wall Street came eventually to an end. Once again the lights blazed all night. Members of the Exchange, their employees, and the employees of the Stock Exchange by now were reaching the breaking point from strain and fatigue. In this condition they faced the task of recording and handling the greatest volume of transactions ever. All of this was without the previous certainty that things might get better. They might go on getting worse. In one house an employee fainted from exhaustion, was revived, and put back to work again.

IV

In the first week the slaughter had been of the innocents. During this second week there is some evidence that it was the well-to-do and the wealthy who were being subjected to a leveling process comparable in magnitude and suddenness to that presided over a decade before by Lenin. The size of the blocks of stock which were offered suggested that big speculators were selling or being sold. Another indication came from the boardrooms. A week before they were crowded, now they were nearly empty. Those now in trouble had facilities for suffering in private.

The bankers met twice on the 29th—at noon and again in the evening. There was no suggestion that they were philosophical. This was hardly remarkable because, during the day, an appalling rumor had swept the Exchange. It was that the bankers' pool, so far from stabilizing the market, was actually selling stocks! The prestige of the bankers had in truth been falling even more rapidly than the market. After the evening session, Mr. Lamont met the press with the disenchanting task of denying that they had been liquidating securities—or participating in a bear raid. After explaining again, somewhat redundantly in view of the day's events, that it was not the purpose of the bankers to maintain a particular level of prices, he concluded: "The group has continued and will continue in a co-operative way to support the market and has not been a seller of stocks." In fact, as later intelligence revealed, Albert H. Wiggin of the Chase was personally short at the time to the tune of some millions. His co-operative support, which if successful would have cost him heavily, must have had an interesting element of ambivalence.

So ended the organized support. The phrase recurred during the next few days, but no one again saw in it any ground for hope. Few men ever lost position so rapidly as did the New York bankers in the five days from October 24 to October 29. The crash on October 24 was the signal for corporations and out-of-town banks, which had been luxuriating in the 10 per cent and more rate of interest, to recall their money from Wall Street. Between October 23 and October 30, as values fell and margin accounts were liquidated, the volume of brokers' loans fell by over a billion. But the corporations and the out-of-town banks responded to the horrifying news from New York— although, in fact, their funds were never seriously endangered—by calling home over two billions. The New York banks stepped into the gaping hole that was left by these summer financiers, and during that first week of crisis they increased their loans by about a billion. This was a bold step. Had the New York banks succumbed to the general fright, a money panic would have been added to the other woes. Stocks would have been dumped because their owners could not have borrowed money at any price to carry them. To prevent this was a considerable achievement for which all who owned stocks should have been thankful. But the banks received no credit. People remembered only that they had bravely undertaken to stem the price collapse and had failed.

Despite a flattering supposition to the contrary, people come readily to terms with power. There is little reason to think that the power of the great bankers, while they were assumed to have it, was much resented. But as the ghosts of numerous tyrants, from Julius Caesar to Benito Mussolini, will testify, people are very hard on those who, having had power, lose it or are destroyed. Then anger at past arrogance is joined with contempt for present weakness. The victim or his corpse is made to suffer all available indignities.

Such was the fate of the bankers. For the next decade they were fair game for congressional committees, courts, the press and the comedians. The great pretensions and the great failures of these days were a cause. A banker need not be popular; indeed, a good banker in a healthy capitalist society should probably be much disliked. People do not wish to trust their money to a hail-fellow-well-met but to a misanthrope who can say no. However, a banker must not seem futile, ineffective, or vaguely foolish. In contrast with the stern power of Morgan in 1907, that was precisely how his successors seemed, or were made to seem, in 1929.

The failure of the bankers did not leave the community entirely without constructive leadership. There was Mayor James J. Walker. Appearing before a meeting of motion picture exhibitors on that Tuesday, he appealed to them to "show pictures which will reinstate courage and hope in the hearts of the people."

V

On the Exchange itself, there was a strong feeling that courage and hope might best be restored by just closing up for a while. This feeling had, in fact, been gaining force for several days. Now it derived support from the simple circumstance that everyone was badly in need of sleep. Employees of some Stock Exchange firms had not been home for days. Hotel rooms in downtown New York were at a premium, and restaurants in the financial area had gone on to a fifteen and twenty-hour day. Nerves were bad, and mistakes were becoming increasingly common. After the close of trading on Tuesday, a broker found a large waste basket of unexecuted orders which he had set aside for early attention and had totally forgotten. One customer, whose margin account was impaired, was sold out twice. A number of firms needed some time to see if they were still solvent. There were, in fact, no important failures by Stock Exchange firms during these days, although one firm had reported itself bankrupt as the result of a clerical error by an employee who was in the last stages of fatigue.

Yet to close the Exchange was a serious matter. It might somehow signify that stocks had lost all their value, with consequences no one could foresee. In any case, securities would immediately become a badly frozen asset. This would be hard on wholly solvent investors who might need to realize on them or use them as collateral. And sooner or later a new "gutter" market would develop in which individuals would informally dispose of stocks to those increasingly exceptional individuals who still wanted to buy them.

In 1929 the New York Stock Exchange was in principle a sovereignty of its members. Apart from the general statutes relating to the conduct of business and the prevention of fraud, it was subject to no important state or federal regulation. This meant a considerable exercise of self-government. Legislation governing the conduct of trading had to be kept under review and enforced. Stocks had to be approved for listing. The building and other facilities of the Exchange had to be managed. As with the United States Congress, most of this work was done in committees. (These, in turn, were dominated by a somewhat smaller group of members who were expected and accustomed to run things.) A decision to close the Exchange had to be taken by the Governing Committee, a body of about forty members. The mere knowledge that this body was meeting would almost certainly have an unfavorable effect on the market.

Nonetheless, at noon on Tuesday, the 29th, a meeting was held. The members of the committee left the floor in twos and threes and went, not to the regular meeting room, but to the office of the President of the Stock Clearing Corporation directly below the trading floor. Some months later, Acting President Whitney described the session with considerable graphic talent. "The office they met in was never designed for large meetings of this sort, with the result that most of the Governors were compelled to stand, or to sit on tables. As the meeting proceeded, panic was raging overhead on the floor. Every few minutes the latest prices were announced, with quotations moving swiftly and irresistibly downwards. The feeling of those present was revealed by their habit of continually lighting cigarettes, taking a puff or two, putting them out and lighting new ones—a practice which soon made the narrow room blue with smoke and extremely stuffy."

The result of these nervous deliberations was a decision to meet again in the evening. By evening the late rally had occurred and it was decided to stay open for another day. The next day a further formula was hit upon. The Exchange would stay open. But it would have some special holidays and then go on short hours and this would be announced just as soon as the market seemed strong enough to stand it.

Many still wanted to close. Whitney said later, although no doubt with some exaggeration, that in the days to come, "the authorities of the Exchange led the life of hunted things, until (eventually) the desirability of holding the market open became apparent to all."

VI

The next day those forces were at work which on occasion bring salvation precisely when salvation seems impossible. Stocks rose wonderfully, miraculously, though still on enormous volume. The *Times* industrials were up 31 points for the day, thus recouping a large part of the terrible losses of the day before. Why this recovery occurred no one will ever know. Organized support can have no credit. Organized re-assurance has a somewhat better claim. On the evening of the 29th, Dr. Julius Klein, Assistant Secretary of Commerce, friend of President Hoover, and the senior apostle of the official economic view, took to the radio to remind the country that President Hoover had said that the "fundamental business of the country" was sound. He added firmly, "The main point which I want to emphasize is the fundamental soundness of (the) great mass of economic activities." On Wednesday, Waddill Catchings, of Goldman, Sachs, announced on return from a western trip that general business conditions were "unquestionably fundamentally sound." (The same, by then, could not unquestionably be said of all Goldman, Sachs.) Arthur Brisbane told Hearst readers: "To comfort yourself, if you lost, think of the people living near Mount Pelee, ordered to abandon their homes."

Most important, perhaps from Pocantico Hills came the first public statement by John D. Rockefeller in several decades. So far as the record shows, it was spontaneous. However, someone in Wall Street— perhaps someone who knew that another appeal to President Hoover to say something specifically encouraging about stocks would be useless—may have realized that a statement from Rockefeller would, if anything, be better. The statement ran: "Believing that fundamental conditions of the country are sound . . . my son and I have for some days been purchasing sound common stocks." The statement was widely applauded, although Eddie Cantor, describing himself as Comedian, Author, Statistician, and Victim, said later, "Sure, who else had any money left?"

The accepted Wall Street explanation of Wednesday's miracle was not the reassurance but the dividend news of the day before. This also, without much question, was somewhat organized. U.S. Steel had declared an extra dividend; American Can had not only declared an extra but had increased its regular dividend. These errant sunbeams were deeply welcome in the dark canyons of lower Manhattan.

Just before the Rockefeller statement arrived, things looked good enough on the Exchange so that Richard Whitney felt safe in announcing that the market would not open until noon the following day (Thursday) and that Friday and Saturday it would stay shut. The announcement was greeted by cheers. Nerves were clearly past the breaking point. On La Salle Street in Chicago a boy exploded a firecracker. Like wildfire the rumor spread that gangsters whose margin accounts had been closed out were shooting up the street. Several squads of police arrived to make them take their losses like honest men. In New York the body of a commission merchant was fished out of the Hudson. The pockets contained $9.40 in change and some margin calls.

VII

At the short session of three hours on Thursday, October 31, well over seven million shares were traded, and the market made another good gain. The *Times* industrials were up 21 points. The weekly return of the Federal Reserve Bank showed a drop in brokers' loans by more than a billion, the largest weekly drop on record. Margin requirements had already been cut to 25 per cent; now the Federal Reserve Banks lowered the rediscount rate from 6 to 5 per cent. The Reserve Bank also launched vigorous open-market purchases of bonds to ease money rates and liberalize the supply of credit. The boom had collapsed; the restraint that had previously been contemplated could now give way to a policy of active encouragement to the market. On all these happy portents the market closed down for Friday, Saturday and Sunday. They were not days of rest. Brokerage offices were fully staffed, and the Exchange floor was open for completion of trades and also for straightening out innumerable misunderstandings and mistakes. It was noted that on Friday a visitor to the galleries could not have told the market was suspended.

The weekend brought one piece of bad news. That was the announcement on Saturday of the failure of the $20,000,000 Foshay enterprises of Minneapolis. Foshay owned utilities in some twelve states, Canada, Mexico, and Central America, and an assortment of hotels, flour mills, banks, manufacturing and retail establishments wherever he had happened to buy them. The 32-story obelisk, commemorating the enterprise, which still dominates the Minneapolis skyline, had been opened with fitting ceremony by Secretary of War James W. Good, only in August. (Secretary Good had referred to it as the "Washington Monument of the Northwest.") By all but the most technical of considerations, Foshay was bankrupt at that festive time. His survival depended on his ability to continue merchandising stock to the public. The market crash eliminated this source of revenue and made him dependent on the wholly inadequate earnings of his enterprises.

On all other fronts the news was all good. Alfred P. Sloan, Jr., President of the General Motors Corporation, said: "Business is sound." The Ford Motor Company emphasized a similar conviction by announcing a general reduction in its prices: ". . . we feel that such a step is the best contribution that could be made to assure a continuation of good business." The Roadster was cut from $450 to $435; the Phaeton from $460 to $440; the Tudor Sedan from $525 to $500. For the three days that the market was closed the papers carried stories of the accumulation of buying orders and, in some indefinable way, stories had a greater ring of conviction than the week before. The market, after all, had closed after an excellent two-day rally. As *Barron's* pointed out, it could now be believed that stocks were selling "ex-hopes and romance." On Monday, the Commercial National Bank and Trust Company took five columns in the *Times* to advertise ". . . our belief and conviction that the general industrial and business condition of the country is fundamentally sound and is essentially unimpaired."

That day the market started on another ghastly slump.

Knowledge Is Safeguard

A GOOD KNOWLEDGE of what happened in 1929 remains our best safeguard against the recurrence of the more unhappy events of those days. Since 1929 we have enacted numerous laws designed to make securities speculation more honest and, it is hoped, more readily restrained. None of these is a perfect safeguard. The signal feature of the mass escape from reality that occurred in 1929 and before—and which has characterized every previous speculative outburst from the South Sea Bubble to the Florida land boom—what that it carried Authority with it. Governments were either bemused as were the speculators or they deemed it unwise to be sane at a time when sanity exposed one to ridicule, condemnation for spoiling the game, or the threat of severe political retribution.

Purely in retrospect it is easy to see how 1929 was destined to be a year to remember. This was not because Mr. Hoover was soon to become President and had inimical intentions toward the market.

Rather, it was simply that a roaring boom was in progress in the stock market and, like all booms, it had to end. On the first of January 1929, it was a simple matter of probability.

The position of the people who had at least a nominal responsibility for what was going on was a complex one. One of the oldest puzzles -of politics is who is to regulate the regulators. But an equally baffling problem, which has never received the attention it deserves, is who is to make wise those who are required to have wisdom.

A bubble can easily be punctured. But to incise it with a needle so that it subsides gradually is a task of no small delicacy. Among those who sensed what was happening in early 1929, there was some hope but no confidence that the boom could be made to subside. The real choice was between an immediate and deliberately engineered collapse and a more serious disaster later on. Someone would certainly be blamed for the ultimate collapse when it came. There was no question whatever as to who would be blamed should the boom be deliberately deflated. (For nearly a decade the Federal Reserve authorities had been denying their responsibility for the deflation of 1920-21.) The eventual disaster also had the inestimable advantage of allowing a few more days, weeks, or months of life. One may doubt if at any time in early 1929 the problem was ever framed in terms of quite such stark alternatives. But however disguised or evaded, these were the choices which haunted every serious conference on what to do about the market.

President Coolidge neither knew nor cared what was going on. A few days before leaving office in 1929, he cheerily observed that things were "absolutely sound" and that stocks were "cheap at current prices."

Now, as throughout history, financial capacity and political perspicacity are inversely correlated. Long-run salvation by men of business has never been highly regarded if it means disturbance in the present. So inaction will be advocated in the present even though it means deep trouble in the future. Here, at least equally with communism, lies the threat to capitalism. It is what causes men who know that things are going quite wrong to say that things are fundamentally sound.

BERNARD
M. BARUCH

Wall Street's Elder Statesman

Bernard Baruch had strong opinions about what went wrong in 1929, which, as the country's elder statesman-financier, he has recounted to several U.S. presidents, along with many other matters.

Baruch was born August 19, 1870 in Camden, South Carolina, a second child of four. He was first educated in a private school but when his family moved to New York in 1881 he was sent to a public school, and later entered the College of the City of New York. His first job was in a firm of dealers in druggist's supplies, where he earned $3 a week.

He began his financial life in 1890, speculating on his own. In 1891 he joined the brokerage firm of A. A. Housman & Co., as a bond salesman and a customer's man. At the beginning of his career, Baruch, like Jesse Livermore, was engaged in "scalping" in the market, i.e. trading in and out for small quick profits. In 1896, at 26, he became a partner in A. A. Housman & Co., at which point Baruch began to emerge as a factor in Wall Street. Three years later he bought a seat on the New York Stock Exchange and became a large market operator.

By 1912, Baruch had become a millionaire, a major name in financial circles and, at 42, was ready to retire from brokerage duties, in order to concentrate on private speculation. In 1916 he was appointed a member of the Advisory Committee for the Council of National Defense, and in 1918 he became chairman of the War Industries Board. This was followed by a series of presidential appointments during World Wars I and II and at the United Nations thereafter.

Even after his retirement from Wall Street, Baruch's opinions on economic and stock matters were continually sought. He wrote for and was interviewed by scores of magazines, and he authored the book *My Own Story* © copyright 1957. Reprinted by permission of Holt, Rinehart & Winston, Inc. in which his colorful career is graphically described.

The Wisdom of
BERNARD M. BARUCH

Madness of the Crowd

THINK THAT the depression of 1929 was due more to a world madness and delusion than anything else. It was somewhat similar to the Tulip Craze, the Mississippi Bubble, and the South Sea Bubble. The world seems to go mad at times, and has extraordinary delusions or crowd madness—as against witches. Or it may take the form of war. The Crusades were such a madness. Or it may take the form, and generally does in modern times, of great speculative madnesses. I think much of the legislation to prevent incompetency and corrupt practices in the sale of securities and regulation of the exchanges is good. The laws ought to be strengthened that will protect the public when they are in these periods of madness such as 1929 and the Florida Boom. That is going to be a difficult thing. But the world has been struck with those things over and over again. Whenever it finds itself in that mess, it turns around to look for an alibi for its own weakness, and its own mistakes. (I made some myself.) Then it also looks for a catharsis.

Whatever men attempt they seem driven to try to overdo.

Some Baruch Trading Philosophy

IN THE STOCK market the first loss is usually the small-est. One of the worst mistakes anyone can make is to hold on blindly and refuse to admit that his judgment had been wrong.

Many a novice will sell something he has a profit in to protect something in which he has a loss. Since the good stock usually has gone down least, or may even show a profit it is psychologically easy to let go. With a bad stock the loss is likely to be very heavy and the impulse is to hold on to it in order to recover what has been lost.

Actually, the procedure one should follow is to sell the bad stock and keep the good stock. With rare exceptions, stocks are high because they are good, and stocks are low because they are of doubtful value.

Occasionally one is **too** close to a stock. In such cases the more one knows about a subject—the more inside information one has—the more likely one is to believe that he or she can outwit the workings of supply and demand.

Experts will step in where even fools fear to tread.

165

No speculator can be right all the time. In fact, if a speculator is correct half of the time he is hitting a good average. Even being right three or four times out of ten should yield a person a fortune if he has the sense to cut his losses quickly on ventures where he has been wrong.

I have found it wise, in fact, to periodically turn into cash most of my holdings and virtually retire from the market. No general keeps his troops fighting all the time; nor does he go into battle without some part of his forces held back in reserve.

Early Days

I GOT A FEW hundred dollars ahead; I would be cleaned out of everything, my original stake included.

I lost not only my own money but some of Father's as well. On one occasion I felt sure that a fortune could be made in an overhead trolley line that ran between the landing and a hotel at Put-in-Bay on a Lake Erie island. The venture had been brought to my attention by a personally charming promoter named John P. Carrothers, whom Father and I had met on the ship returning from Europe in 1890. I was so carried away that I persuaded Father to invest $8,000, a considerable part of his savings in the scheme. Every dollar was lost.

Although Father never reproached me, the loss weighed on my heart. I imagine I took it much harder than Father, who was more concerned with human values than with money.

Not long after the trolley setback, I remarked to Mother that if I had $500 I could make some money in Tennessee Coal and Iron.

"Why don't you ask Father for it?" she urged.

I protested that after the Put-in-Bay disaster, I could not ask him for another penny.

A few days later Father came to me with a check for $500. Memory plays us subtle tricks and I cannot recall whether or not I accepted the money. That detail is obscured by the larger significance of the incident —the profound lift it was to my self-respect to learn that, after I had cost him so much of his earnings, Father still had faith in me.

Unquestionably, Father was psychologist enough to know something of the struggle going on within me. My mind was in a state of balance where the touch of a hand might swerve me in a direction that could determine the whole course of my career.

In such circumstances, some men grow desperate. I grew cautious. I began a habit I was never to forsake—of analyzing my losses to determine where I had made my mistakes. This was a practice I was to develop ever more systematically as my operations grew in size. After each major undertaking—and particularly when things had turned sour —I would shake loose from Wall Street and go off to some quiet place where I could review what I had done and where I had gone wrong. At such times I never sought to excuse myself but was concerned solely with guarding against a repetition of the same error.

Periodic self-examination of this sort is something all of us need, in both private and governmental affairs. It is always wise for individuals and governments to stop and ask whether we should rush on blindly as in the past. Have new conditions arisen which require a change of direction or pace? Have we lost sight of the essential problem and are we simply wasting our energies on distractions? What have we learned that may help us avoid repeating the same old errors? Also, the more we know of our own failings, the easier it becomes to understand other people and why they act as they do.

In those early days it wasn't too difficult to figure out what I was doing that was wrong. There are two principal mistakes that nearly all amateurs in the stock market make.

The first is to have an inexact knowledge of the securities in which one is dealing, to know too little about a company's management, its earnings and prospects for future growth.

The second mistake is to trade beyond one's financial resources, to try to run up a fortune on a shoestring. That was my main error at the outset. I had virtually no "capital" to start with. When I bought stocks I put up so small a margin that a change of a few points would wipe out my equity. What I was really doing was little more than betting whether a stock would go up or down. I might be right sometimes, but any sizable fluctuation would wipe me out.

While I was carrying on these speculations, I had become a bond salesman and customers' man for A. A. Housman & Company. It happened to be a crucial period as far as the country's finances were concerned. The panic of 1893 closed many mills and mines and put into receivership a large part of all the railroads in the country. By 1895, though, one could detect the first promises of better financial weather.

I had never experienced a depression before. But even then I began to grasp dimly that the period of emergence from a depression provides rare opportunities for financial profit.

During a depression people come to feel that better times never will come. They cannot see through their despair to the sunny future that lies behind the fog. At such times a basic confidence in the country's future pays off, if one purchases securities and holds them until prosperity returns.

From what I saw, heard, and read, I know that was exactly what the giants of finance and industry were doing. They were quietly acquiring interests in properties which had defaulted but which would pay out under competent management once normal economic conditions were restored. I tried to do the same thing with my limited means.

The defaulted securities of railroads interested me particularly— partly I suppose, because the romance of railroading had attracted me from childhood when the brakemen on the freight trains waved to me as they passed Grandfather's house in Winnsboro. Then, this was also the period during which the nation's railroads, many of which had been wastefully overbuilt, were being consolidated into more efficient properties.

The problem was to determine which securities would survive these reorganizations. Those that did would become immensely valuable. Those that did not would be junked as worthless.

At first I made mistakes in picking the right securities. This spurred me to study the railroads involved more closely. I compiled a list of the railroads being reorganized whose securities seemed to me likely to prove sound investments. To test myself I jotted down in a little black notebook my expectations for these securities.

One entry I made suggested selling New Haven stock and buying Richmond and West Point Terminal, which was later reorganized into what is now the Southern Railway System. Other comments regarding the Atchison, Topeka and Santa Fe and Northern Pacific showed some foresight. Still another successful forecast in my little black book was a prediction that if Union Pacific were bought at the price then prevailing it would pay 100 per cent on the investment when it came out of receivership and was fully developed.

Baruch's 10 Rules

OTHER PEOPLE'S MISTAKES, I have noticed, often make us only more eager to try to do the same thing. Perhaps it is because in the breast of every man there burns not only that divine spark of discontent but the urge to "beat the game" and show himself smarter than the other fellow. In any case, only after we have repeated these errors for ourselves does their instructive effect sink home.

Being so skeptical about the usefulness of advice, I have been reluctant to lay down any "rules" or guidelines on how to invest or speculate wisely. Still, there are a number of things I have learned from my own experience which might be worth listing for those who are able to muster the necessary self-discipline:

1. Don't speculate unless you can make it a full-time job.
2. Beware of barbers, beauticians, waiters—of anyone— bringing gifts of "inside" information or "tips."
3. Before you buy a security, find out everything you can about the company, its management and competitors, its earnings and possibilities for growth.

171

4. Don't try to buy at the bottom and sell at the top. This can't be done—except by liars.
5. Learn how to take your losses quickly and cleanly. Don't expect to be right all the time. If you have made a mistake, cut your losses as quickly as possible.
6. Don't buy too many different securities. Better have only a few investments which can be watched.
7. Make a periodic reappraisal of all your investments to see whether changing developments have altered their prospects.
8. Study your tax position to know when you can sell to greatest advantage.
9. Always keep a good part of your capital in a cash reserve. Never invest all your funds.
10. Don't try to be a jack of all investments. Stick to the field you know best.

These "rules" mainly reflect two lessons that experience has taught me—that getting the facts of a situation before acting is of crucial importance, and that getting these facts is a continuous job which requires eternal vigilance.

GLENN
G. MUNN

Bear Market Technician

Glenn G. Munn was one of Wall Street's "name" writers during the great boom of the Twenties. A widely followed security analyst for Paine, Webber & Co., he wrote several important technical works and edited the Encyclopedia of Banking and Finance. Munn offered some valuable postmortems on 1929 in his *Meeting the Bear Market,* published by Harper & Bros., 1930.

The Wisdom of
GLENN G. MUNN

"Stocks will find their own level..."

MOTION IS THE first rule of the market. Extremely sensitive to the constant barrage of business news reported by the efficient financial news agencies, and to shifts in floating supply, the stock market is too delicately balanced a mechanism to remain for long on dead center. Almost everything that happens in business has a direct or indirect influence on stock values, and the forces of organized speculation—professional traders, bankers, and investment trusts—are always alert to capitalize changes in the business situation. Beyond the disturbances of purely economic origin are the various sorts of artificial agitation caused by pool manipulation and professional maneuvering. Inertia and stagnation are abhorrent to the speculative fraternity, and conditions within the market itself can be made the basis for price variations when economic motivation is absent.

Stock movements may be classified as (1) primary or cyclical—the major trend movements occupying a period of years and comprehending a complete cycle including a bull and a bear market; (2) secondary—the minor or intermediate swings of weeks' or months' duration in which reactions in a bull market are distinguishable; and (3) tertiary—the superficial daily ripples ruffling the surface of the secondary waves as the secondary waves are superimposed on the primary tides. The primary movements have their source in economic fundamentals, the secondary movements are chiefly technical but economic in part, while the tertiary movements are almost wholly technical. It is with the secondary and tertiary movements that the student of technical action is mainly concerned.

The Minor Swings

NSIGHT INTO THE nature of speculative movements may be had by a rough classification of the intentions of stock owners. Broadly, two classes are distinguishable: (1) stocks owned outright, and (2) the floating supply. Stocks held outright are registered in the name of the owner for the sake of their income and possibilities of appreciation. There is no immediate intention to sell. They are placed in safe deposit boxes, and "off the market." Only potentially do such holdings play a part in the determination of prices. As against stock held for permanent or quasi-permanent investment is the floating supply. This is the balance of the capitalization of a corporation without a permanent owner. Such stock is held in margin accounts, usually against a loan, and is in the name of a broker (street certificates). The floating supply is subject to speculative treatment, and the operations of those who control the shifting floating supply are the determinants of short-swing price fluctuations.

Not all the holders of stock have the same intentions, and a sub-classification of these intentions is here subjoined:

1. Stocks owned outright. (Held for quasi-permanent investment; rarely come on to the market; when sold may be replaced by other issues.)
2. The floating supply. (Held by transient owners.)
   a. Stocks bought with intention of long-pull holding.
   b. Stocks bought with intention of short-swing holding.
   c. Stocks bought by day-to-day (in-and-out) traders.

Speculation for the long pull is founded on the promise of broad primary movements. Speculators so minded base their commitments on fundamentals and analysis. They are not interested in quick trading profits, and from their point of view minor swings are unimportant and day-to-day and week-to-week fluctuations meaningless. But an organized exchange is a daily market and must express itself as a continuous process. No tree grows to heaven in a day, and even in an ebullient market, price advances are never perpendicular. Higher or lower prices may be in the making for the long-pull operator, but the existence of speculators with a trading attitude, willing to accept a few points profits if they accrue within a trading session or overnight, and another group willing to clinch larger profits obtainable within a week or a month, prevent the market from permitting wide gaps in price changes. Continuity is the second law of the market.

Not less than one-fifth and perhaps as much as one-third of the transactions on the stock exchange represent dealings of traders on the floor. Probably no more than 10 per cent of stock exchange members trade exclusively for their own account, but there are many who transact business both for themselves and other members. These are the professional traders who stand ready to take advantage of any item in the news or of changes in technical conditions susceptible of altering a trend. This group is augmented by others, who, though non-members, engage in speculation as a vocation. Since so large a part of total dealings is consummated by those interested in profits from quick turns, daily price variations are seldom extensive in normal markets. A large proportion of professional transactions, indeed, is closed before trading ceases, profit or no profit.

Obviously, the conscious motive of speculators is profits, which may or may not follow. But in their operations, they perform the useful economic function of carrying the floating supply of securities. Profit possibilities are greater in a moving and active market than in an immobile, listless, dormant market. If all speculators were of the long-pull variety, the market would be a dull and colorless exhibition, and for their purposes might be closed until the fruitage they expect has had time to mature. The function of the trading element, then, is to provide a continuous open market, enabling investors (and long-pull holders) to convert their securities into cash at virtually a moment's notice, or to buy in anticipation of an appreciation in values. The trading point of view enlivens the market, affords a basis of operations for investors and long-pull speculative holders, and permits a continuous flow of quotations. It is in this sense, though the ceaseless oscillation of prices composing the tertiary movements seems banal and purposeless, merely reflecting momentary revisions of buyers' and sellers' schedules, that the surface ripples caused by short-run trading are justified.

The attitude of those who are trading-minded is always that if stocks will not move in one direction they must move in the other. If a buying movement on volume, lifting prices a number of points, spends itself, as denoted by diminishing activity on the advance, traders will conclude that the movement will be followed up no further and that prices have temporarily risen as high as they will go. As they take profits and perhaps put out short lines, prices recede. Others may sell, assisting the declining movement. If the selling subsides, and stocks are supported at lower levels, they conclude it is time to cover short lines and to go long of stock. The trading viewpoint is to accept small profits from short swings on the theory that if the capital is turned over frequently, aggregate profits are as great as by assuming a long-pull position.

Trading by the Tape

T HE THEORY OF the technicist is that each price
change, taken in relation to the volume of trading,
has significance—more than that, forecast value. He
assumes that there is a meaning behind each purchase
and sale, and though the tape does not disclose the source
of buying or selling—which admittedly would be helpful
—this is of less importance than the fact of buying or
selling. Nobody buys or sells without some reason though
the reason be impeachable. This is not to say that price
and volume changes as unreeled by the tape can always
be interpreted in a way to permit profitable trades. There
are times when the evidence is negative.

It is also assumed that fundamentals and analysis are
incorporated, or are in process of being incorporated, in
the price. Any new development in a company's affairs,
whether favorable or unfavorable, will begin to register
itself in the price of the stock in advance of the announcement of the news. This is because those in a position first
to know of impending developments will endeavor to
capitalize the information by buying; or, if the news be

adverse, by selling. Consequently, when a stock rises on increasing activity, not otherwise explained, there is valid technical reason for following the move. Conversely, if it declines on increasing volume, the technical signal that it should be sold is worth accepting. Taken in totality, these operaions cause similar changes in average prices.

There are many successful traders who derive inspiration almost exclusively from the revelations of the tape, and the daily history of tape action is graphically delineated in chart form. Fundamentals and analysis are important as background and in predicating long-term movements, and need not be ignored, but for secondary and tertiary movements the tape tells the story to one experienced in interpreting its record. The advantage of guidance by technical action is that the trader need have no preconceived idea of the market's future price path. He need have no pattern for the market to follow. Frequently, fundamentals and analysis suggest movement in one direction, but the immediate short-swing movement is in the opposite. The technicist is not disappointed if the market fails to conform to the course predetermined as logical. He takes his signals from the market itself and does not quarrel with it. As a result, he is in step with the market and has no apologies to make if its behavior is counter to preconceptions

Sponsorship and Support Levels

F EW LISTED STOCKS are so friendless as to be without a godfather. Virtually every important issue is
sponsored by a group (investment bank, investment
trust, speculative pool, an individual or individuals, stabilizing account, or the corporation itself), willing to make
its market. Sponsorship varies in financial power, but is
designed to protect the stock against unjustifiable bear
forays, to maintain a price in consonance with its war-
ranted value as a point of honor with the underwriting
group's offering price, and for the purpose of accumulation and later distribution. The sponsors are in close touch
with the company's progress and presumably in a favored
position to know its real worth.

Sponsorship thus gives rise to support points on declines and resistance points on advances. The detection of
such points is one of the tasks of the technicist. The sponsors have in mind a minimum price at which their stock
should sell under a given set of market conditions, and
are prepared to purchase at such a price should it drop
thereto.

Referring solely to the movement of the averages, a trading area on a high plateau in a bull market almost invariably is an interlude in what later proves to be a resumption of the rise, else the energy required to hold prices within the area would not have been expended. The technical rule is that the line of least resistance is motion, and stocks having risen to a temporary apex, would be more apt to round off and with little hesitation to start downward. Similarly, a trading area at the bottom of a sharp decline is a breathing space to take account of fundamentals. If the decline has gone too far, recovery, if there is to be one, will lose no time in asserting itself. Consequently, a trading area following a declining movement is usually the precursor of a resumption of the fall. Technically, then, a trading area is a compromise since the rule of motion is violated. It is a concession of technical conditions to fundamentals.

What applies to the averages in regard to trading areas is not applicable to individual stocks. Frequently, what appears to be a trading area at the bottom of a decline in an individual stock is a zone of accumulation with the next important movement upward. Similarly, the semblance of a trading area in an individual stock on a high plateau frequently turns out to be a level of distribution with the next move downward.

A trading area offers one type of market situation in which the trader may have his decision made for him with a minimum of risk. Since a trading area is an interruption of the trend, the market will show, by its own action, what the direction will be when the trading market has terminated. Just as soon as the averages break out of their trading range in one direction or the other, the action can be followed almost blindly. Almost invariably, it is a signal for a continuation of that directional change.

Best Trading Vehicles

TRADERS ABLE TO watch the tape incessantly and who are interested in short-swing (perhaps day-to-day) trading profits, should concentrate their operations in those active leaders which vibrate over the widest diurnal arcs. Activity is essential to insure completion of the round turn. More accurately, they will wish to select the stocks showing the greatest daily movements as a percentage of price (and therefore capital requirement).

Some Technical Principles

I N A BULL market there are important reactions, but unless the bull market has been completed, each succeeding reaction fails to reach the low point of its predecessor. If it does, there is a presumption that the bull market has already passed its crest. Similarly, each intermediate advance in a bull market carries farther than the preceding one. Failure of a secondary advance to pass the high point of its predecessor is a presumption, requiring later confirmation, that a bear market is in the making.

Likewise, in a bear market there are important rallies. Until the major decline has been completed, however, each succeeding rally point falls short of the highest position in the immediately preceding rally. When, finally, a rally lifts itself above the next preceding one, there is presumptive, but not conclusive, evidence that the major trend has been reversed.

One month of record-breaking movement in the averages is never followed by another in succession, although the trend may be in the same direction. This holds true in both rising and falling markets. The rapid rise in June, 1929, was followed by a trading market in July. The record-breaking rise in August, 1929, was followed by a decline in September. The unprecedented decline of October, 1929, was followed by an additional, but far less drastic, decline in November.

An almost infallible clue to the end of an intermediate bull swing is the sudden collapse of some popular but overexploited issue. Since 1926, practically every intermediate reaction was heralded by such an incident. In each instance, a sharp decline in Devoe & Reynolds, Manhattan Electric Supply, Bancitaly, Canadian Marconi and Advance Rumely were harbingers of important reactions in this period. Another sign is an unexplained downturn in the entire list.

The culmination of an intermediate or major reaction never appears on heavy trading volume. There may be temporary pauses and recoveries, but so long as activity persists, it is practically certain that bottom has not yet been reached. The conclusion is detected by an evaporation of liquidation in coincidence with a material contraction in sales volume. When diminished turnover is accompanied by narrow price movements, the basal point of the break has been approached and a foundation established for a fresh advance. There is no rule by which to determine the interval that must elapse to start the recovery. It is seldom delayed for long. It will be first suggested by the appearance of strength in a number of leaders or a certain group of stocks that happens to be relatively favorably situated.

In a declining market, when 80 per cent or more of the stocks showing changes for the day are minus three days successively (ignoring issues showing no change for the day), a rally in the nature of a spontaneous automatic rebound must be expected. The normal rally from the low point in a declining phase is from one-third to one-half of the distance lost from the preceding high point. When, in a declining market, stocks are purchased in the climax period, the safe procedure is to dispose of them on the ensuing rally.

A zigzag movement in which stocks travel up and down in a single session without dislocating the general range, is neutral and inconclusive evidence of the next directional change. When price movements are inconclusive, the trader, in an endeavor to detect a favorable buying point, may await one of three developments: (1) A sharp decline of climactic proportions on increasing activity (which should spend itself on the third day); (2) a drying up of the reactionary tendency, as evidenced by dullness and narrow price fluctuations; or (3) the rising of prices to a point just above the last preceding resistance levels through which they were unable to penetrate.

Neither the market as a whole nor an individual stock normally rises perpendicularly even in a bull market; considered from either point of view, the market rarely proceeds in one direction more than five consecutive days without encountering some degree of reaction, however trifling.

Technically, the market tries for continuity. Gaps (when the price range of one day is wholly detached from the preceding day) are against the law of continuity. Unless there is overnight news in explanation, there is always a strong tendency for the gap to be closed, irrespective of the direction. The reason is that an unexplained decline will attract buying by the trading element; a sudden rise induces selling.

Accumulation, especially careful accumulation, is more likely to take place in markets of relatively small volume; distribution on heavy volume.

It is a Wall Street maxim that a short position should be covered in case unfavorable news, other than that expected, permits of this procedure.

Part IV

Sages of the Thirties...

Despite the slow recovery, trading continued on Wall Street. Everything was on a much reduced scale, of course, as compared with the great speculative binge of the Twenties. But even in the Thirties traders tried to take profits out of the market.

To do so, there had to be a refinement of the rules, conceived in the orientation of a depressed market place.

GEORGE SEAMAN .. Compiler of Trading Rules.

RICHARD W. SCHABACKER .. Pioneer of Sophisticated Technical Research.

HAROLD M. GARTLEY .. Master Market Technician.

GEORGE
SEAMAN

Compiler of Trading Rules

One notable attempt at developing new rules, firmly grounded in the speculative techniques of the Twenties and the more somber approaches of the Thirties, was found in *The Seven Pillars of Stock Market Success*, published by Seamans-Blake, Chicago, 1933. The original edition was anonymous, but subsequent editions carried the name of George Seaman. The book included his celebrated "100 Rules" which became standard market philosophy in the 1930's. Many of the "rules" are often referred to in today's market literature, although Seaman is seldom acknowledged as their original compiler.

The Wisdom of
GEORGE SEAMAN

Unchanging Laws of the Market

RULE 1.   In the beginning, trade only in an imaginary way instead of with money. After you have read this book and feel that you have learned a great deal, prove it to yourself by buying and selling stocks **but without money.** Enter every purchase order in a ledger, as though you had given the order to your broker, tabulating a half point for commission and taxes. Execute your buying and selling as though you were playing for real money. Do not fool yourself and do not try to fool your ledger. After a few months of this kind of playing, make out your balance sheet. Figure how many times you were right and how many times you were wrong. If the **times right** exceed the **times wrong** (not how much money you won or lost), go ahead and play for money. Do not play with very much at the beginning. Ten shares is quite sufficient; if you come out ahead this will give you confidence in yourself. Then you can increase your trading to 100 share lots or to any amount within your means.

(Probably each of my readers will have the tendency to think, as I did, that he is different; that he does not have to go through a period of training and apprenticeship. Very quickly I found I was mistaken.)

Rule 2. When you begin to trade make up your mind that a good part of your capital will be lost before you make a success. (That is Wall Street's usual charge for "breaking" you in.) It is only by practice and study that you will learn how to play the market. Naturally, you will make plenty of mistakes. Therefore, if you have, let us say, $10,000.00 at the time of your initiation, figure that you will lose part of it before you make much headway. That is why I strongly urge that in the beginning you trade only in ten share lots rather than in one hundred share lots. Learn the market at the lowest possible tuition fee. You have time to play in 100 or 1,000 share lots after you have learned how to trade. Should you start with 100 or 1,000 share lots, you will not have enough money left after you have learned. **So start low and grow as you go along.**

(In the beginning of your trading career read Rule No. 2. daily. It will give you much comfort and peace and money to play with, when you graduate.)

Rule 3. Do not deal in inactive stocks. Play with live ones. (When you sleep with a dog you awake with fleas.)

Rule 4. Do not hold on to a stock if you see it dropping; it may drop more. You may be able to buy more stock at the bottom for the same money.

(There is no valid reason to hold a stock just because you bought it.)

Rule 5. Do not be overly enthusiastic and permit your prospective profits to run away with you, hoping that stocks will go up still further. **Hope** is your worst enemy in the market. The public usually observes its stocks dropping, hoping against hope that they will advance or make a comeback. But this rarely happens soon enough.

Rule 6. Do not play in low-priced stocks. Keep away from stocks that have not reached a $20 high for a year or so. The best stocks to play with are those from $30 to $130. On higher priced stocks like U. S. Steel or Chrysler, the chances of making money quickly are more certain.

(Always pick a winner.)

Rule 7.   Never cover a margin call. Why put good money after bad? You are not saving anything by putting up more money on your margin. In the final analysis the value of your stock at your broker's is what it can be sold for at market, at the **present moment.** Use your reasoning powers and you will agree you are not helping your situation any, because, if your stock dropped 40% or 50% it may drop still more. You must admit that if you are called upon to put up more margin money it means either that you have bought poor stock, or that you bought at a wrong time. In either case the additional mistake of "hanging on" until the margin bugle blows is fatal, and you should liquidate your purchase. Start trading anew by buying the **right stock** at the **right time.**

(If someone owed you money and you could not collect, would you loan him more money?)

Rule 8.   If you have been "unlucky" in the market, do not try to play with the thought in the back of your mind of making up your losses—forget about them. As a matter of fact, if you have been unlucky for any length of time, the best thing to do is to stop and get away from the market for awhile. Think over what you have done which caused these losses. Perform a post-mortem. When your mind feels rested, and you have forgotten about your losses, you can begin again, but **not with the view of making up your losses.** Play with the view of making money.

Rule 9.   If you have a loss on the market on, let us say, 100 shares, do not play 200 or 300 shares in order to make up your previous losses in a hurry. You may have another and bigger loss than before. Just keep on playing 100 shares as you played on the losing side. Never try to take revenge on the market. You will never do well in that frame of mind. Let me repeat: play the market because you want to make money and because it is ripe for a play, not because you want to make up your losses. Otherwise it will lead you into taking undue chances and usually you will be the loser. The market must be played according to the laws you have learned, and without sentiment.

Rule 10.   Do not jump around from one stock to another thinking the grass is greener in one place than in another. It is not. It is better to play a few stocks and learn their habits well.

Rule 11.   Remember that it takes years to learn how to trade properly and to learn how to interpret the tape. Do not expect to make millions in one week or one year. It takes practice to become perfect.

Rule 12.   Never take the advice or act exclusively on the opinion of any advisory service. I subscribe to about ten and they hardly ever agree. Learn to give yourself your own advice, based on knowledge.

(Why should they know more than you?)

Rule 13.   The best broker is the one who will not give you advice. A good broker should take instructions and let you use your own judgment.

Rule 14.   When you see the market advance, do not rush to buy. This may be the end of the advance and you will be buying at top prices. Wait until a reaction sets in—then buy.

(Those who buy on reactions sell out on advances. Those who buy on advances sell out on reactions.)

Rule 15.   Never ask anybody's advice or think that the next fellow knows more than you. If you follow his advice you may as well give him your money to trade with, which of course, you would not do. Then why ask his advice? Learn to do your own thinking and develop sufficient confidence in yourself to enable you to rely on your own judgment. Solve your problems. In time you will be solving other people's problems.

Rule 16. Do not let anyone influence you when you have made a decision to buy or get out. Act according to your convictions.

Rule 17. Do not trade on "tips" given by friends, by your broker, or on rumors flying around broker's offices.

Rule 18. Change your position quickly if you see that you are wrong. It is better to take a small loss rather than wait until your losses increase. When you buy for a ten point rise, and the stock does not do well, close out at a small profit or loss. Do not stick to a stock just because you bought it. You should be proud of your ability at catching your mistakes in time. A few hours may make all the difference.

(Remember October, 1937.)

Rule 19. Do not buy a stock because the price is low. A stock is only cheap if you can sell it at a higher price. The difference between cheap and expensive is not the **price** but the **time** element. There are times when a stock at $75 is cheap and other times when the same stock at $25 is expensive. To be successful it is not as important to know what to buy as **when** to buy. The price you pay at the "right" time is no criterion so long as you can sell at a higher price.

Rule 20. Do not gamble. Speculation is **not** gambling. A gambler is one who does not know what to do and therefore takes chances. A speculator is one who knows what it is all about, although often he, too, gets "stung." A gambler has little knowledge and bases everything on luck. A speculator who trades according to the laws of the market wins three times out of five and needs no luck.

(If you must satisfy your gambling instincts play solitaire, it is much cheaper.)

Rule 21. Do not over-trade. Always play with sufficient margin so that your broker cannot sell you out. Do not take advantage of any more than half the legal margin allowance, and during uncertain times trade with no margin at all. Pay for your stocks outright. And buy only with part of your capital.

Rule 22.   Do not play with somebody else's money, whether it is your broker's or your friend's, or with money which you can ill-afford to lose.

Rule 23.   If you are attempting to make money in a hurry you will not succeed. There is money in Wall Street for you and if you do not get it today you will get it a week or a month hence. You have a better chance to get it, however, if you wait. Play when the TIME is ripe.

(A hundred yard dash may get you out of breath.)

Rule 24.   Do not be discouraged if you make mistakes. The best traders do. Learn from those mistakes and try not to repeat them. Attempt to find out the underlying cause. When you have thoroughly reasoned out what you did or failed to do, resolve not to make the same error again. Do not place faith in luck, because if you think it is luck that makes the market go up or down you will never be a success- ful trader. The market has its reasons for going up and down. It is up to you to find them out.

(We all make mistakes but only a fool or a weakling repeats them.)

Rule 25.   Be skeptical about any trade that appears to be a dead-sure winner. When you feel one hundred percent certain that you will come out well, that is just the time to look around with a critical eye. Never be **dead sure.** The market may have a lot of surprises in store for you.

(More people get stung by "sure things" than by bees.)

Rule 26.   Do not attempt to "guess" the market. Play only because you have come to definite conclusions by analysis of the situation. Do not arrive at these conclusions without first measuring every angle by fundamental economic conditions, the trend, Dow Theory, and the signals from your charts. When these are in your favor, weigh the news items in your paper to determine if this is the psychological moment to make your purchase.

Rule 27.   Bear in mind always that the market is in the strongest technical position when it is "weak" with prices down and news gloomy. Moreover, it is in an extremely weak position when it appears to be strongest, as when prices are up, business booming and newspapers full of prosperity psychology. Following the theory of cycles, it works out thus: those who are strong have **potential** weakness which must assert itself sooner or later, those that are momentarily weak, possess potential strength.

(Remember what Jesus said about the strength of those who are weak and about the weakness of those who are strong.)

Rule 28.   If you want to come out ahead, do not repeat your mistakes. In that way eventually you will succeed. Remember, also, that the market always gives you a thousand and one opportunities to make new errors. So be on guard!

Rule 29.   It is advisable to play with not more than ten stocks. Study these stocks painstakingly, their actions for years back, their resistance points, and their behavior, so that you may know exactly what they are capable of doing. Ordinarily, what holds good for the entire market, will hold true for your particular stock. Whatever you trade in should be among the ten best sellers on the Exchange. It is advisable to deal only in issues which have a wide market and move rapidly. Select any of the fast leaders for a particular week or month. It is true that at times some stocks have advantages over others, but they are all subject to the same law of supply and demand. There is no reason to play with 100 different stocks, when you can play with a few which you know intimately.

(Remember that the devil you know is better than the devil you do not know.)

Rule 30.   Do not average your stock if it goes against you. Do not buy more of the same stock at a lower price if it has already dropped. Close it out instead.

(A dried up cow goes to the butcher.)

Rule 31. Place your "stops" so that they will be 1/8 below even figures on a "long" buy, and 1/8 above even figures on a "short." Place your stops below resistance points on a "long" buy and above resistance points on a "short" sale.

(Even then they may "gun" for you.)

Rule 32. Your success in speculative operations on the Exchange is based on the following: First, on your ability to determine economic and political conditions, not as they are today, but as they will be three to six months hence. Second, your ability to determine what certain pools and manipulators in Wall Street are doing or intend to do with the stocks they have on hand or with the stocks in the hands of the public. If, after a thorough study of the situation, you decide that Wall Street is interested in buying, then do the same. If, on the contrary, they are disposing of their holdings, sell yours and go short, especially if you detect the move at the top.

Rule 33. To purchase or sell short any stock, begin with the assumption that your profits will be four to five times your risk. If you expect only a two point rise, do not buy. Wait until your analysis shows clearly a possible advance of 8 to 10 points. Then risk two points on a five-to-one shot. This is much better than a one-to-one chance.

(A one-to-one shot is gambling. A five-to-one shot is speculating.)

Rule 34. Money can best be made when buying on the down of a move and then selling close to the top. If you have predetermined by analysis the resistance points on the particular stock you are dealing in, the possibility of error is limited.

Rule 35. Always purchase stocks in the strongest groups. There are times when some groups are stronger than others, when railroads are weak and industrials strong, and when coppers are strong and foods weak. Therefore, always buy in the strongest group. Determine this from the action of the market. The stronger groups will advance further or offer more resistance to decline than the weaker groups. In each group there are always one or two stocks that do better on an average than the group as a whole. That is the stock you should buy for an upward pull. On the other hand, if you wish to play the market short, choose a weak group, one that has not been doing well. Select the weakest stock in that group (the one most sensitive to decline) for a short play.

Rule 36.   Trade evenly. Do not buy 100 shares today and 1000 shares tomorrow. If you trade in 100 share lots do not buy more than 100 shares unless you decide to advance in general your scope of trading. Your percentage of winners or losers will not work out if you vary the amounts from time to time. For example: if out of ten trades in 100 share lots you have had seven winners, and then you play with a 1000 share lot and sustain one loss, this will wipe out all your seven winnings. However, if you stick to 100 share lots and you have a loss, you will have six winners and only one loser.

(Be in balance.)

Rule 37.   The most important thing in the market is the "trend." Do not attempt to trade until you are able to deduce this from a thorough analysis. **Always trade with the trend and not against the trend.** If the trend is doubtful, stay out of the market entirely until the trend is visible, even if it takes weeks or months. You will be well compensated by not trading in a market of which you are in doubt. Money is not made by being in all the time. (In fact that is a good way of losing it.) One or two good trades a month will net you more than trading day in and day out on guess-work.

Rule 38.   Learn to be patient. Guard against hurry-skurry. If you have calculated that your stock will move up a certain number of points and you think that you are correct in your theory, have the patience to wait. Your opportunity may arrive just five minutes after you have sold out your stocks at a lower figure.

(The world might very well have been destroyed in the days of Lot if the good Lord were without patience. So says the Book of Books.)

Rule 39.   Do not permit your opinions about political matters to influence your market judgment. You may have a soft spot for the underdog and sympathize with the New Deal. But during market hours consider President Roosevelt's speeches and actions objectively so that you may gauge every possibility and reaction. Learn to exercise professional judgment and do not allow your political opinions to interfere with your stock market trading.

("When in Rome do as the Romans do.")

Rule 40.   When the tape has been going in a certain direction, either up, or down, and it comes to a stop for a few seconds, that usually signifies that a new chapter is starting. Sometimes it may be a stronger continuation in the same direction. More often, however, it indicates that the market will very soon turn in the opposite direction.

Rule 41.   Remember that the reason stocks go up and down is basically because of **supply and demand.** If there are more buyers than sellers, stocks will go up, even though they were on the downward trend. Some people may wish to sell, but if the people who buy are more numerous and have more money, stocks naturally will go up. When stocks do go up, it is because people want to pay the price. In other words, the demand is greater than the supply. When a point is reached where there are no more buyers at the prices asked, then the demand has diminished. From that point on a decline will take place. With this in mind, act accordingly. When you notice that the supply is greater than the demand and stocks begin to drop, **sell.** You cannot be certain how far they will go down, because you cannot measure how great the supply is and whether the demand will be strong enough to stop this supply. Your most logical move under such circumstances, is to sell. This holds good particularly in an uncertain or down trend market.

205

(There are exceptions to every rule. The prudent trader will break this sound rule under justifiable circumstances.)

Rule 42.   Do not ride up and down with a stock. Although you may have bought with the idea that it will go up ten points, that is no reason why you should wait for the ten points and not take profits beforehand, if they are available. If you bought at 100 with the object of selling at 110 and have followed to 105 (half way) a corrective reaction may be in order. That stock may want to test the 102-103 level. Is there any reason why you should let it ride down on you? The commissions are, approximately, only a half point. The wisest thing to do is to sell at 105, buy back at 102-103-104 or even 105. Do not stay with it while it is reacting as it may go below 100. This gives you the following advantages:

1) A chance to buy for less, thereby making additional profits.
2) Taking no chances while it is slipping on the way down.
3) If the stock should react to 103-104 and then shoot up to 106, it is a safe buy at 106. It has already gone through the reaction and you know that it will go up.

(Remember, you do not marry a stock when you buy, nor do you pay alimony on parting.)

Rule 43.   Watch commodity prices every day, especially wheat and cotton. Take particular note of bank issues. If they go down, most likely all other stocks will go down. The same is true of commodities. A drop in commodity prices usually foretells a drop in stock prices. Another item to watch is foreign selling. During 1937 there was considerable foreign buying and selling. The buying was during the beginning of the year and the selling during the latter part. Many breaks in the market were due to foreign selling.

Rule 44.   It is advisable to place a **time** ultimatum on stocks you buy. If a stock does not come up to your expectations within a certain time, sell, even at a loss. You cannot afford to have your money tied up for too long a period. Meanwhile you may be losing the profits which you could have made if you had invested in other stocks, which are in their technical up move.

Rule 45.   Do not take money out of your business to trade on the market unless your business can unquestionably do without it. Do not play the market with money which will cause you too great anxiety. You will never succeed when you are in that state of mind.

Rule 46.   Do not try to squeeze out the last quarter or half point. If you have made a profit and feel it will not go much higher, it is best to sell and pocket your profits. Potential profits do not mean anything; it is only the money you have after you have sold your stocks that count.

Rule 47.   When you decide to take profits by selling, do it on the up-movement, while the stock is climbing. Do not wait until the movement exhausts itself, as you will then have to sell for one-half or one point less.

(Strike while the iron is hot.)

Rule 48.   When the market is in an **up-trend** and you wish to take advantage of a little shake-out on a reaction, play short, but only with $1/3$ of the amount on the long side. If you purchased 300 shares on the upside, for instance, and decide to sell, dispose of 400 shares. This will mean that you are 100 shares short. When the market has gone down a few points, and you think it will make a turn for a rise, buy 400 shares. This will place you in the position of having covered your 100 short and you will be 300 long. The reverse is true of a down-trend market.

Rule 49.   When buying on a reaction, if the tape moves fast it is best to buy at a stipulated price under the market instead of "at market." Frequently it is advisable to buy or sell "at market," as otherwise you may not get your price and an opportunity may be lost.

Rule 50.   **It is very important** that you know before buying or selling where the next resistance point will be on the averages (Dow-Jones or others) and on the stock you are trading in. For instance: if your records show that there was a good deal of resistance at 102 on Steel you should not buy Steel at 101, as it will certainly sell off at 102 or 103. You should buy at 95; by following it up to 103 and then selling, you can make a profit. The same is true for the Dow-Jones averages. If on previous occasions there was a resistance at 190 on the Dow-Jones averages, sell at 188-189. Buy at 185.

Rule 51.　The chances for covering when playing short are better on a stock with a large number of shares outstanding, such as U. S. Steel. Others with a small issue of shares may jump a point or two between sales. So do not short stocks with limited shares.

Rule 52.　The secret of successful stock market operation is to limit your losses as much as possible. Your profits will pyramid.

Rule 53.　When you see a sharp move on the market it is either short covering on the up-side, or purely technical reaction on the down-side. Do not let these sudden moves tempt you to go in.

Rule 54.　Watch the higher-priced leaders carefully. A lot of maneuvering on smaller issues frequently transpires with a view to advantageous sales, by having the leaders make a smoke-screen demonstration of strength.

Rule 55.　A good time to sell stocks is on a late tape on an up-market. A good time to cover is on a late tape in a down-market.

Rule 56.　It is not good policy to be long and short at the same time. There were occasions during the month of October 1937, when it was logical to assume that industrials might rise and rails decline. However, it is dangerous to play the market that way. It is best to follow the trend. Remember that rails and industrials must eventually confirm one another.

Rule 57.　In the market be neither a bear nor a bull—have no prejudices. Do not love one side more than the other. Play the up-side or the down-side. If the market is on a down-trend play the short side; if the market is on an up-trend, play the long side. Never try to buck the trend of the market because you feel bullish or bearish. Forget your feelings. Go the way the market goes. Float with it, and the tide will carry you in to shore. The public finds it more pleasant to play the upside. They usually buy stocks in order to advance. The fact of the matter is that the short side often is more profitable, and quicker, because when stocks drop they drop rapidly. Be as much at ease trading on the short side as on the long.

Rule 58.   Do not purchase stocks by statistics. The statistical tabulation of a stock does not make it a good or bad buy. It is **now** that counts and not what **has been.** Statistics show only what **has been.** Knowledge of economics is necessary in order to know what is going on **now.** Base your opinion on that and not on statistics. Economics is alive. Statistics are past history—dead documents covered with dust. Quite frequently a stock is in a statistically favorable position, and still it sells lower than the stock which is statistically unsound. **Price is based on supply and demand** not on statistics.

(In a controversy both sides make use of statistics to prove themselves right.)

Rule 59.   Remember that the market may do the unexpected. Therefore, always expect the unexpected—not what you would like it to do. Do not trade by wish-fulfillment.

Rule 60.   Do not buy or sell the first hour of the market, nor at opening prices, unless extraordinary circumstances prevail. After an hour there has usually been a buying and selling period. From these two periods you can decide more readily whether your contemplated action is timely.

The Seven Pillars

There are **SEVEN PILLARS OF STOCK MARKET PRACTICE** necessary for success. The sixty Rules formulated in the foregoing chapters are based on seven cardinal principles which are the main arteries to successful market trading, e.g.,

1. Determine whether the market is in a "bear" or "bull" trend. Then determine further whether it is a major, intermediate, or minor trend.
   TRADE WITH THE TREND!

2. Determine which groups of stocks are the strongest.
   TRADE IN STRONG GROUPS FOR ADVANCE!
   TRADE IN WEAK GROUPS FOR DECLINE!

3. Select the strongest stocks in these particular groups.
   TRADE IN STRONG STOCKS FOR ADVANCE!
   TRADE IN WEAK STOCKS FOR DECLINE!

4. **BUY ONLY ON REACTIONS**—not on advances!
   SELL AND SHORT ONLY ON ADVANCES—not on declines!

5. Place a mental or (if you do not watch the tape) actual stop-loss order of two or three points on your trades.
   BE AT ALL TIMES PROTECTED AGAINST POSSIBLE LOSSES!
   CLOSE OUT WHEN TRADE GOES AGAINST YOU.

6. Protect your profits by stop-loss orders. Let your profits grow when you see your stocks advancing.
   HOLD OUT FOR LARGER PROFITS!

7. Do not hesitate to take your profits; you may be able to re-buy the same stock at lower prices.
   SELL WHEN YOU THINK THE MARKET IS DUE
   FOR A REACTION!
   SELL AT THE TOP * * * NOT AT THE BOTTOM
   BUY AT THE BOTTOM   NOT AT THE TOP
   To capitalize on these rules
   reread
   THE SEVEN PILLARS OF STOCK MARKET SUCCESS

RICHARD W. SCHABACKER

Pioneer of Sophisticated Technical Research

R. W. Schabacker may be unknown to many present day investors; yet, his understanding of the market was awesomely profound and his writings on the market perhaps more prolific and technical than any other of his day. Probably the reason Schabacker is not better known is that he wrote during the early Thirties, when public interest in the stock market was at its lowest ebb in all stock exchange history, and when even Charles Dow himself might not have made much of an impression.

Schabacker, born in 1899 in Erie, Pennsylvania attended Princeton University and was graduated cum laude with a B.A. in 1921.

His early positions were with the Federal Reserve Bank of New York, the Standard Statistics Company (now Standard & Poor's) and the Cleveland *Plain Dealer*. In 1925, Schabacker joined *Forbes Magazine,* became the youngest Financial Editor in its history, and remained there for ten years, until his untimely death in 1935 at the age of 36.

During his short but brilliant career, Schabacker authored three books. His *Stock Market Theory and Practice* (published by B. C. Forbes Publishing Co. in 1930), a massive work of 650 pages, was hailed in the New York *Post* as an "encyclopedia on the stock market, indispensable to any financial library." *Technical Analysis and Market*

Profits was published as a mail order course of lessons in 1932. In 1934 came his *Stock Market Profits,* also published by Forbes.

This body of work by Schabacker is among the most influential ever written on the technical side of the market. Recognized as one of the "greats" by market students, his theories were the basic source material used by Edwards and Magee in their standard technical market works. Schabacker pioneered in the discovery of the chart patterns so widely used by technicians today—"head and shoulders," "double top," "Trendlines," etc.

Schabacker also rated as one of the supreme market forecasters of his time; his published forecasts in September 1929, at the peak of the long Bull market, warned of an "impending major reaction" and advised liquidation of stocks.

The Wisdom of
RICHARD W. SCHABACKER

Characteristics of the End of a Bull Market

(From Stock Market Theory and Practice, B. C. Forbes Pub. Co., 1930)

AFTER FUNDAMENTALS HAVE turned unfavorable the technical strength of the market often carries it on up for a much longer period of time and for much wider gains, and only the technical considerations give much clue, in the final analysis, to the time when the market will actually turn. Excitement is one of the strongest evidences of weakening technical position in such a period. Volume of sales mounts to huge figures, tremendous advances take place in individual and speculative favorites, perhaps sudden collapses of other stocks occur at the same time, interest rates are high and call money soars nervously to abnormal heights. Traders begin to get nervous themselves and warnings appear in the newspapers.

But public enthusiasm and the gambling spirit are aroused. People no longer trade for investment, for yield, for fundamental values, or even for small profits. They buy stocks because they think they are going up rapidly and without regard to asset worth or dividends, earnings, true prospects or dividend yield. Tips and rumors run wild.

216

This stock is going to 500. That one is going up 50 points next week, etc. The stock market "makes the front page" of the newspapers. Everyone is talking stocks. Everyone is in the market or wants to be. And all such circumstances are the most dangerous of symptoms and the very best reasons why the average trader or investor should be selling his stocks rather than buying more. Such circumstances make up the usual picture of the closing days of a long Bull market.

Beginnings of a Bear Market

W HEN THE DISTRIBUTION period is over at the close of any bull market and the major movement has turned downward into the marking down stage or a major bear movement, the tendencies which we have noted in our description of the end of a bull market grow gradually but steadily less potent and less noticeable, finally giving way to just the opposite tendencies, which again go too far the other way at the end of a long bear market.

In the early stages of the bear market, for instance, interest rates are generally still very high, quite often higher than before the bear movement started; business is still satisfactory, or even apparently booming, in individual lines; tips and rumors of a favorable nature are still going around, with frequent sharp recoveries, all perhaps designed to keep the public from becoming discouraged too soon and selling out at comparatively high prices.

As the major bear movement continues interest rates decline, business is poor, commodity prices are often exceptionally low, public confidence is gradually being undermined, earning statements are declining, public interest in the market has dropped away rapidly (at least so far as constructive purchases are concerned), brokers' loans are being reduced, favorable tips and rumors gradually diminish and give way to growing unfavorable ones. Gradually the basic fundamentals are being restored to a more favorable basis, but the public, as usual, sees only the terrific declines, the staggering losses, the growing blackness of the future outlook, just as it saw only the bright side of things while the fundamentals were weakening.

Characteristics of the End of a Bear Market

F INALLY, WHAT IS the picture at the end of the long bear market? Interest rates have been easy for some time, perhaps a year or more, commodity prices are low, wages are far below their previous highs, public buying of all kinds is at low ebb, corporations are trying to liquidate costly inventories and loans, their earnings are poor, even the strongest of companies perhaps showing huge deficits. Dividends are being reduced, failures are on the upgrade, stock prices have dropped for so long that there seems no end.

Now the market "makes the front page" because of its declines instead of its advances. Now the tips and rumors are all on the unfavorable side. This stock is going to have to cut its dividend or pass it. That stock is still too high and is going to drop another 25 points in the next few weeks. This company is on the verge of a receivership and is going bankrupt; that brokerage house is on the ragged edge and likely to join the numerous previous brokerage failures which have already occurred. Even the Twelfth Village Bank is whispered to be in sore difficulties and likely to go under. The country has suffered a death blow. Prosperity may come back some day but it will be a long, hard pull and there is no telling how much further down stocks are going before the turn comes.

What is the result? Just what the insiders are working for. Public confidence is demoralized. The average investor is tied up with his heavy load of stocks accumulated in those rosy days, now seemingly gone forever, when stocks were selling even further above their true asset worth than they are now selling below that worth. The professional speculator, the trader, the wise long swing investor, all have sold their stocks, though perhaps at huge losses, long ago.

Now comes the danger for the long pull investor. Yes, he bought with the idea that nothing could induce him to sell. He was going to hold for long-pull appreciation and pay no attention to intermediate reactions. But now—why, the country is going to the dogs, the stocks that looked so good a year or two ago now look weak enough for receivership. Selling would mean a tremendous loss, but maybe if he sells now he can recoup some of his losses by buying his stocks back later at still lower prices, after things have cleared up a bit.

This is the tragedy of the long-pull investor. It is no exaggeration to say that the greatest amount of public selling is done in such a situation, just when stocks ought to be bought instead of sold, just when inside accumulation is about completed, when the long bear market is about ready to reverse itself into a bull movement. The public usually sells at this seemingly darkest moment, when stocks should be bought for the long-swing, just as it usually buys at the seemingly brightest moment, when long-swing stock holdings ought to be sold.

These pictures may give the reader a rather skeptical outlook on all stock market operations. What they are designed to do is to give him a skeptical attitude toward stock market gossip, publicity and psychology. And if the reader learns from such pictures to discount all he hears as gossip and to base his market activities upon study, experience and fundamental reasoning, then this work will not have been in vain.

Price–Discounting News

B Y THE TIME news regarding a stock is made public such news has generally been discounted in the market and the "cream is off."

Take the example of Kennecott Copper, which raised its dividend from $4 to $5 per share in June, 1929. At the beginning of the year the new stock was selling below 80. Copper prices had been advancing and continued to advance. The presumption was that Kennecott's profits were rising since business was also improving with the advance in prices. The fundamentals, therefore, indicated that when such profits became publicly known the popularity of Kennecott stock would be increased and its market valuation would advance. The dividend increase was generally considered a bullish factor.

We know however, that the real bullish factor was the increase in profits. But most of the advance in the stock from 78 to 105 came before the increase in earnings was made public. To this extent the market had already discounted the increase. The time to buy was at the beginning of the year before such increase had been publicly realized. When the dividend was actually raised in June the stock was already back in the 80's.

The next problem was not how much earnings had increased in 1928, but how much more they would increase in 1929. The future movement of the stock depended no longer on past results but on future earnings. And such future earnings depended largely upon the price of copper and the amount of business done. In April the price of copper declined sharply. To a large degree the price of Kennecott declined along with the price of copper.

But the greatest profits on the short side of the stock went to the insiders or to the students of the situation who could forecast the price of copper and Kennecott's future earnings in advance of the time such factors would influence public selling. By the time the price of copper had declined and the dividend was raised Kennecott had dropped back from a high of around 105 to a price of below 80. Once more profits and not dividends were the chief market factor. And the trader whose campaign in Kennecott was successful was the trader who could look far enough ahead to see what the public attitude would be toward Kennecott a couple of weeks or a couple of months from the time he took his own action in discounting that future popularity.

Since the nature of the general and individual market is to discount the future, **its nature is also to stop discounting when the news is out —when the future has become the present.** There are several theoretical angles of this occurrence, which is a fairly general rule. The truly big traders, the important operators, the professional students, all are the big factors in price fluctuations, prior to public participation. This is the "they" crowd in stock market parlance. "They" are the ones who discount the future. "They" influence the market action of the stock to a considerable degree.

If "they" have been buying the stock and advancing the price to discount announcement of favorable earnings, their natural gesture is to get out of the stock and take their profits when such news becomes public. They held the stock in anticipation of public demand. When the good news is out the public should theoretically, and practically does, step in and buy the stock—generally too late. The best time to sell the stock, therefore, is at the time when this public demand should appear. These important interests, who either have intimate foreknowledge, or accurate foresight, and whom we shall call "insiders," have no further reason for holding their previously purchased stock. "They" have a profit in it and the logical time to sell is while the public is still buying on the good news. The result is the somewhat technical tendency for a stock to react, instead of advance, when a piece of good news comes out.

"Be an Insider"

THE STOCK MARKET is made up, generally, of two large groups, the insiders and the public. The insiders are by far the more intelligent, the more experienced, the more professional, with reference to market affairs. They make more or less a business of making money in the stock market.

It is not necessarily the case that one of these groups must lose in order that the other may win. But in perhaps the majority of cases that is what happens. In any case, the two groups are more likely to be working in diametrically opposite directions. When the insiders are buying stocks they are buying them from the public because they expect to sell them back to the public at higher prices. If the insiders are right the public loses again. Of course, the insiders are by no means always right. They often take losses, and when they do they are generally tremendously larger than the small losses that the public is likely to take.

It cannot, of course, be proven that the insiders are right much more often than the public, but it stands to reason that they are in a better position to do the right thing than is the public. And, likewise, the insiders would hardly continue to give so great a portion of their time to their professional activities if they were not able to make average or fairly consistent profits at the end of successive years.

The author does not mean to give the impression that the public is constantly on the wrong side of the market. It cannot be, for it makes the market in a large degree. The insiders cannot pursue any course very long if they do not have public backing. In the majority of cases both groups, the insiders and the public, are making money. But where there is any sharp differentiation it is more likely that the insiders are on the right side.

And, furthermore, it is important to be one of the insiders, or at least to know what they are doing, because it is that group which generally originates major moves. With better background, greater experience, more practice, and often almost unlimited resources to carry through a campaign, the insider group is very likely to begin discounting the future before the public. Once more, the author does not mean that one must be on the inside to make stock market profits. Far from it, the greatest estates have been built up merely by farsighted investment buying of stocks. But for successful market trading it is an advantage to have the facilities which the insiders have.

The beginner may feel that because he is not the officer of a large corporation, not in the customer's room of a large New York stock exchange commission house, his chances for trading profit are dubious. That is not true. In general, it is true that the corporation officer and the customers' man have opportunities for getting information before it is generally known to the public and they thus have some advantages over the ordinary trader. But such "tips" often go astray, and it is by no means sufficient to rely solely upon such inside information in trading.

As a matter of fact, the author uses the term "insider" to denote not merely this small group which has access to private information, but also to denote the trader who has made a study of trading methods,

226

who is more grounded in fundamental theory and technical practice than the "man in the street." The trader, whether he be corporation president or office boy in a small Western town, whether he work in a New York brokerage office or as a farmhand, becomes one of the "insiders" as soon as he has taken a semi-professional attitude toward the market, has mastered the rudiments of trading and digested the principles set forth in this volume.

The fact that he has done these things means that he is no longer buying and selling stocks "by ear" and in a casual way, as does the public, but that he is making a serious and studious attempt to make something out of stock trading beyond a hobby or an adventurous risk. To just the extent that he leaves this hit-or-miss method of trading and puts true research, analysis and system into his trading, any individual leaves the ranks of the so-called "public" and moves into the group of "insiders."

Both of these groups are so large and the terms so inclusive that there is no way of drawing very definite lines between them. It is only facing facts, however, to disillusion oneself and admit that the inside group is more successful in stock market trading, in the long run, than is the public. That is one of the economic tendencies that justify the writing of such a volume as this. And the reason why the insiders are more successful is not nearly so much because they have inside information as because they have made a science of trading rather than a casual hobby.

Granted, then, that the individual is interested in the stock market for some reason more potent than curiosity, he should study to place himself in this group of semi-professionals. He is doing just that as he reads these lines, but in more specific fashion he must constantly study the action of stocks to determine, if possible, what these insiders are doing. By joining forces with these governing factors he allies himself with them and increases his chances for profit.

Significance of Closing Prices

T HERE IS ONE factor which is perhaps a little more important than much of the Wall Street credo. That is the significance and importance of the closing prices for stocks in general and the more active ones in particular. The active and best-known stocks are generally termed the "market leaders," and their course at any time determines in large measure the course of the "general market." During the five hours of regular trading on the stock exchange the "market" is generally moving either irregularly higher or lower. There are naturally many currents, but by and large there is usually detectable a fairly general tide, be it ebb or flow. The crowds which occupy the chairs in our leading commission houses are to be excused for their so-called indolence, for there is nothing more intriguing than to watch this ceaseless ebb and flow of stock market prices and to try to detect the first signs of faltering in one movement, which may presage the turning into the next counter movement. And, incidentally, while it is not at all necessary for mastering stock market trading, the watching and study of this true market action, right at the source, as it were, is splendid groundwork and a splendid school for the potential trader.

When one of these intermediate currents gets started in the course of a day's trading its own momentum carries it some distance. It may continue for many days with very little set-back but generally there are observable about anywhere from three to a half-dozen such definite alternating currents during a regular trading session. It is natural, therefore, to assume that if the market has lately developed a definite current just before the close of one day, that tendency will continue into the next day's session.

The importance of closing prices is a little stronger than just that, however, due perhaps in large measure to the fact that the public, as it reads the record of the day's trading in the evening papers that night, will judge the day as a whole and the prospects for the future largely by the closing prices rather than by the conflicting movements which have gone on during the earlier trading.

No matter what the definite reason, it is nevertheless true that if there is a well-defined movement on at the close, it is more than an even bet that the next day's market is to be a speedy one, for the closing movement usually carries on in greater strength and for a longer duration of time than the movements which develop and pass out again during the course of the usual day's trading. This is especially true if the previous movements of the day have been erratic, irregular and without any very strong trend. In such case, a strong upward movement at the close is almost sure to presage a good day tomorrow, or at least a good morning.

The exception appears in the practice of window dressing. It requires more experience than book knowledge or theory to differentiate between window dressing at the close of one day's trading, which is not genuine, and the genuine late-day trading movement, which augurs for higher prices tomorrow. The best clue which we can give here is that window dressing occurs generally before a longer holiday and not just overnight, and also the previous point that the late move is more likely to be genuine if it is a fairly strong move, if it reverses the general trend of the day or if it follows a day of high irregularity, without any particular trend predominating.

The Secondary Reaction

W ALL STREET USUALLY expects that after a short recovery a "secondary reaction" will set in, due in part to scared traders who are merely waiting for a little recovery to sell out, and partly to the fact that stock acquired by banking interests for purposes of supporting the market and checking such a fast shake-out is merely for temporary holding and comes back on the market as soon as the decline has been checked. This secondary reaction may go a little lower than the first one, or it may not go quite so far. The latter picture is a much stronger one.

The secondary reaction was fairly dependable in years previous to the last two or three, but in these latter years there has been a tendency for the market to forget such a secondary reaction and to come back fairly steadily from an intermediate reaction. In any case, the best sign that the reaction is over is a further sharp dip in the morning, followed by sharp recovery in the afternoon with total volume of sales for the entire day at relatively high level.

When the major market movement is downward, indicating that a major bear market is in progress, then approximately the opposite rules hold. The major movement is generally indicated by the long-term trend, with the averages moving in the major direction quite steadily but also rather gradually. The intermediate reverses of the major movement are generally much sharper than the major movement itself. In a bull market, therefore, the reactions are short and sharp. In a bear market the recoveries are likewise short and sharp.

In a sharp recovery during a major bear movement, the secondary recovery is not so noticeable and is more likely to be entirely absent. Or at least what secondary recovery there is does not bring average prices back to the higher levels of the original recovery. The end of the recovery is also signalled, however, by sharp advance in the morning, followed by renewed decline in the afternoon and on relatively heavy trading for the entire day.

The Resistance Point

IN THE CASE of an intermediate reaction in a bull market the decline will quite often establish levels of support. A support level is a comparatively narrow price range, anywhere from one to ten points, below which the market, or the individual stock, does not appear disposed to move. A resistance level is a similar range above a stock which limits its advance. The formation of a resistance level or a support point may occupy almost any length of time, from one day to a year or more. The longer the time the level takes to form, the stronger is its indication that the next major movement will be in the opposite direction from that on which the support or resistance has been encountered.

The best picture in which is used the rule not to sell stocks short in a quiet market is when such support levels have been established after a sharp shake-out in a major upward movement. The market may hover near its low levels for a few days. If trading is still heavy, then it is quite possible that the reaction is not over. But if volume of trading shrinks gradually to lower levels with prices hovering irregularly about the support levels the chances are much more than even that the next movement will be a renewal of the upward trend.

When resistance levels are formed after an intermediate recovery in a major bear movement they are not nearly so dependable in indicating that the next move is to be downward, but they are still worthy of consideration. Likewise, the decline in trading at such time is also not so dependable but is likewise a fair indication that the buying power on the recovery has been expended and that the major downward trend is to be resumed.

Wall Street Formula

ONE OF THE "old rules" of Wall Street trading, especially in a bull market, is to "take your losses but let your profits run." It is hardly a rule and there is much to be said on both sides, but in general it is worthy of serious consideration. The theory is that if the trader gets into a stock that declines instead of advancing in a major bull market it cannot be a very good stock, there must be some hidden reason for its decline, that decline may well go further, and he is better out of it and into something that is acting better. One stubborn streak which leads a trader to hold on to a poorly acting stock may eventually wipe out the profits on many successful trades.

On the other hand, if the trader gets into a stock that is truly going up in a bull market a few points profit is not enough and there is no telling how high it may go. Thus he should "let his profits run." The most satisfactory method of limiting any losses to small proportions, of course, is to protect the purchase by a stop-loss order. Such orders must be placed after studying the normal past action of the individual stock, but they are generally set from three to six points below the purchase price. The trader therefore knows that if he is wrong he cannot lose more than the number of "points away" from the purchase where he has placed his stop order, whereas if the stock advances he is constantly accumulating paper profits.

The objections to the rule are that many a day in any bull market sees bear traders, "gunning for stop-loss orders." That is they take advantage of this trading rule and pick on one stock after another, which they strong-arm into a sharp decline. As the stock declines its lower prices catch the stop orders below the market, the automatic selling of these stocks depress the issue still further and the bear traders cover their short sales on this further decline. Thereafter, of course, since the dip was only technical and temporary, the stock rebounds, but the trader who had his stop-loss order caught has lost his position in perhaps a very good stock.

Buying at Support Levels

THERE IS ONE point which needs further treatment in connection with avoiding the disappointments of having stop orders caught in long purchases. This is the practice of buying only at support points, and it affords a much better background for the trading profit-or-loss formula than otherwise. We have previously seen that a resistance level on the up-side, or a support level on the down-side, is a comparatively narrow price range through which the stock, or the general market, does not seem disposed to go. We shall have more to say about such support and resistance levels when we are studying market action by charts, for it is there that resistance points are most easily observed.

It may be noted, however, that some stock has been tending generally upward but has lately had a reaction from its high of 100 to current levels of, say, 75. Suppose that the stock recovers to 90, reacts to 77, recovers to 85, reacts to 74, recovers to 80 and reacts to 75. The limit of the recoveries has not been regular but the limit of the declines has been confined to the support level of around

75. When such a support level is observed it presents a good opportunity to use the profit-or-loss formula. The stock may be bought at around 76, with a stop-loss order at 72. The formula may then be that the trader will either lose four points or win 10. He puts in a coupled order to "Sell at 86 or 72 stop. Coupled. G.T.C."

He may feel fairly sure that the stock will not sink below its support level. If it does he should be glad to be out of the stock, for it would not be a good sign. On the other hand, it is probable that if the stock does not go through its support level on the down-side it will advance to a point where he can accept his formula profit. Of course, if he can do this three times out of five he will make money. The principle of studying resistance points makes the profit-or-loss formula more valuable but it is still a bit too dangerous and automatic to be considered a consistent friend.

Of course, the support level may be used successfully in any type of trading. On theoretical principles, however, it would not be good policy to accept a smaller profit than the limit of possible loss, since the odds would then be definitely against the trader. But profits may be accepted at any time such action is wise in the trader's opinion. He may play for a five point profit or a 10, may use the progressive stop to protect profits or may merely take such profits when the advance seems to have gone far enough. Once more, the method of using one's own judgment rather than depending upon absolute formula is probably most satisfactory from the standpoint of the serious and semi-professional trader.

"Gaps" in Stock Charts

T
HE LAWS OF action and reaction account largely for still another technical chart tendency which is very often valuable, especially in short-turn trading. This is the use of formulae for covering gaps in chart trading. A chart gap or spread is a vertical gap, or open space, between one day's range and the next. It means that the low of one day is higher than the high of the previous day or that the high of one day is lower than the low of the previous day. This results in "open water" or a gap between the two days' ranges. It is easily seen that such a spread results from a sharp jump or drop in the price of a stock.

The theory is that sooner or later the stock will return and "cover" this spread or gap. Usually the spread is covered very soon, perhaps the next day. Sometimes it is not covered for months. In rather rare instances the spread is never covered and, as usual, the rule therefore has its exception. When the spread is not covered it is almost always followed by a very long and profitable major movement in the direction of the original spread.

239

The exception is very important, however, for it comes generally at a particular stage in the market formation and forecasts the beginning of a sharp, long and profitable movement in that direction. This exception is generally found after any of our seven cardinal formations indicating either a major advance or a major decline to follow. Perhaps the most common of these formations, as we have seen before, is the triangle. During the formation of such major pictures there may be many gaps, all of which will be subsequently covered as the major formation progresses toward completion.

As the triangle narrows down to a point, however, or we deduce from our previous experience with the seven major types that the formation of accumulation or distribution is coming to an end, we may begin to expect this exceptional gap formation which, unlike its brothers, is not to be covered. This type of gap constituted the "breaking away" from the previous formation which prophesied the coming move. Whether it be on the up or the down side, it is one of the best indications that the major formation is legitimate in forecasting a major movement and that such major movement has now begun.

It is the stamp of approval on the student's previous analysis of the preceding formation. It is only logical, therefore, to anticipate that, since the looked-for movement is now under way, it will continue rapidly and strongly, and that this primary, or "break away" gap will not be covered, at least not for a good long time to come.

The other important type of gap is that which follows a long straight-away movement in either direction. This is the "exhaustion gap," which is almost a certain indication that the long and major movement is being exhausted and is near its end. This type of gap is almost always covered very shortly after it is made, for it indicates that the previous major movement is giving way to a reversal. Such reversal may be quite long and deep, often amounting to a more or less permanent reversal of the major move. It is a signal to switch to the opposite side of the market from the previous major move, and the fact that the forecasting gap of exhaustion is covered at an early date does not signify that the original direction will again be resumed, or nullify the general warning of further major reversal away from the previous movement.

We now have three chief types of gap. The first is the intermediate, or common gap, formed in ordinary trading, often during formation of one of our seven cardinal pictures, and almost always covered at no very distant future date. Due to the narrow swings accompanying such formations the trader will not make a great deal of money by playing for this common type of gap, though if he is agile, wide-awake, and wants to "scalp" the market, this common gap is almost infallible.

The second type of gap, we have seen, is the "break away" type. It follows the major formation, indicates the beginning of the major move previously forecast by the developing picture of accumulation or distribution, and is very seldom covered. It may be used best to check up on the correctness of the previous analysis, and as the final signal to get aboard for the profitable excursion.

The third type of gap, we have seen, is the "exhaustion" classification. It comes at the end of a long, swift and major movement, indicating the end of that movement and its major reversal. It is, therefore, almost the opposite of the break-away gap, which comes at the beginning of a long and profitable movement. The exhaustion gap is quite accurate and is a good signal that the previous major movement is near its end and that the trader's position should be switched in preparation for another major movement in the opposite direction within the near future.

All three types of gap may be found and used either in an advancing or a declining market, being equally profitable in each case. They are not 100 per cent reliable, but they are among the most accurate and reliable signals which the market student may discern in the study of charts.

The "New Era" Credo

OR AT LEAST a year or two previous to the close of 1929 the cry from the house-tops was this familiar one that "we are in a new era." The laws of cycles, the laws of action and reaction, the basic fundamentals no longer applied because of the New Era—the golden age of American progress. Such statements are misleading because they are always at least partly true. Every period of business expansion or business depression is a new era. Times change and the world moves on. The recent period of prosperity, with the greatest bull market ever recorded in American history, was based upon many factors of a new era. But all the powers of science, of invention, of cost-cutting and labor-saving, of efficient management, co-operation and combination can hardly be expected to overrule the basic laws of supply and demand, of cyclical movements based on excess, and the fundamental theory that inflation in any line does not last forever.

The cry of a "New Era" is heard at the bottom of bear markets as well as the top of bull movements. In the former case it takes the form of argument that the "golden days are gone forever," that the nation's prosperity has passed its peak and that the cream is off of everything. The recent bull market was said to have resulted from a new American era due to our establishment as a creditor nation. The fact unquestionably had merit and served to prolong the bull market, but it did not mean that inflation could be continued indefinitely.

The United States was compared with Great Britain in her early flush of world leadership, but few of those who made the comparison took the time to study the past history of stock movements of that great nation. Unfortunately, the records are not very clear or continuous, but there is sufficient information to show that England went through numerous periods of inflation, based upon the same old cry in those days, of a "New Era" in British industry and world leadership.

HAROLD
M. GARTLEY

Master Market Technician

Harold M. Gartley is one of the illustrious names in the field of technical analysis, having laid the cornerstone for many of the basic concepts used by present day market technicians. His numerous articles and his book classic *Profits in the Stock Market* published in the 1930's are rare collector's items today, seldom seen and eagerly sought by all avid market students.

H. M. Gartley grew up in Newark, New Jersey where he attended the Newark Technical School, then went on to New York University, including the Graduate School where he received his Master's Degree in Business Administration as well as a Bachelor of Commercial Science Degree. He started in Wall Street in 1912 as a board boy and runner—progressed through back office, customers' broker, statistician, (now called security analyst), and finally to a partnership. He owned and conducted his own financial advisory and research organization from 1934 to 1947 with an exclusive clientele consisting of brokerage firms, banks, underwriters, law firms, and substantial investors. Today, Gartley is a Director of the National Securities and Research Corporation, one of the ten largest mutual funds. He is also one of the founders and a former member of the Executive Committee of the New York Society of Security Analysts. His life has been a busy one, including extensive lecture tours on the stock market in addition to conducting private courses for investors.

Since 1947, Gartley has been in the field of financial and shareholder public relations and has since become known as one of the outstanding authorities on the preparation of annual reports and other shareholder documents. He has been an Officer of the Public Relations Society of America, Inc., and today is Chairman of the public relations firm of Gartley & Associates, Inc., at 84 William Street, New York City.

Gartley's contribution to a *Treasury of Wall Street Wisdom*, his famous chapter on Trading Volume is from his famous classic *Profits in the Stock Market,* published and copyrighted by H. M. Gartley, Inc., 76 William Street, New York, a real landmark in technical theory and one of the very few extensive studies on the subject of volume ever published.

The Wisdom of
HAROLD M. GARTLEY

Volume of Trading–A Forecasting Factor

"Is it Volume which causes Price Changes, or do Price Changes cause Volume — the Hen or the Egg, which came first?"

I N THE PRECEDING chapters, the subjects of discussion have been the working tools which applied chiefly to price phenomena. Now we will turn to a study of Volume.

It will be remembered from Chapter I, that Volume and Volume changes were designated as the second of the four elements or factors which are used in the study of stock price trends.

Compared with the amount of material which has been published concerning the theory of price and price changes, which were designated as the first of these four factors, the available published information concerning Volume is indeed small. Many financial writers have referred to the activity on the Stock Exchange (which we call Volume) more or less vaguely but comprehensive analyses are, for the most part, lacking. Perhaps the reason is that a detailed study of volume of trading is a tedious and laborious task, the results of which frequently do not seem worth the effort.

In recent years, the more advanced technical students

and statisticians have been devoting a very substantial part of their time to Volume research and analysis. The relation, or as statisticians term it, the "correlation", of price and price changes with volume and volume changes has occupied an important place in their research efforts. Nevertheless, when they have been published, only a few of their findings appear worthy of attention.

Chiefly, the study of Volume may be classed in the "When to buy or sell" category, although there are times when the activity in an individual stock is helpful in judging the "What" question.

A MEASURE OF SUPPLY AND DEMAND

Theoretically, the reason we study volume is because it is believed that it is a measure of supply of and demand for shares. Some financial writers have referred to volume as a gauge of market pressure. Others have pointed out that it is the quantitative side of stock price analysis.

As a primary principle of economics, it is assumed that if a large number of shares are offered, the price will be depressed; or conversely, if there is a substantial demand for shares, the price will rise. However, a study of the subject indicates that this theory does not always hold during short periods of time, although in the large and long term trends, there is no doubt of its validity.

For example, there are many instances wherein substantial price advances occur accompanied by very small activity, while in other cases substantial price declines develop in the presence of comparative dullness. (This has been especially true since S.E.C. regulation has substituted "thinness of market" for activity.)—And at other times, very substantial turnover is accompanied by very small price advances or declines.

As we study volume, we will find that quite frequently the **negative implications** are the ones from which we gain our most useful conclusions. That is, if a sharp increase occurs in volume, after prices have been rising for some time, and the price advance stops or slows down, we deduce that supply is being encountered; or conversely, if after an extended decline activity shows a definite decrease, the deduction is that offerings have been absorbed.

It is important to point out immediately that the vast majority of volume studies have produced only a few general conclusions. The more deeply one studies the subject, the more evident it becomes that very specific conclusions are quite impossible.

VOLUME AS AN INDICATOR

Every price change occurs as the result of a transaction consisting of the sale and purchase of shares of stock. **The number of shares involved in such a transaction constitutes volume.**

Every transaction is the result of the meeting of demand, on the one hand, with supply on the other. When demand exceeds supply, prices tend to rise. Conversely, when supply exceeds demand, prices tend to fall. Therefore:

1. Volume which occurs during advances may be designated as **"demand volume"**.
2. Volume which occurs during declines may be termed **"supply volume"**.

PRIMARY CONCEPTION

Through long experience, it is generally conceded by technical students that:

1. When a volume tends to increase during price declines, it is a bearish indication.
2. When volume tends to increase during advances, it is a bullish indication.
3. When volume tends to decrease during price declines, it is bullish.
4. When volume tends to decrease during price advances, it is bearish.

It is important to note that the above definitions or premises are concerned with **the changes** in volume. They do not refer to volume at a particular level. The reason for this is that, over long periods of time, the general level of activity so changes that it is not possible to select a permanent base from which to make observations for an indefinite period. Since S.E.C. regulation for instance (July, 1934), there has been a steady decrease in activity, but this has not changed the general implications of volume trends.

HISTORICAL CHARACTERISTICS

Anyone who reads the newspapers knows that in periods of prosperity stock markets are relatively active, while in periods of depression, they are relatively dull. In prosperous times, demand for stocks is stimulated by rising earnings and rising stock prices, and this demand grows increasingly effective as people have more savings available which they use for stock purchases. The supply to meet this demand increases readily enough from the strong boxes of the sophisticated holders, as they sell stocks to take profits and be out of issues which they believe are over-priced, and from corporations issuing additional shares as new flotations are offered to the public.

In periods of depression, volume of trading tends to diminish, because the trend of prices is downward, and the public is never attracted by falling prices. Activity in bear markets arises primarily from the force of liquidation, which starts with a tremendous burst of activity and continues, to a lessening but persistent degree, until the bear market is nearly ended. Early in a major downtrend, such as from November 1929 to April 1930, demand for stocks comes in fair volume from optimistic people who have money to "invest", but as successive waves of liquidation occur their optimism and pocketbooks are steadily depleted, until demand is very low. By that time the force of liquidation is spent, and the extreme dullness of a terminating bear market sets in.

VOLUME AND THE FOUR TRENDS

Let us first examine the record of volume in the four trends, the long term, major, intermediate and minor, and then endeavor to ascertain the usual characteristics of volume in the formation of some of the patterns which serve as working tools in technical study.

THE LONG TERM TREND

A study of the activity at bull market tops and bottoms from 1897 to 1932 indicates that the long term trend of volume was definitely upward in that period. The following table shows the average daily volume of trading at bear market bottoms and bull market tops from the bottom of 1897 to the major upward turn in July, 1932.

AVERAGE DAILY VOLUME

BEAR MARKET BOTTOMS		BULL MARKET TOPS	
Year	Volume	Year	Volume
1897	170,000	1899	500,000
1900	300,000	1901	1,000,000
1903	500,000	1906	1,600,000
1907	500,000	1909	2,000,000
1911	1,000,000	1912	700,000
1914	130,000	1916	1,850,000
1917	600,000	1919	1,700,000
1921	600,000	1923	1,200,000
1923	800,000	1929	4,000,000
1932	600,000		

It will be seen from the above Table that at bull market tops activity increased from an average daily volume of 500,000 in 1899 to an average of 4,000,000 in 1929, an increase of 700 per cent. At bear market bottoms, where public participation is always lacking, the average daily trading increased from 170,000 in 1897 to between 600,000 and 1,000,000 in later years, with the notable exception of the low of 130,000 in December of 1914, when the Stock Exchange was re-opened after a long suspension of trading.

From the Table it will be noted that with the exception of the 1911-1912 comparison, the average daily volume at the culmination of bull markets was several times that at the bottom of previous bear markets, showing that dullness characterizes the end of bear markets and the beginning of bull markets, whereas pronounced activity marks the end of bull markets and the beginning of bear markets. More will be said on this point presently.

The rising trend of volume from 1897 to 1934 is a reflection of the growth of the corporate form of business enterprise, increased public interest in such corporations, the great expansion in security holding effected by the war-time Liberty Loans, the tremendous growth in American industry and wealth, and the spread of stock trading activities to all classes in the latter years of the past decade. Whether S.E.C. regulation will level off this trend only time will tell. Most certainly the curbing of certain types of manipulation will (as long as it lasts) tend to flatten the long term upward trend of activity.

The long term trend of volume can be studied to best advantage on charts which are plotted on a monthly basis.

EFFECT OF REGULATION ON VOLUME

While this "mushrooming" public interest brought hitherto unheard-of activity and prosperity to the Stock Exchange community from 1926 to 1929, it might be said that Wall Street was then "sowing the wind" with little thought that some day it would "reap the whirlwind". When public interest was small, stock market debacles affected only the wealthier classes to any extent Rich Man's Panic of 1907, for example, and there was little outcry. But in 1929-1932, hundreds of thousands of citizens suffered financial paralysis, if not destruction, and others who did not lose directly blamed the depression on the much-publicized stock market. Strong public demand for regulation did not go unheeded by legislators, and while specific changes occasioned by regulation cannot be fully assessed at this writing, it is probable that in the future a repetition of the final stages of the feverish activity of the 1923-1929 bull market is less likely to occur.

If legislative restraints were not applied, the normal long-term trend of volume would no doubt continue upward, for, despite the ravages of the 1929-1932 bear market, trading in the advance of March-July 1933 was tremendous, and activity in May of that year broke all records for that month. But this was prior to the S.E.C.

MAJOR TRENDS

The sequence of volume characteristics in major trends may be summarized as follows:

Bull markets usually start out of the terminating dullness of the preceding bear market. The first intermediate upswing is accompanied by a **crescendo** of activity which continues through the culmination of the advance and the abrupt start of the intermediate correction. (See August and September, 1932, and April to July, 1933.) As the latter proceeds, however, volume diminishes and the correction normally terminates in dullness, from which the next intermediate advance starts (See October 1932, to February 1933). As the bull market progresses, each intermediate advance is apt to occur on bigger volume than the previous one (see 1923-1929). (However, this has not been the case since S.E.C. regulation in 1934. It will be noted that the January-February 1934, April 1936 and March 1937 tops occurred with the long term trend of volume decreasing.) Finally, a long period of heavy trading fails to produce a price rise worth mentioning, and a moderate decline occurs, with volume remaining active. This is the start of the ensuing bear market, as previously mentioned.

Summarizing, it is generally true that:

Bull markets usually begin in pronounced dullness, and end in prolonged, **intensive activity.** (We still have to learn whether or not S.E.C. regulation will permanently change this axiom.)

Bear markets naturally show the opposite tendency, and begin with a fairly moderate decline in prices wherein volume tends to increase instead of to decrease as in bull market price declines. As bearish characteristics develop, fear quickly grows to panic, and selling causes activity to rise to a point where daily trading for a time exceeds any seen in the preceding bull market. The selling climax of the panic produces a rally which shows a tendency to lose volume as prices advance.

Before very long, the major downtrend in prices is resumed, finally running into another selling climax. On this decline, volume increases again, but rarely equals that which appears in the first selling climax. This sequence continues through the bear market, with each climax showing somewhat less volume than the previous one, the tendency of activity to lessen being quite clearly marked.

In time, of course, the force of liquidation becomes spent. Demand, however, is light, because buying power is severely depleted and capital is timid. At this stage of the bear market, which is generally the final one, prices decline but activity is listless. Finally, activity becomes so light that the price trend flattens out and the bear market is about terminated as in July 1932.

Bear markets, therefore, show volume tendencies diametrically opposite to bull markets. They begin in great activity and end in pronounced dullness.

INTERMEDIATE TRENDS

Volume characteristics of intermediate cycles depend upon the prevailing major trend.

In Bull markets, the first major phase, as we have just seen, gains in activity as it progresses. However, volume does not reach a peak simultaneously with the price trend. Rather, the peaks of volume in the major phase usually occur during the mark-ups. At the actual top activity is heavy, but usually it is not as great as on the previous mark-up.

When the over-bought price structure collapses, daily volume rises until it often exceeds anything seen in the preceding major phase. This high volume is temporary, however, and as the corrective phase develops volume tends to dwindle, until dullness is pronounced at the termination of the corrective phase.

Thus, bull market **major phases** occur on **rising volume,** which frequently reaches a maximum on the last mark-up prior to the top. The **corrective phase** following starts in heavy trading, often heavier than any seen in the major phase, but this is soon supplanted by a **steady decline** in activity.

There were some variations in the major phases of the upward cycles of 1935 and 1936. We see that the largest activity between March 1935 and April 1936 was in May, during the first leg of the long rise. Subsequently, although there were periods of expansion, the high levels did not duplicate those of May. However, the characteristic of expanding volume during the markups of the major phase continued. New to bull market phases was the phenomenon shown in June-August 1935, and in March 1936, when activity tended to dwindle while prices advanced. As a matter of fact, the low level of activity during March was a factor which was regarded as quite bullish just prior to the sharp break in April.

In the 1936 rise from an extremely low level of activity in May, it will be noted that there was a steady expansion, although at no time did the total figures rise to levels comparable to those of 1932 and 1933, or for that matter even 1934.

Actually the activity in the 1936-1937 major phase was somewhat smaller than that in the previous 1935-1936 advance.

However, the tendency for volume to expand on markups and contract during price recessions continued as a normal factor. The fact that activity failed to expand to greater size in January of 1937 is an interesting commentary on the effectiveness of regulation in substituting a thin market with wide price fluctuations and low activity for a broad market with substantial activity. Normally at this stage in the 1936-1937 advance the volume in January should have made a peak for the move, such as let us say three or four consecutive days above 3,000,000 shares. The decline in activity in the March-June recession was typical of the corrective phase. It is interesting to note that in the previous correction in April 1936 there was practically no change in activity throughout this short period of three weeks, while prices had more than a 10% setback.

From this discussion we do not conclude that the characteristic volume sequence in a major phase of a bull market is greatly changed by S.E.C. regulation. But the fluctuations are certainly less pronounced, due to lesser activity.

In **bear markets,** the major phase of the first cycle is, of course, the decline which starts the bear market. (See September-November, 1929.) Activity is heavy and rises to a tremendous degree as the selling climax occurs.

The ensuing corrective phase (rally) begins from the climax, but loses activity as it progresses, until the advance practically "dries up" and a new major (downward) phase starts. This gains in velocity and activity as it descends until the selling climax is reached and the corrective rally occurs.

The corrective phase of the first downward cycle in the 1929-1932 bear market stands out as an exception to this general rule. In this case it will be noted that from January through early April, 1930, activity steadily increased.

On the other hand, notice how volume decreased from middle December 1930 to early February 1931. Here again we find an exception, in that activity picked up at the end of a corrective phase (February 7-27, 1931). During this sixteen-day false rally from the apex of the triangle, Wall Street gossip held that the bear market had ended with the December 1930 lows.

Thus, in bear markets, intermediate **major phases** occur on **rising activity** until their selling climaxes initiate **corrective phases.** Remember that there is **one exception**, namely, the major phase of the final bear cycle, wherein volume does **not** increase, but tends to dry up. The first major phase of a bull market, therefore, does **not** come out of heavy trading but out of dullness, and in this phrase volume does **not** dry up as in previous rallies in the bear market, but increases as the rally continues. This important technical factor contributed substantially to the author's shift from a bear to a bull market view early in August 1932.

In the study of intermediate trend volume, it must be understood that the trend of activity for a period of two or three months, or at least several weeks, must be surveyed as a whole. Conclusions concerning intermediate trend volume should not be drawn from the activity during a period of several days.

In the vast majority of cases, the trend of volume in individual issues will closely parallel the market as a whole during major and intermediate trends. On the other hand, there are numerous occasions wherein, for special reasons, the trend of volume over a period of two or three weeks in an individual stock will differ greatly from the market as a whole.

MINOR TREND

Minor trend volume, like minor trend fluctuations, is tricky and often difficult to analyze. For this purpose the trend of hourly volume is very helpful. Safe **general** rules to follow in observing minor trend phenomena are:

1. In **bull market major phases,** volume is more on the upward price movements than the declines, with trading light at the start, but increasing. **As the culmination of the major phase is reached,** volume spreads more evenly over up and down periods until **minor volume is less on rallies than on declines** and the correction begins.

2. In **bull market corrective phases,** volume usually appears on the

downside, but as the correction proceeds, activity lessens and minor trend volume tends to shift from declines to advances.

3. In **bear market major phases,** the tendency at first is only slightly toward increasing activity on declines, but as the price decline develops, volume appears more and more on the downside.

4. In **bear market corrective phases,** the early tendency is toward activity on strength, but as prices advance in the corrective phase, volume tends to grow lighter and occurs more on dips than on rallies.

Generally speaking, the first and last hours in each day are the most active, in all types of markets. This is because in the first half-hour the overnight accumulation of orders are executed, while in the last half-hour professional traders who try not to carry positions overnight "even up" before the closing bell.

HOURLY STUDIES OF MINOR TREND VOLUME

If the technical student desires to make a detailed study of volume, it is essential that intra-day activity be scrutinized constantly. The most convenient way to do this is to observe hourly volume. Since May 19, 1933, the New York Stock Exchange has published the total volume of trading hourly, which permits a more detailed study of volume for the market as a whole. Refined study, however, requires short interval volume data for individual stocks, and these data are not available at the present time unless they are compiled directly from the ticker tape. Such tabulations are extremely laborious. This is probably one important reason why volume research has lagged.

CAUTION

Students are warned that minor trend volume shifts rapidly and must be observed with skepticism. Remember that in minor declines during intermediate advances, volume may quickly develop bearish symptoms, but these can change to bullish indications with lightning rapidity. Conversely, during intermediate declines, volume may suddenly appear bullish, but just as quickly turn bearish. Minor trend volume on daily charts can be very deceptive, but it presents an even more difficult problem to the student who is going beyond daily figures and studying, say, hourly, half-hourly or twenty-minute volume figures. Analyzing volume minute by minute on a moving tape is a job for a veteran. However, with the proper background of experience, close study of this kind often permits early decisions at important turning points.

Before proceeding to a further study of volume characteristics, a discussion of sources of data, and some of the mechanical difficulties in plotting volume may be useful.

SOURCES OF DATA—PLOTTING VOLUME

Each day's individual stock volume is published in the larger metropolitan daily newspapers.

Hourly volume of trading is published on the New York Stock Exchange ticker tape, in *The Wall Street Journal* and other metropolitan dailies. It is very useful in studying the hourly averages. At present, there are no published sources of less than daily volume for individual stocks.

Customarily, chartists plot volume along the lower side of their charts. Some prefer to use bars, while others prefer a line type of plotting.

In studying total market volume many market students prefer to double Saturday volume, on the theory that it is a short day, and if volume is not doubled, meaningless valleys will occur at weekly intervals. Also, doubling volume on Saturdays tends logically to emphasize any substantial increase of activity during the short day.

There is a great difference of opinion as to whether volume should be studied on the ordinary arithmetic scale, or on the ratio, or semi-logarithmic, scale. Students favoring the arithmetic scale argue that the ratio scale, in compressing plotting figures in its higher ranges, just naturally defeats the easy study of volume, in that it is the volume peaks or sharp rises which are significant, and if they are compressed on the semi-logarithmic scale, it is a real handicap.

The other group who favor the semi-logarithmic scale, of which the author is emphatically one, present the counter argument that it is impossible to select a series of convenient arithmetic scales which will permit plotting of the wide ranges necessary in the study of a large number of individual stocks. Most chartists who use arithmetic scales for volume are in the habit of so changing the volume scales on their charts that only a few of the individual stocks they are studying may be compared one with the other. The use of the ratio scale eliminates this difficulty, and makes it possible to make accurate comparisons of the volume of any number of stocks, regardless of wide range in the statistics. Furthermore, the semi-logarithmic volume scale permits the study of volume ratios with the least effort in plotting.

VOLUME AND THE DOW THEORY

In outlining the seven precepts of the Dow Theory in Chapter VII, number six was volume. As outlined by Hamilton, it stated:
". . . When the market is oversold, activity goes dull on declines, and increases on rallies. When the market is overbought, activity goes dull on rallies and increases on declines."

All of the Dow Theorists constantly observe volume phenomena in connection with the other six tenets of the theory. When a previous high or low point is penetrated, they regard the penetration as more significant if it occurs accompanied by an increase in activity. The same is true when the price trend breaks away from either side of a Dow Theory "line". About two-thirds of the published conclusions of Rhea, Collins and Phelps, the contemporary writers concerning the Dow Theory, contain some mention of volume.

Dow Theorists look for volume to be at a high level at the culmination of bull markets, and at a low level at the termination of bear markets. Similarly they expect to see volume at a relatively high point at the end of major phases of intermediate cycles, and conversely at a low level at the end of corrective phases.

Charles Dow himself, in speaking of volume, said:

"In a bull market, dullness is generally followed by an advance; in a bear market, by a decline."

VOLUME AND THE OTHER WORKING TOOLS

In Chapters VIII-XIV, inclusive, frequent mention was made of the relation of volume to the other working tools. In each case, it was emphasized that as volume showed a marked increase in the direction of the trend, as indicated by other technical factors, it was a significant confirmatory signal worthy of note; while conversely, if volume failed to point in the same direction as the trend indicated by the other working tools, there was just reason to question the indications.

With some fear of repeating too much, let us now consider some general relations between volume and the other working tools:

VOLUME AND SUPPLY AND DEMAND AREAS

Briefly, a supply area forms when an advancing trend runs into more supply volume than it can absorb without losing headway. While there is sufficient demand volume to take all offerings, prices rise. When buying power wanes and selling becomes too persistent, either a trading area or a top forms.

Conversely, a demand area forms when a declining trend runs into more demand than is needed to absorb all offerings. As soon as sufficient demand appears to accomplish that, the downward direction of the price trend ceases, and a trading area or bottom forms.

Intermediate demand areas in a bull market are naturally at the end of corrective phases, when activity is at a relatively low level as compared with the previous top, for example. Conversely, the intermediate demand areas in a bear market are at the end of major phases, and in most cases activity is high, usually running into a selling climax.

Intermediate supply areas in a bull market are also at the end of major phases, and are usually accompanied by a substantial increase in activity, as compared with the intermediate low. Conversely, intermediate supply areas in a bear market appear at the tops of intermediate corrections, and are accompanied by less volume than was seen at the previous selling climax intermediate bottoms.

In some cases, there is a tendency for volume to expand during the corrective areas of intermediate cycles in a bear market. A good example of this appears in the period from October 1929 to April 1930.

The final supply area in a bull market, at the end of the last half-cycle, is usually accompanied by sustained activity during both diagonal and horizontal trends, while **the final half-cycle in a bear market** usually develops with activity at an extremely low level in both diagonal and horizontal trends.

As a general proposition, the volume characteristics of minor supply areas in both bull and bear markets, and in both major and corrective phases of intermediate cycles are all about the same. Minor tops in uptrends are usually accompanied by increased volume, and conversely in downtrends, by a drying up of activity.

Minor bottoms in uptrends are usually accompanied by a drying up of activity, and conversely in downtrends, by an increase in volume.

Occasionally, a minor bottom in an uptrend will be accompanied by a sharp increase in activity, as a bull market selling climax forms.

VOLUME AND TRIANGLES

Characteristically, **the triangle pattern is accompanied by a well-defined decrease in volume as it develops to its apex.** This is probably caused by the fact that the initial mark-up or mark-down which forms the third side of the triangle, being a dynamic movement, is accompanied by a sharp increase in volume, which sets up a peak. Then, as price fluctuations narrow down in the formation of the triangle, volume dwindles as uncertainty grows.

Of great importance is the fact that when the price movement breaks away from the apex of a well-defined triangle (remember that only well-marked cases are worth following), if the breakaway is accompanied by an increase in activity, it is less likely to be a false start than in the case of a rally or decline which develops in dullness.

It makes no difference which of the three types (ascending, descending or symmetrical) of triangle may develop—the declining volume characteristic is similar in all three, because it reflects the withdrawing from the market of persons interested in price fluctuations, because of growing uncertainty.

When **dynamite triangles,** covering a period of from three to five days develop, particularly in individual stocks, if there is a sharp step-up in activity early on the day when the price trend breaks away from the apex, it is a fairly reliable sign of a good buying or selling signal, according to the direction of the price trends.

VOLUME AND TREND LINES

When an important trend line is penetrated, it frequently happens that volume increases immediately after the penetration. It is likely that

264

in recent years no small part of such volume arises from the activities of technical students who take positions promptly as the penetration occurs. When their guesses prove wrong, the volume soon dwindles and remains quiet. If their forecast is correct, volume continues at an active pace.

As most important trend lines, both intermediate and major, are penetrated during or by means of a mark-up or mark-down, it is to be expected that activity at such penetrations will increase as compared with that immediately preceding such an area. Where penetrations occur as a result of a sidewise movement, volume is likely to be notably small. Such penetrations are usually of doubtful significance.

Horizontal trend lines are usually penetrated on dull volume, with activity picking up if the move is important and continuing at a low level if the move is a false one.

VOLUME AND MOVING AVERAGES

In the penetration of moving averages applied to the price trend, particularly those used in connection with intermediate trend observation, a sharp step-up in volume is a sound confirmation of the importance of a penetration. As most of the more significant moving average penetrations occur as sharp mark-ups or sharp mark-downs, it is quite logical to see an increase in volume either coincident with the penetration, or a day or two following.

Volume phenomena in connection with the penetration of the minor trend moving averages are not sufficiently reliable to be very significant. There are many cases where a minor trend moving average is penetrated sharply for an hour or two, accompanied by an increase in hourly volume, which later prove to be false penetrations so that commitments made upon them prove unprofitable.

VOLUME AND GAPS

Experience shows that when an important gap occurs in the general price structure, as reflected in the composite and major group averages, volume increases sharply in the first hour's trading on that day. If the gap occurs at a point in the trend where a breakaway, measuring or exhaustion gap might be expected, its importance is emphasized if activity increases in the first hour. **If the price movement breaks out from a triangle wtih a gap and heavy volume, the move is likely to be even more significant.**

An upside breakaway gap is usually the point at which the notable increase in volume begins after trading has dwindled at a bottom. Upside measuring gaps more frequently than not appear in the price trend when volume has already increased substantially. Thus, they frequently occur without any notable increase in activity. Upside exhaustion gaps are almost always accompanied by a burst of volume which misleads the untrained observer to believe that the top is still much higher. As the exhaustion gap is usually part of the final mark-up formation, substantial trading is to be expected as it occurs.

The volume which accompanies the downside breakaway gap varies, and is not a dependable sign. In some declines, volume, already at a high level, increases sharply as the first part of the mark-down which follows a top gets under way. In other cases where downside gaps occur, activity slows down, giving a temporary bullish pattern. It is not until prices continue their decline that the volume increases to its characteristic peak in the reversal mark-down. Downside measuring and exhaustion gaps are almost always accompanied by a substantial increase in volume.

Before proceeding to a discussion of the refinements of volume studies, some emphasis should be directed to the phenomena of volume in connection with selling climaxes, which occur in both bull and bear markets but more often in bear markets.

To the trained technical student, the selling climax represents such an excellent opportunity to make stock market profits that it is important for the reader to be aware of the conditions which usually attend a selling climax.

SELLING CLIMAX BOTTOMS

The sequence of events in a selling climax, particularly in a bear market, is fairly consistent, and may be summarized as follows:

1. After the market has declined for some time, it closes at the bottom on a given day with ample evidence that the decline is not over. The news is preponderantly bearish, things look badly and appear to be getting worse, the "Street" is blue, customers' men suggest many specific reasons why prices should go lower.
2. On the next morning, there is a gap on the downside, substantial selling, prices fading away, thin bids, specialists with little on the "buy" side of their books.
3. On the tape—5,000 shares of this leader and that—possibly at substantial concessions, but often at only small concessions from previous prices. Frequently, reports come up from the floor indicating that one or more leading stocks, such as Steel, Chrysler, Telephone, or du Pont "are offered for a bid".
4. Then practically without warning, large blocks of the same stock are very much in demand, advancing half and full points, sometimes two points, between sales.
5. This advance often carries to the close, with no important setbacks and with heavy volume on the upside, quite contrary to its behavior in the preceding decline.
6. At the end of the day a study of the day's trading almost always shows an unmistakable sequence that confirms the intra-day phenomena.

These are the marks of a selling climax.

The last intermediate bottom at the end of the last half-cycle in a bear market is, of course, different from its predecessors in that it has bull market characteristics, chief of which is the tendency of volume to dry up on declines. Also, when fairly extended corrections (advances) are under way in bear markets, minor bottoms frequently occur on slackening volume, but these characteristics are counter to the underlying trend.

There is a real and difficult practical problem in connection with getting the most out of a selling climax, particularly for the average person who is interested in the market as a sideline, and thus finds the majority of his time engaged by his regular business. Briefly, the problem is this:

A selling climax is a phenomenon which often occurs in the course of two or three trading hours. The low prices are reached in hectic trading with markets in many stocks changing rapidly so that a bid or asked quotation of one moment is no good in the next.

The most advantageous purchases have to be made when selling has reached its peak, usually sometime in the first two hours of that day. Remember that the selling climax is an excellent example of mob psychology operating to its own discomfort. Because nearly everyone interested in stock prices is bearish at the same time on the morning of a selling climax day, bids are few and far between, and prices drop a half, one, or even two points between sales.

It is a matter of mere guesswork or chance if the average individual happens to pick a price somewhere near the bottom in the case of an individual stock during a selling climax. In most cases, open orders placed below the market do not offer a means of getting in at the right place, because it is anyone's guess as to where the panic of a selling climax will carry an individual stock level, before the recovery sets in.

In planning purchases in a selling climax, it is important that the trader keep clearly in mind that a point or two in the purchase price won't make much difference (except in low priced issues), because the rebound from the selling climax is likely to retrace one-third or one-half of the decline which preceded it. But this does not mean that a careful effort should not be made to make purchases somewhere near the bottom.

Probably one of the best methods available to the average trader is to assume that when prices have dropped sharply in the first two hours, and reports are coming up from the floor that leading stocks are offered for a bid, the time is ripe to make purchases.

Perhaps a peculiar experience which the author witnessed may help the reader to make some well-timed purchases in a future selling climax. When leaders were offered for a bid on the morning of a day which appeared as a possible selling climax day, orders placed one-half or one point above the last sale in two different selling climaxes in the 1929-1932 bear market obtained better executions than market orders for the same stocks, placed at the same time. It seems like an irrational procedure, but in a selling climax the bid and asked fluctuate so rapidly, that a buyer stands a far better chance of getting a good purchase price, when the selling climax is at its height, by being willing to pay up a little from the last sale. This margin provides the broker on the floor with a peculiar psychological stimulus which, in many actual cases in the past (believe it or not, Ripley), obtained mighty good executions.

Above, it was stated that there are selling climaxes in bull markets. These usually appear at the end of the corrective phase in a bull market cycle. They are not so pronounced as in the case of a bear market, because the force of liquidation is less acute, due to the fact that if the underlying major trend is upward the large bulk of stocks are being comfortably held for the long pull.

Nevertheless, the selling climax in a bull market provides one of the best opportunities for the stock trader to take his intermediate trend long positions. Worthwhile knowledge of these bull market selling climaxes may be obtained by studying the October 21, 1933 and July 26, 1934 reversals as well as the situations of April 28, May 13 and June 14, 1937.

There is no exact counterpart of the selling climax bottom, in the way of a buying climax top. Although it is true that many intermediate tops are accompanied by sustained activity at a high level, volume does not run up to a new high peak as it does in a selling climax bottom. There is no frenzied buying which compares with the panic selling during a selling climax. Probably this is because there is no force which makes people buy stocks, such as the relentless force of liquidation which often makes even the strongest holders sell their stocks in a bear market.

Usually, at the top of the major phase of an upward cycle, the trend of volume shows a tendency to flatten out, even though it is at a high level, as prices show a stubbornness to move forward any further. For example, look at the July 1933 top. In the case of the high points in April 1936 and March 1937, we see a definite tendency for volume to decrease preceding the high point. This definite decrease in activity prior to these two intermediate high points in the current bull market was a factor which threw many technical students off the track in judging the nearness of an intermediate correction. It still remains to be determined as to whether S.E.C. regulation, in reducing total volume of trading, has changed the typical high level of volume which usually exists in the several weeks prior to the beginning of a bull market intermediate correction.

VOLUME OF THE MAJOR AND MINOR GROUPS

Some students attempt to divide the study of total volume, and make observations of the aggregate daily and weekly volume in various groups of stocks, such as the Dow Jones 30 Industrials, 20 Rails and 20 Utilities. Others further subdivide the study of volume by observing the volume figures for minor groups, such for example the Herald-Tribune average of 15 Manufacturing, 10 Oils, or 6 Steel Stocks et cetera, for which the daily figures are published.

Although the author has made very comprehensive price studies concerning minor groups, no equally complete studies of minor group volume have as yet been attempted, because of the voluminous computations necessary in making a comprehensive survey of group volume for a sufficient period of time to provide worthwhile conclusions. Those readers who may desire to conduct a broad research program might well focus their attention toward the study of minor group volume, particularly by means of volume ratios, about which we will learn more later.

A study of group volume of the major and minor groups is undoubtedly useful, in that it contributes more detailed data with which to apply the premises suggested above. But it is the author's considered opinion that unless one has ample time, the study involves more work than it is worth, particularly because numerous experiments have shown that unless major and minor group volume figures are reduced to some standard, by means of ratios or logarithms, their value is decidedly limited.

REFINED AND MORE ADVANCED STUDIES OF VOLUME

Up to this point, all of our considerations of the volume of trading in shares of stock may be designated as studies, conclusions and premises based upon the statistics "in the raw". As many market students become more experienced, they soon find that the wide fluctuations in volume figures tend to confuse volume studies, to such an extent that precise conclusions are quite impossible.

Among the numerous methods which have been employed by statisticians and stock market students, for the purpose of eliminating the difficulties which arise as the result of these fluctuations, those which have come to the attention of the author may be classified in four general categories, as follows:

1. **Moving Averages of Volume,** wherein fluctuations in activity are smoothed out, in order to observe their trends more closely. Chiefly, these studies have been with 5-10 day moving averages of daily volume and 4-6 week moving averages of weekly volume.
2. **Volume Ratios,** wherein daily and weekly volume figures for individual stocks are expressed as percentages of the total trading in the market, and studied in these terms.
3. **Correlations of Volume and Price,** wherein the two phenomena are in some way combined to make related observations. The methods used in doing this are numerous, with the observations quite varied. Some are simple; others very intricate. In some cases

price and volume are multiplied while in others volume is divided by price or price change.

4. **Special Group Studies,** wherein the volume of investment stocks and/or speculative stocks is studied in relation to the total trading.

MOVING AVERAGE OF VOLUME

Following the publication of hourly volume figures by the Stock Exchange in May 1933, technical students began to make hourly comparisons of activity in order to supplement their daily studies. The fluctuations in hourly volume were found to be so wide however anywhere from 40,000 to 3,320,000 shares; the range from January 2, 1936 to July 31, 1937 was between 40,000 and 1,020,000, the latter figure being reached on March 3, 1937, that some method was necessary to smooth out the rapidly moving curve. Naturally, the moving average was the first instrument employed. Because daily studies of volume were so commonly used, a five-hour (one-day) moving average was adopted by the author.

On *Chart 13** is a 5-hour **moving average** of hourly volume used with the 15-stock aggregate plotted at 20-minute intervals. This 5-hour moving average is obtained by adding the volume for five consecutive hours and dividing by 5. When a new hourly figure is available, the earliest figure in the previous five figures is dropped and the new one added, the total is again divided by 5 and so on. The plotting is made at the end of the 5-hour period.

Moving averages of volume show a smoothed curve of the trend of activity and permit more trustworthy identification of volume trends. This smoothed curve shows an even distribution of the day's volume. When the actual volume line appears above or below the moving average line, the resulting peaks of valleys are considered relatively more significant than during the periods when volume and its 5-hour moving average are much alike.

*This refers to a chart that is no longer available.

If a substantial peak above the moving average accompanies a price advance, it is reasonable to assume that important progress is being made through substantial resistance, and further gains are indicated. If on the other hand a peak accompanies a decline, increased supply is indicated, and a further recession may be expected.

Conversely, if a peak forms and prices strike supply and fail to progress despite excessive volume, a top may be forming. Or if a price decline is checked despite a volume peak, demand is indicated and a bottom may be forming. It is suggested that this method be observed at great length before commitments are based upon it. Decidedly, it is a minor trend study for the advanced student.

VOLUME RATIOS

As the stock market student progresses in his learning, he finds that relative figures are almost always more useful than raw data (actual figures). The more advanced observers thus study not only actual volume of trading in a stock for a given period, but also the ratio or per cent which that volume represents of the total volume of trading. If both series are plotted on the same scale, it is advantageous to use lines rather than bars, although some chartists prefer to use bars for the actual volume and a line for the volume ratio, both plotted on the same scale. **(The study of volume ratios applies specifically to individual stock observation.)**

WHY VOLUME RATIOS ARE IMPORTANT

Let us illustrate the reasoning why volume ratios are a necessary refinement in the study of individual stock volume by considering the simple tabulation which follows:

CHRYSLER	TOTAL MARKET VOLUME	PER CENT OF TOTAL VOLUME (VOLUME RATIO)
150,000	1,500,000	10.0
100,000	1,000,000	10.0
150,000	1,000,000	15.0

If 150,000 shares of Chrysler are traded on a particular day when the total market volume is 1,500,000, the ratio would be 150,000/1,500,-000, or .10, meaning that the trading in Chrysler was 10 per cent of the total trading on that day.

If, on the next day 100,000 shares of Chrysler were traded, and the total market volume decreased to 1,000,000 shares, the activity in Chrysler would still be 10 per cent, and there would be no relative change in the activity in Chrysler, notwithstanding the fact that there had been an actual change from 150,000 to 100,000 shares, or a decrease of 33$^{1}/_{3}$ per cent. As the total volume in the market was decreased by the same amount, there was not a relative change in Chrysler activity. It merely followed the market.

But if, on the other hand, on the third day the trading in Chrysler totaled 150,000 while the total volume remained at 1,000,000 the percentage of trading in Chrysler would have advanced from 10 per cent to 15 per cent, or an increase of 50 per cent over the previous day. This would be construed as very significant, because the trading in Chrysler would have been relatively **more active,** while the total trading **remained the same.**

The value of volume ratios lies in the fact that they show the relative trend of volume. To the uninformed observer, an increase in the volume of trading looks significant, regardless of whether it is in line with the fluctuation apparent in the market as a whole. To the trained observer, volume is significant only when it shows a change in relation to the total volume.

The study of relative volume by means of ratios (percentages of total volume) is particularly important when a noticeable peak or valley or trend in the ratio is apparent coincident with some other technical factor, which may be confirmed or denied by the action of volume—for example, a breakaway from a triangle, the penetration of a trend line, or the breaking of a previous high or low point.

A study of several hundred volume ratios, over a period of several years, clearly shows that there is no significant peak in actual volume which does not show up in relative volume (the ratio to the total trading). On the other hand, there are numerous occasions where a notable increase or decrease is not discernible in the raw figures, which is clearly apparent in the relative figures. That is, there are many occasions where the raw figures show nothing significant, while the ratio figures develop important indications; but there are no occasions where a significant indication shows itself in the raw figures which is not equally apparent in the refined data.

If this writer had his choice of watching charts of the actual volume figures, or charts showing the ratio of volume figures, he would select the ratios and drop the actual figures, unless trading operations were large enough to require a knowledge of the actual number of shares traded. Some of the corporate investors and very large individual investors of necessity must follow the actual figures in order to plan their accumulation and distribution because the number of shares they buy and sell is large enough to influence the market. The same is true of some of the large investment counsel organizations.

One of the advantages of using volume ratios instead of the actual figures for volume is that they can be plotted on arithmetic charts without any of the difficulties of changing arithmetic scales. Ordinarily, the daily trading in the 700-800 most active stocks varies in the range from about .05 per cent to 10 per cent. Although this range at first seems very wide, it is relatively small compared with the range of actual figures, which vary from 100 shares to 300,000—400,000 shares a day.

ONE GREAT VALUE OF VOLUME RATIOS

Perhaps the greatest value, however, in studying volume ratios ver-

sus the raw figures is that when they develop a peak comparable to the highest two or three peaks in the previous year or two, an important development in the price trend is almost always under way; whereas in the raw figures, numerous peaks which appear to the eye as possibly important are of no significance whatsoever.

Usually, in the course of 18 months, in a fairly active stock there will only be three or four important peaks in a volume ratio; 7 out of 10 such peaks will be signals of importance to the technical student, whereas during the same time period, 15 or 20 peaks, of which only a third or a half later prove to be of importance, will develop in the actual volume line.

PRICE-VOLUME CORRELATION
PRICE-VOLUME STUDIES—CORRELATION
OF VOLUME AND PRICE

The discussion from this point to where the summary begins is presented for those readers who are interested in some of the research developments in price-volume relations, being employed by more advanced students. The vast majority of the studies in this category require considerable labor in their preparation, and unless they are used in connection with the operation of a large trading fund, they are hardly worth the effort involved.

THE EARLIEST PRICE-VOLUME CHART

For years market students have toyed with the idea that a given amount of advance or decline in price could be measured in terms of turnover or volume. The premise usually adopted is that in an advance, for example, if for each one point of rise 10,000 shares are traded, supply is being encountered as soon as 20,000-30,000 shares are traded with a rise of only one point or less. At first this system of measurement

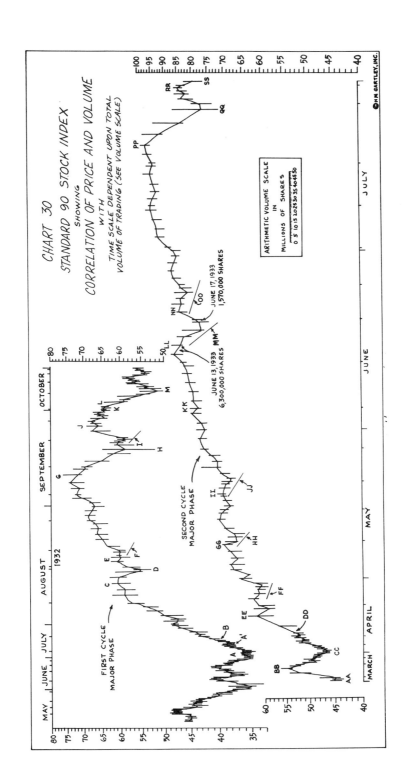

CHART 30

STANDARD 90 STOCK INDEX

SHOWING

CORRELATION OF PRICE AND VOLUME

WITH

TIME SCALE DEPENDENT UPON TOTAL
VOLUME OF TRADING (SEE VOLUME SCALE)

ARITHMETIC VOLUME SCALE
IN
MILLIONS OF SHARES
0 5 10 15 20 25 30 35 40 45 50

©H.M.GARTLEY, INC.

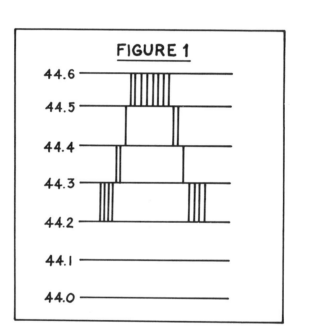

FIGURE 1

appears very logical, simple and direct. But when it is studied for a while, it is quickly found that there are many occasions where the method falls down badly and causes many losses if used alone in actual trading.

Essentially, most of the price-volume studies are devices which have grown out of an old type of bar chart used before 1900 by tape-readers. If a trader were operating then in Steel, he would watch the tape for all the shares traded in the stock. When a sale of 100 shares came out, at 44.2, he drew a vertical line at the 44.2 level on his chart, as illustrated in Figure 1. If the next sale was 300 shares at the same price, he drew three more lines at the 44.2 level. Following this, let us say, 200 shares of Steel sold at 44.3, 100 at 44.4, and 500 at 44.5. The trader then drew two lines at the 44.3 level, one line at the 44.4, and five lines at 44.5 as shown.

Three more sales of 100 shares each were then made at 44.5; 100, 100 at 44.4; 100 at 44.3; 300, 100 at 44.2. For each 100 shares sold, the trader drew a line at the appropriate price level, securing the graph illustrated. This type of chart enabled the trader to recognize important supply and demand areas by the volume which occurred at such levels. In the example cited here, Steel was obviously in supply at 44.5.

THE PRINCIPLE APPLIED TO THE STANDARD 90 STOCK INDEX

An interesting example of graphic correlation of price change and volume is given on *Chart* 30. The series in the upper left-hand corner shows high, low and closing prices (closing prices connected by continuous line) for the Standard Statistics 90-stock average from May to October, 1932. This period covers the bear market low, the major phase of the first intermediate cycle, and the early part of the correction of this major phase. The lower series shows the major phase of the second intermediate cycle, from March to July 1933. Both series are plotted on the same ratio price scale.

TIME SCALE BASED ON VOLUME

The reader will immediately note that, unlike the usual high, low and last bar chart, the bar plottings on *Chart 30* appear at unequal intervals on the time scale.

This is because the bars were spaced in relation to volume rather than to predetermined horizontal time units, customarily standing for a day. The usual spacing assigned to a time unit was given to the unit of 1,000,000 shares of total activity, as indicated on the Arithmetic Volume scale shown at the lower right-hand side of the Chart. On June 13, 1933, for example, 6,300,000 shares were sold. The high, low and last bar for this day is plotted, not one unit of horizontal distance to the right of the bar representing the price range for June 12, as in ordinary daily interval bar plotting, but 6.3 units of horizontal space, representing 6.3 millions of shares of volume. In the same way, the volume on June 17 was 1,570,000 shares. The high, low and last bar for that day is plotted 1.57 units of horizontal space to the right of the bar standing for June 16. The plotting thus combines price and trading activity in one series.

INTERPRETATION OF CHART 30

In order to interpret *Chart 30,* it is necessary to recall the following axioms about volume, stated in somewhat different phraseology than in the early part of this Chapter:

1. When prices are **rising** and volume is **increasing,** the advance is impressive. Conversely, if prices are **rising** and volume is **decreasing,** the advance is questionable.
2. When prices are **falling,** and volume is **increasing,** the decline is impressive. Conversely, when prices are **falling** and volume is **decreasing,** the decline is questionable.
3. If an advance halts, or if little progress is made on the up-side, with activity **large,** a possible **top** is signaled.

4. If a decline halts, or if little progress is made on the down-side, with activity large, a possible **bottom** is signaled.

All experienced students view the market with these axioms in mind. With the customary chart showing daily price range in one series and volume in another at the bottom of the chart, it is necessary to correlate the two series with the eye, in order to apply these volume axioms. In *Chart 30,* however, both price and volume phenomena are graphed in one series.

In July 1932, at the bottom of the bear market, it will be noted that stocks traded in a narrow range or Dow Theory "line" (A) on very light volume, denoted by the close spacing between the bars. Shortly after this line was broken on the up-side, volume picked up (the spaces widened), giving evidence that the breakout was probably important. A slight recession occurred between A and B and volume declined, giving a bullish signal (the spacing between the bars contracted again at A^1). This was confirmed following B, when activity increased on the sharp mark-up (spacings expanded). Throughout the mark-up from A to C, volume continued to expand. At C, volume was very large, and little progress was made on the up-side, indicating the nearby possibility of a reversal.

On the decline from C to D, however, volume tended to dry up, suggesting the end of a reaction. When prices rebounded to E, volume again picked up, but decreased on the set-back to F, once more signalling strength. From F to G volume continued heavy, but the price gain was smaller proportionate to that made from A to E.

The increased space between the high and low bars, together with the slowing up of the advance, clearly indicated that the market was running into supply. At G, activity was extremely great, with no price gains, and the forecast correction to H on high volume followed. After the bottom at H had formed, volume decreased on the small reaction which took place at I. This bullish indication was confirmed by an expansion of volume on the rally to J. Further confirmation developed as activity dwindled from J to K, but the down-side break at L on high volume abruptly reversed this bullish signal, and gave indications that the corrective phase was to continue. At M, volume again tended to dry up, suggesting the possibility that the corrective phase was over.

From M on the upper series to AA on the lower series, there occurred a long trading area on relatively light volume. Volume signals during this period were relatively unimportant.

In the lower series, after the formation of the low at AA in March 1933, activity increased sharply on the advance to BB following the Bank Holiday. This increase compares with point B in the upper series, except that in the lower series the expansion of volume was pronounced. On the decline from the top at BB to CC, activity dwindled, denoting strength. The rally from CC was marked with a gradual increase in volume until the previous high (BB) was approached at DD, when volume expanded sharply on the upward penetration to give an important buying signal. The decline in volume on the small reactions from EE to FF confirmed the signal, and additional bullish evidence was furnished by the tendency of volume to dry up on the declines from GG to HH and II to JJ.

From JJ to KK, volume expanded on the rally, but from KK to LL the advance slowed up on increasing volume, indicating the possibility of a nearby reaction. The high volume from LL to MM was decidedly bearish, for, unlike the previous reactions to CC, FF, HH and JJ, activity increased on the decline. Subsequently, however, volume again increased on the rally to NN, and declined slightly on the reaction to OO, giving bullish indications which were justified by the advance from OO. As the top PP was reached, high volume continued with virtually no price gains, and the market broke sharply to QQ on an avalanche of selling. This situation compares with that in the upper series from G to H, in September 1932. On the rebound from QQ to RR, volume declined, continuing the bearish indication.

Thus, on *Chart 30,* which combines price movement and activity in one series, we are able to see fairly consistent phenomena from which deductions as to important market reversals can be made.

In the period from June 1933 to August 1937, covering practically four years, during which two complete bull market cycles made their appearance, the volume characteristics shown on *Chart 30* were not duplicated, although a study of the previous 36 years shows that the phenomena covering the period 1932 and 1933 were repeated time and again.

It is this author's opinion that as long as S.E.C. regulation controls manipulation comparably to the period 1935-1937, it is possible that a study like that shown on *Chart 30* will be of small value.

TRENDOGRAPHS—A FURTHER REFINEMENT

Figures 2-6 inclusive show a further development of a price-volume correlation study. They illustrate what is probably the greatest current development of graphic correlation of price and volume, and show the work of Mr. E. S. Quinn, Vice-President of Investographs, Inc.* Trendographs, Inc., a division of Investographs, Inc., publishes a series of 60 such charts which are issued weekly. The reproductions were furnished and presented with the permission of Mr. Quinn.

The studies which Quinn has made of price-volume correlations of individual stocks are employed as part of a comprehensive program of studying volume in the market as a whole. He begins with consideration of the relation of volume in certain investment and speculative groups, for the purpose of determining what we have termed the "When" to buy or sell question. He then carries the study through a process of examining the individual volume characteristics, both actual and relative, of a picked group of stocks, to the point where the price-volume relation of these stocks is made the basis of answering the "What" question.

But let Mr. Quinn tell his own story, in the following quotations which he has kindly furnished the author.

*31 Gibbs Street, Rochester, New York

QUINN'S GENERAL PHILOSOPHY

"Trendograph procedure is founded upon the proposition that rising prices follow investment buying of values; that declines are caused by gambling in intangibles.

"Whenever the sales price of an article in general demand descends to the point where a sufficient number of prospective purchasers recognize its **fundamental, economic** value and would rather own the article than the cash required to buy it, it will not go lower. This reasoning holds whether the article in question is real estate, commodities, stocks or anything else. But there is a significant distinction here which should be understood. It is economic values which provide a base—**not** speculative possibilities.

"Similarly, whenever the price of an article exceeds its fundamental value, either on the basis of reproduction cost or intrinsic investment or economic value, its market position is weak and its price cannot be long maintained.

"A familiar practical example is represented in the Florida land boom of some years ago. Before prices started to rise so spectacularly, properties could be acquired at figures reasonably close to basic values and, just so long as the spread between prices and values was small, the land situation was sound.

"As Florida became a fad, however, and prices sky-rocketed far beyond the levels of values, it was impossible to secure adequate returns on land investments. People were buying properties not because they wanted to keep them, but solely in the hope of selling out to someone else for more money than they paid. Financing loans could not be supported and it was only a question of time before the inevitable collapse occurred.

"Other well known instances include the unsuccessful attempt of Brazil to hold the price of coffee at levels which were economically unsound and Britain's effort to peg the price of rubber, both of which

284

brought disastrous results. Another example, equally doomed to fail-ure, is the program our Government is carrying on currently in trying to maintain the price of cotton above world market values.

"When a general market decline is in progress, it will continue, irre-spective of previously held conceptions of values, until prices reach the point where they represent values at that time, under the new condi-tions which then prevail. When a sufficient number of interested per-sons recognize the existence of sound values, prices will not decline further because such offerings as are made will be absorbed, so that the trend will be reversed and prices will rise. The natural question here is: 'How can one know with reasonable accuracy when stock prices are forming a "value" base?' The answer to this is found in analysis of the character of general trading, which discloses whether stocks are largely being purchased for value or for speculation.

"We know that the point has been reached where true values are being recognized, when value stock, such as American Telephone, Union Carbide, Allied Chemical, Woolworth and others like them, are being bought. Their purchase is not being stimulated because of their speculative appeal because, normally, they are slow movers and, per-centagewise, gain less than the market as a whole in a general advance. They are being acquired because, at current yields and according to balance sheet values, they are worth more than the cash required to purchase them. Moreover, as a class, the individuals who buy these stocks are not speculatively inclined in the sense that they do not make their purchases on borrowed money. They pay outright for their shares. Such purchases at such times are economically right and supply the force which stops market declines.

"Concentration of trading in investment stocks means that there has been a proportionate shrinkage of transactions in speculative shares. Lack of offerings in the latter classification is evidence that such neces-sitous liquidation as may have been overhanging the market, as the de-cline originally got under way, has been completed; that accounts which were vulnerable have either been sold out or strengthened. Obviously, when speculative holdings are no longer being pressed for sale and there is an active demand for investment stocks, the market is basically healthy and prices will not go lower.

"After the market has formed a base and starts to rise, it will continue its forward move until prices run too far ahead of intrinsic values, whereupon it will fall of its own weight. Here, too, we recognize the approach to a turning point by analyzing the relationship between investment and speculative trading in the market as a whole.

"As the market moves ahead, investment stocks become less attractive, so that the demand for them begins to taper off. And this demand becomes proportionately less as prices move further away from values. Somewhere in this phase the small gamblers start coming in, attracted by the gains they have been watching from day to day. Their number is legion—and their lack of knowledge of market affairs is nearly as great. Their combined purchases carry prices still higher. But while they are buying, so-called wise money is being withdrawn. Soon the stock market loses its character as a common ground for the exchange of values for currency. It becomes a meeting place for gamblers, big and little, whose purchases are largely made on borrowed money, purely in the hope of quick, easy profits. Such purchases, because of their temporary nature, constitute a constant threat to the health of the market as a whole because, on the first sign of serious price-weakness, dumping begins. As the decline continues, it compels added selling for the protection of margins and thus feeds on itself until weakly-held accounts are cleaned up and prices reach the point where values establish a new base.

"These are the economic principles used in measuring the degree of underlying strength or weakness of the market. The actual selection of stocks to be used is made from observation of the performance of individual issues.

PRICE-VOLUME FACTORS MUST BE RELATIVE

"The proper analysis of the operation of the law of supply and demand within individual stocks serves two essential purposes. Not only does it reveal the trend of public interest; it also discloses whether such interest is favorable or unfavorable. In Trendograph charts, a study of supply and demand is employed as a means of showing the trend and character of public interest in the various stocks.

"The volume of trading in any particular stock will normally represent a certain percentage of the volume of trading in the market as a whole. This is an axiom which many chartists, who base their conclusions upon absolute volume, have entirely overlooked. Seeing volume in a stock increase substantially, they look for some reason to buy or sell, not realizing that if general volume has increased in proportion, the situation is of no significance.

"Obviously, a stock which merely drifts along, consuming only its normal volume of trading from day to day, is without particular public or private interest and for this reason does not offer good trading prospects. But when any stock shows a large increase in relative volume; when it suddenly begins to consume more than its usual percentage of total trading, only one conclusion can be drawn. Some individual or group has decided—and their judgment is being backed up by their own cash—that the stock is selling either too high or too low.

"This leads to two conclusions. First, **that it is impossible to interpret the meaning of volume fluctuations in a stock unless these are tied up percentagewise with total market volume.**

"Second—and this is important—**the percentage relationship provides a means of recognizing instantly any unusual activity in a stock.** Whether such unusual activity is buying or selling may be determined by considering the coincident price action.

"Just as volume in a single stock must be considered in relation to total trading, price movements of individual stocks are misleading except as they are compared with the trend of the market as a whole.

Simply because a stock may gain 2% in value in a day is not necessarily favorable—It is if the market as a whole gained 1%. It is not if the market as a whole has gained 3%. Similarly, it is not necessarily unfavorable if a stock declines 2% on a given day. If the market at the same time lost 5%, then the stock is showing strength merely in resisting the general decline.

CONSTRUCTION OF THE TRENDOGRAPH CHARTS

"In a standard Trendograph chart (see Figures 2-6 inclusive) the upper rectangles coordinate daily price ranges, vertically, and relative volume, horizontally. Wide rectangles mean greater relative volume; narrow ones, less. Since relative volume is the interest-indicator, we look for any sudden broadening out in the horizontal dimensions of the rectangles. If, on increased activity, a stock moves ahead of the market, a plain indication is given that the demand for that stock is greater than the supply as compared with the relationship of these forces in the market as a whole. This, under certain conditions, would be interpreted as a buying signal, particularly if underlying conditions in the general market are favorable.

"To permit direct comparison of relative price movements, two connected, irregular lines are superimposed upon the pattern of the price-volume chart of the stock. The heavy line is the general market as represented by the daily changes in the sum of the three Dow Jones averages—Industrials, Railroads and Utilities. This combined average provides the basis upon which all relative price movements in individual stocks are computed. The lighter, broken line gives the trend of average stock prices in the specific industrial group classifications (such as Agricultural Implements, Chemicals, etc.), to which each stock is assigned. Accordingly, it is possible at a glance to analyze price action in any given stock, both with respect to the general market and its particular group.

"The supplementary chart is really more important than the price-

288

volume curve which it supports. The zero line represents the market 'straightened out'. The black vertical bars, extending both upward and downward from it, provide a breakdown of the daily price action of the stock in comparison with the price action of the market as a whole. The vertical distance of a bar above the line shows the percentage by which the price of the stock exceeded the averages on a given day; comparative losses are reflected below the line. The width of these bars indicates relative volume.

"The cross-hatched (shaded) areas between the vertical lines, marking calendar weeks, show the net percentage gains and losses of the stock, by weeks, in excess of the market.

"In practical use, it will be found that the upper section of the Trendograph chart is valuable principally as a means of gaining an accurate perspective of both near term and long term price habits and volume characteristics. Obviously, if a particular stock displays a constant repetition of price-volume habits throughout rallies and declines and at tops and bottoms, a knowledge of these factors is most useful in predicting what the future might bring.

"The lower section of the chart form provides a detailed breakdown of comparative action, which is another way of saying a representation of the daily operation of supply and demand. This section of the chart is used in analyzing current action in order to determine whether or not the underlying condition of a stock is strong or weak.

VOLUME HABITS OF STOCKS AT TOPS AND BOTTOMS

"Stocks are like people in that they have varying and, in many cases, definitely established habits. It is for this reason that Trendograph charts going back to January 1932 have been prepared. By studying these, one is able to recognize what a given stock normally does at tops and bottoms and in rallies and declines, and is thus in a position to attempt a forecast of future action which is almost certain to be more accurate than if this knowledge were not available.

"As has already been explained, the general market forms a base under pressure of investment buying; tops are seen to the accompaniment of gambling in intangible speculations. In the practical use of Trendograph procedure, analysis of the current position of a stock usually begins with consideration of its relative-volume characteristics at tops and bottoms.

"Accordingly, in an investment stock, we recognize the approach to a base and a buying level, while market prices are still declining, when we see our charted rectangles begin to expand horizontally, evidencing increased investment demand. Once a purchase has been made, we watch volume as the general market moves ahead. When volume begins to shrink, we know we must begin to think about selling, because the operation of the law of supply and demand is telling us that intrinsic value has become questionable. Re-purchases of investment stocks are not made until relative activity again broadens out after a decline. Trendograph charts of many investment stocks over a period of years show that American Can, American Telephone, du Pont, U. S. Steel, Union Pacific and others display a surprising consistency in volume characteristics. Relative volume expands as such stocks approach buying areas and narrows down at tops.

"In similar fashion, we follow the general swings in a speculative stock, except that the opposite interpretation applies. The approach to a buying point can be seen as volume dries up, indicating a lack of selling pressure. A purchase is made as soon as price action shows the stock to be in a position to rise. As our stock advances, again we watch volume, but this time we look for increased activity as an indication of the probable termination of the advance and get ready to sell. Striking examples of small volume bottoms and large volume tops are seen in Trendograph charts of Columbia Gas & Electric, Douglas Aircraft, Electric Bond & Share, Montgomery Ward, U. S. Smelting and others.

"While up to this point our discussion of volume habits at tops and bottoms has been confined to the two general classifications of investment and speculative issues, we have, for greater accuracy, divided our index of the stocks we cover into five groups. The majority of the first two groups comprise investment stocks; groups 3 and 4, speculative stocks. The symbols, in parentheses, designate volume characteristics. The groups are as follows:

GROUP 1 (I) With but rare exceptions relative volume broadens out at bottoms and dries up at tops.

GROUP 2 (I-T) Relative volume shows a **tendency** to broaden out at bottoms and dry up at tops.

GROUP 3 (S) With but rare exceptions relative volume of stocks in this group dries up at bottoms and broadens out at tops.

GROUP 4 (S-T) Relative volume shows a **tendency** to dry up at bottoms and broaden out at tops.

GROUP 5 (X) This group has no marked volume characteristics.

According to the latest classification (August 1937), the 60 stocks which Mr. Quinn regularly studies are classified in the above categories as follows:

"The segration outlined above is based entirely upon observation of the charted volume habits of the various stocks; not upon analysis of balance sheets as a means of determining, fundamentally, whether a given stock should be classed as investment or speculative. The reason for this is that some stocks, which are of investment nature, when judged by their balance sheets alone, display speculative volume habits throughout certain phases of the business cycle. Similarly, some speculative stocks, which under certain conditions are lacking in speculative appeal, occasionally show investment volume characteristics for an extended period. Because volume habits of all stocks are not fixed, a permanent list is not published.

"As has already been mentioned, volume does not expand in **all** investment stocks as bases are being formed—nor does activity broaden in **all** speculative issues as tops are being approached. Public interest frequently ignores some stocks so that they do not perform in their customary manner. By appraising the relationship of trading from day

ACCORDING TO THE LATEST CLASSIFICATION (AUGUST 1937), THE 60 STOCKS WHICH MR. QUINN REGULARLY STUDIES ARE CLASSIFIED AS FOLLOWS:

GROUP 1 (I)	GROUP 2 (I-T)	GROUP 3 (S)	GROUP 4 (S-T)	GROUP 5 (X)
With but rare exceptions relative volume broadens out at bottoms and dries up at tops.	Relative volume shows a **tendency** to broaden out at bottoms and dry up at tops.	With but rare exceptions relative volume of stocks in this group dries up at bottoms and broadens out at tops.	Relative volume shows a **tendency** to dry up at bottoms and broaden out at tops.	This group has no marked volume characteristics.
Amer. Can	(I)	(S)	(S-T)	(X)
Amer. Telephone	(I-T)	Amer. Radiator	Allis Chalmers	Case
Corn Products	Allied Chemical	Amer. Smelting	Amer. Rolling M.	Consol. Edison
du Pont	Amer. Tobacco B	Anaconda	Briggs	Gen. Electric
Great Northern	Atchison	Balt. & Ohio	Celanese	Pennsylvania
Union Pacific	Stand. Oil of N.J.	Bendix	Chrysler	Phillips Pete.
U. S. Steel	Union Carbide	Beth. Steel	Com. Solvents	Sears Roebuck
Woolworth	Western Union	Columbia Gas	Gen. Motors	
		Dome Mines	Int. Harvester	
		Douglas	Int. Nickel	
		Elec. Auto-Lite	Johns Manville	
		Elec. Bond & Sh.	Loew's	
		Goodyear	Stand. Brands	
		Int. Telephone	Westinghouse	
		Kennecott		
		Mont. Ward		
		Nat. Distillers		
		N.Y. Central		
		North American		
		Packard		
		Pullman		
		Radio		
		Schenley		
		Sperry		
		United Aircraft		
		United Corp.		
		U.S. Smelting		

to day in groups of investments and groups of speculations, an adequate check is provided on individual stock action. Accordingly, purchase of an investment stock should normally require that it be reflecting increased relative volume as indicative of an active investment demand and that the general market as healthy. A speculative stock is not acquired until small relative volume shows that selling pressure has subsided and the market as a whole is ready to move ahead—

"Determination of selling points depends, in general, upon a similar check. If one is carrying an investment stock in which relative volume has dried up significantly, it is frequently wise to dispose of it. Lack of current interest suggests that further gains will probably be small. Likewise, speculative stocks are let go when volume broadens out to the point where a typical top formation is recognized. Whether increased activity in group 5 represents accumulation or distribution is usually determined by noting whether the Pressure Indicator is appraising the general market as strong or weak."

The author has chosen five sample Trendograph charts,* taken from Quinn's work, with the idea of generally illustrating the five categories into which Mr. Quinn divides the group of individual stocks.

In Figure 2, which shows Union Pacific, we see a stock which Quinn rates as an (I) or Investment issue, characteristically having large activity at bottoms (A) and small activity at tops (B). Although only a short period of time (March 14-October 3, 1936) is shown on this chart, a study of the previous several years shows exactly the same characteristics.

In Figure 3 we see an illustration of a Trendograph chart of American Tobacco B, which is rated as an (IT) or Investment Tendency issue. Somewhat like Union Pacific, American Tobacco B has a habit of having larger volume at bottoms (A and C) and smaller volume at tops (B), although at times this stock has fairly heavy volume at high points. Thus it cannot be given a rating as a wholly investment issue, on the basis of large volume at low points and small volume at high points.

*This refers to a chart that is no longer available.

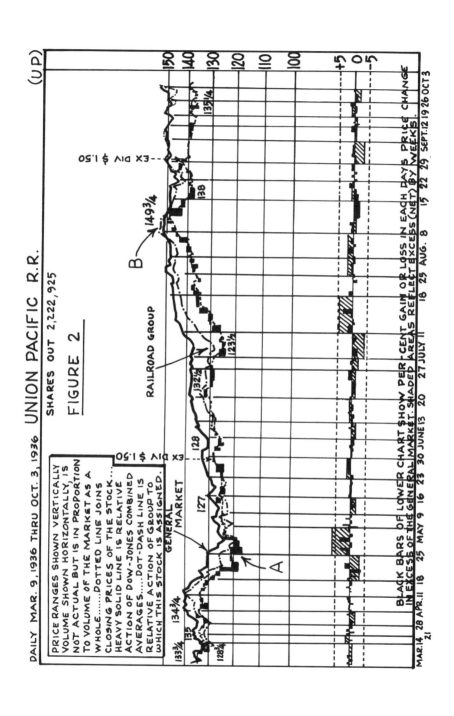

DAILY MAR. 9, 1936 THRU OCT. 3, 1936 UNION PACIFIC R.R. (UP)

SHARES OUT 2,22,925

FIGURE 2

PRICE RANGES SHOWN VERTICALLY
VOLUME SHOWN HORIZONTALLY, IS
NOT ACTUAL BUT IS IN PROPORTION
TO VOLUME OF THE MARKET AS A
WHOLE......DOTTED LINE JOINS
CLOSING PRICES OF THE STOCK...
HEAVY SOLID LINE IS RELATIVE
ACTION OF DOW-JONES COMBINED
AVERAGES......DOT-DASH LINE IS
RELATIVE ACTION OF GROUP TO
WHICH THIS STOCK IS ASSIGNED.

RAILROAD GROUP

GENERAL MARKET

B ← 149¾

EX DIV $ 1.50

EX DIV $ 1.50

A

135¾
135
133¾
128¾
127
128
132½
123½
138
135¾

150
140
130
120
110
100

+5
0
-5

BLACK BARS OF LOWER CHART SHOW PER CENT GAIN OR LOSS IN EACH DAY'S PRICE CHANGE
IN EXCESS OF THE GENERAL MARKET. SHADED AREAS REFLECT EXCESS (NET) BY WEEKS.

MAR.14 28 APR.11 18 25 MAY 9 16 23 30 JUNE13 20 27 JULY11 18 25 AUG. 8 15 22 29 SEPT.12 19 26 OCT 3
21

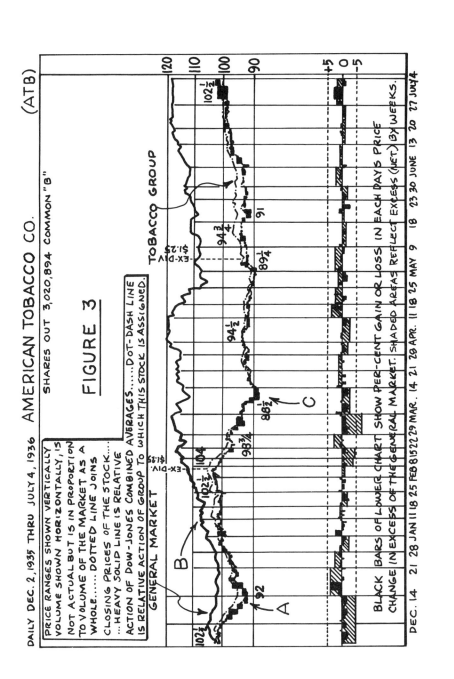

AMERICAN TOBACCO CO. (ATB)

DAILY DEC. 2, 1935 THRU JULY 4, 1936

SHARES OUT 3,020,894 COMMON "B"

FIGURE 3

PRICE RANGES SHOWN VERTICALLY, VOLUME SHOWN HORIZONTALLY, IS NOT ACTUAL BUT IS IN PROPORTION TO VOLUME OF THE MARKET AS A WHOLE......DOTTED LINE JOINS CLOSING PRICES OF THE STOCK..... ...HEAVY SOLID LINE IS RELATIVE ACTION OF DOW-JONES COMBINED AVERAGES.....DOT-DASH LINE IS RELATIVE ACTION OF GROUP TO WHICH THIS STOCK IS ASSIGNED.

TOBACCO GROUP

GENERAL MARKET

BLACK BARS OF LOWER CHART SHOW PER-CENT GAIN OR LOSS IN EACH DAYS PRICE CHANGE IN EXCESS OF THE GENERAL MARKET. SHADED AREAS REFLECT EXCESS (NET) BY WEEKS.

DEC. 14 21 28 JAN 11 18 25 FEB 8 15 22 29 MAR. 14 21 28 APR. 11 18 25 MAY 9 18 23 30 JUNE 13 20 27 JU\y4

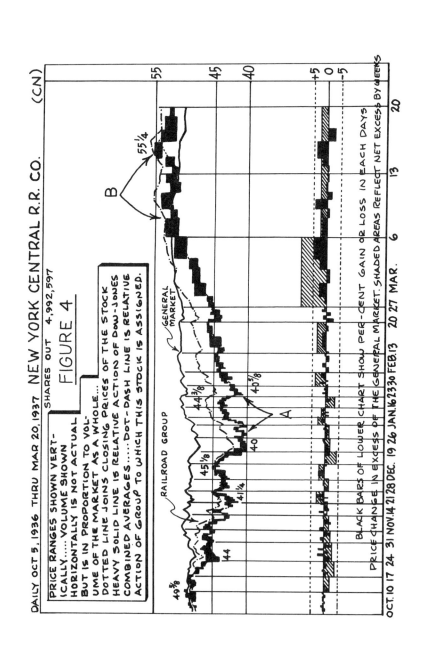

DAILY OCT 5, 1936 THRU MAR 20, 1937 NEW YORK CENTRAL R.R. CO. (CN)

SHARES OUT 4,992,597

FIGURE 4

PRICE RANGES SHOWN VERT-
ICALLY.... VOLUME SHOWN
HORIZONTALLY IS NOT ACTUAL
BUT IS IN PROPORTION TO VOL-
UME OF THE MARKET AS A WHOLE...
DOTTED LINE JOINS CLOSING PRICES OF THE STOCK
HEAVY SOLID LINE IS RELATIVE ACTION OF DOW-JONES
COMBINED AVERAGES..... DOT-DASH LINE IS RELATIVE
ACTION OF GROUP TO WHICH THIS STOCK IS ASSIGNED.

BLACK BARS OF LOWER CHART SHOW PER-CENT GAIN OR LOSS IN EACH DAYS
PRICE CHANGE IN EXCESS OF THE GENERAL MARKET. SHADED AREAS REFLECT NET EXCESS BY WEEKS

GENERAL
MARKET

RAILROAD GROUP

B

55¼

A

49⅝
44
45⅛
41¼
40
44¼
44⅜
40⅝

55
45
40

+5
0
-5

OCT.10 17 24 31 NOV.14 21 28 DEC. 19 26 JAN.16 23 30 FEB.13 20 27 MAR. 6 13 20

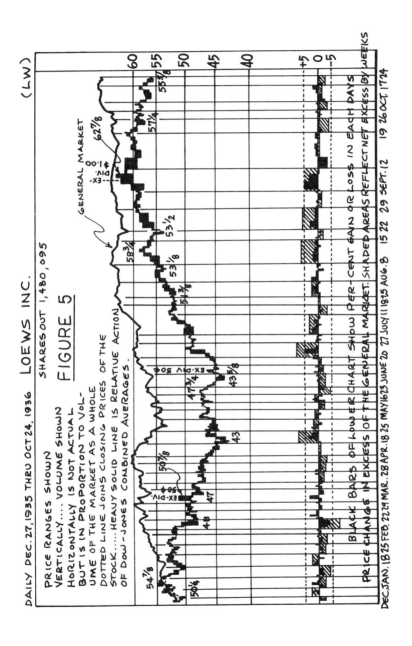

DAILY DEC.27,1935 THRU OCT 24, 1936   LOEWS INC.   (LW)

SHARES OUT 1,480,095

FIGURE 5

PRICE RANGES SHOWN
VERTICALLY.....VOLUME SHOWN
HORIZONTALLY IS NOT ACTUAL
BUT IS IN PROPORTION TO VOL-
UME OF THE MARKET AS A WHOLE
DOTTED LINE JOINS CLOSING PRICES OF THE
STOCK......HEAVY SOLID LINE IS RELATIVE ACTION
OF DOW-JONES COMBINED AVERAGES.

GENERAL MARKET

BLACK BARS OF LOWER CHART SHOW PER-CENT GAIN OR LOSS IN EACH DAYS
PRICE CHANGE IN EXCESS OF THE GENERAL MARKET. SHADED AREAS REFLECT NET EXCESS BY WEEKS

DEC.JAN. 18 25 FEB. 22 29 MAR. 28 APR. 18 25 MAY16 23 JUNE 20 27 JULY11 18 25 AUG. 8 15 22 29 SEPT. 12 19 26 OCT. 17 24

The chart of New York Central, which is shown on Figure 4, shows a stock rated by Quinn as a typical (S) or Speculative issue, which it truly is, with light volume at bottoms (A) and high volume at tops (B). Perhaps no better sample of a speculative issue could be used than this particular "Hope" Rail stock.

The chart of Loew's is provided as an example of the group which Mr. Quinn classifies as the (S-T) Speculative Tendency group. Lows may be expected in Loew's on light volume (no pun intended) while tops are likely to appear on large volume. But the phenomenon is not consistent although it is quite worth watching.

In Figure 6, which reflects some of the fluctuations in Consolidated Edison, we see a picture which Mr. Quinn classifies as in the (X) group, which has no marked volume characteristics. In this case it will be noted that both tops and bottoms seem to form without any notable increase in activity, as shown by the horizontal width of the rectangles showing the volume tendencies.

Continuing his interpretation, Mr. Quinn states further.

BUYING AND SELLING POINTS IN INDIVIDUAL STOCKS

"Naturally, background charts of various stocks must be studied to provide a means of studying and classifying the various issues according to their velocity characteristics in rallies and declines and their volume habits at tops and bottoms. With a knowledge of these factors, as market prices are declining, purchases are determined upon in the following manner:

"Where stocks of investment caliber are to be acquired, the charted record for various issues in this category are studied on three points.

1. Has price performance during the past year or more been satisfactory in comparison with the rest of the market?
2. From a price standpoint has the stock stood up better-than-usual in the last decline?
3. Has relative volume expanded to the point where one may reasonably conclude that this particular stock is one of those which

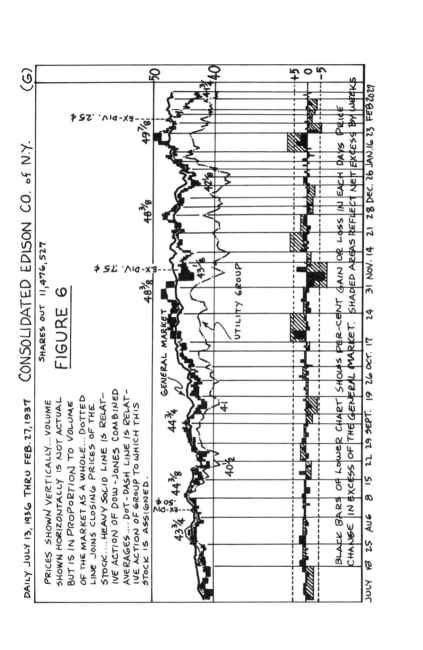

DAILY JULY 13, 1936 THRU FEB. 27, 1937   CONSOLIDATED EDISON CO. of N.Y.   (G)

SHARES OUT 11,476,527

FIGURE 6

PRICES SHOWN VERTICALLY....VOLUME
SHOWN HORIZONTALLY IS NOT ACTUAL
BUT IS IN PROPORTION TO VOLUME
OF THE MARKET AS A WHOLE...DOTTED
LINE JOINS CLOSING PRICES OF THE
STOCK.....HEAVY SOLID LINE IS RELAT-
IVE ACTION OF DOW-JONES COMBINED
AVERAGES.....DOT-DASH LINE IS RELAT-
IVE ACTION OF GROUP TO WHICH THIS
STOCK IS ASSIGNED.

GENERAL MARKET

UTILITY GROUP

BLACK BARS OF LOWER CHART SHOWS PER-CENT GAIN OR LOSS IN EACH DAYS PRICE
CHANGE IN EXCESS OF THE GENERAL MARKET. SHADED AREAS REFLECT NET EXCESS BY WEEKS

is being singled out as representing better-than-average value?

If the answer to these three questions is in the affirmative, purchases may be made with reasonable assurance.

"A similar procedure is followed in determining upon the purchase of speculative stocks except with respect to point No. 3. Speculative stocks normally make bottoms to the accompaniment of small relative volume, as a consequence, we look for a significant narrowing down in our rectangles as evidence of lack of selling pressure. It is important, too, in studying the record for approximately the past year to determine whether or not it embraces a period of major distribution at a level above that at which the stock is currently priced. Where a condition of this kind exists, an approach to the past distribution area in all probability encounters so much supply as seriously to impair the forward move (lower tops). Points of major distribution are recognized by extreme width in the daily rectangles.

"When the general price trend turns upward after a base has been formed, speculative stocks are purchased as so-called 'buying signals' are seen. These develop under increased activity and favorable price action and usually are found within a single day's performance.

"If, after a decrease in relative volume in a decline, activity broadens out on a single day to the accompaniment of a percentage increase in price greater than that seen in the market as a whole, we can conclude (a) that there is a trend on interest toward this stock, and (b) that this increased interest is favorable. Usually, but not always, relative volume in a dependable buying signal will be greater than in any of the five preceding days.

"The three following rules appear to embrace most of the fundamentals necessary for profitable operation:

"Rule No. 1—A buying point is usually indicated when relative volume shows an appreciable increase accompanied by a reasonably proportionate increase in the price of the stock in excess of the average.

"Rule No. 2—A stop-loss order should be placed below the closing price of the stock on the first day following that in which it shows
a price loss on the average of any extent at all, accompanied by relative volume equal to 50% or more of that which has gone immediately before.

"Rule No. 3—A stop-loss order should be placed below the closing price of a stock on the first day following that in which the stock
gained little on the average despite unusually large relative volume.

"Observation suggests that stops should be placed about 10% below
closing prices for low-priced stocks and about 5% for high-priced
stocks. 'Open' stop orders should always be used. Placing stops too
close behind an active issue is likely to take you out on the bottom of
a small recession.

"The comparative price gain one should look for depends upon the
stock's velocity characteristics. If it is a fast mover, a comparatively
large gain in excess of the market—say, 5% or more—should be seen.
Just what this percentage should be can best be determined by checking the past record and noting those patterns which later on proved to
have been dependable.

"Those who are carrying investment stocks watch relative volume as
prices advance. In a major move, it will frequently be found that one
issue, upon reaching certain levels, will lose its following, as evidenced
by a continued decrease in relative activity. If the market is still strong,
funds in such issues can often be switched advantageously to other
situations which have been late in getting started, but currently are
showing a more active investment demand. When, however, the point
is reached where the market is given over largely to speculation all
investment stocks should either be sold or profits protected with stop-
loss orders.

"In speculative stocks we know that tops normally are seen to the
accompaniment of a broadening out in relative volume. Just so long
as this widening out in the charted rectangles is supported by **propor-**

tionate comparative price gains, it may be assumed that the supply-demand situation is satisfactory. As the time approaches when, perhaps under still greater activity, comparative price gains are insignificant or lacking, then it is obvious that the supply-demand relationship has deteriorated and profit taking is impeding a continuation of the advance.

"Under these conditions, if the market as a whole appears to be reasonably healthy, it is usually desirable to protect profits with stops or to switch funds to other speculative situations in which supply has not yet been encountered."

There is no question about the fact that Quinn's studies of price-volume relations represent research of considerable importance.

He has developed an index which he calls a "Pressure Indicator", for the purpose of measuring the relation of supply and demand, with the object of determining the technical position of the market as a whole. This was first published in 1933, and during 1934 and 1935 it had a fairly good record of accuracy in forecasting the important intermediate turning points. But at the April 1936 and the March 1937 highs the index failed to forecast growing weakness prior to substantial declines. And so in May of 1937 Quinn revised his "Pressure Indicator" and published an entirely new index, which as yet has not been tested by a period of actual market practice. This revised "Pressure Indicator" appears to present a considerable problem in interpretation, and for that reason this author chooses to withhold judgment on its value.

The general approach of the Trendograph chart, as illustrated in Figures 2-6, must be credited as a sound one, but unless the trader subscribes to the service and receives each week the 60 individual charts, the labor involved in making a chart of this kind for any substantial number of stocks is extensive, and unless the trader has a substantial interest in a few particular issues the effort involved is great. Nevertheless, the method evolved by Quinn of studying the price-volume relation may certainly be credited as one of the greatest advances in the field.

OTHER VOLUME STUDIES

Before proceeding to a brief summary of the subject of Volume let us consider it from several other angles. Earlier in the Chapter, it was noticed that some market students attempt to study what might be called price-volume velocity by relating price changes and volume mathematically.

The usual method, it was noted, is to divide volume by price change, with the idea of finding out what amount of volume is required for a given gain or loss in price.

The theory of these studies is that when an advance meets a preponderance of supply volume the upward changes, or advances, will be accompanied by an increased amount of turnover as compared with the amount of advance; and declines will be accompanied by an increased turnover. Conversely, the theory is that during a price decline, when an increase in activity does not result in a proportionate decline in price, a bottom is not far away.

Let us examine Figure 7, as an illustration of the principle. Unfortunately, as noted previously, these studies do not show uniform phenomena.

Figure 7, shows the hourly price movements from September 4 to September 21, 1935, inclusive. The upper series of black bars drawn downward toward the price trend represent those hours which were declines; while the lower series of bars drawn upward to the price trend designate those hours in which there were price advances. Both series of black bars show the relative amount of volume as compared with the price change, which is obtained by dividing the hourly volume in each successive case by the net change in price, and plotting the resulting quotients in the top series, if they represent minuses or declines, and in the bottom series if they represent pluses or advances.

Although this particular illustration shows the hourly index, the same principle may be applied to daily or weekly charts. The formula consists of two simple steps in arithmetic: (1) find the price change, desig-

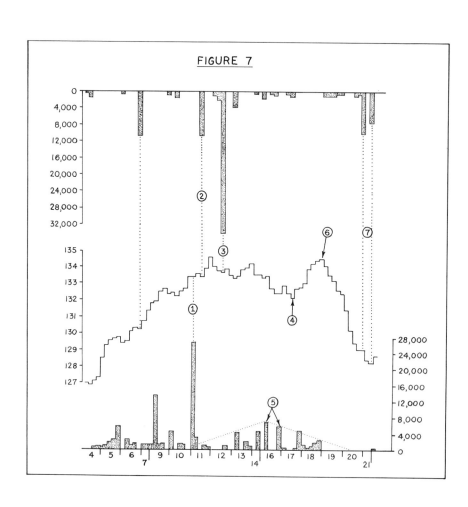

FIGURE 7

nating it minus or plus, and (2) divide it into the volume for the time period (hourly, daily, weekly), and plot the figure so obtained on a center line graph, from figures below it. The arrangement in Figure 7 is a convenient one.

Now let us look at Figure 7. Here we see an advance from the first hour September 4 to the last hour September 11, a decline from that point to the third hour September 17. This was followed by a short advance to the last hour September 18, and finally there was a decline to the first hour September 21.

The questions which arise are: Did this statistical study show evidence of the top at the last hour on September 11; the bottom in the third hour September 17; the top in the last hour September 18; and the low point in the last hour September 21.

The phenomena we see in Figure 7 are typical of such studies. Dotted lines have been projected from the bars showing significant volume-price changes to the price line. It is interesting to note that as the advance from September 4 reached the high on September 11, substantial volume on the upside at (1) failed to result in a proportionate increase in price to that in previous hours.

Also, as this top was reached, there were two occasions when there were substantial increases in volume (2 and 3), when price declines occurred just before and at the top. Together, these signalled a turn.

So far, so good—the theory outlined above appears correct. But let us take the low which terminated the decline from September 11 to September 17. Theoretically, we might have seen here, in the middle hour of September 17, at (4), some increase in volume, as shown by black bars at the top, without comparable price recession. Instead, all that the chart showed was a moderate increase of activity during two price advances (5), several hours before the bottom.

Next, according to the theory, we should have seen some increase in volume, as shown in the lower series, as the top of September 18 was reached (6) indicating that activity was increasing without price advance, or conversely that during minor declines, volume was increasing, as might have been seen in the upper series. Actually, there was no important indication.

The bottom on September 21 was signalled somewhat better, in that after a steady decline, in the last hour September 18, when the majority of price changes were downward, there was a substantial increase in volume proportionate to price change, in the fourth hour September 20 and the first hour September 21, (7) which helped to signal the upside reversal.

The shortcoming of this type of study is that sometimes it produces valuable indications, of a reversal point, and at other times a turning point goes without any indications whatsoever.

VOLUME AND FIGURE CHARTS

With the exception of some minor trend charts, wherein the volume is accumulated and plotted for every fluctuation of ⅛ in an individual stock, volume is seldom studied in connection with figure charts, except where the figure chartist refers to a bar chart of the market as a whole.

Many figure chart students contend that volume is an unreliable indicator, and that the price trend shows all that they need. But perhaps the chief reason why figure chart students do not employ a study of volume is because it is almost impossible to plot it on a figure chart.

"NEVER SELL A DULL MARKET SHORT"

This is an old Wall Street axiom, which we hear more often in bear markets than in bull markets. It is **not,** by any means, always true. Let us take Figures 8 and 9 to illustrate our point. In the case shown in Figure 8, volume goes dull, or dries up on a reaction in an uptrend, and

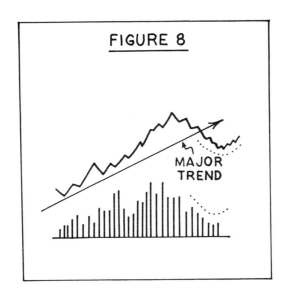

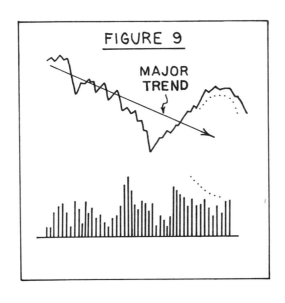

the axiom holds true only too well. But in the case of Figure 9, volume goes dull after a correction on the upside has spent itself, just before a downtrend is resumed. The latter case is typical of not only the minor trends in bear markets, but also the corrective phases of bear market intermediate cycles. Upon several occasions in the 1929-1932 bear market, the first minor reaction from the intermediate tops was accompanied by a decrease in activity just as some of the best selling opportunities developed.

It might be good practice never to sell a dull market short in a corrective decline of an upward trend, but many opportunities would be lost by not selling a dull market short after a corrective rally in a bear market. The importance of the axiom appears to depend upon the direction of the major trend.

Thus, we may profitably amend the axiom, and say: "Never sell a dull market short in a major upward trend." Let us take as two examples, periods during 1932. In the last week of March, just before the three-months' trading area was broken, and the drastic decline which ended with the July bottoms of 1932 developed, the market was exceedingly dull, and the trader had every reason to believe that the floor of the trading area had been reached. That dullness might easily have been interpreted as a bullish signal, indicating that a rise from the floor of this trading area might ensue. Instead, a terrific decline developed.

Let us look at another case in the first ten days of July, 1932 when the bear market ended. Here is a case where, unlike March, the dullness was one of the most important signals of a coming advance which turned out to be a major reversal.

If we lay down the new axiom as a general rule which has exceptions, we might also say, conversely: "Never buy a dull bear market".*

---

*Fred S. McClafferty, in his "A Course in Trading," published by the Wetsel Market Bureau, suggested these variations of the original axiom, which appear to be very sound.

SUMMARY

Although many pages have been spent in discussing the subject of Volume, and it has been reviewed from many different angles, we can reduce its practical use for the average reader to a few simple ideas, which we may summarize as follows:

1. Avoid inactive stocks, unless you are interested chiefly in the long term trend, because their thin markets make it almost impossible to conduct advantageous trading. (S.E.C. regulation has emphasized this axiom.)

2. If you are interested in the minor trend, by all means confine your trading to the leading issues which are included in the 50 most active stocks, over a period of the preceding year.

3. Never neglect the consideration of volume. If an active stock becomes inactive, do not continue to trade in it.

4. Stocks of companies with small capitalizations are not necessarily the best trading mediums. They are often very volatile issues which have thin markets and move rapidly. Successful trading in such issues depends on keeping one's eyes glued to the tape. Large capitalizations are not necessarily a drawback to the trader. General Motors and U. S. Steel are good examples of this contention.

5. Remember that the relative changes in volume are far more important than the actual changes, because all during an active period the trading in almost every stock expands.

6. When a volume ratio, which represents true relative volume, rises to a sharp peak as compared with its performance for a year or eighteen months previously, if an advance or decline of two or three weeks has been under way, look for a turning point. On the other hand, if the price trend of a leading stock has been moving sidewise, and suddenly resumes a diagonal direction, if the volume ratio rises sharply it is usually a good signal that a new diagonal trend of importance is under way. If

the move is up, buy the stock on the next reaction. If the move is down, sell the stock on the next rally.

7. Remember that various stocks have different characteristics at reversal points. As a general proposition, a speculative issue will show increased activity during a rise, and a peak of volume preceding or near a top. Conversely, it will show a decrease in activity during a price decline, and a low level of trading near a bottom (in a bull market).

   As a general proposition, investment stocks will show a tendency for activity to increase in a decline, and reach a peak near a bottom, while conversely, activity in investment stocks tends to decrease in price advances, and be at a relatively low level compared with the general market volume, when tops are reached. However, these characteristics are not permanent or unchanging, thus the volume characteristics of various stocks must be scrutinized constantly to see possible changes.

8. After a long decline has taken place and the price trend begins to rise, an increase of volume on minor rallies and a decrease on minor declines is of important bullish significance. Conversely, after an extended advance, a decrease of volume on minor rallies and an increase on minor declines is of important bearish significance.

9. As a general rule, volume decreases during a bear market and increases during a bull market. The peaks of volume in bull markets appear **just preceding** the intermediate tops, near the end of major phases. The highest points of volume are seldom at exactly the top levels.

10. During a corrective phase of a bull market, one of the characteristics in judging its termination is a steady decrease in volume, with activity at a low level as the correction reaches its termination, just before the resumption of the major uptrend.

11. In bear markets, selling climaxes are accompanied by a sharp increase in volume, as panic reaches its peak. During rallies in

bear markets (corrective phases), volume shows a tendency to decrease from the high level of the selling climax, but will frequently rise at the top of the corrective phase.

12. Whenever a trend line or moving average, or the upper or lower limit of a Dow Theory "line", or a previous high or low is penetrated, an increase in volume is considered a confirming factor. If the breakaway from the apex of a triangle is accompanied by an increase in activity, it is less likely to be a false one than a movement which occurs on dullness.

Part V

Contemporary Wisdom

It was a long, hard climb, but in the prosperous years following World War II the market finally began to stir the imagination of the public again. It took the Industrials 25 years—until 1954—to recover their 1929 levels. The Rails and Utilities were even slower; it took them 35 years—until 1964—to come back to 1929 levels. In many ways, Wall Street of the Fifties and Sixties started out as a safer and saner place than it had been in the frenzied Twenties. While it still retained many of its old habits and customs, it learned some new tricks. Thus, the contemporary market sages, speaking from their present vantage point, command the special attention of a new generation of investors attempting the age-old profit-making strategies.

BENJAMIN GRAHAM . . The Father of Fundamental Analysis.

HUMPHREY NEILL . . Wall Street Contrarian.

GERALD M. LOEB . . "The Wizard of Wall Street".

GARFIELD A. DREW . . Columbus of the Odd-Lot Theory.

ROBERT D. EDWARDS and JOHN MAGEE . . Master Chart Interpreters.

DR. LEO BARNES . . Collector of Profitable Stock Market Ideas.

BENJAMIN GRAHAM

The Father of Fundamental Security Analysis

It may seem strange to newcomers that anyone still living could merit the label "Father of Security Analysis" when individual stocks have been studied for some 175 years in this country. Yet it is true, for Benjamin Graham is generally credited with the first really penetrating brand of almost scientific security analysis. His concepts are source material for today's fundamental analysis.

As were a surprising number of "greats" in the investment world, Benjamin Graham was born in London, on May 9, 1894. But unlike the others, he was brought to the USA as an infant, in 1895 (and naturalized in 1921).

After gaining a BS degree at Columbia in 1914, at the age of 20, he began working for Newburger, Henderson and Loeb, where he remained until 1923. From 1921-1923 he was a junior partner in the firm (achieving this rank at the age of 27), where he managed investment portfolios.

In 1945, he became president of the Graham-Newman Corporation. Among other posts he has held: director, Government Employees Insurance Co., governor, New York Institute of Finance (where he lectured on security analysis), and more recently, Regents Professor of Finance, University of California at Los Angeles.

But it is in his written works that Graham has made his real mark on Wall Street. His *Security Analysis,* now in its fourth edition, (McGraw-Hill), is the definitive work in its field. In both this book and his more popular *Intelligent Investor,* Graham takes a pro-investment line to stock purchase. He frowns on stock speculation, feeling that there are no sound principles to guide the speculator in the market.

The Wisdom of
BENJAMIN GRAHAM

Stock Selection

(From "THE INTELLIGENT INVESTOR," revised
edition, copyright 1949, 1954 by Harper & Bros.
Reprinted by permission of Harper & Row, Inc.,
Publishers.)

THE SELECTION OF common stocks for the portfolio of the defensive investor is a relatively simple matter. Here we would suggest four rules to be followed:

(1) There should be adequate though not excessive diversification. This might mean a minimum of ten different issues and a maximum of about thirty.

(2) Each company selected should be large, prominent, and conservatively financed. Indefinite as these adjectives must be, their general sense is clear.

(3) Each company should have a long record of continuous dividend payments. The acid test is the payment of dividends during the great depression years, 1931-33. We are reluctant, however, to include 1931-33 dividend payments as a positive requirement here. It would mean carrying the test of investment quality too far backward into the past and thus into circumstances that may no longer be sufficiently relevant to future probabilities. As a logical compromise we would suggest the requirement of continuous dividend payments beginning at least in 1936. This would cover the period now generally referred to as "pre-war."

(4) The price paid for each should be reasonable in relation to its average earnings for the last five years or longer. We would recommend a price not to exceed twenty times such earnings. (Until a record of post-war earnings has been established, we suggest also a price not to exceed twenty-five times the 1936-40 earnings.) This would protect the investor against the common error of buying good stocks at high levels of the general market. It would also bar the purchase, even in normal markets, of a number of fine issues which sell at unduly high prices in anticipation of greatly increased future earnings. We feel that such common stocks are not appropriate for the defensive investor who should not be called upon to use the judgment and foresight necessary to avoid errors in this field.

Investment Company Shares

THE INVESTOR WITH a common stock fund of under $15,000 would be well advised to acquire his list indirectly, through the medium of investment company shares. Most of the shares now being purchased are issued by so-called "open end" companies, which sell their securities continuously through distributing organizations. The price charged includes a mark-up for selling costs, which tend to run about eight per cent of the value of the underlying assets. The shares may be sold back to the company at any time at the then asset value.

Rules for the Appraisal of Common Stocks

(1) The appraised value is determined by (a) estimating the earning power, (b) applying thereto a suitable multiplier, and (c) adjusting, if necessary, for asset value.

(2) The earning power should ordinarily represent an estimate of average earnings for the next five years.

(3) The above estimate should be developed preferably from a projection of the dollar volume and the profit margin. The starting point is the actual exhibit over some period in the past. Under conditions existing in early 1949 there is no "normal period" of past years which can be accepted as a direct measure of future earning power. However, an averaging of the results of an unusually good period and a subnormal period might be acceptable, i.e., giving 50 per cent weight to the 1936-40 average after taxes and 50 per cent weight to 1947-48 or 1946-48.

(4) When figures of earlier years enter into the calculation, proper adjustment should be made for subsequent changes in capitalization.

(5) The multiplier should reflect prospective longer term changes in earnings. A multiplier of 12 is suitable for stocks with neutral prospects. Increases or decreases from this figure must depend on the judgment and preferences

of the appraiser. In all but the most exceptional cases, however, the maximum multiplier should be 20 and the minimum should be 8.

(6) If the tangible-asset value is less than the earning-power value (earning power times multiplier), the latter may be reduced by some arbitrary factor to reflect this deficiency. Our suggested factor is as follows: Deduct one-quarter of the amount by which the earning-power value exceeds twice the asset value. (This permits a 100 per cent premium over tangible assets without penalty.)

(7) If the net-current-asset value exceeds the earning-power value, the latter may be increased by 50 per cent of the excess to give the final appraised value.

(8) Where extraordinary conditions prevail—such as war profits or war restrictions, or a temporary royalty or rental situation—the amount of the total probable gain or loss per share due to such conditions should be estimated and added to, or subtracted from, the appraised value as determined without considering the abnormal conditions.

(9) Where the capitalization structure is highly speculative—that is, where the total of senior securities is disproportionately large—then the value of the entire enterprise should first be determined as if it had common stock only. This value should be apportioned between the senior securities and the common stock on a basis which recognizes the going-concern value of the senior claims. (Note difference between this treatment and a valuation based on dissolution rights of the senior securities.) If an adjustment is needed for extraordinary conditions, as referred to in (8), this should be made in the total enterprise value, not on a per-share-of common basis.

(10) The more speculative the position of the common stock—for whatever reason—the less practical dependence can be accorded to the appraised value found.

(11) Appraised values should be taken as a definite guide to current purchase or sale only if they exceed or fall below the market price by at least one-third. In other cases they may be useful as a supplemental fact in analysis and investment decisions.

Investment in Giant Enterprises

N 1947 *Business Week* ran a little article on the "Billion Dollar Club," in which it referred to American businesses with either assets or sales exceeding $1 billion. In addition to thirty-one banks and insurance companies there were six railroads, three utilities, and nine industrials in this category, as follows:

Railroads: Atchison, B. & O., N. Y. Central, Pennsylvania, Southern Pacific, and Union Pacific.

Utilities: American Tel. & Tel., Commonwealth & Southern, and Consolidated Edison of N.Y.

Industrials: Armour, Great Atlantic & Pacific, Du Pont, General Motors, Sears Roebuck, Standard Oil of N.J., Swift, U.S. Steel.

All of these enterprises have achieved enormous size, and by that token they have presumably made a great success. But how successful are they from the standpoint of the investor? We must first supply our definition of success in this context:

"A successful listed company is one which earns sufficient to justify an average valuation of its shares in excess of the invested capital behind them."

This means that to be really successful (or prosperous) the company must have an earning power value which exceeds the amount invested by and for the stockholder. In the aggregate the industrial issues listed on the New York Stock Exchange sold for more than book value in 1947, and this was true for about three-quarters of the companies in the Dow-Jones Industrial List. The companies in the "billion-dollar club," however, do not show up so well. Only four of the industrials, one of the utilities, and none of the rails sold on the average in 1947 as high as book value. Similarly, most of these issues sold at lower prices in 1947 than they did in 1927. Far from showing the dynamic qualities of growth issues, the group as a whole was unable to maintain its market position vis-a-vis common stocks generally.

If similar data were compiled for the nineteen banking institutions in the billion-dollar class, we are sure they would fail to meet our tests of prosperous operation from the stockholder's standpoint.

It is evident from this analysis that the biggest companies are not the best companies to invest in. (Federal Trade Commission data on the percentage earned on invested capital support this conclusion.) It is equally true that small-sized companies are not suited to the needs of the average investor, although there may be remarkable opportunities in individual concerns in this field. There is some basis here for suggesting that defensive investors show preference to companies in the asset range between $50 million and $250 million, although we have no idea of propounding this as a hard-and-fast rule.

HUMPHREY NEILL

Wall Street Contrarian

Thinking along "unfashionable" lines has always had a certain following. But the leading exponent of Contrary Opinion with regard to the market in the postwar world has been Humphrey Neill.

If the nation thinks peace, he is likely to think war; if the nation thinks war he may think peace. It is not just "opposite" thinking, but rather a refined process and a re-refining to see if what is expected to happen is truly LIKELY to happen. It's an art.

Humphrey Bancroft Neill was born January 21, 1895 in Buffalo, New York. His first writing efforts were in the field of advertising. He has been an economic journalist and business writer most of his life. He lays no claim to being a professional economist; rather prefers to consider himself a socio-economic journalist.

Sometime after he had established the theory on contrary thinking in a formal fashion in 1940, he began publishing, at irregular intervals, an opinion letter. In 1949 it became a fortnightly affair called the Fraser-Neill Letter (together with James L. Fraser).

The service proclaims to discuss business, finance and socio-economics, but in fact it also covers any and all pertinent matters and dwells frequently on the stock market. Politics is a regular subject visitor also. The service is published in Wells, Vermont.

The Wisdom of
HUMPHREY NEILL

Thoughts on the Contrary Opinion Approach

BECAUSE A CROWD does not think but acts on impulses, public opinions are frequently wrong. By the same token because a crowd is carried away by feeling, or sentiment, you will find the public participating enthusiastically in various manias **after** the mania has got well under momentum. This is illustrated in the stock market. The crowd—the public—will remain indifferent when prices are low and fluctuating but little. The public is attracted by activity and by the movement of prices. It is especially attracted by **rising** prices. Thus, in former days a "crowd" could be tempted into the market when a manipulator made a stock active and pushed its price higher.

Is the public wrong **all the time?**

The answer is, decidedly, "No." The public is perhaps right more of the time than not. In stock-market parlance, the public is right **during** the trends but wrong at both ends!

One can assert that the public is usually wrong at junctures of events and at terminals of trends.

328

So, to be cynical, you might say, "Yes, the public is always wrong when **it pays to be right**—but is far from wrong in the meantime.

It is to be noted that the use of contrary opinions will frequently result in one's being rather **too** far ahead of events. A contrary opinion will seldom "time" one's conclusions accurately.

If one relies on the Theory of Contrary Opinion for accurate timing of his decisions he frequently will be disappointed.

Having concentrated for many years on the study of the Theory of Contrary Opinion (and having put my thoughts on paper), I believe it is correct to say that the theory is more valuable in **avoiding** errors in forecasting than in employing it for definite forecasting.

* * * * * *

Let us quickly define that harsh word "gregarious." It means "associating together in herds"—from the Latin word for "Flock."

One of the books found helpful in a study of the art of contrary thinking is *Instincts of the Herd in Peace and War,** by William Trotter. The author bases his sociological thesis on "gregarious man," or the herd instincts in us humans. He asserts that "man is a gregarious animal in literal fact, that he is as essentially gregarious as the bee and the ant, the sheep, the ox, and the horse . . . and that his (man's) conduct furnished incontestable proof of this thesis, which is thus an indispensable clue to any inquiry into the intricate problems of human society.

Very briefly, with the risk of lifting thoughts out of context let us extract Trotter's summary of the more obvious gregarious characteristics we display:

(1) Man is intolerant and fearful of solitude—physical or mental. (I think we all recognize this general characteristic. The vast majority of people dislike to be alone. If we have to spend a day all by ourselves, most of us become bored with our own company within the first hour.)

(2) He is more sensitive to the voice of the herd than to any other

---

*Published by Ernest Benn, Ltd., London.

influence. (This, of course, is the theory of "Following the crowd.")

(3) He is subject to passions of the pack in his mob violence and the passions of the herd in panics. (Economic panics reflect this characteristic also.)

(4) He is remarkably susceptible to leadership. (One immediately thinks of Hitler or Napoleon, but history books contain countless stories of mob leadership.)

(5) His relations with his fellows are dependent upon the recognition of him as a member of the herd. (Here we get into the psychological excuses for "popularity contests," and into the field of modern personnel work and into the new science of "human relations in industry.")

If the habit of contrary thinking does no more than to teach us to develop our own resources—**and to like to be alone occasionally**—it would be worth while; because when alone we might fall into the habit of actually thinking through a given subject, instead of taking the other fellow's word for it. (As one writer has said: If you cannot think through a subject you're through thinking.) If we can learn to think we shall indeed be a member of the **minority!** An aid to thinking is found by taking prominent assertions and allowing your mind to roam over all the "opposites" and "alternates" you can think of. I call this ruminating (or chewing the cud).

This question bobs up constantly: What **is** this theory of contrary opinion?

The reply may be stated in a word: It is a "way" of thinking, but, let me add, let's not overweigh it! Let us give it its proper weight.

Law of Universal Inequality

WHEN THE SOCIAL falsifiers, with their pernicious propaganda, try to make us believe that there should be full equality among everybody, let us contrary realists take heed of Pareto's Law of Universal **In**-equality.

Vilfredo Pareto (1848-1923) was a brilliant engineer, born in Paris of Italian parentage. His discovery of the "distribution of incomes" became known as Pareto's Law while the graphic representation of his law is known as the Pareto Curve.

According to Carl Snyder, Pareto's Law states, in simplest terms, "that the larger incomes are received by comparatively few people, the number with low incomes are more numerous, and as the incomes decrease the number receiving these lower incomes steadily increases in a very smooth curve.

"If we represent graphically by logarithms the various levels of income and the number of persons in receipt of each level of income, the 'curve' so drawn will be a straight line (with minor discrepancies at the extremes of the curve)."

Of what good is Pareto's Law you may be asking yourself. Everyone knows there are millions more poor people than rich ones.

The basic concept that is so important in this law is that those nations which have developed the largest wealthy classes also have the highest standard of living among **all** the population. A moment's reflection on the comparison between, say China and the United States will emphasize this.

Moreover, any long-run **lowering** of the incomes of the top groups will **decrease** the incomes of those all the way down to the bottom. Perhaps it would be clearer to say that any shrinkage in the large income groups would cause a lowering of the standard of living of the groups below. (Short run income decreases, due to temporary heavy taxation, are not considered.)

So, when the social experimenters talk to you about equalizing incomes you can turn to Pareto's Law and demonstrate that if incomes are equalized they will be equalized at **low** levels—and, further, that as time passes the standard of living will sink to the levels of those nations which have relatively few rich.

General welfare is derived from **more** crumbs falling off the **increasing numbers** of wealthy tables; not by taking away the tables and making everybody eat at a trough.

Is the Public Always Wrong in the Market?

THIS QUESTION COMES up repeatedly during any discussion of the contrary theory. It is natural that it should come up, because the idea of money-making the easy way is a popular pastime. And of course it's a fallacy!

Perhaps no undertaking is more difficult than playing the stock market. Only a tiny fraction of those who attempt this "easy way to riches" ever succeed. What defeats them is a little matter of inherent characteristics. (1) A few persons are endowed with the money-making attribute (this, to my mind, you're born with; and if you haven't got it, you'd better forget it! I believe people either have a "money mind" or they haven't); (2) Additionally various human traits stand in the way of this pleasant method of getting rich without working for it, such as the emotional drawbacks of fear, hope, greed, wishful-thinking, and so on.

From these references you can see why the public is wrong so frequently in the stock market. However, a fairly correct, generalized reply to the question in the heading above might be expressed this way:

The "Crowd" has always been found to be wrong when it counted most to be right. This is a bit quippish; a more sedate reply would be that the crowd is wrong at the **terminals** of trends, but it is right, on the average, **during** the trends.

You find the public aiding and "pushing" the trends (up and down) —more actively when the stock market is going up than when it is in a prolonged bear trend. The public loses heart quickly when prices continue to slide off. Thus, we find public selling often increasing as the slide deepens; until finally, near the bottom "when all hope is lost" people dump their stocks—at a time when they should be picking up the bargains.

One might suppose from this that a simple formula of acting in a contrary manner would make it easy to rake in the profits.

However, those traits of human nature have to be dealt with, and they are obstinate obstructionists indeed! Above all, what makes it practically impossible to beat the game is the trait of IMPATIENCE.

Advice on Trading

THIS COUNSEL MAY be the most important I can suggest: trade alone. Close your mind to the opinions of others; pay no attention to outside influences. Disregard reports, rumors, and idle board-room chatter. If you are going to trade actively, and are going to employ your own judgment, then for heaven's sake, stand or fall by your own opinions.

If we all would trade only when the trend is definitely indicated and then patiently wait until the action signifies the probable termination of the move, how much larger our profits would be! Six to twelve successful trades a year, based upon the important, intermediate trends will return far greater profits than countless attempts within the minor fluctuations, whereby a large number of losses must ensue and where profits will be small.

GERALD
M. LOEB

The Wizard of Wall Street

Gerald M. Loeb wrote a book that probably has had more printings since its first edition in 1937 than any book in the history of U. S. financial literature. In that book, as in all his pronouncements he puts forth his basic philosophy that **"FINANCIAL SAFETY LIES ONLY IN DOING THE RIGHT THING WITH MONEY . . . FORGET DIVIDENDS . . . LOOK TO CAPITAL GAINS."**

Loeb was born in 1899 in San Francisco, where he was educated. At 21 he began as a bond salesman for a retail bond dealer in San Francisco. The job lasted only three days because Loeb couldn't sell a share of a security he didn't believe in. His next job was with a NYSE firm in San Francisco, directing people to a customers' man. But many mistook him for a salesman so he took orders and built up 85 customers in 9 months. He put in a 14-hour day, working and studying.

From the start Loeb was his own best customer. One of his principles: "You can't sell anything to anybody if you can't sell it first to yourself." Though employed in the bond department, his interest was heavily in stocks. He wrote signed articles for the San Francisco *Call* and *Post* and other newspapers starting in 1921; they achieved a wide following.

After nine months he left this job (for somewhat similar

reasons to his first quitting), and became San Francisco manager of the Statistical Department of E. F. Hutton and Co. (at the age of 22) taking his 85 customers with him. But before starting the job he went to New York—though he couldn't afford it—to see Wall Street and make contacts. This furthered his career immeasurably. He came back from New York to the west coast brimming with information that would prove to be of great value to his clients.

In 1924 young Loeb returned to New York to stay. Eventually, he rose to partnership in E. F. Hutton and Co., in the course of which he became a millionaire, trading for his own and his customers' accounts. He is constantly asked, by a varied range of publications, for his opinion on the health of the market. If Wall Street has any royalty, G. M. Loeb is one of the leading blue bloods; if not indeed a pretender to the throne.

Loeb's foremost book is *The Battle for Investment Survival,* which has been referred to for so long that people just call it *The Battle.* In 1960 he authored a very slim but useful volume entitled *Loeb's Checklist for Buying Stocks.* Both are published by Simon & Schuster, Publishers.

The Wisdom of
GERALD M. LOEB

Trends and Psychology

(FROM "THE BATTLE FOR INVESTMENT SURVIVAL," 1935)

THERE IS ROOM for much improvement in the average run of statistical analysis attempting to appraise the value of a particular issue. Most of the time the figures considered are not, in my opinion, the useful and vital ones at all, and generally the whole method of approach is academic and theoretical, neglecting fundamental trends which are far more important than statistics on individual issues.

In my opinion, the primary factor in securing market profits lies in sensing the general trend. Are we in a deflation or inflation period? If the former, I would hardly bother to analyze most equities. I have known people to go to the expense of securing a thorough field report on a company, complete except for proper consideration of market factors, buying the stock because of the report and later losing a fortune in it at a time when a market study would have suggested that all equities should be avoided. And I have seen individuals make a great deal of money buying, without much study of individual issues, the leading stocks under circumstances that suggested a fall in money and a rise in shares. Thus effort should be concentrated first on deciding the trend and next in seeking out the most responsive stocks.

I certainly feel that it is more feasible to try to follow profitably a trend upwards or downwards than to attempt to determine the price level. I do not think anyone really knows when a particular security is "cheap" or "dear" in the sense that cheapness would occur around a real market bottom and dearness around a real top. For example, shares have a habit of sometimes seeming dear in the early stages of an advance, and later at far higher levels new and unexpected developments often make them seem cheap again. There is no rule about it.

I have seen stocks make bottoms when they seemed so cheap that one actually mistrusted one's intelligence, and I have seen bottoms reached at times that suggested to the majority that the shares in question were actually a good short sale. The reverse is true for bull-market tops. The money that has been lost "feeling" for the bottom or top never has been generally appreciated. The totals, if they could be known, must be staggering. Naturally we are concerned only with factors influencing security prices that are open to successful interpretation. It would be satisfying always to buy on the bottom and sell on the top, but as we do not know how to determine the bottoms and tops and would lose too much trying to guess, then of course it is only logical to turn our attention to those profitable methods we might actually learn to follow.

The most important single factor in shaping security markets is public psychology. This is really another reason why I am not particularly impressed with academic calculations purporting to show what this or that stock should be worth unless due regard is given to market factors. I feel that the psychology which leads people to pay forty times net (to use that yardstick for an example) for a stock under one set of conditions and refuse to buy the same shares under another set of conditions at ten times is such a powerful and vital price-changing factor that it can overshadow actual earnings trends as an influence on stock prices.

On Tape Reading

IN MY OPINION, far and away the most important thing to master in Wall Street is the tape. It is possible to see only the tape, and nothing else, and make a lot of money. It is a safety valve and automatic check on everything you do if you understand how to read it.

My strong belief in this point of view is another compelling reason for my early insistence on active listed leaders. The best means for judging the rest is simply not at hand. Dealing in outside stocks or bonds without benefit of an active quoted auction market is like firing a steam boiler without a safety valve, or running a train with the signal system out of order. I marvel at the courage of those who do it, but on reflection realize they don't know their danger. I am talking from experience. I have seen the ups and downs of thousands of accounts.

The way to learn to read the tape is to try it. Try it, one stock at a time, with small positions. A very few will have the advantage of knowing someone who understands it. Most of the books and courses (excepting a very few) are theoretical.

One must realize that tape reading and chart reading and all the systems based on using the market's own current action as a forecast of its future are today pretty widespread. I mean by that, practically everyone has a smattering knowledge of them. Of course, what everyone knows isn't worth knowing.

The appearance of each transaction on the tape adds, as it properly should, its mite to determining the market price. One person sees a transaction and thinks it's put there for a reason, so he ignores it or does the opposite of what he feels its appearance is intended to suggest. Another perhaps also thinks he recognizes its character, but feels, coming as it did, that the "sponsorship" is strong and worth following in its current stages anyway. And a third never heard of a transaction occurring for any reason except that someone wanted to buy or sell. He draws still another conclusion. How different is the result than in other lines where things are concealed instead of being brought out into the open.

In any event, the first thing to learn about tape reading is the ability to see the difference between indications recorded on good buying or selling and those which are the result of light-waisted action. This is not any easy thing to do, but is nevertheless essential. Anything one does on the tape is revealing to one who can read it. In the old days, so-called "manipulation," that is, trying to make buyers and sellers react in a common way, was revealing. The good manipulator knew that the very impression he painted on the tape to draw some buying power would generate a certain amount of selling from those who could really understand what they saw.

There are times when one will see "poor buying." But if it is just the start, one might want to follow right along as it sometimes takes months to fill all the outside buy orders once the public gets the bit in its teeth. On the other hand, at the point where every last elevator boy is in stocks, then additional desultory "poor buying" would be a bad thing to follow indeed.

My main point is to develop a realistic attitude; 99.99% and more of those who try to deal in Wall Street think they are right and the tape is wrong. But it's the tape that is watched by both the margin clerk and the tax collector. Stocks that are high and going higher are a good buy. Stocks that are "cheap" and growing cheaper don't interest me from a buying angle.

Statistics, mentioned above, are useful at times and have their place. Sometimes stocks are deadlocked. Statistics are useful in helping to suggest (along with other things) which way they may break out of that sidewise zone. However, I class the tape first and indispensable, and, second, accurate information from brokers and banks on the kinds and amount of buyers, sellers, loans, etc. Then come statistics and all the rest.

1929 Experiences

ACK IN 1929 I had the "privilege" of seeing a very extensive report on a listed corporation. I think it was reputed to have cost $10,000. It was bound in leather. The people who had this compiled bought a lot of the stock analyzed and lost a fortune doing it. Why? Because they stressed individual statistics instead of the tape and because they made several other common mistakes such as forgetting the importance of correct "timing."

At a time like 1929 no real tape reader would have committed an error like this. I actually bought a client 10,000 Radio at 110 as I recall it. I thought it was going straight up. It didn't and we were out at 109.

I saw the top in 1929 and sold stocks in time. It came about, as well as I can recall, something like this: All stocks, of course, did not reach their best prices simultaneously. The issues we traded in not only changed during the year but also narrowed in number. Thus, as this stock and that began to "act" badly, I was switching into those that still acted well. This of itself would eventually result in getting us out altogether. But there were other signs. Ordinary statistics were of no use. Steel common looked cheap enough above 250 on earnings of above $25 a share.

The vogue those days was investment trusts. One house had a special reputation along that line. I forget, but I think it was their third issue. If any new issue (or old one for that matter) should have been a success, that was it. But shortly after the offering it was supported by a "syndicate bid." Well, if ever there was a sign of a market that was overbought here it was. If people couldn't or wouldn't buy that, what could or would they buy? Of course, that wasn't all. There were brokers trying to keep clients from buying more stocks because they couldn't finance them. It was things like this, that told the top of the market. And after the top, the tape told the tale of 1930 and 1931 when the oracles were saying all the way down that everything was OK again.

"Better Late _____ *"*

THERE IS NO rule about anything in the stock market save perhaps one. That rule is that the key to market tops and bottoms or the key to market advances or declines will never work more than once. The lock, so to speak, is always changed. Therefore, a little horse sense is far more useful than a lot of theory.

However, in a broad way the averages work in favor of those that assume the trend in being will continue until proven changed. This applies both for the company in question, industrially speaking, and price trend of a stock, tape-wise.

"Never argue with the tape" is one saying worth thinking about.

In order for the trend in being to change direction there has to be a change in the influences that caused the trend in the first place. Those that can detect this change before it occurs and becomes generally evident are gifted with powers of analysis and foresight of the very highest order. For most of us detecting the change after it has occurred but before it has proceeded too far is still a very profitable and to many an attainable goal. I think on the average it is better for most of us to be **late and sure** than to be early and doubtful. Many, who thought that various levels on the way down after 1929 to 1932 were buying or turning points, lost the most. The late buyer who came in after 1933 and up quite a bit from the bottom, did quite all right.

Technical Observations

THE **first** new highs for the year after a weak spell usually mean a lot. After scores of shares have been making new highs, the addition of new ones is meaningless.

Volume of trading is also an important factor. It is difficult to define in positive terms. If you are driving a car you can get to your destination more quickly at 50 m.p.h. than at 10 m.p.h. But you may wreck the car at 100 m.p.h. In a similar way increasing volume on an advance up to a point is bullish and decreasing volume on a rally is bearish, but in both cases only up to a point. There are a great many varying circumstances. Experience is the best teacher. Observe the variation in volume, and in time you will learn what it indicates.

GARFIELD
A. DREW

Columbus of the Odd-Lot Theory

One of the most widely accepted technical methods of measuring stock market sentiment is the Odd Lot Index. It was not always so. The man chiefly responsible for their popularization, refinement and interpretation, the Christopher Columbus of the Odd Lot Theory, is Garfield Albee Drew.

Drew was born October 8, 1903, to an old New England family, in Dedham, Massachusetts. He went to Wall Street after graduation from Harvard in 1926, sat out the 1929 crash and early years of depression as a bond statistician. He was later employed by Babson's United Business Service in Boston, and during this period "discovered" odd lots.

In 1940 he published his first treatise on odd lot research and received so many letters from interested investors that he expanded his research into a book. The reception to the book was so gratifying that he set up his own investment service in 1949 with the odd lot concept as its base. He keeps an office in Boston but does most of his work at his home in Newton Center, Massachusetts.

On his choice for a location he said: "What's the point of being in Wall Street? Out here you're aloof from the scuttlebutt, the emotions and social entanglements of life in a financial district." He spends most of his time in sport clothes.

Time magazine called him "The Small Investor's Boswell," and his market philosophy has been widely quoted on the nation's financial pages.

Drew wrote *New Methods for Profits in the Stock Market* in 1941, for Metcalf Press in Boston. Revised editions have been issued since. Most of the passages here from Drew lore are to be found in this volume.

The Wisdom of
GARFIELD A. DREW

The Odd Lotters

(FROM "NEW METHODS FOR STOCK MARKET PROFIT," 1941)

THE TRADING PUBLIC is ordinarily most interested in **this** day, **this** week, and **this** month. It is far more concerned with market movements than with intrinsic values. Business prospects, earnings, and dividends mean little in comparison with a ten point rally or decline, and it is in its largely futile attempts to "catch" these moves perfectly that the public is "wrong."

To go back, a second and more important factor usually missed on odd lot trading is that—because it is essentially a speculative "quick-turn" affair—its volume is always directly proportional to the total volume of trading. Therefore, it is not the number of shares bought or sold on balance that is important, but the proportions of buying or selling to each other.

Most important, however, is the fact that **THE TREND OF SENTIMENT AS INDICATED BY THE ODD LOT BALANCE OF TRADING IS MORE IMPORTANT THAN THE SIDE ON WHICH THE BALANCE LIES.**

Both of the comments quoted above drew their conclusions from whether a buying or selling balance actually existed prior to any given market movement, and disregarded entirely the significance of changes in the size of either balance. To illustrate, odd lot trading will be well on the buying side at the bottom of a drastic decline, but it will be proportionately less so than it was on the way down. The weekly balances never show a preponderance of selling around important bottoms, although on a few individual days there may be such a balance. Primarily, it is always just a matter of less buying. The converse is true with respect to odd lot selling on a top, although here there will be more times when an actual buying balance exists.

These conclusions were derived from a statistical usage of the daily odd lot purchases and sales (available continuously since March, 1936) which will be described later. However, they are also borne out by the monthly data employed by the Brookings Institution which found that on the more important trends the odd lot public invariably bought on declines. Its action on advances was about equally divided between buying and selling.

Thus, although the public is never "wrong" in the sense that it buys around every bottom, it is almost invariably wrong in that it buys proportionately less at the bottom than it did on the way down. Similarly, as an advance progresses toward its peak, selling may either become less or change to actual buying. A change of sentiment on the part of the public after any market trend has become well established is almost always just the opposite of what it should be.

On Stocks and Cash

T HE AVERAGE INVESTOR likes to keep his money "working" for as large a return as possible, and ordinarily abhors what he feels is the futility of holding cash or the equivalent (such as high-grade, short-term bonds). What he fails to realize is that, in a period of declining stock prices, cash which is allocated to common stocks is actually an appreciating asset. If an investor sells a stock at 100, holds the proceeds of the sale until the price reaches 50, and then reinvests in the same issue, his money has doubled in terms of that stock since he can buy with the same amount of dollars twice as many shares as he sold.

The "Industry Group" Approach

I T HAS BEEN pointed out that if the right industries could be selected, it would be possible always to be invested in common stocks which were in a rising price trend. Even in the devastating bear market of 1929-1932, gold stocks were an exception to the rule of declining prices. All other things being equal, a business depression benefits gold producers because the full production can be sold at a fixed price, while costs go down. Thus, the investor would have enjoyed a constantly increasing value who had bought steels in 1915, switched into merchandising stocks in 1918, oils in 1919, rails in 1920, utilities in 1922, electrical equipments in 1926, gold shares in 1929, liquor shares in 1932, silver shares in 1933, automobiles in 1935, aircrafts in 1938-39, railroads in 1941, amusements in 1945, oils in 1946, and no doubt **something** in 1948.

Using hindsight, it is easy to see what could have been done in this respect. In practice, it obviously involves putting all investment eggs in one basket. Few would dare to go to this extreme. Secondly, it involves a tremendous amount of one sort of "forecast"—in fact, a far more difficult type of forecast than is ordinarily the case with "timing." To buy gold stocks in 1929, for example, the investor would have had to foresee a long business depression of considerable severity. At the other extreme, he might have sold on the basis of the Dow Theory or some other trend method, content merely to wait until the trend proved to have changed and without any attempt to foresee exactly what might happen.

Growth Stocks

T HE THIRD APPROACH which eliminates timing attempts to solve the problem of confining all purchases to "growth stocks" on the comfortable theory that, whatever happens to them temporarily in declining markets, they will always go ahead to new highs afterward. Growth stocks are the equities of companies whose earnings have demonstrated underlying long-term growth and give indications of continued secular growth in the future.

As a group, chemicals have been the most outstanding example of "growth stocks" within the last two decades. The 1929 investor in Monsanto Chemical at its high (equivalent for the present stock) of 13½, for example, suffered during the next three years when the price dropped to 2¼, but he saw it recover to his cost in 1933, reach new highs at 36 and 40 in 1937 and 1940, drop again to 22 in 1942, and hit a new all-time high at 64 in 1946-47. Basically, this reflected a long-term expansion in sales and earnings, due to the exploitation of new discoveries and products by an exceptionally able management. Conversely, the stocks of some older and more mature companies like U.S. Steel, American Telephone, and General Electric have never since come anywhere near their 1929 highs.

There are obvious advantages in the theory of growth stock investment, but there are still many risks in that some unforeseen element may change the growth factor, or so great a premium may be paid for it that the anticipated new highs do not materialize, to say nothing of the fact that a severe business depression and bear market would—temporarily at least—make the picture look extremely sick.

Like Monsanto, the outstanding "growth stocks" of the last twenty years sold at higher prices in 1937 than in 1929 and at higher prices in 1946 than in 1937, but how many could have been initially selected? Few investors had ever heard of Monsanto in 1929, and if they believed in the long-term future of the chemical industry would have been much more likely to have selected duPont. As an individual organization, it was simply farther along the road to maturity at that time.

The point is that "growth stocks" are seldom outstandingly attractive by the time their growth qualities are widely recognized. This may conceivably be true of the chemicals today. The potentialities of the industry have been so widely touted for several years that the investor at present price levels for the stocks of the leading companies is already paying a considerable premium for those potentialities. Stocks of even the most promising companies frequently sell at levels which only the remote future can justify, and at times discount even the future beyond the point of ultimate realization. Price-to-earnings ratios of 20 or 25 for some chemical stocks are, in effect, already discounting a doubling of earnings at the potential peak that may or may not materialize. Even if it does, the stocks would not necessarily be worth then more than they are selling for now, since the attainment of earnings maturity would not justify the same high price-to-earnings ratios that now exist. Hence, to invest most successfully in growth companies, one must recognize them for what they are—or will be—well ahead of the crowd and thus buy only at a reasonable price.

None of the foregoing comments is intended to disparage the "growth stock" approach. It is a more practical solution than the attempt always to be in the exceptional industry group. On the other hand, as a long-term program, it is a difficult one for the individual investor or even the professional analyst because it is likely to require the most intimate and continuous knowledge of companies and managements as well as industry prospects. The individual probably has a better chance with "timing," because the assumption is not justified that growth stock investment is the best answer on the ground that "forecasting" is impossible. Granting that mistakes will inevitably be made in dealing with the price swings, it is certainly questionable whether there is not just as much room for error in attempting to pick growth stocks at the right time and price.

On the Technical Approach

EVEN THE FUNDAMENTALISTS who decry "technical market timing" say that purchases should only be made when the general price level is low and then sold when the level is high "as judged by objective standards"—something that is likely to result in very poor timing indeed. How high is high? Stocks seemed irrationally "high" in 1927 to experienced investors, but during the next two years they went much higher. Similarly, they seemed "low" in 1931, but they soon after sold at one-third of their average price of that year.

There have been frequent occasions when technical analysis was the **only** thing that could possibly have given the correct answer to the future trend of the market. This was true, for example, in the spring of 1946. If any investor had then possessed a crystal ball which would have shown him what corporate earnings were to be a year later, he could only have concluded that stock prices would be considerably higher. Instead, they were substantially lower in the face of record earnings and dividends.

There was nothing in the "fundamentals"—either in 1946 or 1947—to explain why prices had collapsed in the meantime. But there was considerable evidence of a weak **technical** situation in the market beforehand. . . . It did not seem to make sense, but it was there. The investor who acted on technical grounds did not need to concern himself with **why** the market should seem to be acting irrationally, whereas the analyst of business facts and possibilities—unable to find a "reason"—was forced to conclude that the market could not do what it actually did.

On Predicting the Averages

IN EARLY MAY, 1946, a well-known financial editor asked five specialists in railroad securities to tell him where they thought the Dow-Jones Railroad Average —then around 63—would be in three months, six months, and twelve months. The independent answers of all five were surprisingly close for each period of time, but the average level predicted compared as follows with the facts.

	Average Predicted Level	Actual Level
After three months	65.4	62
After six months	83.4	50
After twelve months	106.0	43

Thus, for the prediction covering one year, there was actually a decline of nearly 32% as against an anticipated gain of more than 68%. Now, the point is that the analysts polled were not amateurs carried away by bullish enthusiasm. Their forecasts were based on sober, expert appraisal of what railroad earning power would be, and in this respect, they were entirely correct.

But, to predict a market level involves another type of forecast. It is necessary not only to estimate future earnings correctly, but in addition to form an opinion as to how those earnings will be appraised by future buyers and sellers. In other words, will investment psychology be pessimistic or optimistic? The particular group involved here not unnaturally assumed that railroad stocks would continue to sell in the same relationship to earnings that prevailed at the time they were making their calculations. For that reason only, their forecast of market prices proved to be entirely wrong.

Price Earnings Ratios and Psychology

N A BROAD sense, the experience of the past ten years has very clearly demonstrated that the price-to-earnings ratio is a much more important factor than the actual level and/or trend of earnings themselves. Since the ratio is determined by investment psychology, the study of technical market action has, on the whole, been more fruitful than fundamental analysis. As in the case of the railroad analysts, it was quite possible to be perfectly correct in estimating future earnings, but entirely wrong on the level of stock prices at the same time.

From 1938 to 1948, earnings and stock prices pursued different courses. The reasons for the diverse trends are quite understandable, but it should nevertheless have been an illuminating experience for the businessman investor accustomed to an orthodox relationship.

Corporate profits were at their lowest ebb in 1938 when the Dow-Jones Industrial Average rose to nearly 160—a level not seen again until 1945. Profits more than doubled, however, from 1938 through 1941 in reflection of war and "defense" orders, but because of the war background, stock prices pursued a downward course. Excess profits taxes and—later—strikes and material shortages brought about a generally declining trend in earnings during the 1942-46 period, but stock prices rose in anticipation of the high postwar profits which actually materialized by 1947. Again conforming to contrary and apparently illogical behavior, however, the stock market dropped in 1946-47 as corporate earnings rose sharply. Investor psychology swung to the view that such earnings were just too good to last.

ROBERT D. EDWARDS

and

JOHN MAGEE

Master Chart Interpreters

Whether investors are individually pro or anti-charts they can probably agree on one point: the best source book and authority on chart interpretation is a work by Edwards and Magee.

Edwards is related to R. W. Schabacker, who was the first man to spell out chart patterns in early Wall Street years.

John Magee, a close friend and disciple of Edwards, is a graduate of Massachusetts Institute of Technology and initially approached the stock market from an engineering point of view.

Specializing in horticulture at Cornell, Robert Edwards worked for a time for W. Atlee Burpee of Philadelphia. When his brother-in-law, R. W. Schabacker, died in the late 1930's, Edwards took over the management of the Schabacker Institute. In 1941 he came to Springfield, Massachusetts, where he worked for 10 years as Senior Technician for the Stock Trend Service, a position which was later filled by John Magee.

With Magee, he went over the work of Schabacker and added to it using the basic material as a foundation for a refined and greatly expanded statement of technical theory, which became "Technical Analysis of Stock Trends," the definitive volume on the subject, which in its successive revisions and re-publications had, by 1964, reached the fourteenth printing of its fourth edition.

On leaving Springfield in 1951, Edwards moved to South Carolina, where he became a teacher of science at the Georgetown High School with which he is still connected.

John Magee has remained in the investment field. He is president of John Magee, Inc., Springfield, Massachusetts, which maintains daily charts of most listed stocks on the New York and American Stock Exchanges. Copies of these are supplied on request to clients, and they form the foundation of a stock advisory service. The organization also publishes books, and produces chart paper and supplies for market technicians.

Magee has written a number of articles for national publications, has lectured and conducted seminars in his subjects, and was a member of the faculty of the Springfield Evening Adult Schools for eight years, teaching a course on "The Semantics of Wall Street."

The Wisdom of
EDWARDS AND MAGEE

An Outline of the Technical Approach

T IS EASY, in a detailed study of the many and fascinating phenomena which stock charts exhibit, to lose sight of the fact that they are only the rather imperfect instruments by which we hope to gauge the relative strength of supply and demand, which in turn exclusively determines what way, how fast and how far a stock will go.

Remember that in this work it doesn't in the least matter what **creates** the supply and the demand. The fact of their existence and the balance between them are all that count. No man, no organization (and we mean this **verbatim et literatim**) can hope to know and accurately to appraise the infinity of factual data, mass moods, individual necessities, hopes, fears, estimates and guesses which, with the subtle alterations ever proceeding in the general economic framework, combine to generate supply and demand. But the summation of all these factors is reflected virtually instantaneously in the market.

The technical analyst's task then is to interpret the action of the market itself—to read the flux in supply and demand mirrored therein. For this task, charts are the most satisfactory tools thus far devised. Lest you become enrapt, however, with the mechanics of the chart—the minutiae of daily fluctuations—ask yourself constantly, "What does this action really mean in terms of supply and demand?"

Judgment is required, and perspective, and a constant reversion to first principles. A chart, as we have said and should never forget, is not a perfect tool; it is not a robot; it does not give all the answers quickly, easily and positively, in terms that anyone can read and translate at once into certain profit.

We have examined and tested exhaustively many technical theories, systems, indexes and devices which have not been discussed in this book, chiefly because they tend to short-circuit judgment to seek the impossible by a purely mechanical approach to what is very far indeed from a purely mechanical problem. The methods of chart analysis which have been presented herein are those which have proved most useful because they are relatively simple and for the most part, easily rationalized, because they stick closely to first principles; because they are of a nature that does not lead us to expect too much of them; because they supplement each other and work well together.

Let us review these methods briefly. They fall roughly into four categories:

PART I

The area patterns or formations of price fluctuation which, with their concomitant volume, indicate an important change in the supply-demand balance. They can signify consolidation, a recuperation or gathering of strength for renewed drive in the **same direction** as the trend which preceded them. Or they can indicate reversal, the playing out of the forces formerly prevailing and the victory of the opposing force, resulting in a new drive in the **reverse direction.** In either case, they may be described as periods during which energy is brewed or pressure built up to propel prices in a move (up or down) which can be turned to profit. Some of them provide an indication as to how far their pressure will push prices.

These chart formations, together with volume, furnish the technician with most of his "get in" and many of his "get out" signals.

Volume, which has not been discussed in this book as a feature apart from price action and which cannot, in fact, be utilized as a technical guide by itself, deserves some further comment. Remember that it is **relative,** that it tends naturally to run higher near the top of a Bull Market than near the bottom of a Bear Market. Volume "follows the trend"; i.e., it increases on rallies and decreases on reactions in an over-all up trend, and vice-versa. But use this rule judiciously; do not place too much dependence on the showing of a few days, and bear in mind that **even in a Bear Market** (except during panic moves) there is always a slight tendency for activity to pick up on rises. **("Prices can fall of their own weight, but it takes buying to put them up.")**

A notable increase in activity, as compared with previous days or weeks, may signify either the beginning (breakout) or the end (climax) of a move, temporary or final. (More rarely it may signify a "shake-out.") Its meaning in any given case can be determined by its relation to the price pattern.

PART II

Trend and trendline studies, which supplement area patterns as a means of determining the general direction in which prices are moving and of detecting changes in direction. Although lacking in many cases the nice definition of area formations, they may frequently be used for "get in" and "get out" purposes in short-term trading, and they provide a defense against premature relinquishment of profitable long-term positions.

PART III

Support and resistance levels created by the previous trading and investing commitments of others. They may serve to indicate where it should pay to take a position, but their more important technical function is to show where a move is likely to slow down or end, at what level it should encounter a sudden and important increase in supply or demand as the case may be.

Before entering a trade, look both to the pattern of origin for an indication of the power behind the move and to the history of support resistance for an indication as to whether it can proceed without difficulty for a profitable distance. Support resistance studies are especially useful in providing "cash in" or "switch" signals.

PART IV

Broad market background, including the Dow Theory. Do not scorn this time-tested device for designating the (presumed) prevailing Major trend of the market. Its signals are "late" but, with all its faults (and one of these is the greatly augmented following it has acquired in recent years, resulting in a considerable artificial stimulation of activity at certain periods), it is still an invaluable adjunct to the technical trader's kit of tools.

The general characteristics of the various stages in the stock market's great Primary Bull and Bear cycles should never be lost to view. This brings us back to the idea of **perspective** which we emphasized as essential to successful technical analysis at the beginning of our summary. It is true that you cannot buy or sell "the market"; you can deal only in individual stocks. But that stock which does not to some degree follow the Major trend of the market as a whole is an extraordinary exception. More money has been lost by buying perfectly good stocks in the later and most exciting phases of a Bull Market and then selling them, perhaps from necessity in the discouraging conditions prevailing in a Bear Market than from all other causes combined!

So, keep your perspective on the broad market picture. The basic economic tide is one of the most important elements in the supply-demand equation for each individual stock. It may pay to buck "the public" but it does not pay ever to buck the real underlying trend.

Major Bull and Bear Markets have recurred in fairly regular pattern throughout all recorded economic history and there is no reason to suppose that they will not continue to recur for as long as our present system exists. It is well to keep in mind that caution is in order whenever stock prices are at historically high levels, and that purchases will usually work out well eventually when they are at historically low levels.

DR. LEO
BARNES

Collector of Profitable Stock Market Ideas

Professor, analyst, editor, and author, Dr. Leo Barnes is one of America's best known contemporary writers on finance and investment. At the time this is published he is Professor and Chairman of the Department of Finance and Investments at The School of Business of Hofstra University, and is also a member of the Editorial Board of *Business Economics,* the journal of the National Association of Business Economists. He has taught and lectured in his chosen field at Johns Hopkins, Brown, Rutgers, the City University of New York and the New School for Social Research, and has also been engaged as a consultant on investments and economics for many large corporations.

Dr. Barnes is widely known as the author and compiler of *Your Investments,* one of the best selling stock market books of the past decade, and also authored *Buying Guide to Mutual Funds and Investment Companies* (five editions 1956-60), *Handbook for Business Forecasting* (1950), and was a contributor to the *Encyclopedia of Stock Market Techniques* (1963), the *Business Finance Handbook* (1953), and is a frequent contributor to the Financial Analyst's Journal. Just prior to his present post at Hofstra University, he was chief economist for Prentice Hall, Inc.

The Wisdom of
DR. LEO BARNES

How to Beat Market Swings by Formula Plans

(FROM "YOUR INVESTMENTS," 1966 EDITION)

ORMULA PLANS ARE designed in advance for automatic buying and selling action when the predetermined signals are given. In most forms, they compel caution in bull markets and bravery in bear markets. They automatically (even if only partially) achieve the investment target of buying cheap and selling dear. They impel you to sell as prices rise and force you to buy as prices decline.

Formula plans can definitely improve the batting average of most investors. While they deliberately avoid maximum **theoretical** profits, they more than make up for this by substantially cutting potential losses. Only the exceptional investor or speculator can hope to outperform a good formula plan **in the long run.**

Many different formula plans have been introduced, developed, and perfected since 1937. In this chapter, you will find typical examples of more popular and useful formula plans. You will also find some simplifications and modifications of such plans that will make them easier to use. You will probably be able to tailor at least one plan for your own use.

CONSTANT DOLLAR FORMULA PLANS

This is the simplest type of formula plan. It is probably also the least effective. You simply decide in advance how many **dollars** you wish to have invested in stocks. Then, if the market rises, at predetermined time intervals (say quarterly), you sell stocks to reduce your holdings to that dollar value. If the market declines, you buy stocks to raise your holdings to that dollar value. When you sell stocks, you either buy bonds with the proceeds or put the money in a savings account.

This method is obviously easy, but gains are very limited.

CONSTANT RATIO PLANS

In this type of plan, you decide in advance what per cent of your investment funds should be in stocks—say 40%, 50%, 60%, or 70%. Then, at predetermined time intervals, you sell or buy stocks to restore or maintain the predetermined ratio of stocks regardless of the level of stock prices.

EXAMPLE: You start with an investment fund of $15,000. You decide that you should keep 60% of it (or $9,000 to start) in good quality common stocks, and the remaining 40% of it (or $6,000 to start) partly in E bonds and partly in savings and loan accounts. You buy accordingly.

After six months, you find that the stock market has risen, so that the total value of your fund is $2,000 more, or $17,000. Your stocks are now worth $11,000. That is roughly 65% of $17,000. Therefore, you must sell $800 worth of stocks to reduce your holdings to $10,200, or 60% of $17,000. You then put more in savings and loan accounts with the $800 (less commissions and taxes).

You thus have salted away some of your bull market profits, but also have kept some of them invested for a possible further gain. And, because you have bought more fixed income investments, you are not as vulnerable to a decline.

Suppose, however, that your $15,000 investment fund was set up just before the market took a turn for the worse. In six months, instead of rising in value by $2,000 it declines by that amount. Your total fund is now worth only $13,000. Your stocks are now valued at $7,000, 54% of $13,000.

Under your constant ratio formula, you must now buy $800 more of stocks to bring your stockholdings up to $7,800, or 60% of $13,000. You use some of your savings and loan funds to do this.

You do it no matter how scared you are that the market is going to drop some more. When you are following a formula plan, you soon learn to regard falling prices as a chance to buy more stocks at a lower price to help make up paper losses.

WHEN TO ADJUST PORTFOLIOS

How often do you change your portfolio to restore the predecided stock ratio? Obviously, you do not want to do it too often. If you do, you cut your profits short and run up your commissions and taxes excessively. Therefore, in practice, before restoring your stock ratio, you should wait until the value of your total fund has increased or decreased by at least 10%. Many followers of this simple formula approach prefer to wait for a 15% or 20% move.

If you are an inexperienced investor, the constant ratio plan is probably a good jumping-off point for formula-type investing—with part of your funds only. It will work only in a complete market cycle—both down and up. It will work well only if that cycle included some comparatively wide swings. It does not make much money on narrower fluctuations. To take advantage of smaller price shifts, various variable ratio formula plans have been developed.

VARIABLE RATIO PLANS

Under such plans, the percentage of stocks in a fund is stepped up as stock prices decline and lowered as stock prices rise. For example, at bull market peaks, you are only 5-10% in stocks, 90-95% in bonds.

At bear market bottoms you are 90-95% in stocks, only 5-10% in bonds.

This obviously gives better results than the constant ratio plan. You have bought substantially more stock at low prices and sold substantially more stock at high prices. For this reason, it is mathematically certain that a variable ratio plan will do better than either the average investor or the "buy-and-hold-forever" investor—but only as long as the stock market continues to fluctuate around some central average.

There are four main problems you face in setting up a variable ratio formula plan. You can best understand the whole technique if you think about these problems.

1. How to get the central stock price average? Any variable ratio formula plan revolves around the central average or median market price selected. How do you determine it? Do you use historical price ranges? Or do you rely on average price-earnings ratios, average price-dividend ratios, or average stock-bond yield spreads?

2. What stock-bond ratios? What ratios of stocks and bonds (or, more generally, aggressive securities and defensive investments) should be maintained at estimated market highs, market lows, and average market levels? For example, are you 50% in stocks and 50% in bonds at the estimated average? A more conservative ratio? A more speculative ratio?

3. How many price zones? How many different price zones or percentage ratios or steps should you set up? Do you have price zones for every 5% change in ratios, every 10%, or every 20%?

4. How often to buy and sell? When and how often do you buy or sell securities to achieve the indicated ratios? Do you buy or sell as soon as a particular step is reached, or do you wait? Do you have different rules for changing ratios in bull markets and in bear markets?

DETERMINING THE CENTRAL STOCK PRICE AVERAGE

Successful operation of a variable ratio formula plan depends largely on the selection of a properly located average or median zone. If—for example, because of either runaway or creeping inflation—stock market prices zoom far above your selected median and never return, your formula plan will quickly become utterly obsolete. You will be completely in bonds or cash and never permitted to get back into stocks. On the other hand, should your averages zone be placed too high, your formula plan will be operating on a more speculative basis than you originally intended. The first predicament has often happened; the latter, rarely if ever.

Three kinds of answers to this basic problem have been developed over the past 20-plus years.

THE HISTORICAL APPROACH

Here the middle zone is set in terms of stock price patterns of the past, presumably with more attention paid to the recent past. No long-term growth trend in stock prices is assumed. In the depression '30's, before World War II and after the stock market debacle of 1929, such an approach was natural.

What has happened to formula plans using this approach? A dramatic answer is given by the fate of one of the first variable ratio formula plans—that of Vassar College, started in 1938. Under its zoning timetable, the fund was supposed to be completely out of stocks and completely in bonds when the Dow-Jones Industrial average hit the (post 1929) historically high level of 206. That point was reached in 1945 and, in its old form, the fund would not have bought since then.

THE GROWTH OR TREND APPROACH

To overcome the error of the strictly historical approach illustrated above, it is here assumed that the stock market is in a definite long-term upward trend. Therefore, the central zone of a formula plan should be higher each year, in step with the long-term trend.

An example of this approach is the "Seven Step Variable Ratio Plan," several formulations of which have been used by the Keystone Custodian Funds of Boston.

The original plan was based on 1897-1941 experience, which showed stock prices rising an average of 3% per year. When this pace of increase turned out to be inadequate for the bull market of the fifties, a second plan was developed in terms of an average stock price gain of 4.4% per year, based on 1933-1957 experience.

But even this pace of gain was unable to keep up with the bull market of the late fifties and early sixties. So a third formula plan, based on 1946-1957 experience of an average 8.2% gain in stock prices per year, came into force.

Even under this most generous formulation, in late 1964 investors would have been 80-90% in bonds or other defensive holdings, and only 10-20% in common stocks.

THE RATIO OR "CASUAL" APPROACH

The growth approach, like the historical approach it supplanted, is still open to the criticism that it relies too much on historical stock price levels. The fact that stock averages have risen an average of 3% per year—or 8% per year—for many years is no guarantee that they will continue to do so. What's more, in any single year, stocks could rise or fall 25% or more, rather than rise 3% or 8%. Therefore, any plan tied directly to specific price ranges is not fully satisfactory. It cannot achieve maximum year-to-year results.

What is needed is a means of tying a formula plan to the determinants of stock prices, rather than to stock prices themselves. In this way, if the factors determining stock prices change—because of inflation, the growing importance of institutional investment, some basic change in investor psychology, or for any other reason—the formula plan will not be automatically and swiftly outmoded.

This is the essence of the ratio or "casual" approach to formula planning. Here the central price zone is geared not to price levels as such, but to some measure which, it is believed, determines, reflects, or anticipates the level of stock prices.

Favorite measures that have been used for this purpose include latest reported overall dividend yields and price-earnings ratios. Alternatively, price-cash-flow ratios could be employed. Or a strictly economic (rather than financial) measure—like the level of total national product (GNP)—could be utilized.

It is even possible that a formula plan could be geared to some strictly technical yardstick rather than a basic value measure. A single favored technical indicator could be used. It probably would be more fruitful, however, to link a formula plan with some consensus of a number of technical indicators.

To illustrate formula plans based on all these possible variations, and to facilitate your own formula planning, we have drawn up three alternative plans—each geared to overall dividend yields, price-earnings ratios, price-cash-flow ratios, and a consensus of technical indicators— that seem suitable for market conditions in 1966-68.

The difference among the three plans shown on the inside back cover is highlighted by the nature of the portfolios they called for in September 1965, when the Dow-Jones industrial average was about 935, the DJIA price-earnings ratio about 18 to 1, and its price-cash-flow ratio about 10.5 to 1. Under the ultra-conservative plan, you would have been down to 35% in stocks and 65% in bonds, cash, or cash equivalents. Under the conservative plan, your stock-bond ratio would be 50-50. Under the moderately speculative plan, you would have been 65% in stocks, 35% in bonds, cash, or equivalents.

Other, more complicated standards have also been developed for formula plans based on the ratio or casual approach. Perhaps the one which has achieved the greatest public interest is that of Graham, Dodd, and Cottle in their *Security Analysis* (fourth edition, 1962).

The authors work out a central annual value for the Dow-Jones industrials in terms of average earnings of the 30 D-J stocks for the previous 10 years, capitalized on a basis equivalent to 1.33 times the recent yield of top-grade bonds. In earlier editions, Mr. Graham had called for capitalizing stocks at twice the yield of high-grade bonds.

Even with the current more generous capitalization for stocks, fair price levels under the formula were far below actual stock prices near the end of 1965, and would have called for the sale of all common stock holdings. Indeed, the formula would have missed the entire 1961-65 bull market.

CONSERVATIVE OR SPECULATIVE STOCK-BOND RATIOS

Ratios can be varied all the way from 100% stocks at estimated bear market lows to 100% bonds at estimated bull market highs. For any plan, you have to work out a range table similar to those exemplified in the plans on the inside back cover, indicating the ratios of defensive and aggressive investments in your portfolios in the seven zones.

A crucial test of your conservative or speculative approach occurs at the estimated average or median price range or bracket, around which you assume stock market prices will fluctuate. In such a median bracket, the ultraconservative investor may decide to be 65% in bonds and 35% in stocks. The moderately conservative investor may decide to be 50% in both bonds and stocks. A more speculative investor may choose to be only 35% in defensive securities and 65% in common stocks at the center point.

It is instructive, however, to note the conclusions of a careful study of variable ratio formula plans made by the First National Bank of Birmingham, Alabama, under the direction of Mr. Charles F. Zukoski, Jr. The study examined the relative results over the 25-year period from 1924 to 1950 with different stock-bond ratios at the median range. This span of years covers both the incredible speculative boom of 1929 and the equally incredible bust of 1932-33.

Conclusion of the study: The larger the per cent of common stocks required by the formula at the median range, the greater the capital appreciation and income received over the whole 25-year period. What's more, within the 25 years, funds using higher stock ratios did not fall in value below those using lower stock ratios—even in the depression years of 1932-33 or in the sharp market breaks of 1937 and 1942.

HOW TO IMPROVE FORMULA PLAN RESULTS

The very essence of formula plans is to sell out most stocks well before bull market peaks and buy most stocks well before bear market bottoms.

This bothers many investment managers. They would like to sell more stocks in the higher zones 6 and 7, near bull market peaks; and buy more stocks in zones 1 and 2, near bear market bottoms. Undoubtedly this would improve results for the formula over a complete bull and bear market cycle.

Since you are supposed to be operating under an automatic formula, however, you cannot be asked to use your judgment to decide whether a bull market or bear market trend will continue. But there are some supplementary rules and techniques for riding the trend a little longer:

1. Wait a month or two before buying or selling. Do not act on the very first day called for by your formula. Wait to confirm the trend. This is probably a good formula rule—if the exact waiting period is specified and not left to the investor's judgment, and if it is not too long.

2. Act at the mid-point of the zone, not at the top or bottom. This is another delaying tactic. Actually, all it does is to shift the action points called for by a formula up or down.

3. Use stop-loss orders. When your formula stock selling point is reached in a rising market, put in a stop order to sell a few points below the current market level. Then, if the up-trend continues, you have not sold stocks too soon.

In the opposite direction, when your formula stock buying point is reached in a declining market, you put in a stop order to buy a few points above the current market. Then, if the down-trend continues, you have not bought stocks too soon.

In practice, this device can become a virtual abandonment of the variable ratio formula plan—unless the stop-loss point is placed very close to the current market level. Indeed, an entirely different "technical" technique, based on the continuous use of stop orders, has been developed.

4. Change stock-bond ratios if necessary. Suppose you find that your formula plan is out of step with the actualities of current stock prices, earnings and dividends—that, as has been the case for many earlier formula plans, you have been too conservative. How and when do you change your stock-bond ratios? To change your zoning plan at or near the top of a bull market is not very effective. The reason is that you are largely out of stocks anyhow. To invest very heavily in stocks at such a high level of the market is risky.

It is much more effective to make a zoning change when the market drops into the middle or lower zones of your plan. At that time you will be more substantially invested in stocks, which will then appreciate in the subsequent market rise.

HOW TO SELECT SECURITIES FOR FORMULA PLANS

Formula plans are essentially timing formulas, not formulas for selecting stocks and bonds. They are formulas for when, not for what. Yet the purpose of formula plans is to minimize the need and occasion for both judgment and emotionally influenced decisions. Therefore, the securities you plan to buy and sell under a formula plan should as far as possible be designated—or at least described or defined—in advance.

HOW TO SELECT STOCKS TO BUY OR SELL

In theory, it is possible for a formula plan to use almost any one of many techniques for selecting securities. You can use either the fundamental or technical approach, buy only market leaders or only market laggards, only growth stocks or only income stocks, and so on. Whatever method of selection you use, it is usually wise to concentrate on a specific eligible list of securities from which buying selections will be made.

Some larger formula plans buy all the 65 stocks in the Dow-Jones composite average. Others concentrate on a dozen or so leading blue chips only. Still others choose from among "The Favorite Fifty" of the experts. Still others choose from among even larger diversified lists, such as the 100 top institutional favorites.

Some formula funds make a practice of buying volatile, high-leverage stocks in the lower buying zones but less volatile ones in the higher buying zones. Correspondingly, they sell the more volatile ones first in zones above the median. This practice will increase capital gain over the entire cycle.

If you are attracted by the formula approach but have not too much time for security selection, consider investing in several representative closed-end investment companies or similarly diversified mutual funds.